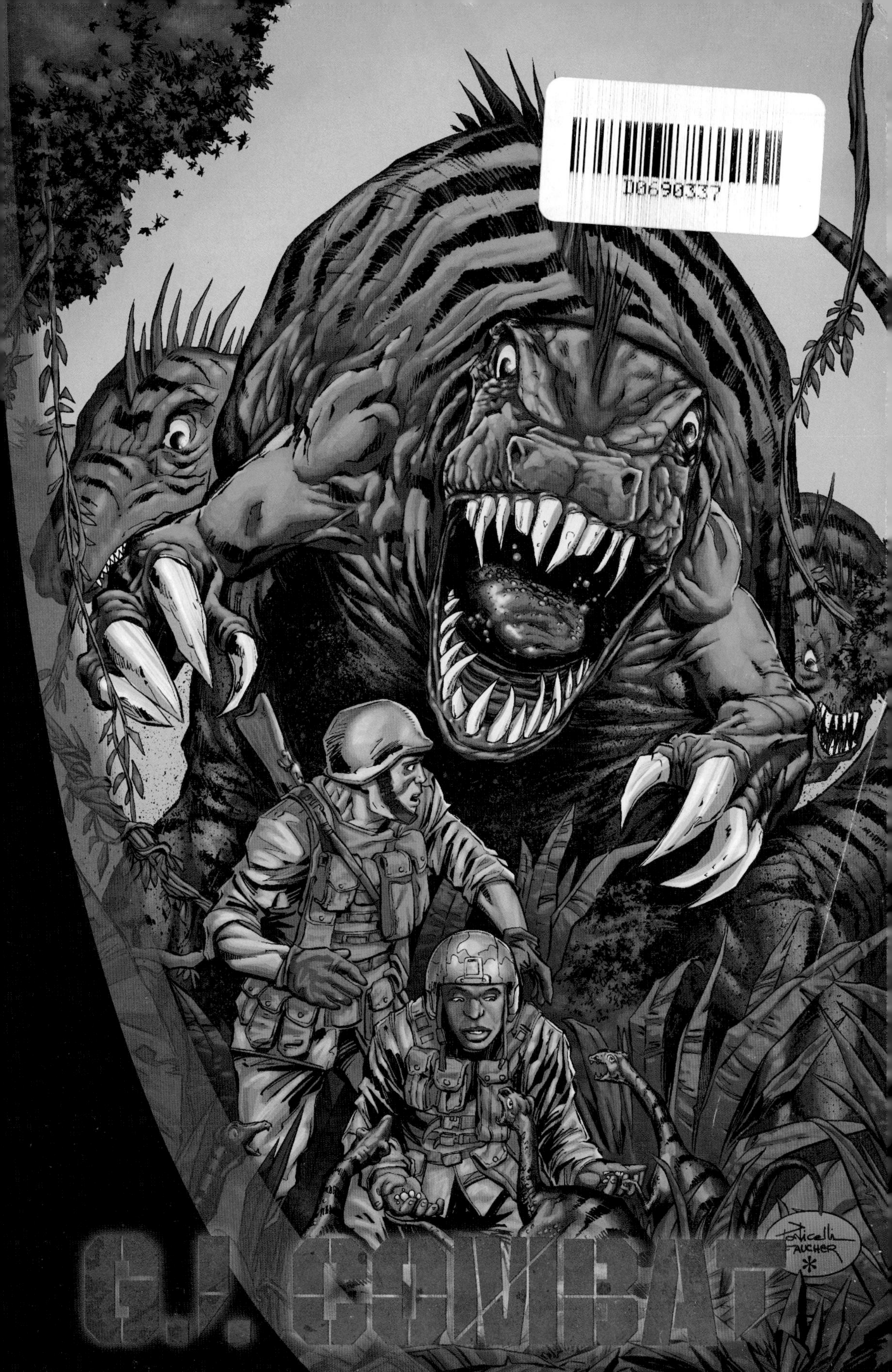

G.I. COMBAT

VOLUME 1 THE WAR THAT TIME FORGOT

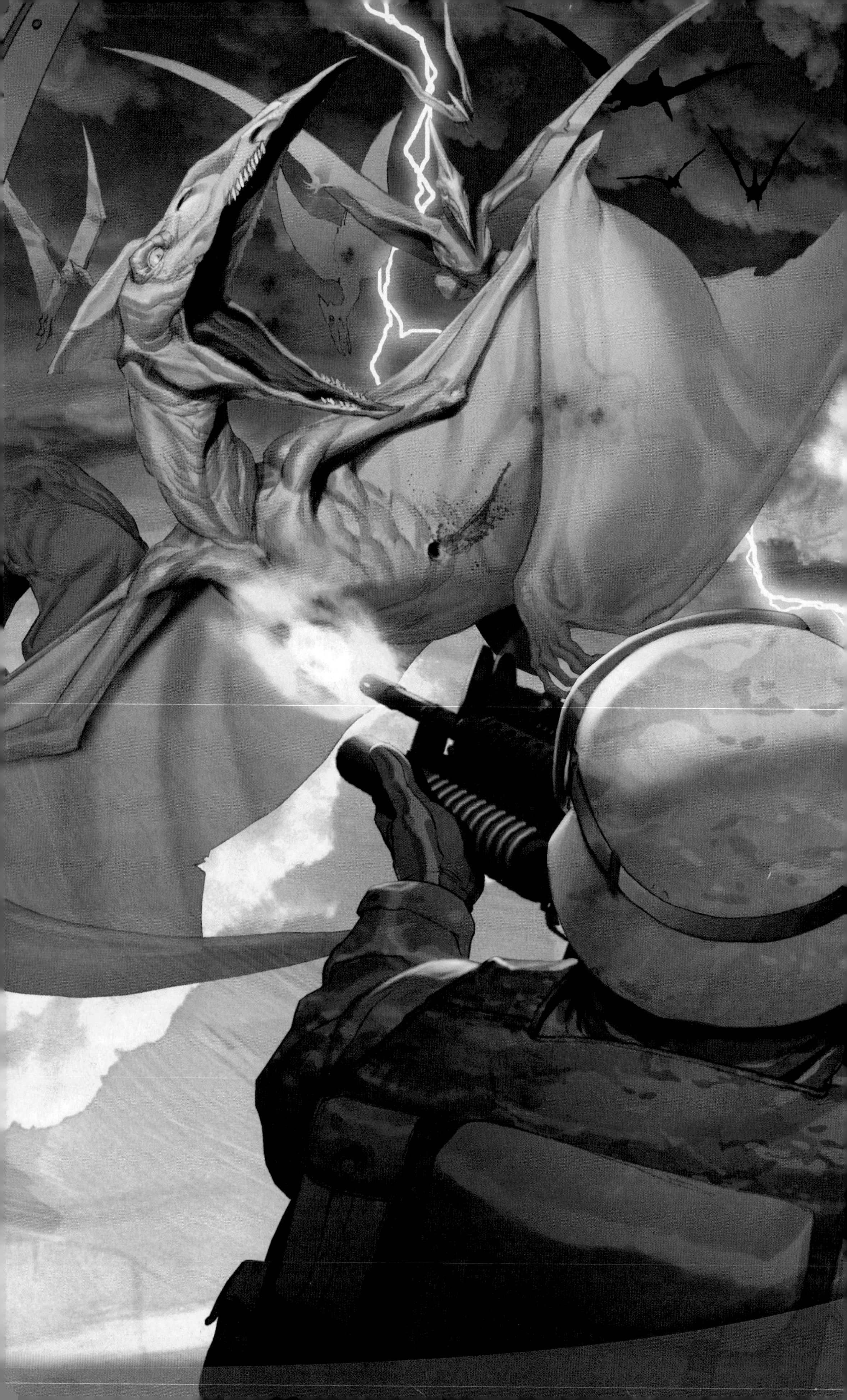

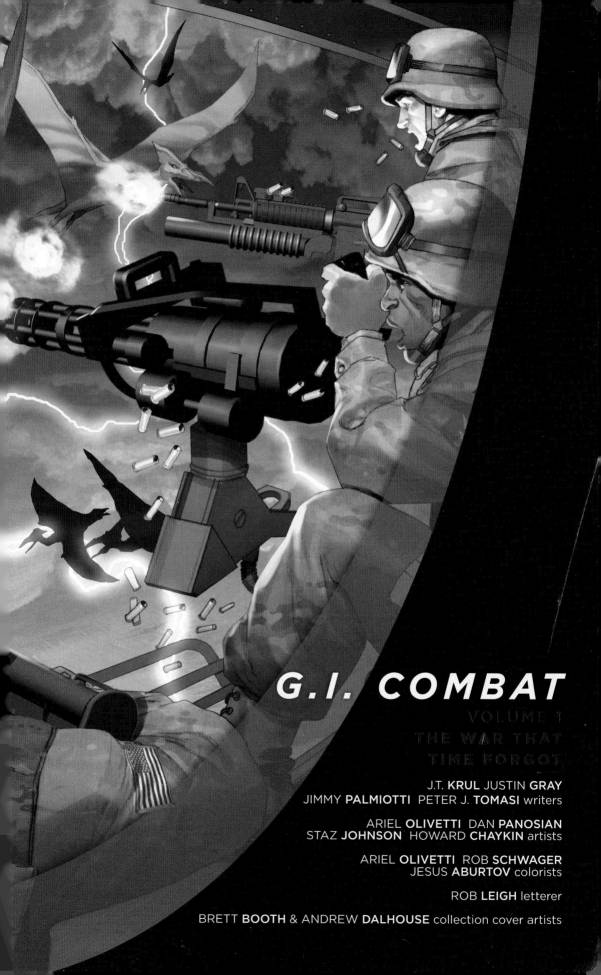

G.I. COMBAT

VOLUME 1
THE WAR THAT
TIME FORGOT

J.T. **KRUL** Justin **GRAY**
JIMMY **PALMIOTTI** PETER J. **TOMASI** writers

ARIEL **OLIVETTI** DAN **PANOSIAN**
STAZ **JOHNSON** HOWARD **CHAYKIN** artists

ARIEL **OLIVETTI** ROB **SCHWAGER**
JESUS **ABURTOV** colorists

ROB **LEIGH** letterer

BRETT **BOOTH** & ANDREW **DALHOUSE** collection cover artists

JOEY CAVALIERI Editor – Original Series KATE STEWART Assistant Editor – Original Series
ROBIN WILDMAN Editor ROBBIN BROSTERMAN Design Director – Books ROBBIE BIEDERMAN Publication Design

BOB HARRAS VP – Editor-in-Chief

DIANE NELSON President DAN DIDIO and JIM LEE Co-Publishers GEOFF JOHNS Chief Creative Officer
JOHN ROOD Executive VP – Sales, Marketing and Business Development AMY GENKINS Senior VP – Business and Legal Affairs
NAIRI GARDINER Senior VP – Finance JEFF BOISON VP – Publishing Operations MARK CHIARELLO VP – Art Direction and Design
JOHN CUNNINGHAM VP – Marketing TERRI CUNNINGHAM VP – Talent Relations and Services
ALISON GILL Senior VP – Manufacturing and Operations HANK KANALZ Senior VP – Digital
JAY KOGAN VP – Business and Legal Affairs, Publishing JACK MAHAN VP – Business Affairs, Talent
NICK NAPOLITANO VP – Manufacturing Administration SUE POHJA VP – Book Sales
COURTNEY SIMMONS Senior VP – Publicity BOB WAYNE Senior VP – Sales

G.I. COMBAT VOLUME 1: THE WAR THAT TIME FORGOT

DC Comics, 1700 Broadway, New York, NY 10019
A Warner Bros. Entertainment Company.
Printed by RR Donnelley, Salem, VA, USA. 2/22/13. First Printing.
ISBN: 978-1-4012-3853-7

Library of Congress Cataloging-in-Publication Data

Palmiotti, Jimmy, author.
G.I. Combat. Volume 1, The War That Time Forgot / Jimmy Palmiotti, Justin Gray, J.T. Krul, Ariel Oliveti.
pages cm
"Originally published in single magazine form in G.I. Combat 0-7."
ISBN 978-1-4012-3853-7
1. Graphic novels. I. Gray, Justin, author. II. Krul, J. T., author. III. Olivetti, Ariel, illustrator. IV. Title. V. Title: War that time forgot.
PN6728.G16P35 2013
741.5'973—dc23
2012046006

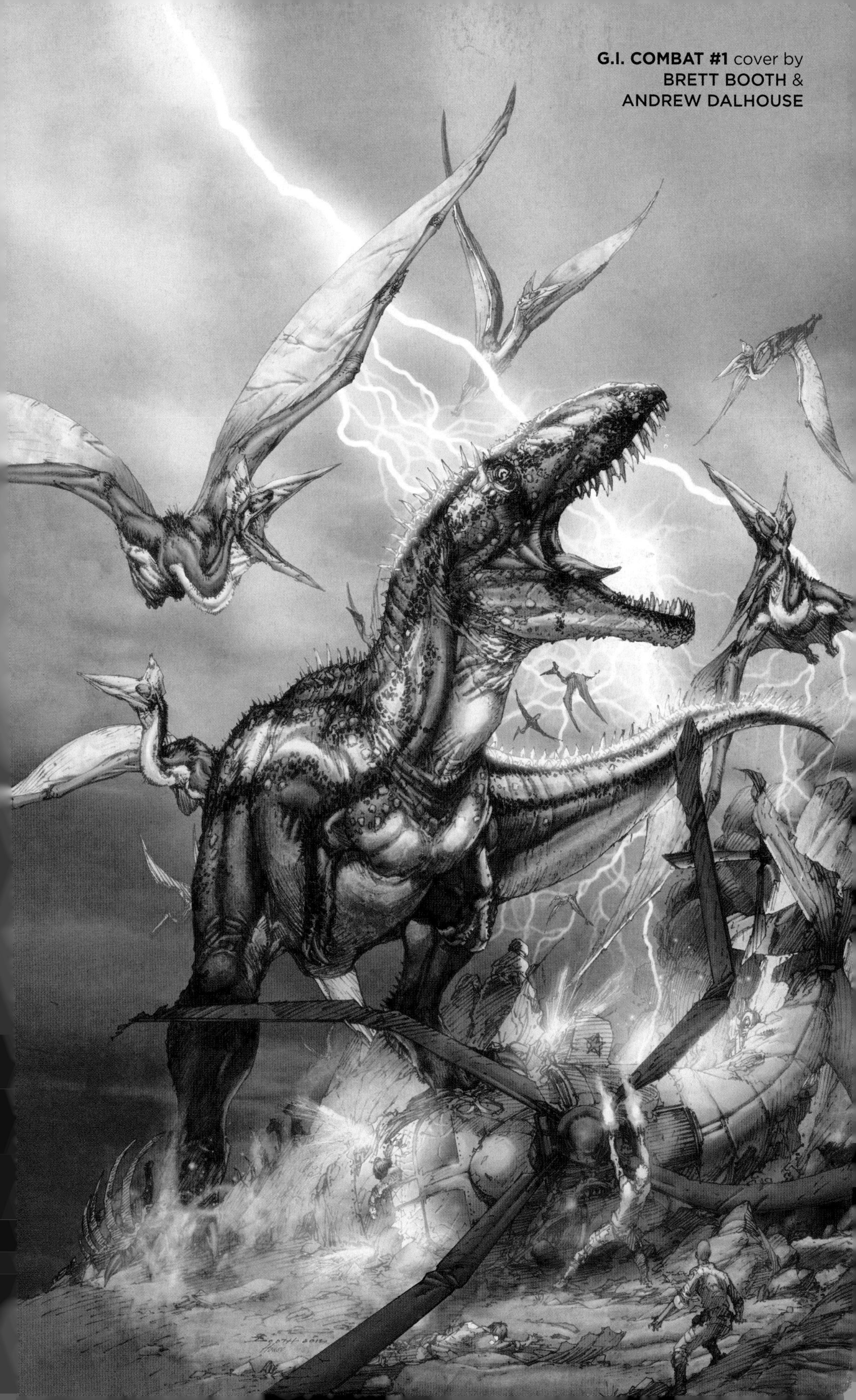

G.I. COMBAT #1 cover by
BRETT BOOTH &
ANDREW DALHOUSE

THE WAR THAT TIME FORGOT

J.T. KRUL writer

ARIEL OLIVETTI artist

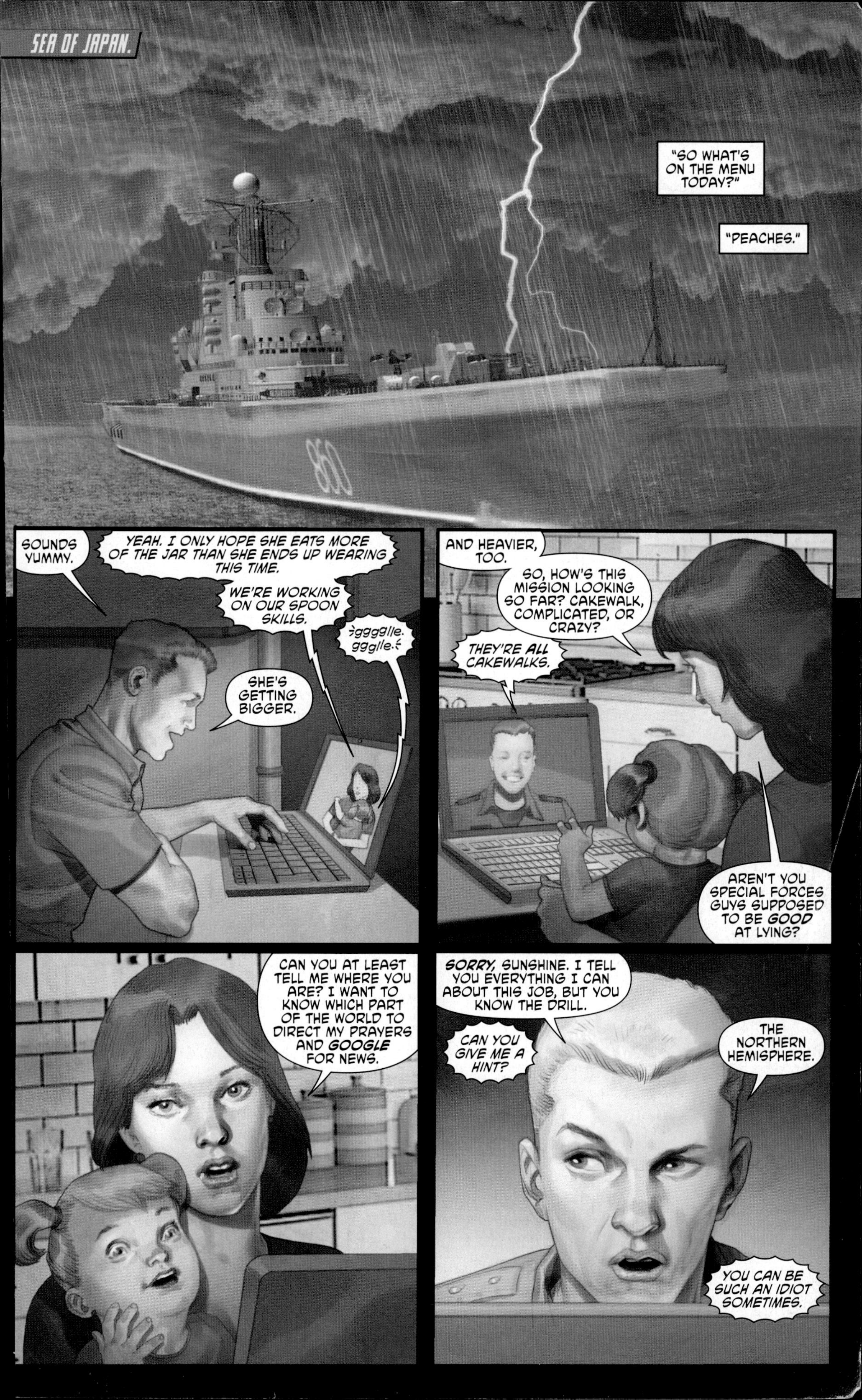
SEA OF JAPAN.
"SO WHAT'S ON THE MENU TODAY?"
"PEACHES."
SOUNDS YUMMY.
YEAH. I ONLY HOPE SHE EATS MORE OF THE JAR THAN SHE ENDS UP WEARING THIS TIME.
WE'RE WORKING ON OUR SPOON SKILLS.
ggggle. ggglle.
SHE'S GETTING BIGGER.
AND HEAVIER, TOO.
SO, HOW'S THIS MISSION LOOKING SO FAR? CAKEWALK, COMPLICATED, OR CRAZY?
THEY'RE ALL CAKEWALKS.
AREN'T YOU SPECIAL FORCES GUYS SUPPOSED TO BE GOOD AT LYING?
CAN YOU AT LEAST TELL ME WHERE YOU ARE? I WANT TO KNOW WHICH PART OF THE WORLD TO DIRECT MY PRAYERS AND GOOGLE FOR NEWS.
SORRY, SUNSHINE. I TELL YOU EVERYTHING I CAN ABOUT THIS JOB, BUT YOU KNOW THE DRILL.
CAN YOU GIVE ME A HINT?
THE NORTHERN HEMISPHERE.
YOU CAN BE SUCH AN IDIOT SOMETIMES.

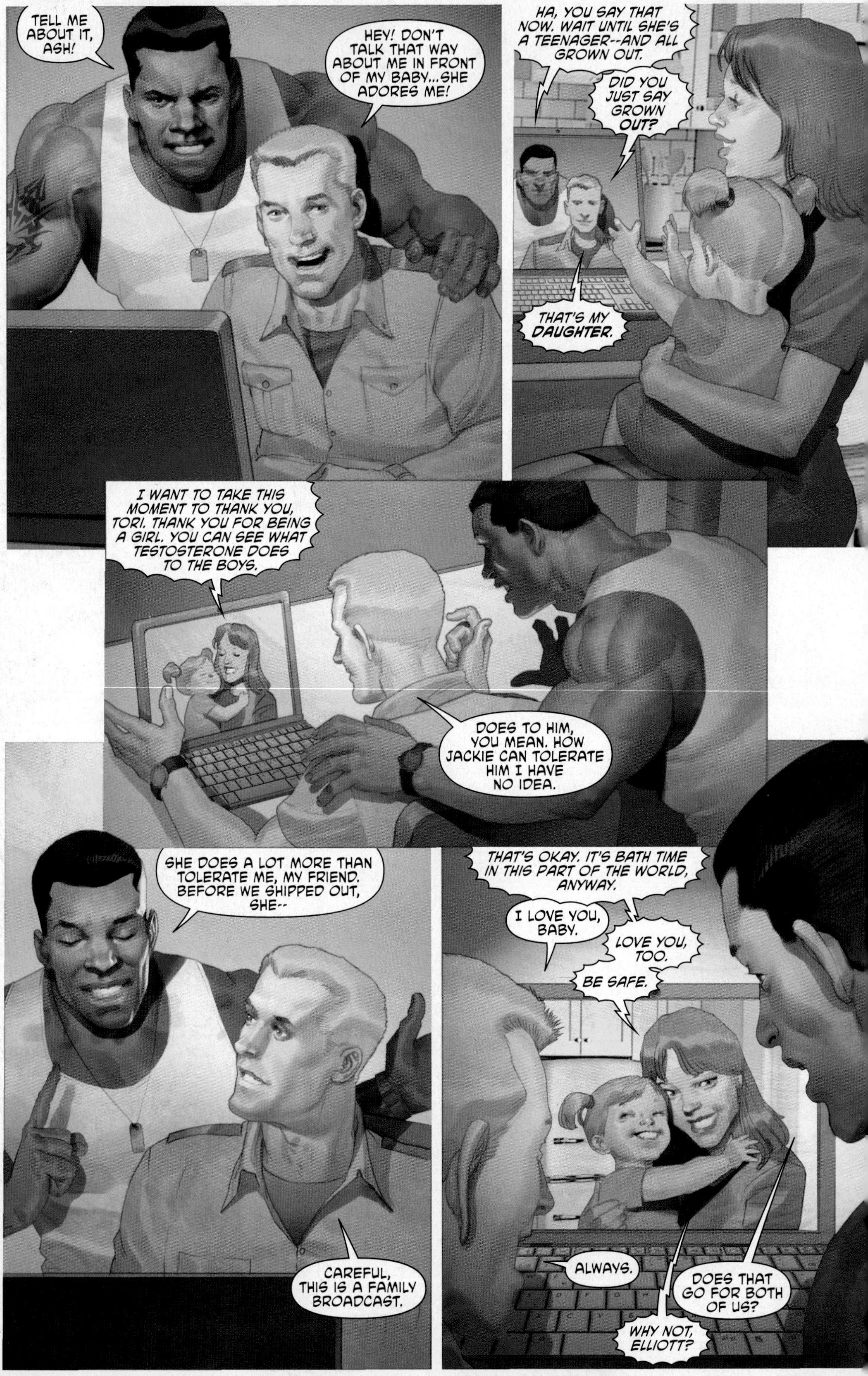
TELL ME ABOUT IT, ASH!
HEY! DON'T TALK THAT WAY ABOUT ME IN FRONT OF MY BABY...SHE ADORES ME!
HA, YOU SAY THAT NOW. WAIT UNTIL SHE'S A TEENAGER--AND ALL GROWN OUT.
DID YOU JUST SAY GROWN OUT?
THAT'S MY DAUGHTER.
I WANT TO TAKE THIS MOMENT TO THANK YOU, TORI. THANK YOU FOR BEING A GIRL. YOU CAN SEE WHAT TESTOSTERONE DOES TO THE BOYS.
DOES TO HIM, YOU MEAN. HOW JACKIE CAN TOLERATE HIM I HAVE NO IDEA.
SHE DOES A LOT MORE THAN TOLERATE ME, MY FRIEND. BEFORE WE SHIPPED OUT, SHE--
CAREFUL, THIS IS A FAMILY BROADCAST.
THAT'S OKAY. IT'S BATH TIME IN THIS PART OF THE WORLD, ANYWAY.
I LOVE YOU, BABY.
LOVE YOU, TOO.
BE SAFE.
ALWAYS.
DOES THAT GO FOR BOTH OF US?
WHY NOT, ELLIOTT?

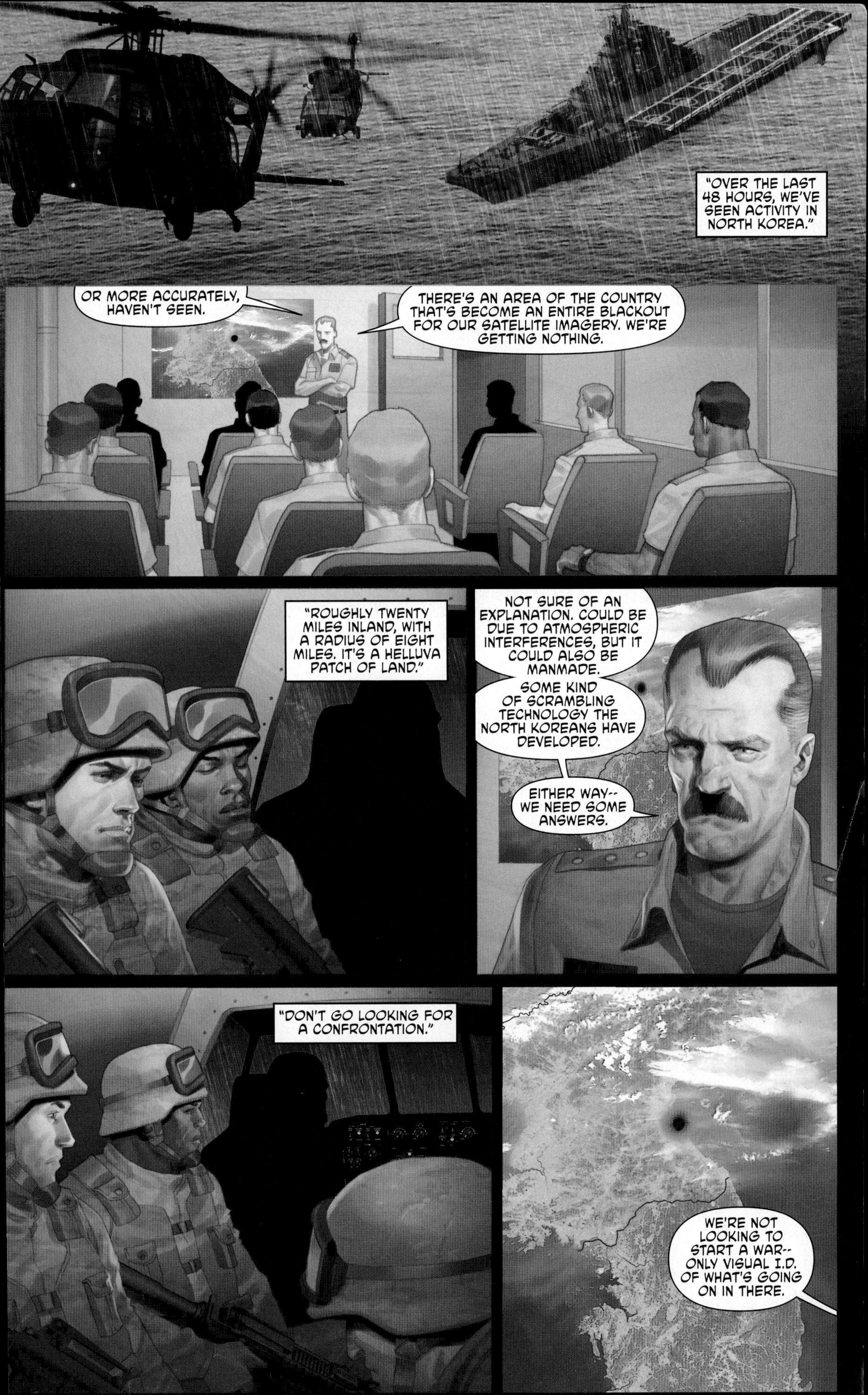
"OVER THE LAST 48 HOURS, WE'VE SEEN ACTIVITY IN NORTH KOREA."
OR MORE ACCURATELY, HAVEN'T SEEN.
THERE'S AN AREA OF THE COUNTRY THAT'S BECOME AN ENTIRE BLACKOUT FOR OUR SATELLITE IMAGERY. WE'RE GETTING NOTHING.
"ROUGHLY TWENTY MILES INLAND, WITH A RADIUS OF EIGHT MILES. IT'S A HELLUVA PATCH OF LAND."
NOT SURE OF AN EXPLANATION. COULD BE DUE TO ATMOSPHERIC INTERFERENCES, BUT IT COULD ALSO BE MANMADE.
SOME KIND OF SCRAMBLING TECHNOLOGY THE NORTH KOREANS HAVE DEVELOPED.
EITHER WAY-- WE NEED SOME ANSWERS.
"DON'T GO LOOKING FOR A CONFRONTATION."
WE'RE NOT LOOKING TO START A WAR-- ONLY VISUAL I.D. OF WHAT'S GOING ON IN THERE.

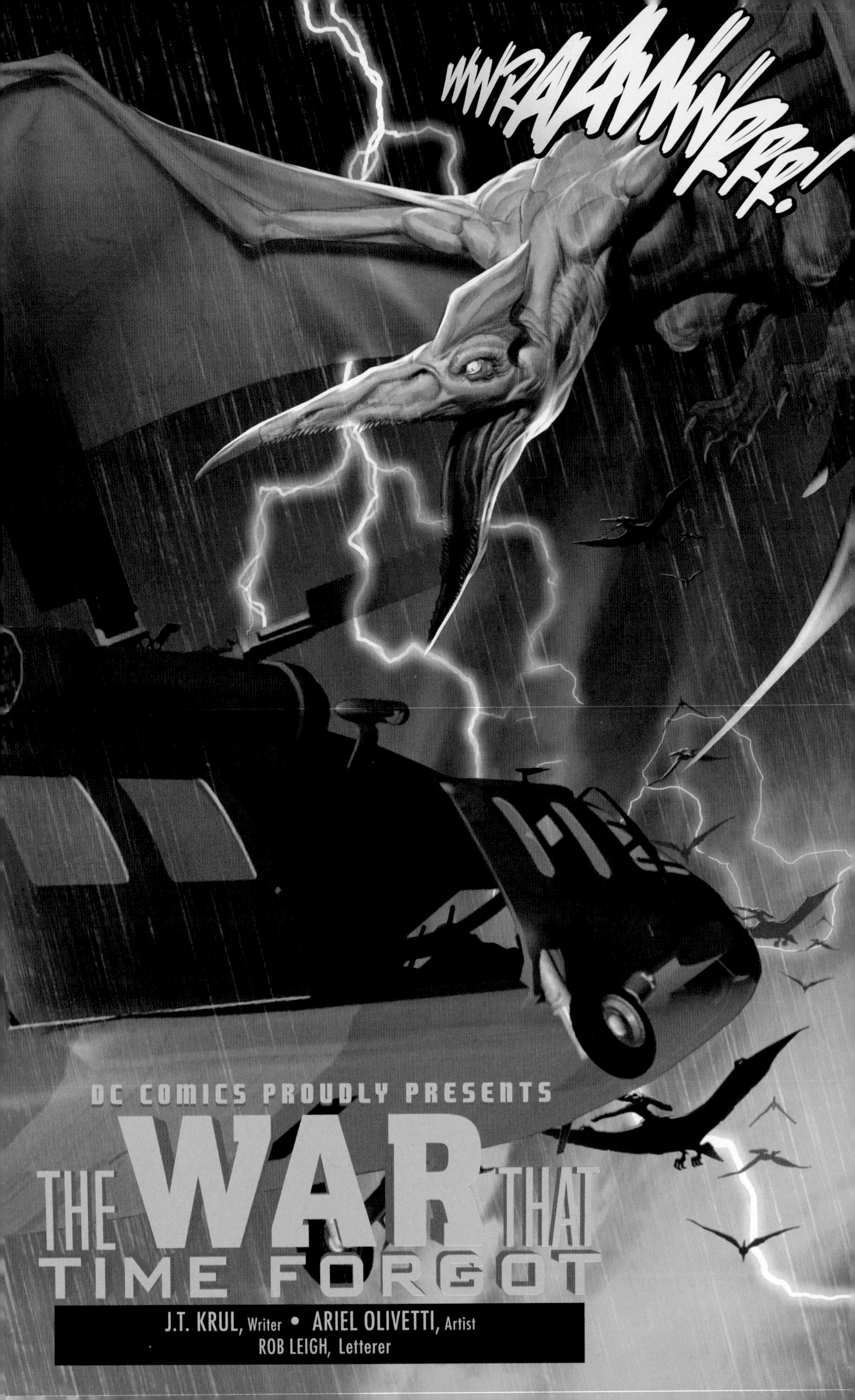

DC COMICS PROUDLY PRESENTS
THE WAR THAT TIME FORGOT
J.T. KRUL, Writer • ARIEL OLIVETTI, Artist
ROB LEIGH, Letterer

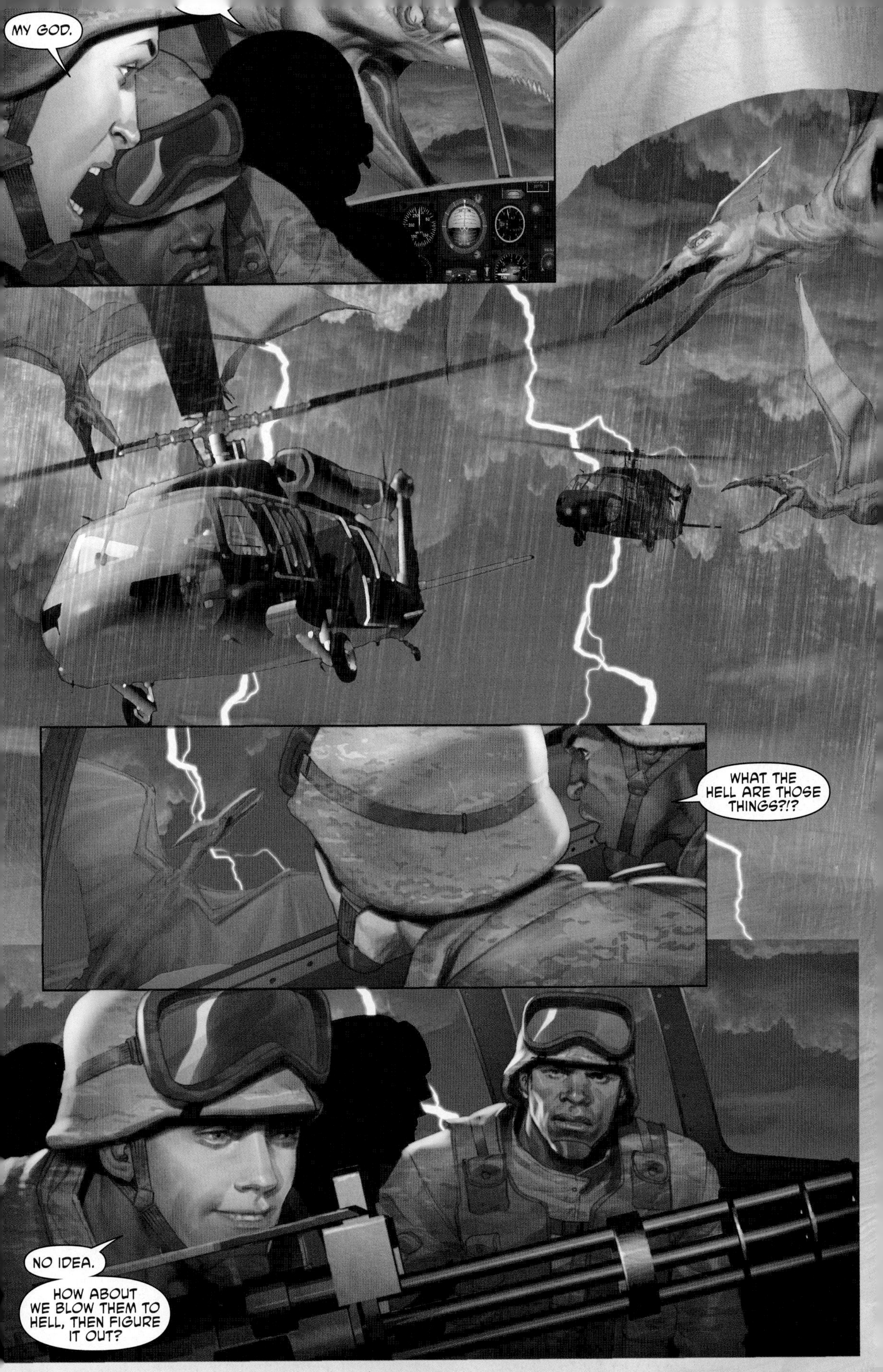
MY GOD.
WHAT THE HELL ARE THOSE THINGS?!?
NO IDEA.
HOW ABOUT WE BLOW THEM TO HELL, THEN FIGURE IT OUT?

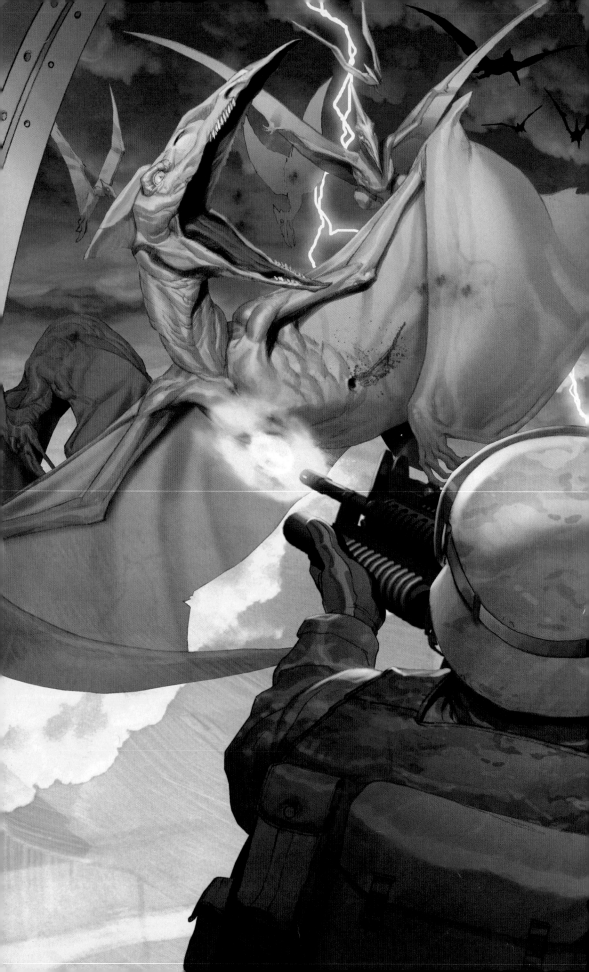

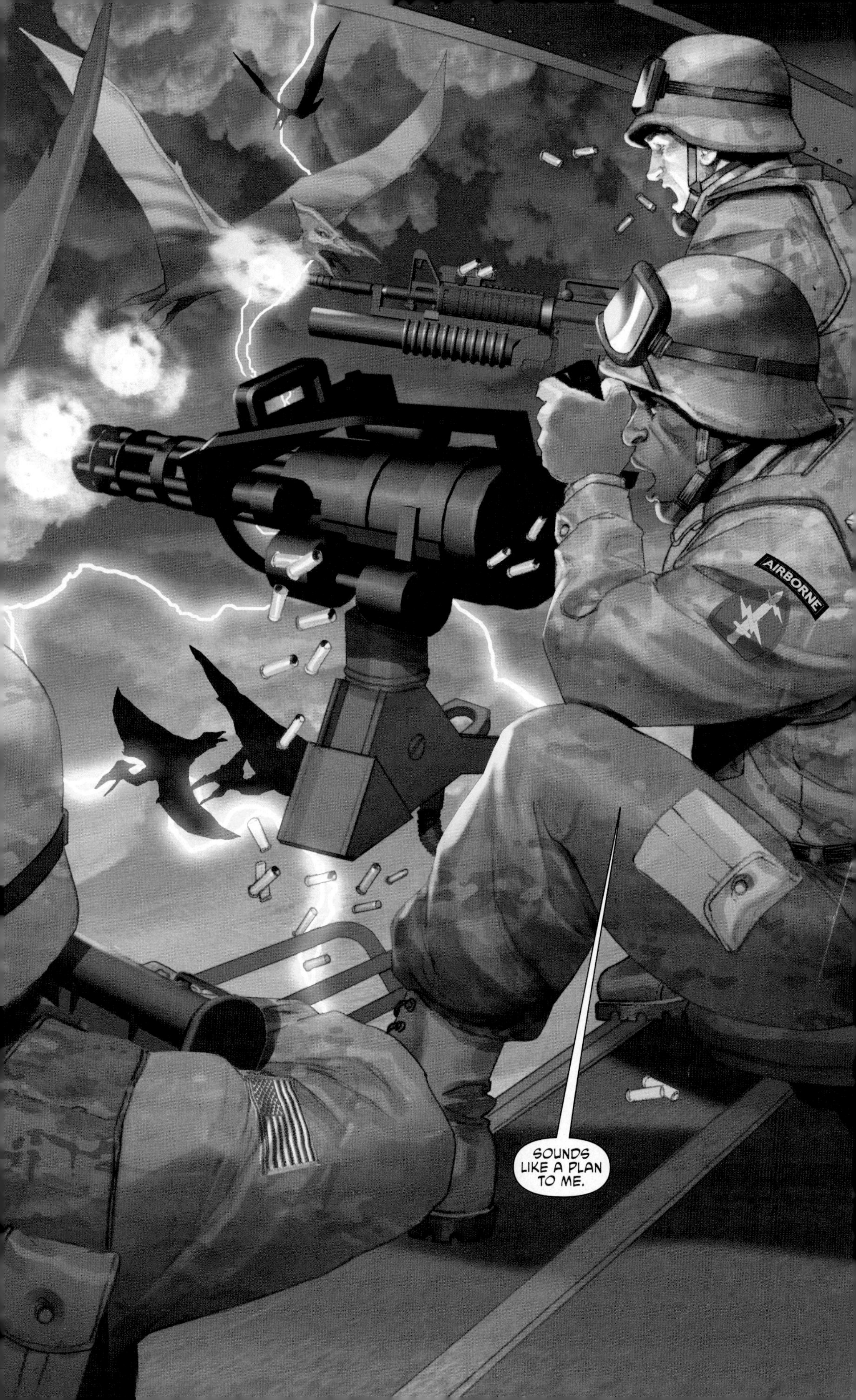
AIRBORNE
SOUNDS LIKE A PLAN TO ME.

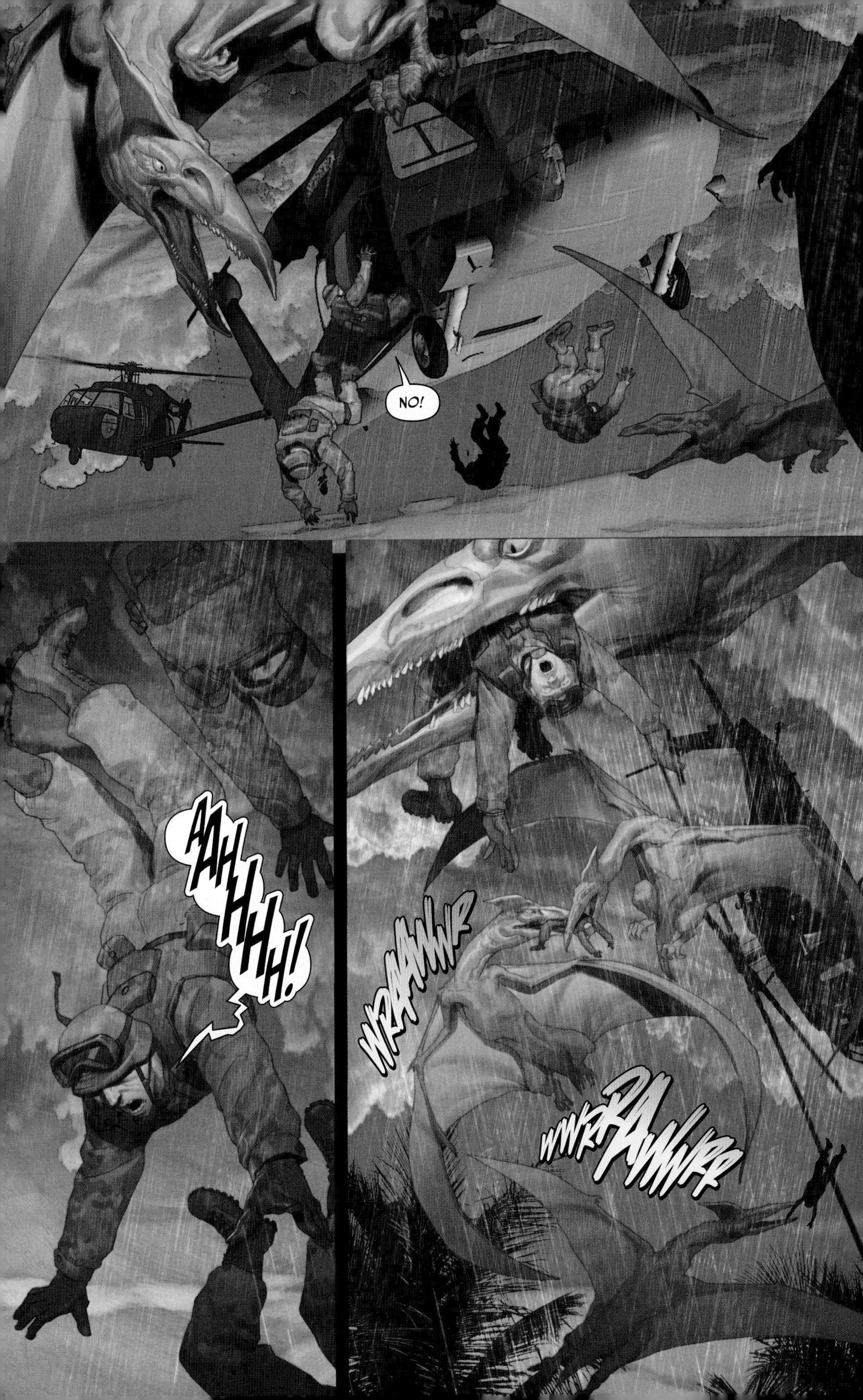
NO!
AAAHHHHH!
WRRAAWWR
WWRRAWWRR

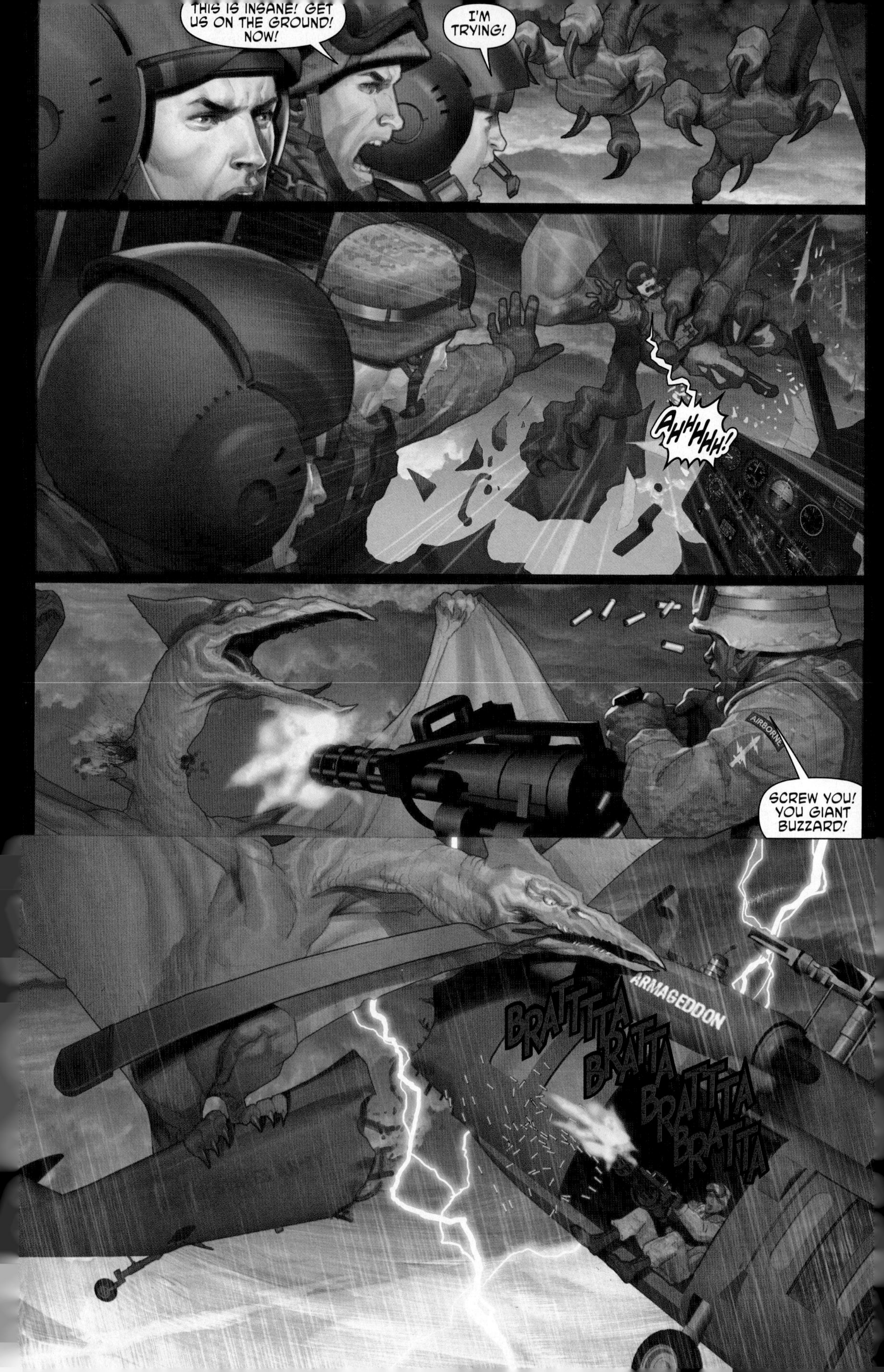
THIS IS INSANE! GET US ON THE GROUND! NOW!
I'M TRYING!
AHHHHH!
AIRBORNE
SCREW YOU! YOU GIANT BUZZARD!
ARMAGEDDON
BRATTTTA
BRATTA
BRATTTTA
BRATTA
BRATTTA

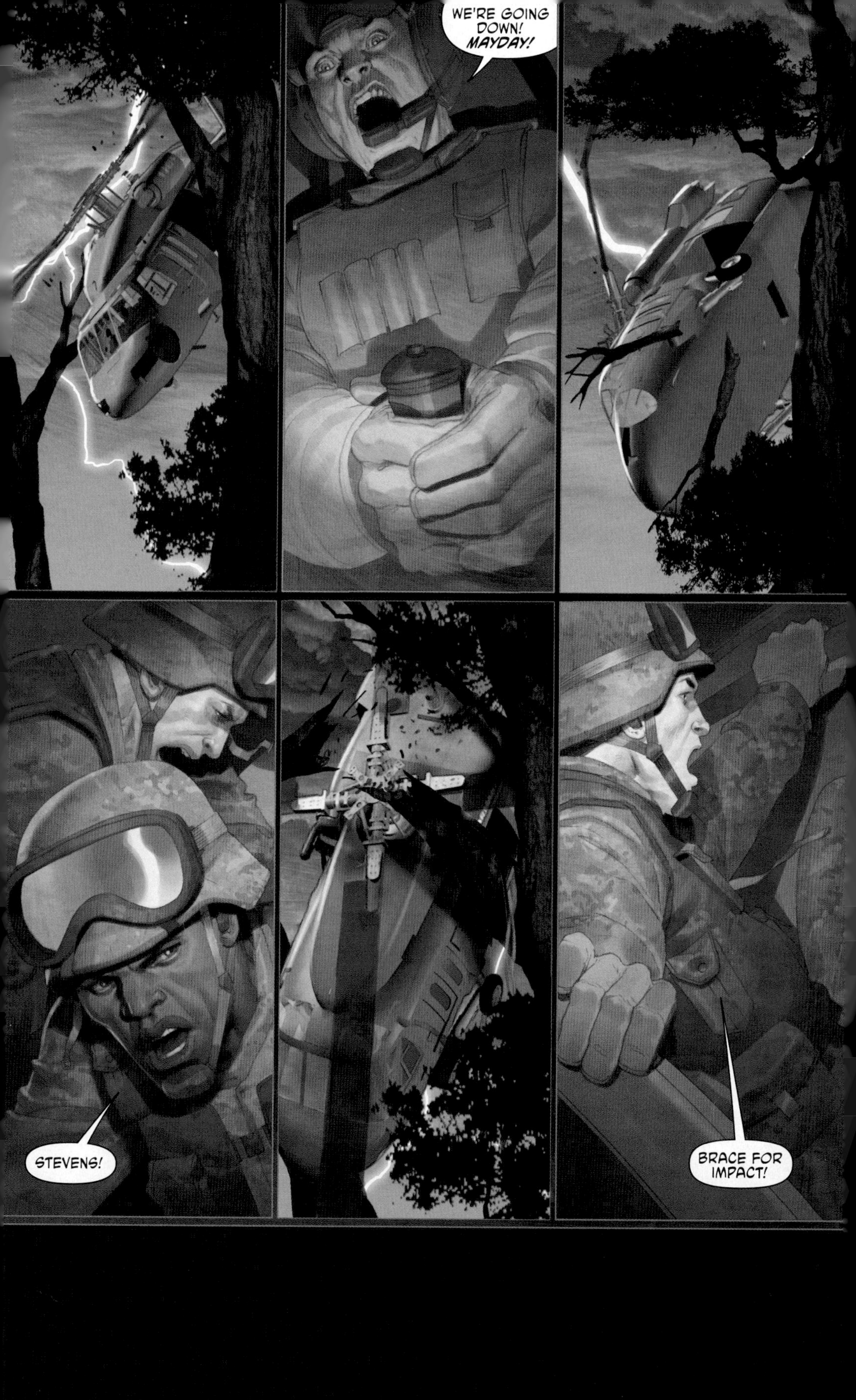
WE'RE GOING DOWN! MAYDAY!
STEVENS!
BRACE FOR IMPACT!

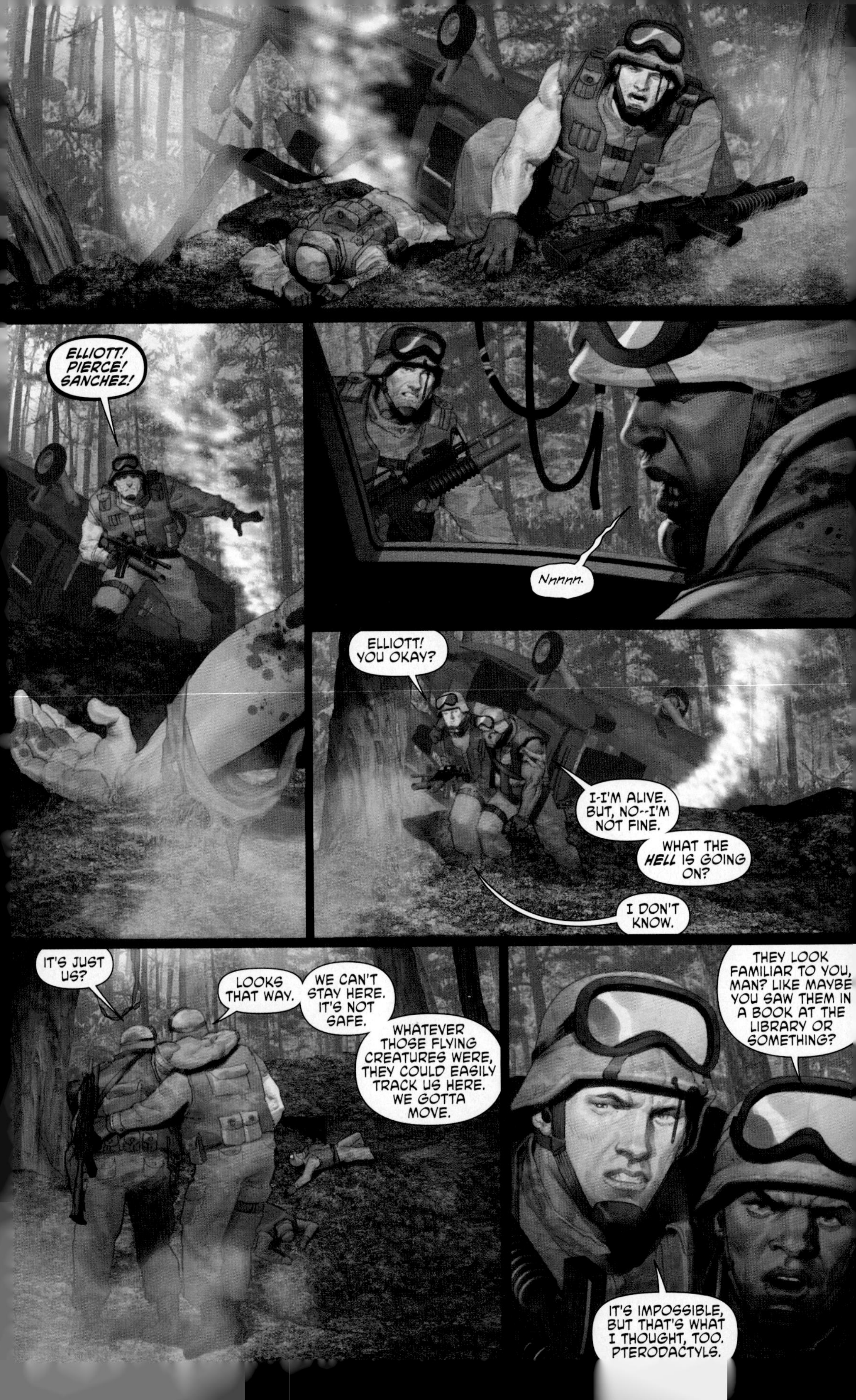
ELLIOTT! PIERCE! SANCHEZ!
Nnnnn.
ELLIOTT! YOU OKAY?
I-I'M ALIVE. BUT, NO--I'M NOT FINE.
WHAT THE HELL IS GOING ON?
I DON'T KNOW.
IT'S JUST US?
LOOKS THAT WAY.
WE CAN'T STAY HERE. IT'S NOT SAFE.
WHATEVER THOSE FLYING CREATURES WERE, THEY COULD EASILY TRACK US HERE. WE GOTTA MOVE.
THEY LOOK FAMILIAR TO YOU, MAN? LIKE MAYBE YOU SAW THEM IN A BOOK AT THE LIBRARY OR SOMETHING?
IT'S IMPOSSIBLE, BUT THAT'S WHAT I THOUGHT, TOO. PTERODACTYLS.

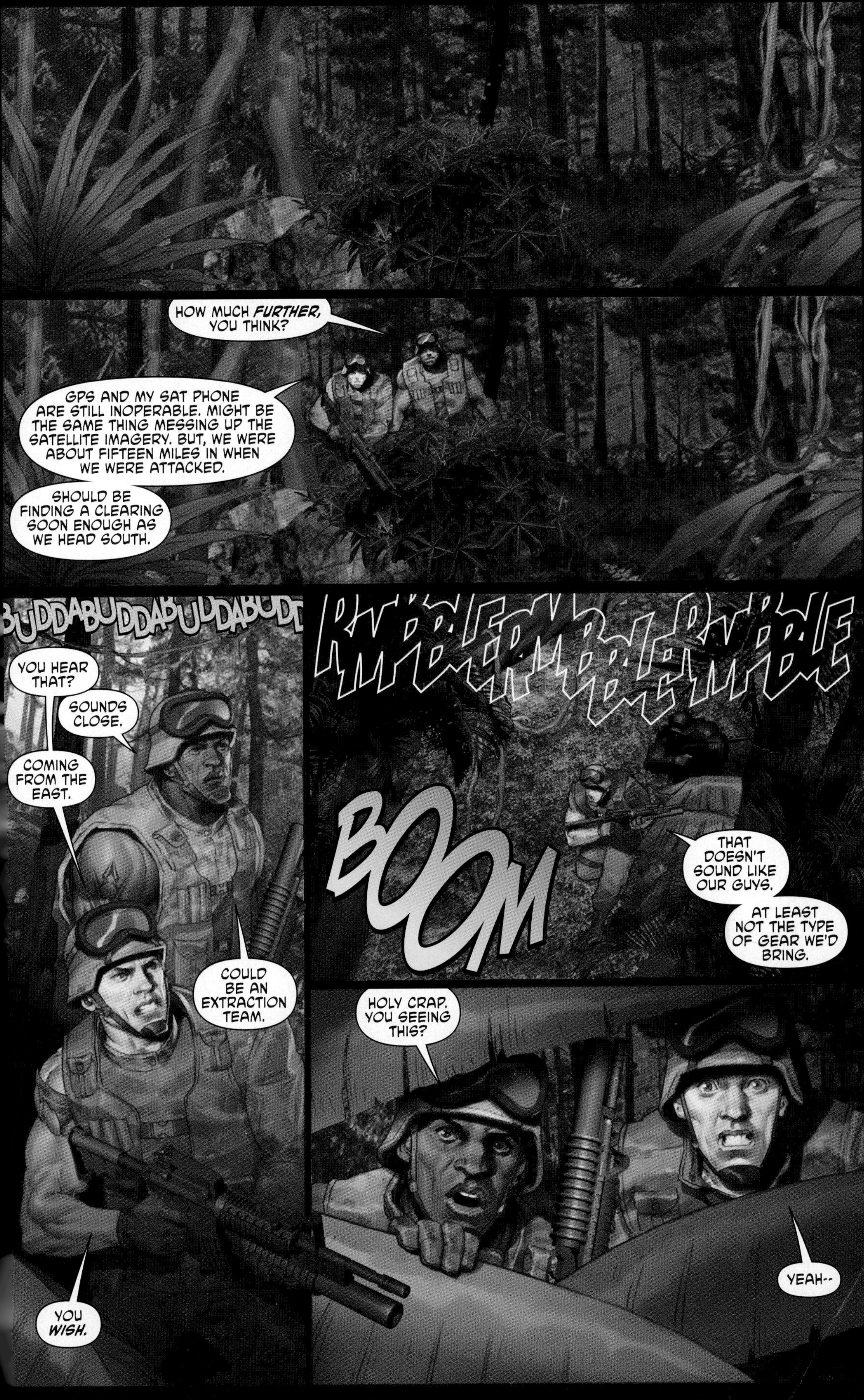
HOW MUCH *FURTHER*, YOU THINK?
GPS AND MY SAT PHONE ARE STILL INOPERABLE. MIGHT BE THE SAME THING MESSING UP THE SATELLITE IMAGERY. BUT, WE WERE ABOUT FIFTEEN MILES IN WHEN WE WERE ATTACKED.
SHOULD BE FINDING A CLEARING SOON ENOUGH AS WE HEAD SOUTH.
BUDDABUDDABUDDABUDD
YOU HEAR THAT?
SOUNDS CLOSE.
COMING FROM THE EAST.
COULD BE AN EXTRACTION TEAM.
YOU *WISH*.
BOOM
THAT DOESN'T SOUND LIKE OUR GUYS.
AT LEAST NOT THE TYPE OF GEAR WE'D BRING.
HOLY CRAP. YOU SEEING THIS?
YEAH--

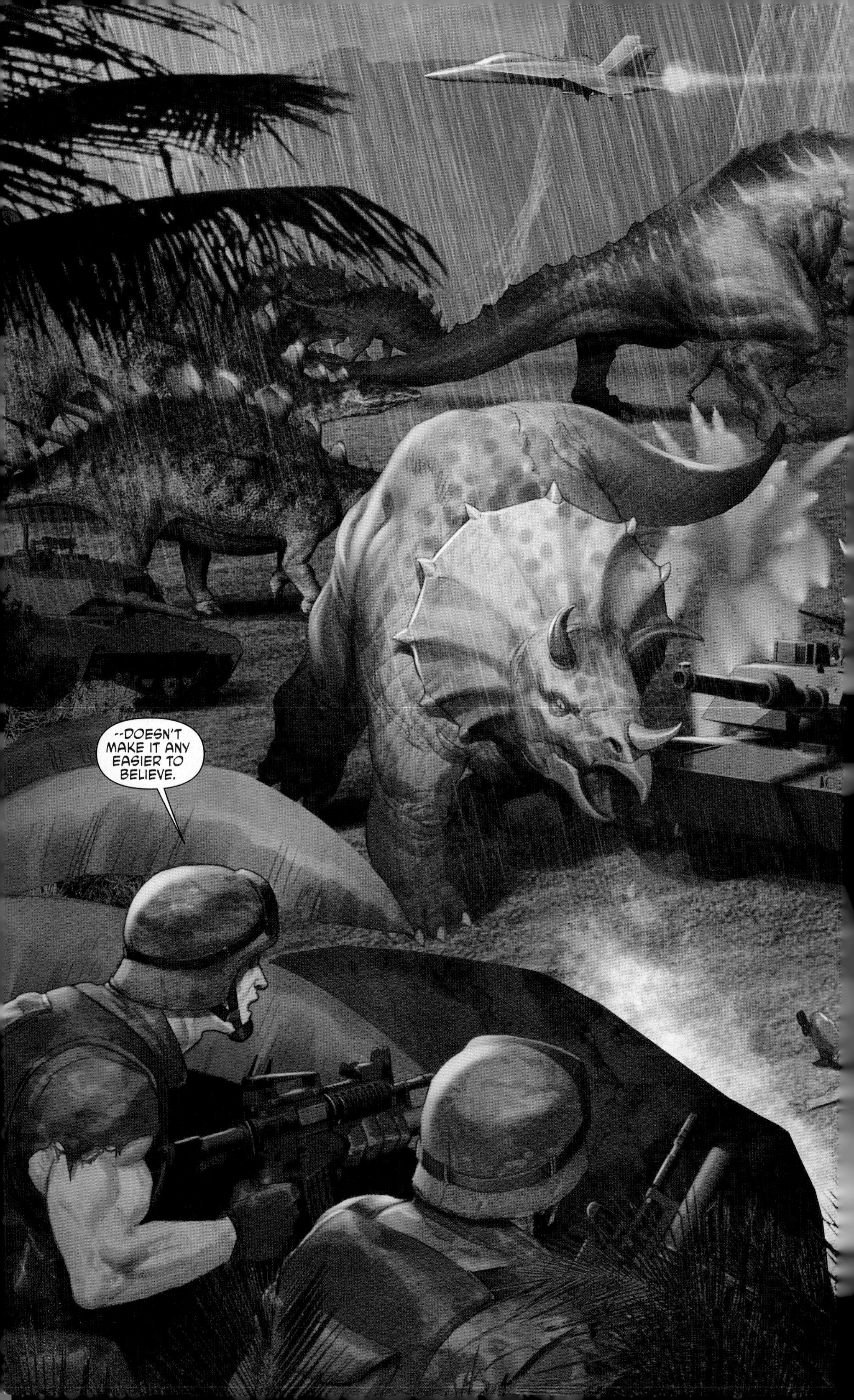
--DOESN'T MAKE IT ANY EASIER TO BELIEVE.

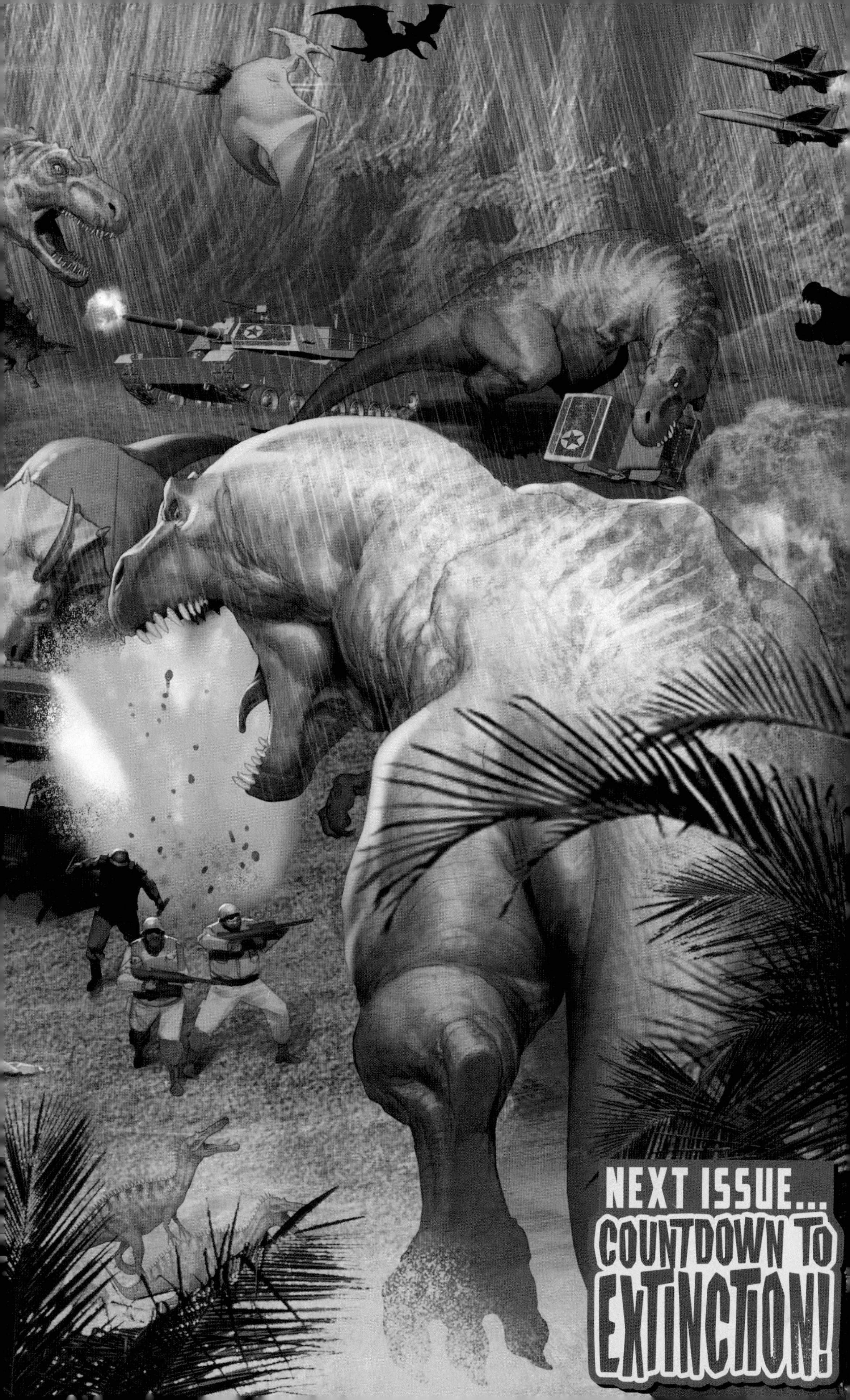
NEXT ISSUE...
COUNTDOWN TO EXTINCTION!

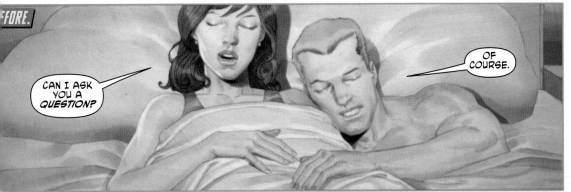

CAN I ASK YOU A *QUESTION?*

OF COURSE.

OW DO YOU O IT? *KILL* PEOPLE?

I MEAN--I KNOW OW YOU CAN DO IT. BUT IS IT...*HARD?* KILLING ANOTHER HUMAN BEING?

I'M SORRY. FORGET I ASKED. IT'S *STUPID.*

NO. IT'S NOT STUPID.

I JUST DON'T THINK I COULD DO IT.

I DON'T LIKE KILLING PEOPLE. AND NEVER LOOK FORWARD TO IT.

I KNOW THAT.

BUT SOMETIMES YOU HAVE TO. AND THAT'S WHEN THE *TRAINING* KICKS IN.

LIKE TURNING A SWITCH...LIKE A *MACHINE?* GOING ON AUTOPILOT?

ACTUALLY... THE *OPPOSITE.*

IN THE THICK OF IT, ANY THREAT IS SIMPLY WHAT I HAVE TO GO THROUGH TO GET BACK HOME.

AN *OBSTACLE* BETWEEN US.

AND *NOTHING'S* GOING TO KEEP ME AWAY.

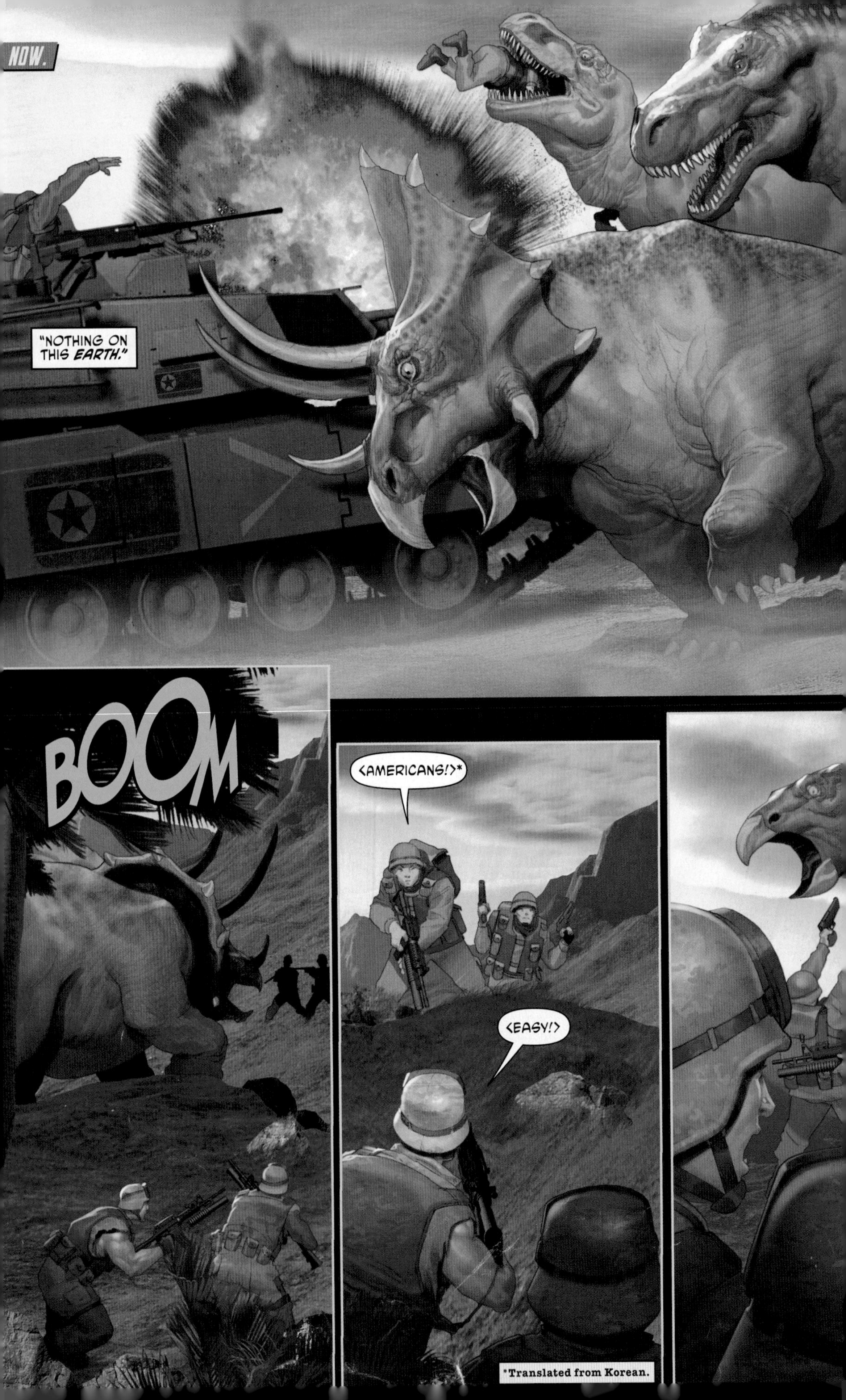
NOW.
"NOTHING ON THIS *EARTH.*"
BOOM
<AMERICANS!>*
<EASY!>
*Translated from Korean.

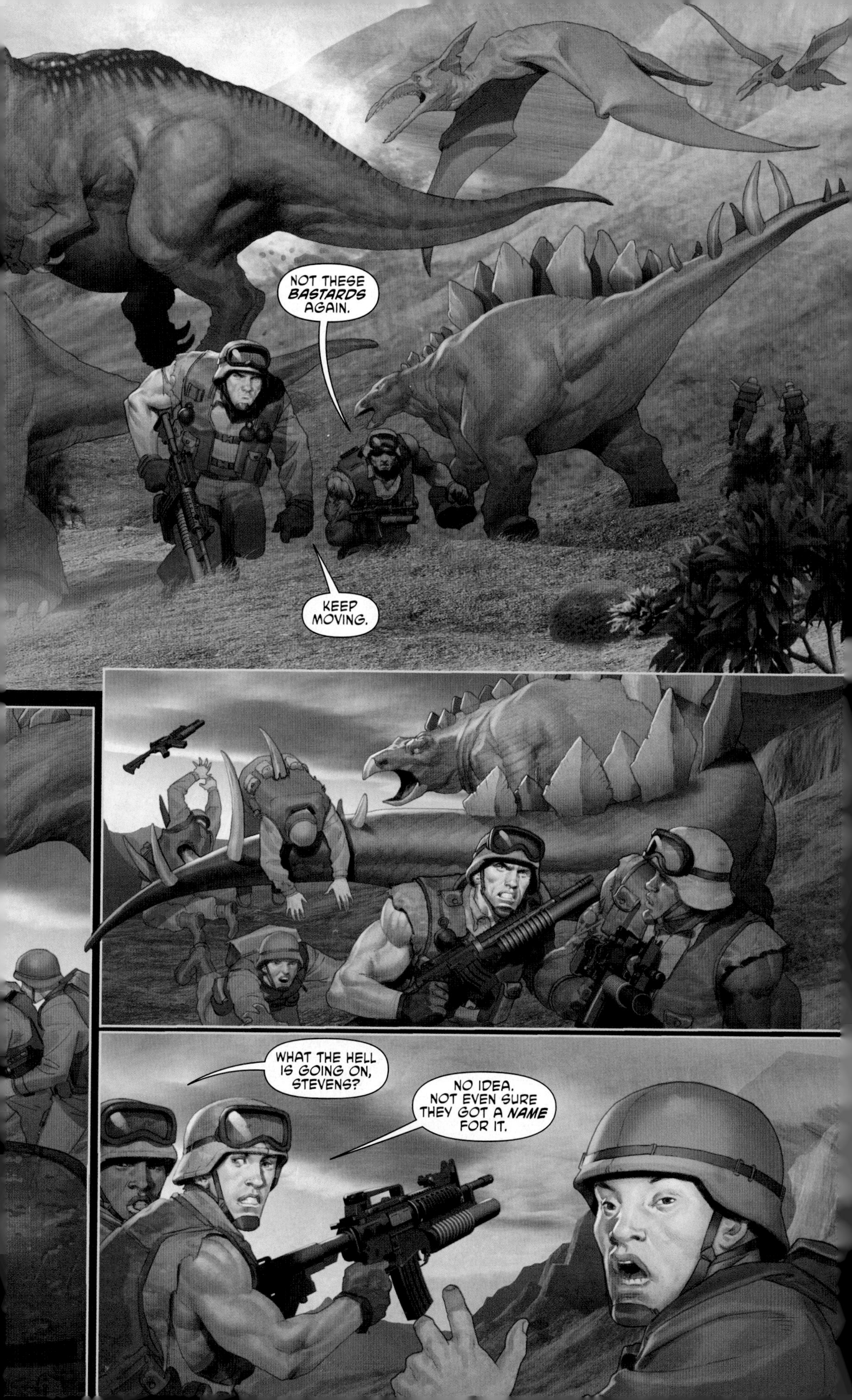
NOT THESE *BASTARDS* AGAIN.
KEEP MOVING.
WHAT THE HELL IS GOING ON, STEVENS?
NO IDEA. NOT EVEN SURE THEY GOT A *NAME* FOR IT.

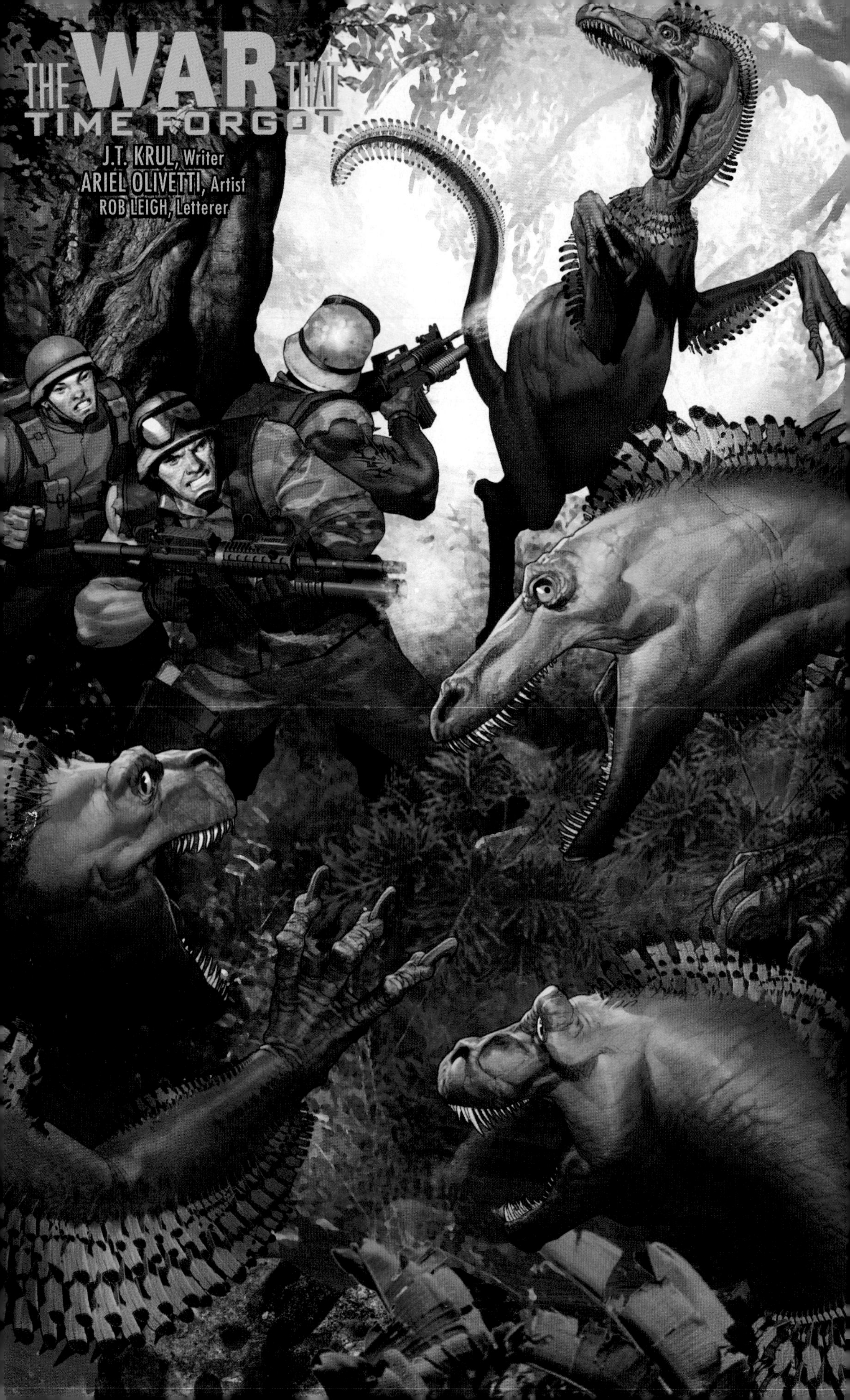
THE WAR THAT TIME FORGOT
J.T. KRUL, Writer
ARIEL OLIVETTI, Artist
ROB LEIGH, Letterer

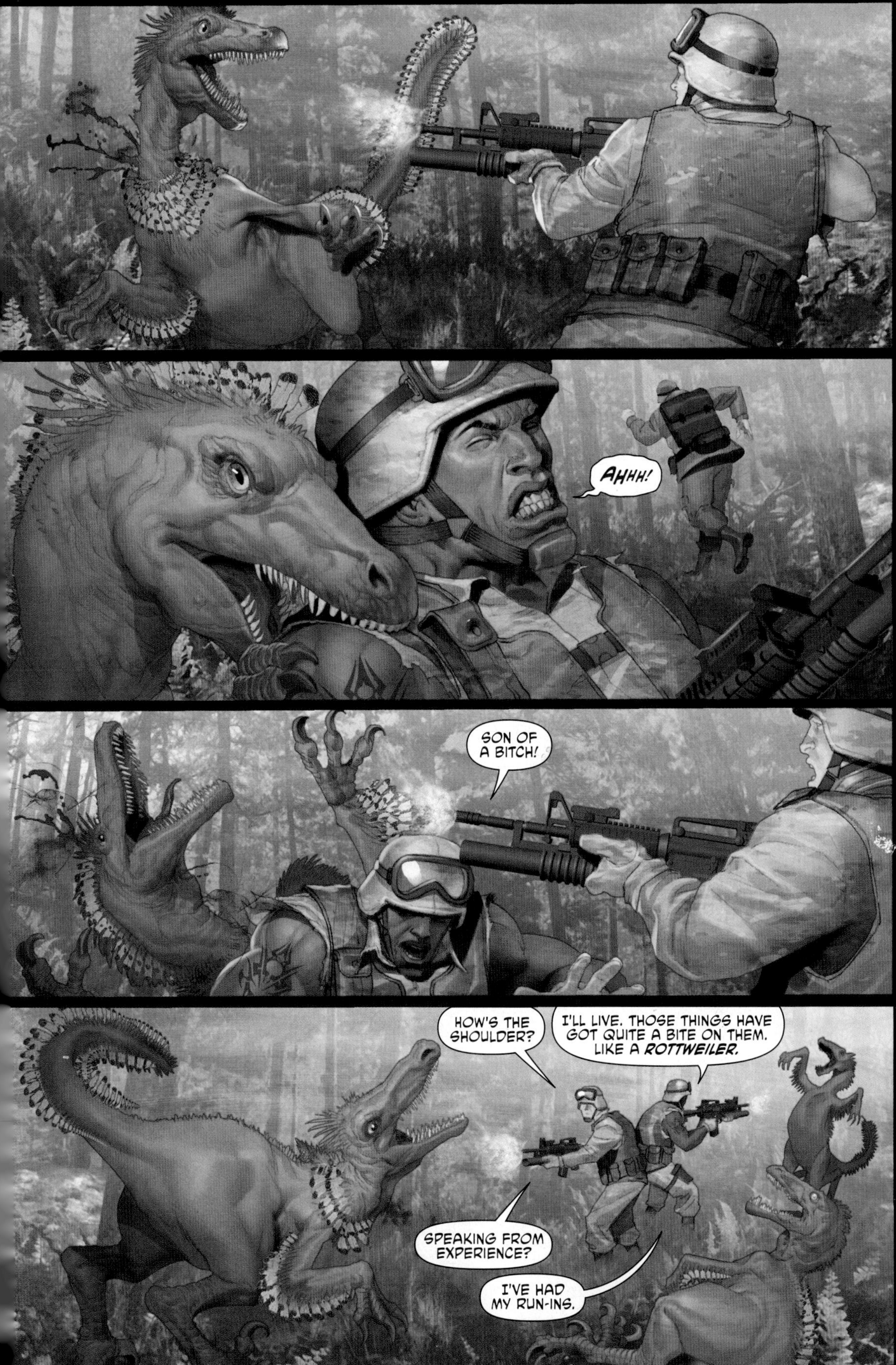
AHHH!
SON OF A BITCH!
HOW'S THE SHOULDER?
I'LL LIVE. THOSE THINGS HAVE GOT QUITE A BITE ON THEM. LIKE A ROTTWEILER.
SPEAKING FROM EXPERIENCE?
I'VE HAD MY RUN-INS.

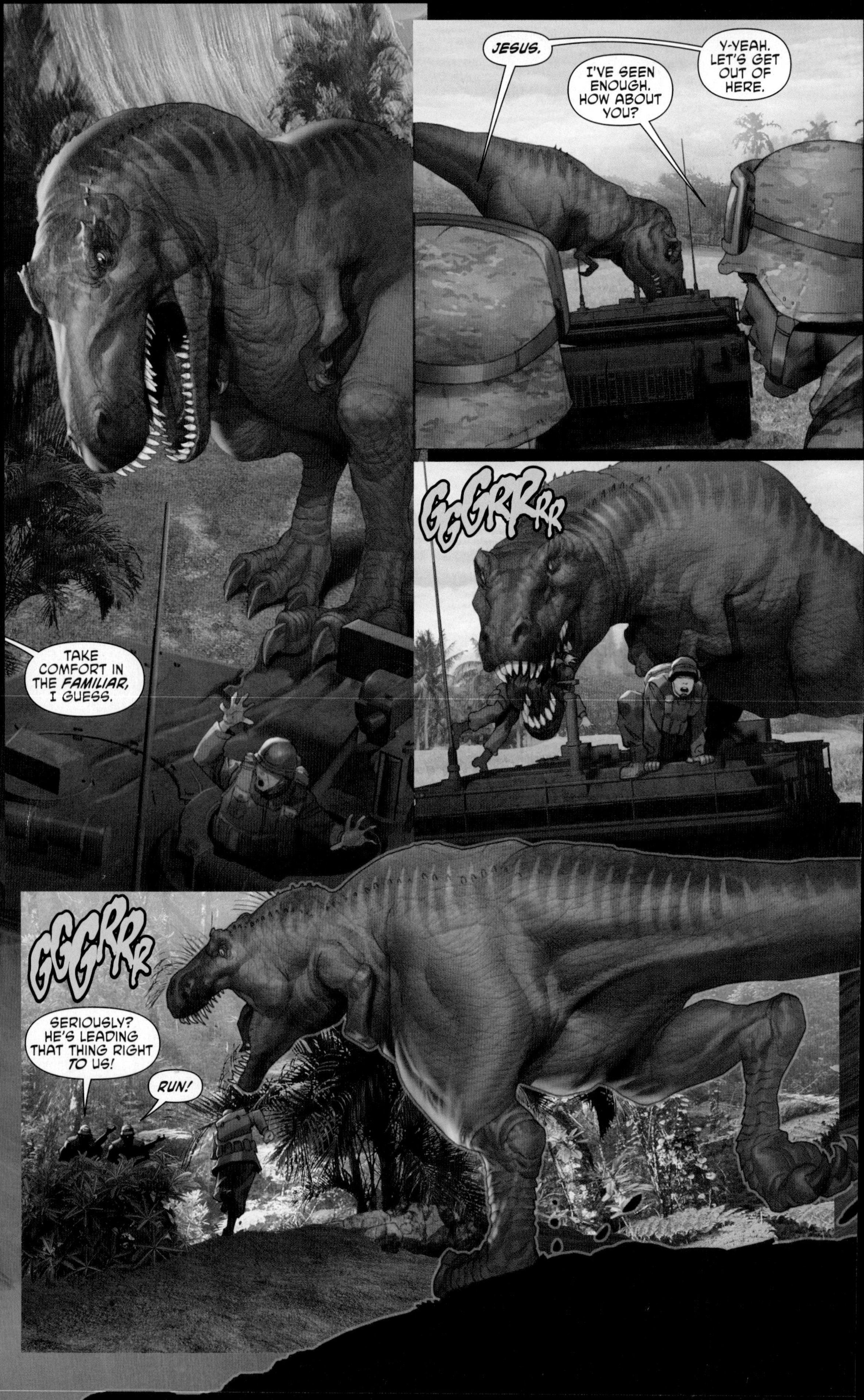
TAKE COMFORT IN THE FAMILIAR, I GUESS.
JESUS.
I'VE SEEN ENOUGH. HOW ABOUT YOU?
Y-YEAH. LET'S GET OUT OF HERE.
GGGRRRR
GGGRRR
SERIOUSLY? HE'S LEADING THAT THING RIGHT TO US!
RUN!

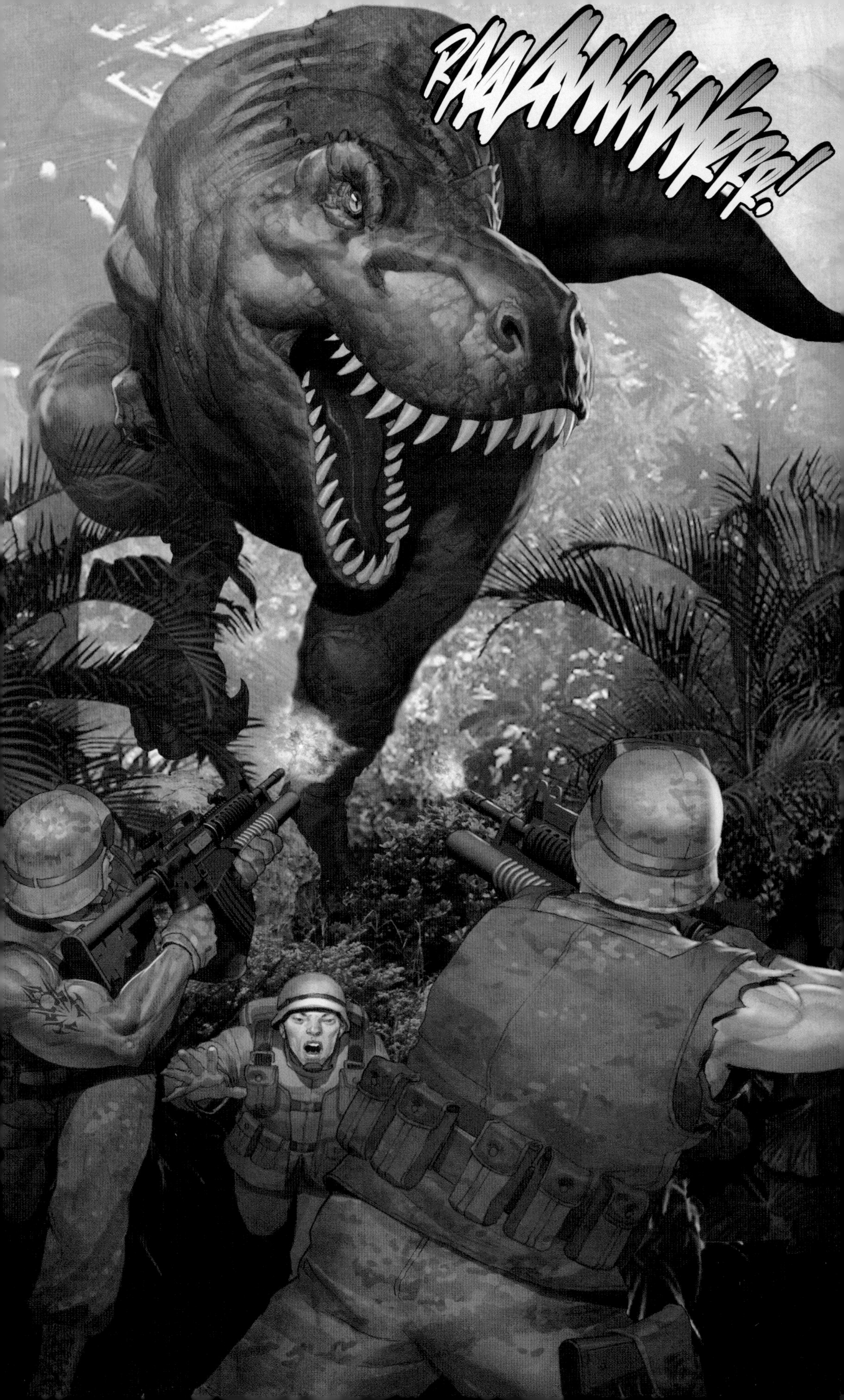

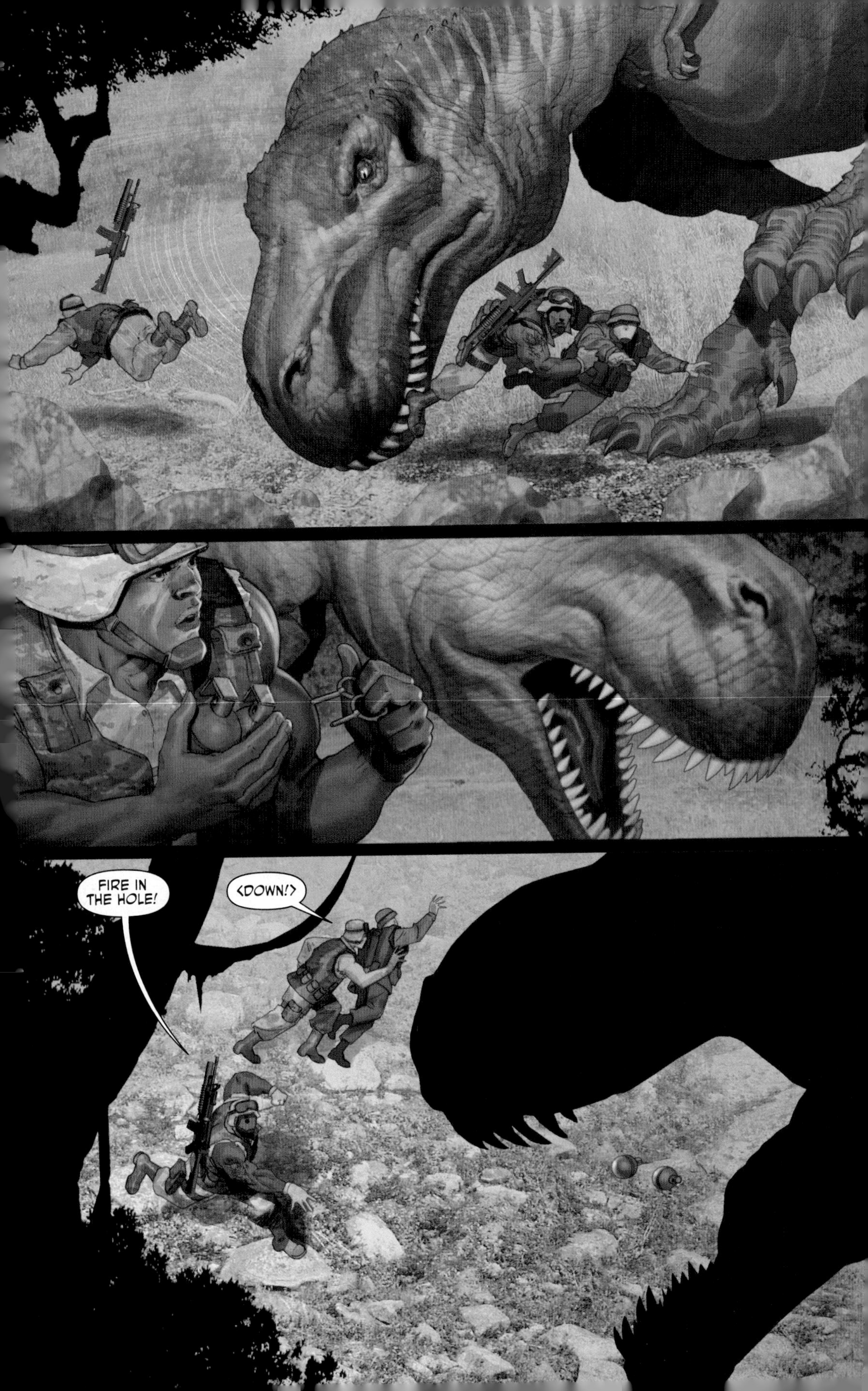
FIRE IN THE HOLE!
<DOWN!>

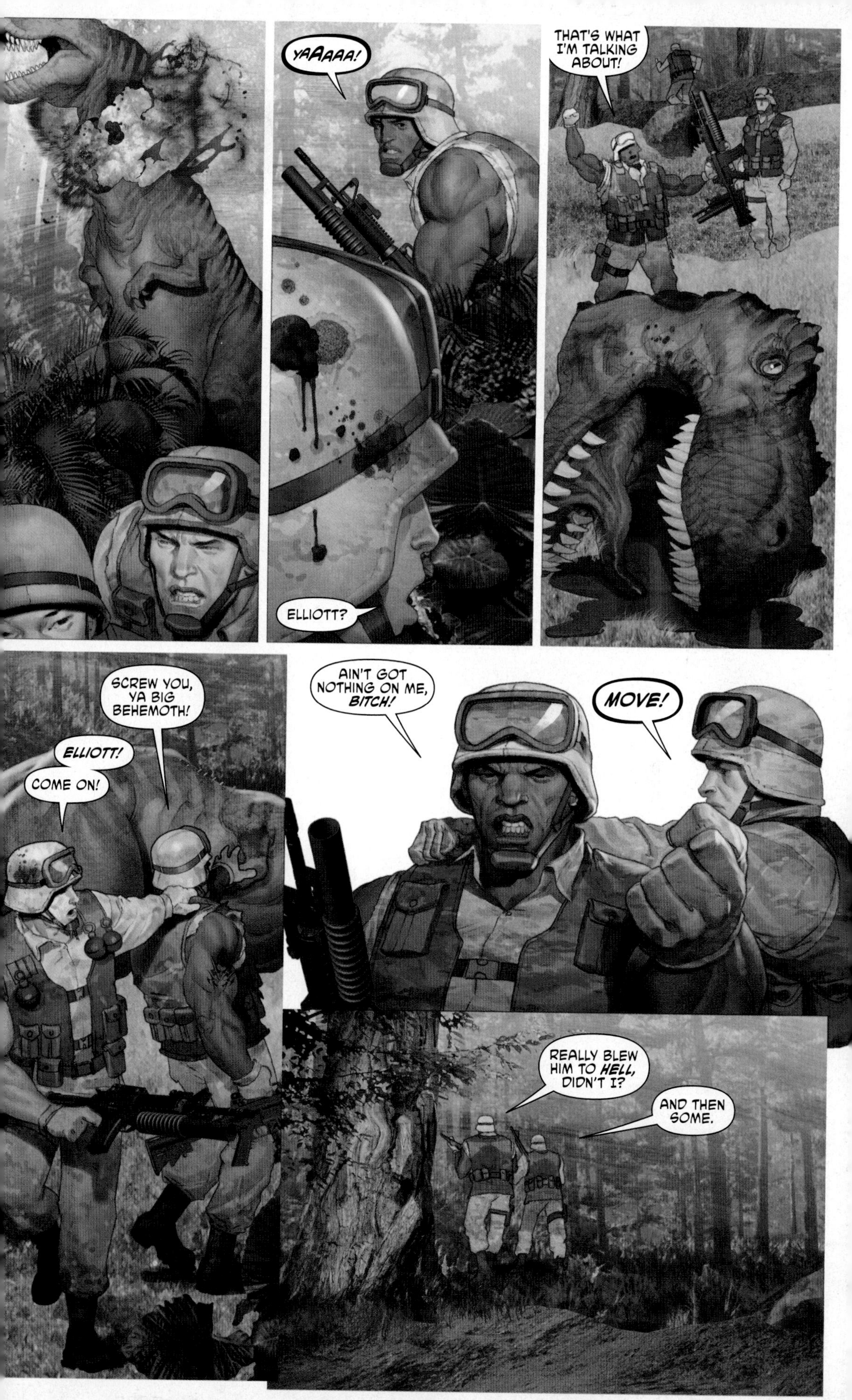
YAAAAA!
ELLIOTT?
THAT'S WHAT I'M TALKING ABOUT!
SCREW YOU, YA BIG BEHEMOTH!
ELLIOTT!
COME ON!
AIN'T GOT NOTHING ON ME, BITCH!
MOVE!
REALLY BLEW HIM TO HELL, DIDN'T I?
AND THEN SOME.

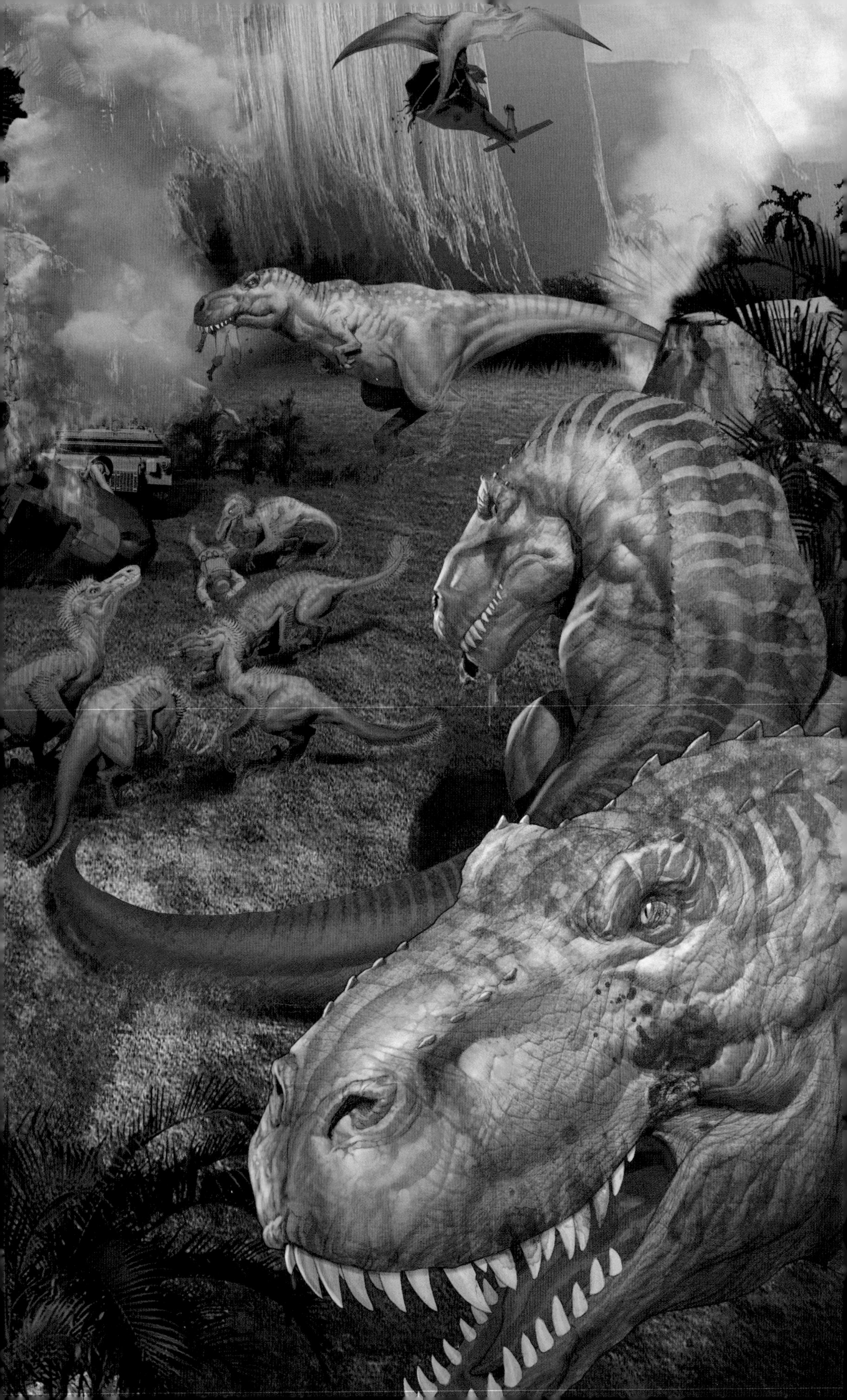

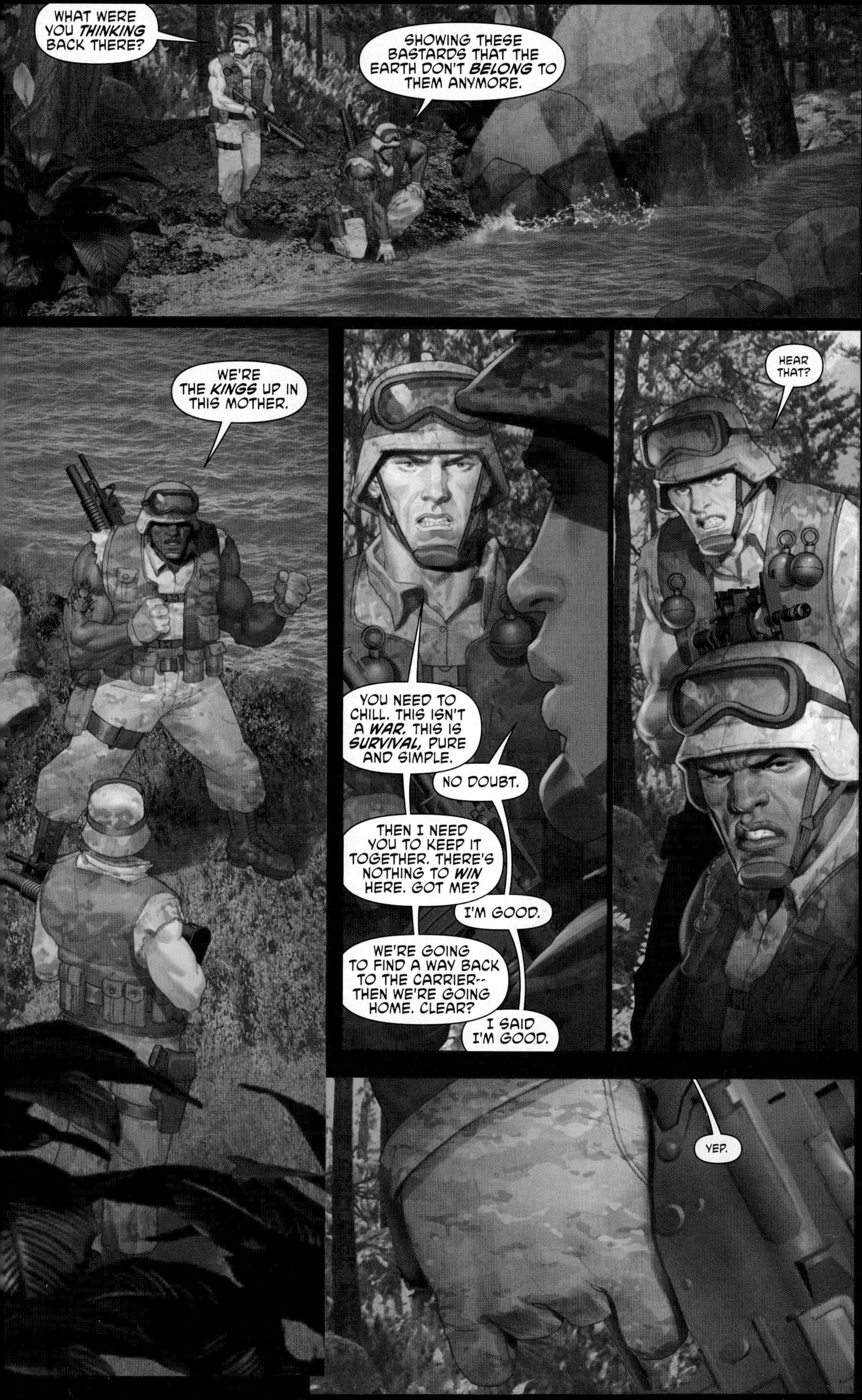

WHAT WERE YOU *THINKING* BACK THERE?
SHOWING THESE BASTARDS THAT THE EARTH DON'T *BELONG* TO THEM ANYMORE.
WE'RE THE *KINGS* UP IN THIS MOTHER.
YOU NEED TO CHILL. THIS ISN'T A *WAR.* THIS IS *SURVIVAL,* PURE AND SIMPLE.
NO DOUBT.
THEN I NEED YOU TO KEEP IT TOGETHER. THERE'S NOTHING TO *WIN* HERE. GOT ME?
I'M GOOD.
WE'RE GOING TO FIND A WAY BACK TO THE CARRIER-- THEN WE'RE GOING HOME. CLEAR?
I SAID I'M GOOD.
HEAR THAT?
YEP.

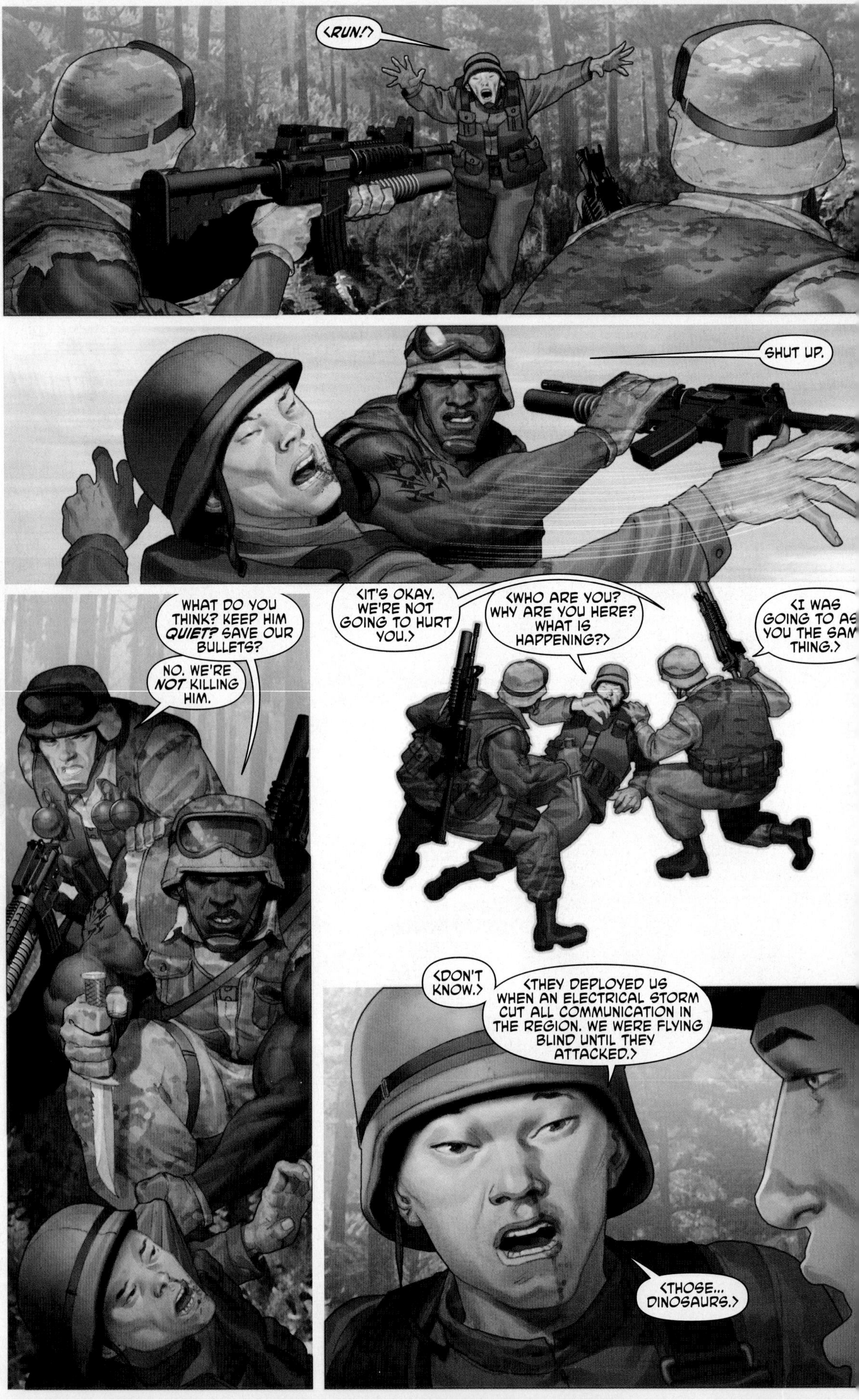
<RUN!>
SHUT UP.
WHAT DO YOU THINK? KEEP HIM QUIET? SAVE OUR BULLETS?
NO. WE'RE NOT KILLING HIM.
<IT'S OKAY. WE'RE NOT GOING TO HURT YOU.>
<WHO ARE YOU? WHY ARE YOU HERE? WHAT IS HAPPENING?>
<I WAS GOING TO AS YOU THE SAM THING.>
<DON'T KNOW.>
<THEY DEPLOYED US WHEN AN ELECTRICAL STORM CUT ALL COMMUNICATION IN THE REGION. WE WERE FLYING BLIND UNTIL THEY ATTACKED.>
<THOSE... DINOSAURS.>

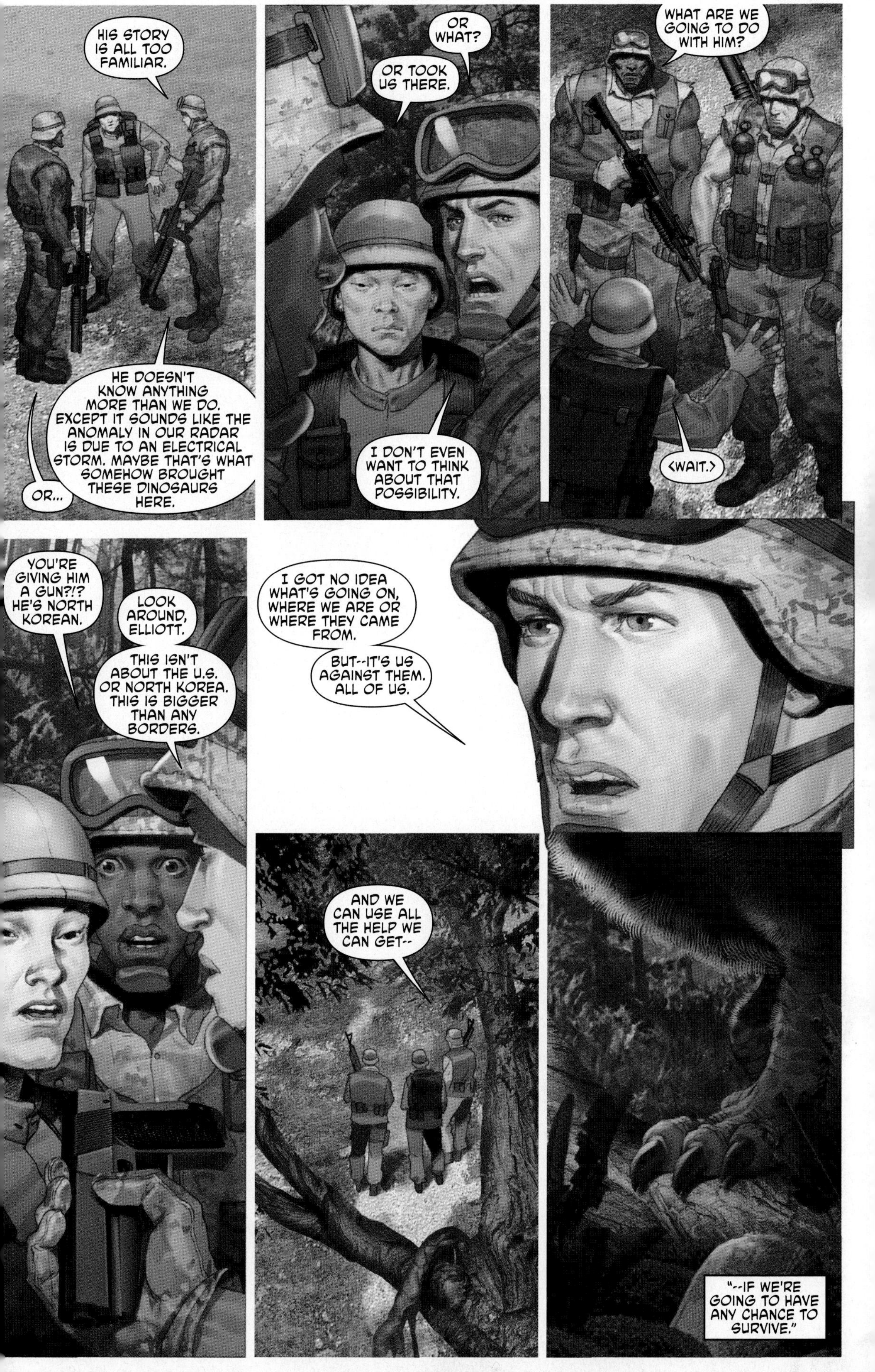
HIS STORY IS ALL TOO FAMILIAR.
HE DOESN'T KNOW ANYTHING MORE THAN WE DO. EXCEPT IT SOUNDS LIKE THE ANOMALY IN OUR RADAR IS DUE TO AN ELECTRICAL STORM. MAYBE THAT'S WHAT SOMEHOW BROUGHT THESE DINOSAURS HERE.
OR...
OR WHAT?
OR TOOK US THERE.
I DON'T EVEN WANT TO THINK ABOUT THAT POSSIBILITY.
WHAT ARE WE GOING TO DO WITH HIM?
<WAIT.>
YOU'RE GIVING HIM A GUN?!? HE'S NORTH KOREAN.
LOOK AROUND, ELLIOTT.
THIS ISN'T ABOUT THE U.S. OR NORTH KOREA. THIS IS BIGGER THAN ANY BORDERS.
I GOT NO IDEA WHAT'S GOING ON, WHERE WE ARE OR WHERE THEY CAME FROM.
BUT--IT'S US AGAINST THEM. ALL OF US.
AND WE CAN USE ALL THE HELP WE CAN GET--
"--IF WE'RE GOING TO HAVE ANY CHANCE TO SURVIVE."

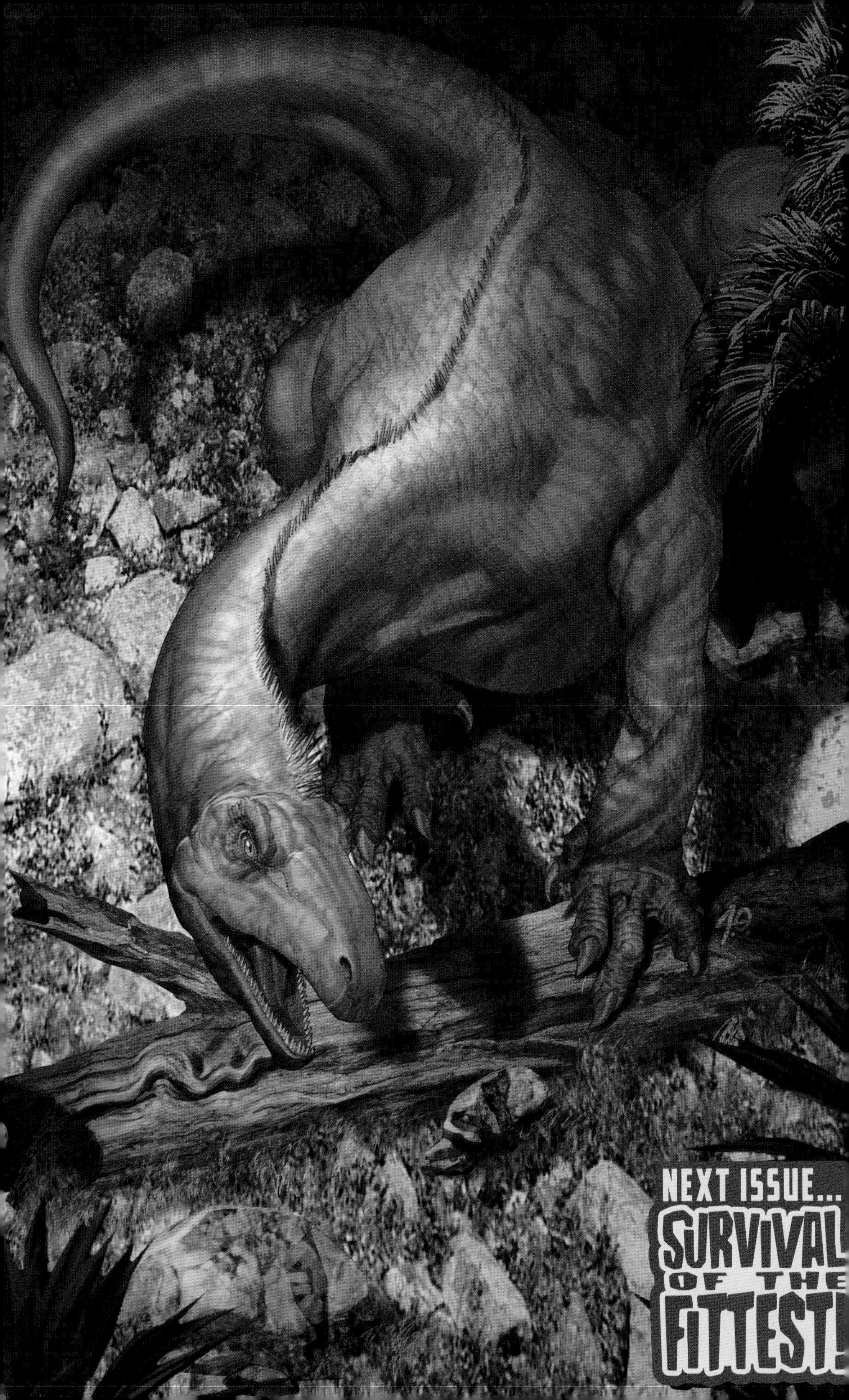
NEXT ISSUE...
SURVIVAL OF THE FITTEST!

OKAY. ALL CLEAR.

LET'S GO.

WHAT HAVE YOU GOT THERE?

HEY, BABE.

FOUND THIS LITTLE GUY WANDERING AROUND THE TRASH OUTSIDE THE MARKET.

NO COLLAR. NO TAGS. NO NOTHING.

NO WAY. MANGY THING. PROBABLY CRAWLING WITH GERMS.

AW, DON'T BE LIKE THAT, JACKIE. POOR GUY'S BEEN ON THE STREET FOR A WHILE. JUST NEEDS A GOOD BATH.

YOU THINK SO, *huh?*

GIVE HIM A CHANCE--

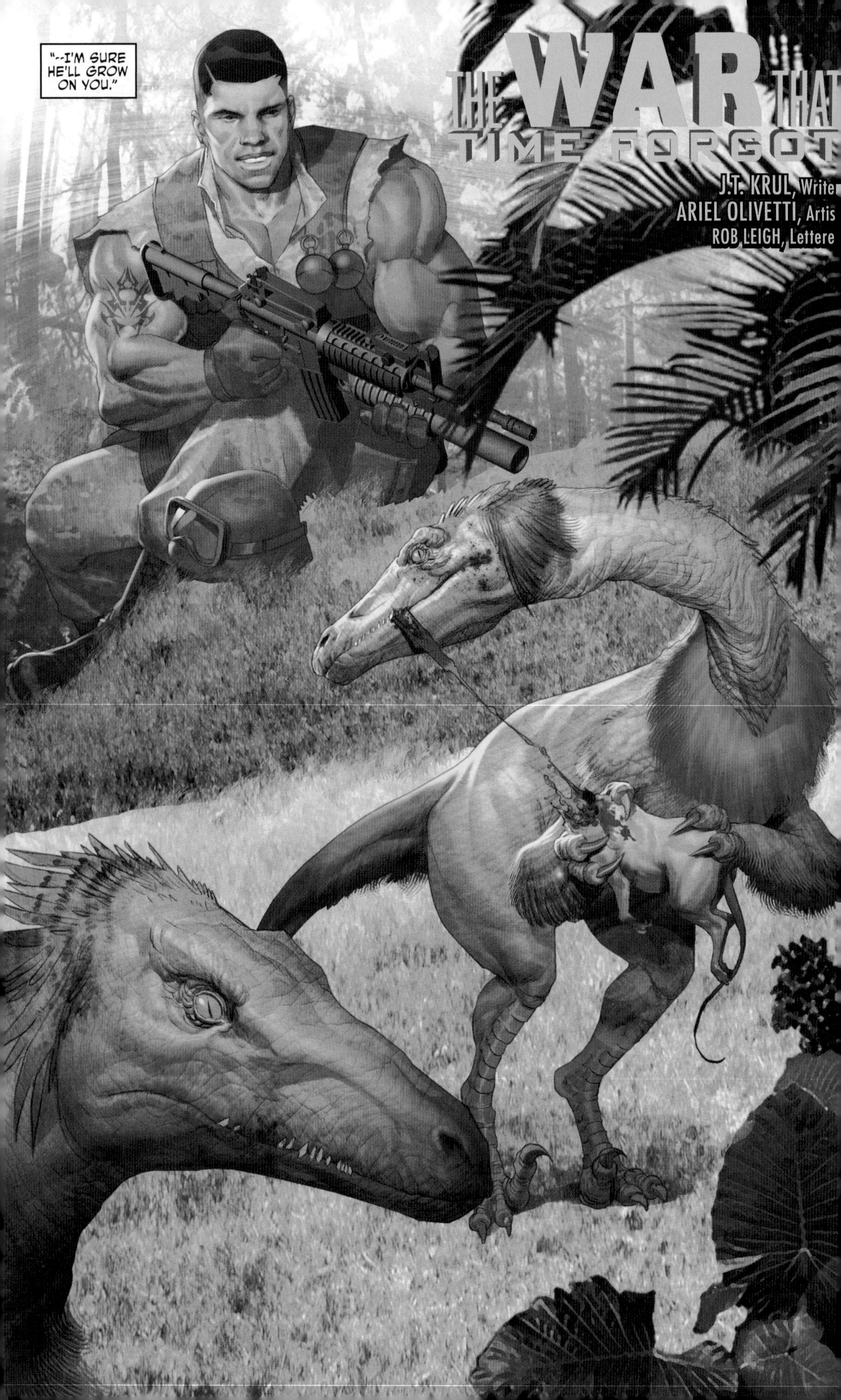
"--I'M SURE HE'LL GROW ON YOU."
THE WAR THAT TIME FORGOT
J.T. KRUL, Write
ARIEL OLIVETTI, Artis
ROB LEIGH, Lettere

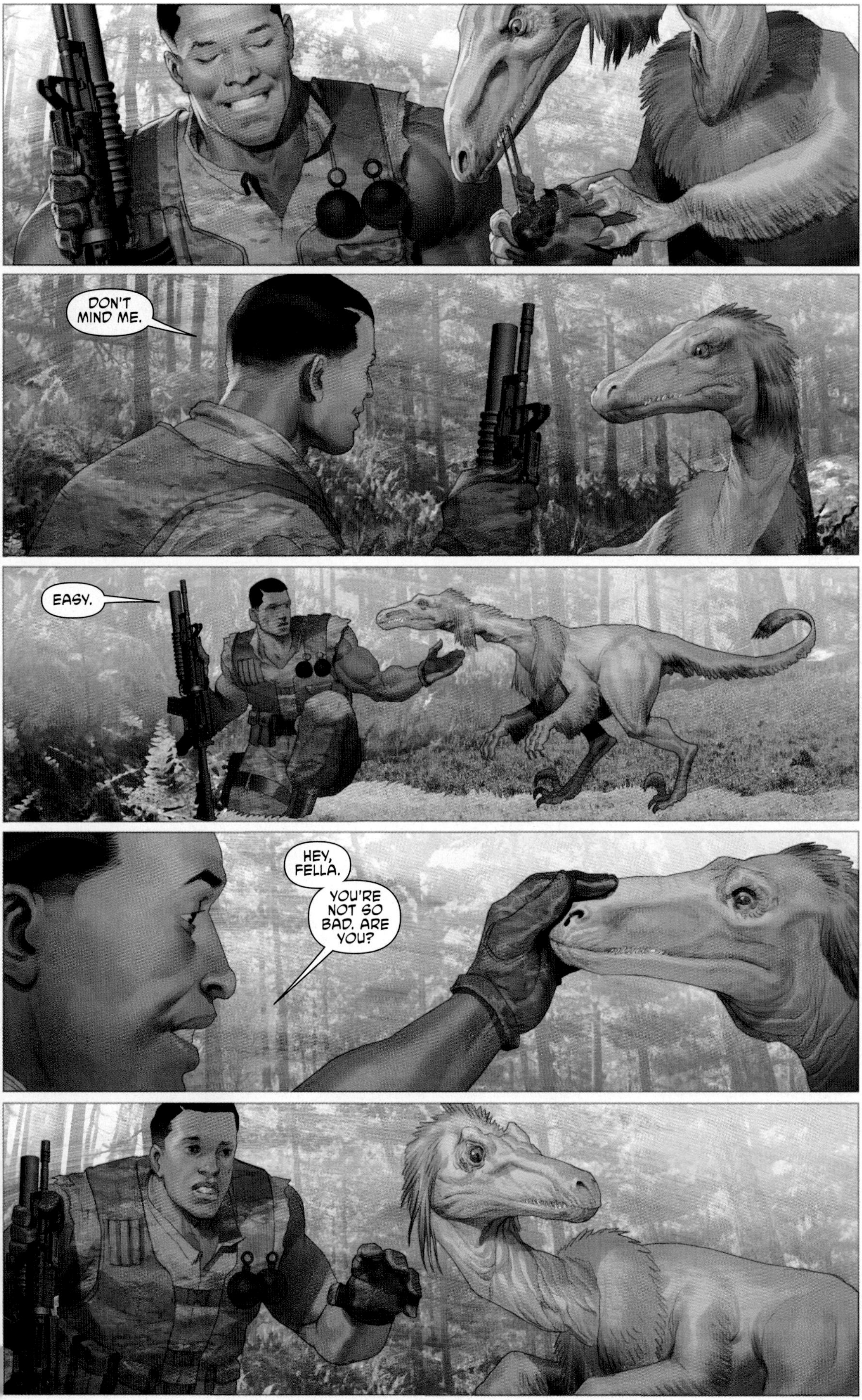
DON'T MIND ME.
EASY.
HEY, FELLA.
YOU'RE NOT SO BAD. ARE YOU?

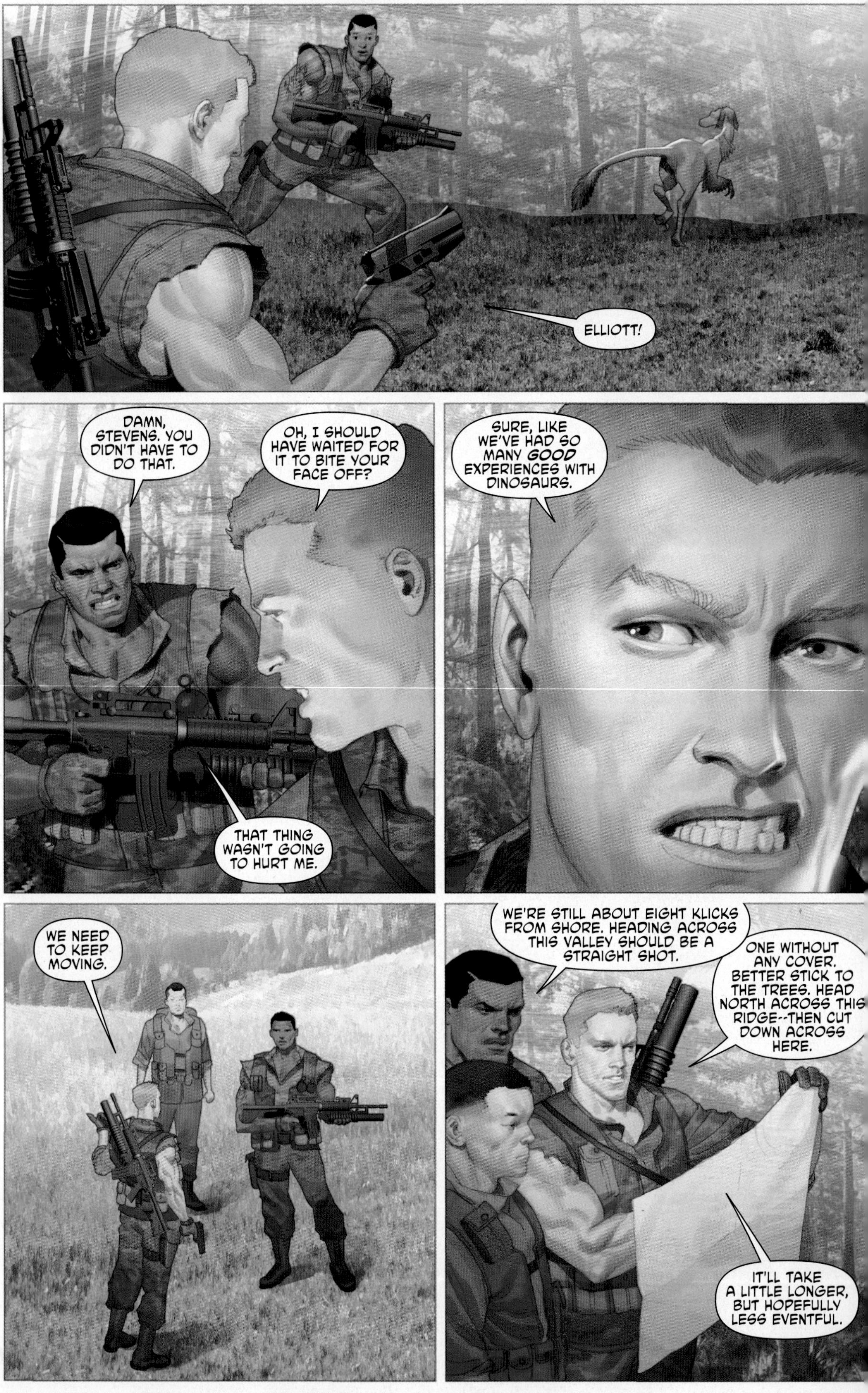
ELLIOTT!
DAMN, STEVENS. YOU DIDN'T HAVE TO DO THAT.
OH, I SHOULD HAVE WAITED FOR IT TO BITE YOUR FACE OFF?
THAT THING WASN'T GOING TO HURT ME.
SURE, LIKE WE'VE HAD SO MANY GOOD EXPERIENCES WITH DINOSAURS.
WE NEED TO KEEP MOVING.
WE'RE STILL ABOUT EIGHT KLICKS FROM SHORE. HEADING ACROSS THIS VALLEY SHOULD BE A STRAIGHT SHOT.
ONE WITHOUT ANY COVER. BETTER STICK TO THE TREES. HEAD NORTH ACROSS THIS RIDGE--THEN CUT DOWN ACROSS HERE.
IT'LL TAKE A LITTLE LONGER, BUT HOPEFULLY LESS EVENTFUL.

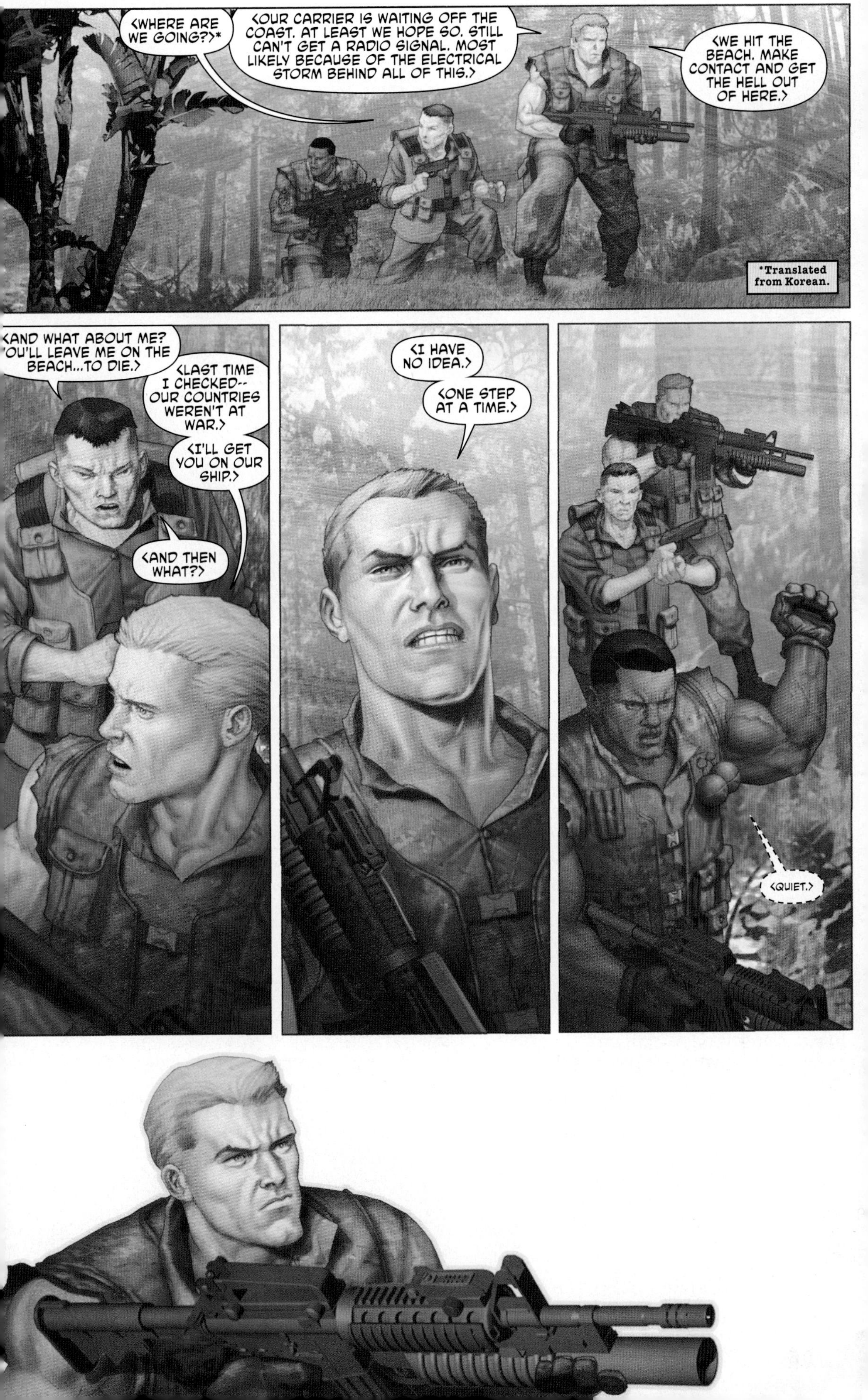
<WHERE ARE WE GOING?>*
<OUR CARRIER IS WAITING OFF THE COAST. AT LEAST WE HOPE SO. STILL CAN'T GET A RADIO SIGNAL. MOST LIKELY BECAUSE OF THE ELECTRICAL STORM BEHIND ALL OF THIS.>
<WE HIT THE BEACH. MAKE CONTACT AND GET THE HELL OUT OF HERE.>
*Translated from Korean.
<AND WHAT ABOUT ME? 'OU'LL LEAVE ME ON THE BEACH...TO DIE.>
<LAST TIME I CHECKED-- OUR COUNTRIES WEREN'T AT WAR.>
<I'LL GET YOU ON OUR SHIP.>
<AND THEN WHAT?>
<I HAVE NO IDEA.>
<ONE STEP AT A TIME.>
<QUIET.>

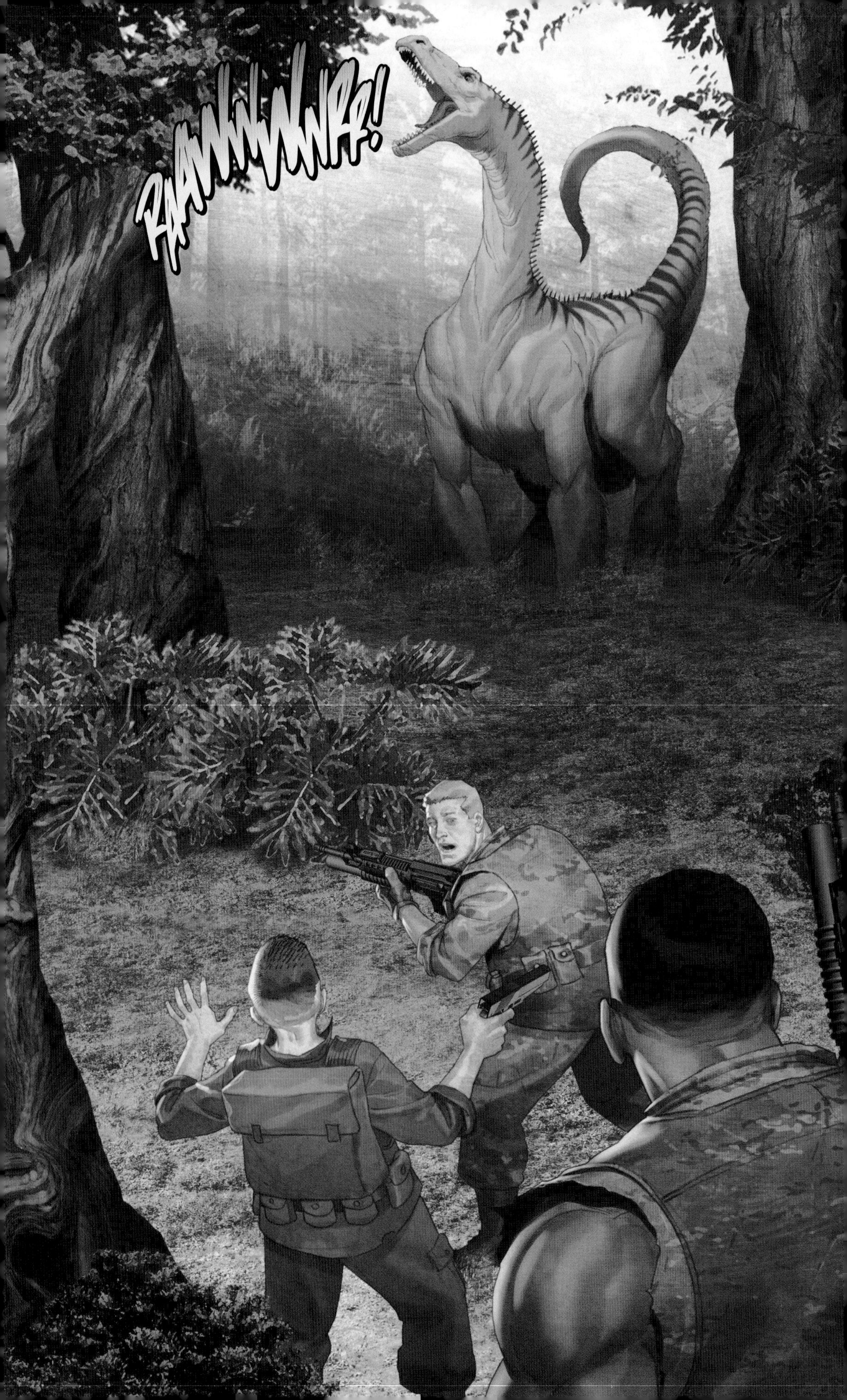
RRAWWWWWRR!

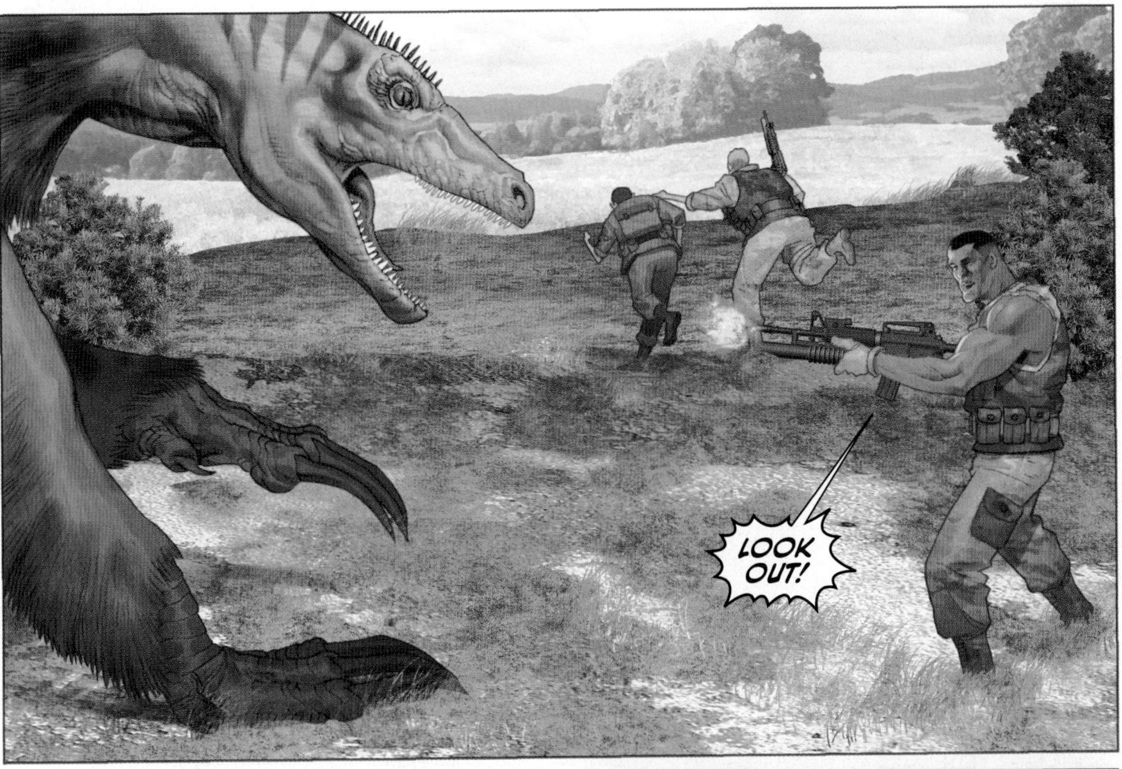
LOOK OUT!

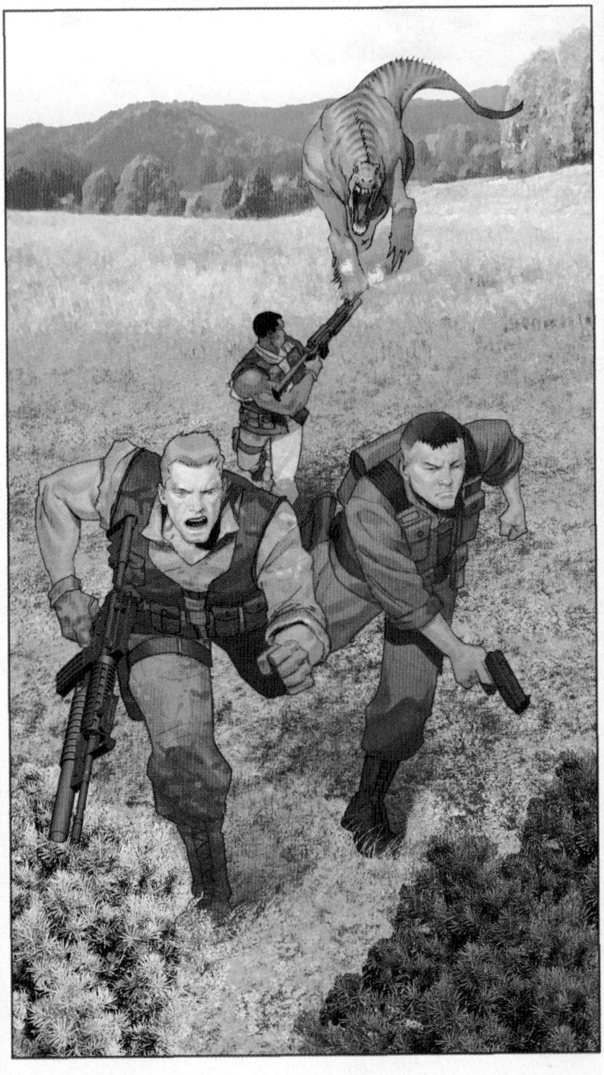

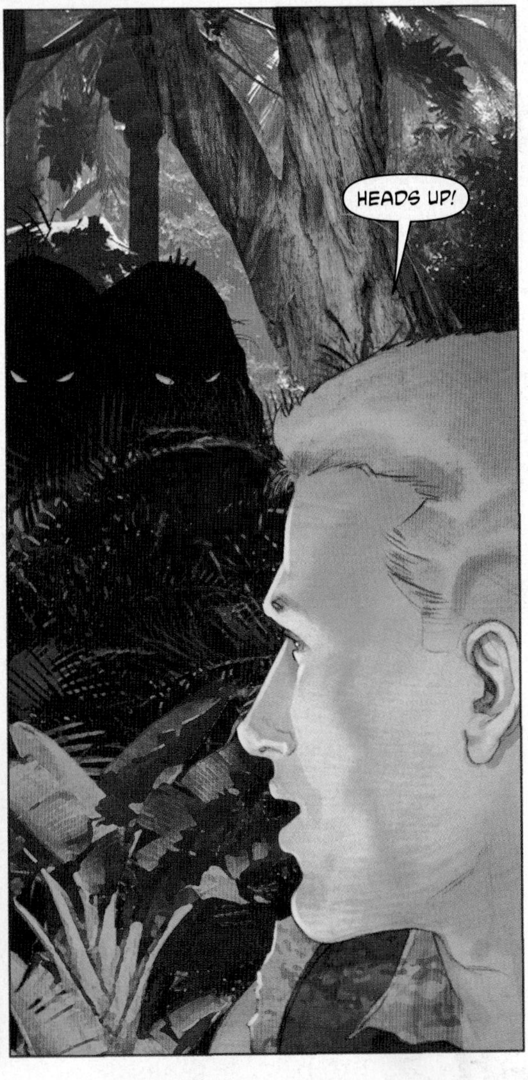
HEADS UP!

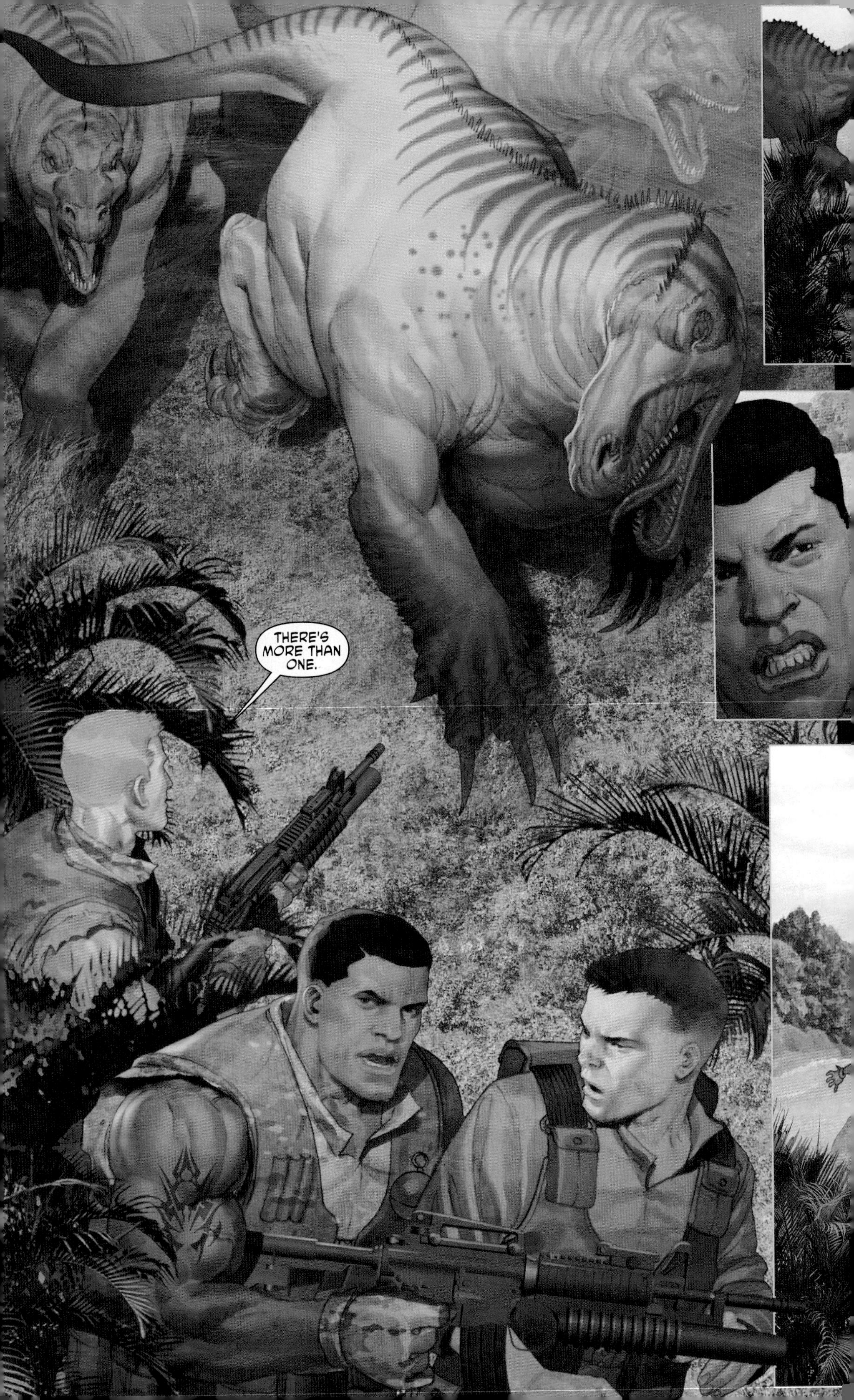
THERE'S MORE THAN ONE.

YOU GOT ANY MORE GRENADES?

WANT ME TO TAKE HIM OUT THE WAY I BROUGHT THE T. REX DOWN?

WORKED, DIDN'T IT?

YOU BETTER HAUL ASS.

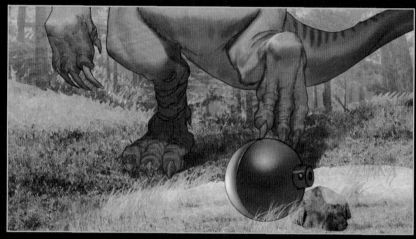

WHOOOM

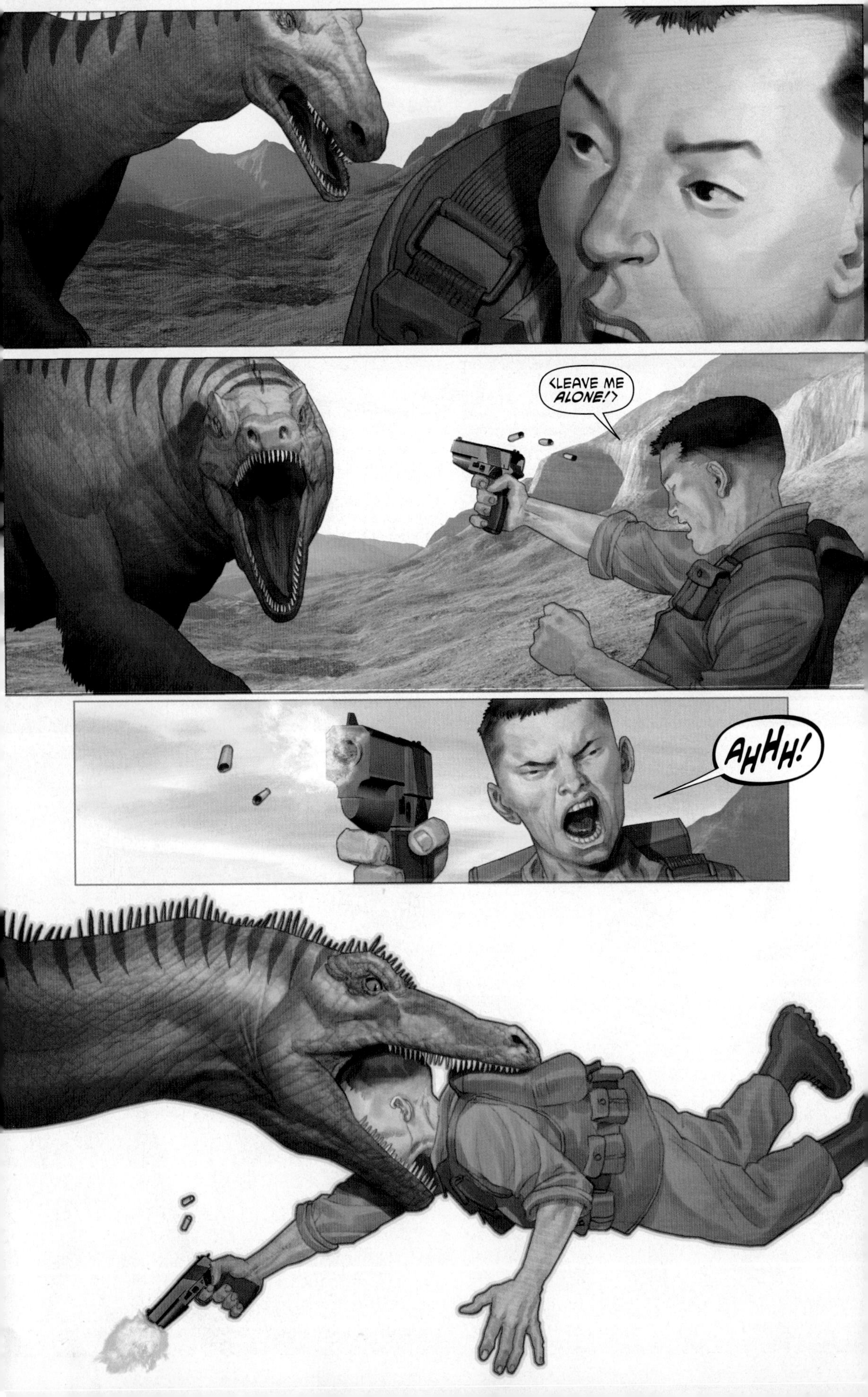
<LEAVE ME ALONE!>
AHHH!

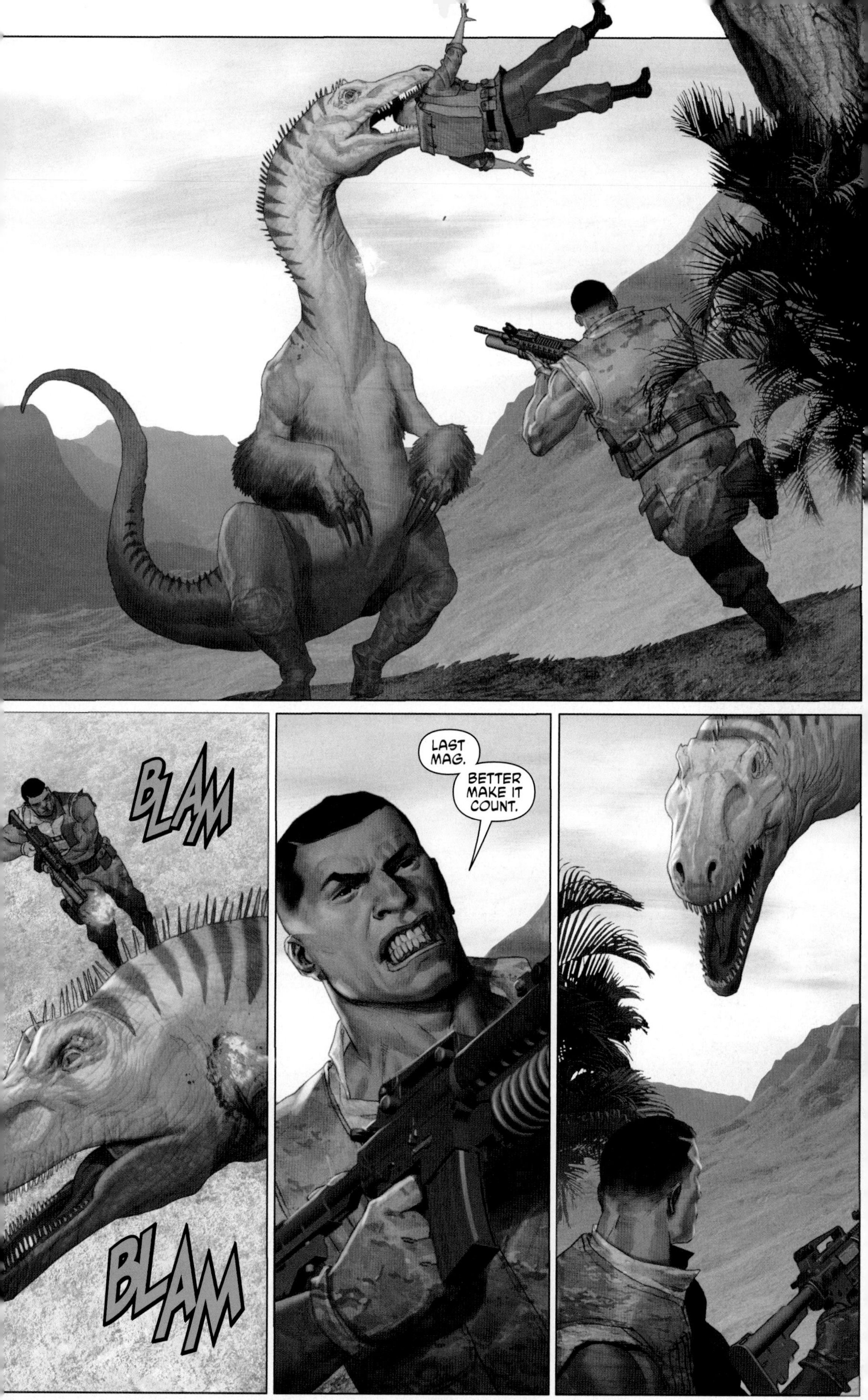
BLAM
BLAM
LAST MAG.
BETTER MAKE IT COUNT.

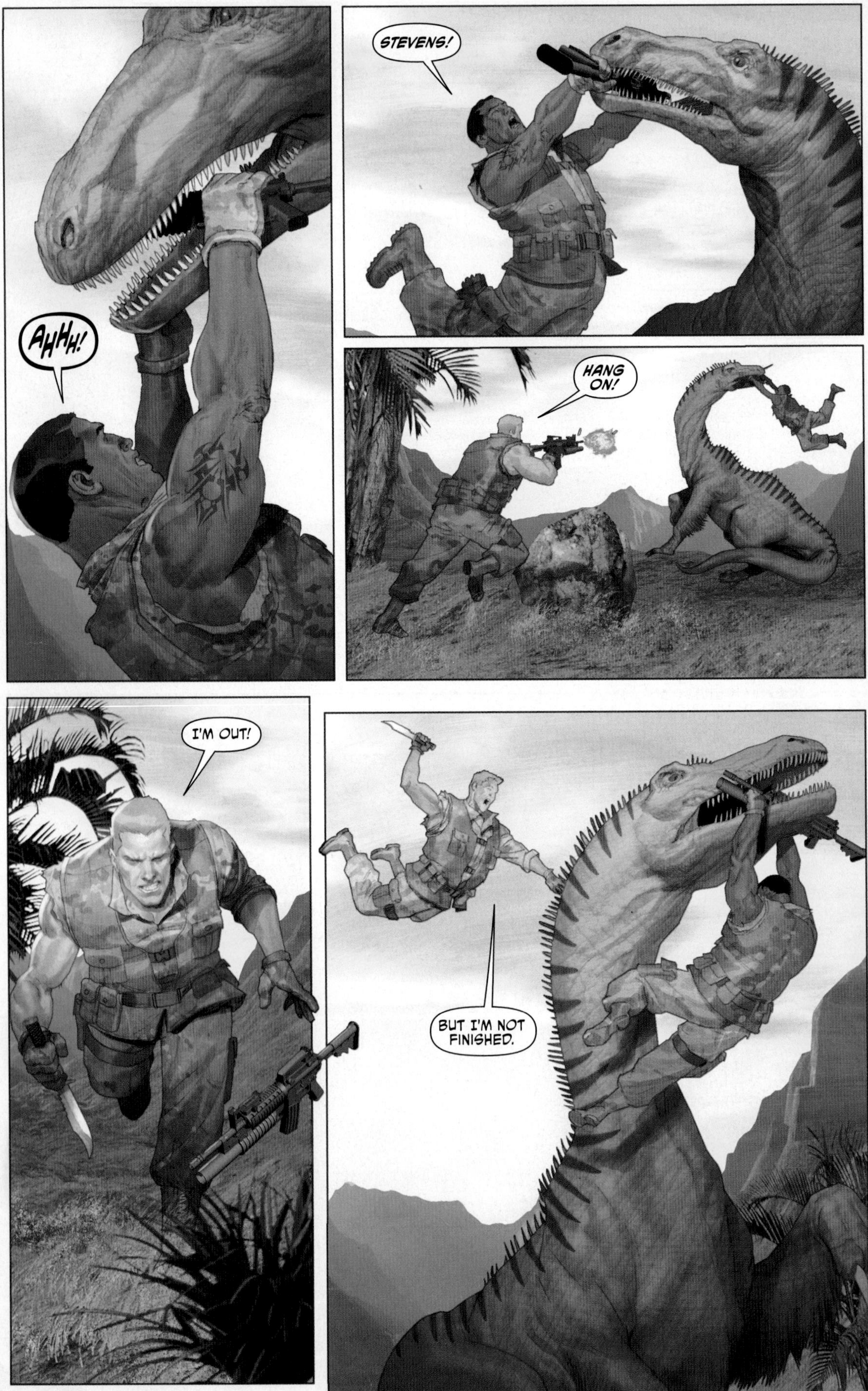
AHHH!
STEVENS!
HANG ON!
I'M OUT!
BUT I'M NOT FINISHED.

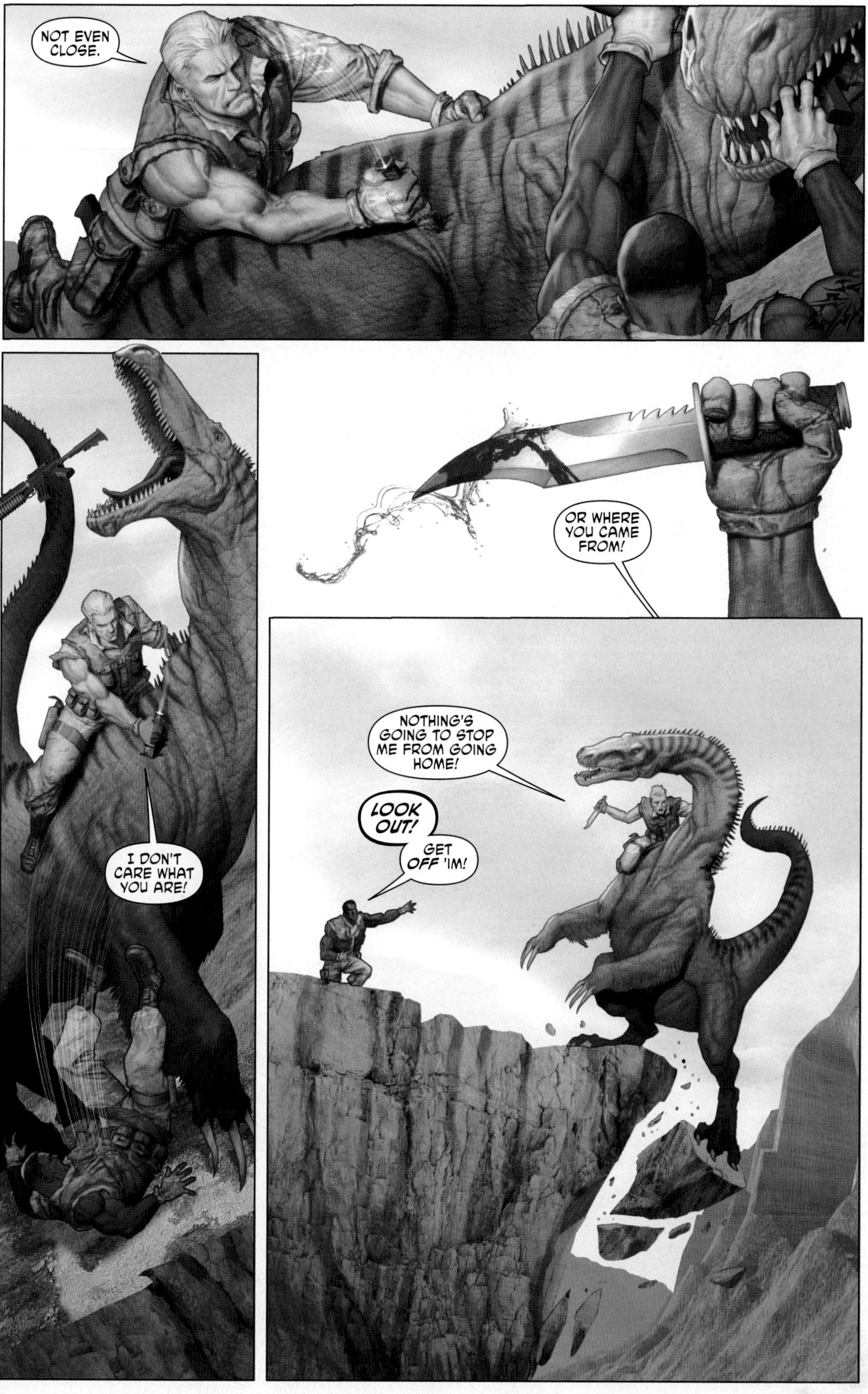
NOT EVEN CLOSE.
I DON'T CARE WHAT YOU ARE!
OR WHERE YOU CAME FROM!
NOTHING'S GOING TO STOP ME FROM GOING HOME!
LOOK OUT!
GET OFF 'IM!

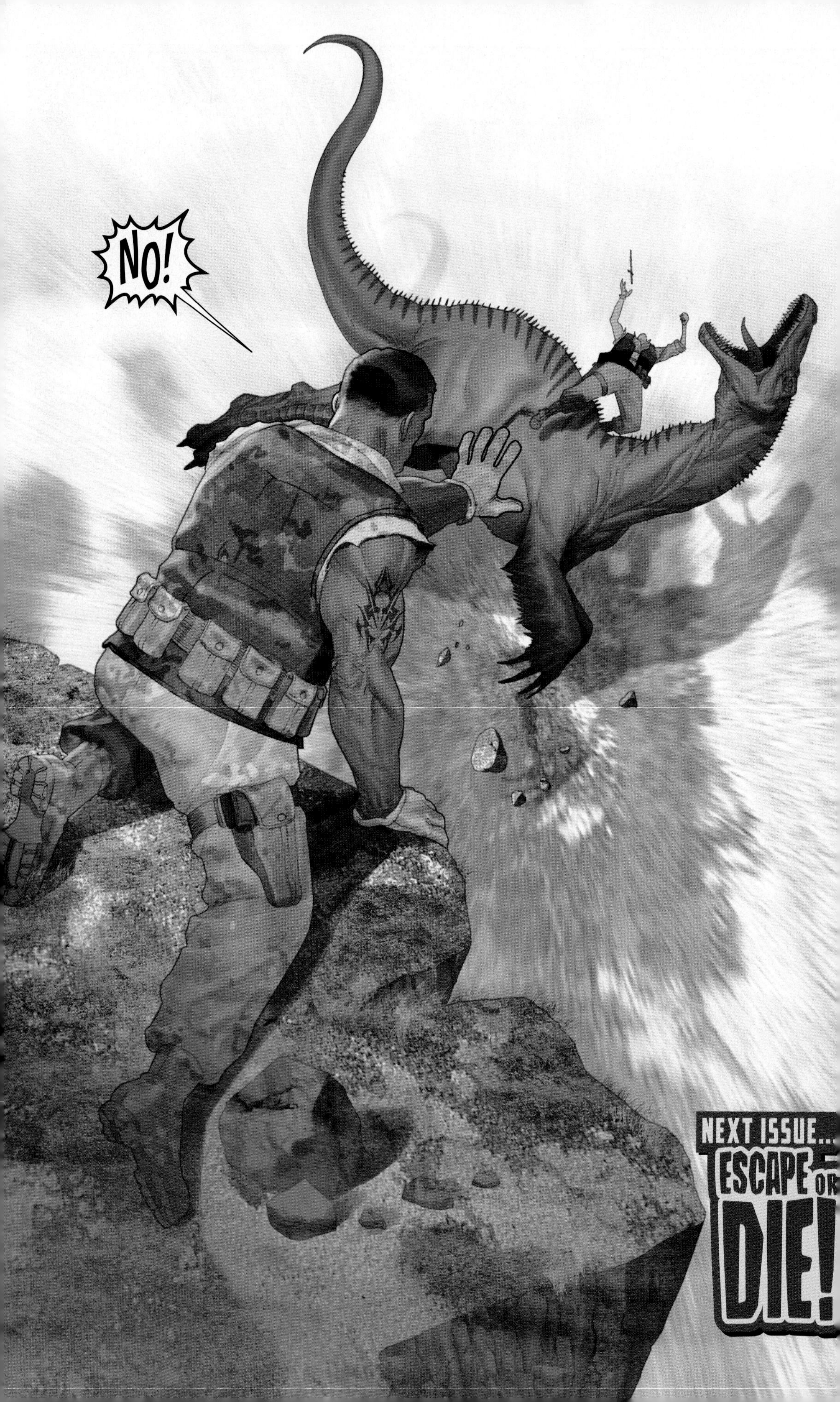
NO!
NEXT ISSUE...
ESCAPE OR DIE!

SORRY ABOUT THAT.

CAN'T BLAME YOURSELF.

SEEMS LIKE EVERY TIME WE HIT A BAR, THERE'S ALWAYS SOME JACKASS LOOKING TO PROVE HIMSELF--TAKE ON THE BIGGEST GUY IN THE ROOM.

IT'S YOUR GENES, ELLIOTT.

GUESS I COULD LAY OFF THE GYM FOR A BIT. TRY TO SLOUCH MORE.

SCREW THAT. IT'S THEIR PROBLEM.

STILL. NOT THE KIND OF QUIET NIGHT YOU PROMISED ASHLEY, I BET.

SHE'LL UNDERSTAND. SHE ALWAYS DOES. THAT'S WHY I MARRIED HER.

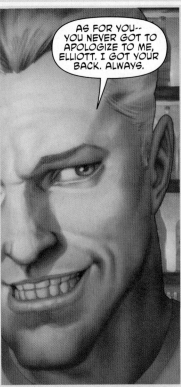

AS FOR YOU-- YOU NEVER GOT TO APOLOGIZE TO ME, ELLIOTT. I GOT YOUR BACK. ALWAYS.

DITTO, BROTHER.

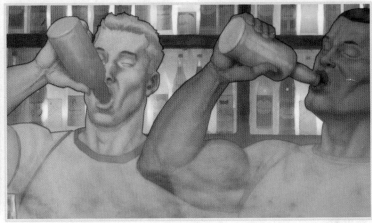

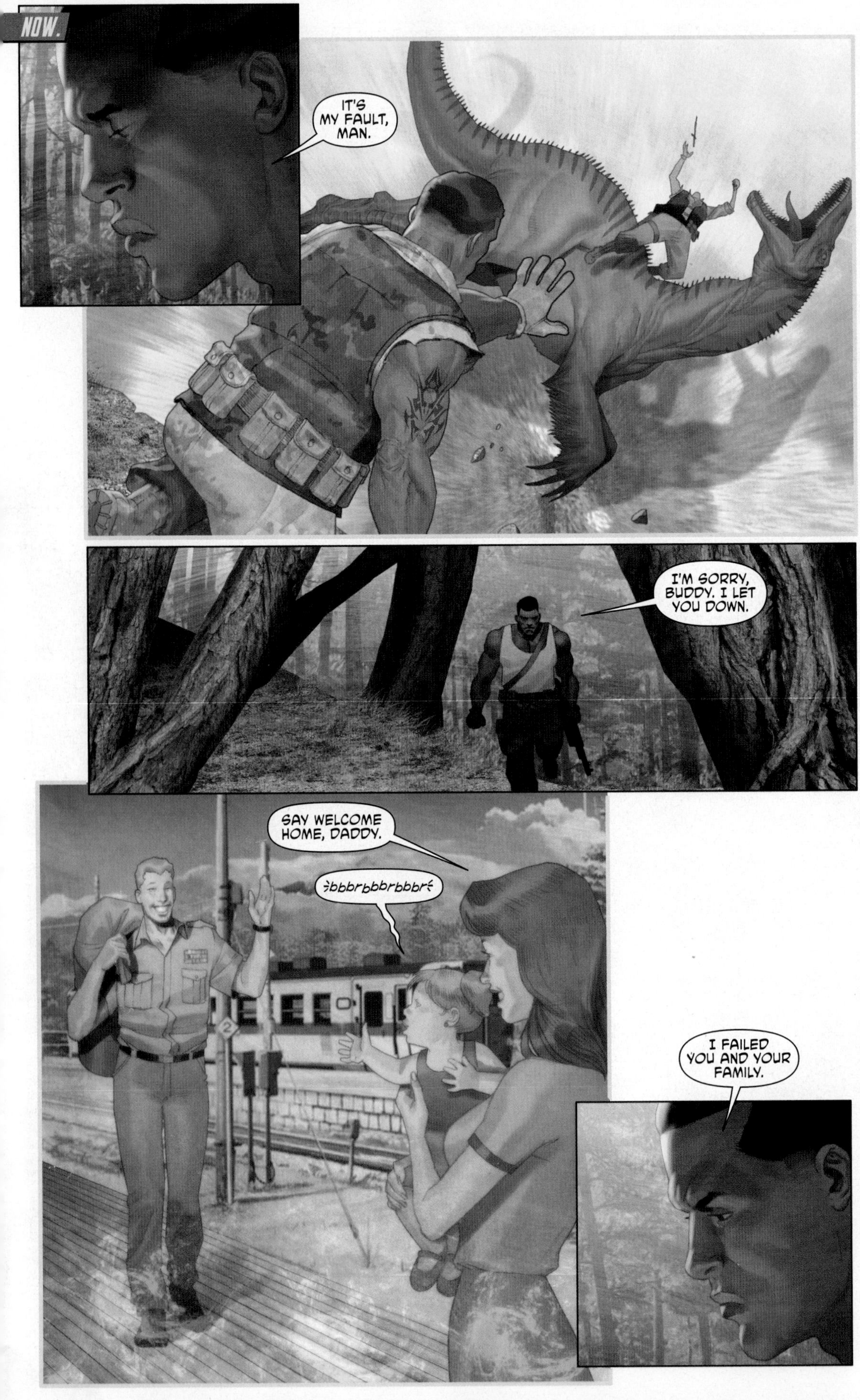
NOW.
IT'S MY FAULT, MAN.
I'M SORRY, BUDDY. I LET YOU DOWN.
SAY WELCOME HOME, DADDY.
bbbrbbbrbbbr
I FAILED YOU AND YOUR FAMILY.

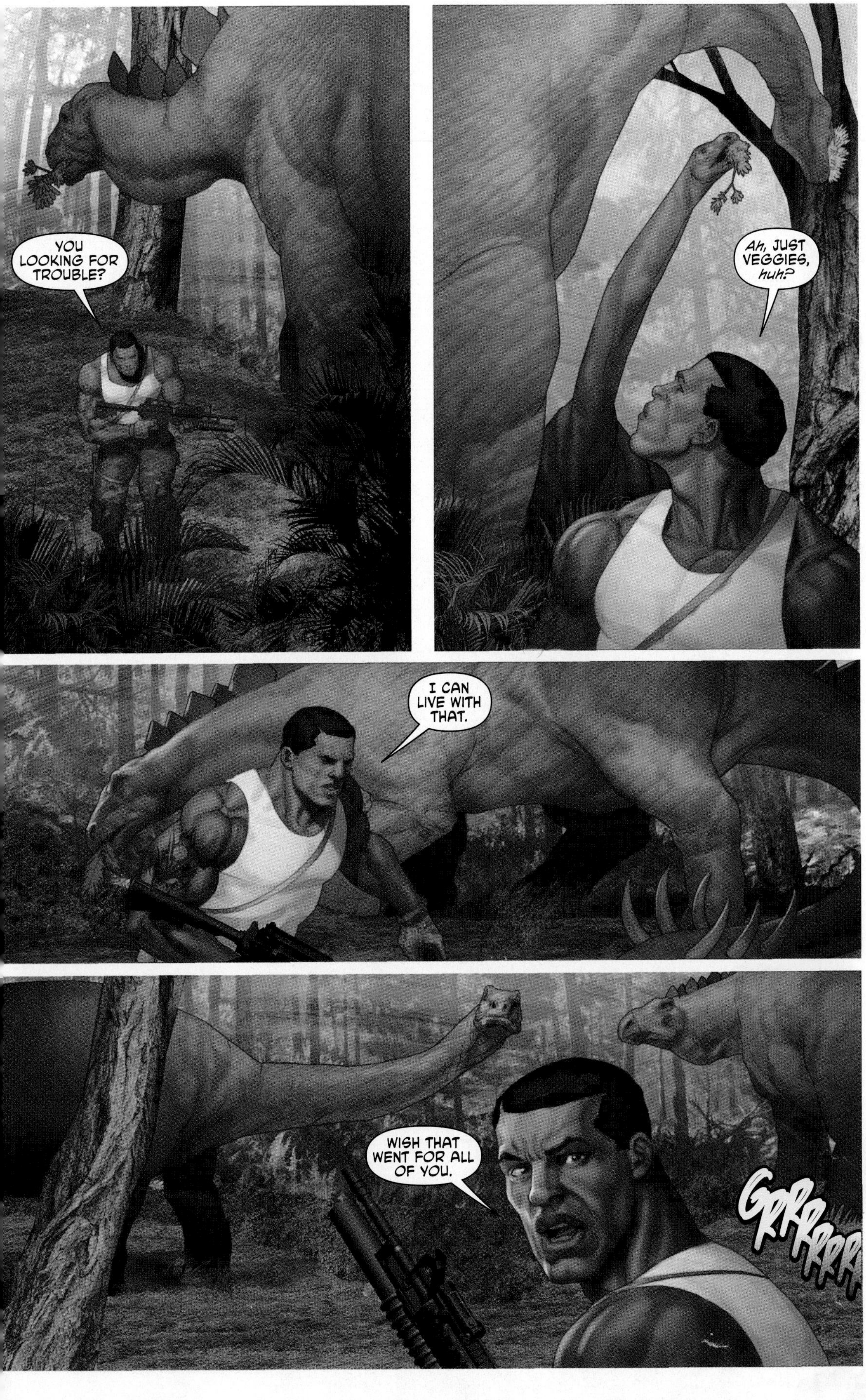
YOU LOOKING FOR TROUBLE?
Ah, JUST VEGGIES, huh?
I CAN LIVE WITH THAT.
WISH THAT WENT FOR ALL OF YOU.
GRRRRRR

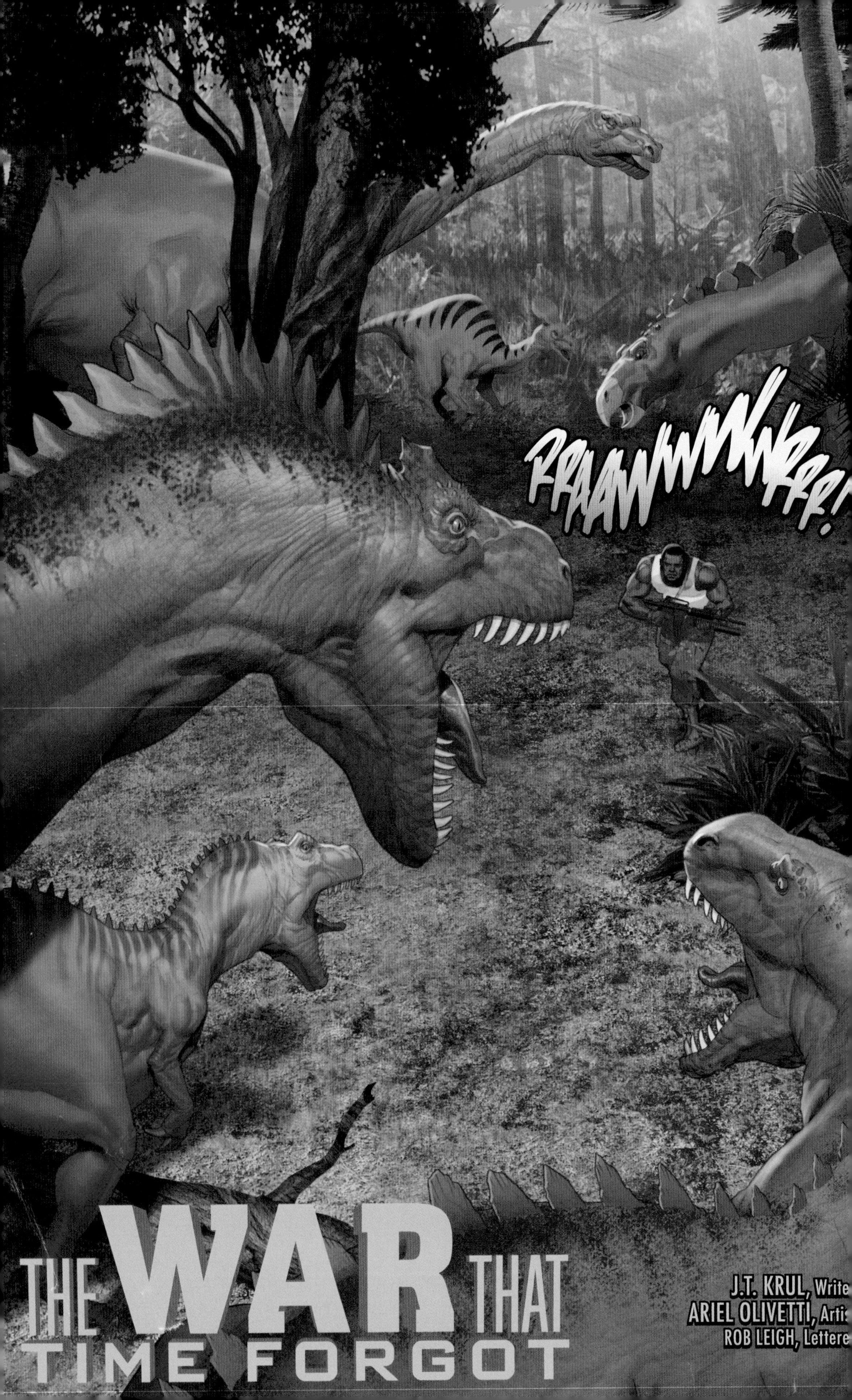
RRAAWWWWKRRR!
THE WAR THAT TIME FORGOT
J.T. KRUL, Write
ARIEL OLIVETTI, Arti
ROB LEIGH, Lettere

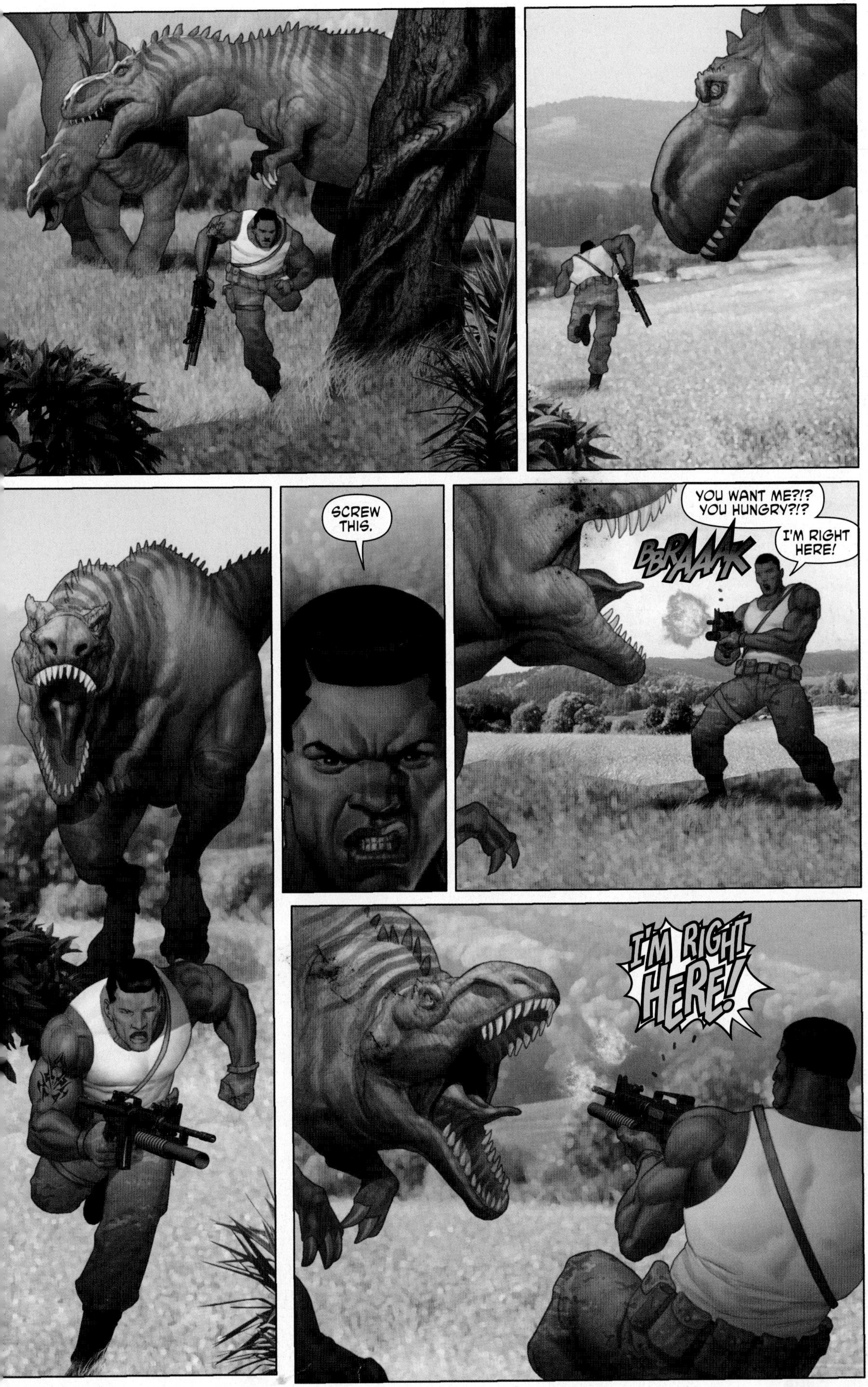
SCREW THIS.
YOU WANT ME?!? YOU HUNGRY?!?
BBRAAAK
I'M RIGHT HERE!
I'M RIGHT HERE!

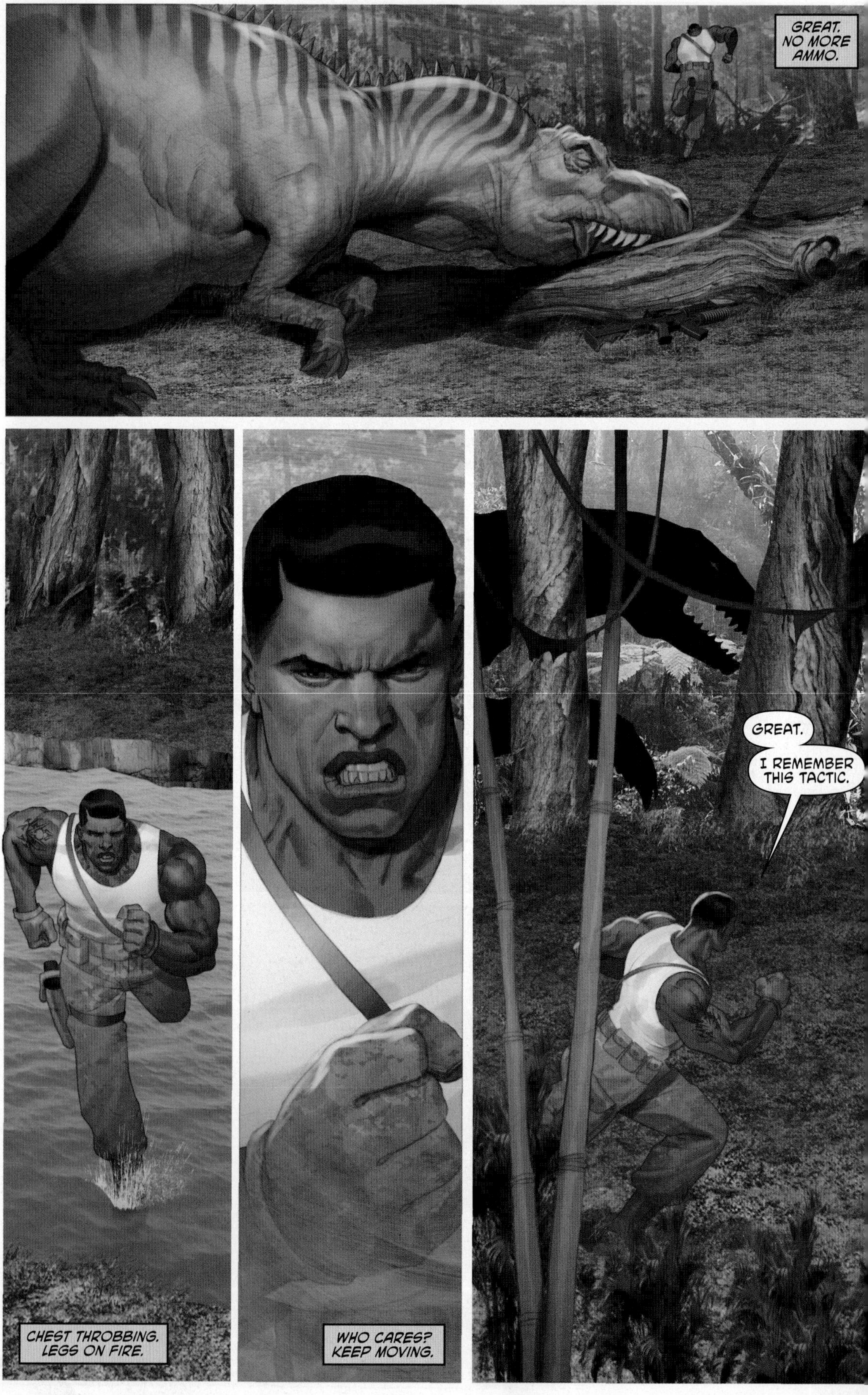
GREAT. NO MORE AMMO.
CHEST THROBBING. LEGS ON FIRE.
WHO CARES? KEEP MOVING.
GREAT.
I REMEMBER THIS TACTIC.

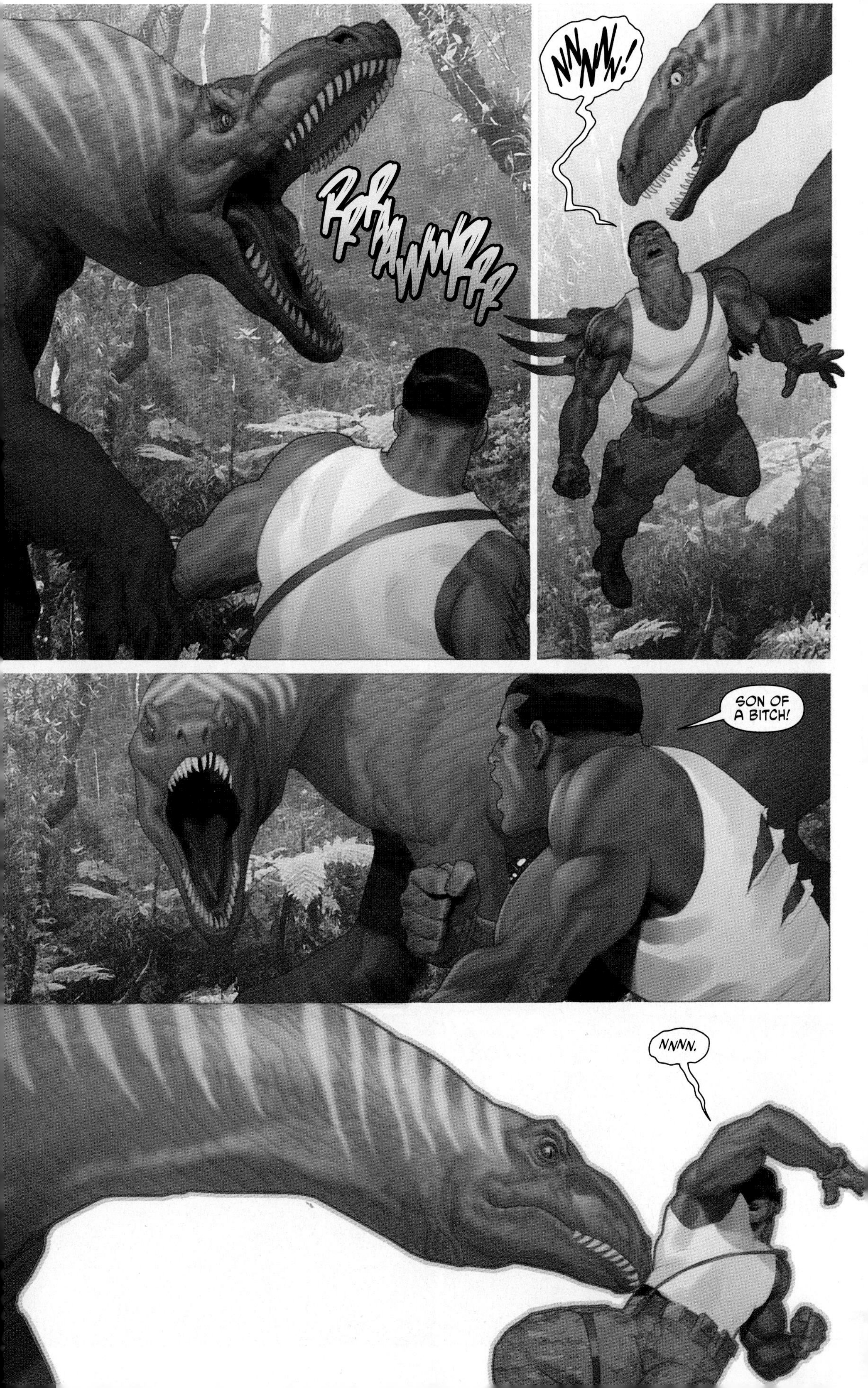
RRRAWWRRR
NNNNN!
SON OF A BITCH!
NNNN.

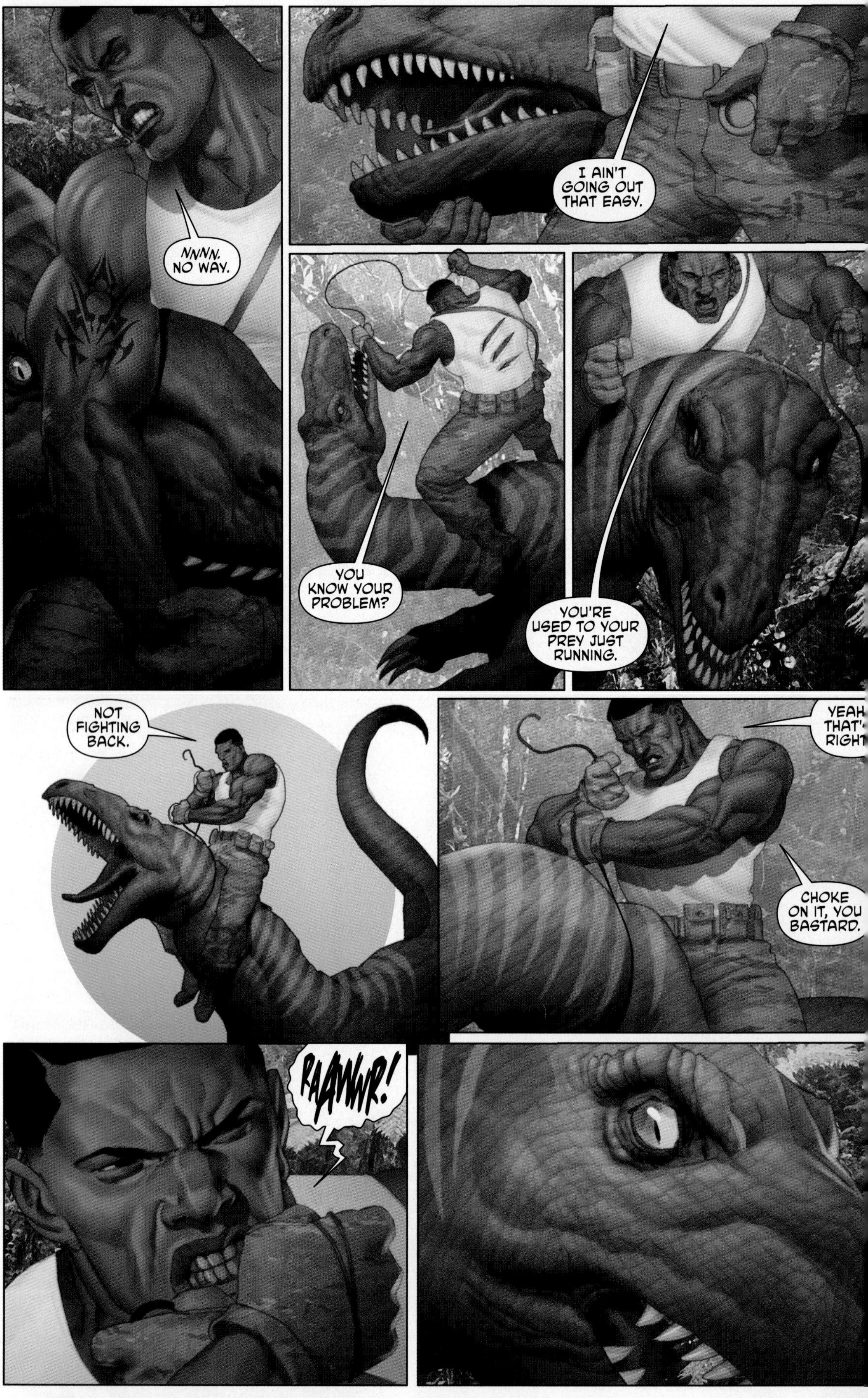
NNNN.
NO WAY.
I AIN'T
GOING OUT
THAT EASY.
YOU
KNOW YOUR
PROBLEM?
YOU'RE
USED TO YOUR
PREY JUST
RUNNING.
NOT
FIGHTING
BACK.
CHOKE
ON IT, YOU
BASTARD.
RAAWWR!

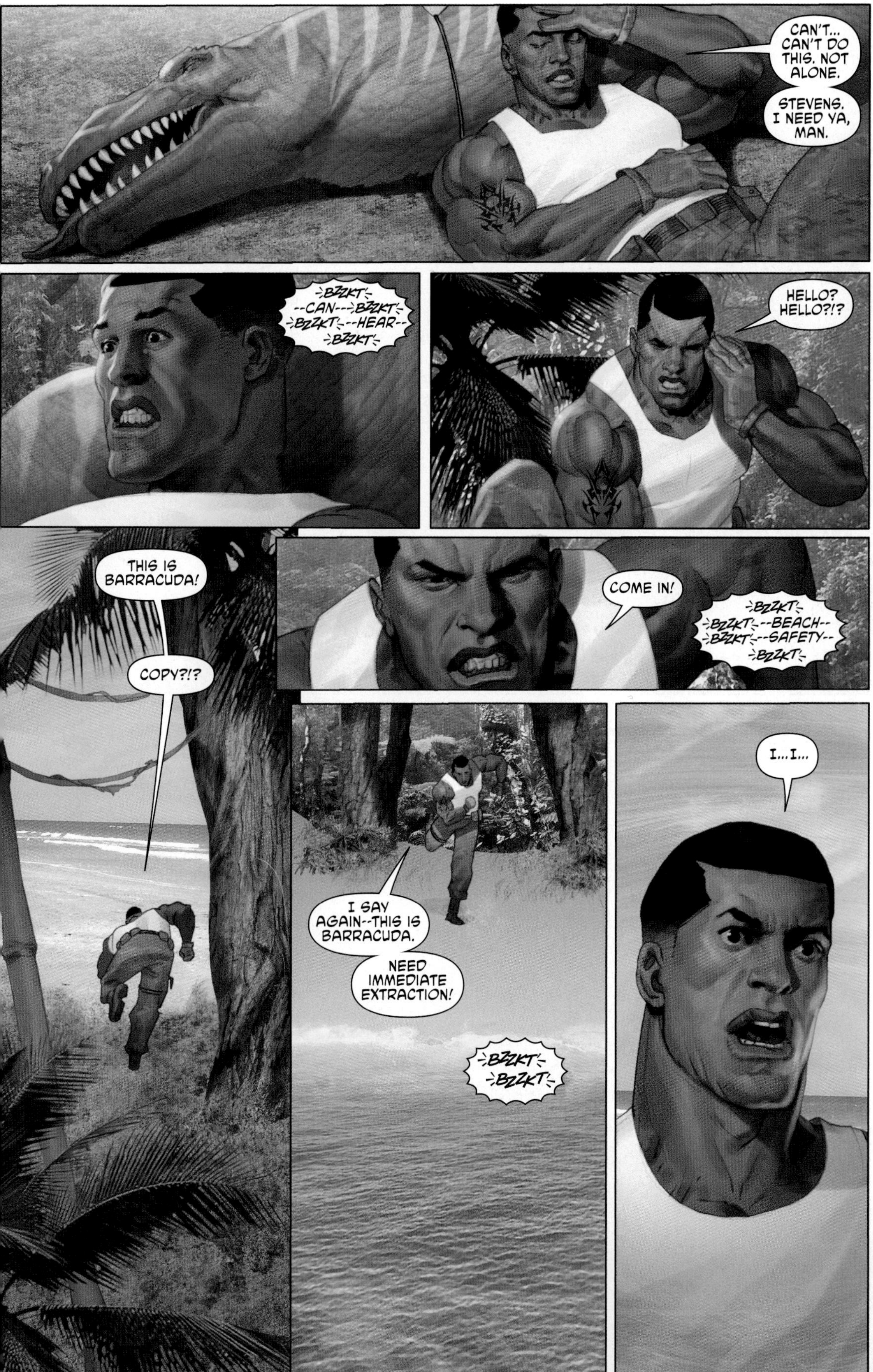
CAN'T... CAN'T DO THIS. NOT ALONE.
STEVENS. I NEED YA, MAN.
-BZZKT- --CAN-- -BZZKT- -BZZKT- --HEAR-- -BZZKT-
HELLO? HELLO?!?
THIS IS BARRACUDA!
COPY?!?
COME IN!
-BZZKT- -BZZKT- --BEACH-- -BZZKT- --SAFETY-- -BZZKT-
I SAY AGAIN--THIS IS BARRACUDA.
NEED IMMEDIATE EXTRACTION!
-BZZKT- -BZZKT-
I...I...

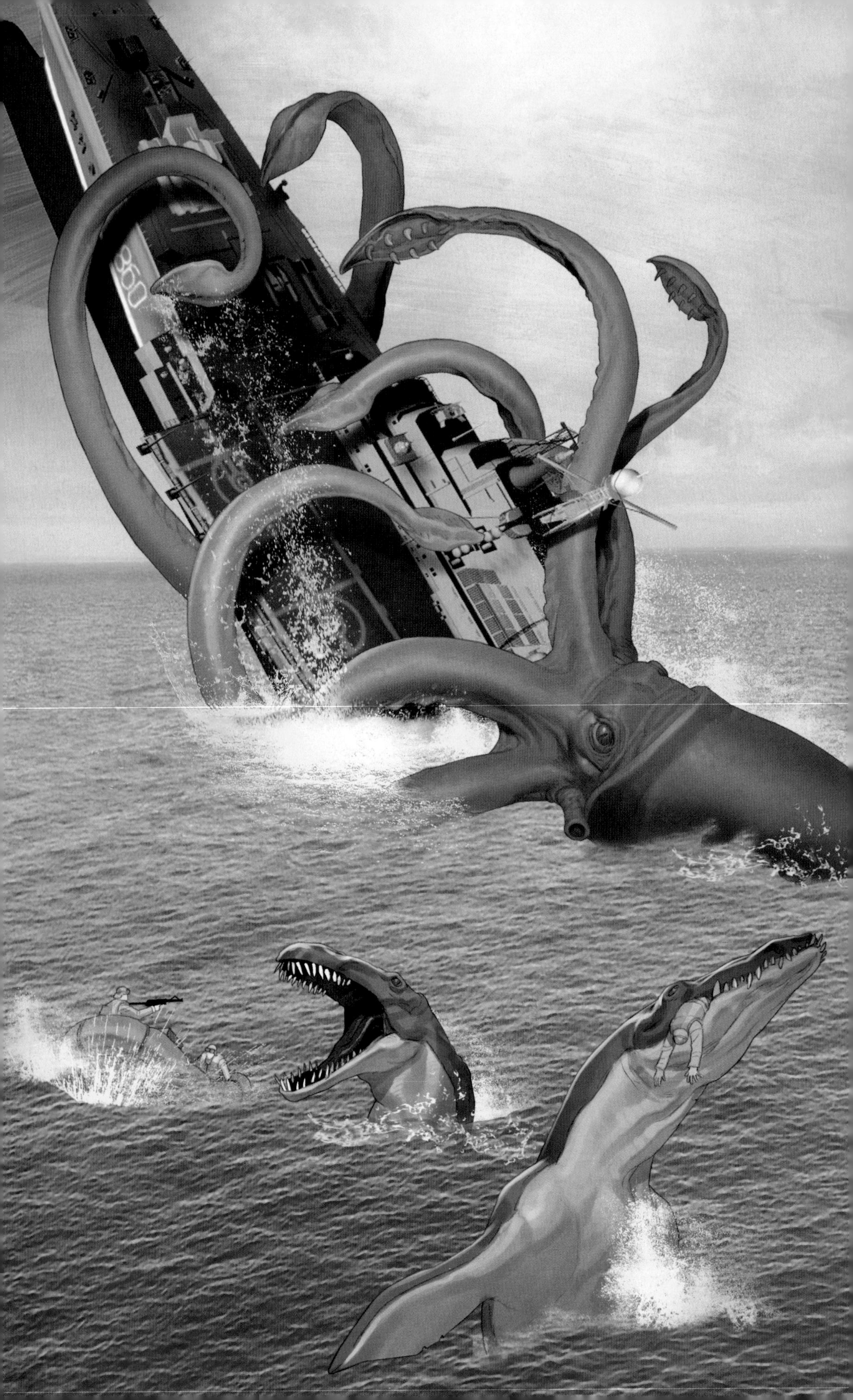
360

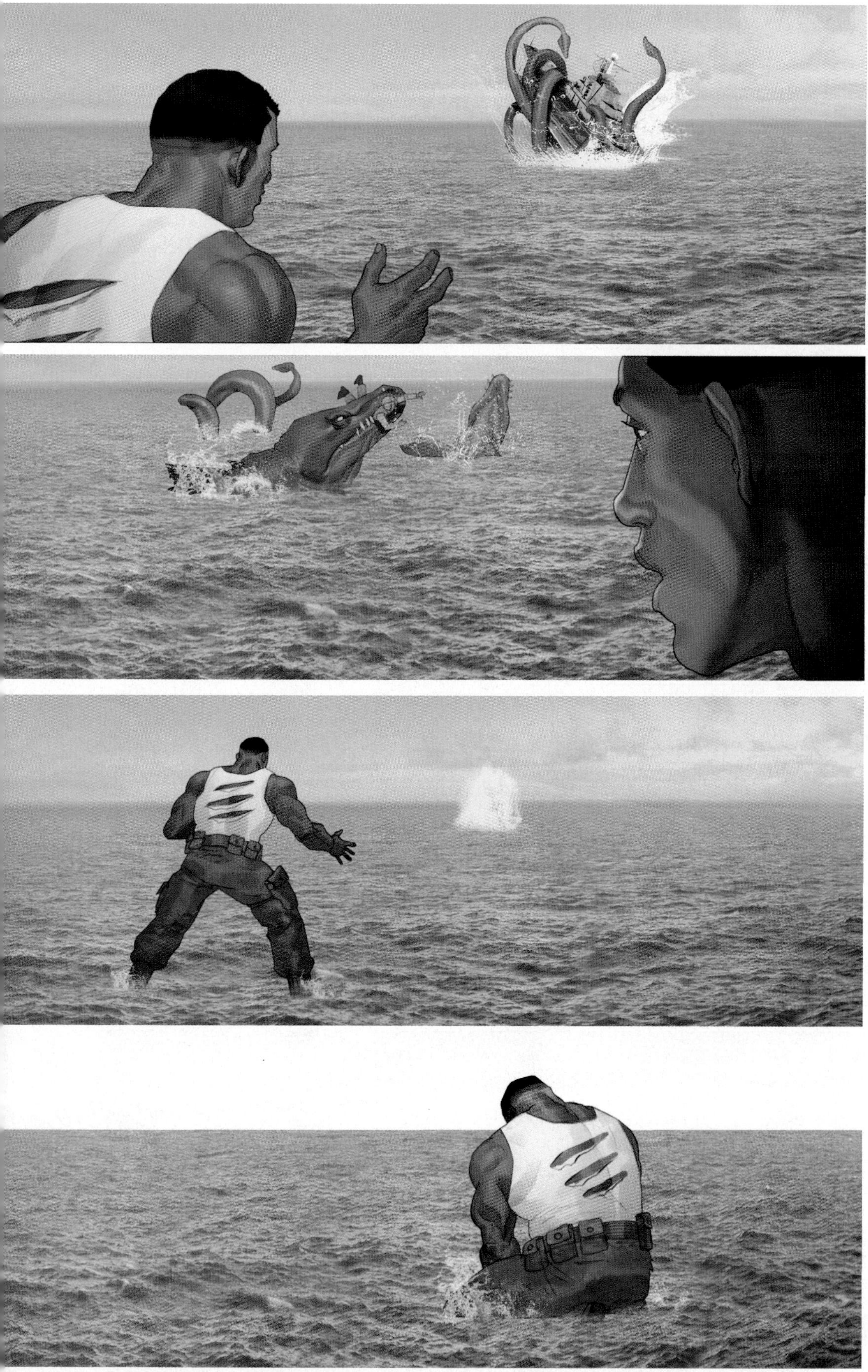

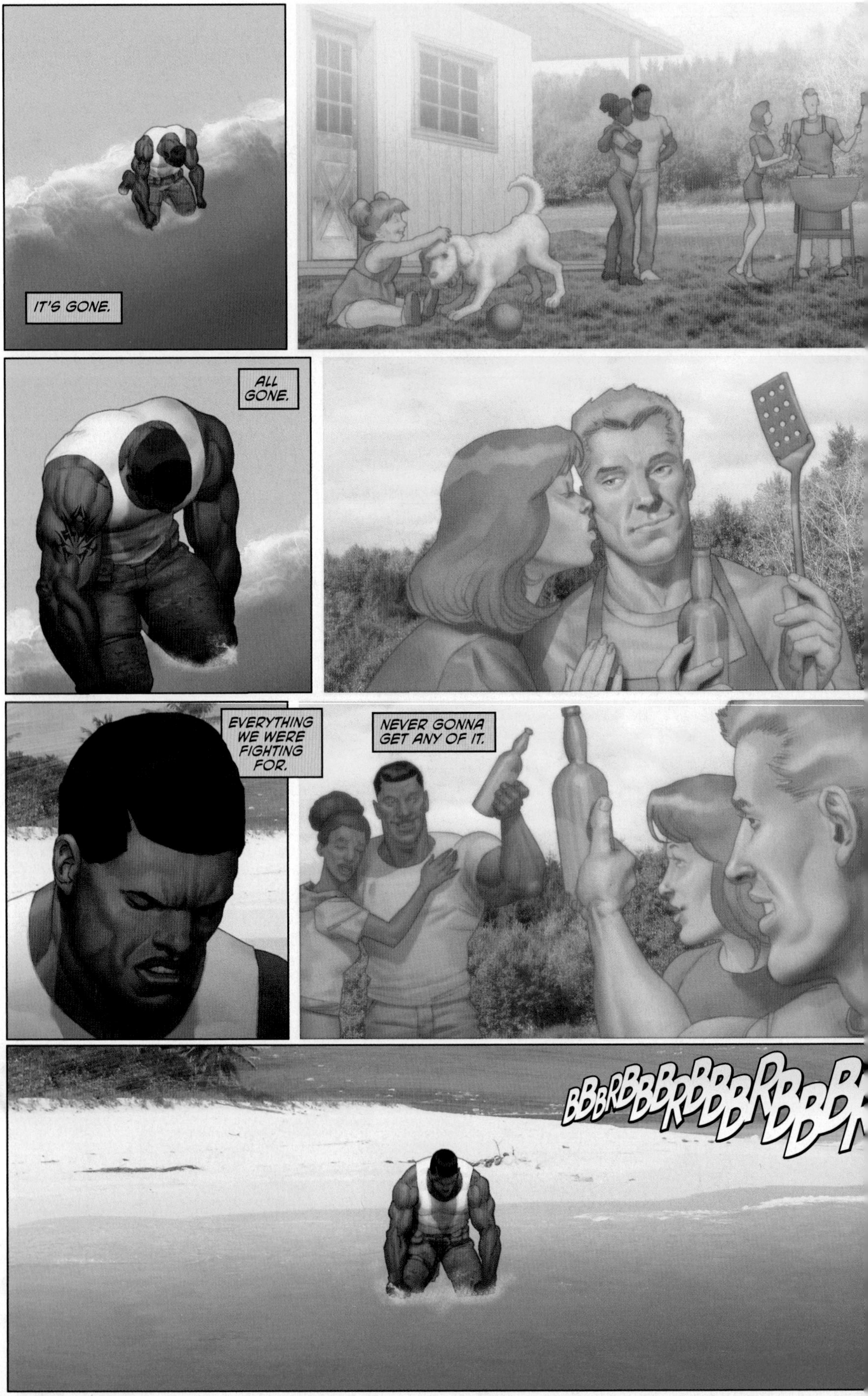
IT'S GONE.
ALL GONE.
EVERYTHING WE WERE FIGHTING FOR.
NEVER GONNA GET ANY OF IT.
BBBRBBBRBBBRBBBR

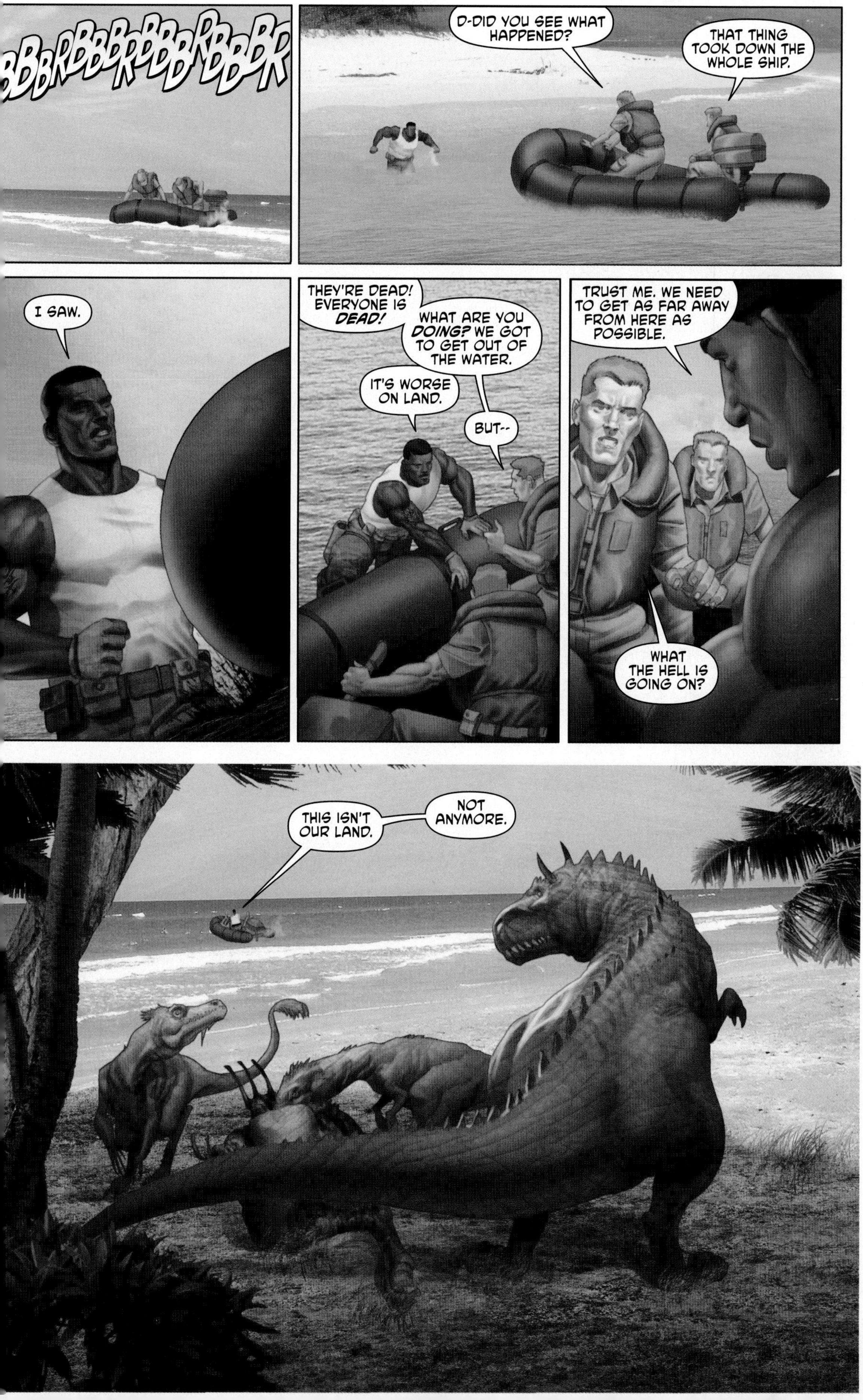
BBBRBBBRBBBRBBBR
D-DID YOU SEE WHAT HAPPENED?
THAT THING TOOK DOWN THE WHOLE SHIP.
I SAW.
THEY'RE DEAD! EVERYONE IS DEAD!
WHAT ARE YOU DOING? WE GOT TO GET OUT OF THE WATER.
IT'S WORSE ON LAND.
BUT--
TRUST ME. WE NEED TO GET AS FAR AWAY FROM HERE AS POSSIBLE.
WHAT THE HELL IS GOING ON?
THIS ISN'T OUR LAND.
NOT ANYMORE.

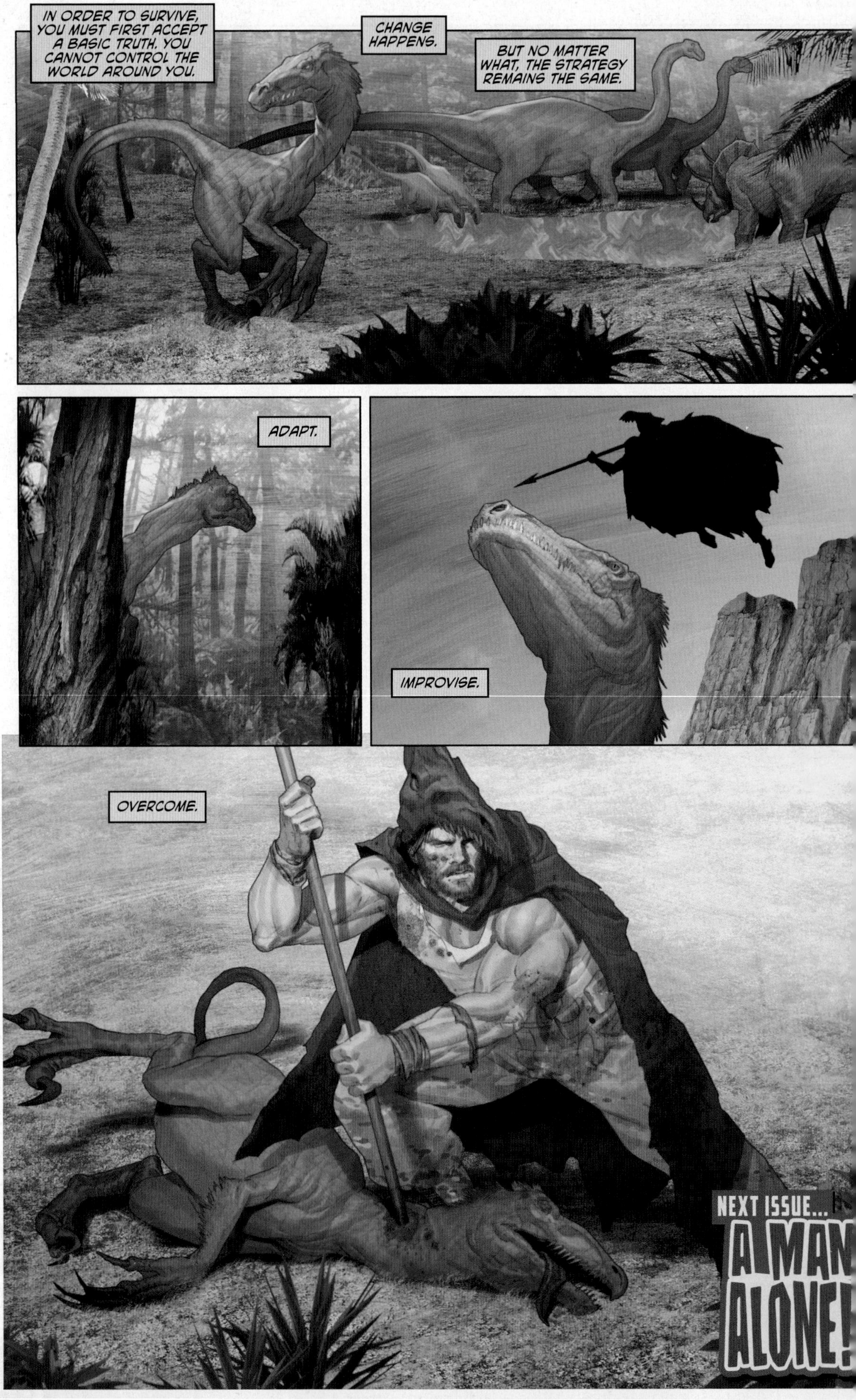
IN ORDER TO SURVIVE, YOU MUST FIRST ACCEPT A BASIC TRUTH. YOU CANNOT CONTROL THE WORLD AROUND YOU.
CHANGE HAPPENS.
BUT NO MATTER WHAT, THE STRATEGY REMAINS THE SAME.
ADAPT.
IMPROVISE.
OVERCOME.
NEXT ISSUE...
A MAN ALONE!

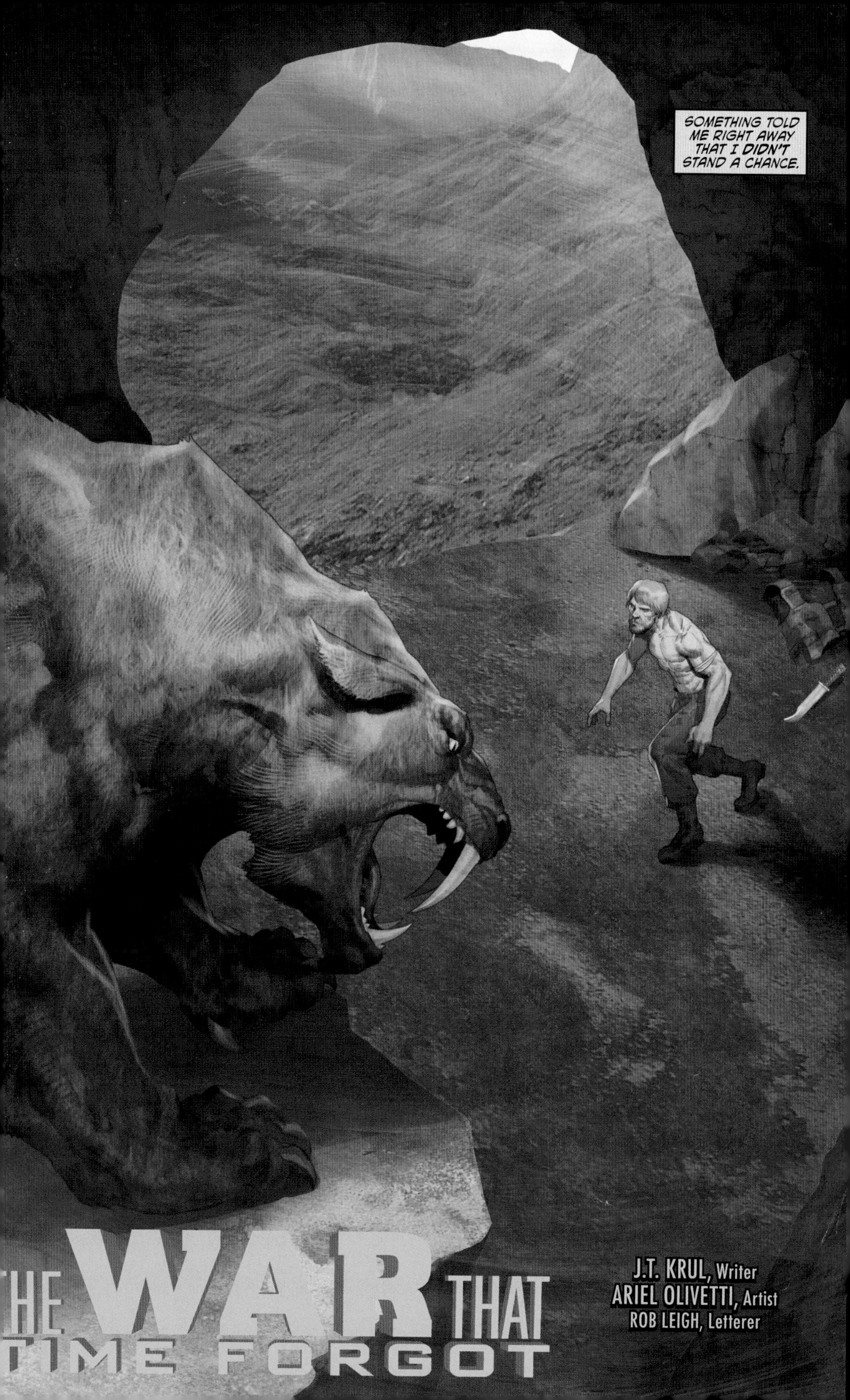
SOMETHING TOLD ME RIGHT AWAY THAT I DIDN'T STAND A CHANCE.
THE WAR THAT TIME FORGOT
J.T. KRUL, Writer
ARIEL OLIVETTI, Artist
ROB LEIGH, Letterer

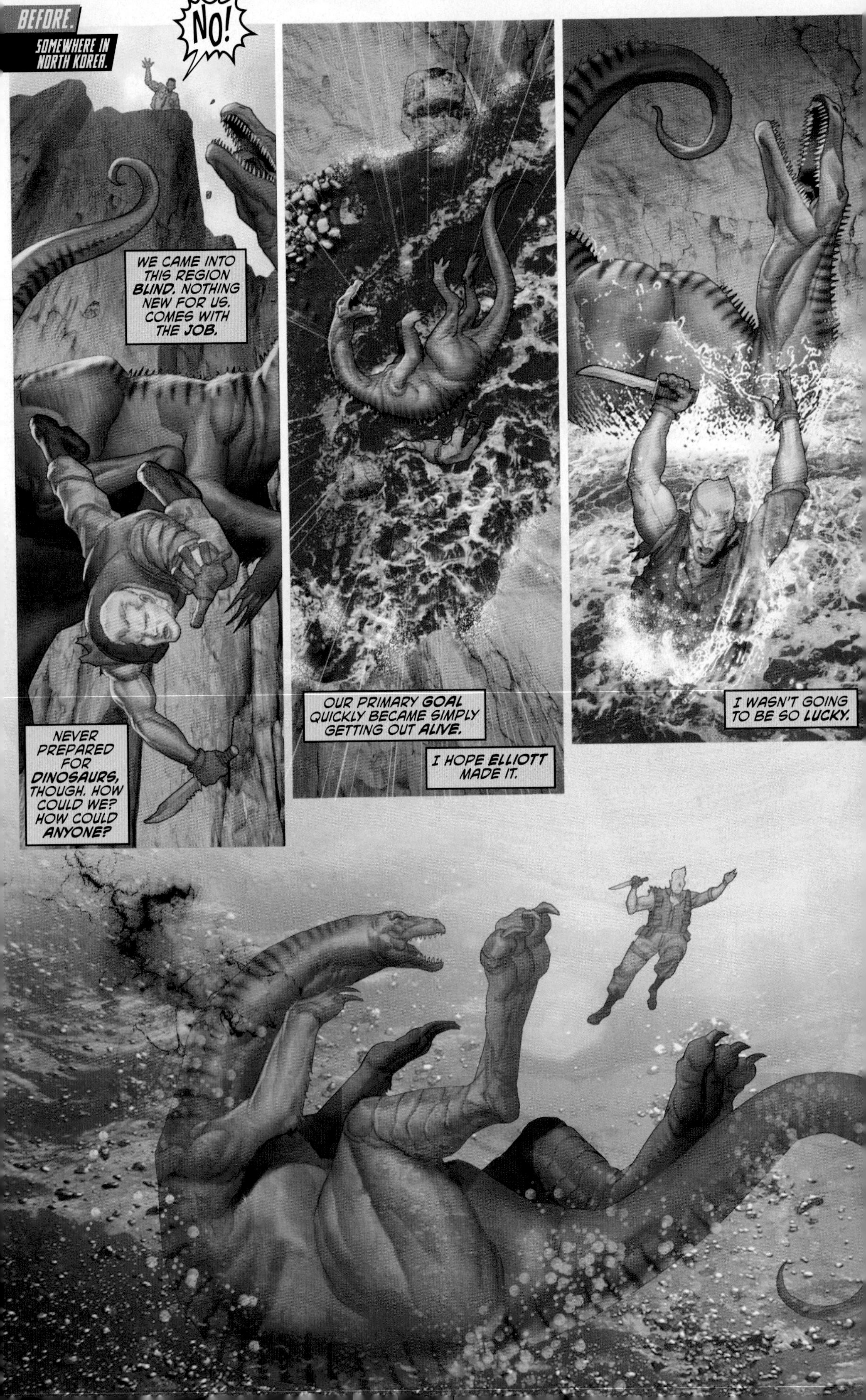
BEFORE.
SOMEWHERE IN NORTH KOREA.
NO!
WE CAME INTO THIS REGION BLIND. NOTHING NEW FOR US. COMES WITH THE JOB.
NEVER PREPARED FOR DINOSAURS, THOUGH. HOW COULD WE? HOW COULD ANYONE?
OUR PRIMARY GOAL QUICKLY BECAME SIMPLY GETTING OUT ALIVE.
I HOPE ELLIOTT MADE IT.
I WASN'T GOING TO BE SO LUCKY.

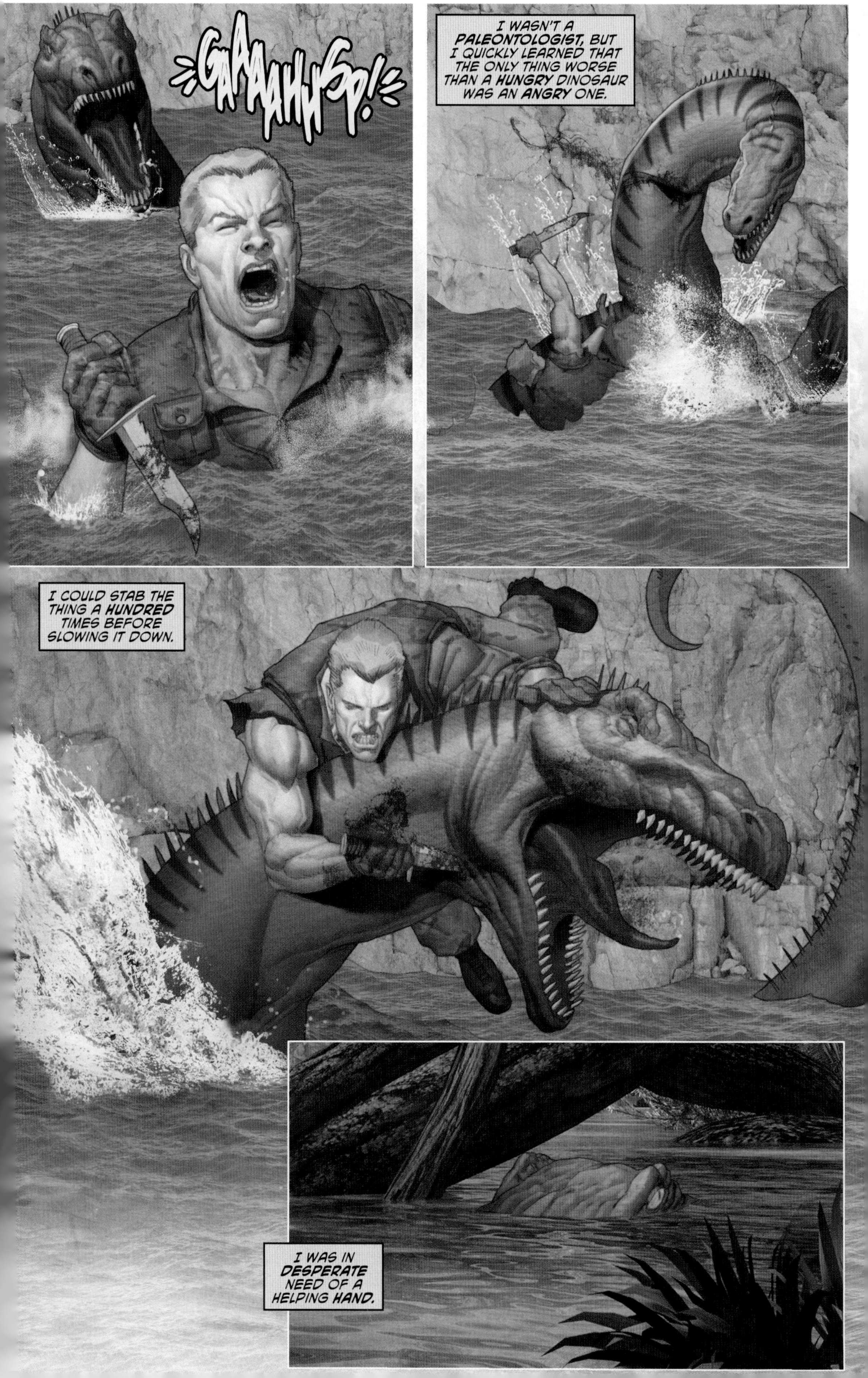
GAAAAHHUSP!
I WASN'T A PALEONTOLOGIST, BUT I QUICKLY LEARNED THAT THE ONLY THING WORSE THAN A HUNGRY DINOSAUR WAS AN ANGRY ONE.
I COULD STAB THE THING A HUNDRED TIMES BEFORE SLOWING IT DOWN.
I WAS IN DESPERATE NEED OF A HELPING HAND.

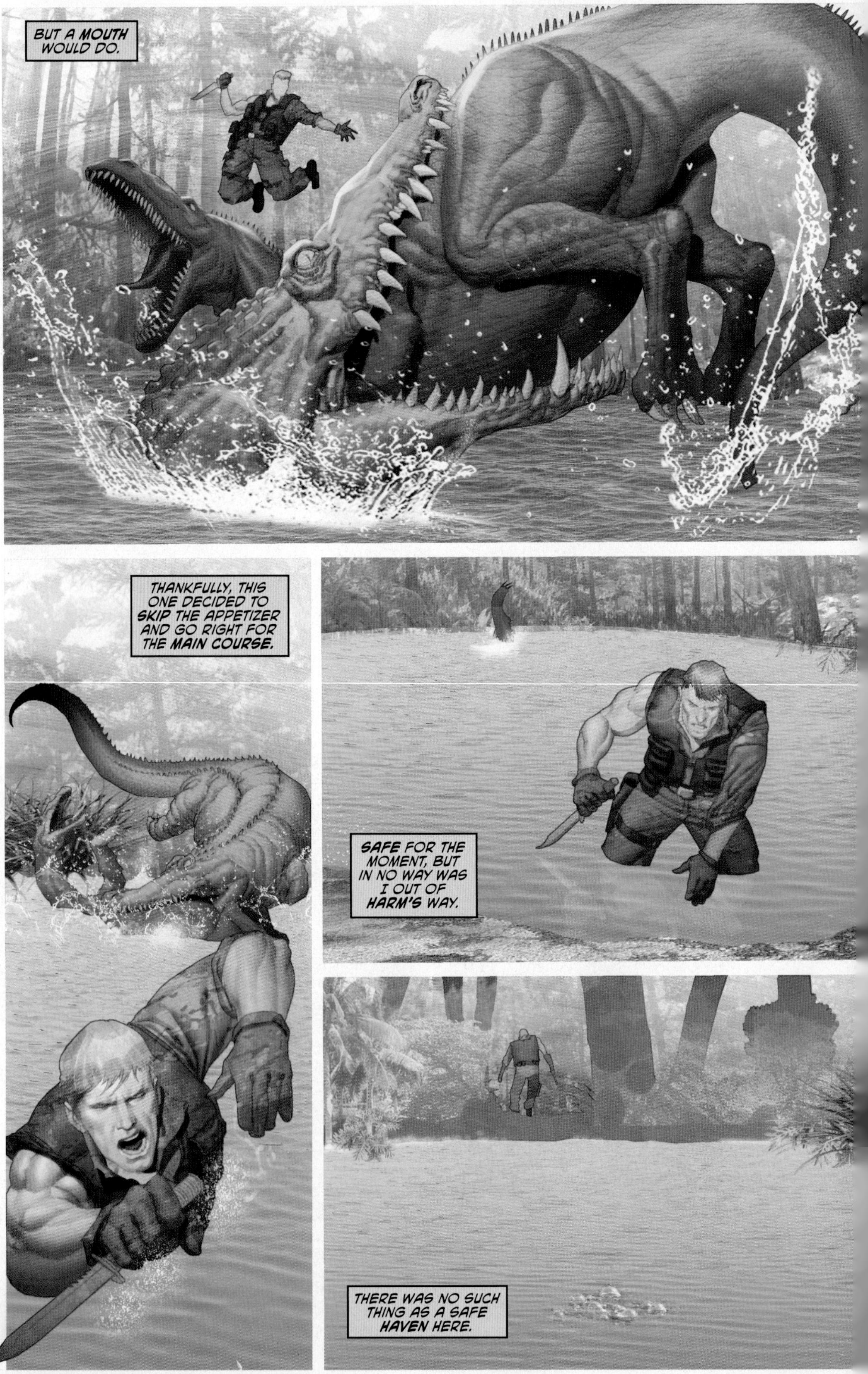
BUT A MOUTH WOULD DO.
THANKFULLY, THIS ONE DECIDED TO SKIP THE APPETIZER AND GO RIGHT FOR THE MAIN COURSE.
SAFE FOR THE MOMENT, BUT IN NO WAY WAS I OUT OF HARM'S WAY.
THERE WAS NO SUCH THING AS A SAFE HAVEN HERE.

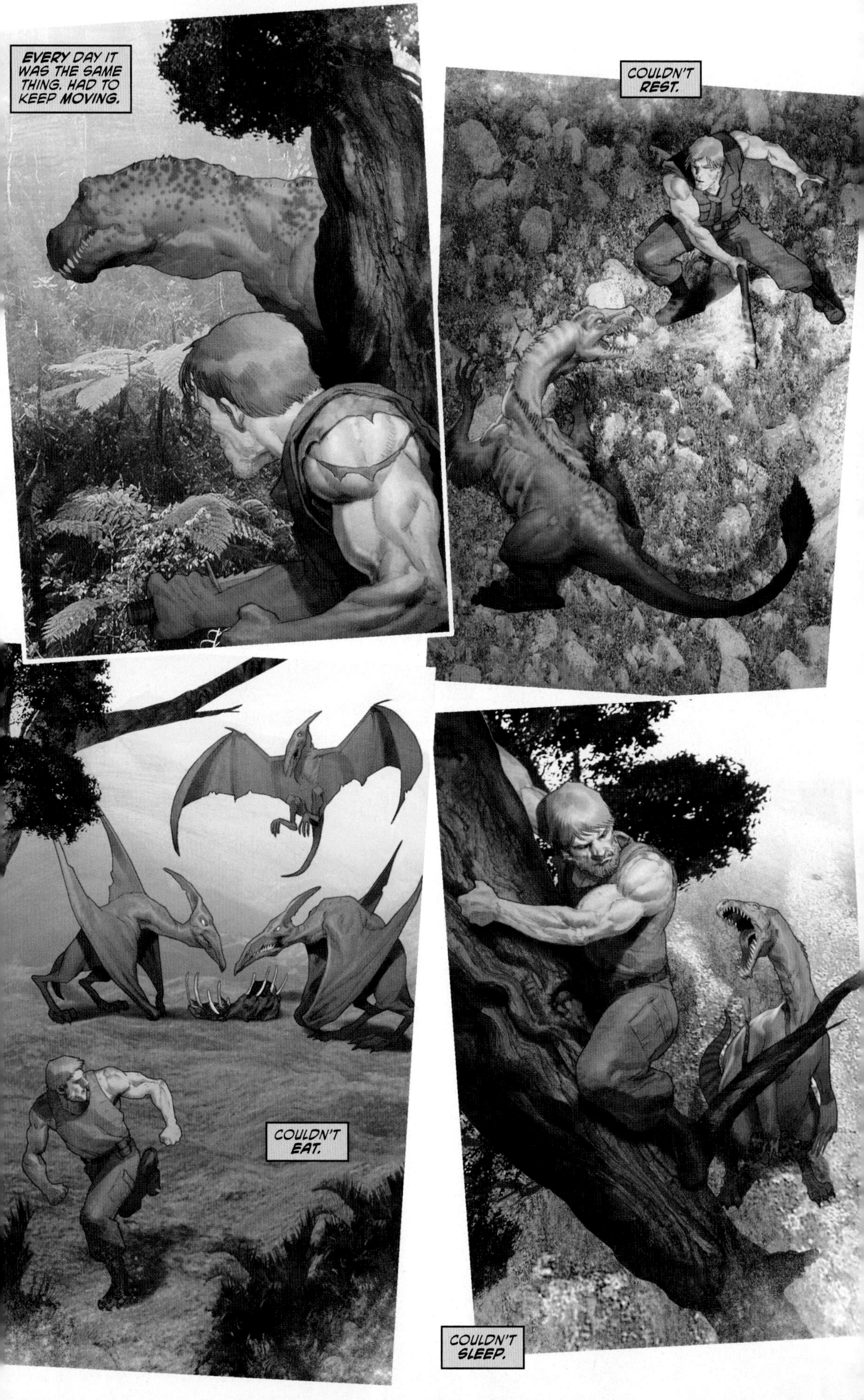
EVERY DAY IT WAS THE SAME THING. HAD TO KEEP MOVING.
COULDN'T REST.
COULDN'T EAT.
COULDN'T SLEEP.

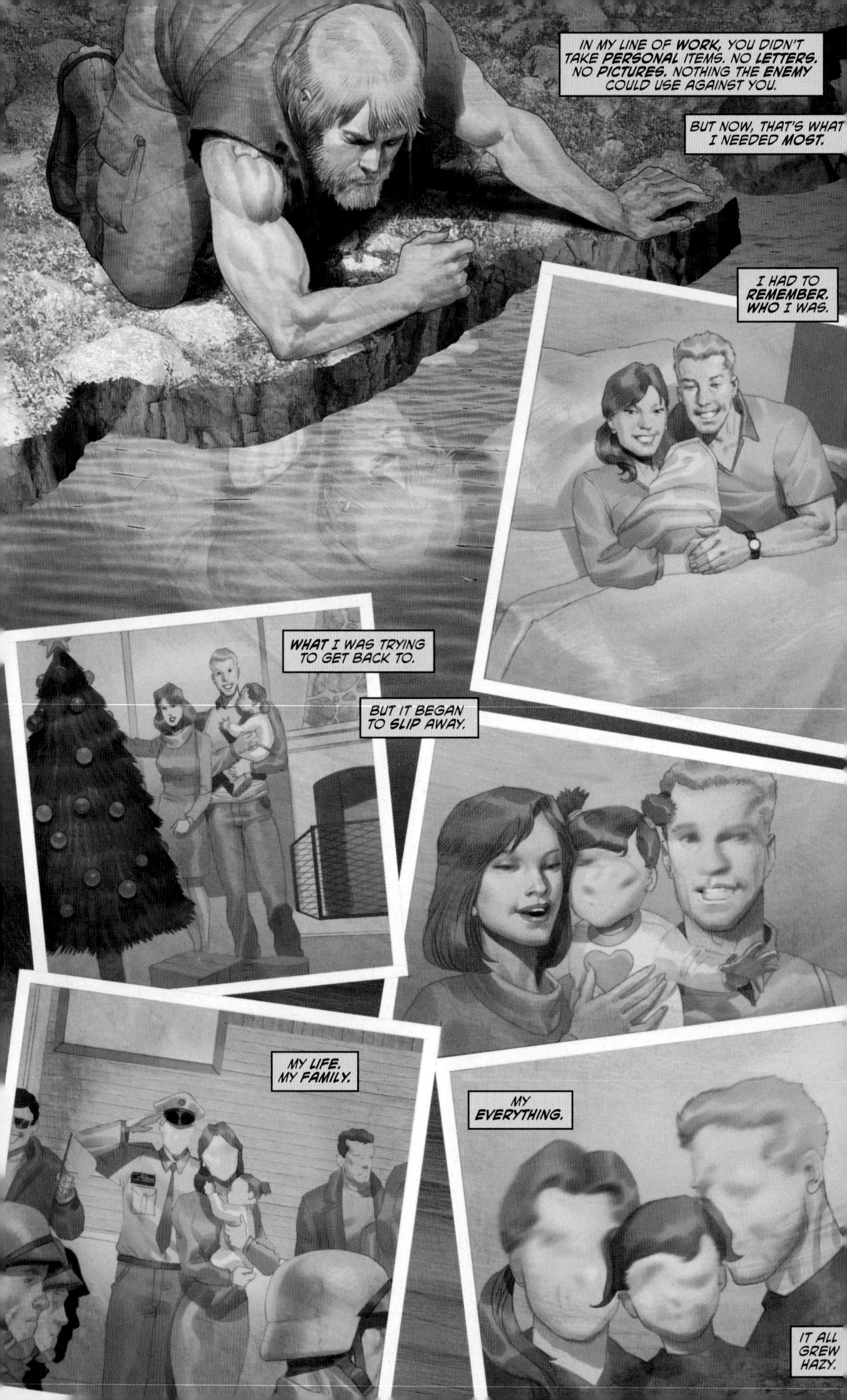
IN MY LINE OF WORK, YOU DIDN'T TAKE PERSONAL ITEMS. NO LETTERS. NO PICTURES. NOTHING THE ENEMY COULD USE AGAINST YOU.
BUT NOW, THAT'S WHAT I NEEDED MOST.
I HAD TO REMEMBER. WHO I WAS.
WHAT I WAS TRYING TO GET BACK TO.
BUT IT BEGAN TO SLIP AWAY.
MY LIFE. MY FAMILY.
MY EVERYTHING.
IT ALL GREW HAZY.

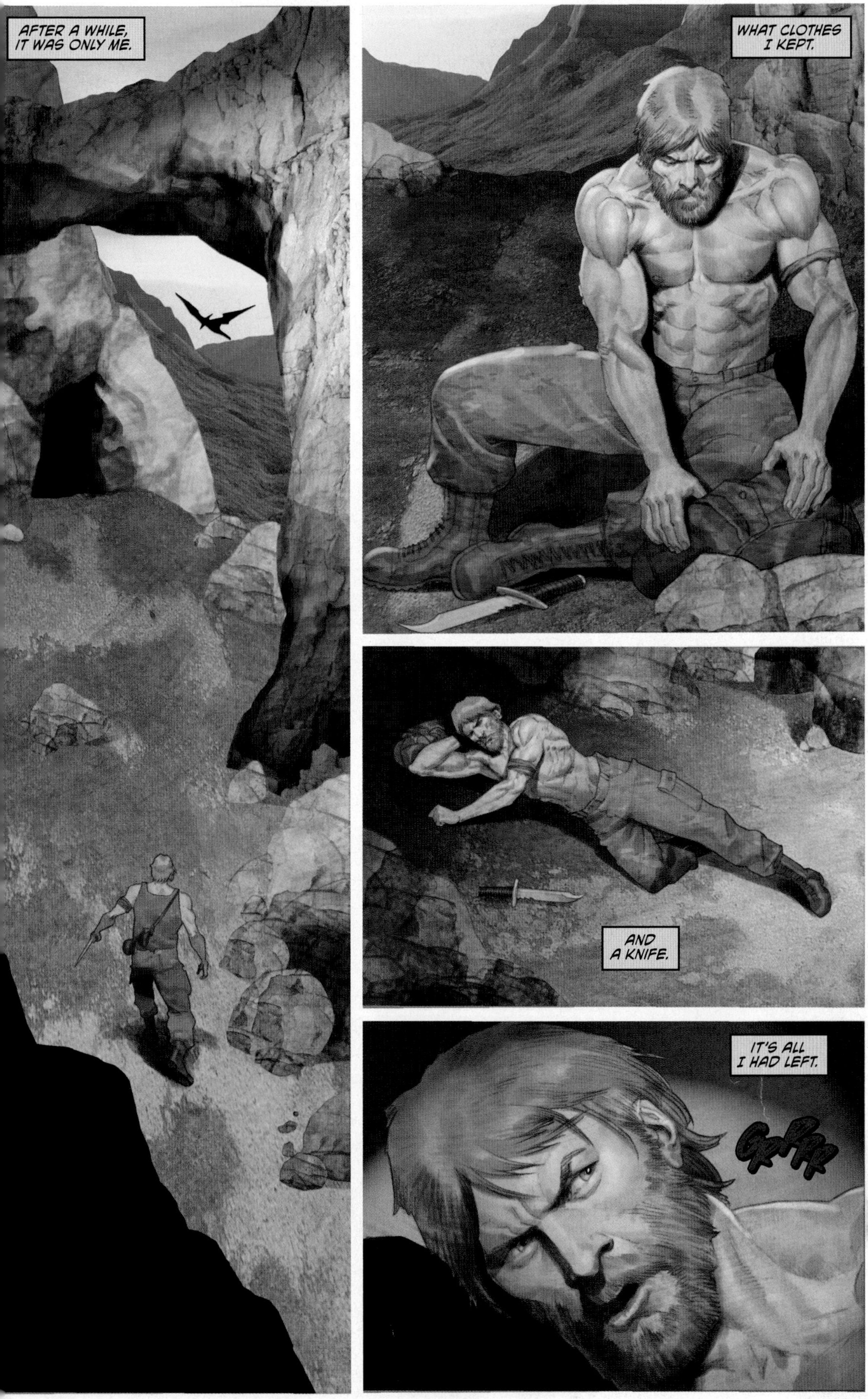
AFTER A WHILE, IT WAS ONLY ME.
WHAT CLOTHES I KEPT.
AND A KNIFE.
IT'S ALL I HAD LEFT.
GRRRR

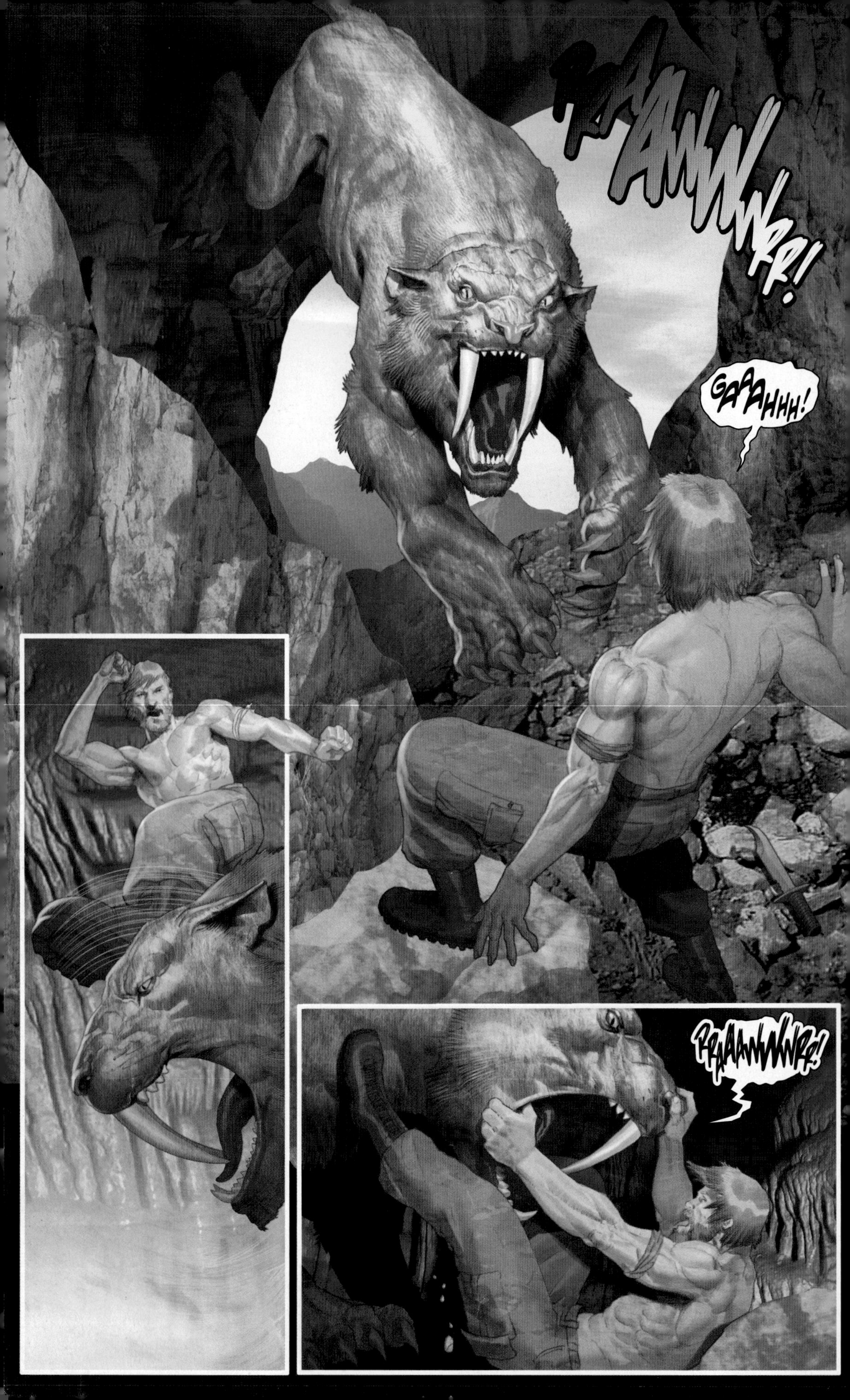

RRAAAWWRR!
GAAAAHHH!
RRAAAWWWRR!

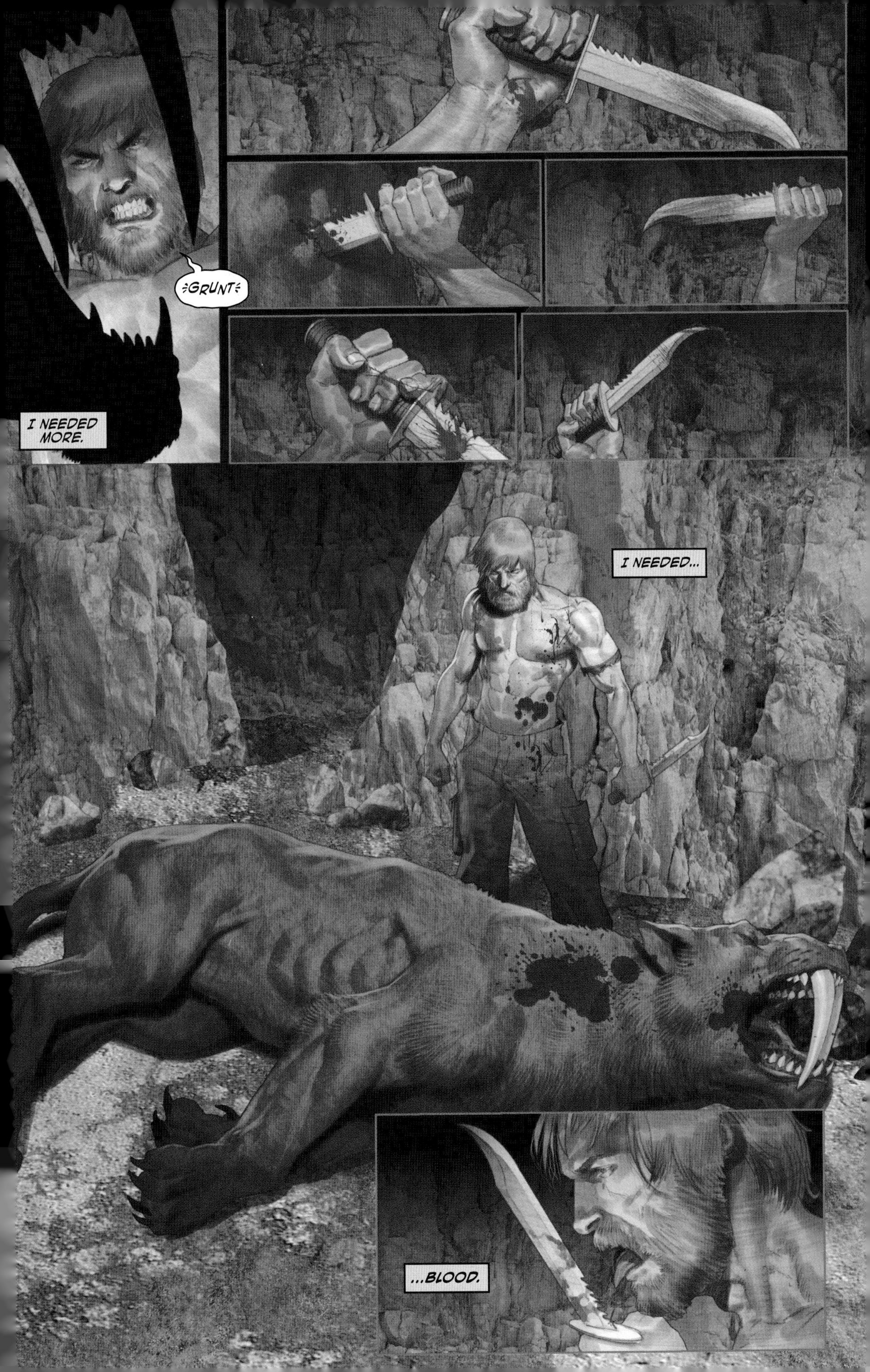
GRUNT
I NEEDED MORE.
I NEEDED...
...BLOOD.

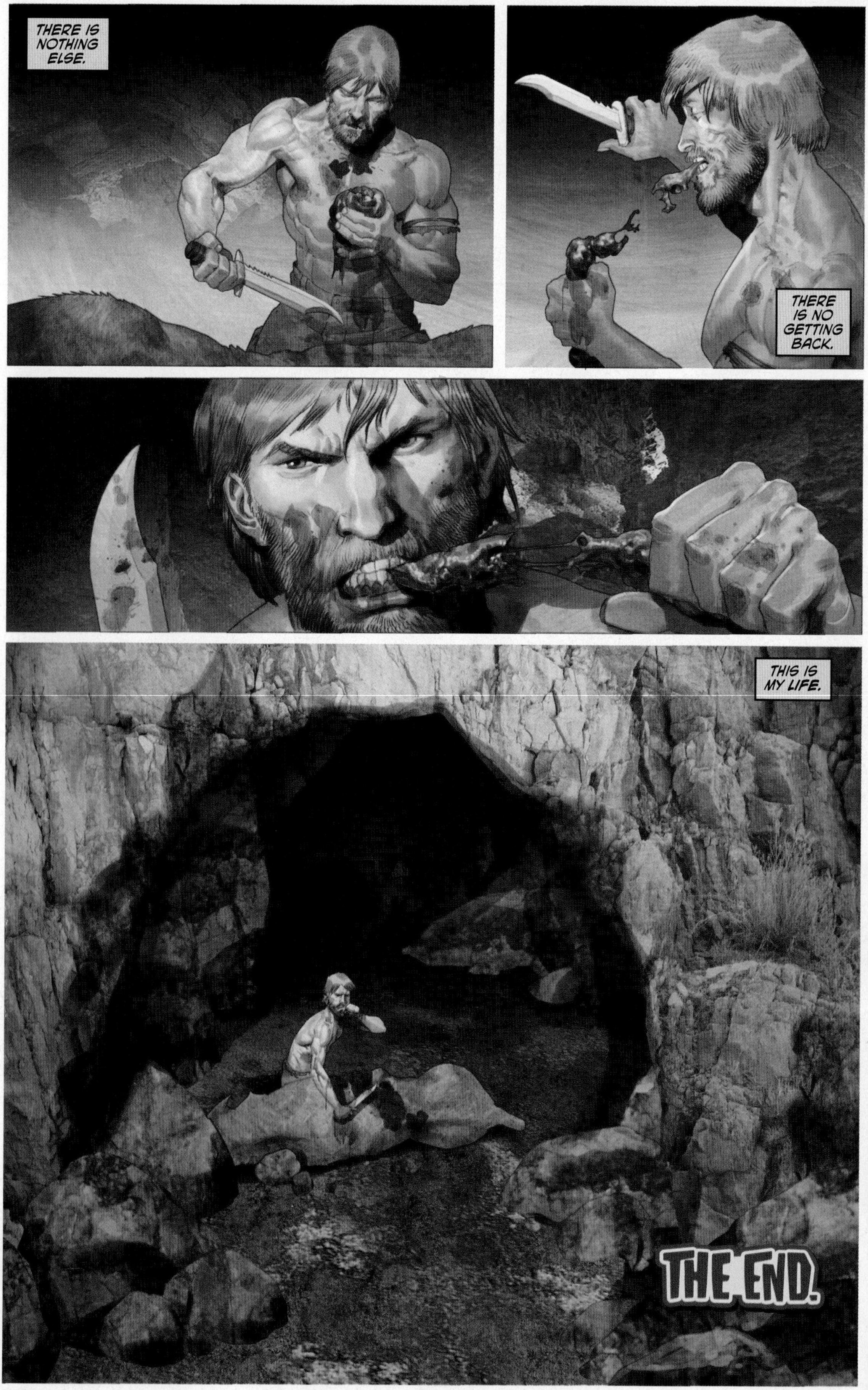
THERE IS NOTHING ELSE.
THERE IS NO GETTING BACK.
THIS IS MY LIFE.
THE END.

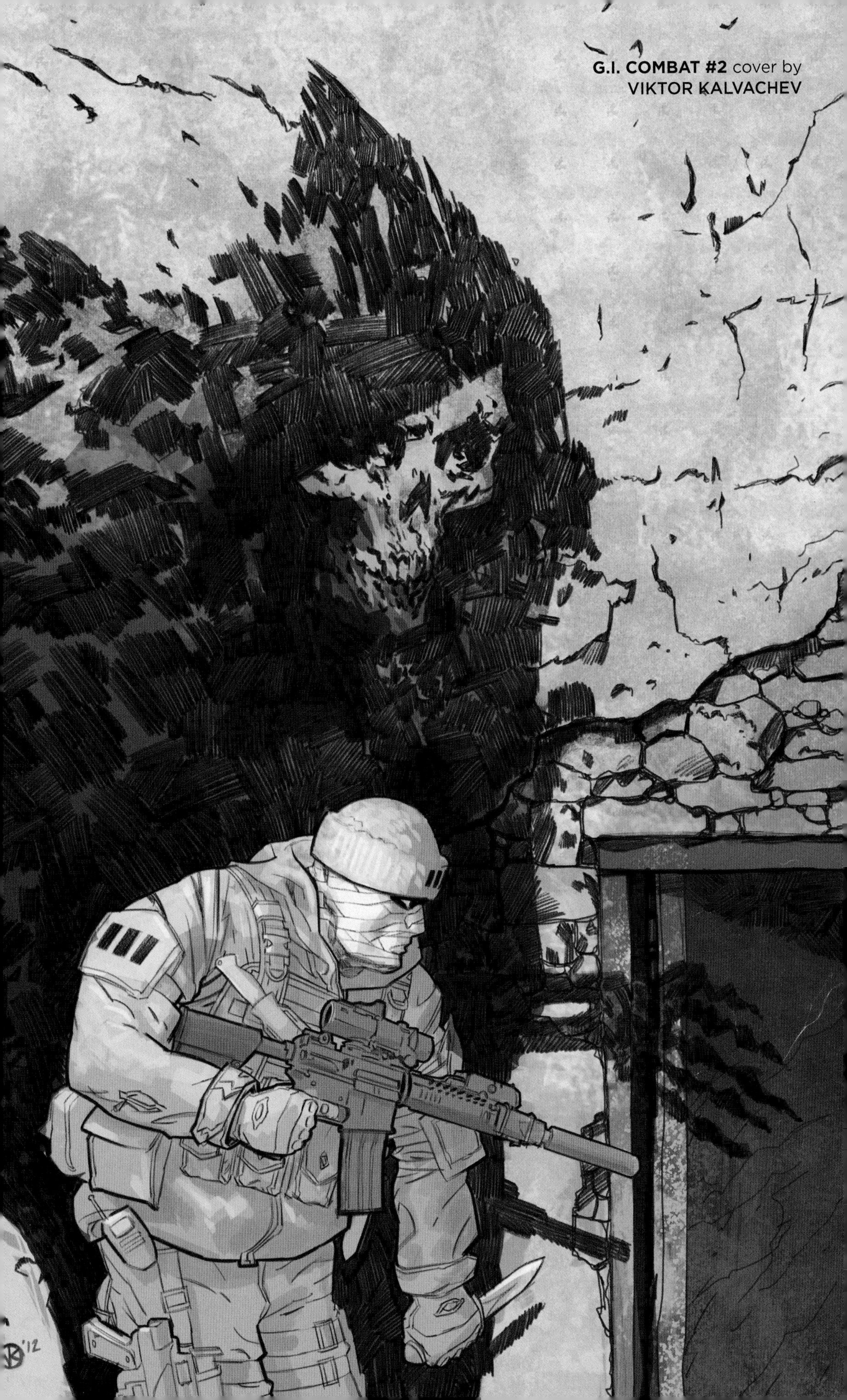

G.I. COMBAT #2 cover by
VIKTOR KALVACHEV

THE UNKNOWN SOLDIER

JUSTIN GRAY & **JIMMY PALMIOTTI** writers

DAN PANOSIAN & **STAZ JOHNSON** artists

THE UNKNOWN SOLDIER

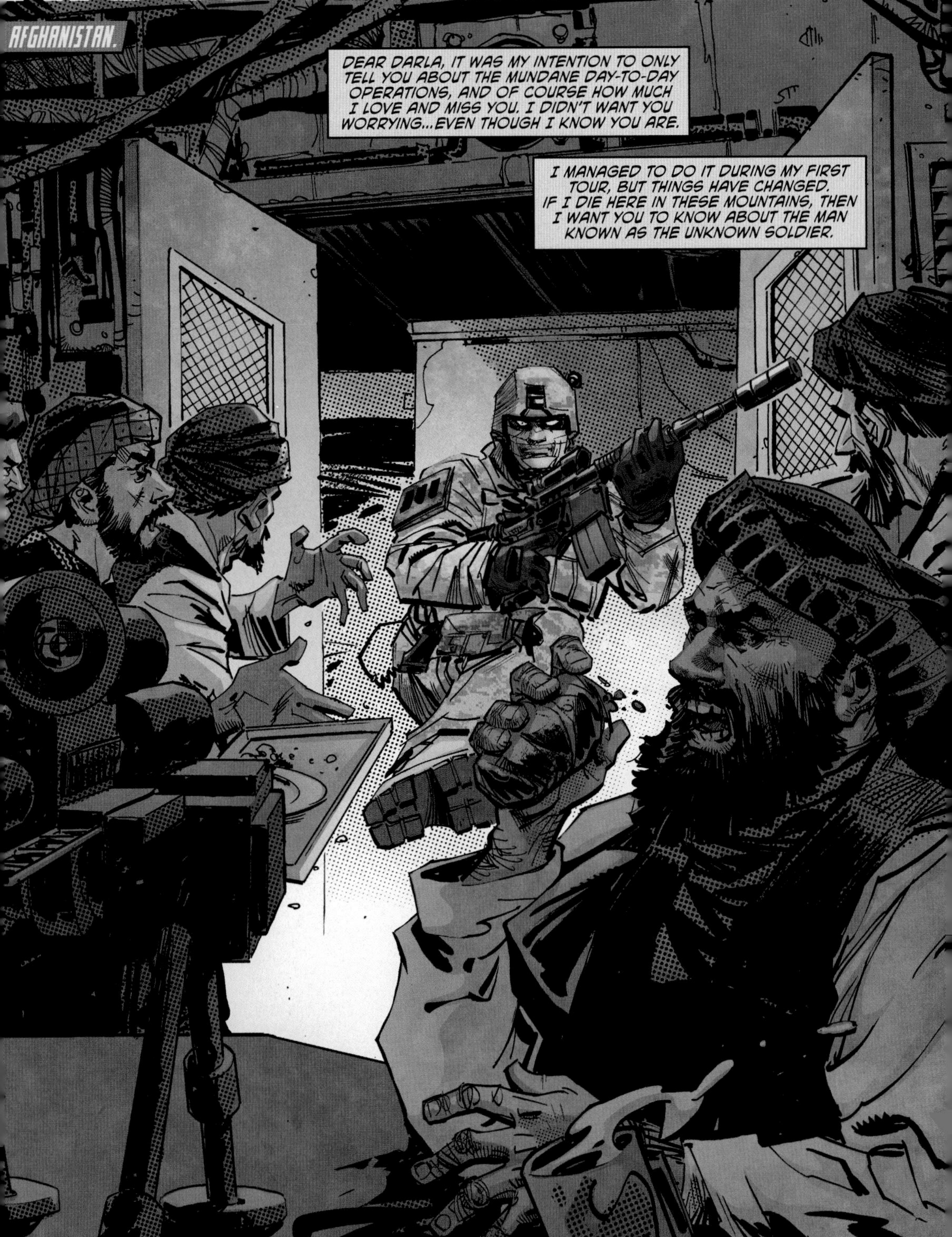
AFGHANISTAN.
DEAR DARLA, IT WAS MY INTENTION TO ONLY TELL YOU ABOUT THE MUNDANE DAY-TO-DAY OPERATIONS, AND OF COURSE HOW MUCH I LOVE AND MISS YOU. I DIDN'T WANT YOU WORRYING...EVEN THOUGH I KNOW YOU ARE.
I MANAGED TO DO IT DURING MY FIRST TOUR, BUT THINGS HAVE CHANGED. IF I DIE HERE IN THESE MOUNTAINS, THEN I WANT YOU TO KNOW ABOUT THE MAN KNOWN AS THE UNKNOWN SOLDIER.

JUSTIN GRAY and JIMMY PALMIOTTI
DAN PANOSIAN
ROB SCHWAGER
ROB LEIGH

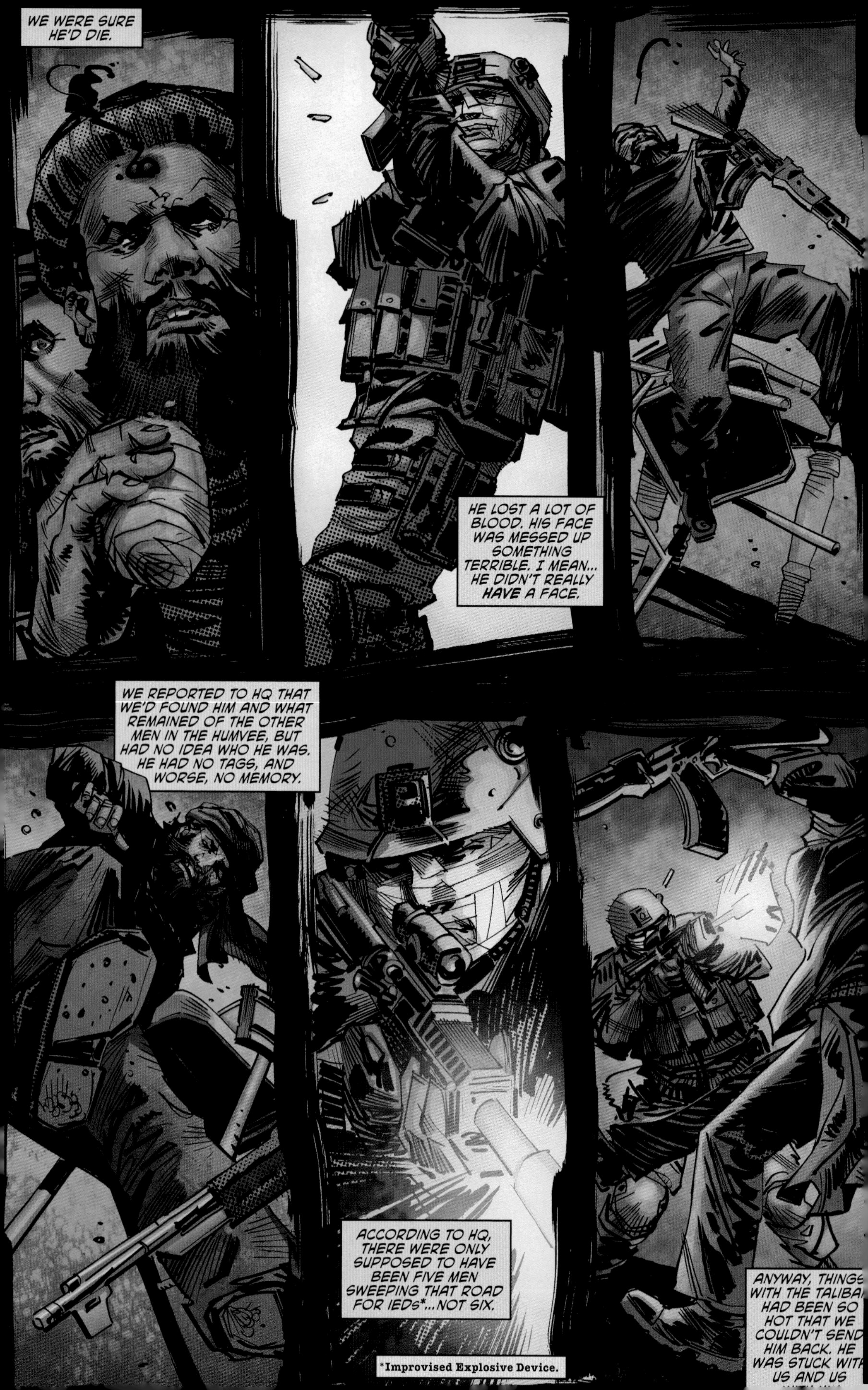
WE WERE SURE HE'D DIE.
HE LOST A LOT OF BLOOD. HIS FACE WAS MESSED UP SOMETHING TERRIBLE. I MEAN... HE DIDN'T REALLY HAVE A FACE.
WE REPORTED TO HQ THAT WE'D FOUND HIM AND WHAT REMAINED OF THE OTHER MEN IN THE HUMVEE, BUT HAD NO IDEA WHO HE WAS. HE HAD NO TAGS, AND WORSE, NO MEMORY.
ACCORDING TO HQ, THERE WERE ONLY SUPPOSED TO HAVE BEEN FIVE MEN SWEEPING THAT ROAD FOR IEDs*...NOT SIX.
ANYWAY, THINGS WITH THE TALIBA HAD BEEN SO HOT THAT WE COULDN'T SEND HIM BACK. HE WAS STUCK WITH US AND US
*Improvised Explosive Device.

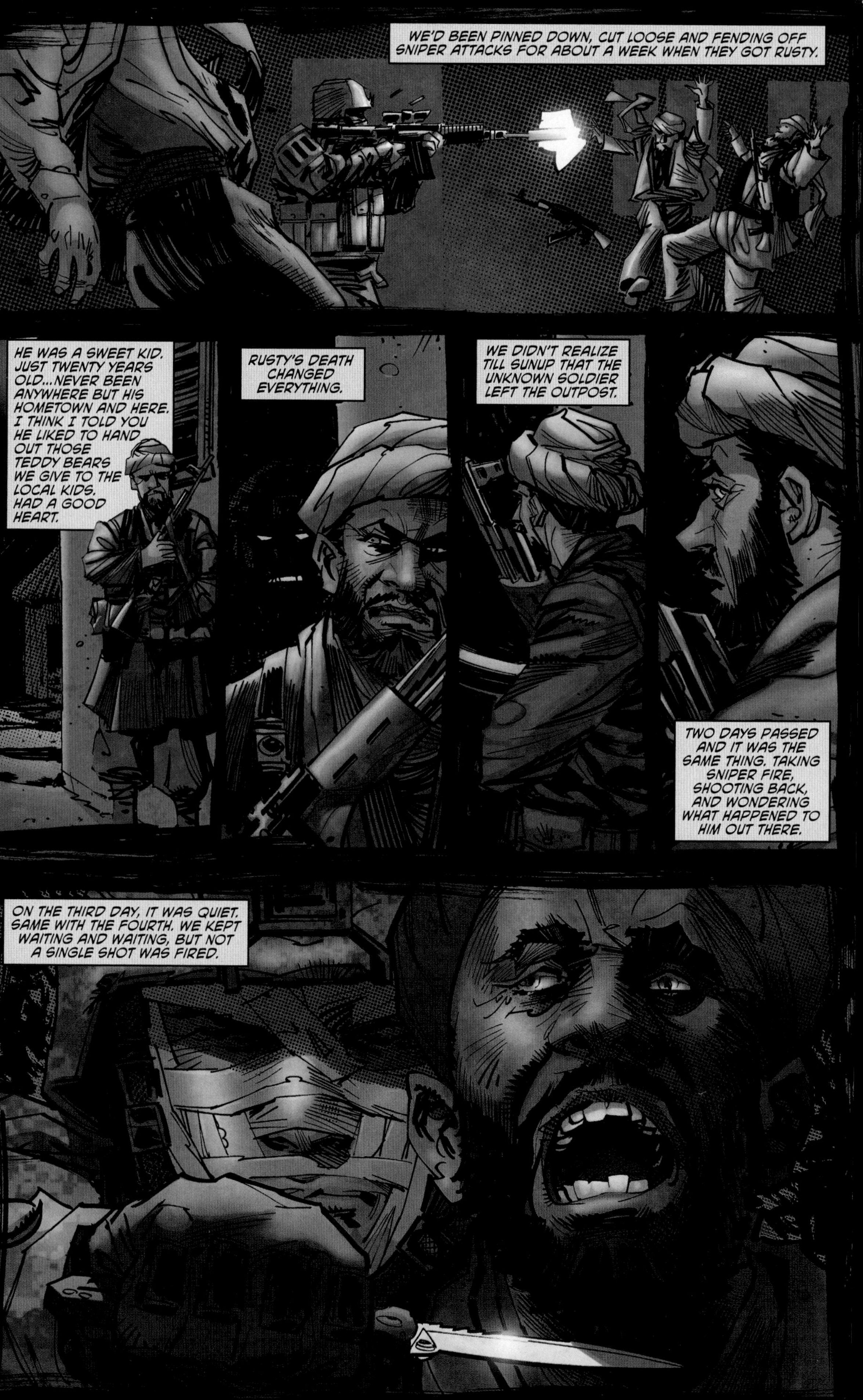
WE'D BEEN PINNED DOWN, CUT LOOSE AND FENDING OFF SNIPER ATTACKS FOR ABOUT A WEEK WHEN THEY GOT RUSTY.
HE WAS A SWEET KID. JUST TWENTY YEARS OLD...NEVER BEEN ANYWHERE BUT HIS HOMETOWN AND HERE. I THINK I TOLD YOU HE LIKED TO HAND OUT THOSE TEDDY BEARS WE GIVE TO THE LOCAL KIDS. HAD A GOOD HEART.
RUSTY'S DEATH CHANGED EVERYTHING.
WE DIDN'T REALIZE TILL SUNUP THAT THE UNKNOWN SOLDIER LEFT THE OUTPOST.
TWO DAYS PASSED AND IT WAS THE SAME THING. TAKING SNIPER FIRE, SHOOTING BACK, AND WONDERING WHAT HAPPENED TO HIM OUT THERE.
ON THE THIRD DAY, IT WAS QUIET. SAME WITH THE FOURTH. WE KEPT WAITING AND WAITING, BUT NOT A SINGLE SHOT WAS FIRED.

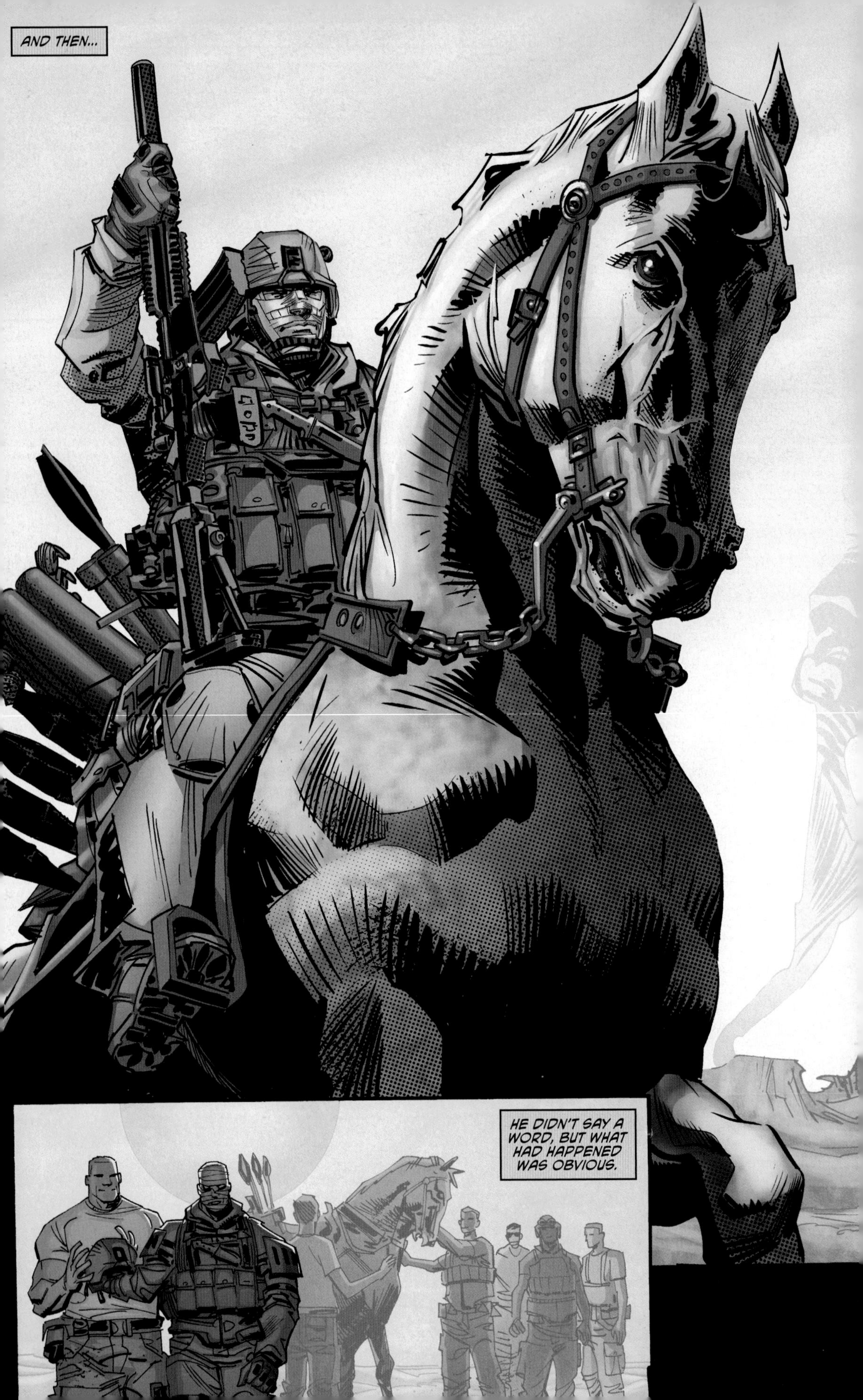
AND THEN...
HE DIDN'T SAY A WORD, BUT WHAT HAD HAPPENED WAS OBVIOUS.

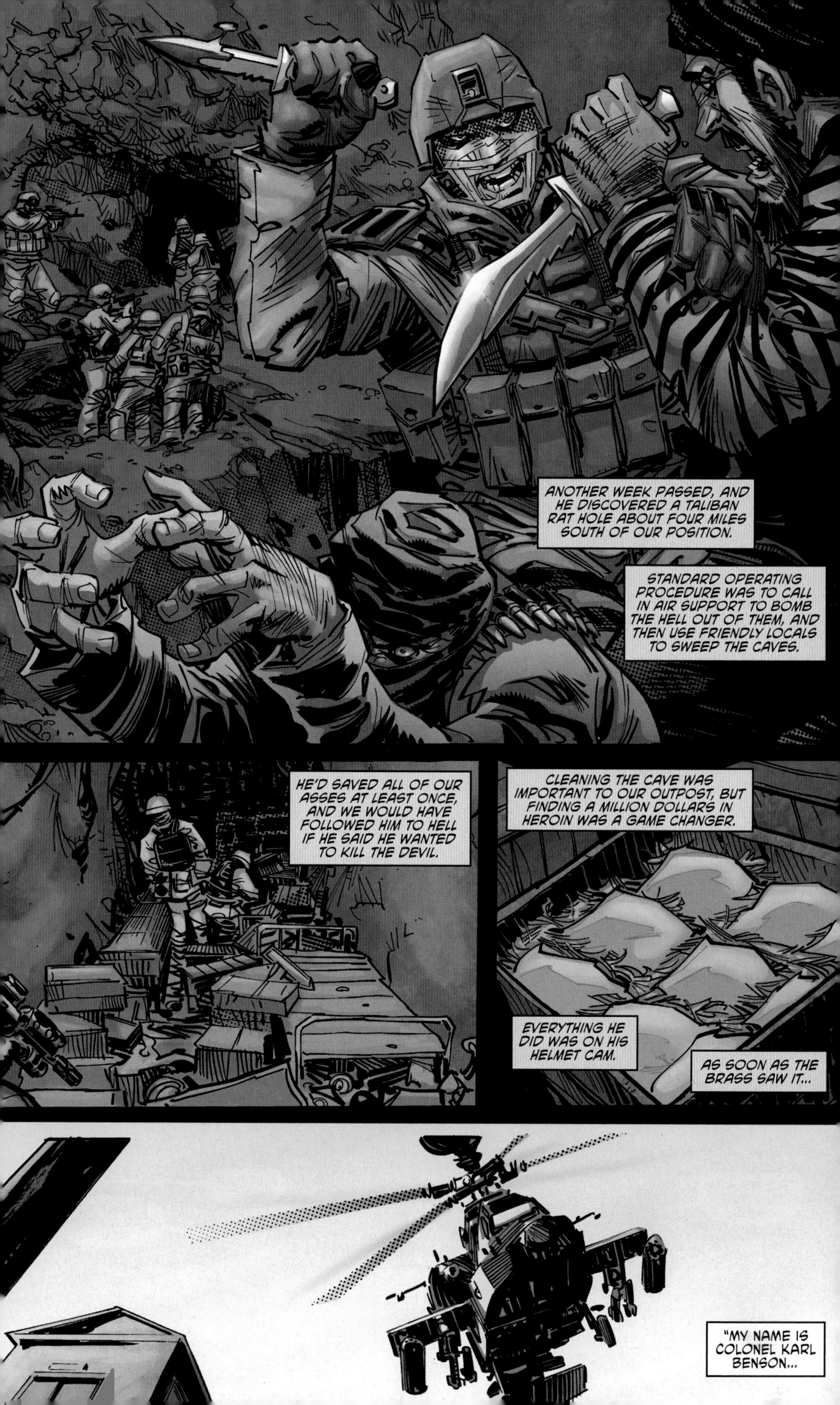
ANOTHER WEEK PASSED, AND HE DISCOVERED A TALIBAN RAT HOLE ABOUT FOUR MILES SOUTH OF OUR POSITION.
STANDARD OPERATING PROCEDURE WAS TO CALL IN AIR SUPPORT TO BOMB THE HELL OUT OF THEM, AND THEN USE FRIENDLY LOCALS TO SWEEP THE CAVES.
HE'D SAVED ALL OF OUR ASSES AT LEAST ONCE, AND WE WOULD HAVE FOLLOWED HIM TO HELL IF HE SAID HE WANTED TO KILL THE DEVIL.
CLEANING THE CAVE WAS IMPORTANT TO OUR OUTPOST, BUT FINDING A MILLION DOLLARS IN HEROIN WAS A GAME CHANGER.
EVERYTHING HE DID WAS ON HIS HELMET CAM.
AS SOON AS THE BRASS SAW IT...
"MY NAME IS COLONEL KARL BENSON...

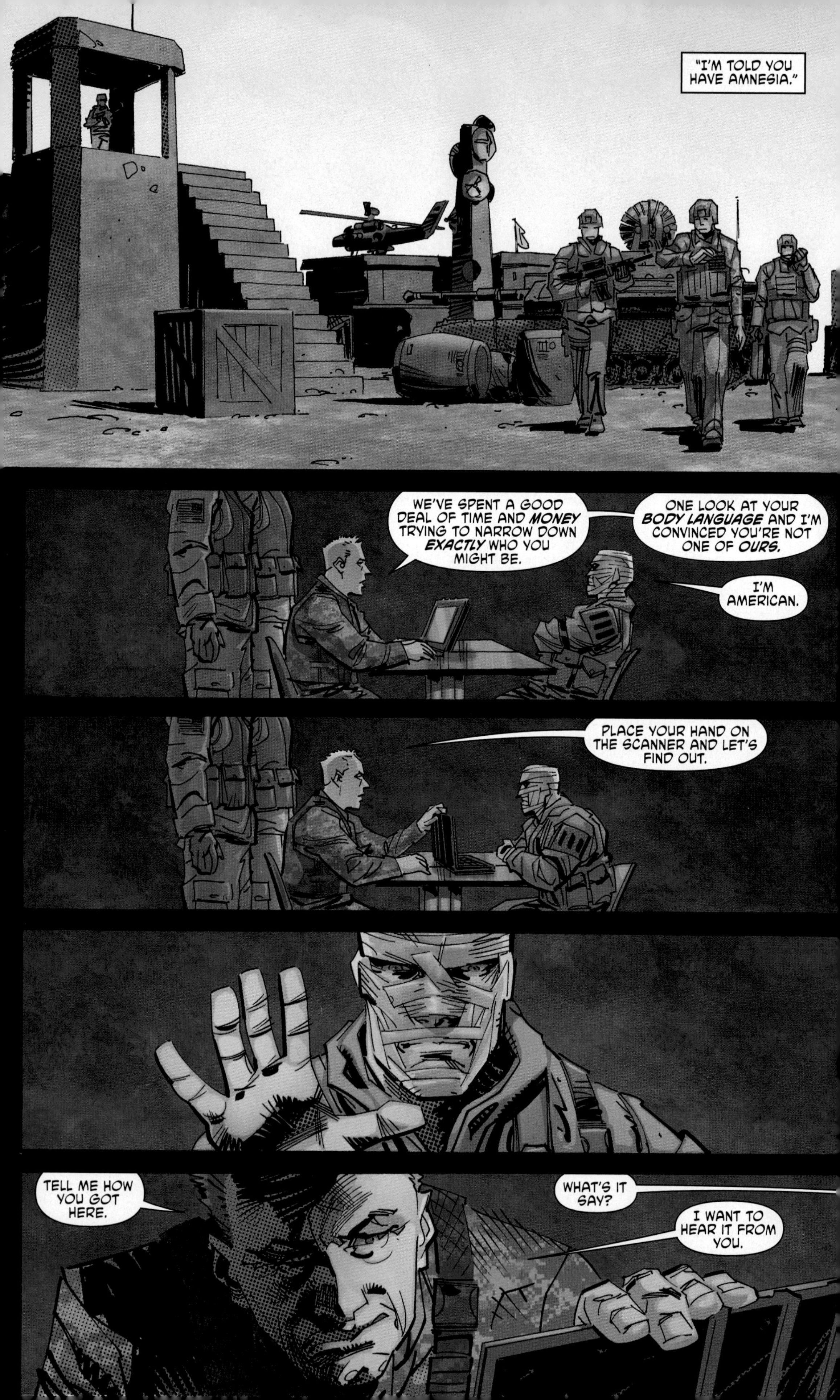
"I'M TOLD YOU HAVE AMNESIA."
WE'VE SPENT A GOOD DEAL OF TIME AND MONEY TRYING TO NARROW DOWN EXACTLY WHO YOU MIGHT BE.
ONE LOOK AT YOUR BODY LANGUAGE AND I'M CONVINCED YOU'RE NOT ONE OF OURS.
I'M AMERICAN.
PLACE YOUR HAND ON THE SCANNER AND LET'S FIND OUT.
WHAT'S IT SAY?
I WANT TO HEAR IT FROM YOU.
TELL ME HOW YOU GOT HERE.

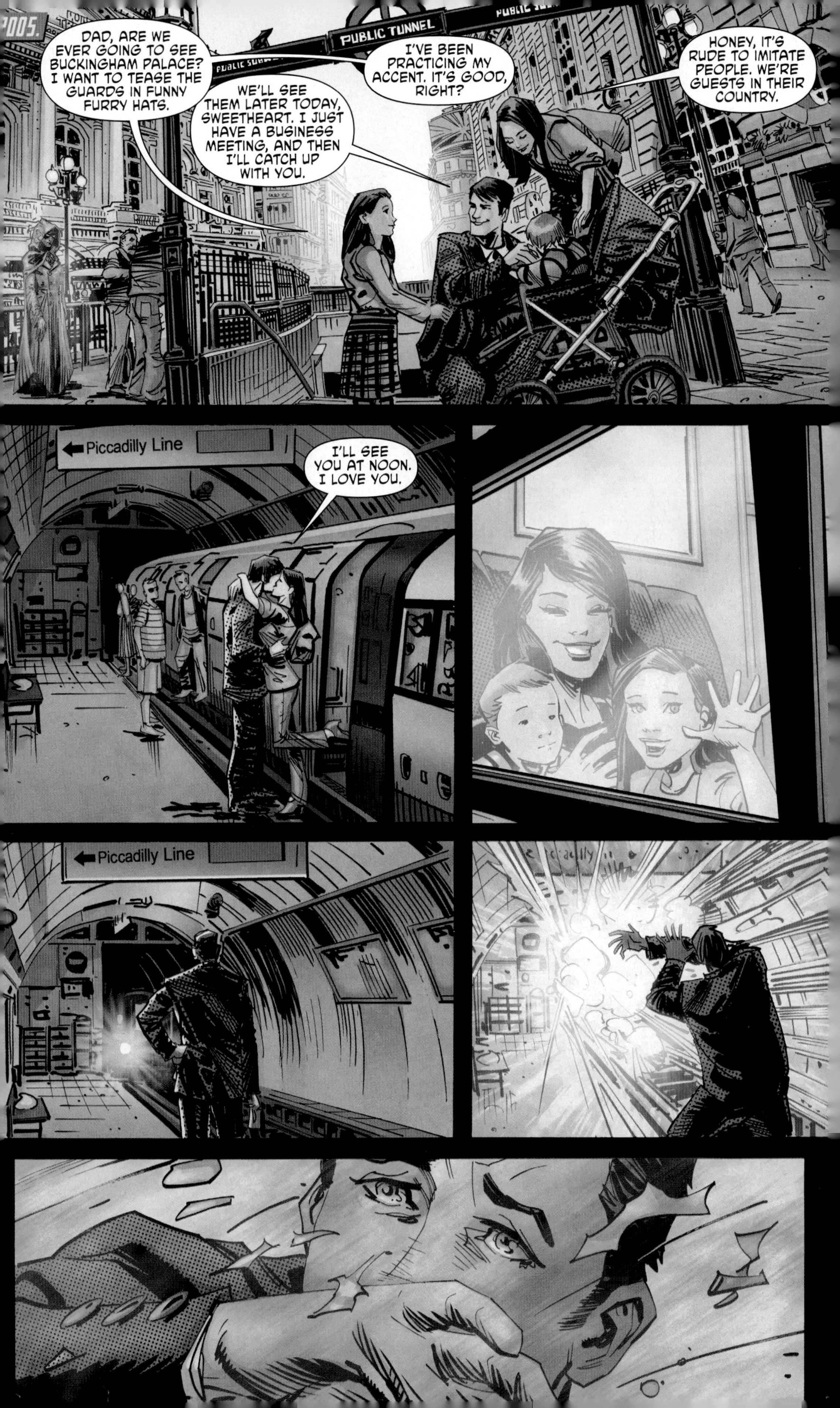
2005.
PUBLIC TUNNEL
DAD, ARE WE EVER GOING TO SEE BUCKINGHAM PALACE? I WANT TO TEASE THE GUARDS IN FUNNY FURRY HATS.
WE'LL SEE THEM LATER TODAY, SWEETHEART. I JUST HAVE A BUSINESS MEETING, AND THEN I'LL CATCH UP WITH YOU.
I'VE BEEN PRACTICING MY ACCENT. IT'S GOOD, RIGHT?
HONEY, IT'S RUDE TO IMITATE PEOPLE. WE'RE GUESTS IN THEIR COUNTRY.
Piccadilly Line
I'LL SEE YOU AT NOON. I LOVE YOU.
Piccadilly Line

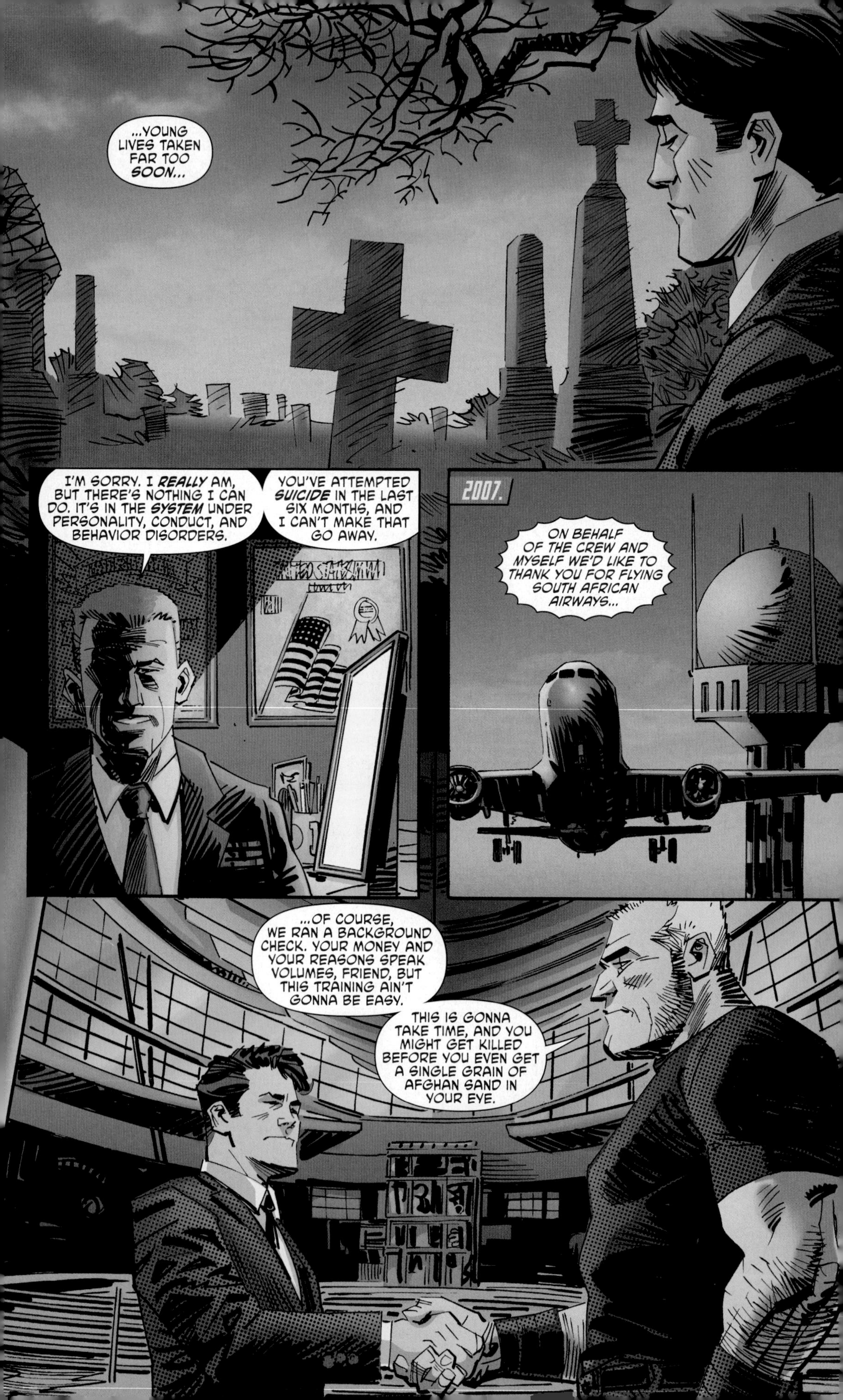
...YOUNG LIVES TAKEN FAR TOO *SOON*...
I'M SORRY. I *REALLY* AM, BUT THERE'S NOTHING I CAN DO. IT'S IN THE *SYSTEM* UNDER PERSONALITY, CONDUCT, AND BEHAVIOR DISORDERS.
YOU'VE ATTEMPTED *SUICIDE* IN THE LAST SIX MONTHS, AND I CAN'T MAKE THAT GO AWAY.
2007.
ON BEHALF OF THE CREW AND MYSELF WE'D LIKE TO THANK YOU FOR FLYING SOUTH AFRICAN AIRWAYS...
...OF COURSE, WE RAN A BACKGROUND CHECK. YOUR MONEY AND YOUR REASONS SPEAK VOLUMES, FRIEND, BUT THIS TRAINING AIN'T GONNA BE EASY.
THIS IS GONNA TAKE TIME, AND YOU MIGHT GET KILLED BEFORE YOU EVEN GET A SINGLE GRAIN OF AFGHAN SAND IN YOUR EYE.

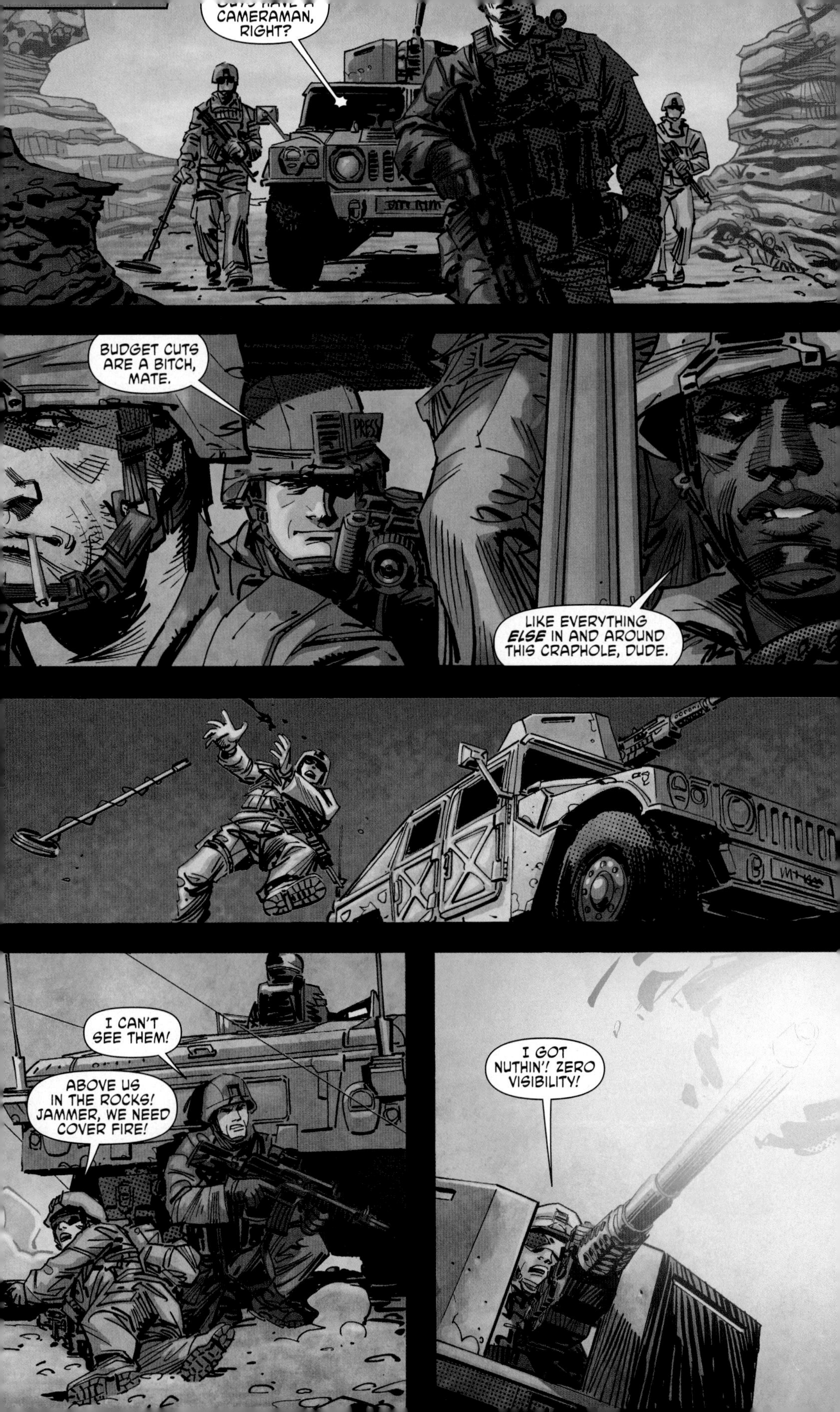
CAMERAMAN, RIGHT?
BUDGET CUTS ARE A BITCH, MATE.
LIKE EVERYTHING *ELSE* IN AND AROUND THIS CRAPHOLE, DUDE.
I CAN'T SEE THEM!
ABOVE US IN THE ROCKS! JAMMER, WE NEED COVER FIRE!
I GOT NUTHIN'! ZERO VISIBILITY!

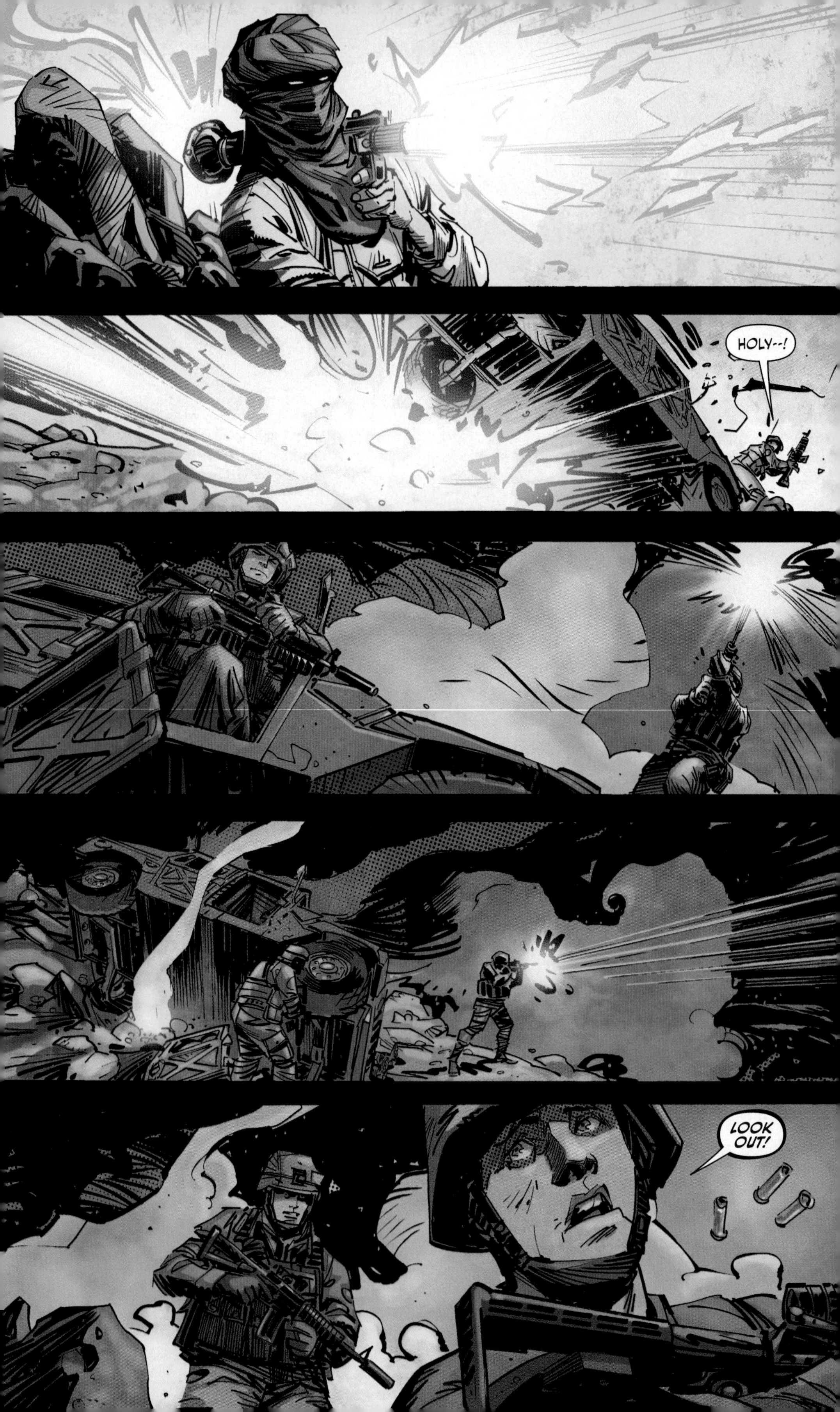
HOLY--!
LOOK OUT!

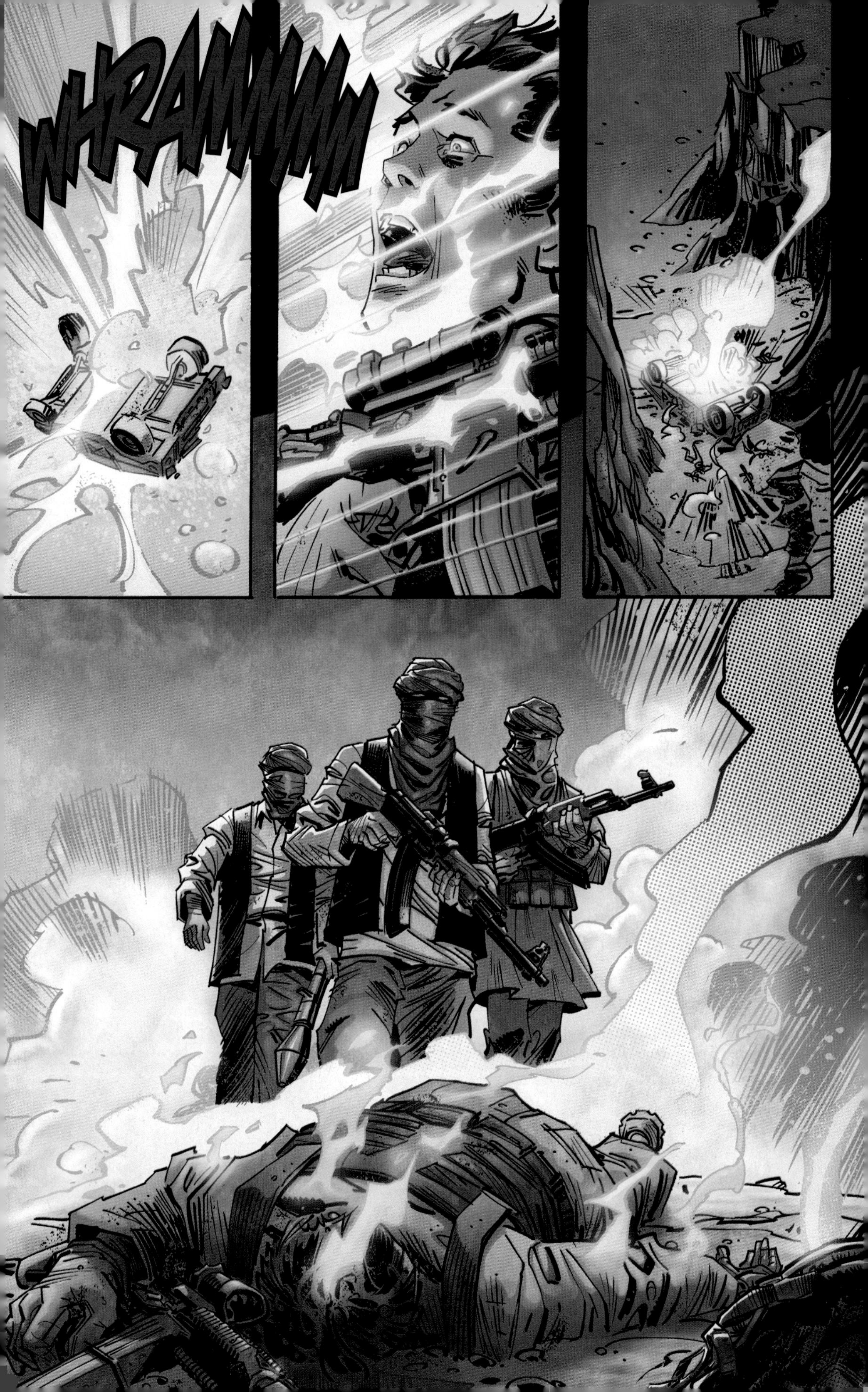
WHRAMMMMM

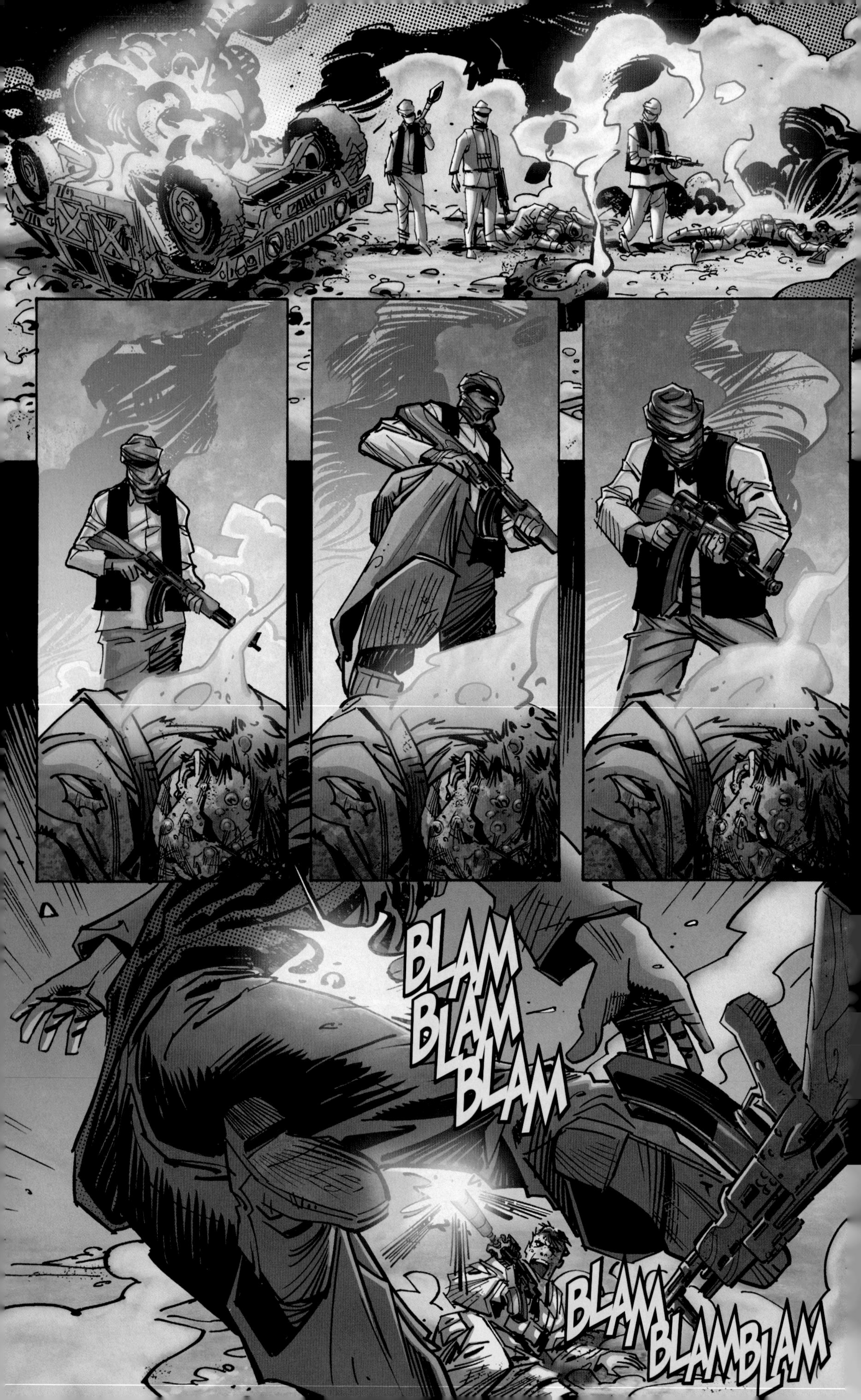
BLAM
BLAM
BLAM
BLAM
BLAMBLAM

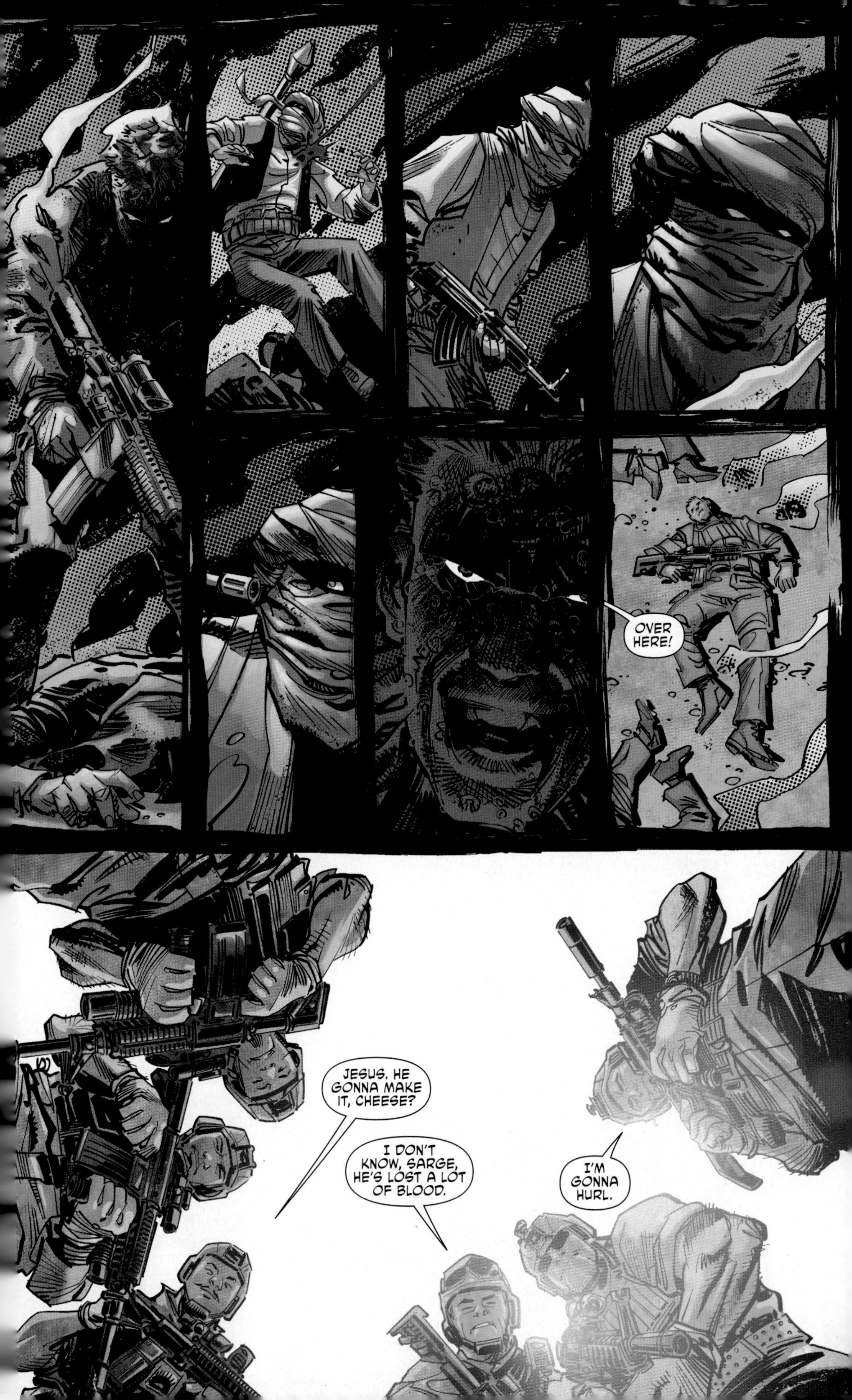
OVER HERE!
JESUS. HE GONNA MAKE IT, CHEESE?
I DON'T KNOW, SARGE, HE'S LOST A LOT OF BLOOD.
I'M GONNA HURL.

AND HERE YOU ARE, A SUICIDAL MURDER MACHINE LOOKING TO AVENGE HIS FAMILY BY ANY MEANS NECESSARY.

TRUTH IS... NO MATTER HOW MANY OF THESE ZEALOTS YOU KILL, YOUR FAMILY ISN'T COMING BACK.

SO WHAT NOW?

IF IT WERE UP TO ME, I'D BE DAMN GLAD TO HAVE YOU ON OUR TEAM, BUT IT SEEMS THE INTELLIGENCE COMMUNITY BACK IN WASHINGTON HAS TAKEN AN INTEREST IN YOU.

WHAT DOES THAT MEAN?

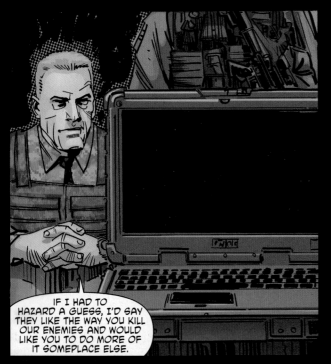

IF I HAD TO HAZARD A GUESS, I'D SAY THEY LIKE THE WAY YOU KILL OUR ENEMIES AND WOULD LIKE YOU TO DO MORE OF IT SOMEPLACE ELSE.

YOU'RE BEING RECRUITED. THAT'S ALL I KNOW.

NEXT
GLOBA
WARRIN

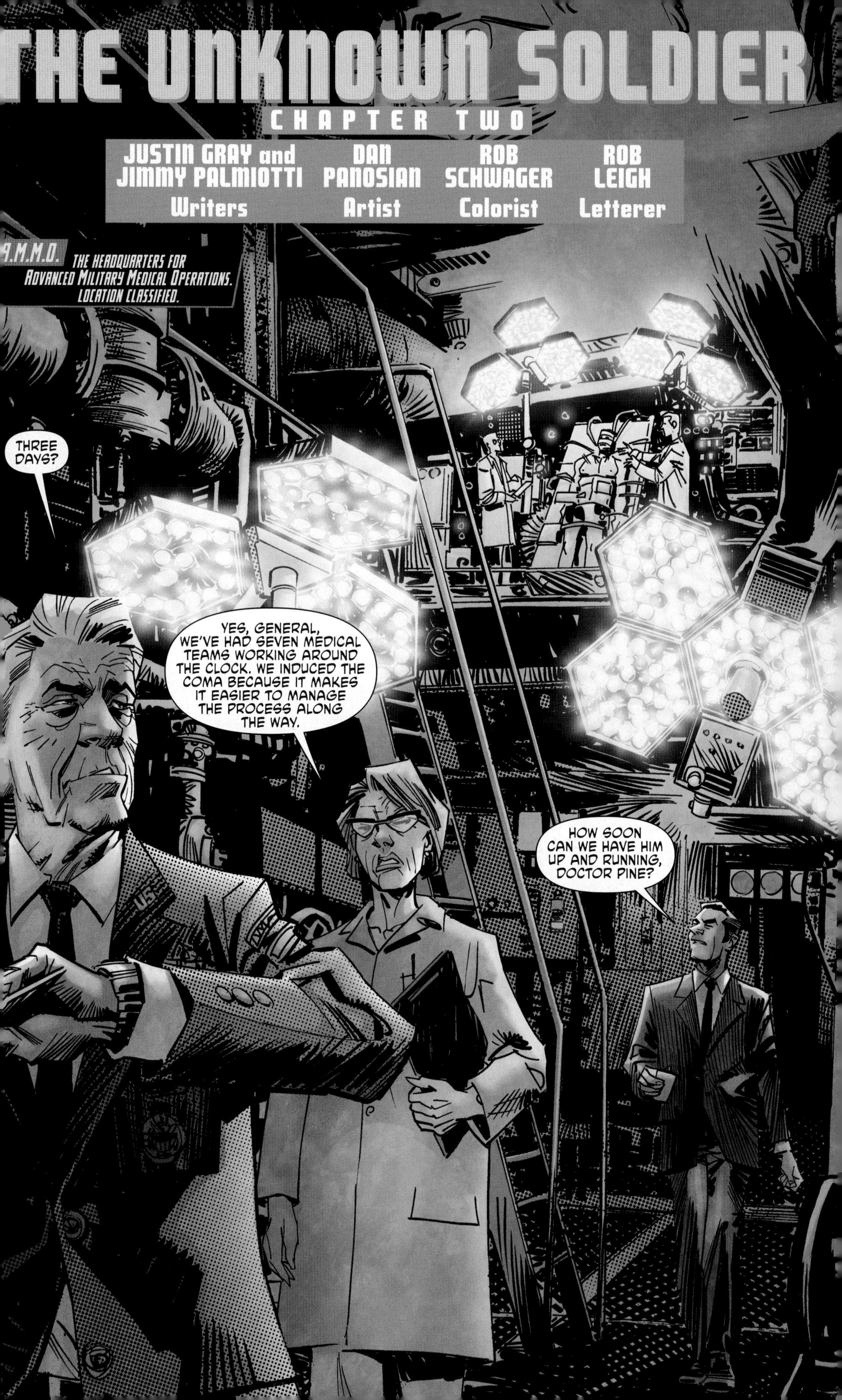
THE UNKNOWN SOLDIER
CHAPTER TWO
JUSTIN GRAY and JIMMY PALMIOTTI Writers
DAN PANOSIAN Artist
ROB SCHWAGER Colorist
ROB LEIGH Letterer
A.M.M.O. THE HEADQUARTERS FOR ADVANCED MILITARY MEDICAL OPERATIONS. LOCATION CLASSIFIED.
THREE DAYS?
YES, GENERAL, WE'VE HAD SEVEN MEDICAL TEAMS WORKING AROUND THE CLOCK. WE INDUCED THE COMA BECAUSE IT MAKES IT EASIER TO MANAGE THE PROCESS ALONG THE WAY.
HOW SOON CAN WE HAVE HIM UP AND RUNNING, DOCTOR PINE?

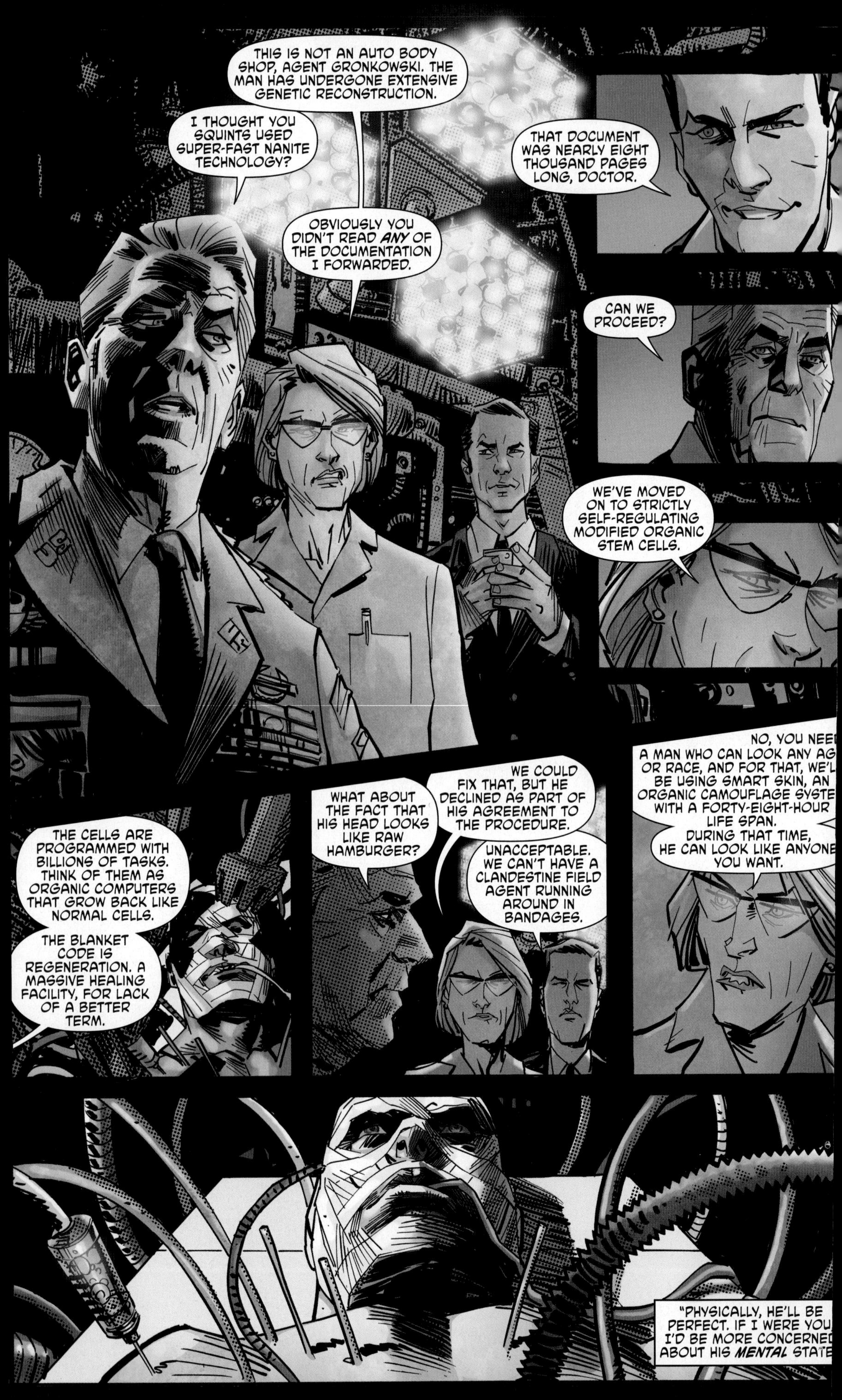
I THOUGHT YOU SQUINTS USED SUPER-FAST NANITE TECHNOLOGY?
THIS IS NOT AN AUTO BODY SHOP, AGENT GRONKOWSKI. THE MAN HAS UNDERGONE EXTENSIVE GENETIC RECONSTRUCTION.
OBVIOUSLY YOU DIDN'T READ *ANY* OF THE DOCUMENTATION I FORWARDED.
THAT DOCUMENT WAS NEARLY EIGHT THOUSAND PAGES LONG, DOCTOR.
CAN WE PROCEED?
WE'VE MOVED ON TO STRICTLY SELF-REGULATING MODIFIED ORGANIC STEM CELLS.
THE CELLS ARE PROGRAMMED WITH BILLIONS OF TASKS. THINK OF THEM AS ORGANIC COMPUTERS THAT GROW BACK LIKE NORMAL CELLS.
THE BLANKET CODE IS REGENERATION. A MASSIVE HEALING FACILITY, FOR LACK OF A BETTER TERM.
WHAT ABOUT THE FACT THAT HIS HEAD LOOKS LIKE RAW HAMBURGER?
WE COULD FIX THAT, BUT HE DECLINED AS PART OF HIS AGREEMENT TO THE PROCEDURE.
UNACCEPTABLE. WE CAN'T HAVE A CLANDESTINE FIELD AGENT RUNNING AROUND IN BANDAGES.
NO, YOU NEE A MAN WHO CAN LOOK ANY AG OR RACE, AND FOR THAT, WE'L BE USING SMART SKIN, AN ORGANIC CAMOUFLAGE SYSTE WITH A FORTY-EIGHT-HOUR LIFE SPAN.
DURING THAT TIME, HE CAN LOOK LIKE ANYONE YOU WANT.
"PHYSICALLY, HE'LL BE PERFECT. IF I WERE YOU I'D BE MORE CONCERNE ABOUT HIS *MENTAL* STAT

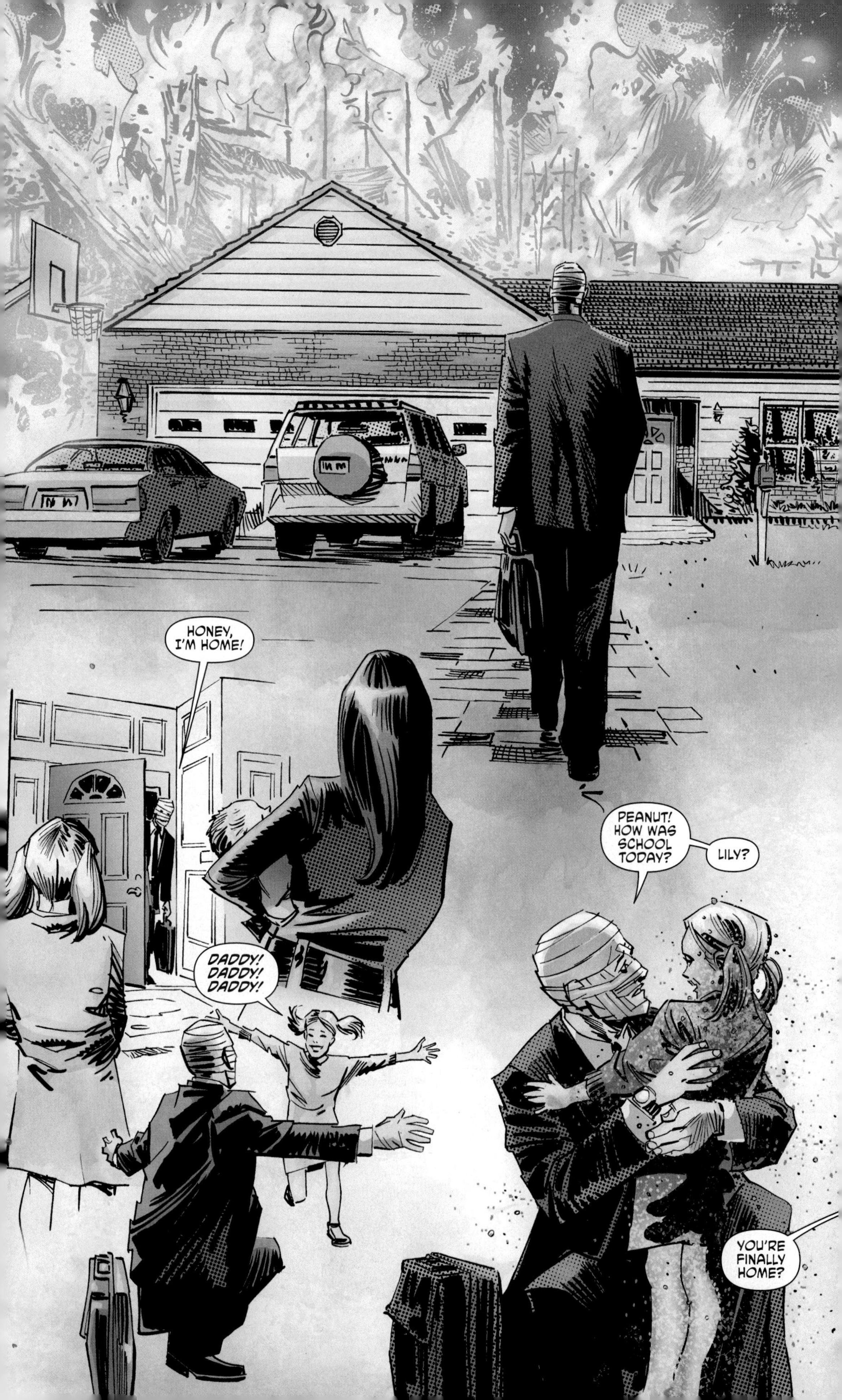
HONEY, I'M HOME!
DADDY! DADDY! DADDY!
PEANUT! HOW WAS SCHOOL TODAY?
LILY?
YOU'RE FINALLY HOME?

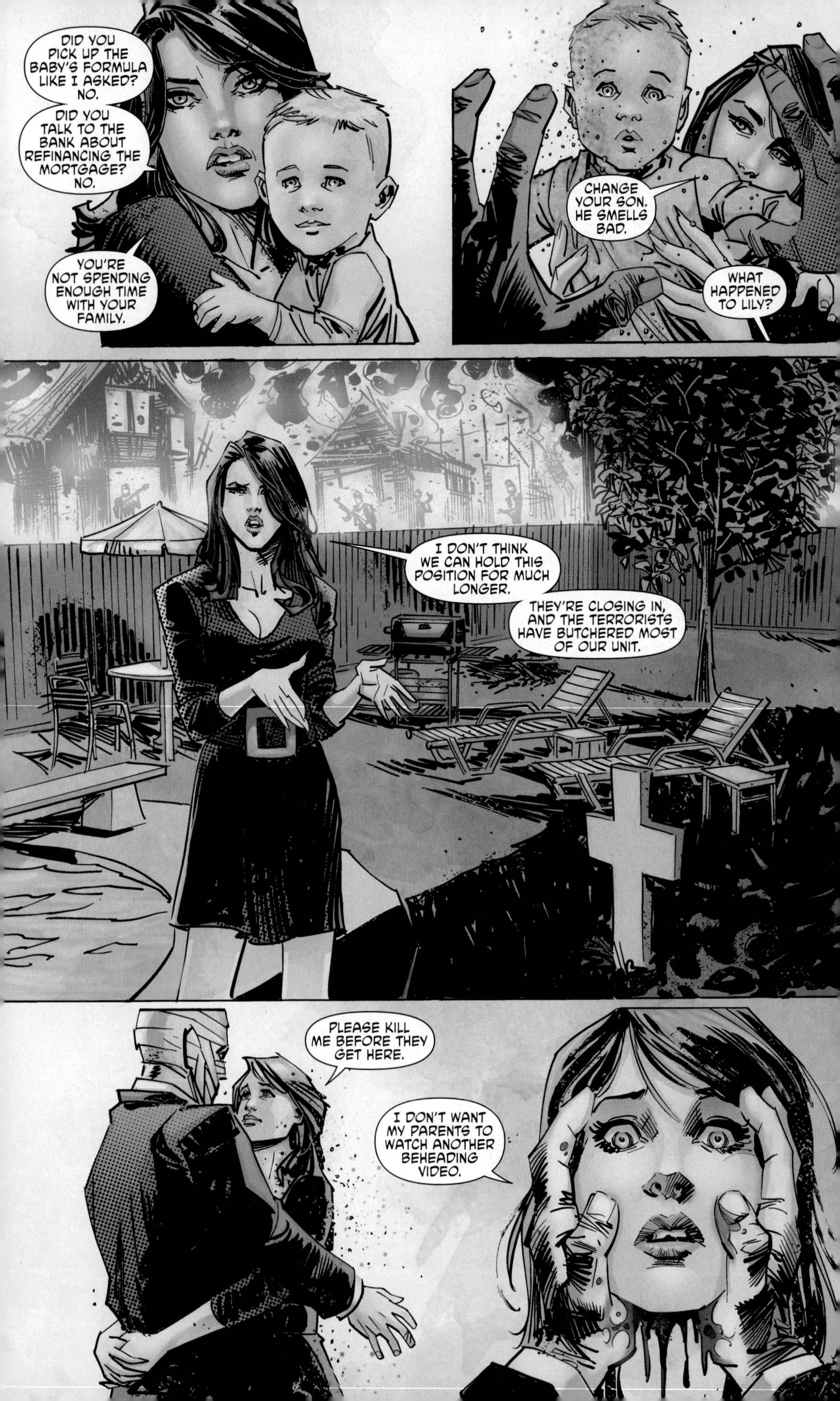
DID YOU PICK UP THE BABY'S FORMULA LIKE I ASKED? NO.
DID YOU TALK TO THE BANK ABOUT REFINANCING THE MORTGAGE? NO.
YOU'RE NOT SPENDING ENOUGH TIME WITH YOUR FAMILY.
CHANGE YOUR SON. HE SMELLS BAD.
WHAT HAPPENED TO LILY?
I DON'T THINK WE CAN HOLD THIS POSITION FOR MUCH LONGER.
THEY'RE CLOSING IN, AND THE TERRORISTS HAVE BUTCHERED MOST OF OUR UNIT.
PLEASE KILL ME BEFORE THEY GET HERE.
I DON'T WANT MY PARENTS TO WATCH ANOTHER BEHEADING VIDEO.

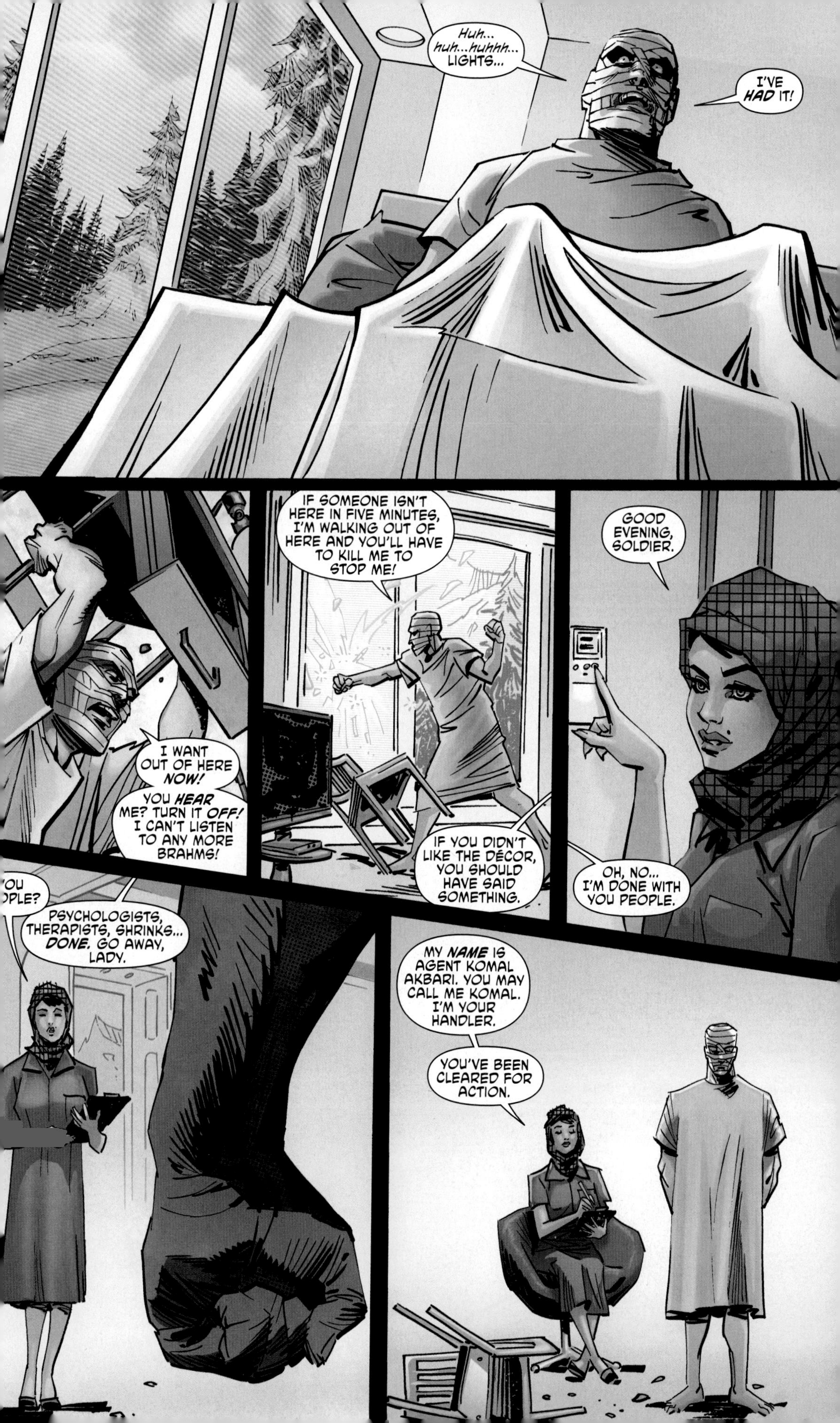
Huh... huh...huhhh... LIGHTS...
I'VE HAD IT!
I WANT OUT OF HERE NOW!
YOU HEAR ME? TURN IT OFF! I CAN'T LISTEN TO ANY MORE BRAHMS!
IF SOMEONE ISN'T HERE IN FIVE MINUTES, I'M WALKING OUT OF HERE AND YOU'LL HAVE TO KILL ME TO STOP ME!
IF YOU DIDN'T LIKE THE DÉCOR, YOU SHOULD HAVE SAID SOMETHING.
GOOD EVENING, SOLDIER.
OH, NO... I'M DONE WITH YOU PEOPLE.
YOU PEOPLE?
PSYCHOLOGISTS, THERAPISTS, SHRINKS... DONE. GO AWAY, LADY.
MY NAME IS AGENT KOMAL AKBARI. YOU MAY CALL ME KOMAL. I'M YOUR HANDLER.
YOU'VE BEEN CLEARED FOR ACTION.

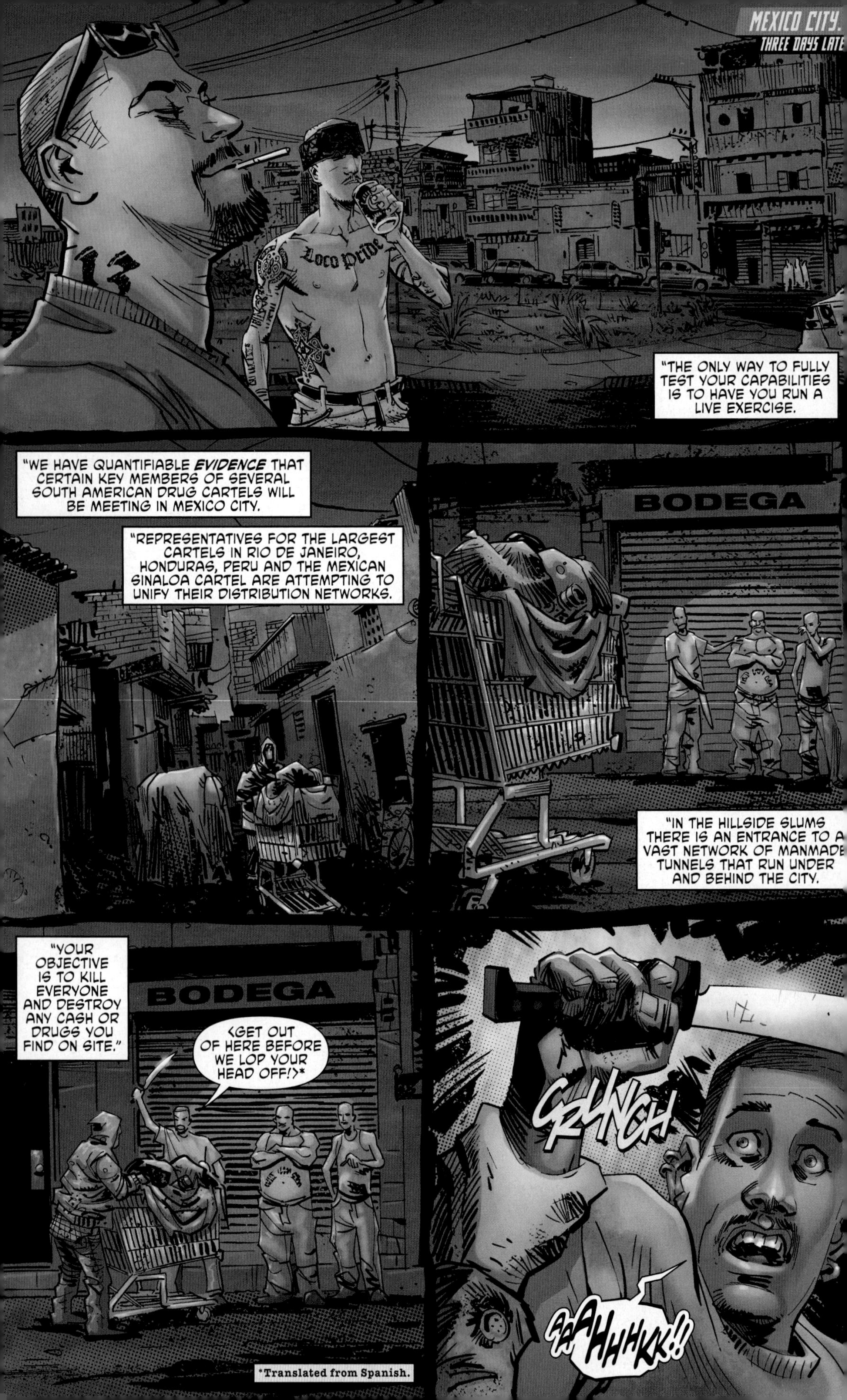

MEXICO CITY.
THREE DAYS LATE
Loco Pride
"THE ONLY WAY TO FULLY TEST YOUR CAPABILITIES IS TO HAVE YOU RUN A LIVE EXERCISE.
"WE HAVE QUANTIFIABLE *EVIDENCE* THAT CERTAIN KEY MEMBERS OF SEVERAL SOUTH AMERICAN DRUG CARTELS WILL BE MEETING IN MEXICO CITY.
"REPRESENTATIVES FOR THE LARGEST CARTELS IN RIO DE JANEIRO, HONDURAS, PERU AND THE MEXICAN SINALOA CARTEL ARE ATTEMPTING TO UNIFY THEIR DISTRIBUTION NETWORKS.
BODEGA
"IN THE HILLSIDE SLUMS THERE IS AN ENTRANCE TO A VAST NETWORK OF MANMADE TUNNELS THAT RUN UNDER AND BEHIND THE CITY.
"YOUR OBJECTIVE IS TO KILL EVERYONE AND DESTROY ANY CASH OR DRUGS YOU FIND ON SITE."
BODEGA
<GET OUT OF HERE BEFORE WE LOP YOUR HEAD OFF!>*
*Translated from Spanish.
CRUNCH
AAAHHHKK!!

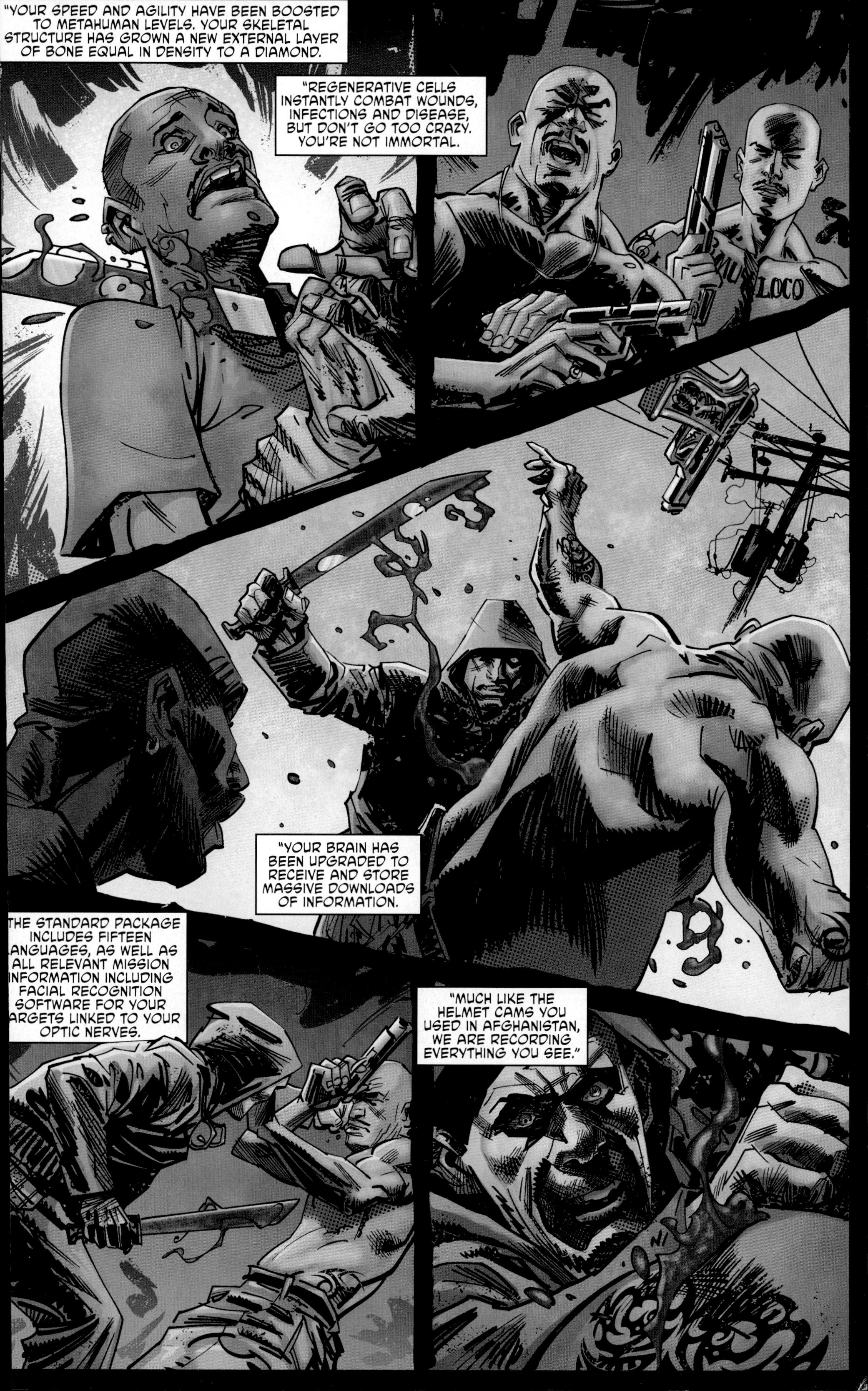
"YOUR SPEED AND AGILITY HAVE BEEN BOOSTED TO METAHUMAN LEVELS. YOUR SKELETAL STRUCTURE HAS GROWN A NEW EXTERNAL LAYER OF BONE EQUAL IN DENSITY TO A DIAMOND.
"REGENERATIVE CELLS INSTANTLY COMBAT WOUNDS, INFECTIONS AND DISEASE, BUT DON'T GO TOO CRAZY. YOU'RE NOT IMMORTAL.
LOCO
"YOUR BRAIN HAS BEEN UPGRADED TO RECEIVE AND STORE MASSIVE DOWNLOADS OF INFORMATION.
THE STANDARD PACKAGE INCLUDES FIFTEEN LANGUAGES, AS WELL AS ALL RELEVANT MISSION INFORMATION INCLUDING FACIAL RECOGNITION SOFTWARE FOR YOUR TARGETS LINKED TO YOUR OPTIC NERVES.
"MUCH LIKE THE HELMET CAMS YOU USED IN AFGHANISTAN, WE ARE RECORDING EVERYTHING YOU SEE."

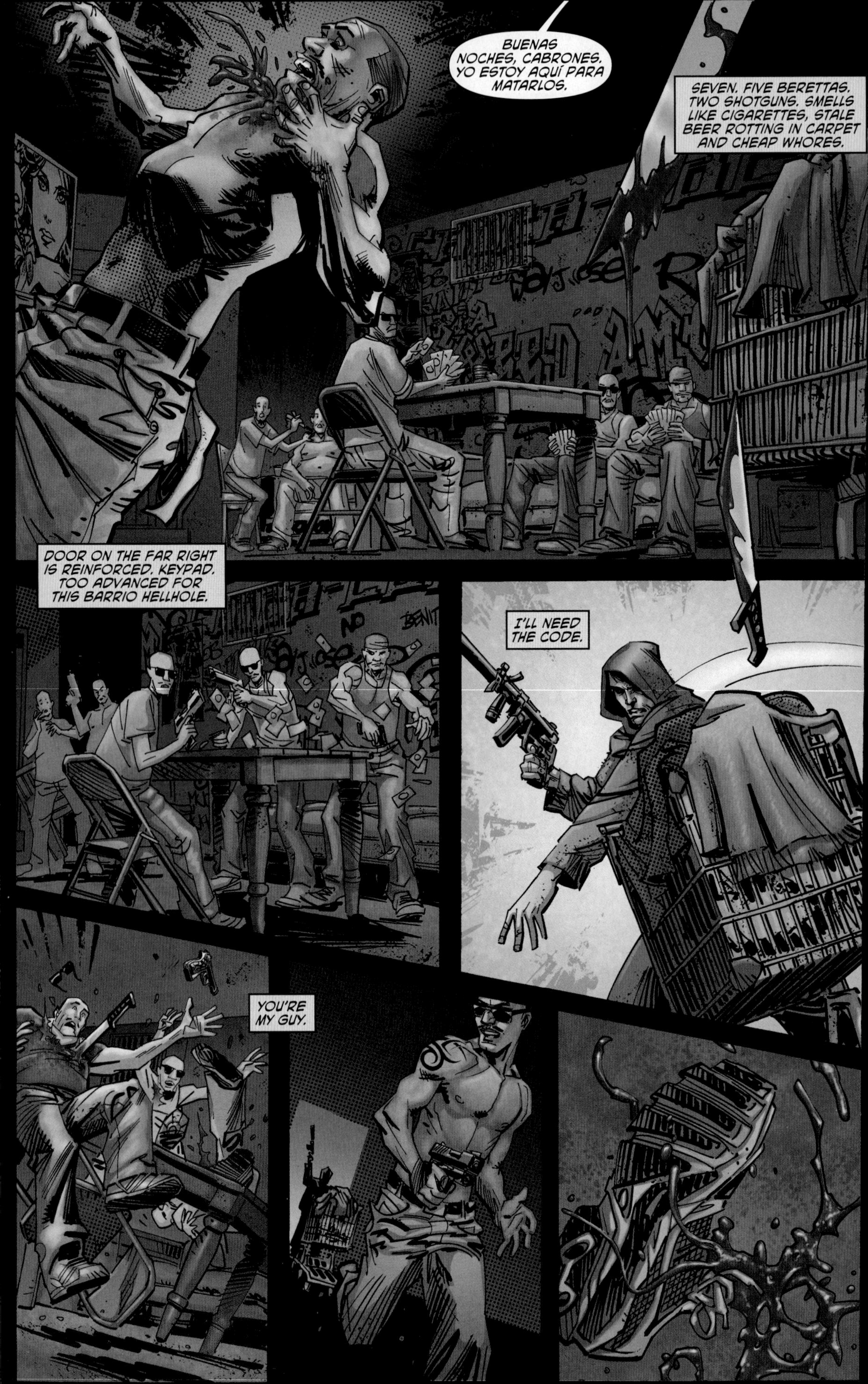
BUENAS NOCHES, CABRONES. YO ESTOY AQUÍ PARA MATARLOS.
SEVEN. FIVE BERETTAS. TWO SHOTGUNS. SMELLS LIKE CIGARETTES, STALE BEER ROTTING IN CARPET AND CHEAP WHORES.
DOOR ON THE FAR RIGHT IS REINFORCED. KEYPAD. TOO ADVANCED FOR THIS BARRIO HELLHOLE.
I'LL NEED THE CODE.
YOU'RE MY GUY.

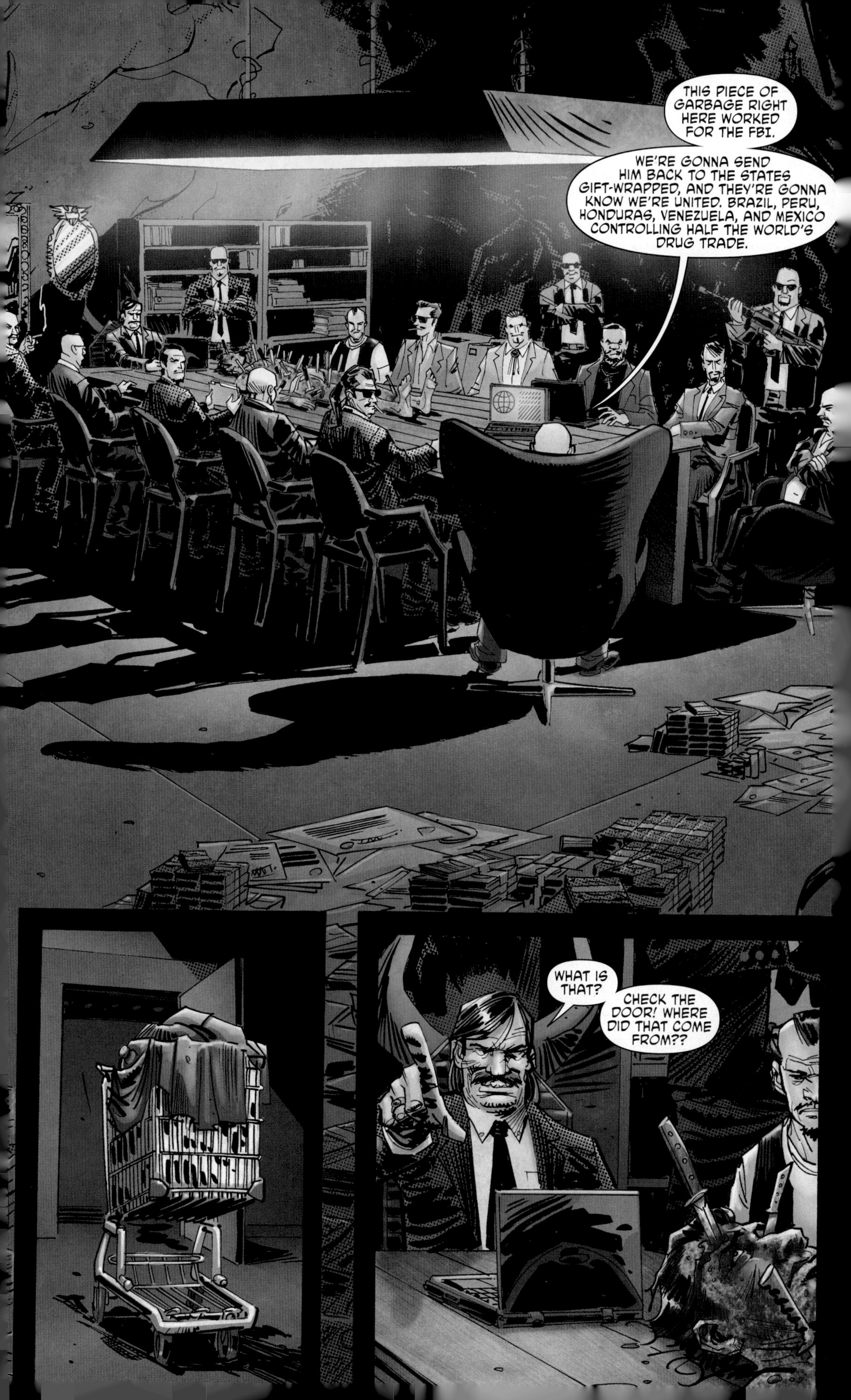
THIS PIECE OF GARBAGE RIGHT HERE WORKED FOR THE FBI.
WE'RE GONNA SEND HIM BACK TO THE STATES GIFT-WRAPPED, AND THEY'RE GONNA KNOW WE'RE UNITED. BRAZIL, PERU, HONDURAS, VENEZUELA, AND MEXICO CONTROLLING HALF THE WORLD'S DRUG TRADE.
WHAT IS THAT?
CHECK THE DOOR! WHERE DID THAT COME FROM??

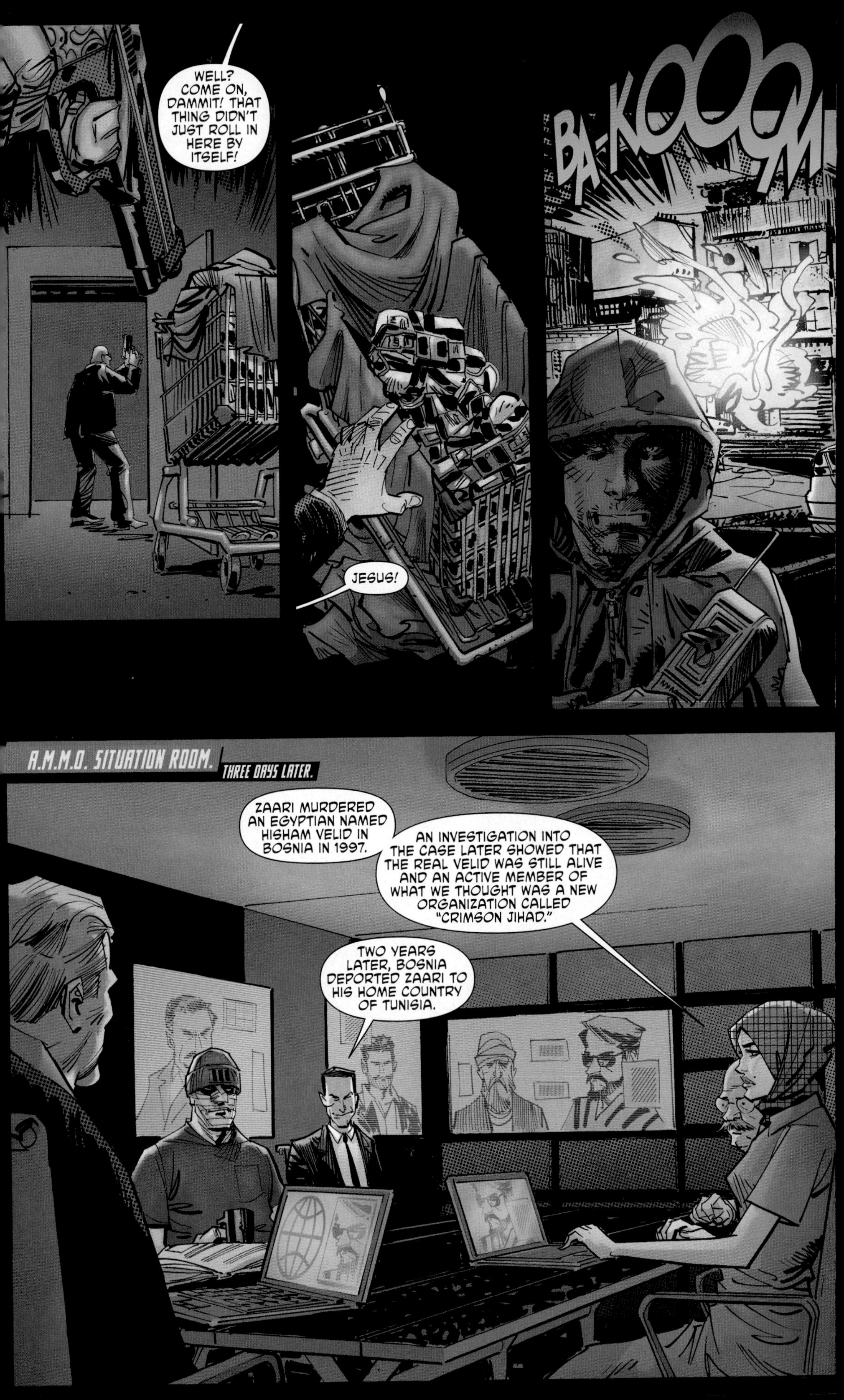
WELL? COME ON, DAMMIT! THAT THING DIDN'T JUST ROLL IN HERE BY ITSELF!
JESUS!
BA-KOOOM
A.M.M.O. SITUATION ROOM.
THREE DAYS LATER.
ZAARI MURDERED AN EGYPTIAN NAMED HISHAM VELID IN BOSNIA IN 1997.
AN INVESTIGATION INTO THE CASE LATER SHOWED THAT THE REAL VELID WAS STILL ALIVE AND AN ACTIVE MEMBER OF WHAT WE THOUGHT WAS A NEW ORGANIZATION CALLED "CRIMSON JIHAD."
TWO YEARS LATER, BOSNIA DEPORTED ZAARI TO HIS HOME COUNTRY OF TUNISIA.

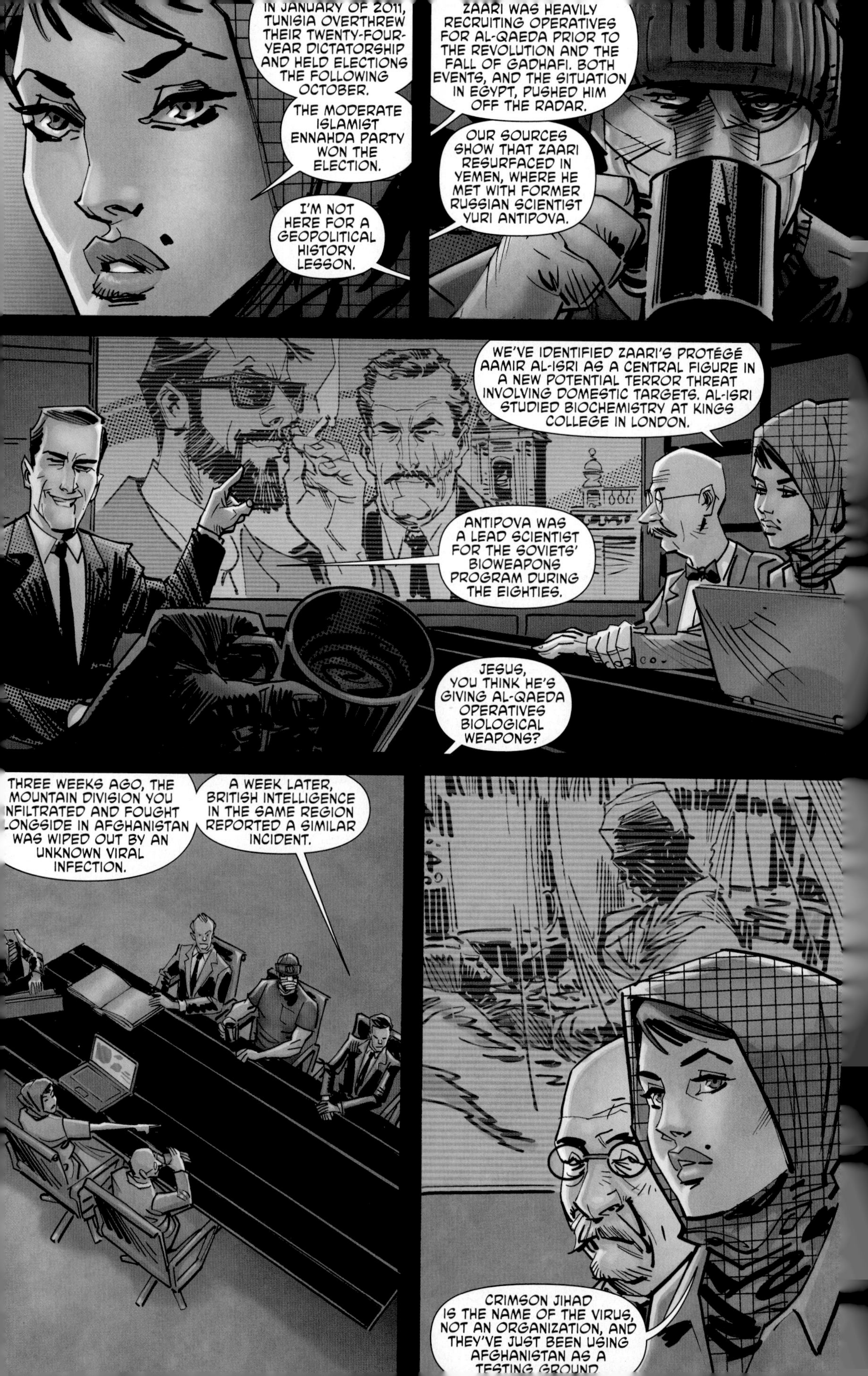
IN JANUARY OF 2011, TUNISIA OVERTHREW THEIR TWENTY-FOUR-YEAR DICTATORSHIP AND HELD ELECTIONS THE FOLLOWING OCTOBER.
THE MODERATE ISLAMIST ENNAHDA PARTY WON THE ELECTION.
I'M NOT HERE FOR A GEOPOLITICAL HISTORY LESSON.
ZAARI WAS HEAVILY RECRUITING OPERATIVES FOR AL-QAEDA PRIOR TO THE REVOLUTION AND THE FALL OF GADHAFI. BOTH EVENTS, AND THE SITUATION IN EGYPT, PUSHED HIM OFF THE RADAR.
OUR SOURCES SHOW THAT ZAARI RESURFACED IN YEMEN, WHERE HE MET WITH FORMER RUSSIAN SCIENTIST YURI ANTIPOVA.
WE'VE IDENTIFIED ZAARI'S PROTÉGÉ AAMIR AL-ISRI AS A CENTRAL FIGURE IN A NEW POTENTIAL TERROR THREAT INVOLVING DOMESTIC TARGETS. AL-ISRI STUDIED BIOCHEMISTRY AT KINGS COLLEGE IN LONDON.
ANTIPOVA WAS A LEAD SCIENTIST FOR THE SOVIETS' BIOWEAPONS PROGRAM DURING THE EIGHTIES.
JESUS, YOU THINK HE'S GIVING AL-QAEDA OPERATIVES BIOLOGICAL WEAPONS?
THREE WEEKS AGO, THE MOUNTAIN DIVISION YOU NFILTRATED AND FOUGHT LONGSIDE IN AFGHANISTAN WAS WIPED OUT BY AN UNKNOWN VIRAL INFECTION.
A WEEK LATER, BRITISH INTELLIGENCE IN THE SAME REGION REPORTED A SIMILAR INCIDENT.
CRIMSON JIHAD IS THE NAME OF THE VIRUS, NOT AN ORGANIZATION, AND THEY'VE JUST BEEN USING AFGHANISTAN AS A TESTING GROUND

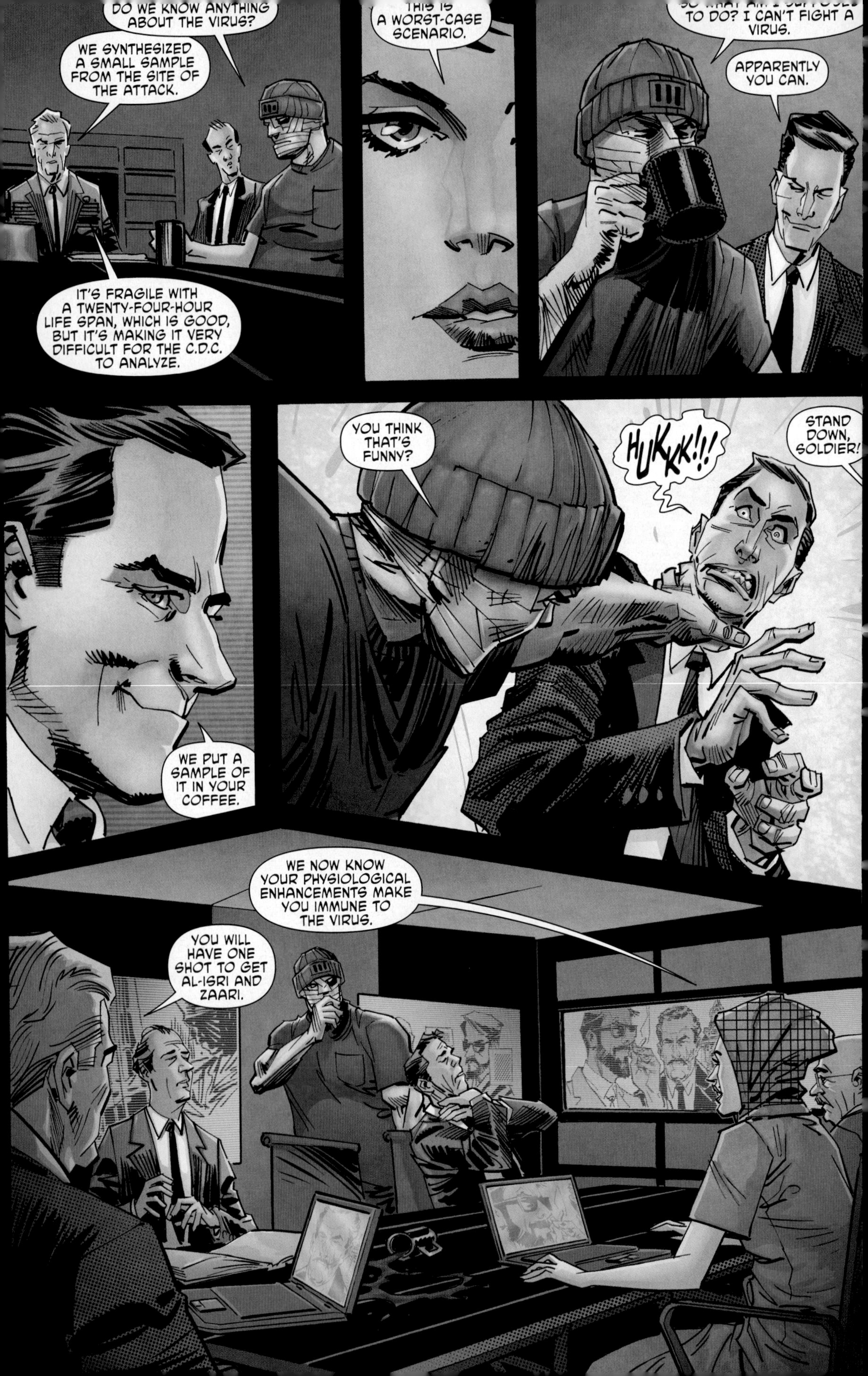
DO WE KNOW ANYTHING ABOUT THE VIRUS?
WE SYNTHESIZED A SMALL SAMPLE FROM THE SITE OF THE ATTACK.
IT'S FRAGILE WITH A TWENTY-FOUR-HOUR LIFE SPAN, WHICH IS GOOD, BUT IT'S MAKING IT VERY DIFFICULT FOR THE C.D.C. TO ANALYZE.
THIS IS A WORST-CASE SCENARIO.
TO DO? I CAN'T FIGHT A VIRUS.
APPARENTLY YOU CAN.
WE PUT A SAMPLE OF IT IN YOUR COFFEE.
YOU THINK THAT'S FUNNY?
HUKKK!!!
STAND DOWN, SOLDIER!
WE NOW KNOW YOUR PHYSIOLOGICAL ENHANCEMENTS MAKE YOU IMMUNE TO THE VIRUS.
YOU WILL HAVE ONE SHOT TO GET AL-ISRI AND ZAARI.

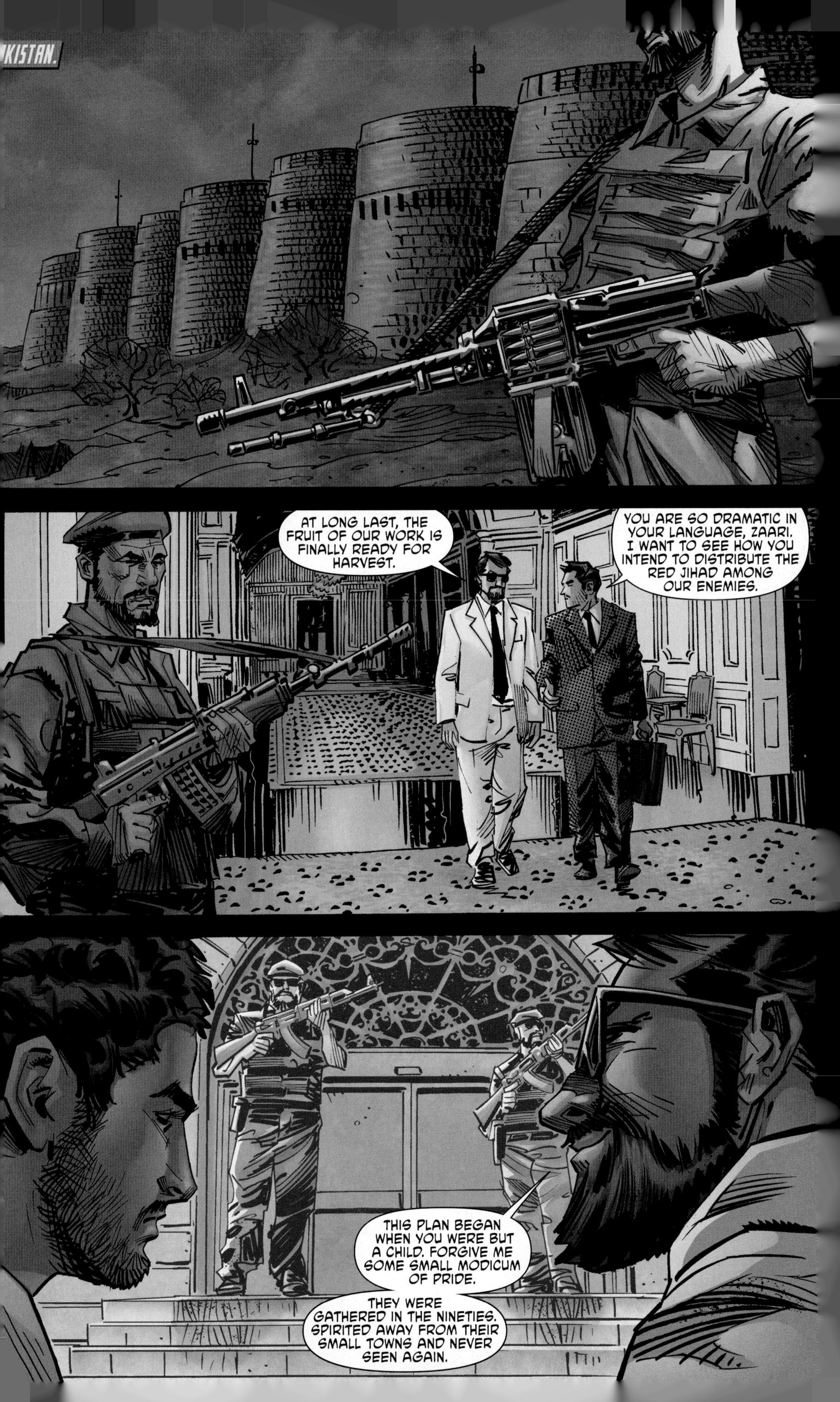
KISTAN.
AT LONG LAST, THE FRUIT OF OUR WORK IS FINALLY READY FOR HARVEST.
YOU ARE SO DRAMATIC IN YOUR LANGUAGE, ZAARI. I WANT TO SEE HOW YOU INTEND TO DISTRIBUTE THE RED JIHAD AMONG OUR ENEMIES.
THIS PLAN BEGAN WHEN YOU WERE BUT A CHILD. FORGIVE ME SOME SMALL MODICUM OF PRIDE.
THEY WERE GATHERED IN THE NINETIES. SPIRITED AWAY FROM THEIR SMALL TOWNS AND NEVER SEEN AGAIN.

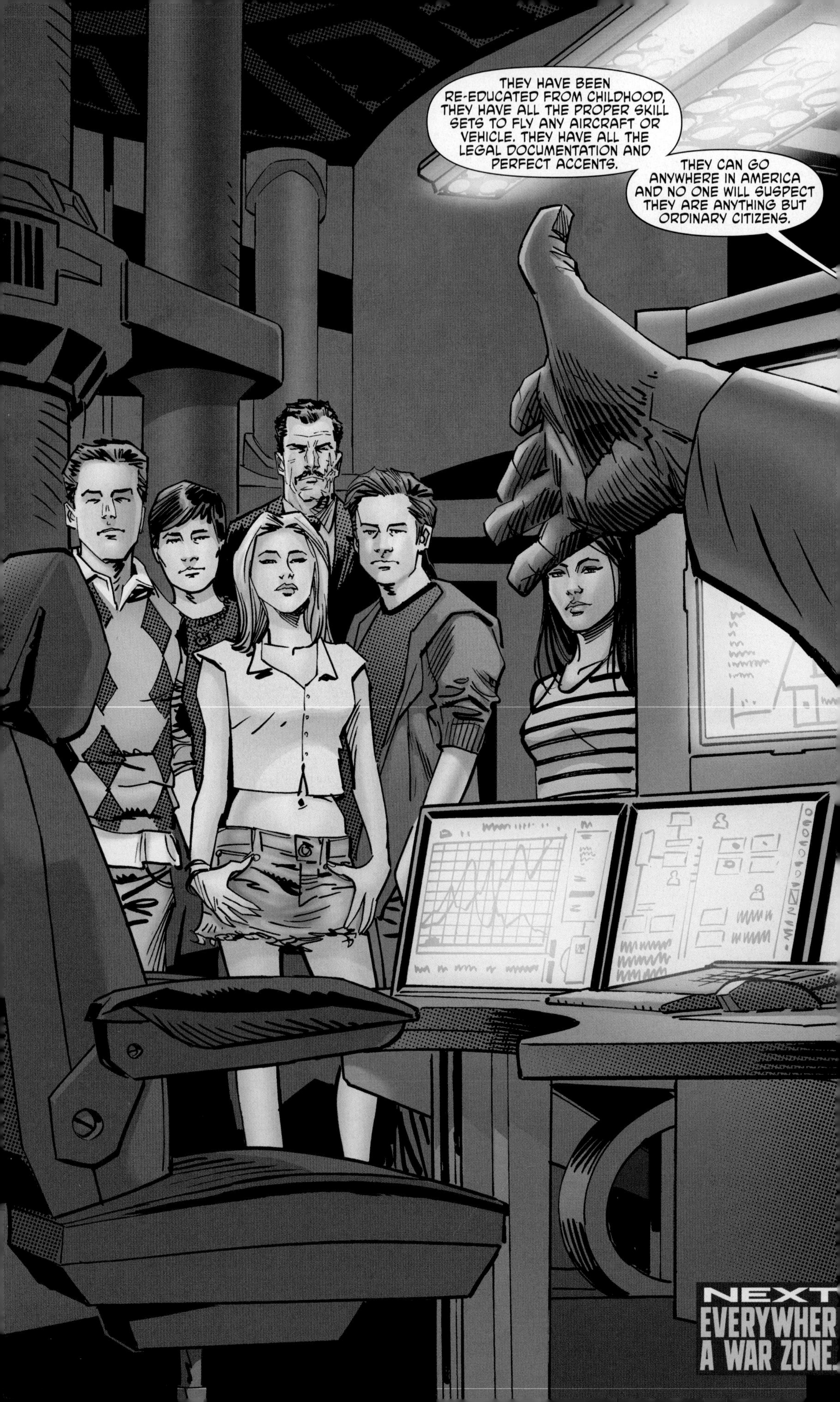
THEY HAVE BEEN RE-EDUCATED FROM CHILDHOOD, THEY HAVE ALL THE PROPER SKILL SETS TO FLY ANY AIRCRAFT OR VEHICLE. THEY HAVE ALL THE LEGAL DOCUMENTATION AND PERFECT ACCENTS.
THEY CAN GO ANYWHERE IN AMERICA AND NO ONE WILL SUSPECT THEY ARE ANYTHING BUT ORDINARY CITIZENS.
NEXT
EVERYWHER
A WAR ZONE.

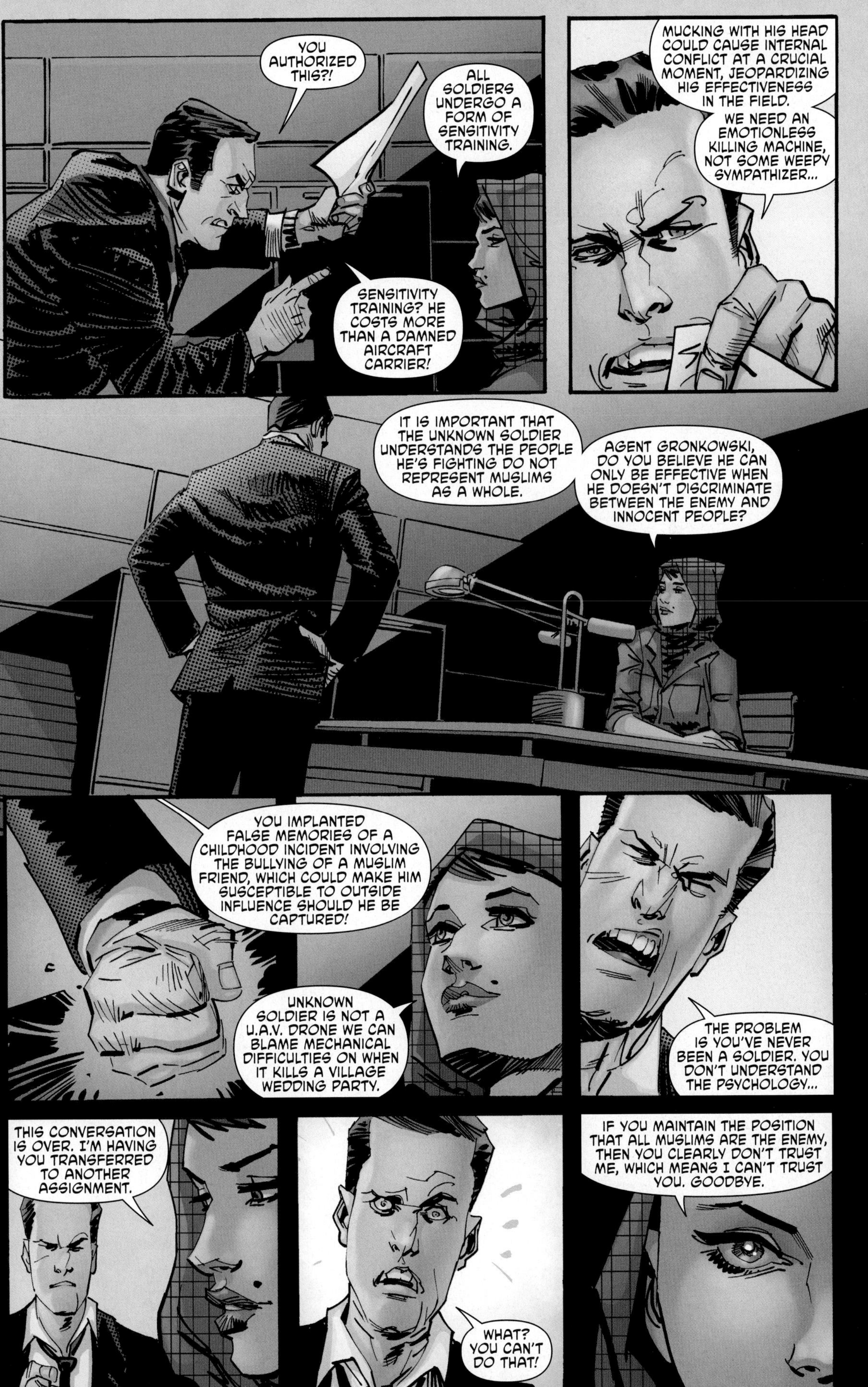
YOU AUTHORIZED THIS?!
ALL SOLDIERS UNDERGO A FORM OF SENSITIVITY TRAINING.
SENSITIVITY TRAINING? HE COSTS MORE THAN A DAMNED AIRCRAFT CARRIER!
MUCKING WITH HIS HEAD COULD CAUSE INTERNAL CONFLICT AT A CRUCIAL MOMENT, JEOPARDIZING HIS EFFECTIVENESS IN THE FIELD.
WE NEED AN EMOTIONLESS KILLING MACHINE, NOT SOME WEEPY SYMPATHIZER...
IT IS IMPORTANT THAT THE UNKNOWN SOLDIER UNDERSTANDS THE PEOPLE HE'S FIGHTING DO NOT REPRESENT MUSLIMS AS A WHOLE.
AGENT GRONKOWSKI, DO YOU BELIEVE HE CAN ONLY BE EFFECTIVE WHEN HE DOESN'T DISCRIMINATE BETWEEN THE ENEMY AND INNOCENT PEOPLE?
YOU IMPLANTED FALSE MEMORIES OF A CHILDHOOD INCIDENT INVOLVING THE BULLYING OF A MUSLIM FRIEND, WHICH COULD MAKE HIM SUSCEPTIBLE TO OUTSIDE INFLUENCE SHOULD HE BE CAPTURED!
UNKNOWN SOLDIER IS NOT A U.A.V. DRONE WE CAN BLAME MECHANICAL DIFFICULTIES ON WHEN IT KILLS A VILLAGE WEDDING PARTY.
THE PROBLEM IS YOU'VE NEVER BEEN A SOLDIER. YOU DON'T UNDERSTAND THE PSYCHOLOGY...
THIS CONVERSATION IS OVER. I'M HAVING YOU TRANSFERRED TO ANOTHER ASSIGNMENT.
WHAT? YOU CAN'T DO THAT!
IF YOU MAINTAIN THE POSITION THAT ALL MUSLIMS ARE THE ENEMY, THEN YOU CLEARLY DON'T TRUST ME, WHICH MEANS I CAN'T TRUST YOU. GOODBYE.

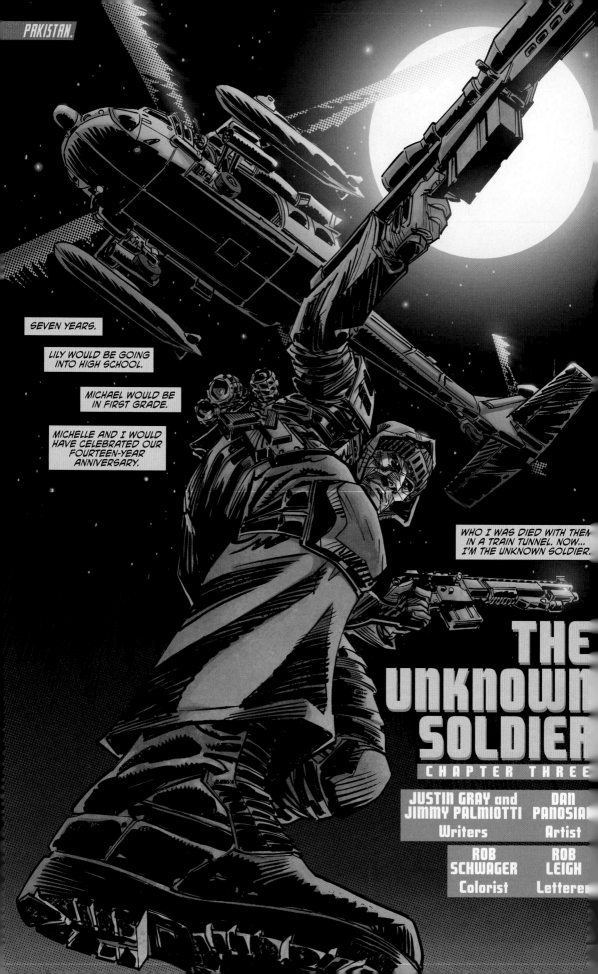

PAKISTAN.

SEVEN YEARS.

LILY WOULD BE GOING INTO HIGH SCHOOL.

MICHAEL WOULD BE IN FIRST GRADE.

MICHELLE AND I WOULD HAVE CELEBRATED OUR FOURTEEN-YEAR ANNIVERSARY.

WHO I WAS DIED WITH THEM IN A TRAIN TUNNEL. NOW... I'M THE UNKNOWN SOLDIER.

THE UNKNOWN SOLDIER
CHAPTER THREE

JUSTIN GRAY and JIMMY PALMIOTTI
Writers

DAN PANOSIAN
Artist

ROB SCHWAGER
Colorist

ROB LEIGH
Letterer

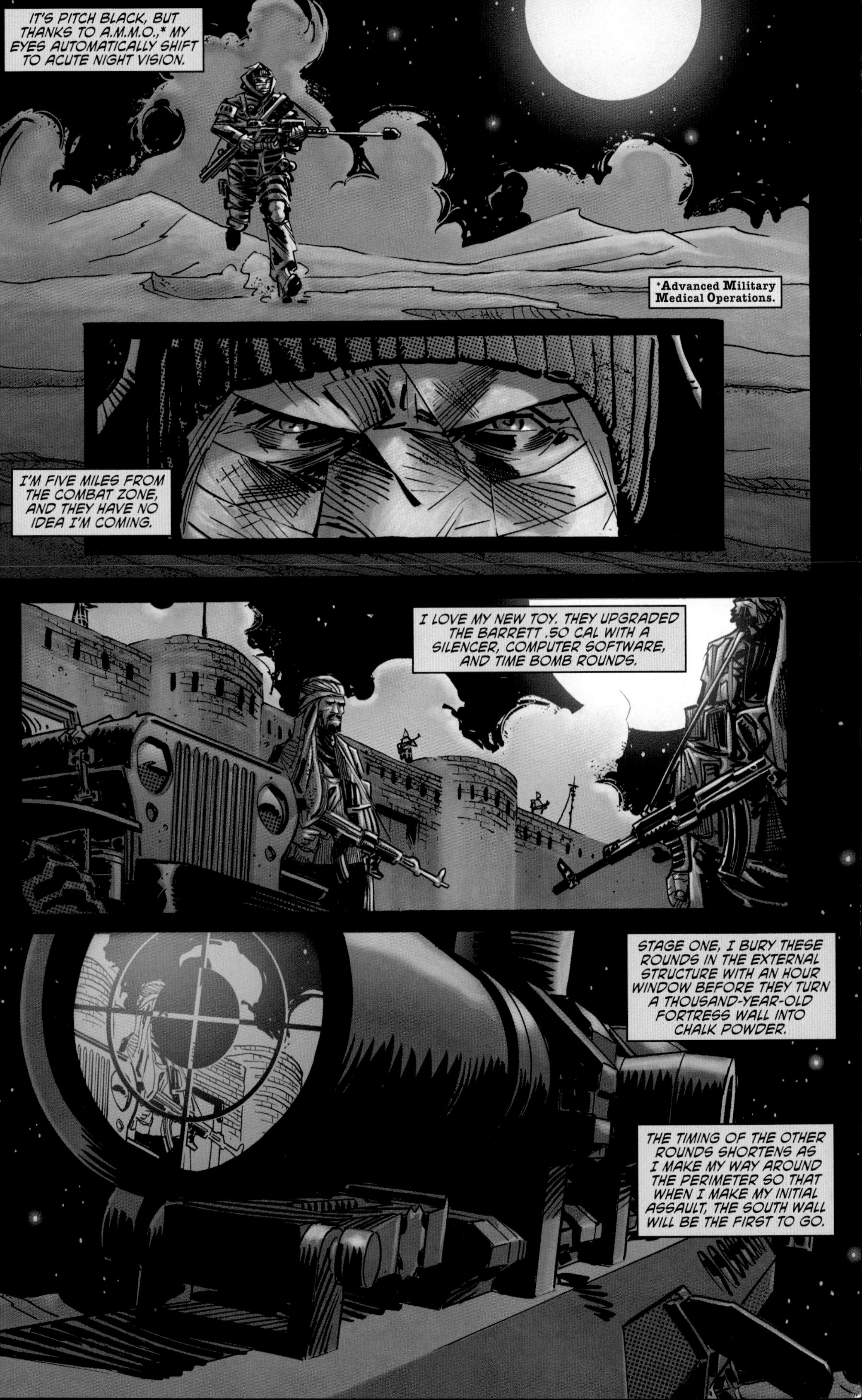
IT'S PITCH BLACK, BUT THANKS TO A.M.M.O.,* MY EYES AUTOMATICALLY SHIFT TO ACUTE NIGHT VISION.
*Advanced Military Medical Operations.
I'M FIVE MILES FROM THE COMBAT ZONE, AND THEY HAVE NO IDEA I'M COMING.
I LOVE MY NEW TOY. THEY UPGRADED THE BARRETT .50 CAL WITH A SILENCER, COMPUTER SOFTWARE, AND TIME BOMB ROUNDS.
STAGE ONE, I BURY THESE ROUNDS IN THE EXTERNAL STRUCTURE WITH AN HOUR WINDOW BEFORE THEY TURN A THOUSAND-YEAR-OLD FORTRESS WALL INTO CHALK POWDER.
THE TIMING OF THE OTHER ROUNDS SHORTENS AS I MAKE MY WAY AROUND THE PERIMETER SO THAT WHEN I MAKE MY INITIAL ASSAULT, THE SOUTH WALL WILL BE THE FIRST TO GO.

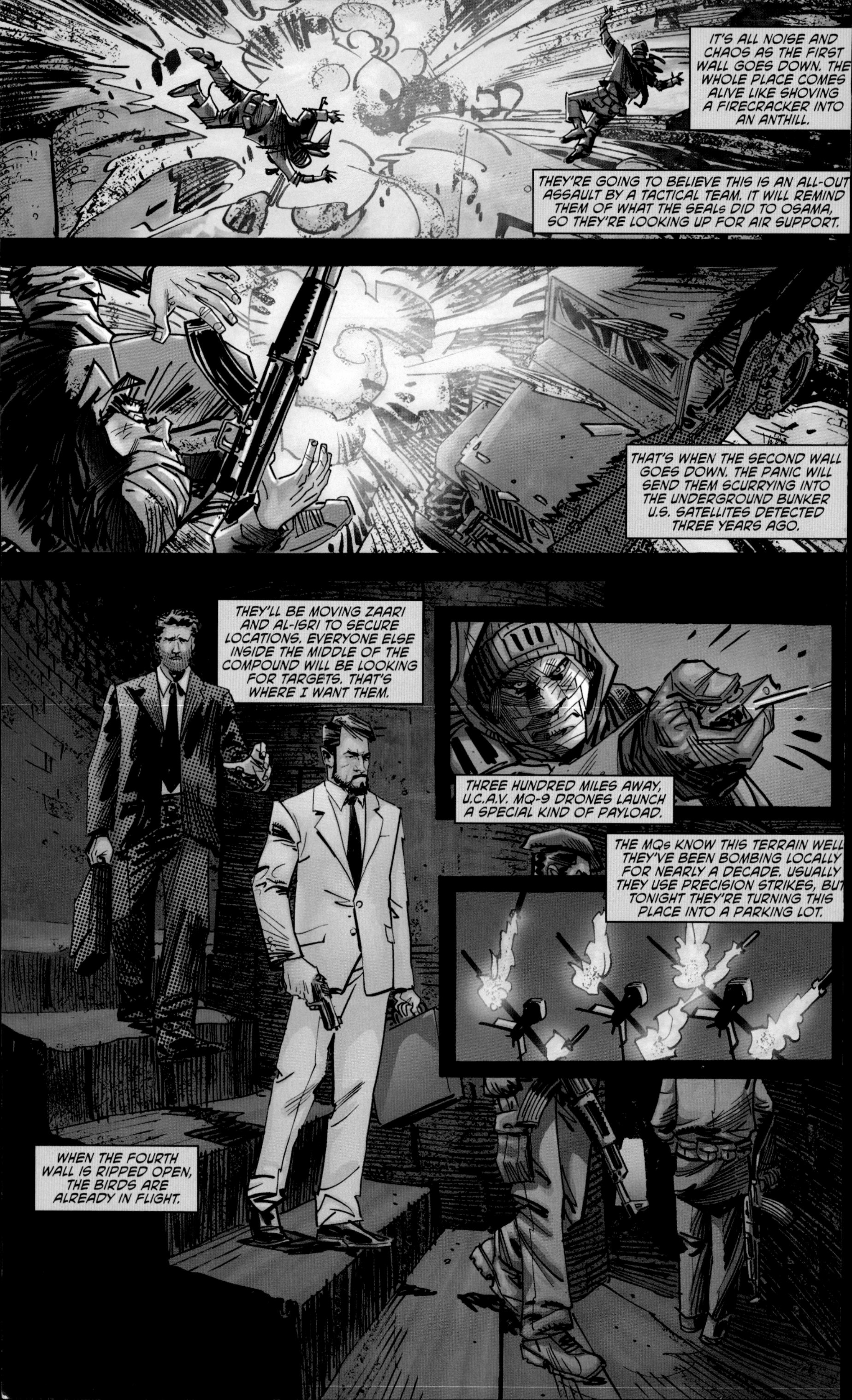
IT'S ALL NOISE AND CHAOS AS THE FIRST WALL GOES DOWN. THE WHOLE PLACE COMES ALIVE LIKE SHOVING A FIRECRACKER INTO AN ANTHILL.
THEY'RE GOING TO BELIEVE THIS IS AN ALL-OUT ASSAULT BY A TACTICAL TEAM. IT WILL REMIND THEM OF WHAT THE SEALs DID TO OSAMA, SO THEY'RE LOOKING UP FOR AIR SUPPORT.
THAT'S WHEN THE SECOND WALL GOES DOWN. THE PANIC WILL SEND THEM SCURRYING INTO THE UNDERGROUND BUNKER U.S. SATELLITES DETECTED THREE YEARS AGO.
THEY'LL BE MOVING ZAARI AND AL-ISRI TO SECURE LOCATIONS. EVERYONE ELSE INSIDE THE MIDDLE OF THE COMPOUND WILL BE LOOKING FOR TARGETS. THAT'S WHERE I WANT THEM.
THREE HUNDRED MILES AWAY, U.C.A.V. MQ-9 DRONES LAUNCH A SPECIAL KIND OF PAYLOAD.
THE MQs KNOW THIS TERRAIN WELL. THEY'VE BEEN BOMBING LOCALLY FOR NEARLY A DECADE. USUALLY THEY USE PRECISION STRIKES, BUT TONIGHT THEY'RE TURNING THIS PLACE INTO A PARKING LOT.
WHEN THE FOURTH WALL IS RIPPED OPEN, THE BIRDS ARE ALREADY IN FLIGHT.

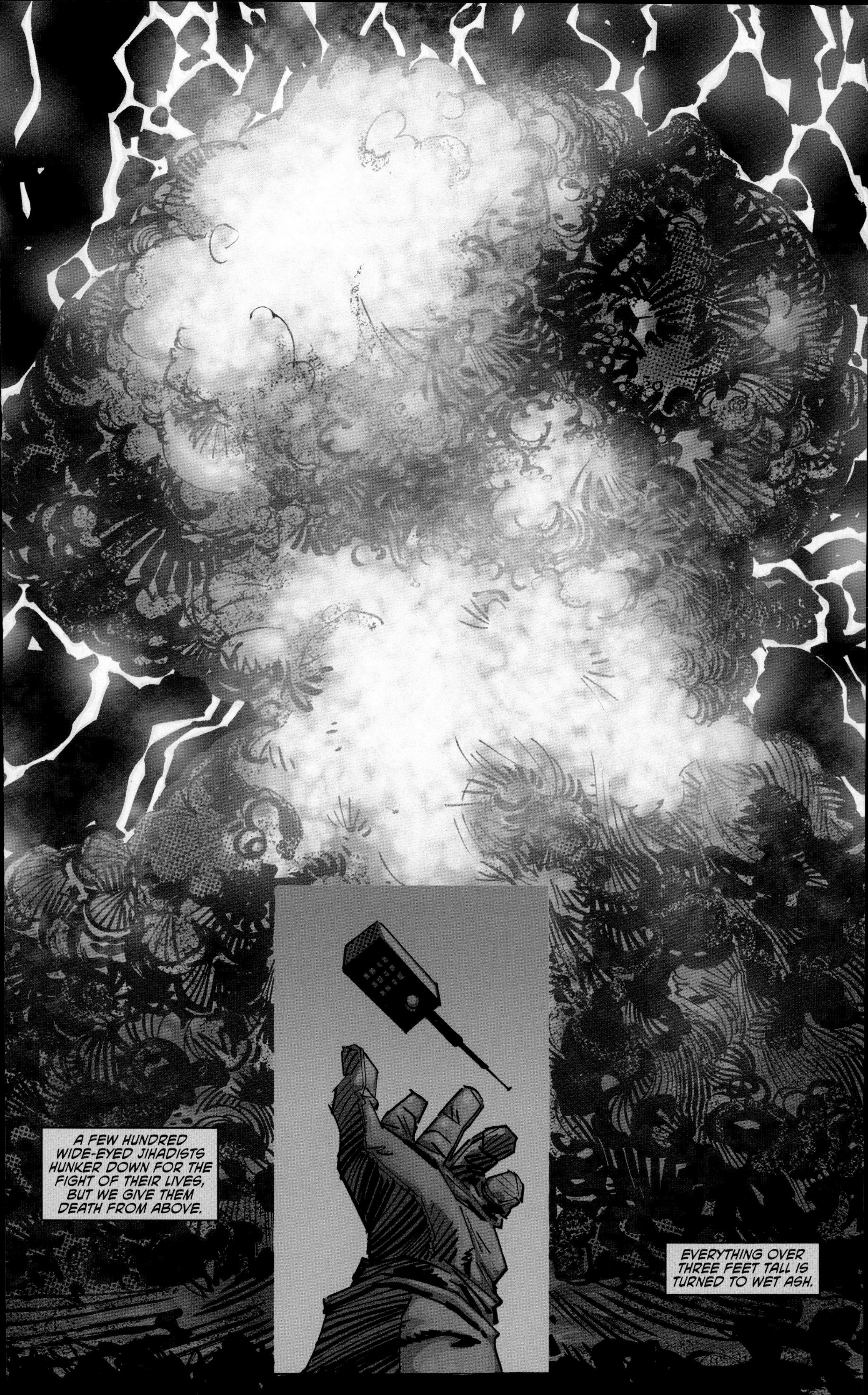
A FEW HUNDRED WIDE-EYED JIHADISTS HUNKER DOWN FOR THE FIGHT OF THEIR LIVES, BUT WE GIVE THEM DEATH FROM ABOVE.
EVERYTHING OVER THREE FEET TALL IS TURNED TO WET ASH.

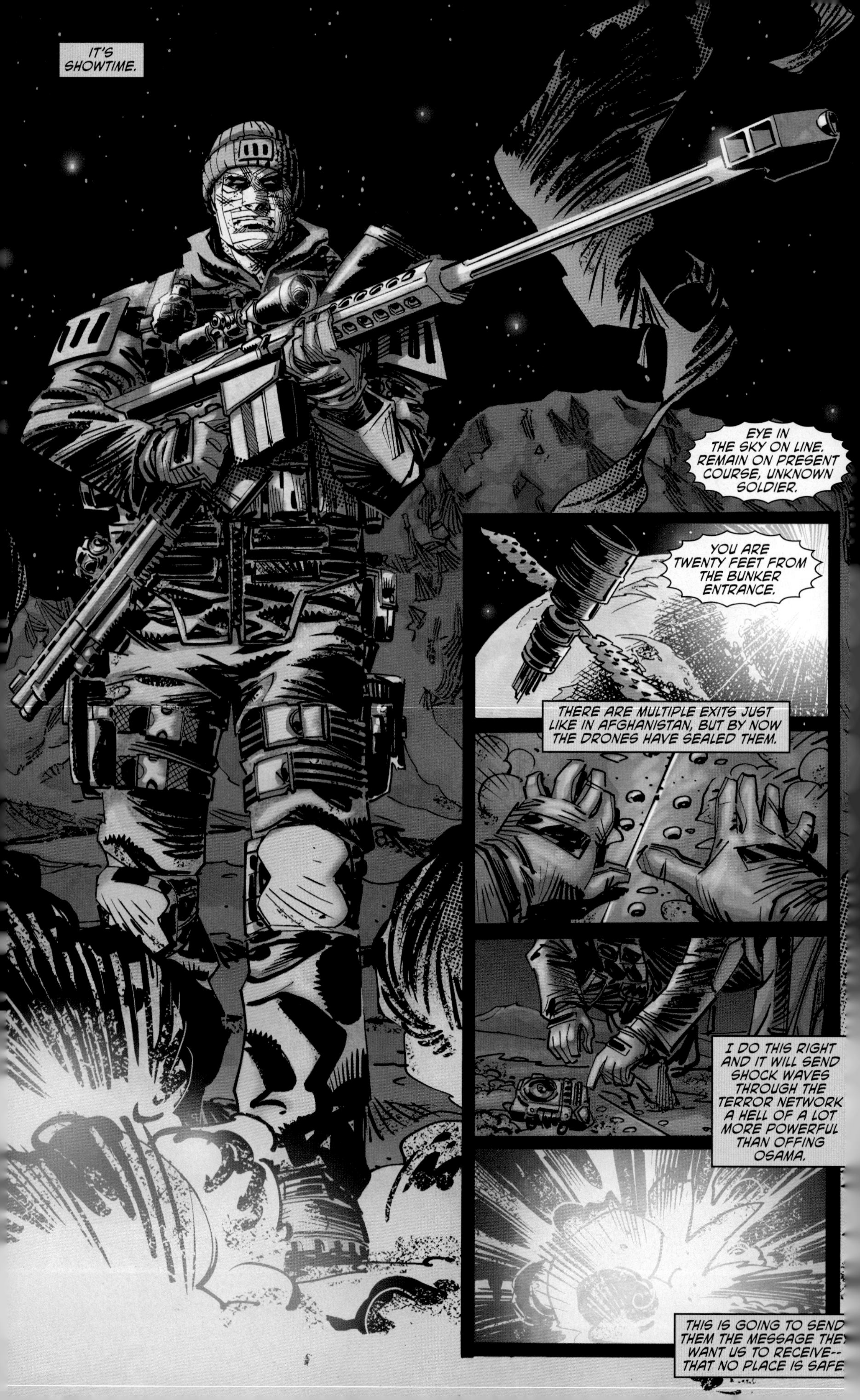
IT'S SHOWTIME.
EYE IN THE SKY ON LINE. REMAIN ON PRESENT COURSE, UNKNOWN SOLDIER.
YOU ARE TWENTY FEET FROM THE BUNKER ENTRANCE.
THERE ARE MULTIPLE EXITS JUST LIKE IN AFGHANISTAN, BUT BY NOW THE DRONES HAVE SEALED THEM.
I DO THIS RIGHT AND IT WILL SEND SHOCK WAVES THROUGH THE TERROR NETWORK A HELL OF A LOT MORE POWERFUL THAN OFFING OSAMA.
THIS IS GOING TO SEND THEM THE MESSAGE THEY WANT US TO RECEIVE-- THAT NO PLACE IS SAFE

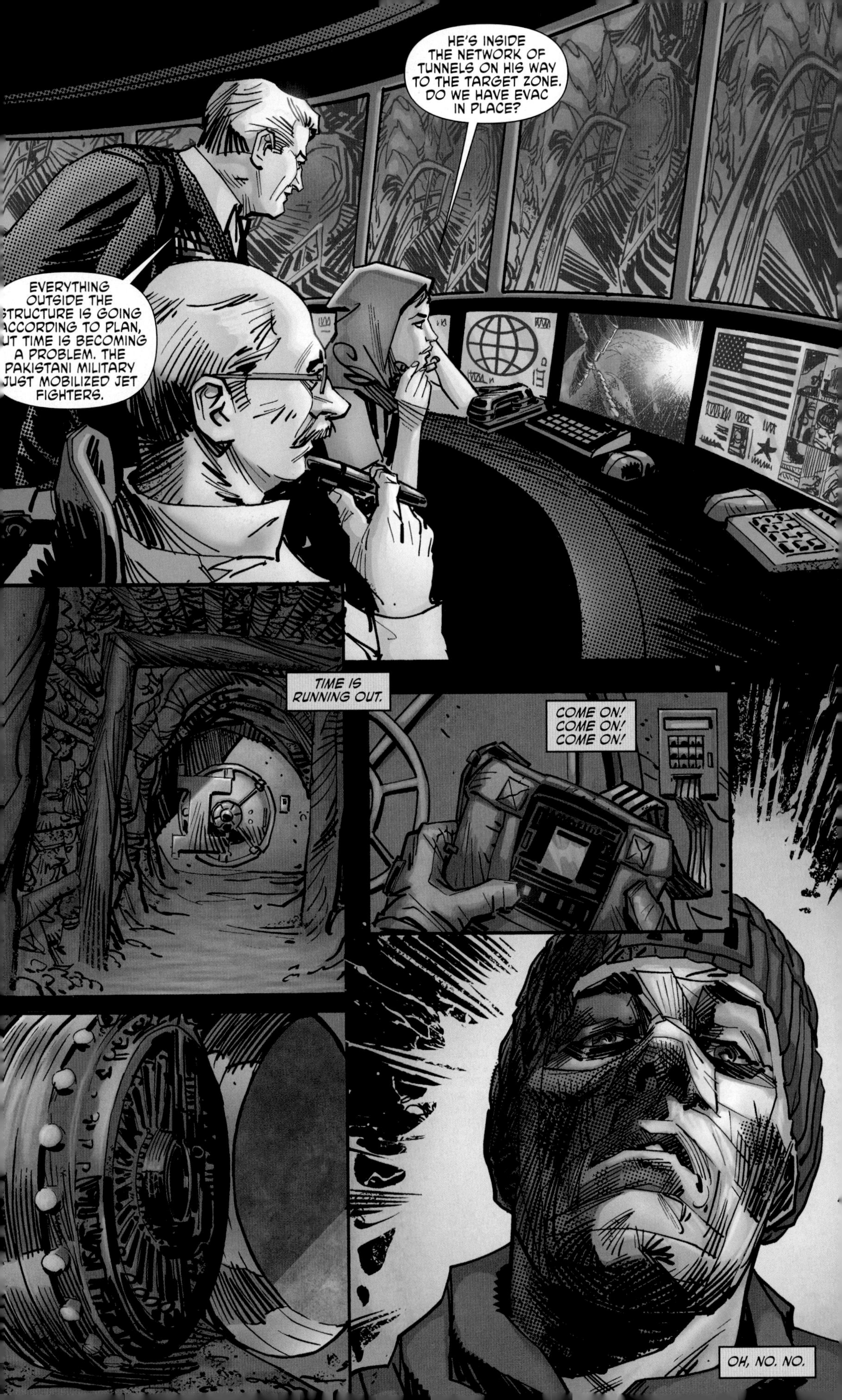

HE'S INSIDE THE NETWORK OF TUNNELS ON HIS WAY TO THE TARGET ZONE. DO WE HAVE EVAC IN PLACE?
EVERYTHING OUTSIDE THE STRUCTURE IS GOING ACCORDING TO PLAN, UT TIME IS BECOMING A PROBLEM. THE PAKISTANI MILITARY JUST MOBILIZED JET FIGHTERS.
TIME IS RUNNING OUT.
COME ON! COME ON! COME ON!
OH, NO. NO.

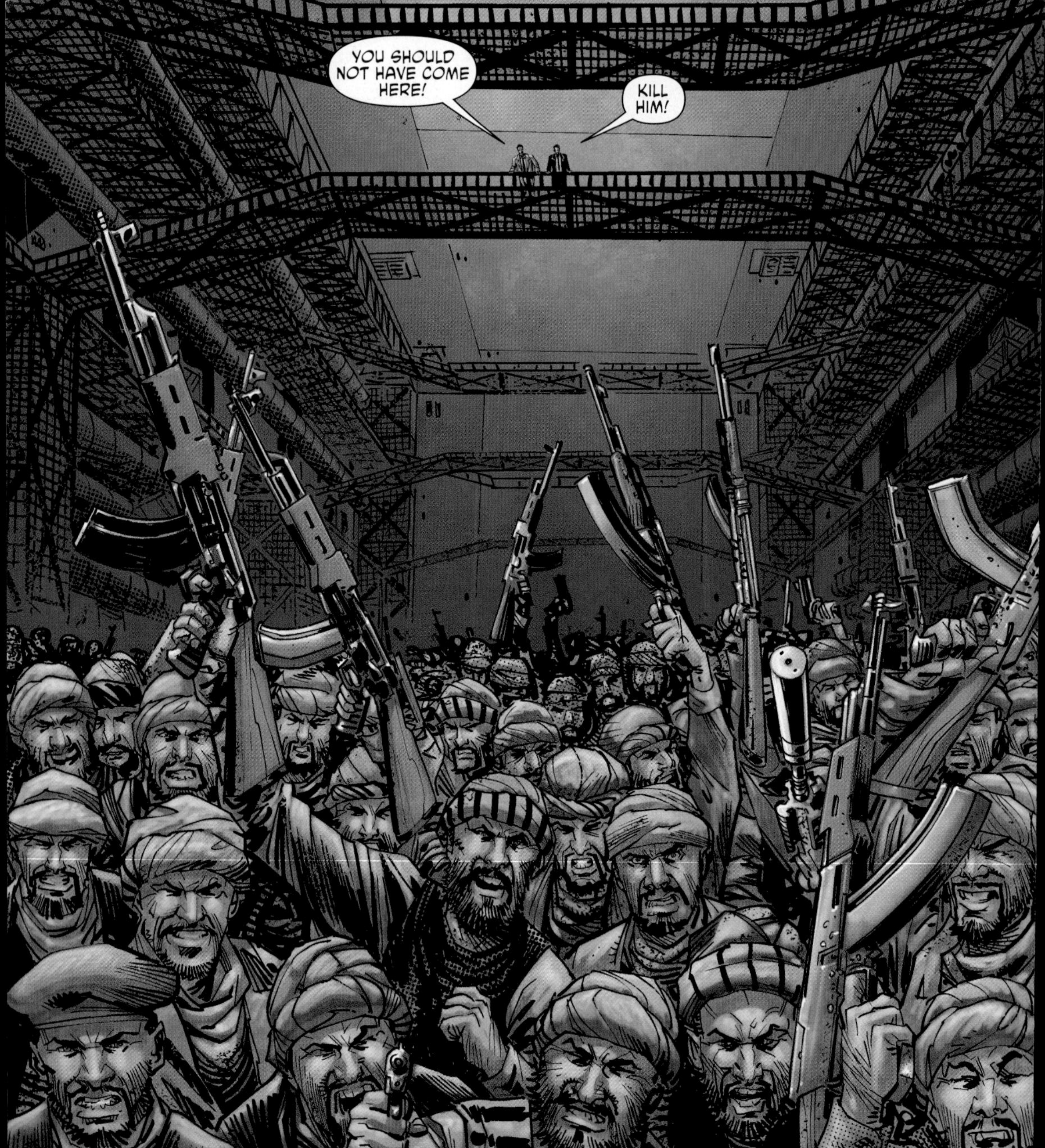
YOU SHOULD NOT HAVE COME HERE!
KILL HIM!

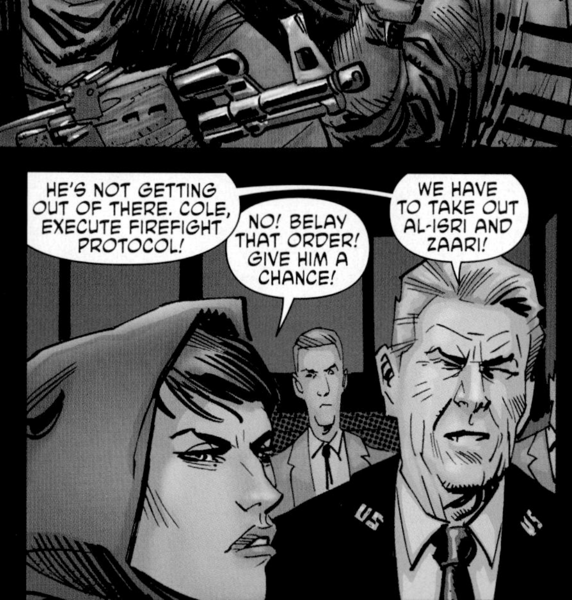
HE'S NOT GETTING OUT OF THERE. COLE, EXECUTE FIREFIGHT PROTOCOL!
NO! BELAY THAT ORDER! GIVE HIM A CHANCE!
WE HAVE TO TAKE OUT AL-ISRI AND ZAARI!

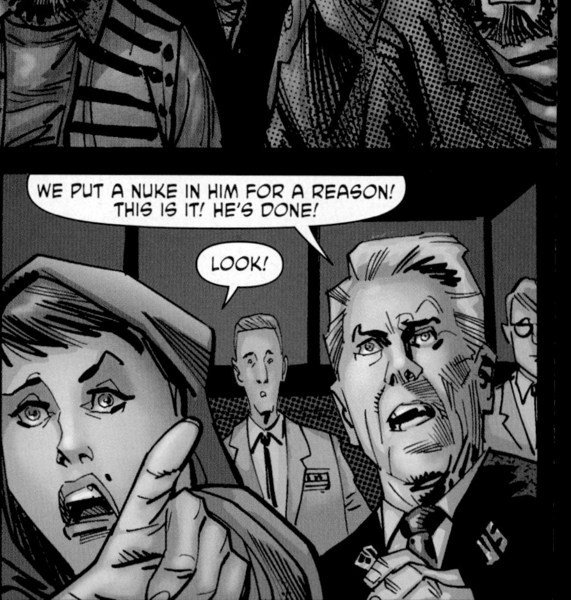
WE PUT A NUKE IN HIM FOR A REASON! THIS IS IT! HE'S DONE!
LOOK!

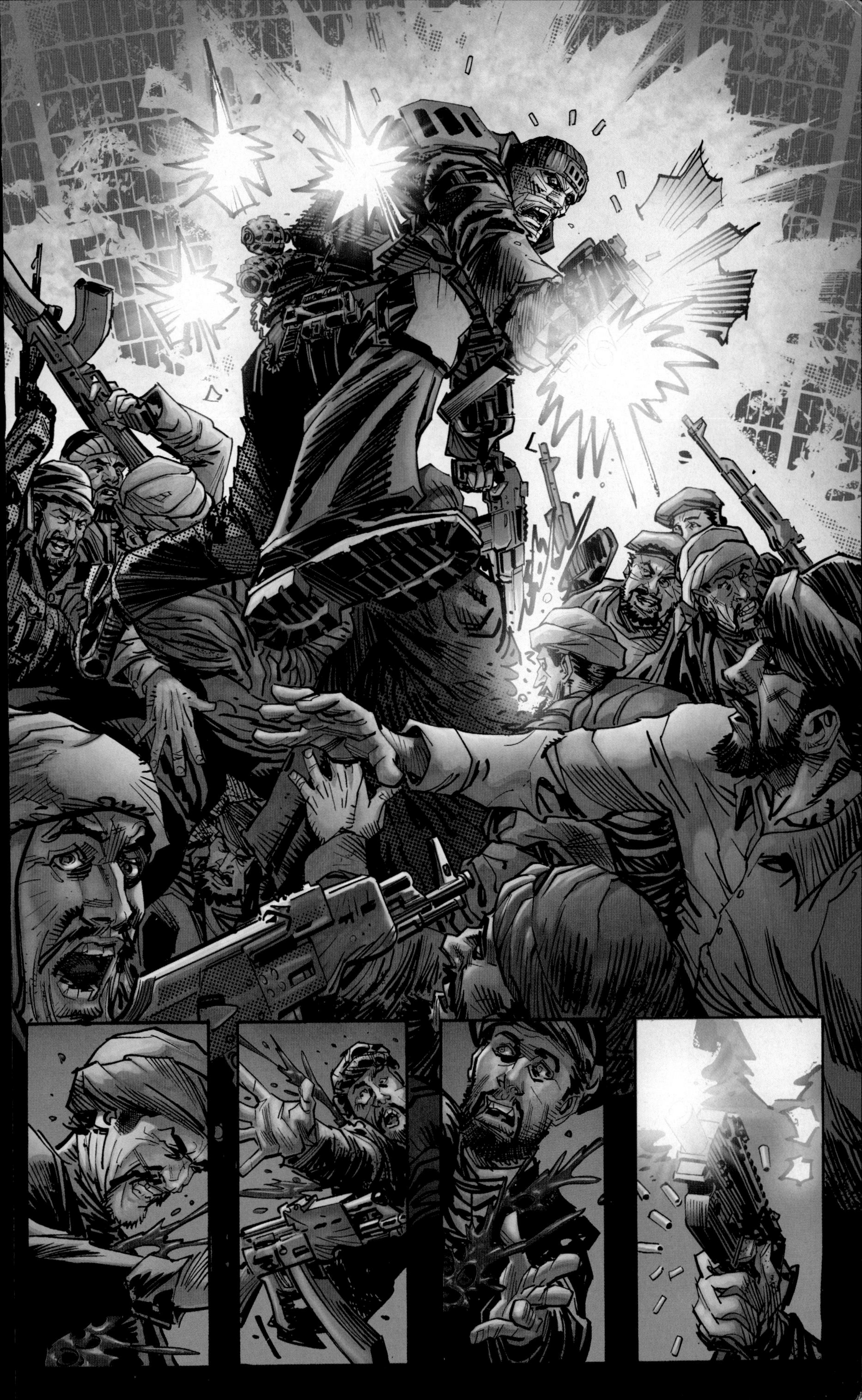

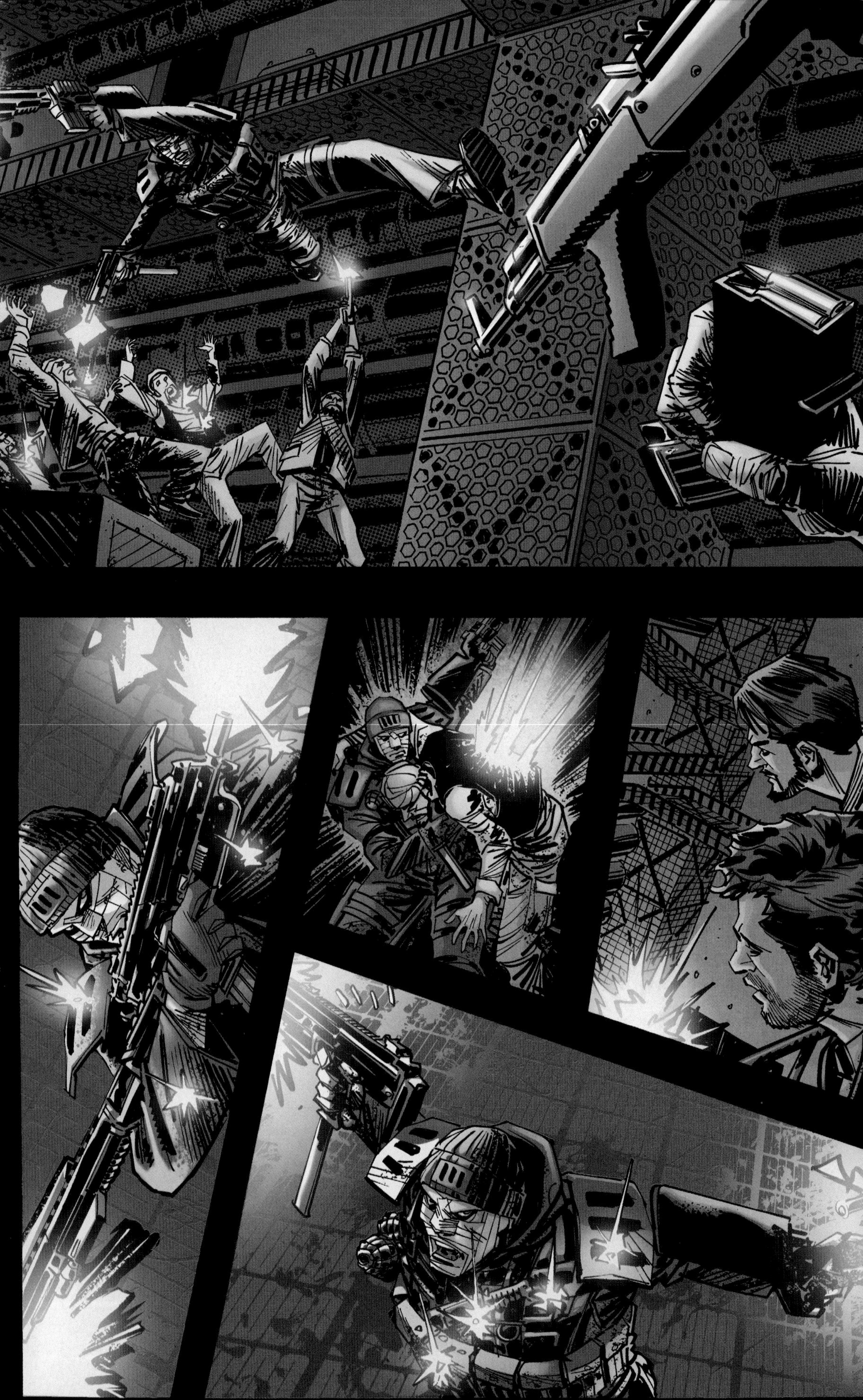

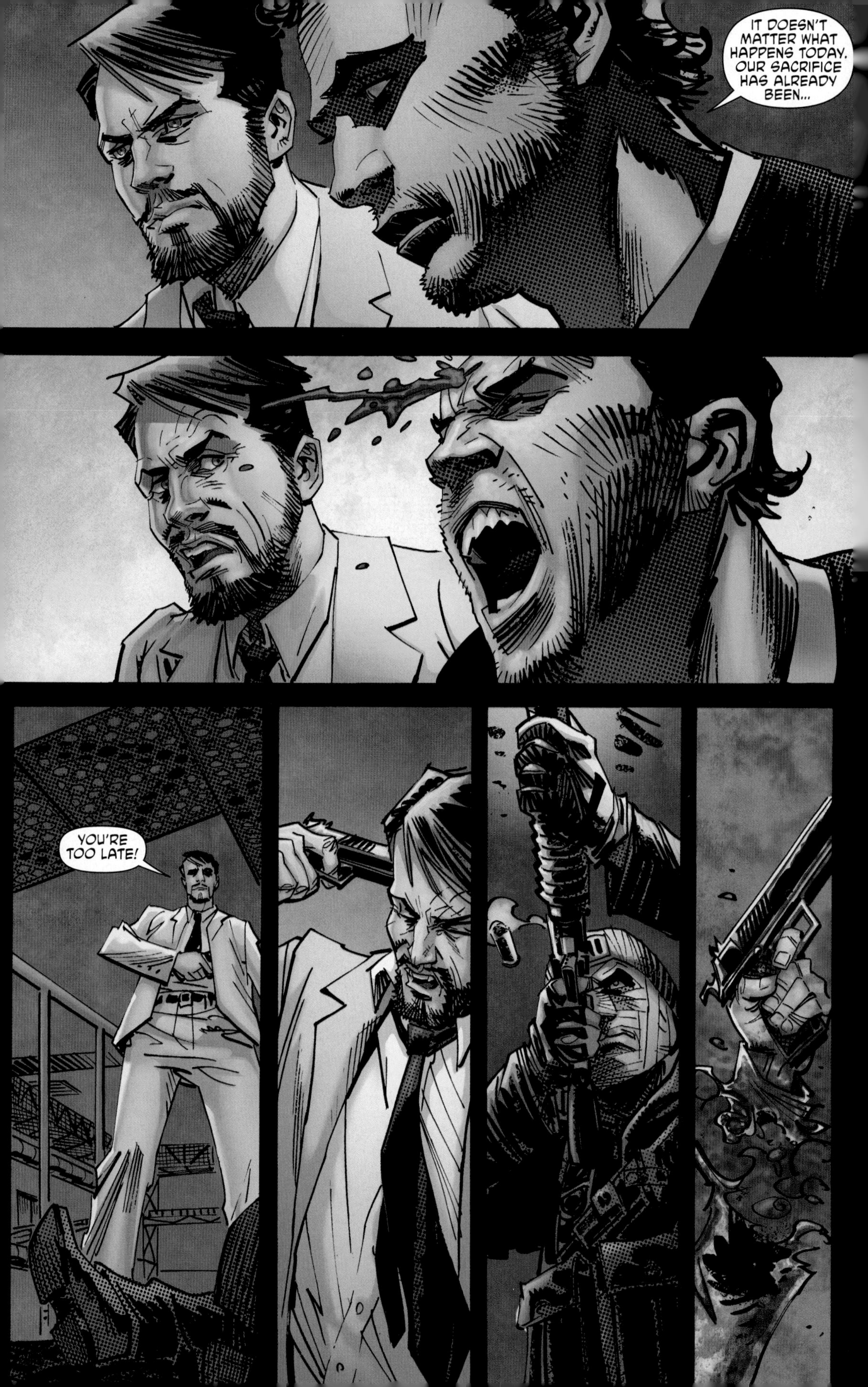
IT DOESN'T MATTER WHAT HAPPENS TODAY. OUR SACRIFICE HAS ALREADY BEEN...
YOU'RE TOO LATE!

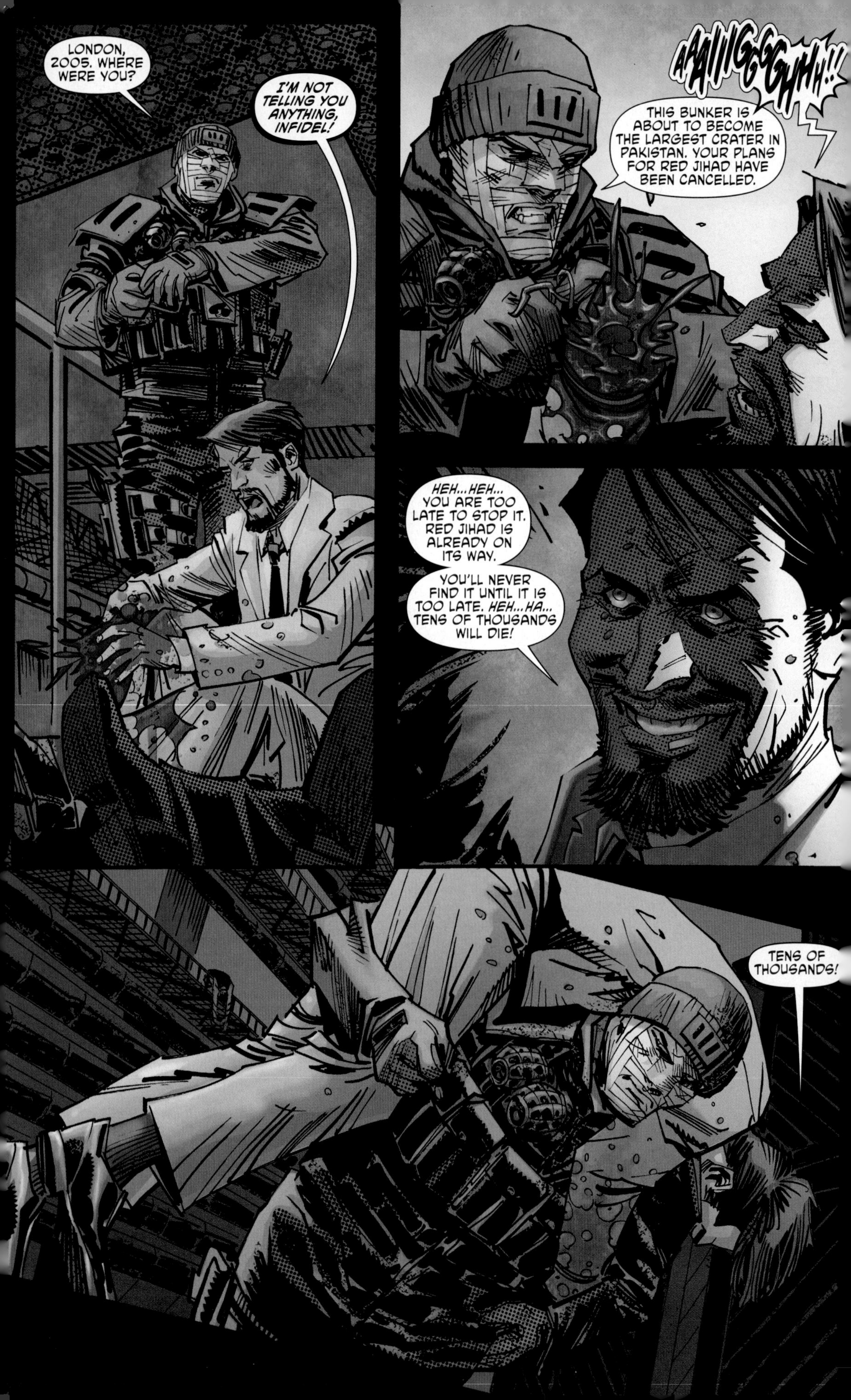
LONDON, 2005. WHERE WERE YOU?
I'M NOT TELLING YOU ANYTHING, INFIDEL!
AAAAIIIGGGGHHH!!
THIS BUNKER IS ABOUT TO BECOME THE LARGEST CRATER IN PAKISTAN. YOUR PLANS FOR RED JIHAD HAVE BEEN CANCELLED.
HEH...HEH... YOU ARE TOO LATE TO STOP IT. RED JIHAD IS ALREADY ON ITS WAY.
YOU'LL NEVER FIND IT UNTIL IT IS TOO LATE. HEH...HA... TENS OF THOUSANDS WILL DIE!
TENS OF THOUSANDS!

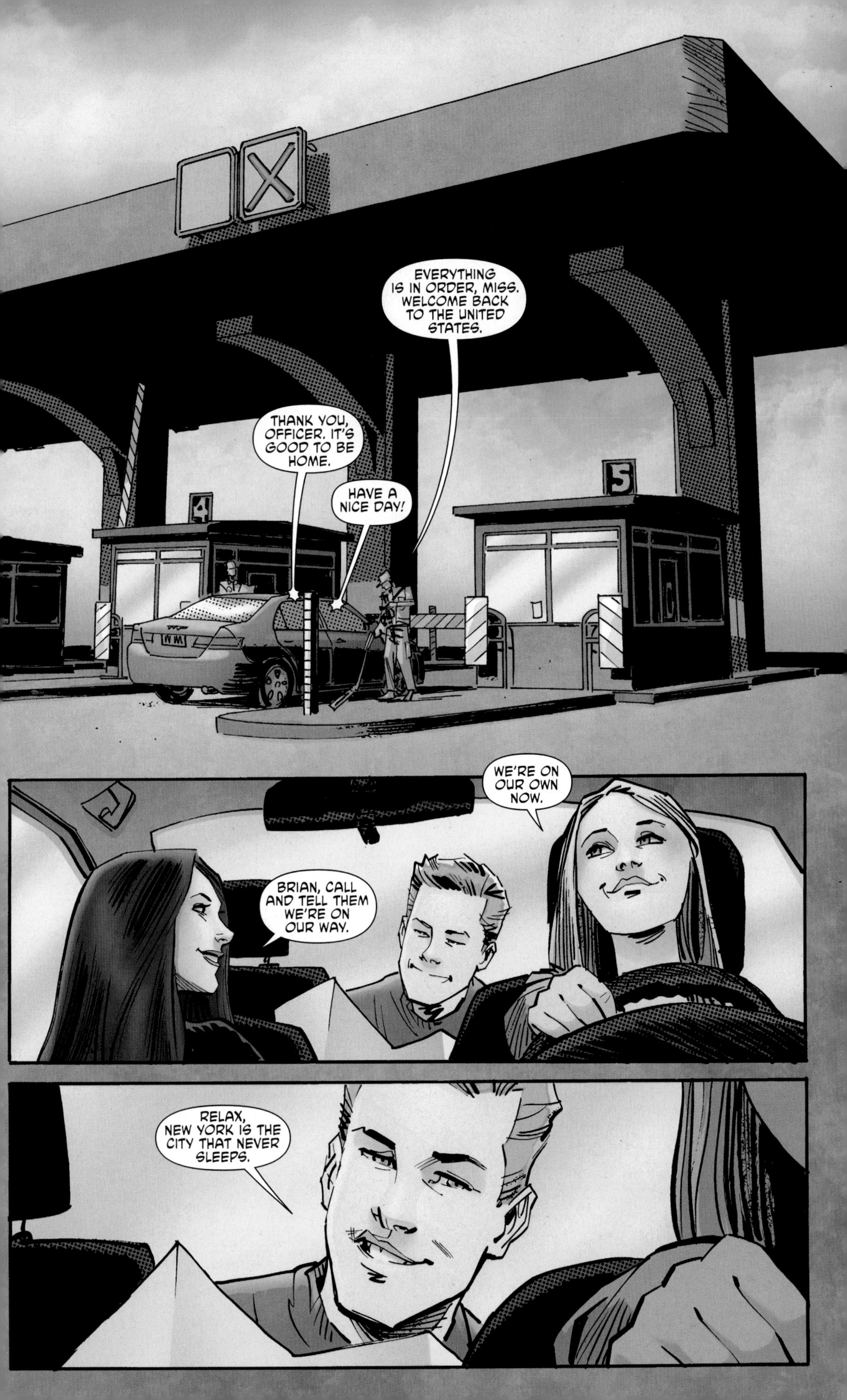

EVERYTHING IS IN ORDER, MISS. WELCOME BACK TO THE UNITED STATES.
THANK YOU, OFFICER. IT'S GOOD TO BE HOME.
HAVE A NICE DAY!
4
5
WE'RE ON OUR OWN NOW.
BRIAN, CALL AND TELL THEM WE'RE ON OUR WAY.
RELAX, NEW YORK IS THE CITY THAT NEVER SLEEPS.

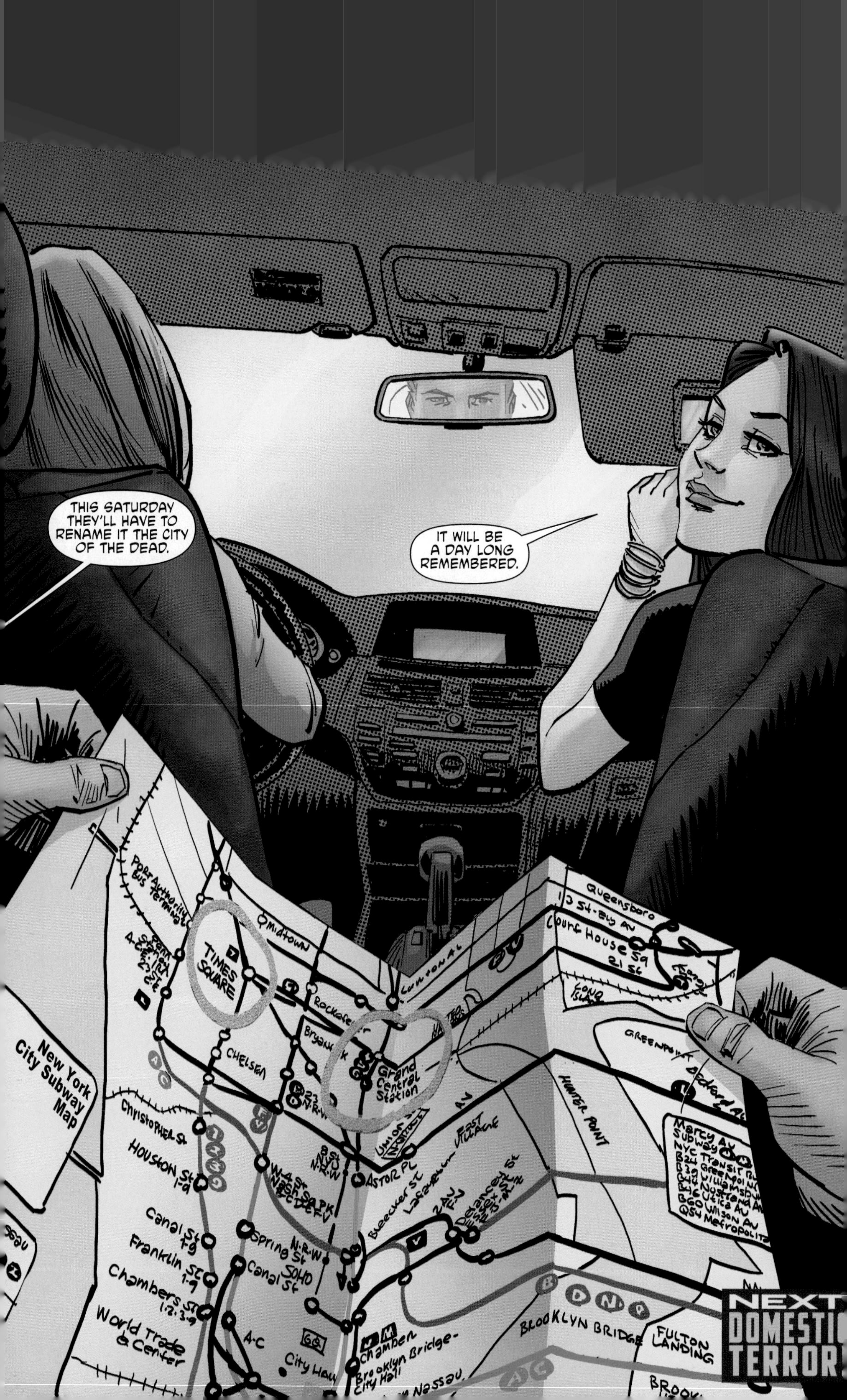
THIS SATURDAY THEY'LL HAVE TO RENAME IT THE CITY OF THE DEAD.
IT WILL BE A DAY LONG REMEMBERED.
New York City Subway Map
TIMES SQUARE
Grand Central Station
CHELSEA
BROOKLYN BRIDGE
FULTON LANDING
NEXT
DOMESTIC TERROR

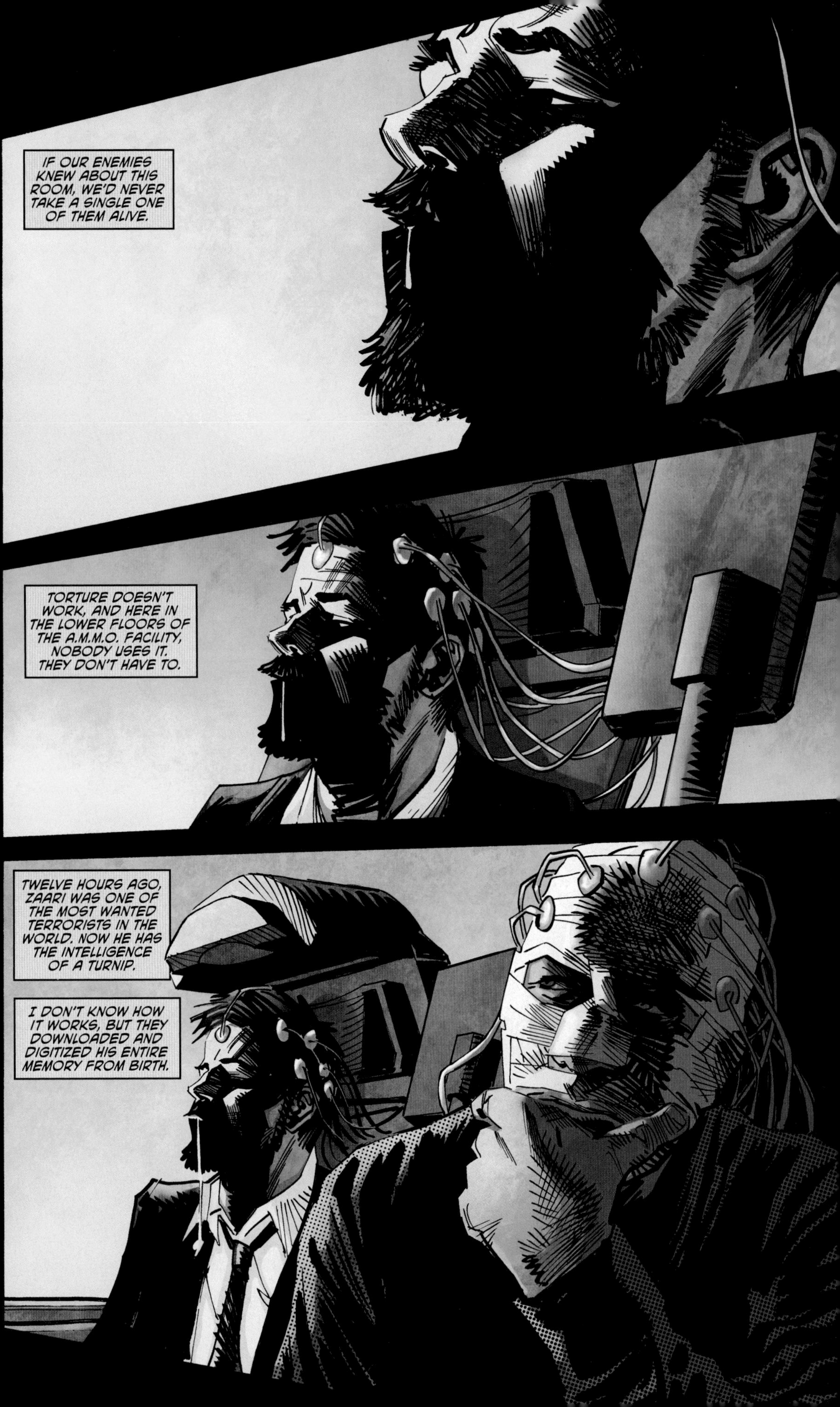
IF OUR ENEMIES KNEW ABOUT THIS ROOM, WE'D NEVER TAKE A SINGLE ONE OF THEM ALIVE.
TORTURE DOESN'T WORK, AND HERE IN THE LOWER FLOORS OF THE A.M.M.O. FACILITY, NOBODY USES IT. THEY DON'T HAVE TO.
TWELVE HOURS AGO, ZAARI WAS ONE OF THE MOST WANTED TERRORISTS IN THE WORLD. NOW HE HAS THE INTELLIGENCE OF A TURNIP.
I DON'T KNOW HOW IT WORKS, BUT THEY DOWNLOADED AND DIGITIZED HIS ENTIRE MEMORY FROM BIRTH.

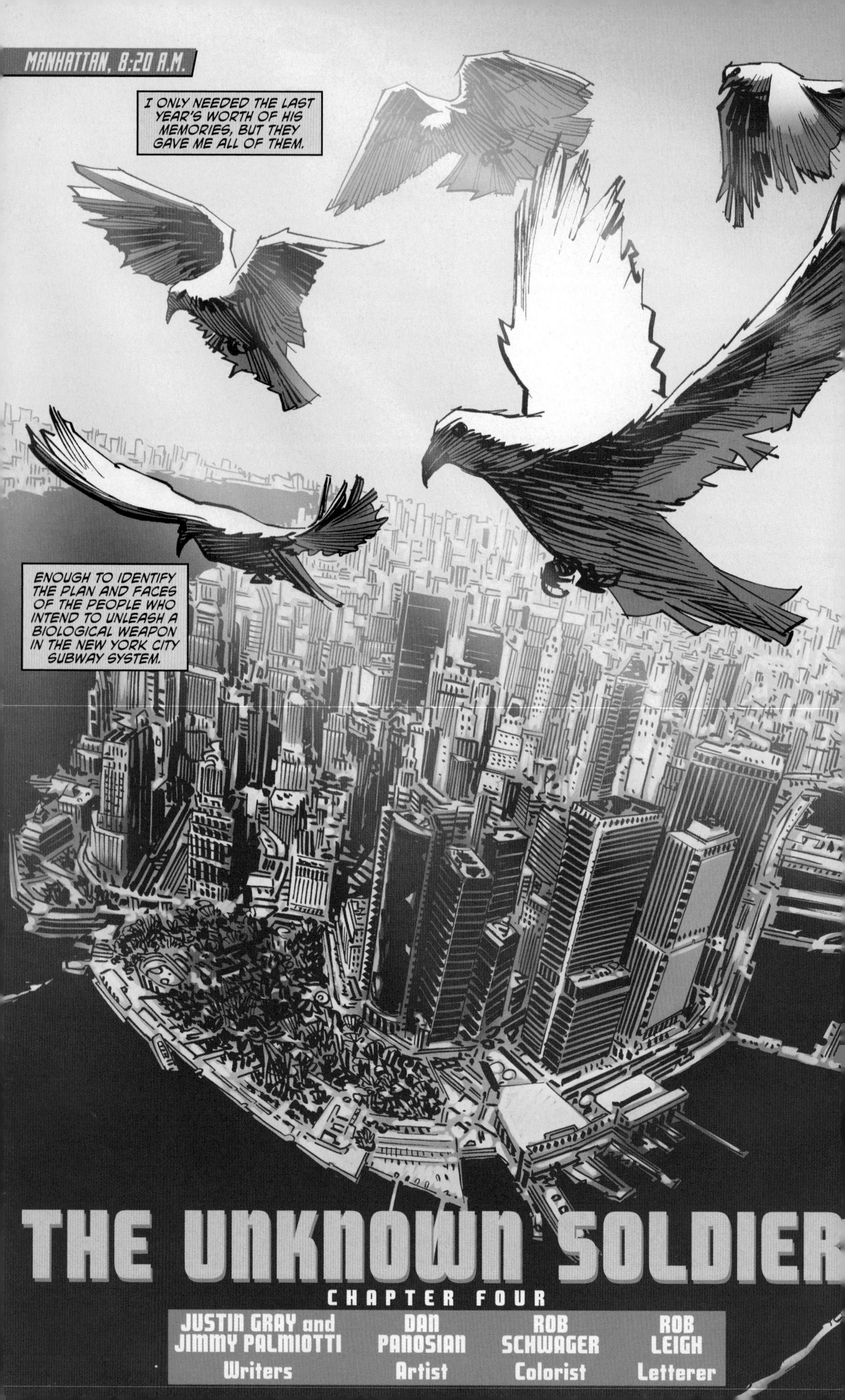
MANHATTAN, 8:20 A.M.
I ONLY NEEDED THE LAST YEAR'S WORTH OF HIS MEMORIES, BUT THEY GAVE ME ALL OF THEM.
ENOUGH TO IDENTIFY THE PLAN AND FACES OF THE PEOPLE WHO INTEND TO UNLEASH A BIOLOGICAL WEAPON IN THE NEW YORK CITY SUBWAY SYSTEM.
THE UNKNOWN SOLDIER
CHAPTER FOUR
JUSTIN GRAY and JIMMY PALMIOTTI Writers
DAN PANOSIAN Artist
ROB SCHWAGER Colorist
ROB LEIGH Letterer

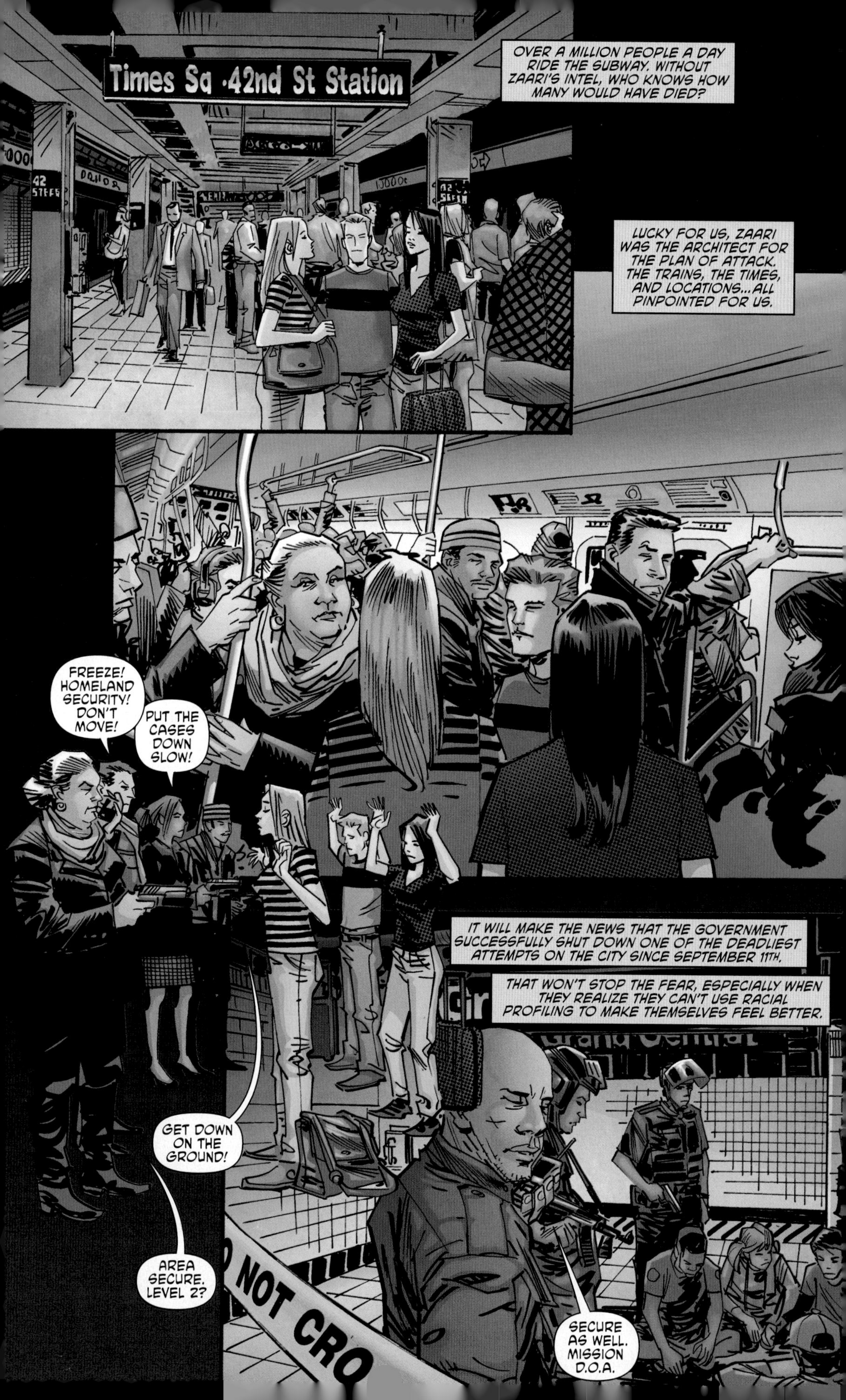
Times Sq ·42nd St Station
OVER A MILLION PEOPLE A DAY RIDE THE SUBWAY. WITHOUT ZAARI'S INTEL, WHO KNOWS HOW MANY WOULD HAVE DIED?
LUCKY FOR US, ZAARI WAS THE ARCHITECT FOR THE PLAN OF ATTACK. THE TRAINS, THE TIMES, AND LOCATIONS...ALL PINPOINTED FOR US.
FREEZE! HOMELAND SECURITY! DON'T MOVE!
PUT THE CASES DOWN SLOW!
IT WILL MAKE THE NEWS THAT THE GOVERNMENT SUCCESSFULLY SHUT DOWN ONE OF THE DEADLIEST ATTEMPTS ON THE CITY SINCE SEPTEMBER 11TH.
THAT WON'T STOP THE FEAR, ESPECIALLY WHEN THEY REALIZE THEY CAN'T USE RACIAL PROFILING TO MAKE THEMSELVES FEEL BETTER.
GET DOWN ON THE GROUND!
AREA SECURE. LEVEL 2?
SECURE AS WELL. MISSION D.O.A.

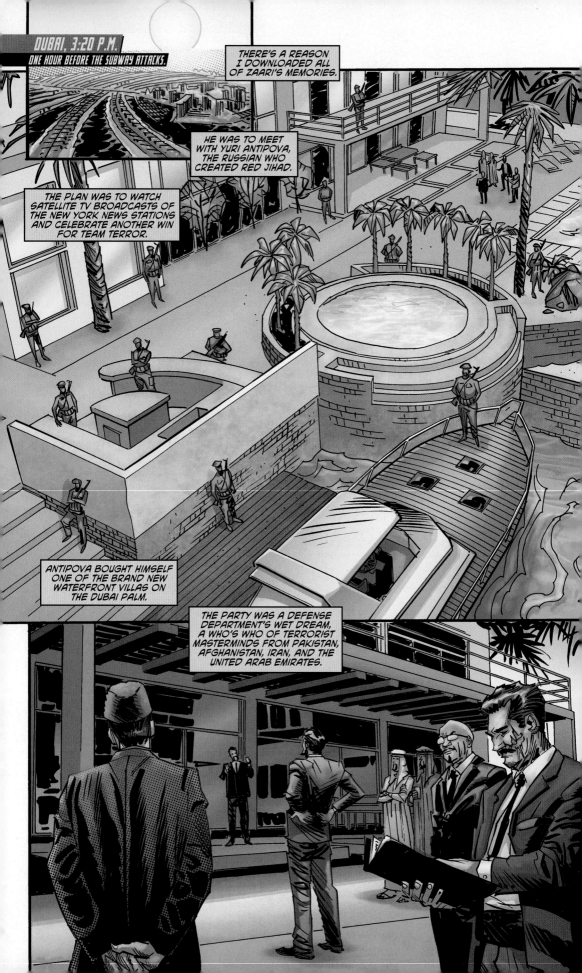

DUBAI, 3:20 P.M.
ONE HOUR BEFORE THE SUBWAY ATTACKS.

THERE'S A REASON I DOWNLOADED ALL OF ZAARI'S MEMORIES.

HE WAS TO MEET WITH YURI ANTIPOVA, THE RUSSIAN WHO CREATED RED JIHAD.

THE PLAN WAS TO WATCH SATELLITE TV BROADCASTS OF THE NEW YORK NEWS STATIONS AND CELEBRATE ANOTHER WIN FOR TEAM TERROR.

ANTIPOVA BOUGHT HIMSELF ONE OF THE BRAND NEW WATERFRONT VILLAS ON THE DUBAI PALM.

THE PARTY WAS A DEFENSE DEPARTMENT'S WET DREAM, A WHO'S WHO OF TERRORIST MASTERMINDS FROM PAKISTAN, AFGHANISTAN, IRAN, AND THE UNITED ARAB EMIRATES.

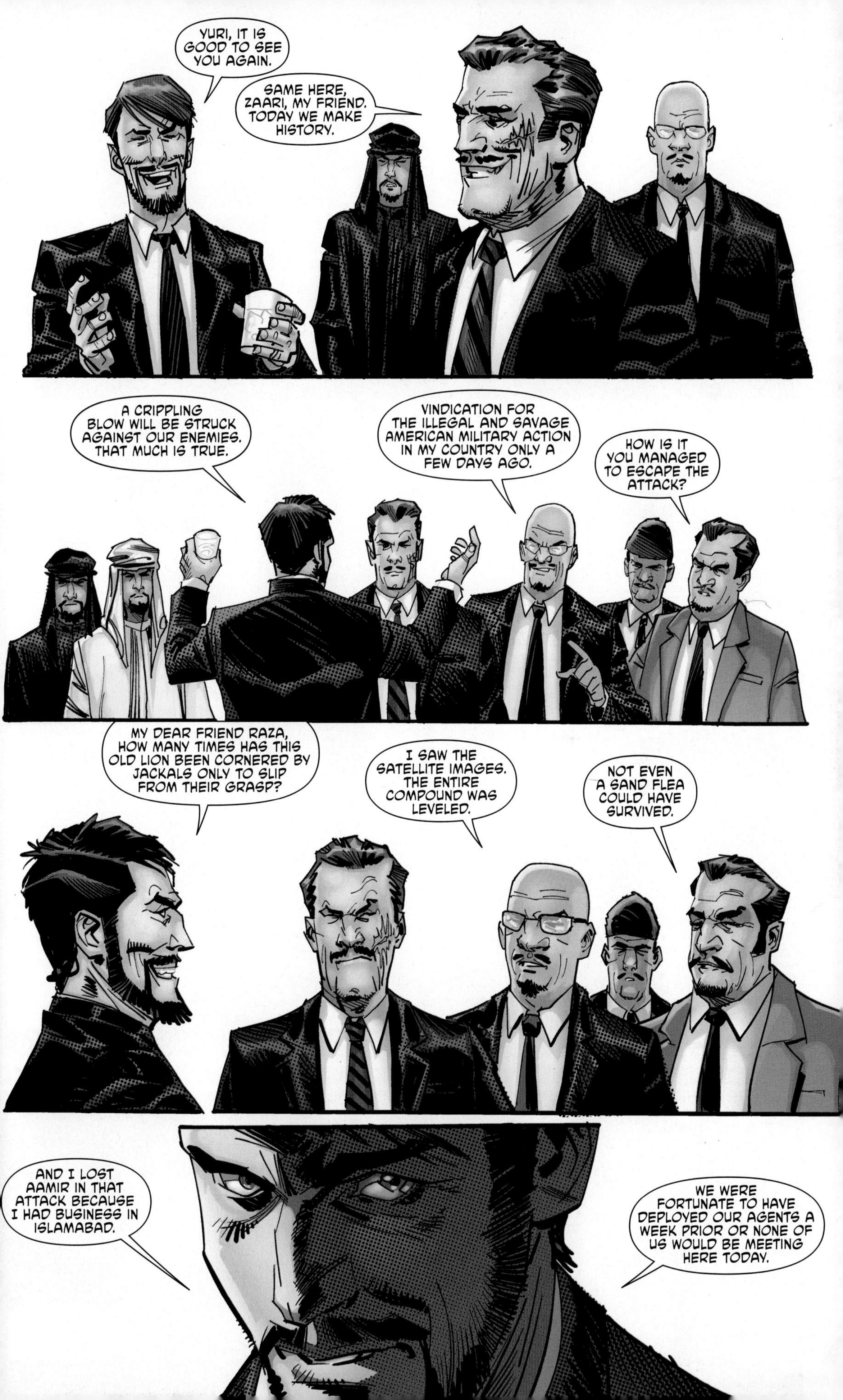
YURI, IT IS GOOD TO SEE YOU AGAIN.
SAME HERE, ZAARI, MY FRIEND. TODAY WE MAKE HISTORY.
A CRIPPLING BLOW WILL BE STRUCK AGAINST OUR ENEMIES. THAT MUCH IS TRUE.
VINDICATION FOR THE ILLEGAL AND SAVAGE AMERICAN MILITARY ACTION IN MY COUNTRY ONLY A FEW DAYS AGO.
HOW IS IT YOU MANAGED TO ESCAPE THE ATTACK?
MY DEAR FRIEND RAZA, HOW MANY TIMES HAS THIS OLD LION BEEN CORNERED BY JACKALS ONLY TO SLIP FROM THEIR GRASP?
I SAW THE SATELLITE IMAGES. THE ENTIRE COMPOUND WAS LEVELED.
NOT EVEN A SAND FLEA COULD HAVE SURVIVED.
AND I LOST AAMIR IN THAT ATTACK BECAUSE I HAD BUSINESS IN ISLAMABAD.
WE WERE FORTUNATE TO HAVE DEPLOYED OUR AGENTS A WEEK PRIOR OR NONE OF US WOULD BE MEETING HERE TODAY.

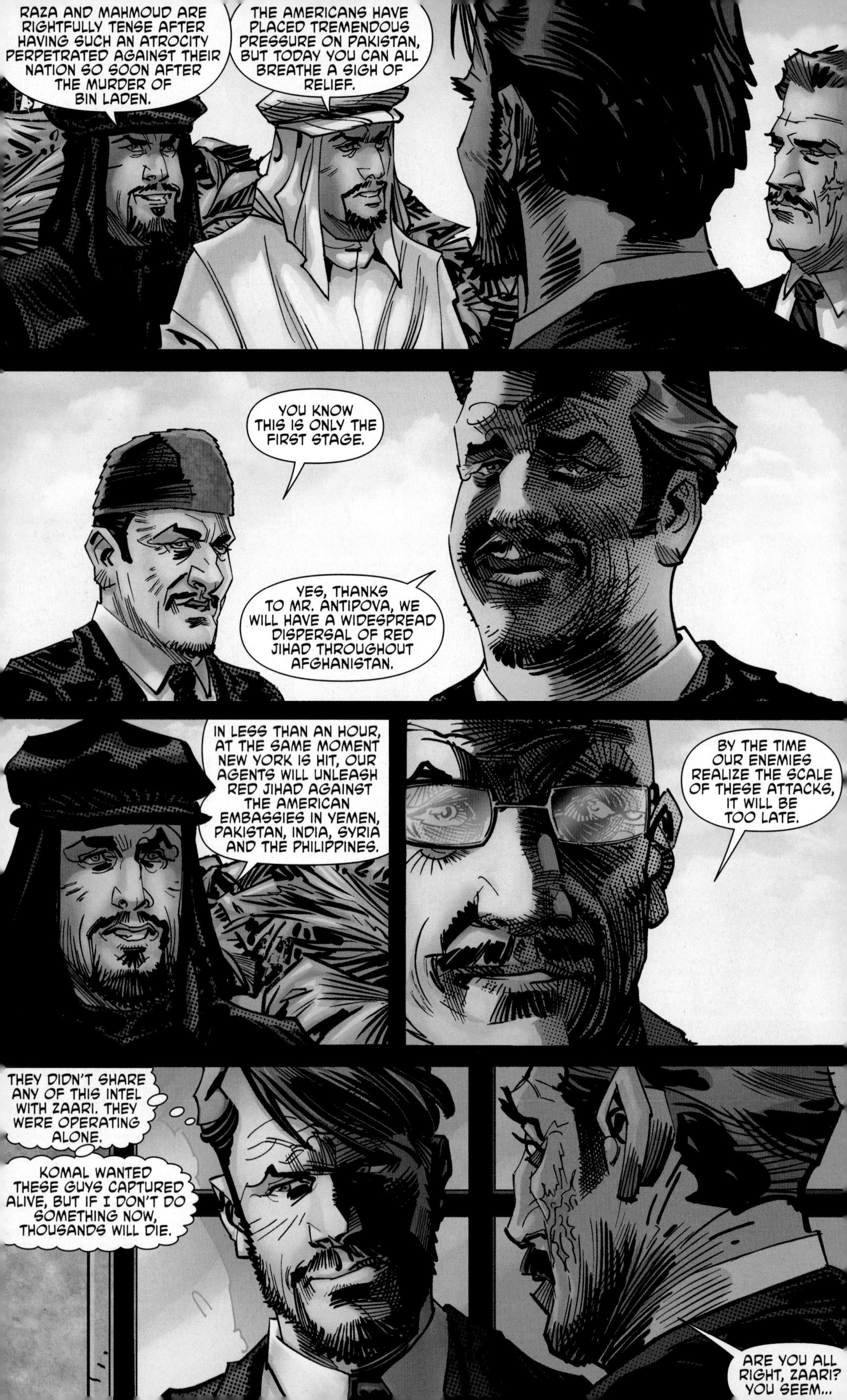
RAZA AND MAHMOUD ARE RIGHTFULLY TENSE AFTER HAVING SUCH AN ATROCITY PERPETRATED AGAINST THEIR NATION SO SOON AFTER THE MURDER OF BIN LADEN.
THE AMERICANS HAVE PLACED TREMENDOUS PRESSURE ON PAKISTAN, BUT TODAY YOU CAN ALL BREATHE A SIGH OF RELIEF.
YOU KNOW THIS IS ONLY THE FIRST STAGE.
YES, THANKS TO MR. ANTIPOVA, WE WILL HAVE A WIDESPREAD DISPERSAL OF RED JIHAD THROUGHOUT AFGHANISTAN.
IN LESS THAN AN HOUR, AT THE SAME MOMENT NEW YORK IS HIT, OUR AGENTS WILL UNLEASH RED JIHAD AGAINST THE AMERICAN EMBASSIES IN YEMEN, PAKISTAN, INDIA, SYRIA AND THE PHILIPPINES.
BY THE TIME OUR ENEMIES REALIZE THE SCALE OF THESE ATTACKS, IT WILL BE TOO LATE.
THEY DIDN'T SHARE ANY OF THIS INTEL WITH ZAARI. THEY WERE OPERATING ALONE.
KOMAL WANTED THESE GUYS CAPTURED ALIVE, BUT IF I DON'T DO SOMETHING NOW, THOUSANDS WILL DIE.
ARE YOU ALL RIGHT, ZAARI? YOU SEEM...

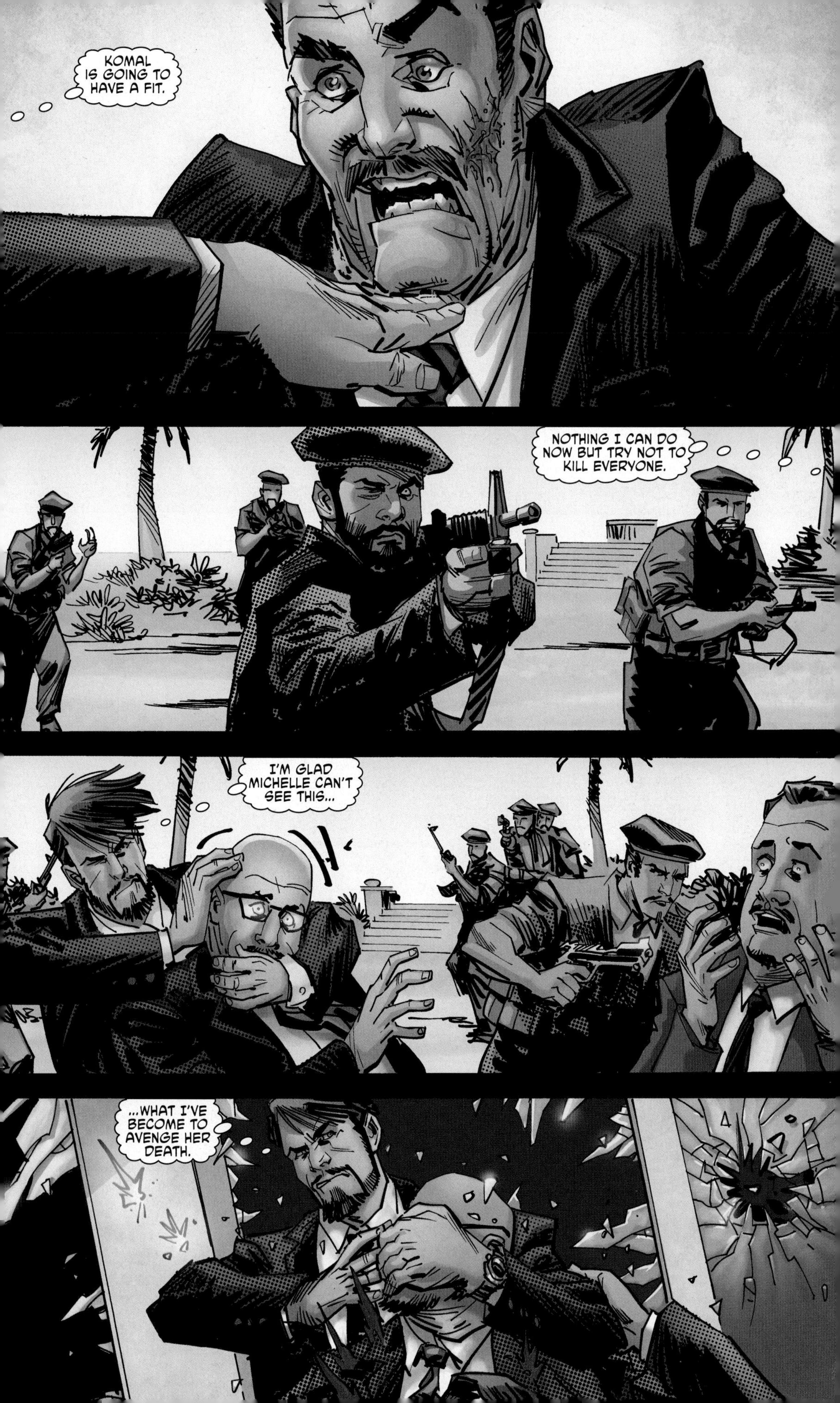

KOMAL IS GOING TO HAVE A FIT.
NOTHING I CAN DO NOW BUT TRY NOT TO KILL EVERYONE.
I'M GLAD MICHELLE CAN'T SEE THIS...
...WHAT I'VE BECOME TO AVENGE HER DEATH.

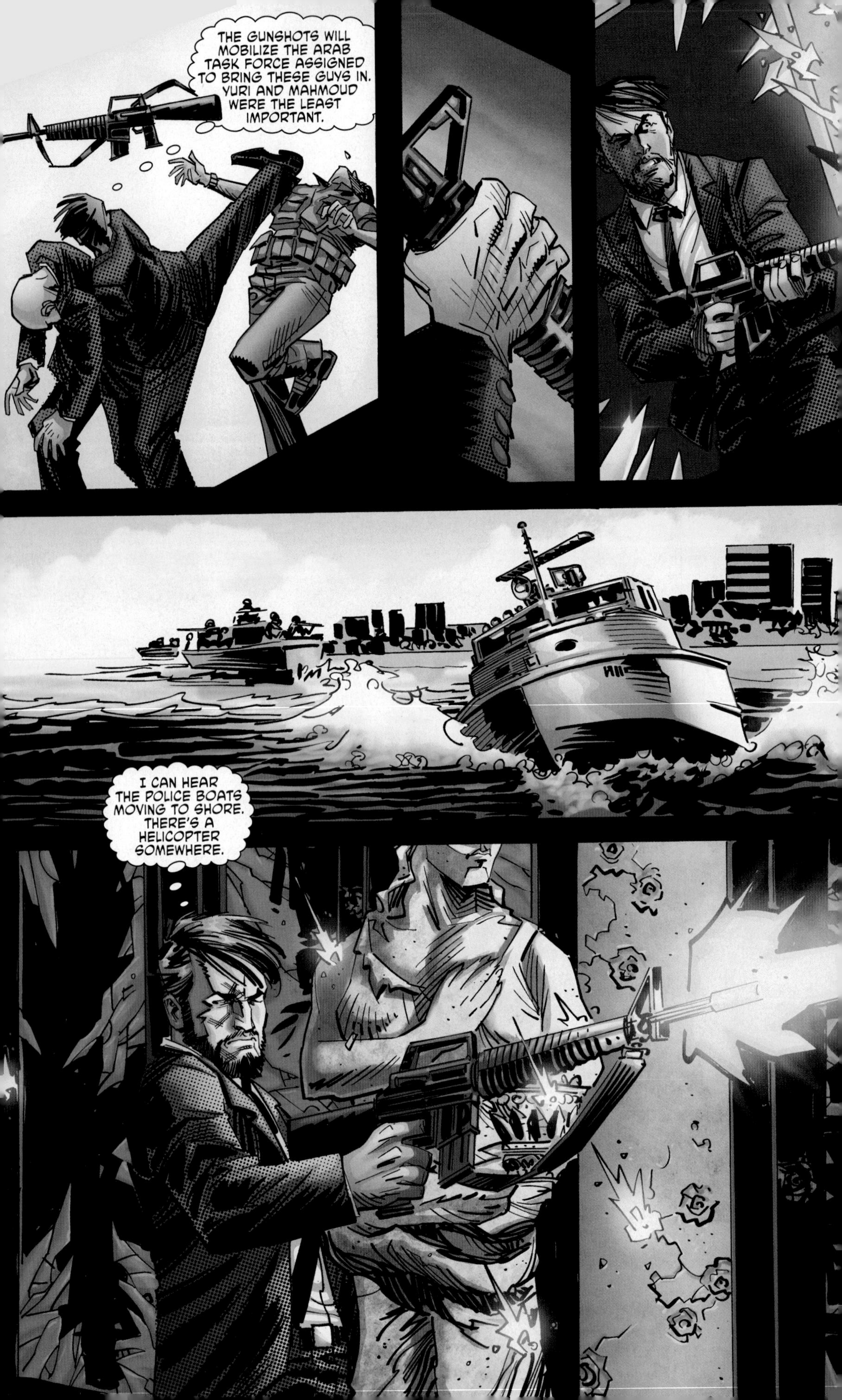
THE GUNSHOTS WILL MOBILIZE THE ARAB TASK FORCE ASSIGNED TO BRING THESE GUYS IN. YURI AND MAHMOUD WERE THE LEAST IMPORTANT.
I CAN HEAR THE POLICE BOATS MOVING TO SHORE. THERE'S A HELICOPTER SOMEWHERE.

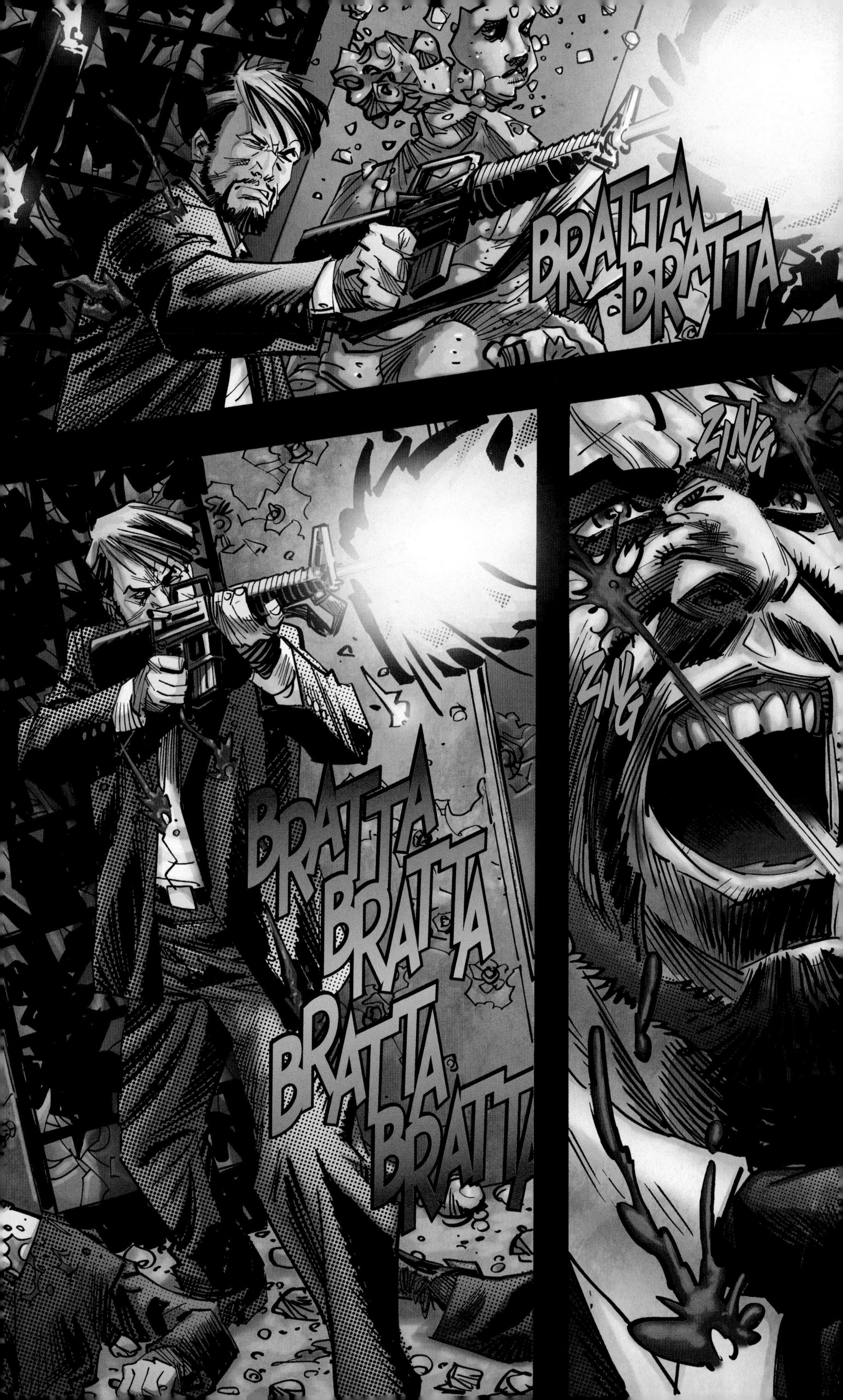
BRATTA BRATTA
BRATTA
BRATTA
BRATTA
BRATTA
ZING
ZING

THIS MASK IS USELESS NOW. JUST BLOCKING MY VISION.

BRATTA BRATTABRATTA BRATTA

KPOW KPOW

ZIING

BRATTA BRATT BRATTA BR

TCHOW TCHOW TCHOW

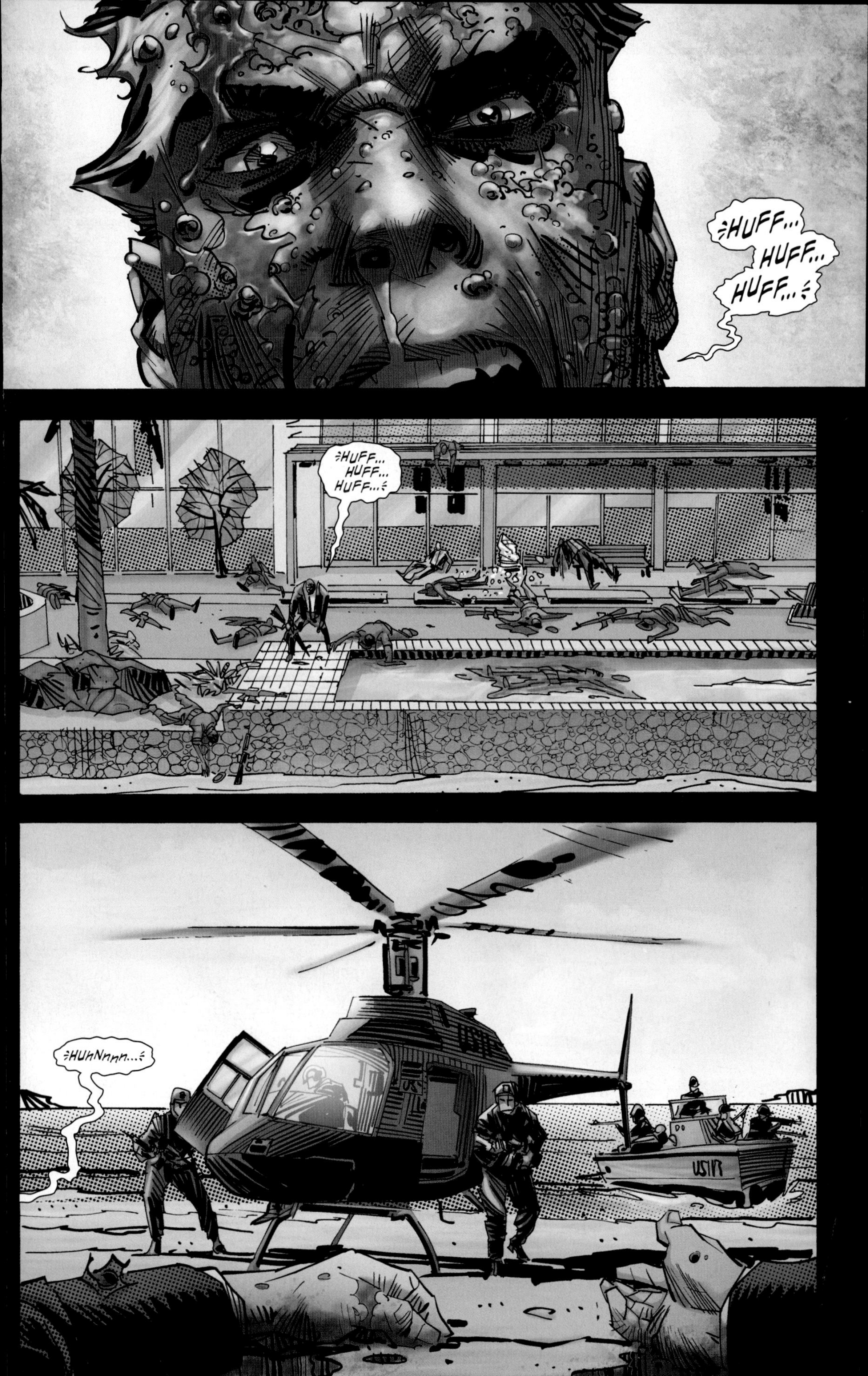
HUFF... HUFF... HUFF...
HUFF... HUFF... HUFF...
HUHNnnn...

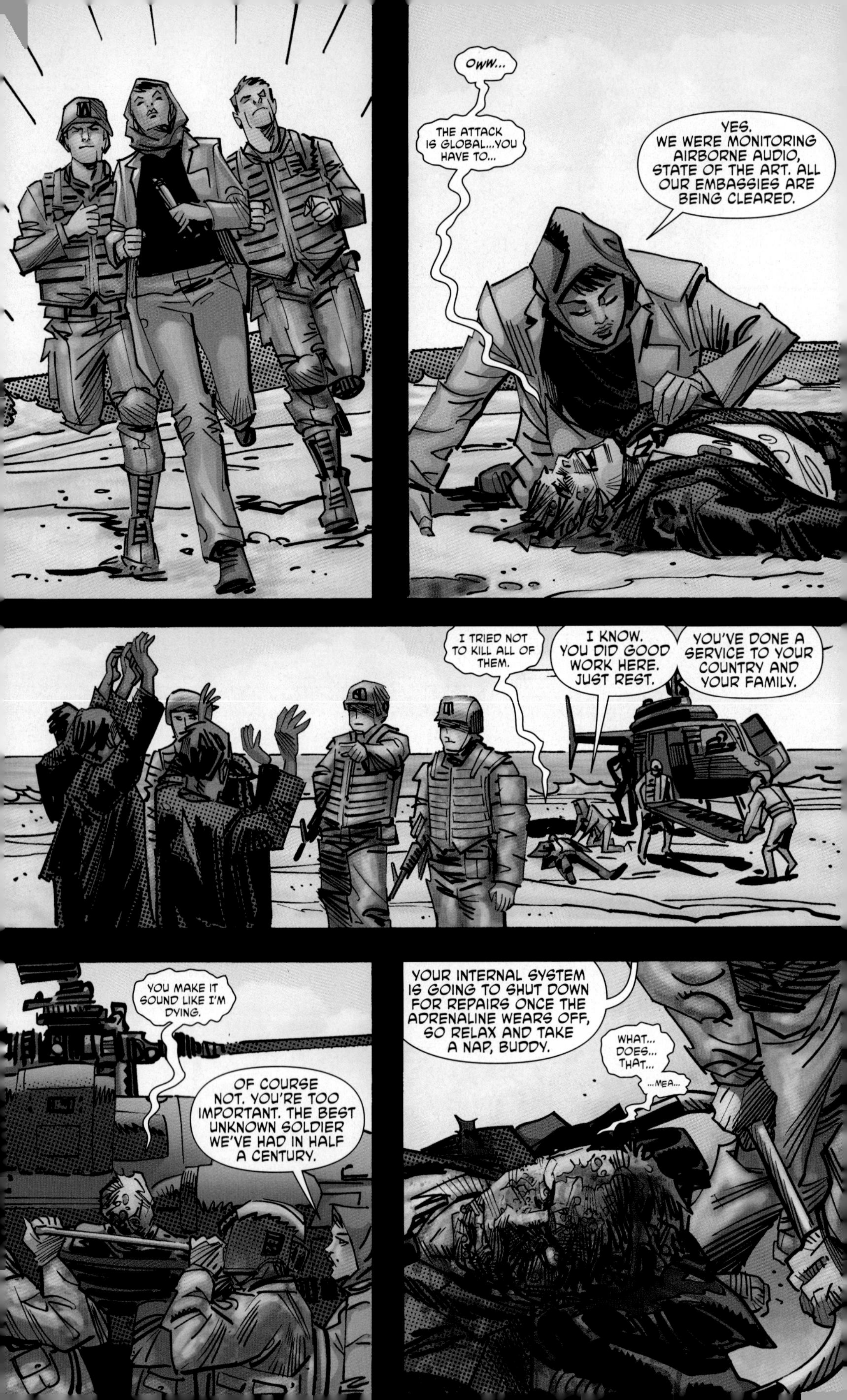
OWW...
THE ATTACK IS GLOBAL...YOU HAVE TO...
YES. WE WERE MONITORING AIRBORNE AUDIO, STATE OF THE ART. ALL OUR EMBASSIES ARE BEING CLEARED.
I TRIED NOT TO KILL ALL OF THEM.
I KNOW. YOU DID GOOD WORK HERE. JUST REST.
YOU'VE DONE A SERVICE TO YOUR COUNTRY AND YOUR FAMILY.
YOU MAKE IT SOUND LIKE I'M DYING.
OF COURSE NOT. YOU'RE TOO IMPORTANT. THE BEST UNKNOWN SOLDIER WE'VE HAD IN HALF A CENTURY.
YOUR INTERNAL SYSTEM IS GOING TO SHUT DOWN FOR REPAIRS ONCE THE ADRENALINE WEARS OFF, SO RELAX AND TAKE A NAP, BUDDY.
WHAT... DOES... THAT...
...MEA...

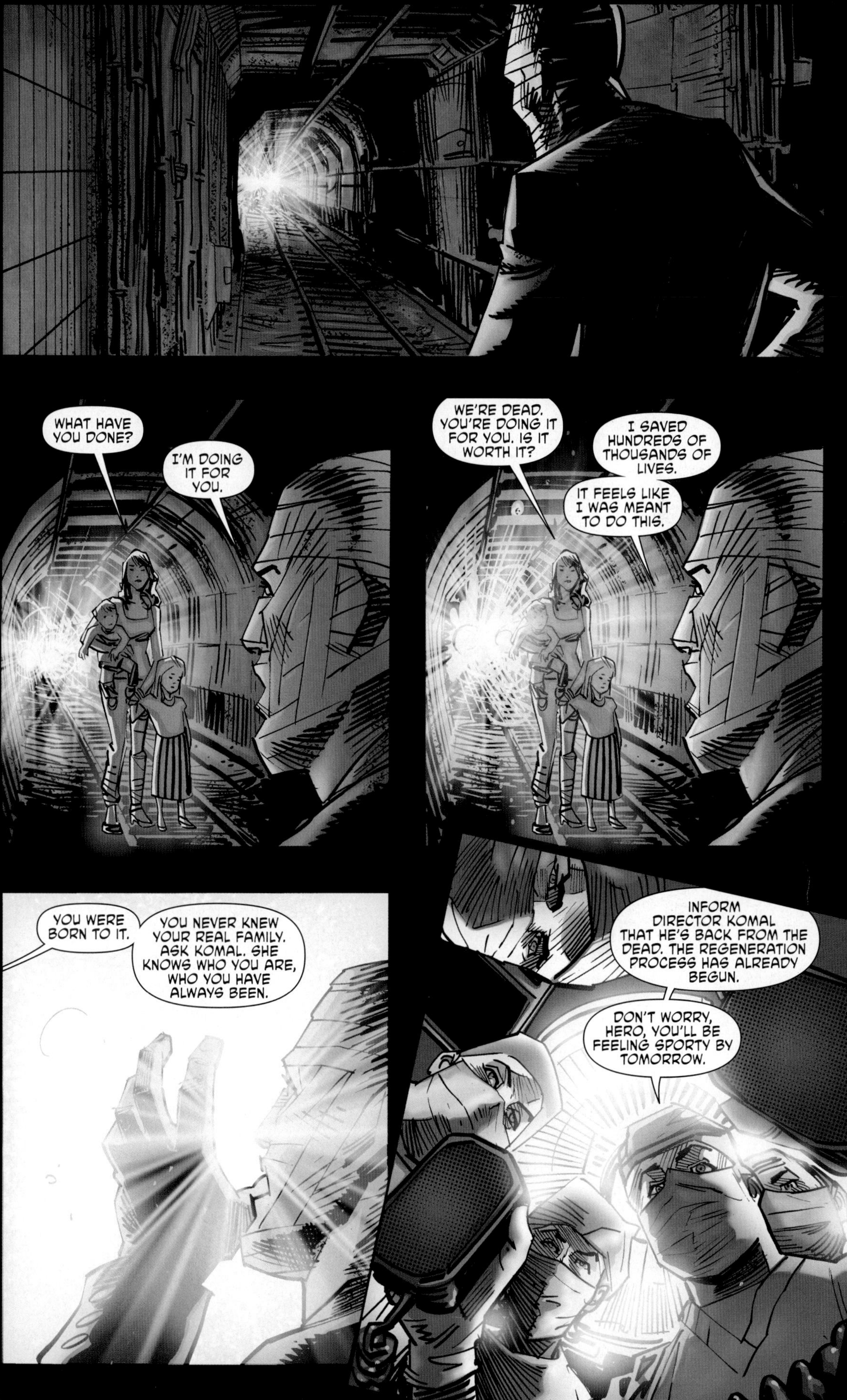
WHAT HAVE YOU DONE?
I'M DOING IT FOR YOU.
WE'RE DEAD. YOU'RE DOING IT FOR YOU. IS IT WORTH IT?
I SAVED HUNDREDS OF THOUSANDS OF LIVES.
IT FEELS LIKE I WAS MEANT TO DO THIS.
YOU WERE BORN TO IT.
YOU NEVER KNEW YOUR REAL FAMILY. ASK KOMAL. SHE KNOWS WHO YOU ARE, WHO YOU HAVE ALWAYS BEEN.
INFORM DIRECTOR KOMAL THAT HE'S BACK FROM THE DEAD. THE REGENERATION PROCESS HAS ALREADY BEGUN.
DON'T WORRY, HERO, YOU'LL BE FEELING SPORTY BY TOMORROW.

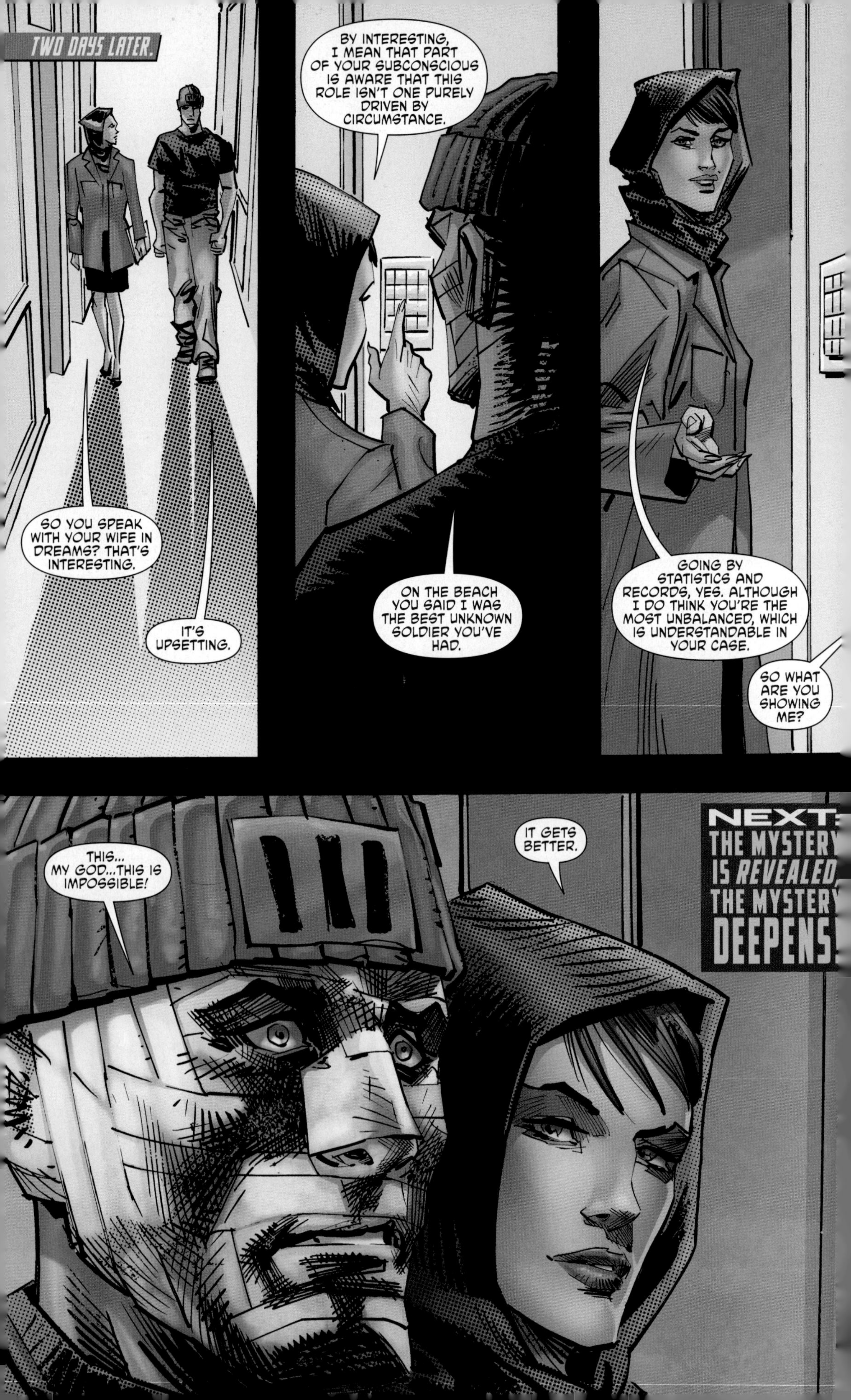
TWO DAYS LATER.
SO YOU SPEAK WITH YOUR WIFE IN DREAMS? THAT'S INTERESTING.
IT'S UPSETTING.
BY INTERESTING, I MEAN THAT PART OF YOUR SUBCONSCIOUS IS AWARE THAT THIS ROLE ISN'T ONE PURELY DRIVEN BY CIRCUMSTANCE.
ON THE BEACH YOU SAID I WAS THE BEST UNKNOWN SOLDIER YOU'VE HAD.
GOING BY STATISTICS AND RECORDS, YES. ALTHOUGH I DO THINK YOU'RE THE MOST UNBALANCED, WHICH IS UNDERSTANDABLE IN YOUR CASE.
SO WHAT ARE YOU SHOWING ME?
THIS... MY GOD...THIS IS IMPOSSIBLE!
IT GETS BETTER.
NEXT: THE MYSTERY IS *REVEALED*. THE MYSTERY DEEPENS!

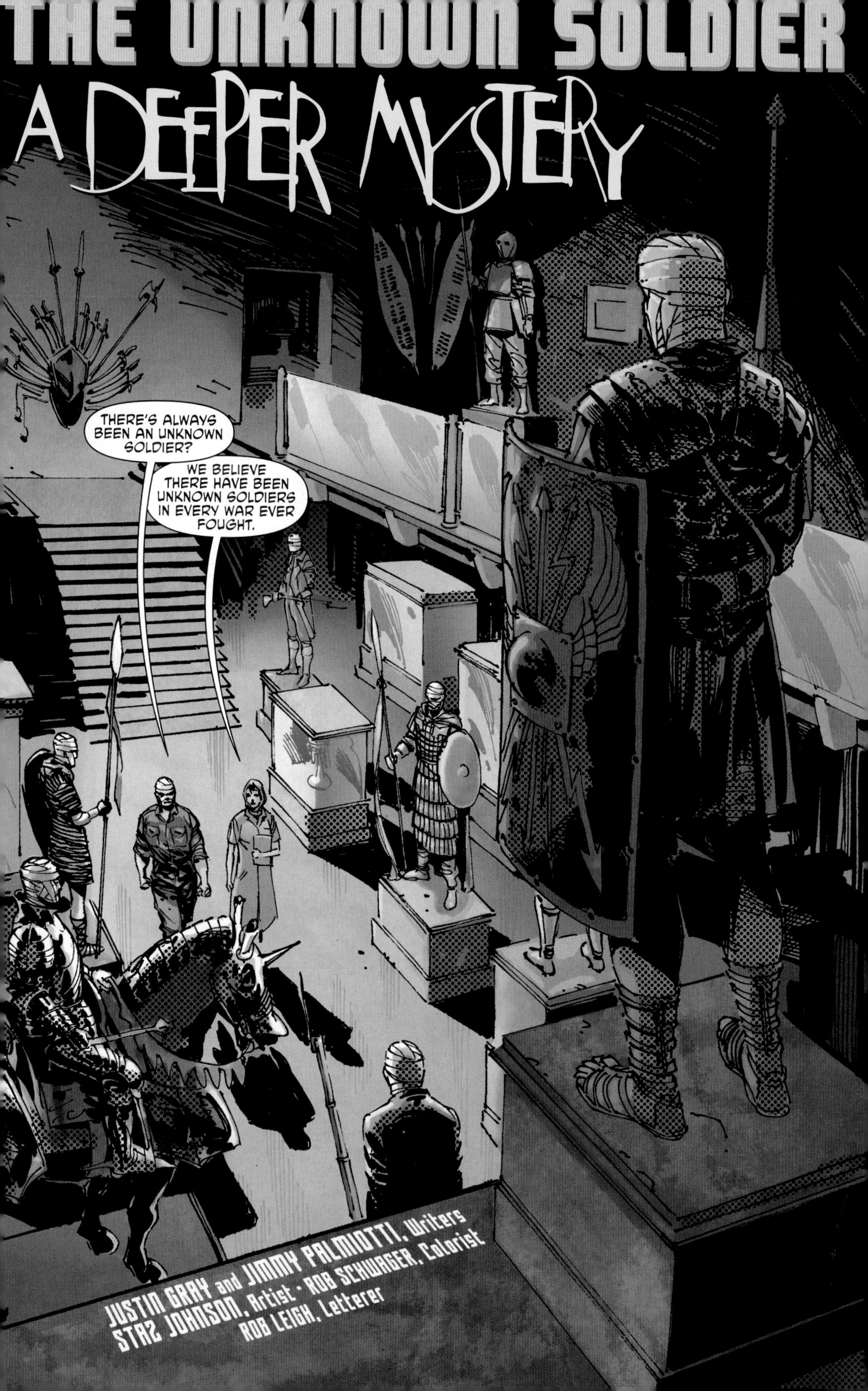
THE UNKNOWN SOLDIER
A DEEPER MYSTERY
THERE'S ALWAYS BEEN AN UNKNOWN SOLDIER?
WE BELIEVE THERE HAVE BEEN UNKNOWN SOLDIERS IN EVERY WAR EVER FOUGHT.
JUSTIN GRAY and JIMMY PALMIOTTI, Writers
STAZ JOHNSON, Artist · ROB SCHWAGER, Colorist
ROB LEIGH, Letterer

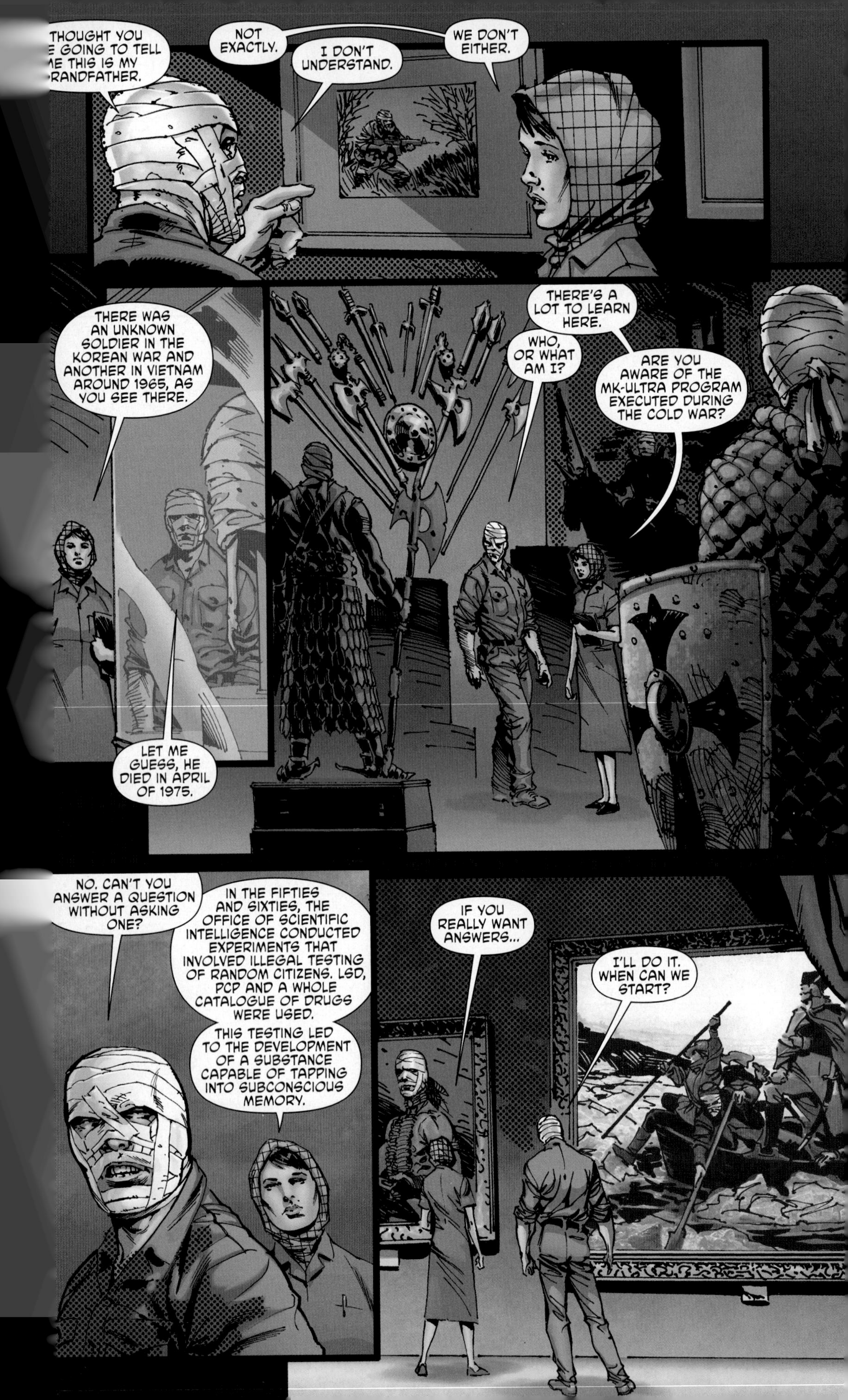
THOUGHT YOU
E GOING TO TELL
ME THIS IS MY
RANDFATHER.
NOT EXACTLY.
I DON'T UNDERSTAND.
WE DON'T EITHER.
THERE WAS AN UNKNOWN SOLDIER IN THE KOREAN WAR AND ANOTHER IN VIETNAM AROUND 1965, AS YOU SEE THERE.
LET ME GUESS, HE DIED IN APRIL OF 1975.
WHO, OR WHAT AM I?
THERE'S A LOT TO LEARN HERE.
ARE YOU AWARE OF THE MK-ULTRA PROGRAM EXECUTED DURING THE COLD WAR?
NO. CAN'T YOU ANSWER A QUESTION WITHOUT ASKING ONE?
IN THE FIFTIES AND SIXTIES, THE OFFICE OF SCIENTIFIC INTELLIGENCE CONDUCTED EXPERIMENTS THAT INVOLVED ILLEGAL TESTING OF RANDOM CITIZENS. LSD, PCP AND A WHOLE CATALOGUE OF DRUGS WERE USED.
THIS TESTING LED TO THE DEVELOPMENT OF A SUBSTANCE CAPABLE OF TAPPING INTO SUBCONSCIOUS MEMORY.
IF YOU REALLY WANT ANSWERS...
I'LL DO IT. WHEN CAN WE START?

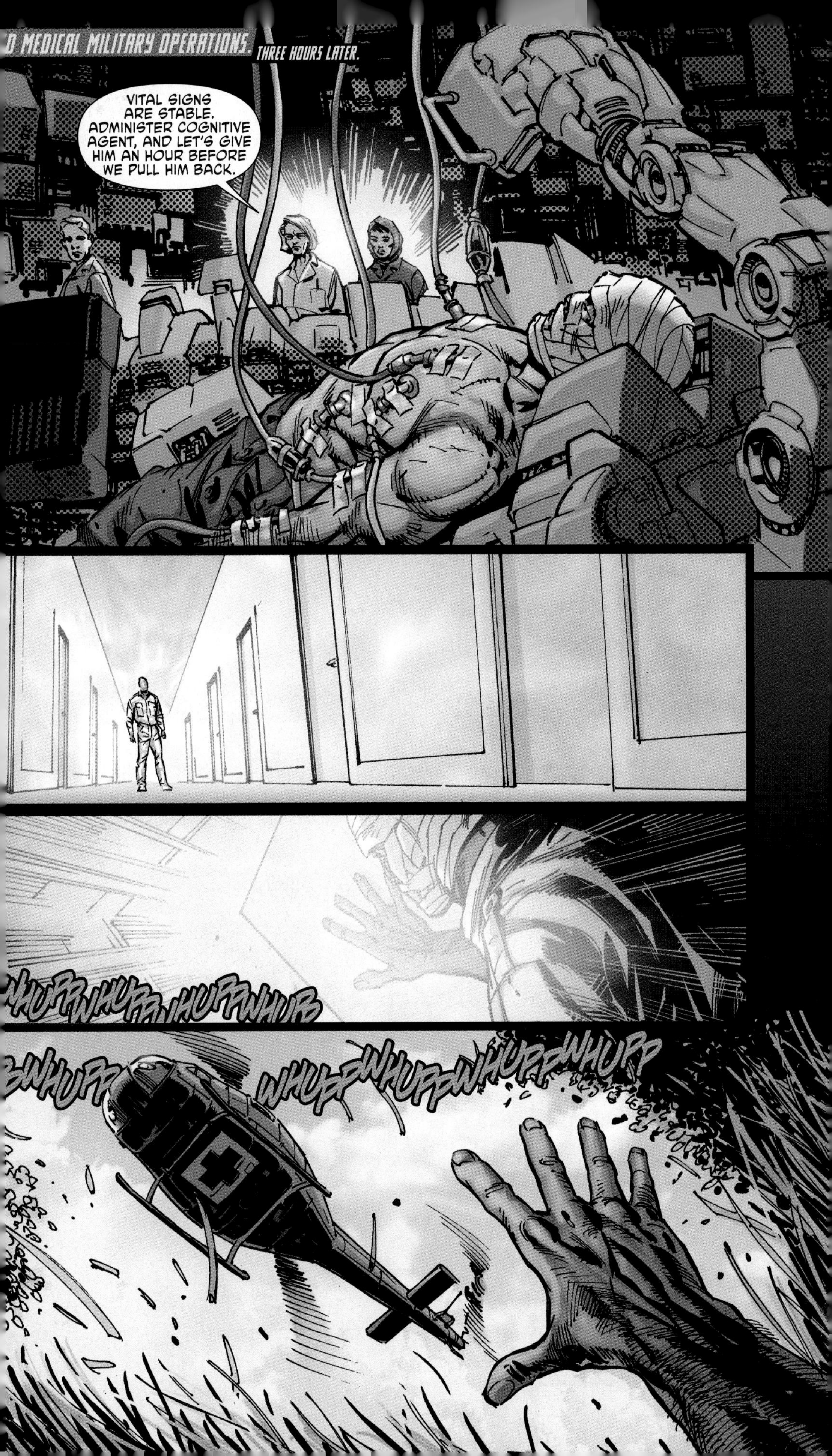

...D MEDICAL MILITARY OPERATIONS.
THREE HOURS LATER.
VITAL SIGNS ARE STABLE. ADMINISTER COGNITIVE AGENT, AND LET'S GIVE HIM AN HOUR BEFORE WE PULL HIM BACK.
WHUPPWHUPPWHUPPWHUPP
WHUPP
WHUPPWHUPPWHUPPWHUPP

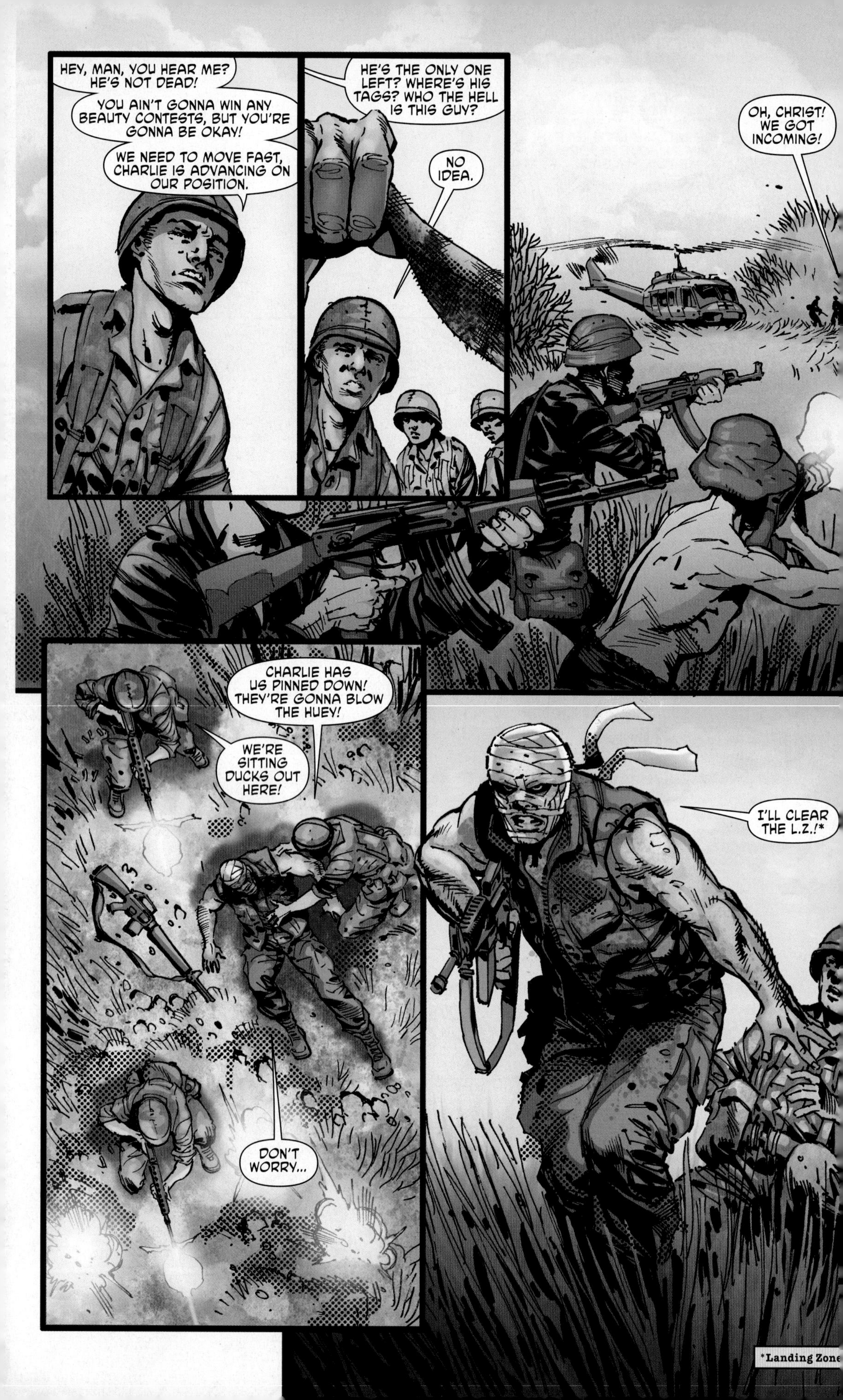

HEY, MAN, YOU HEAR ME? HE'S NOT DEAD!
YOU AIN'T GONNA WIN ANY BEAUTY CONTESTS, BUT YOU'RE GONNA BE OKAY!
WE NEED TO MOVE FAST, CHARLIE IS ADVANCING ON OUR POSITION.
HE'S THE ONLY ONE LEFT? WHERE'S HIS TAGS? WHO THE HELL IS THIS GUY?
NO IDEA.
OH, CHRIST! WE GOT INCOMING!
CHARLIE HAS US PINNED DOWN! THEY'RE GONNA BLOW THE HUEY!
WE'RE SITTING DUCKS OUT HERE!
DON'T WORRY...
I'LL CLEAR THE L.Z.!*
*Landing Zone

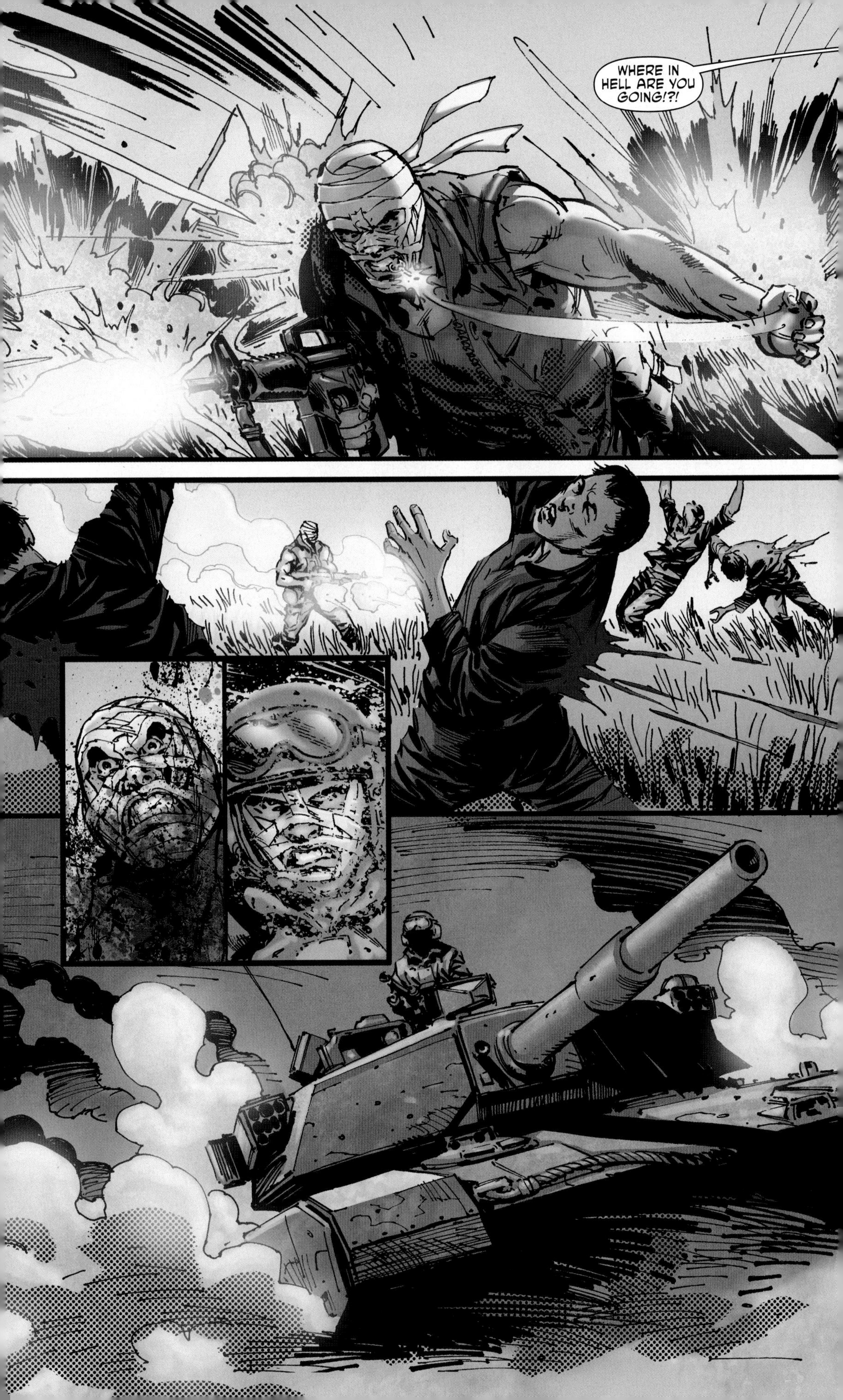
WHERE IN
HELL ARE YOU
GOING!?!

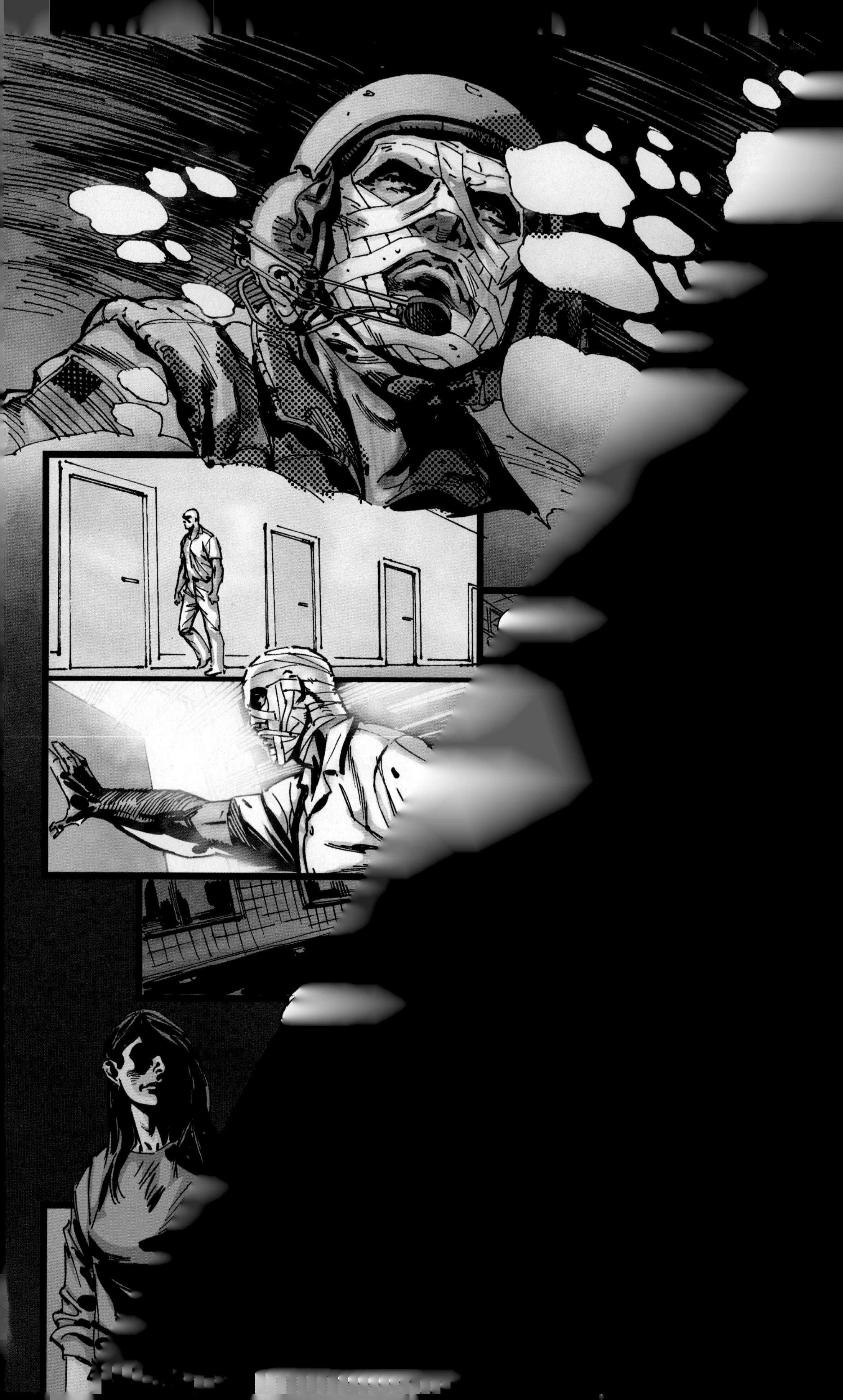

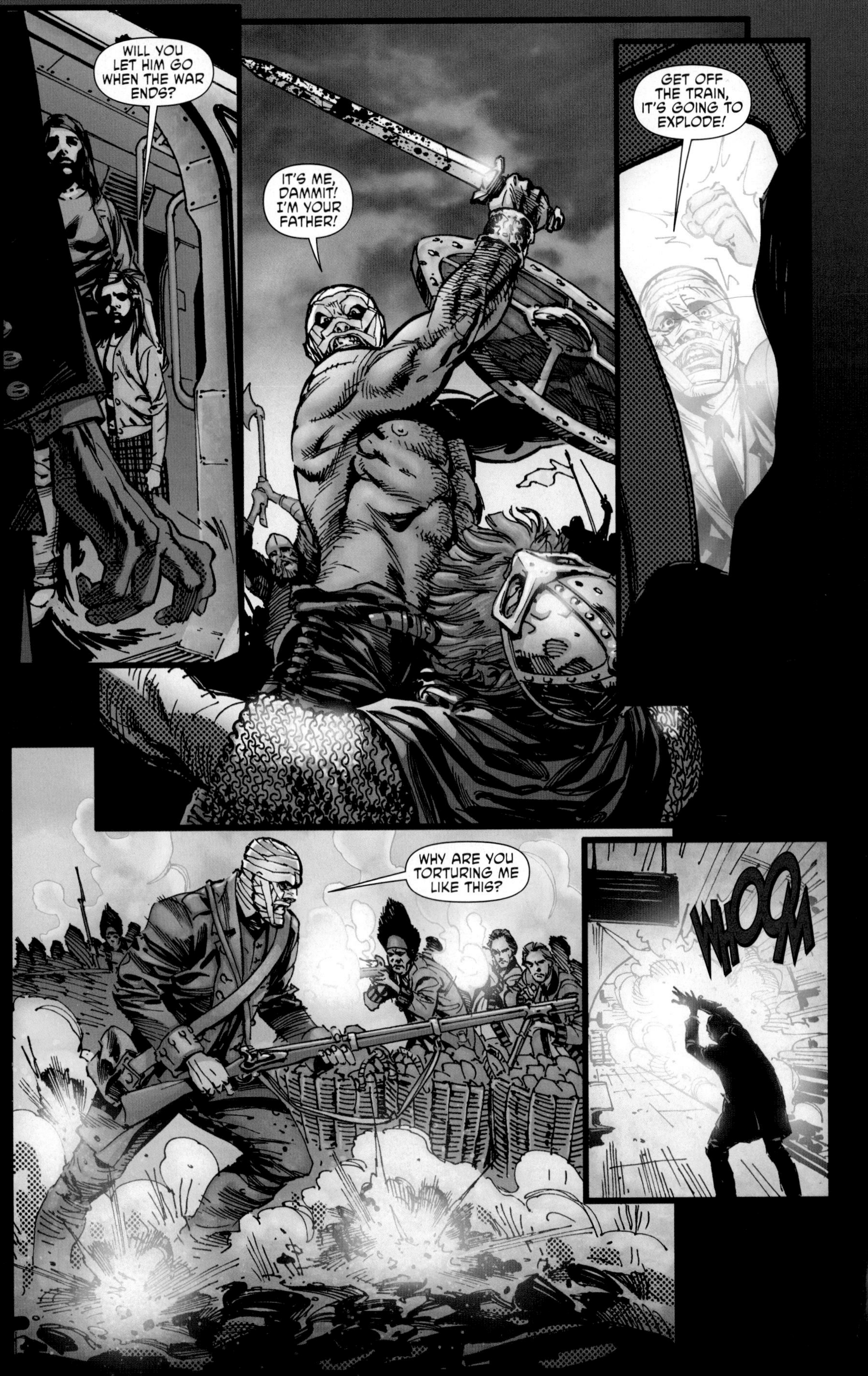
WILL YOU LET HIM GO WHEN THE WAR ENDS?
IT'S ME, DAMMIT! I'M YOUR FATHER!
GET OFF THE TRAIN, IT'S GOING TO EXPLODE!
WHY ARE YOU TORTURING ME LIKE THIS?
WHOOM

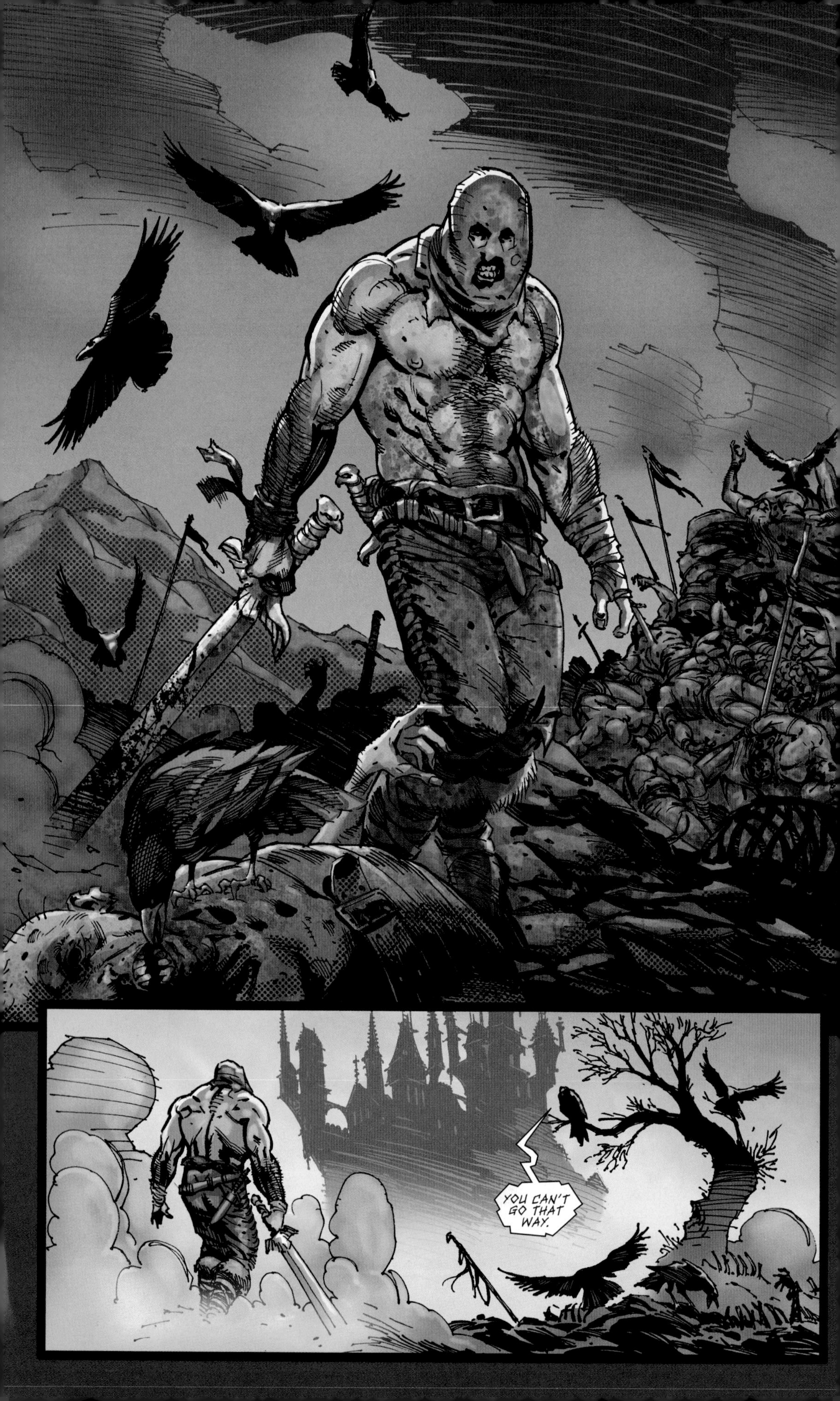
YOU CAN'T GO THAT WAY.

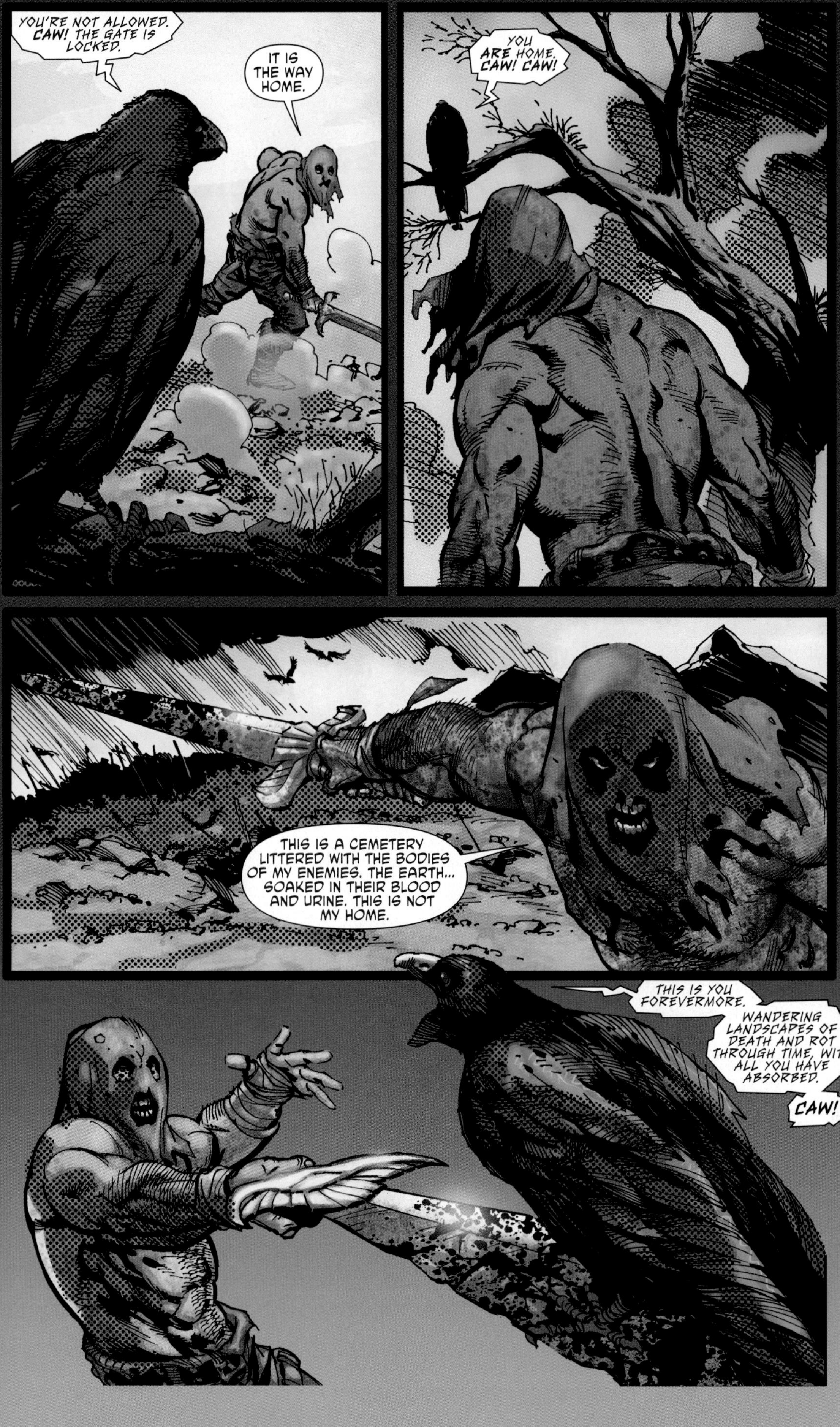
YOU'RE NOT ALLOWED. CAW! THE GATE IS LOCKED.
IT IS THE WAY HOME.
YOU ARE HOME. CAW! CAW!
THIS IS A CEMETERY LITTERED WITH THE BODIES OF MY ENEMIES. THE EARTH... SOAKED IN THEIR BLOOD AND URINE. THIS IS NOT MY HOME.
THIS IS YOU FOREVERMORE.
WANDERING LANDSCAPES OF DEATH AND ROT THROUGH TIME, WITH ALL YOU HAVE ABSORBED.
CAW!

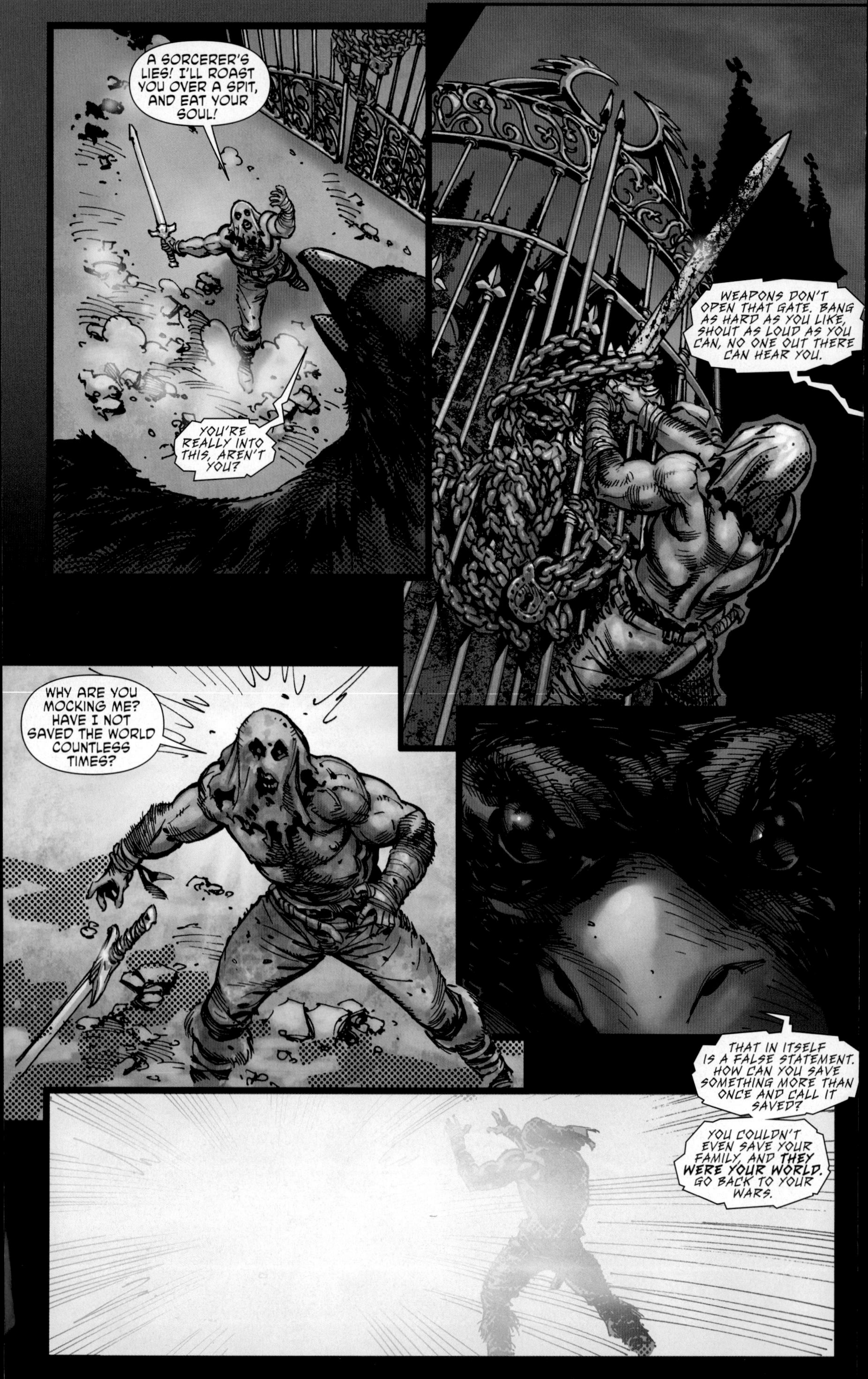
A SORCERER'S LIES! I'LL ROAST YOU OVER A SPIT, AND EAT YOUR SOUL!
YOU'RE REALLY INTO THIS, AREN'T YOU?
WEAPONS DON'T OPEN THAT GATE. BANG AS HARD AS YOU LIKE, SHOUT AS LOUD AS YOU CAN, NO ONE OUT THERE CAN HEAR YOU.
WHY ARE YOU MOCKING ME? HAVE I NOT SAVED THE WORLD COUNTLESS TIMES?
THAT IN ITSELF IS A FALSE STATEMENT. HOW CAN YOU SAVE SOMETHING MORE THAN ONCE AND CALL IT SAVED?
YOU COULDN'T EVEN SAVE YOUR FAMILY, AND **THEY WERE YOUR WORLD.** GO BACK TO YOUR WARS.

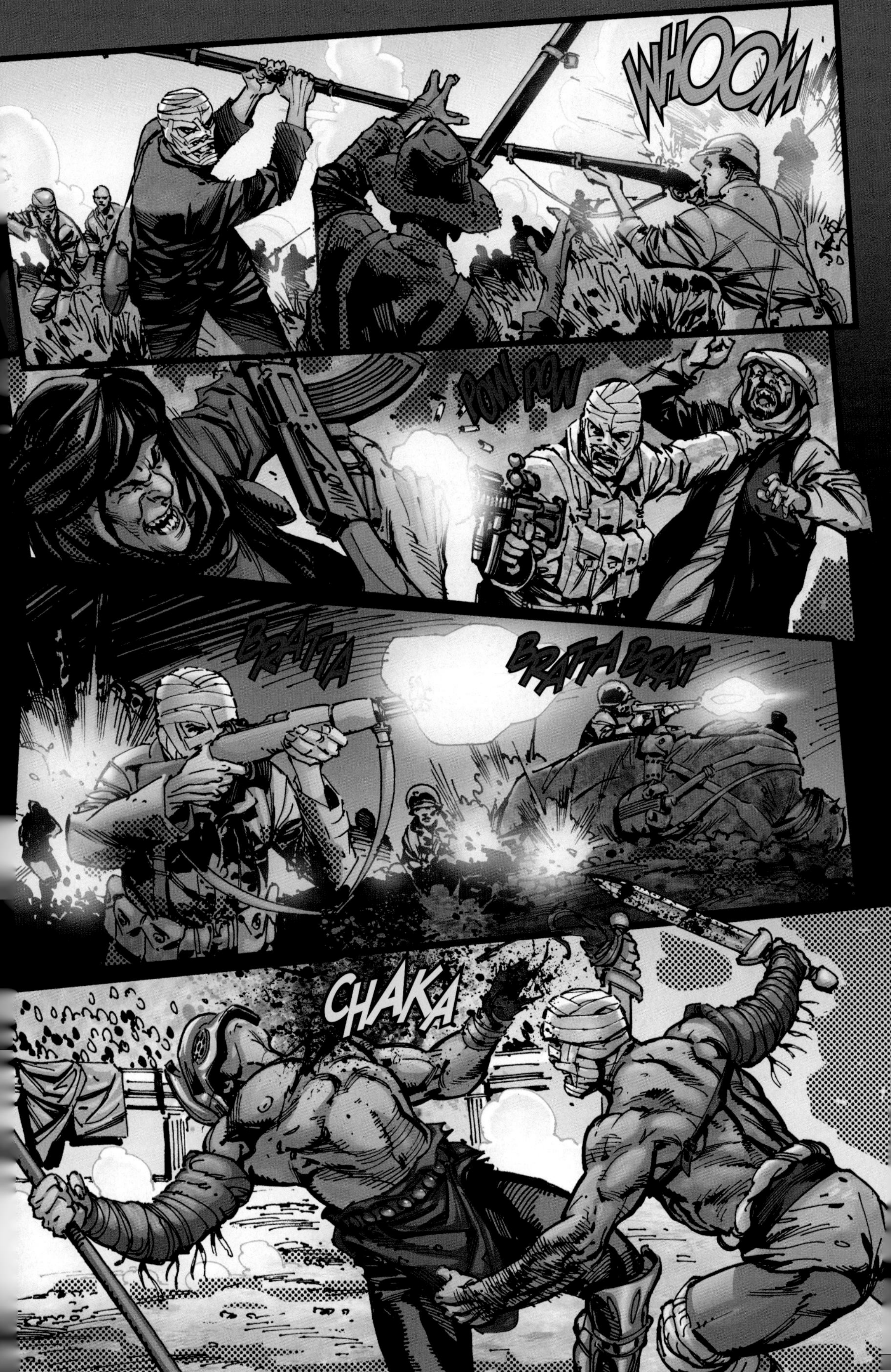
WHOOM
POW POW
BRATTA
BRATTA BRAT
CHAKA

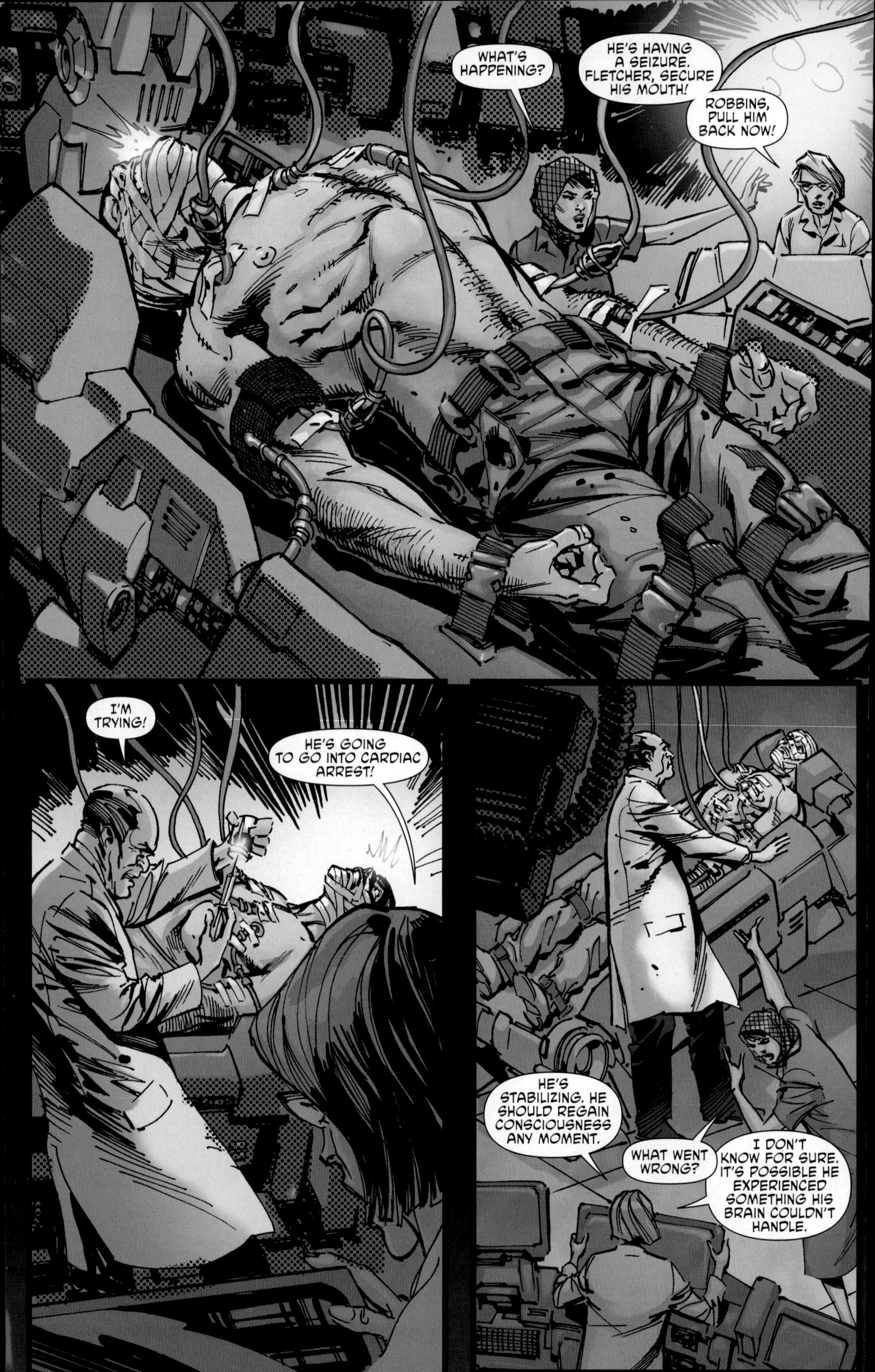
WHAT'S HAPPENING?
HE'S HAVING A SEIZURE. FLETCHER, SECURE HIS MOUTH!
ROBBINS, PULL HIM BACK NOW!
I'M TRYING!
HE'S GOING TO GO INTO CARDIAC ARREST!
HE'S STABILIZING. HE SHOULD REGAIN CONSCIOUSNESS ANY MOMENT.
WHAT WENT WRONG?
I DON'T KNOW FOR SURE. IT'S POSSIBLE HE EXPERIENCED SOMETHING HIS BRAIN COULDN'T HANDLE.

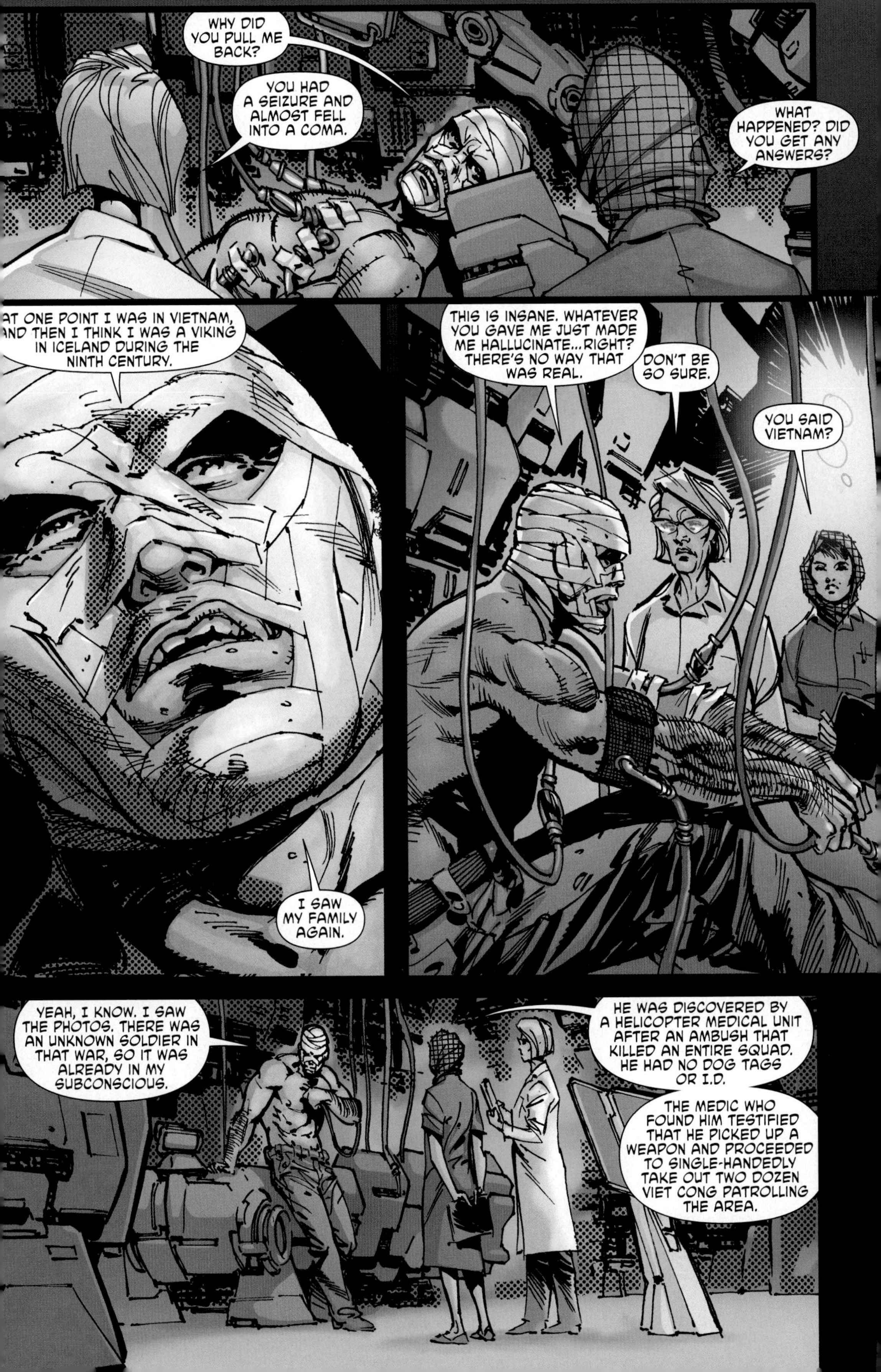
WHY DID YOU PULL ME BACK?
YOU HAD A SEIZURE AND ALMOST FELL INTO A COMA.
WHAT HAPPENED? DID YOU GET ANY ANSWERS?
AT ONE POINT I WAS IN VIETNAM, AND THEN I THINK I WAS A VIKING IN ICELAND DURING THE NINTH CENTURY.
I SAW MY FAMILY AGAIN.
THIS IS INSANE. WHATEVER YOU GAVE ME JUST MADE ME HALLUCINATE...RIGHT? THERE'S NO WAY THAT WAS REAL.
DON'T BE SO SURE.
YOU SAID VIETNAM?
YEAH, I KNOW. I SAW THE PHOTOS. THERE WAS AN UNKNOWN SOLDIER IN THAT WAR, SO IT WAS ALREADY IN MY SUBCONSCIOUS.
HE WAS DISCOVERED BY A HELICOPTER MEDICAL UNIT AFTER AN AMBUSH THAT KILLED AN ENTIRE SQUAD. HE HAD NO DOG TAGS OR I.D.
THE MEDIC WHO FOUND HIM TESTIFIED THAT HE PICKED UP A WEAPON AND PROCEEDED TO SINGLE-HANDEDLY TAKE OUT TWO DOZEN VIET CONG PATROLLING THE AREA.

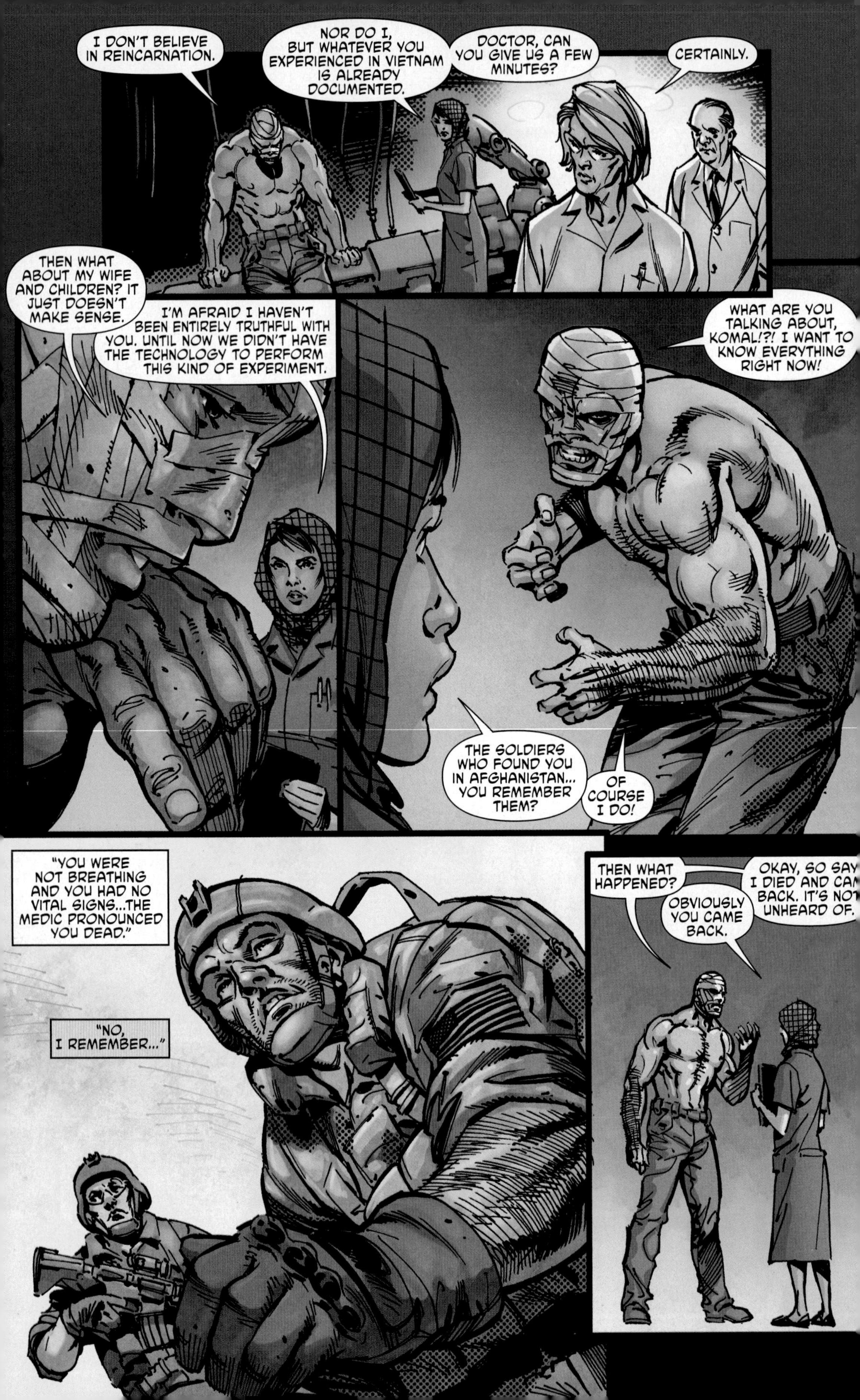

I DON'T BELIEVE IN REINCARNATION.
NOR DO I, BUT WHATEVER YOU EXPERIENCED IN VIETNAM IS ALREADY DOCUMENTED.
DOCTOR, CAN YOU GIVE US A FEW MINUTES?
CERTAINLY.
THEN WHAT ABOUT MY WIFE AND CHILDREN? IT JUST DOESN'T MAKE SENSE.
I'M AFRAID I HAVEN'T BEEN ENTIRELY TRUTHFUL WITH YOU. UNTIL NOW WE DIDN'T HAVE THE TECHNOLOGY TO PERFORM THIS KIND OF EXPERIMENT.
WHAT ARE YOU TALKING ABOUT, KOMAL!?! I WANT TO KNOW EVERYTHING RIGHT NOW!
THE SOLDIERS WHO FOUND YOU IN AFGHANISTAN... YOU REMEMBER THEM?
OF COURSE I DO!
"YOU WERE NOT BREATHING AND YOU HAD NO VITAL SIGNS...THE MEDIC PRONOUNCED YOU DEAD."
"NO, I REMEMBER..."
OKAY, SO SAY I DIED AND CAME BACK. IT'S NOT UNHEARD OF.
OBVIOUSLY YOU CAME BACK.
THEN WHAT HAPPENED?

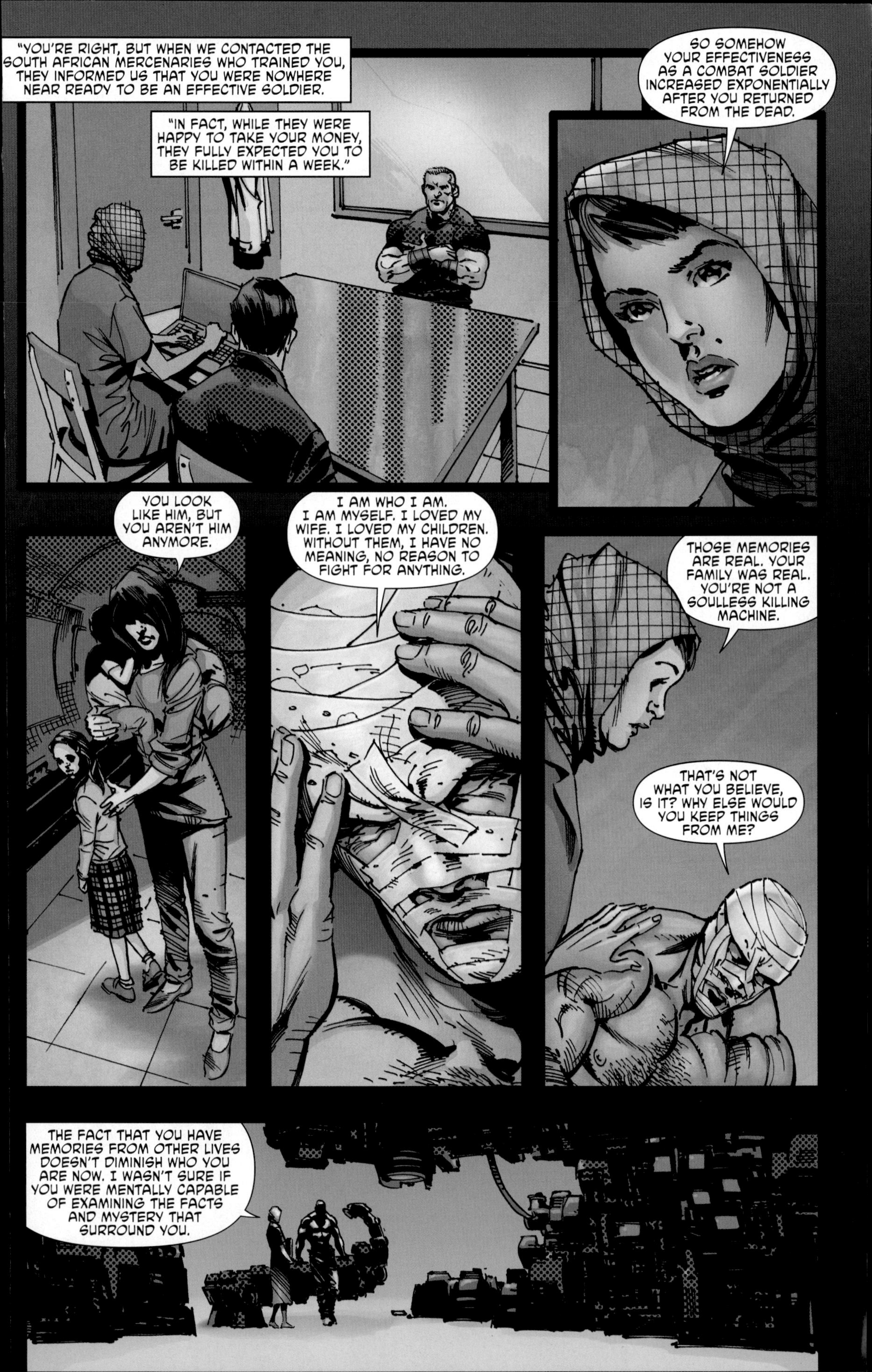
"YOU'RE RIGHT, BUT WHEN WE CONTACTED THE SOUTH AFRICAN MERCENARIES WHO TRAINED YOU, THEY INFORMED US THAT YOU WERE NOWHERE NEAR READY TO BE AN EFFECTIVE SOLDIER.
"IN FACT, WHILE THEY WERE HAPPY TO TAKE YOUR MONEY, THEY FULLY EXPECTED YOU TO BE KILLED WITHIN A WEEK."
SO SOMEHOW YOUR EFFECTIVENESS AS A COMBAT SOLDIER INCREASED EXPONENTIALLY AFTER YOU RETURNED FROM THE DEAD.
YOU LOOK LIKE HIM, BUT YOU AREN'T HIM ANYMORE.
I AM WHO I AM. I AM MYSELF. I LOVED MY WIFE. I LOVED MY CHILDREN. WITHOUT THEM, I HAVE NO MEANING, NO REASON TO FIGHT FOR ANYTHING.
THOSE MEMORIES ARE REAL. YOUR FAMILY WAS REAL. YOU'RE NOT A SOULLESS KILLING MACHINE.
THAT'S NOT WHAT YOU BELIEVE, IS IT? WHY ELSE WOULD YOU KEEP THINGS FROM ME?
THE FACT THAT YOU HAVE MEMORIES FROM OTHER LIVES DOESN'T DIMINISH WHO YOU ARE NOW. I WASN'T SURE IF YOU WERE MENTALLY CAPABLE OF EXAMINING THE FACTS AND MYSTERY THAT SURROUND YOU.

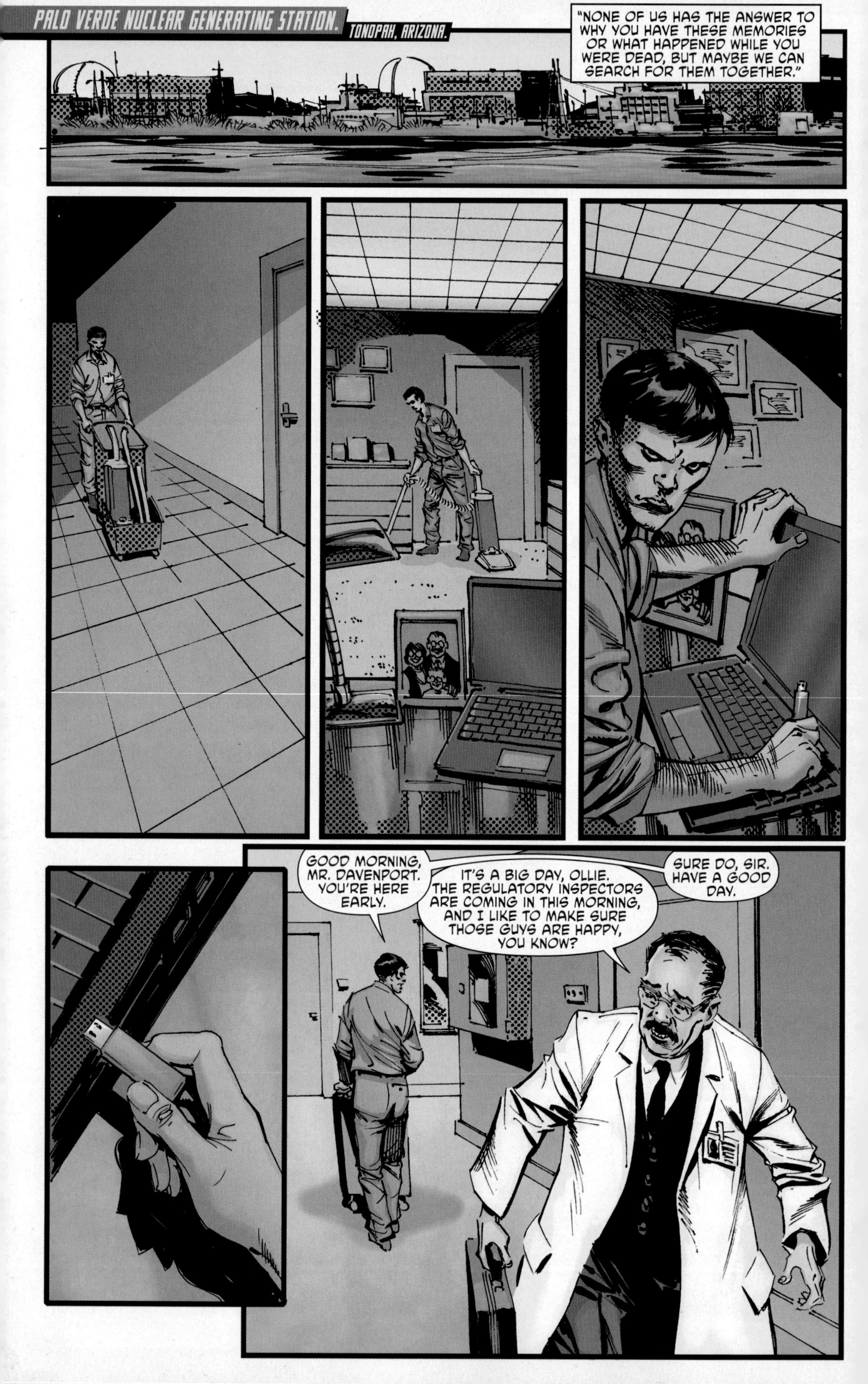
PALO VERDE NUCLEAR GENERATING STATION.
TONOPAH, ARIZONA.
"NONE OF US HAS THE ANSWER TO WHY YOU HAVE THESE MEMORIES OR WHAT HAPPENED WHILE YOU WERE DEAD, BUT MAYBE WE CAN SEARCH FOR THEM TOGETHER."
GOOD MORNING, MR. DAVENPORT. YOU'RE HERE EARLY.
IT'S A BIG DAY, OLLIE. THE REGULATORY INSPECTORS ARE COMING IN THIS MORNING, AND I LIKE TO MAKE SURE THOSE GUYS ARE HAPPY, YOU KNOW?
SURE DO, SIR. HAVE A GOOD DAY.

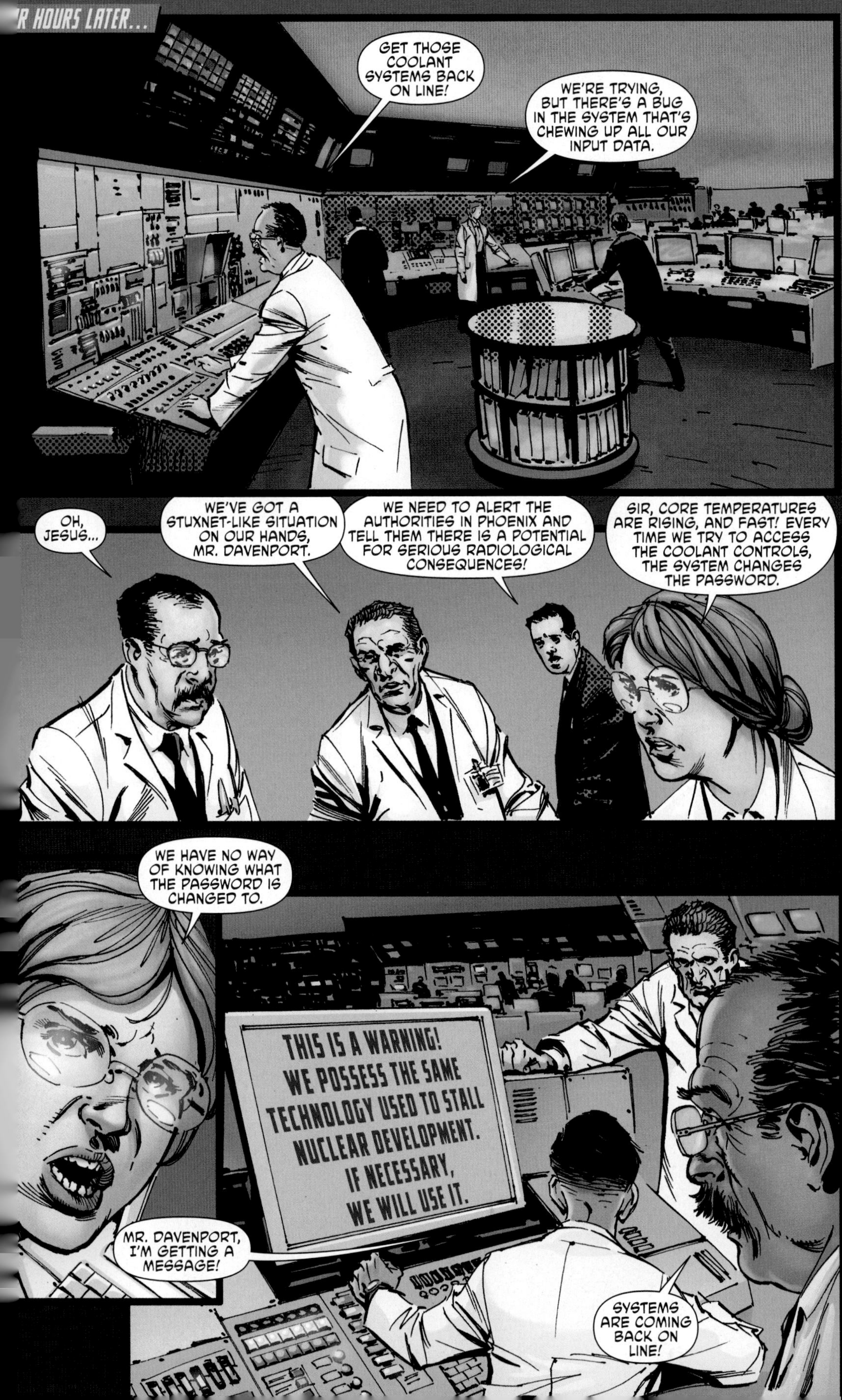
R HOURS LATER...
GET THOSE COOLANT SYSTEMS BACK ON LINE!
WE'RE TRYING, BUT THERE'S A BUG IN THE SYSTEM THAT'S CHEWING UP ALL OUR INPUT DATA.
OH, JESUS...
WE'VE GOT A STUXNET-LIKE SITUATION ON OUR HANDS, MR. DAVENPORT.
WE NEED TO ALERT THE AUTHORITIES IN PHOENIX AND TELL THEM THERE IS A POTENTIAL FOR SERIOUS RADIOLOGICAL CONSEQUENCES!
SIR, CORE TEMPERATURES ARE RISING, AND FAST! EVERY TIME WE TRY TO ACCESS THE COOLANT CONTROLS, THE SYSTEM CHANGES THE PASSWORD.
WE HAVE NO WAY OF KNOWING WHAT THE PASSWORD IS CHANGED TO.
THIS IS A WARNING! WE POSSESS THE SAME TECHNOLOGY USED TO STALL NUCLEAR DEVELOPMENT. IF NECESSARY, WE WILL USE IT.
MR. DAVENPORT, I'M GETTING A MESSAGE!
SYSTEMS ARE COMING BACK ON LINE!

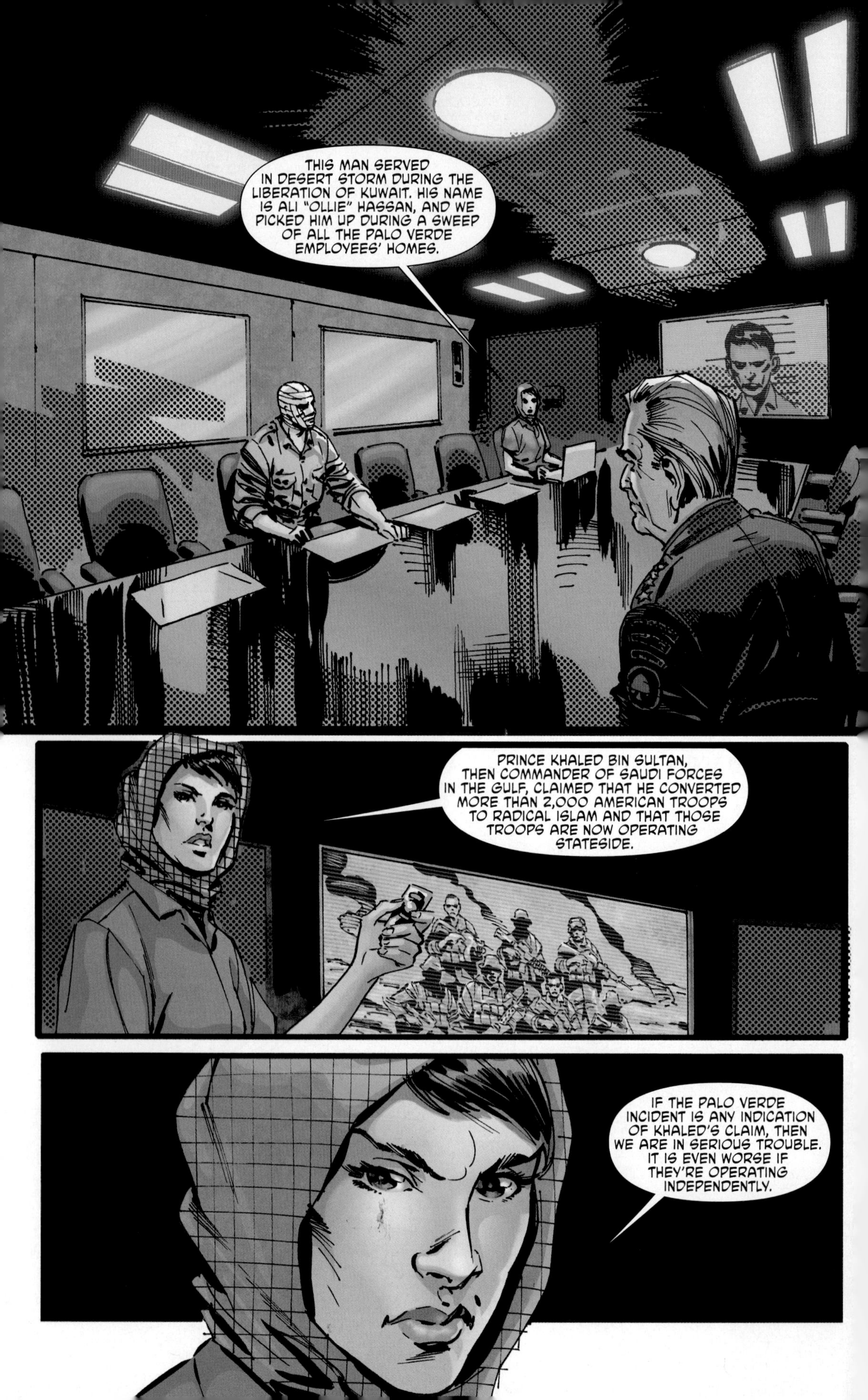
THIS MAN SERVED IN DESERT STORM DURING THE LIBERATION OF KUWAIT. HIS NAME IS ALI "OLLIE" HASSAN, AND WE PICKED HIM UP DURING A SWEEP OF ALL THE PALO VERDE EMPLOYEES' HOMES.
PRINCE KHALED BIN SULTAN, THEN COMMANDER OF SAUDI FORCES IN THE GULF, CLAIMED THAT HE CONVERTED MORE THAN 2,000 AMERICAN TROOPS TO RADICAL ISLAM AND THAT THOSE TROOPS ARE NOW OPERATING STATESIDE.
IF THE PALO VERDE INCIDENT IS ANY INDICATION OF KHALED'S CLAIM, THEN WE ARE IN SERIOUS TROUBLE. IT IS EVEN WORSE IF THEY'RE OPERATING INDEPENDENTLY.

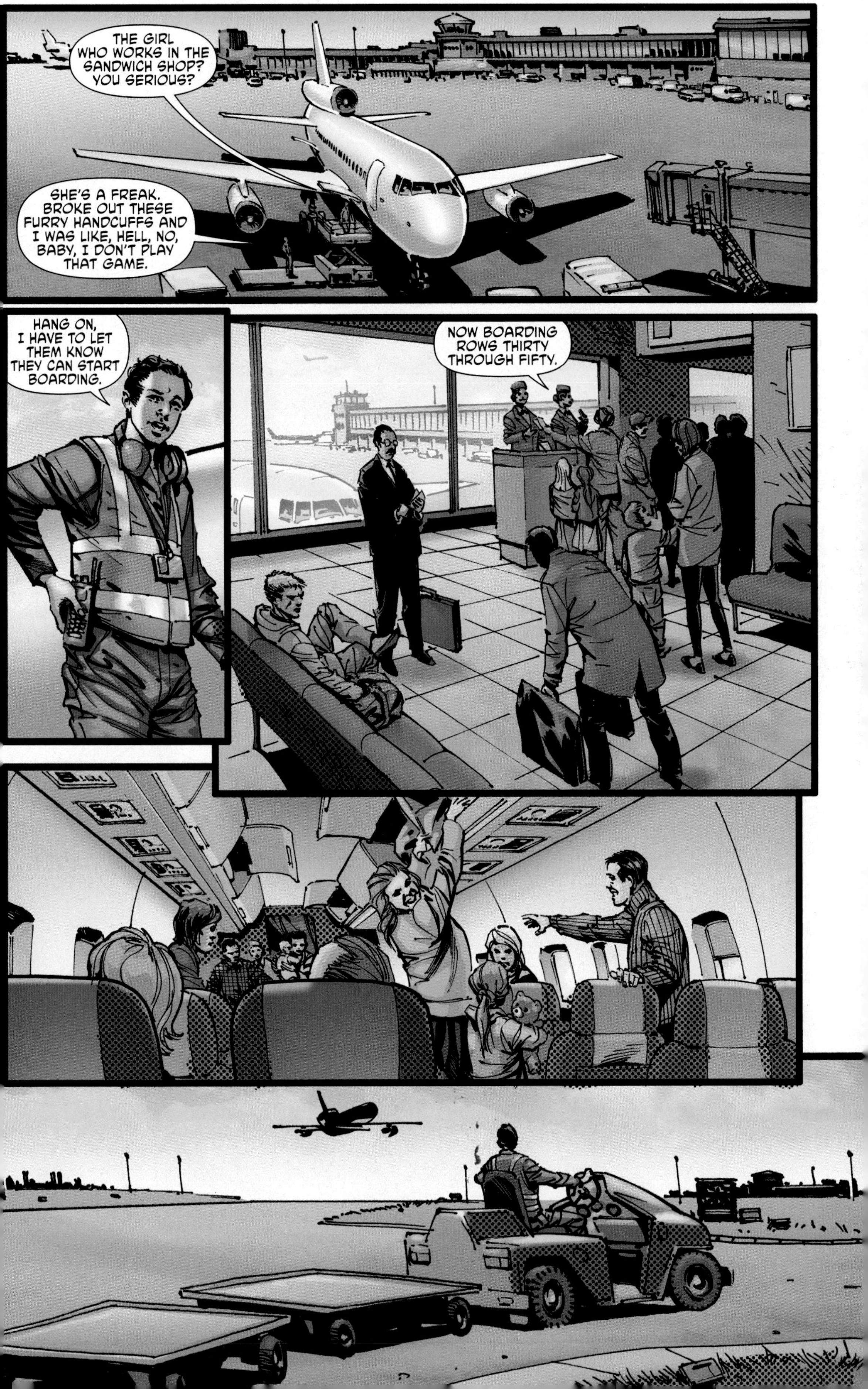
THE GIRL WHO WORKS IN THE SANDWICH SHOP? YOU SERIOUS?
SHE'S A FREAK. BROKE OUT THESE FURRY HANDCUFFS AND I WAS LIKE, HELL, NO, BABY, I DON'T PLAY THAT GAME.
HANG ON, I HAVE TO LET THEM KNOW THEY CAN START BOARDING.
NOW BOARDING ROWS THIRTY THROUGH FIFTY.

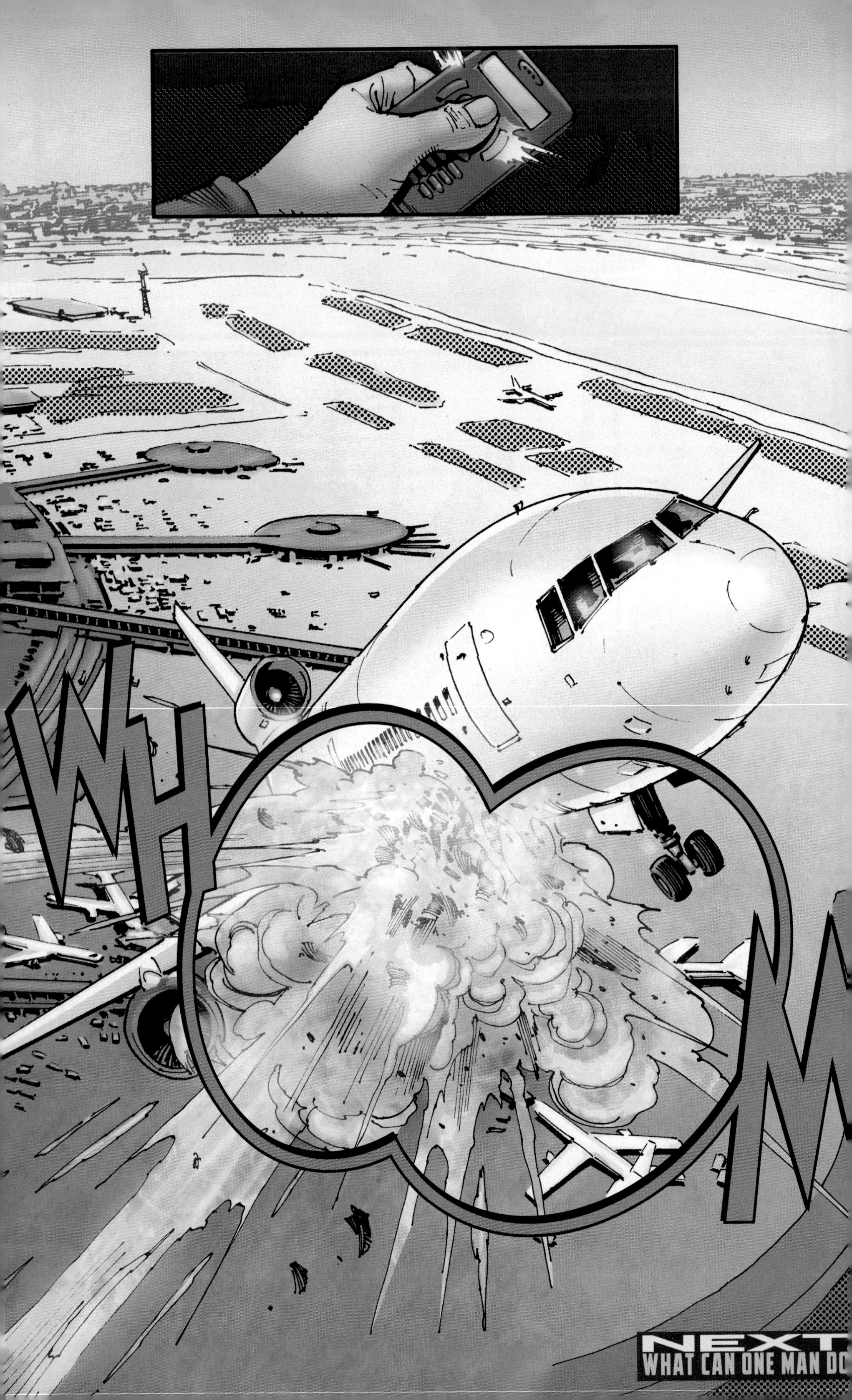
WHOOM
NEXT
WHAT CAN ONE MAN DO

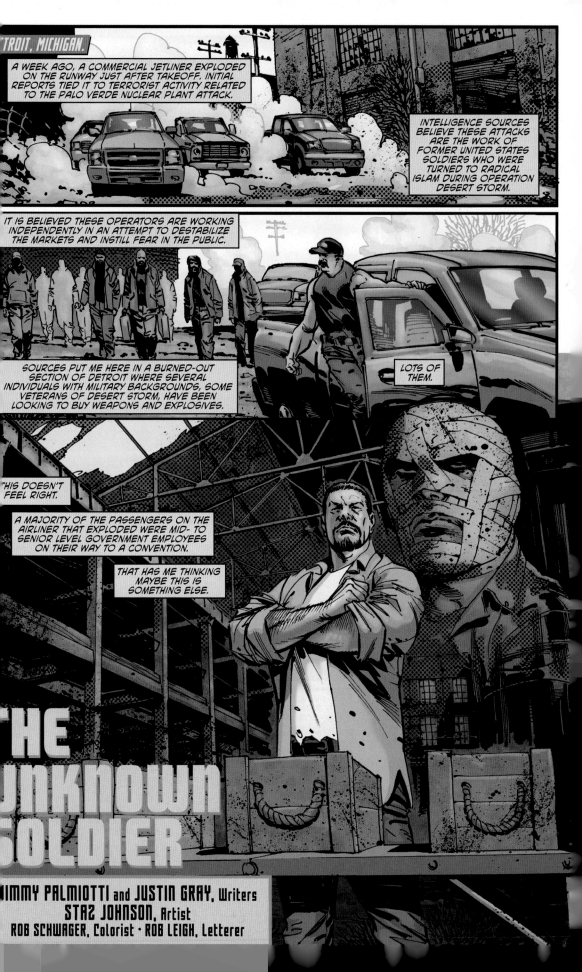

DETROIT, MICHIGAN.

A WEEK AGO, A COMMERCIAL JETLINER EXPLODED ON THE RUNWAY JUST AFTER TAKEOFF. INITIAL REPORTS TIED IT TO TERRORIST ACTIVITY RELATED TO THE PALO VERDE NUCLEAR PLANT ATTACK.

INTELLIGENCE SOURCES BELIEVE THESE ATTACKS ARE THE WORK OF FORMER UNITED STATES SOLDIERS WHO WERE TURNED TO RADICAL ISLAM DURING OPERATION DESERT STORM.

IT IS BELIEVED THESE OPERATORS ARE WORKING INDEPENDENTLY IN AN ATTEMPT TO DESTABILIZE THE MARKETS AND INSTILL FEAR IN THE PUBLIC.

SOURCES PUT ME HERE IN A BURNED-OUT SECTION OF DETROIT WHERE SEVERAL INDIVIDUALS WITH MILITARY BACKGROUNDS, SOME VETERANS OF DESERT STORM, HAVE BEEN LOOKING TO BUY WEAPONS AND EXPLOSIVES.

LOTS OF THEM.

THIS DOESN'T FEEL RIGHT.

A MAJORITY OF THE PASSENGERS ON THE AIRLINER THAT EXPLODED WERE MID- TO SENIOR LEVEL GOVERNMENT EMPLOYEES ON THEIR WAY TO A CONVENTION.

THAT HAS ME THINKING MAYBE THIS IS SOMETHING ELSE.

THE UNKNOWN SOLDIER

JIMMY PALMIOTTI and JUSTIN GRAY, Writers
STAZ JOHNSON, Artist
ROB SCHWAGER, Colorist · ROB LEIGH, Letterer

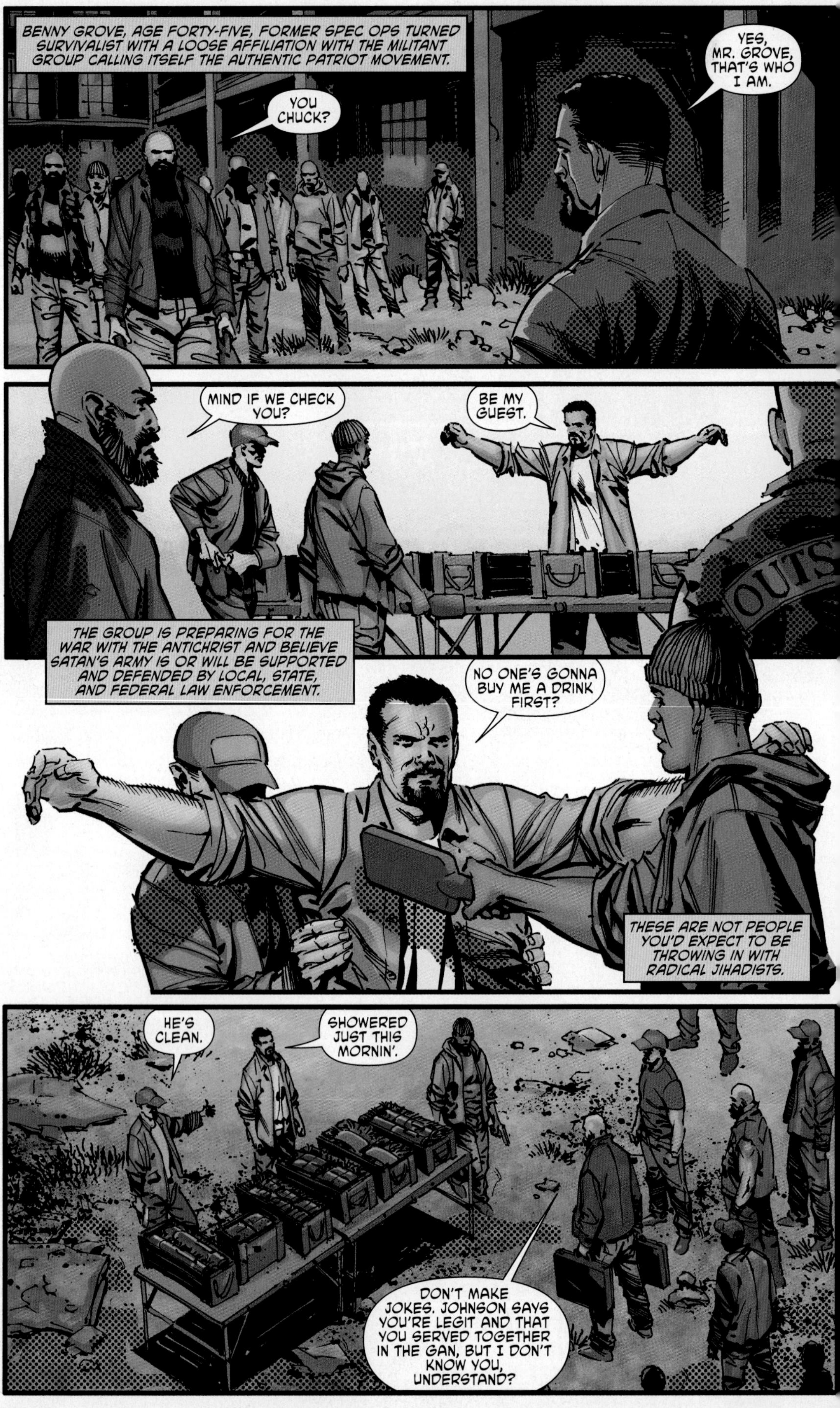

BENNY GROVE, AGE FORTY-FIVE, FORMER SPEC OPS TURNED SURVIVALIST WITH A LOOSE AFFILIATION WITH THE MILITANT GROUP CALLING ITSELF THE AUTHENTIC PATRIOT MOVEMENT.
YOU CHUCK?
YES, MR. GROVE, THAT'S WHO I AM.
MIND IF WE CHECK YOU?
BE MY GUEST.
OUTS
THE GROUP IS PREPARING FOR THE WAR WITH THE ANTICHRIST AND BELIEVE SATAN'S ARMY IS OR WILL BE SUPPORTED AND DEFENDED BY LOCAL, STATE, AND FEDERAL LAW ENFORCEMENT.
NO ONE'S GONNA BUY ME A DRINK FIRST?
THESE ARE NOT PEOPLE YOU'D EXPECT TO BE THROWING IN WITH RADICAL JIHADISTS.
HE'S CLEAN.
SHOWERED JUST THIS MORNIN'.
DON'T MAKE JOKES. JOHNSON SAYS YOU'RE LEGIT AND THAT YOU SERVED TOGETHER IN THE GAN, BUT I DON'T KNOW YOU, UNDERSTAND?

I GET THAT, AND IT'S COOL.

I DON'T KNOW YOU EITHER, AND SITTIN' HERE IN THE MIDDLE OF D-TROIT WITH CRATES FULL OF C-4 MAKES IT HARD TO TRUST ANYBODY YOU'RE JUST MEETIN' FOR THE FIRST TIME.

WHERE'D YOU GET THESE?

YOU HEAR ABOUT SUNNY MARQUEZ'S LITTLE DEAL WITH THE MEXICANS?

SURE, HE WAS USING LICENSED FIREARMS DEALERS TO SELL GUNS TO STRAW BUYERS, WHO TRANSFERRED THEM TO THE MOB IN MEXICO.

MY COUSIN LIVES DOWN IN ARIZONA. YOU CAN SAY WE'RE RUNNIN' A NATIONAL CAMPAIGN.

I HEAR ABOUT YOUR NEED FROM JOHNSON, AND I CALL MY COUSIN. HE DIVERTS A SHIPMENT AND REROUTES THE WEAPONS NORTH TO ME SO I CAN SELL THEM TO YOU.

ARE THESE PART OF THAT STUFF OBAMA PULLED DOWN NEAR RIO RICO? BECAUSE IF THEY ARE, THEN WE'RE DONE HERE.

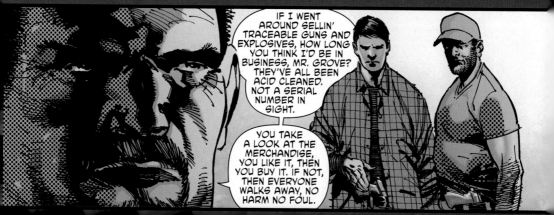

IF I WENT AROUND SELLIN' TRACEABLE GUNS AND EXPLOSIVES, HOW LONG YOU THINK I'D BE IN BUSINESS, MR. GROVE? THEY'VE ALL BEEN ACID CLEANED. NOT A SERIAL NUMBER IN SIGHT.

YOU TAKE A LOOK AT THE MERCHANDISE, YOU LIKE IT, THEN YOU BUY IT. IF NOT, THEN EVERYONE WALKS AWAY, NO HARM NO FOUL.

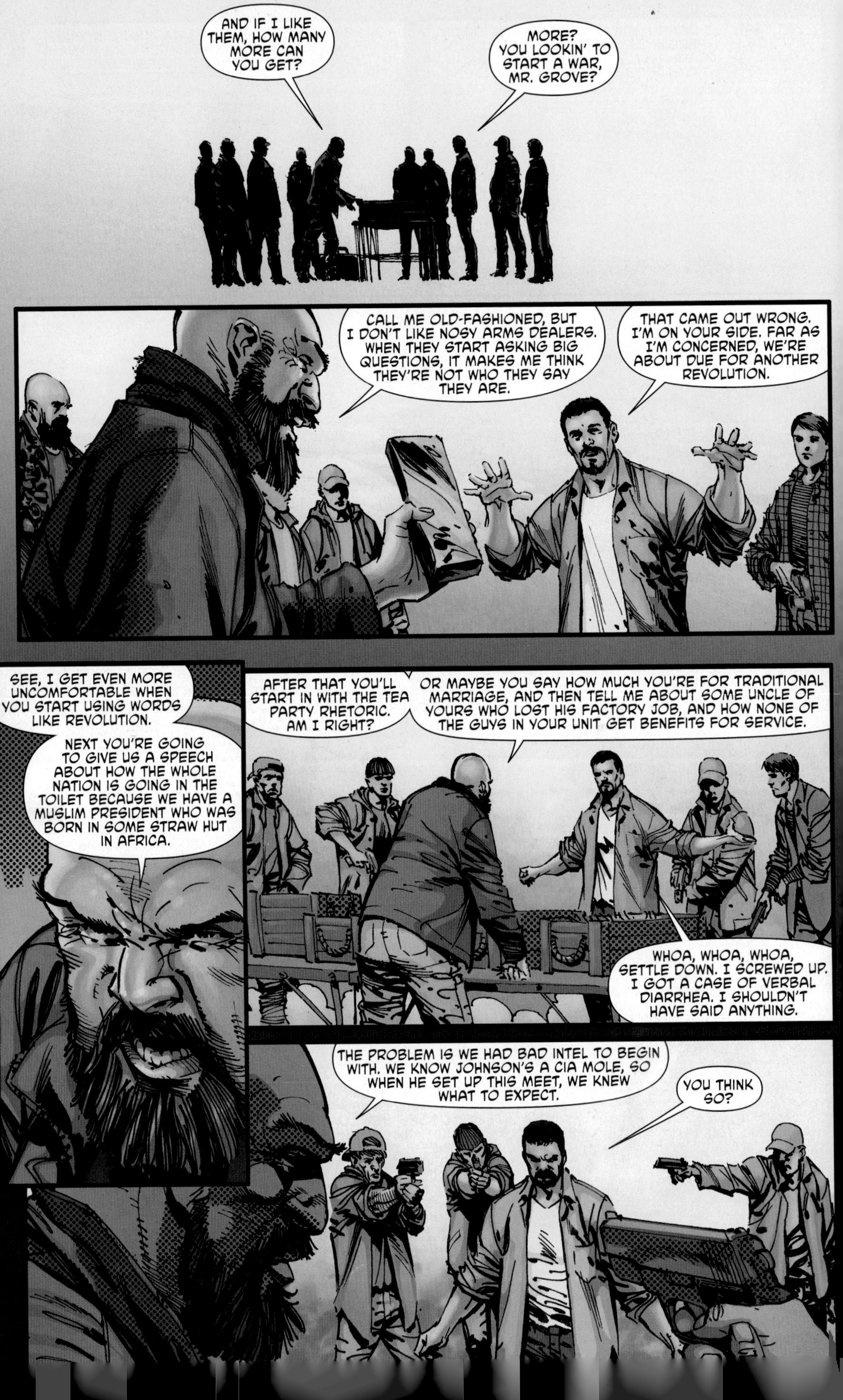
AND IF I LIKE THEM, HOW MANY MORE CAN YOU GET?
MORE? YOU LOOKIN' TO START A WAR, MR. GROVE?
CALL ME OLD-FASHIONED, BUT I DON'T LIKE NOSY ARMS DEALERS. WHEN THEY START ASKING BIG QUESTIONS, IT MAKES ME THINK THEY'RE NOT WHO THEY SAY THEY ARE.
THAT CAME OUT WRONG. I'M ON YOUR SIDE. FAR AS I'M CONCERNED, WE'RE ABOUT DUE FOR ANOTHER REVOLUTION.
SEE, I GET EVEN MORE UNCOMFORTABLE WHEN YOU START USING WORDS LIKE REVOLUTION.
NEXT YOU'RE GOING TO GIVE US A SPEECH ABOUT HOW THE WHOLE NATION IS GOING IN THE TOILET BECAUSE WE HAVE A MUSLIM PRESIDENT WHO WAS BORN IN SOME STRAW HUT IN AFRICA.
AFTER THAT YOU'LL START IN WITH THE TEA PARTY RHETORIC. AM I RIGHT?
OR MAYBE YOU SAY HOW MUCH YOU'RE FOR TRADITIONAL MARRIAGE, AND THEN TELL ME ABOUT SOME UNCLE OF YOURS WHO LOST HIS FACTORY JOB, AND HOW NONE OF THE GUYS IN YOUR UNIT GET BENEFITS FOR SERVICE.
WHOA, WHOA, WHOA, SETTLE DOWN. I SCREWED UP. I GOT A CASE OF VERBAL DIARRHEA. I SHOULDN'T HAVE SAID ANYTHING.
THE PROBLEM IS WE HAD BAD INTEL TO BEGIN WITH. WE KNOW JOHNSON'S A CIA MOLE, SO WHEN HE SET UP THIS MEET, WE KNEW WHAT TO EXPECT.
YOU THINK SO?

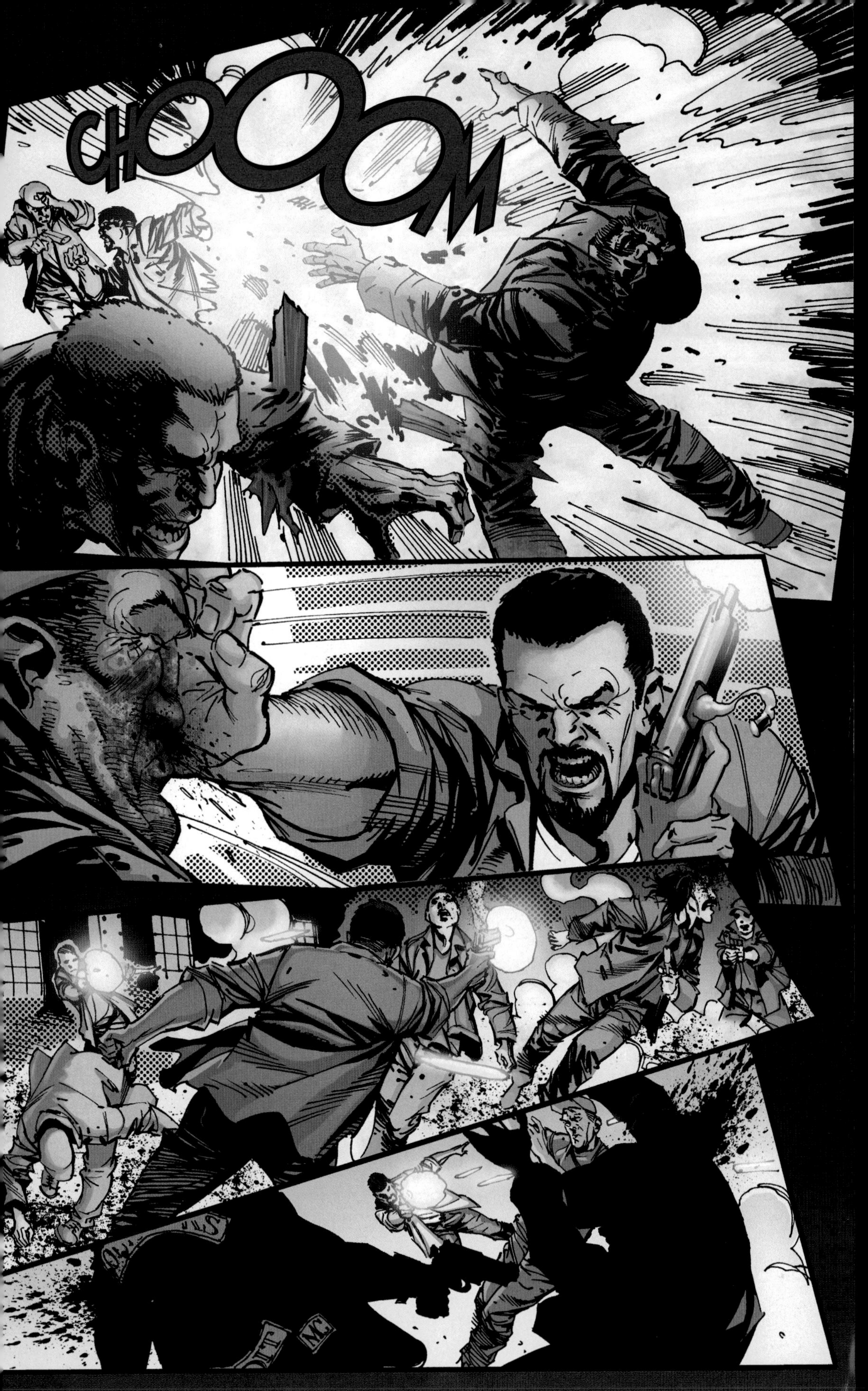
CHOOOOM

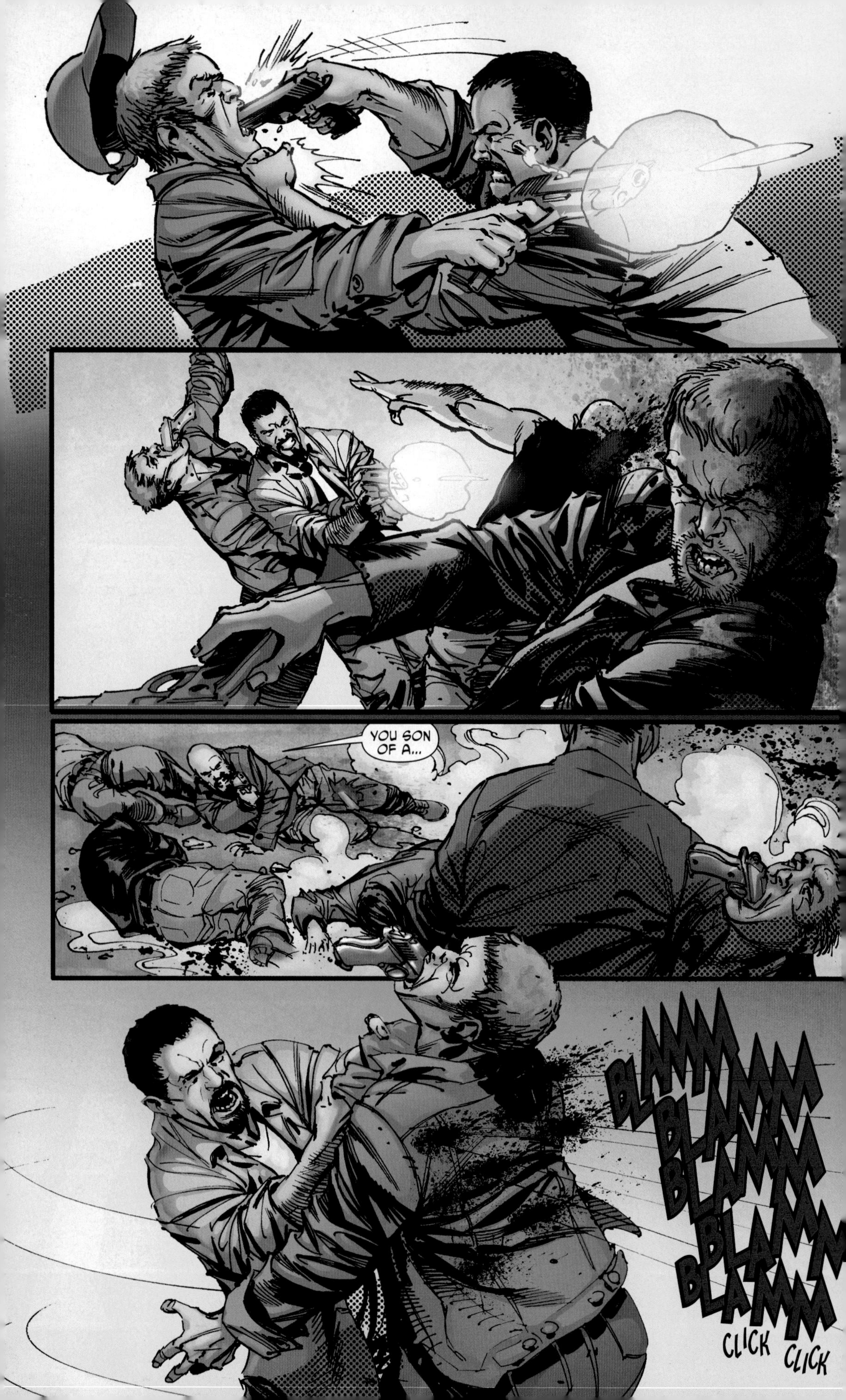
YOU SON OF A...
BLAMM BLAMM BLAMM BLAMM BLAMM
CLICK CLICK

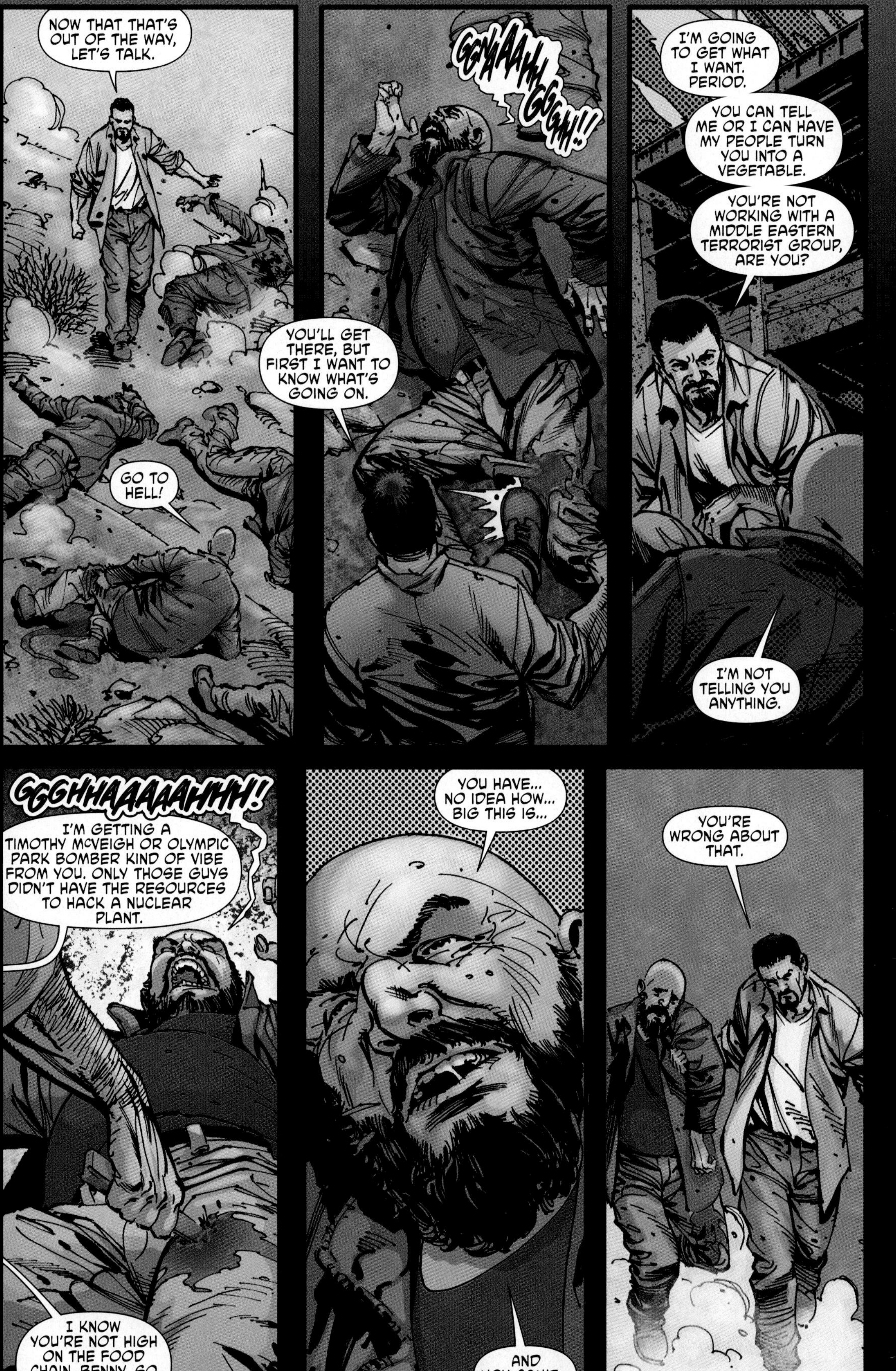
NOW THAT THAT'S OUT OF THE WAY, LET'S TALK.
GO TO HELL!
GGNNAAAHHGGGHH!!
YOU'LL GET THERE, BUT FIRST I WANT TO KNOW WHAT'S GOING ON.
I'M GOING TO GET WHAT I WANT. PERIOD.
YOU CAN TELL ME OR I CAN HAVE MY PEOPLE TURN YOU INTO A VEGETABLE.
YOU'RE NOT WORKING WITH A MIDDLE EASTERN TERRORIST GROUP, ARE YOU?
I'M NOT TELLING YOU ANYTHING.
GGGHHAAAAAHHH!
I'M GETTING A TIMOTHY McVEIGH OR OLYMPIC PARK BOMBER KIND OF VIBE FROM YOU. ONLY THOSE GUYS DIDN'T HAVE THE RESOURCES TO HACK A NUCLEAR PLANT.
I KNOW YOU'RE NOT HIGH ON THE FOOD CHAIN, BENNY, SO I'M WILLING TO CUT A DEAL.
YOU HAVE... NO IDEA HOW... BIG THIS IS...
AND YOU CAN'T... STOP IT...
YOU'RE WRONG ABOUT THAT.

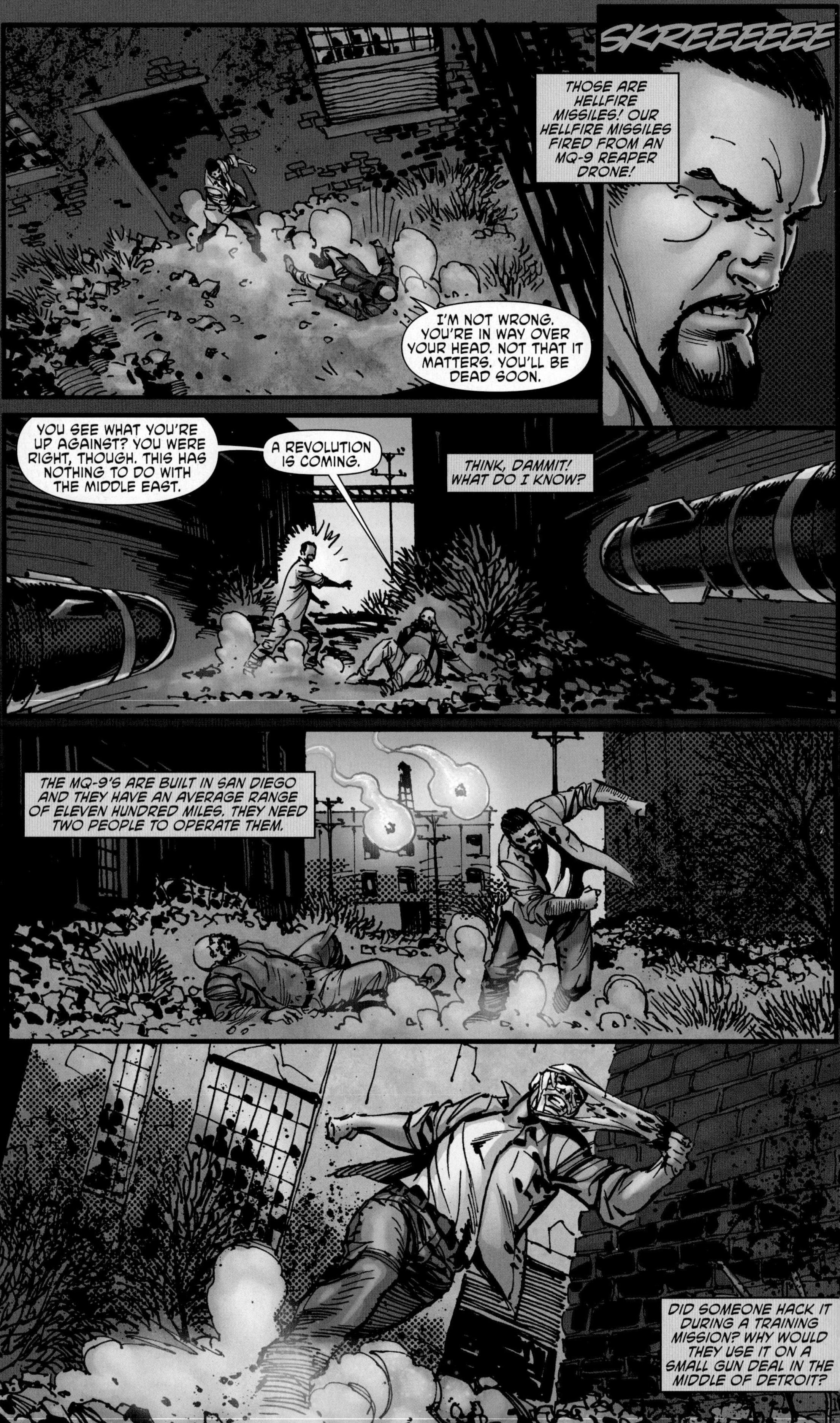
SKREEEEEEE
THOSE ARE HELLFIRE MISSILES! OUR HELLFIRE MISSILES FIRED FROM AN MQ-9 REAPER DRONE!
I'M NOT WRONG. YOU'RE IN WAY OVER YOUR HEAD. NOT THAT IT MATTERS. YOU'LL BE DEAD SOON.
YOU SEE WHAT YOU'RE UP AGAINST? YOU WERE RIGHT, THOUGH. THIS HAS NOTHING TO DO WITH THE MIDDLE EAST.
A REVOLUTION IS COMING.
THINK, DAMMIT! WHAT DO I KNOW?
THE MQ-9'S ARE BUILT IN SAN DIEGO AND THEY HAVE AN AVERAGE RANGE OF ELEVEN HUNDRED MILES. THEY NEED TWO PEOPLE TO OPERATE THEM.
DID SOMEONE HACK IT DURING A TRAINING MISSION? WHY WOULD THEY USE IT ON A SMALL GUN DEAL IN THE MIDDLE OF DETROIT?

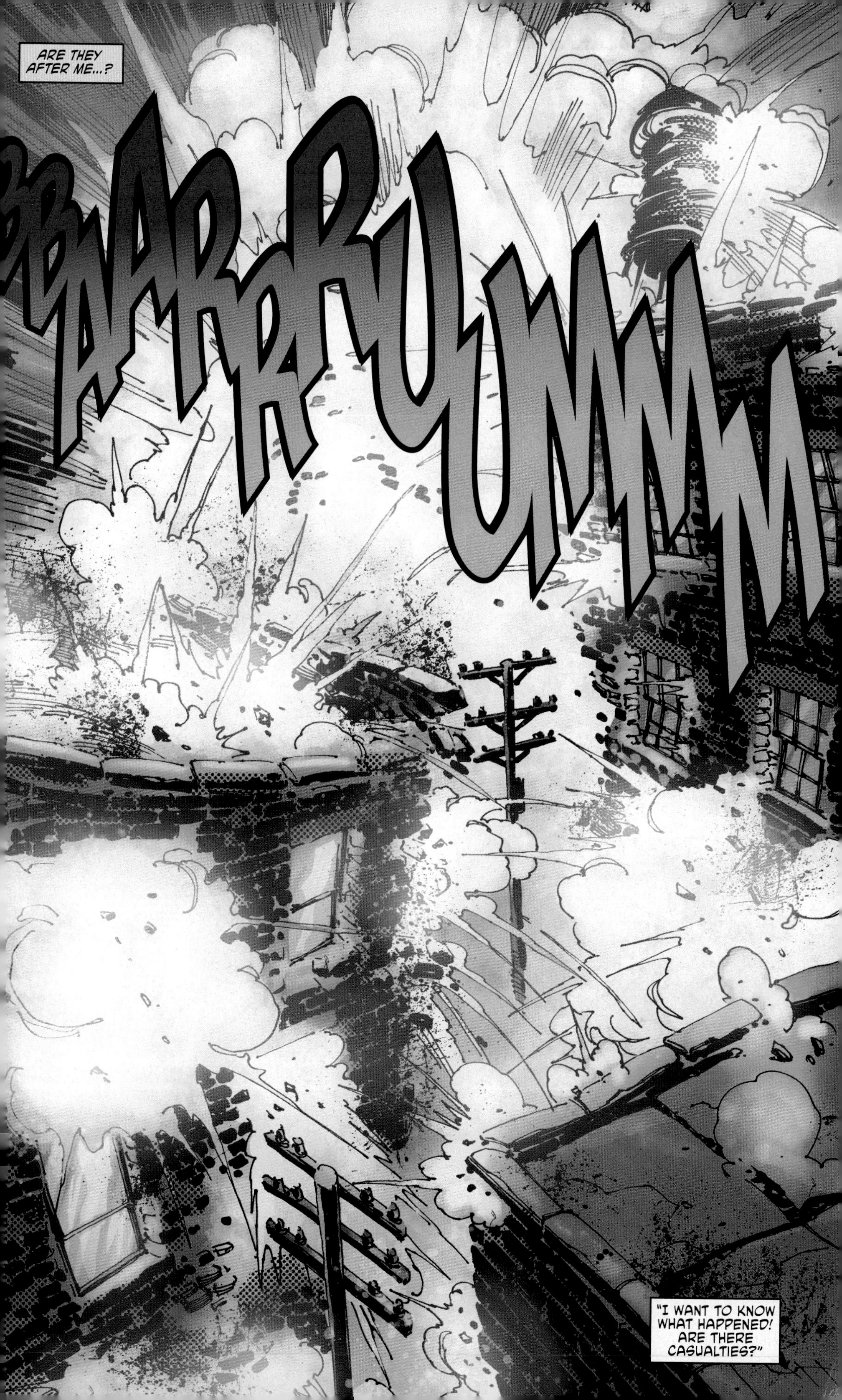
ARE THEY AFTER ME...?
BBARRRUMMM
"I WANT TO KNOW WHAT HAPPENED! ARE THERE CASUALTIES?"

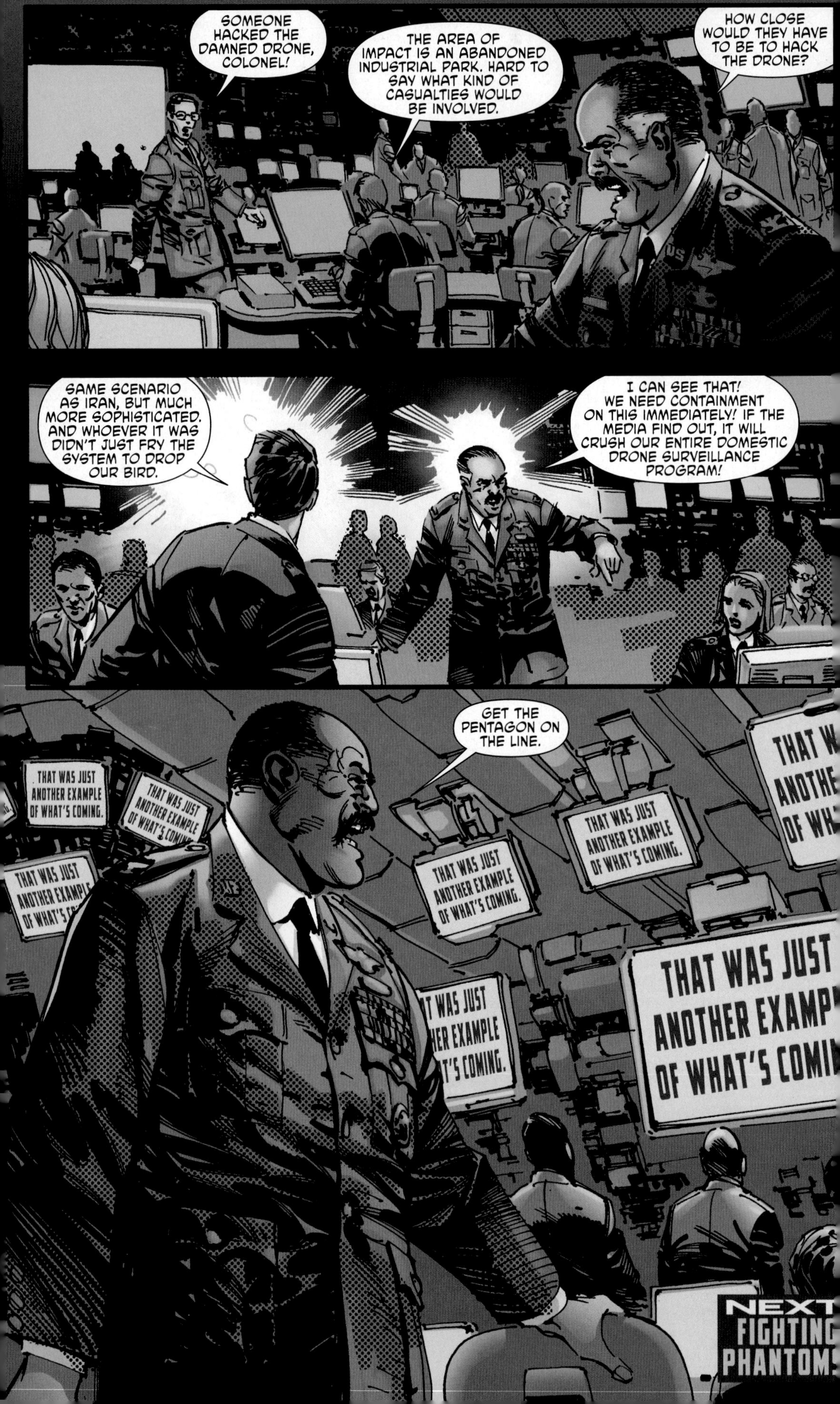
SOMEONE HACKED THE DAMNED DRONE, COLONEL!
THE AREA OF IMPACT IS AN ABANDONED INDUSTRIAL PARK. HARD TO SAY WHAT KIND OF CASUALTIES WOULD BE INVOLVED.
HOW CLOSE WOULD THEY HAVE TO BE TO HACK THE DRONE?
SAME SCENARIO AS IRAN, BUT MUCH MORE SOPHISTICATED. AND WHOEVER IT WAS DIDN'T JUST FRY THE SYSTEM TO DROP OUR BIRD.
I CAN SEE THAT! WE NEED CONTAINMENT ON THIS IMMEDIATELY! IF THE MEDIA FIND OUT, IT WILL CRUSH OUR ENTIRE DOMESTIC DRONE SURVEILLANCE PROGRAM!
GET THE PENTAGON ON THE LINE.
THAT WAS JUST ANOTHER EXAMPLE OF WHAT'S COMING.
THAT WAS JUST ANOTHER EXAMPLE OF WHAT'S COMING.
THAT WAS JUST ANOTHER EXAMPLE OF WHAT'S COMING.
THAT WAS JUST ANOTHER EXAMPLE OF WHAT'S COMING.
NEXT FIGHTING PHANTOM

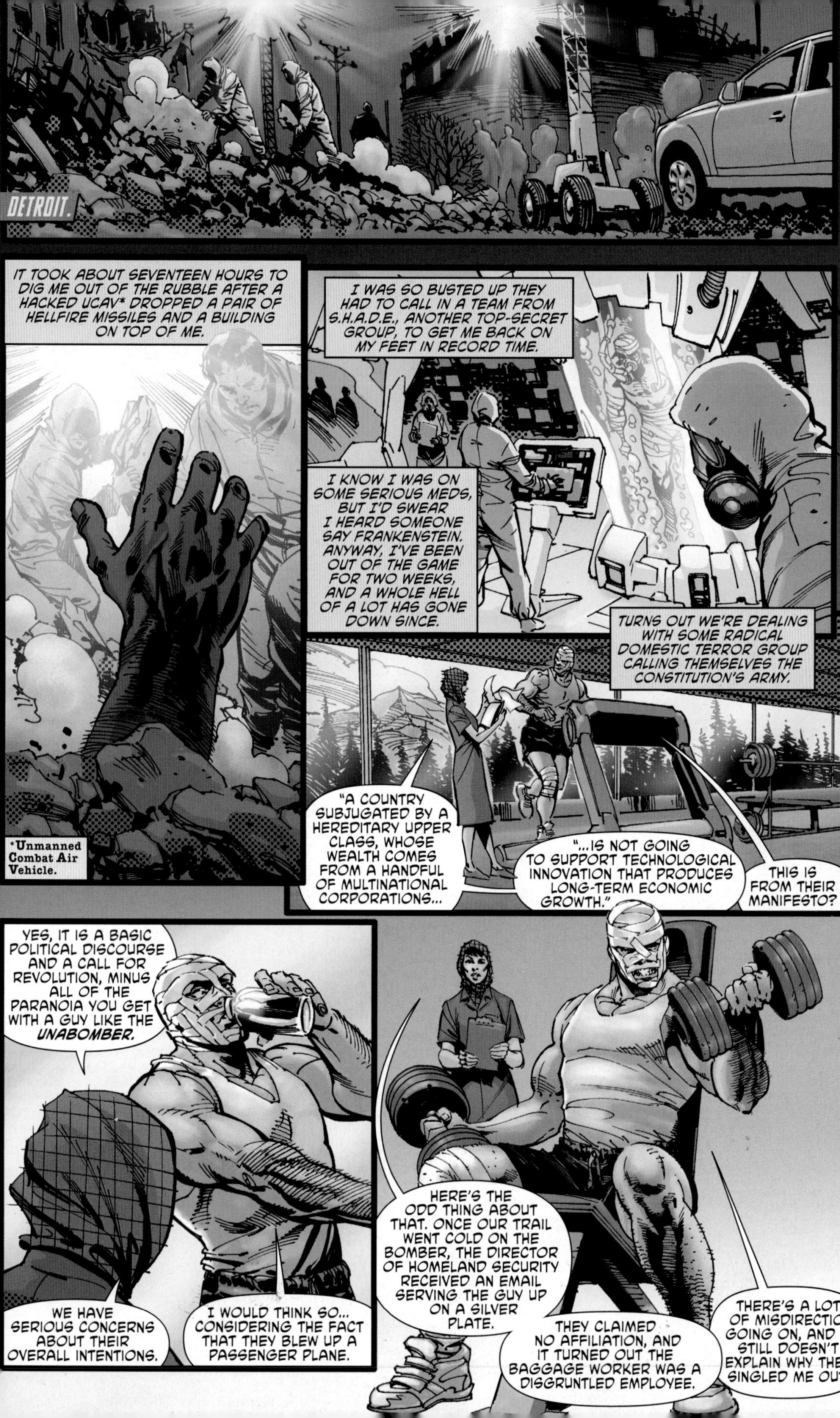
DETROIT.
IT TOOK ABOUT SEVENTEEN HOURS TO DIG ME OUT OF THE RUBBLE AFTER A HACKED UCAV* DROPPED A PAIR OF HELLFIRE MISSILES AND A BUILDING ON TOP OF ME.
*Unmanned Combat Air Vehicle.
I WAS SO BUSTED UP THEY HAD TO CALL IN A TEAM FROM S.H.A.D.E., ANOTHER TOP-SECRET GROUP, TO GET ME BACK ON MY FEET IN RECORD TIME.
I KNOW I WAS ON SOME SERIOUS MEDS, BUT I'D SWEAR I HEARD SOMEONE SAY FRANKENSTEIN. ANYWAY, I'VE BEEN OUT OF THE GAME FOR TWO WEEKS, AND A WHOLE HELL OF A LOT HAS GONE DOWN SINCE.
TURNS OUT WE'RE DEALING WITH SOME RADICAL DOMESTIC TERROR GROUP CALLING THEMSELVES THE CONSTITUTION'S ARMY.
"A COUNTRY SUBJUGATED BY A HEREDITARY UPPER CLASS, WHOSE WEALTH COMES FROM A HANDFUL OF MULTINATIONAL CORPORATIONS...
"...IS NOT GOING TO SUPPORT TECHNOLOGICAL INNOVATION THAT PRODUCES LONG-TERM ECONOMIC GROWTH."
THIS IS FROM THEIR MANIFESTO?
YES, IT IS A BASIC POLITICAL DISCOURSE AND A CALL FOR REVOLUTION, MINUS ALL OF THE PARANOIA YOU GET WITH A GUY LIKE THE UNABOMBER.
WE HAVE SERIOUS CONCERNS ABOUT THEIR OVERALL INTENTIONS.
I WOULD THINK SO... CONSIDERING THE FACT THAT THEY BLEW UP A PASSENGER PLANE.
HERE'S THE ODD THING ABOUT THAT. ONCE OUR TRAIL WENT COLD ON THE BOMBER, THE DIRECTOR OF HOMELAND SECURITY RECEIVED AN EMAIL SERVING THE GUY UP ON A SILVER PLATE.
THEY CLAIMED NO AFFILIATION, AND IT TURNED OUT THE BAGGAGE WORKER WAS A DISGRUNTLED EMPLOYEE.
THERE'S A LOT OF MISDIRECTION GOING ON, AND IT STILL DOESN'T EXPLAIN WHY THEY SINGLED ME OUT.

THAT'S EVEN STRANGER, BECAUSE YOU WEREN'T IN A DIRECT POSITION TO THREATEN THEM, ARMED WITH WHAT LITTLE INFORMATION YOU MIGHT HAVE GOTTEN FROM BENNY GROVE.

MAYBE IT WAS A CASE OF TRYING TO KILL TWO BIRDS WITH ONE STONE.

THEY GOT TO HACK THE UCAV AND PUT ON A DISPLAY OF THEIR POWER, WHILE GETTING RID OF ME IN THE PROCESS.

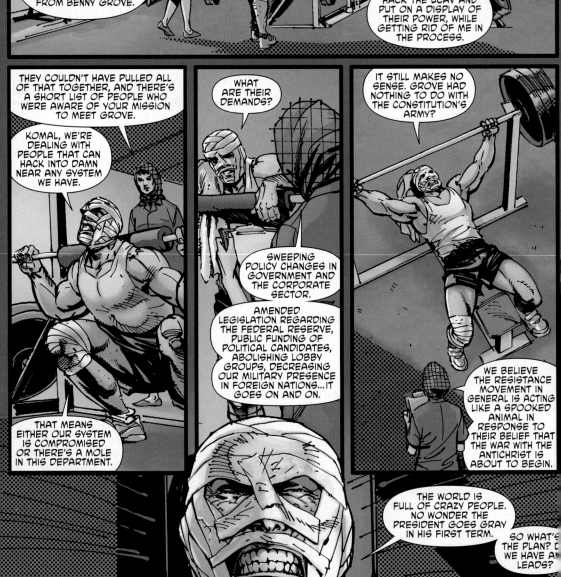

THEY COULDN'T HAVE PULLED ALL OF THAT TOGETHER, AND THERE'S A SHORT LIST OF PEOPLE WHO WERE AWARE OF YOUR MISSION TO MEET GROVE.

KOMAL, WE'RE DEALING WITH PEOPLE THAT CAN HACK INTO DAMN NEAR ANY SYSTEM WE HAVE.

THAT MEANS EITHER OUR SYSTEM IS COMPROMISED OR THERE'S A MOLE IN THIS DEPARTMENT.

WHAT ARE THEIR DEMANDS?

SWEEPING POLICY CHANGES IN GOVERNMENT AND THE CORPORATE SECTOR.

AMENDED LEGISLATION REGARDING THE FEDERAL RESERVE, PUBLIC FUNDING OF POLITICAL CANDIDATES, ABOLISHING LOBBY GROUPS, DECREASING OUR MILITARY PRESENCE IN FOREIGN NATIONS...IT GOES ON AND ON.

IT STILL MAKES NO SENSE. GROVE HAD NOTHING TO DO WITH THE CONSTITUTION'S ARMY?

WE BELIEVE THE RESISTANCE MOVEMENT IN GENERAL IS ACTING LIKE A SPOOKED ANIMAL IN RESPONSE TO THEIR BELIEF THAT THE WAR WITH THE ANTICHRIST IS ABOUT TO BEGIN.

THE WORLD IS FULL OF CRAZY PEOPLE. NO WONDER THE PRESIDENT GOES GRAY IN HIS FIRST TERM.

SO WHAT'S THE PLAN? D WE HAVE A LEADS?

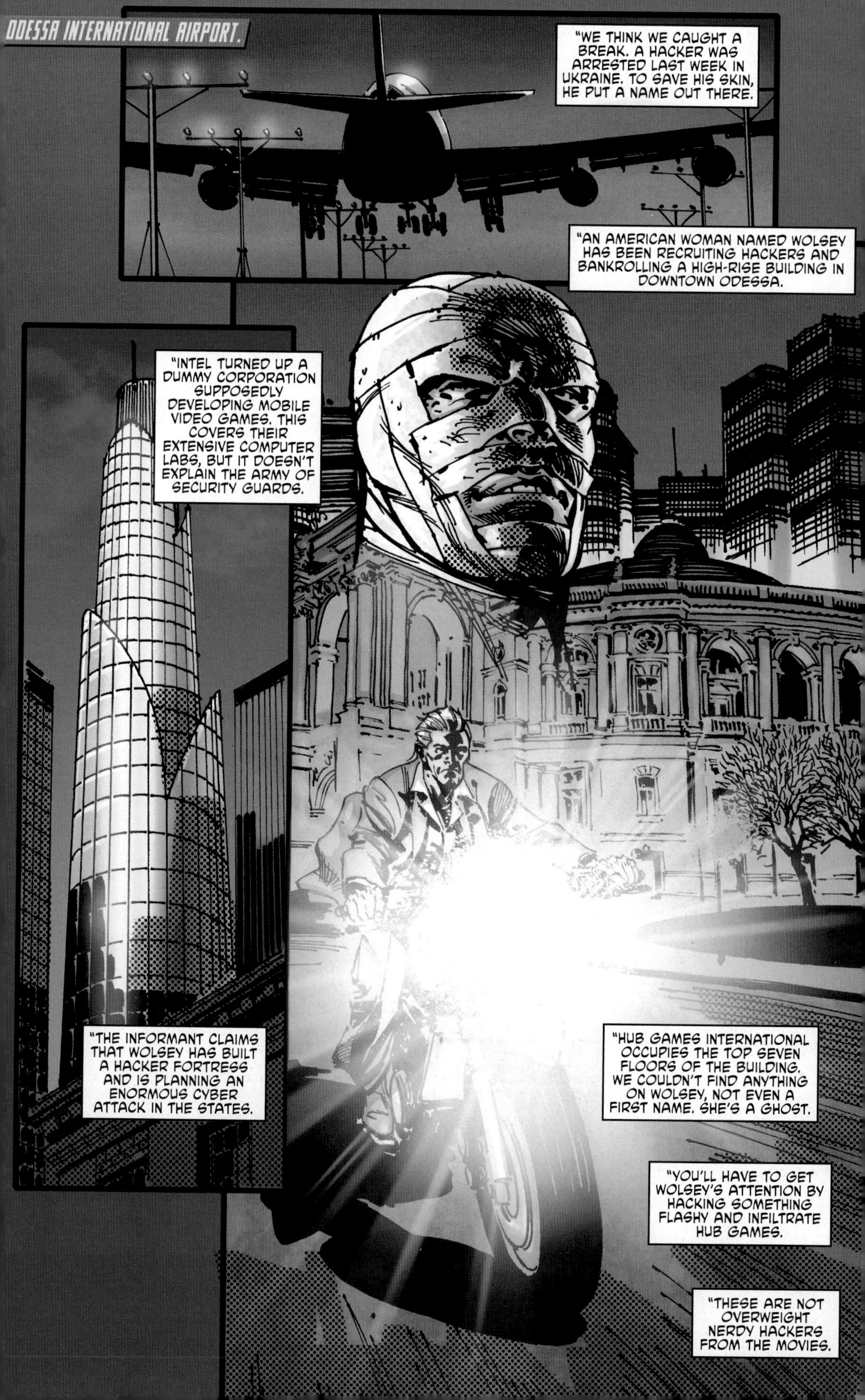
ODESSA INTERNATIONAL AIRPORT.
"WE THINK WE CAUGHT A BREAK. A HACKER WAS ARRESTED LAST WEEK IN UKRAINE. TO SAVE HIS SKIN, HE PUT A NAME OUT THERE.
"AN AMERICAN WOMAN NAMED WOLSEY HAS BEEN RECRUITING HACKERS AND BANKROLLING A HIGH-RISE BUILDING IN DOWNTOWN ODESSA.
"INTEL TURNED UP A DUMMY CORPORATION SUPPOSEDLY DEVELOPING MOBILE VIDEO GAMES. THIS COVERS THEIR EXTENSIVE COMPUTER LABS, BUT IT DOESN'T EXPLAIN THE ARMY OF SECURITY GUARDS.
"THE INFORMANT CLAIMS THAT WOLSEY HAS BUILT A HACKER FORTRESS AND IS PLANNING AN ENORMOUS CYBER ATTACK IN THE STATES.
"HUB GAMES INTERNATIONAL OCCUPIES THE TOP SEVEN FLOORS OF THE BUILDING. WE COULDN'T FIND ANYTHING ON WOLSEY, NOT EVEN A FIRST NAME. SHE'S A GHOST.
"YOU'LL HAVE TO GET WOLSEY'S ATTENTION BY HACKING SOMETHING FLASHY AND INFILTRATE HUB GAMES.
"THESE ARE NOT OVERWEIGHT NERDY HACKERS FROM THE MOVIES.

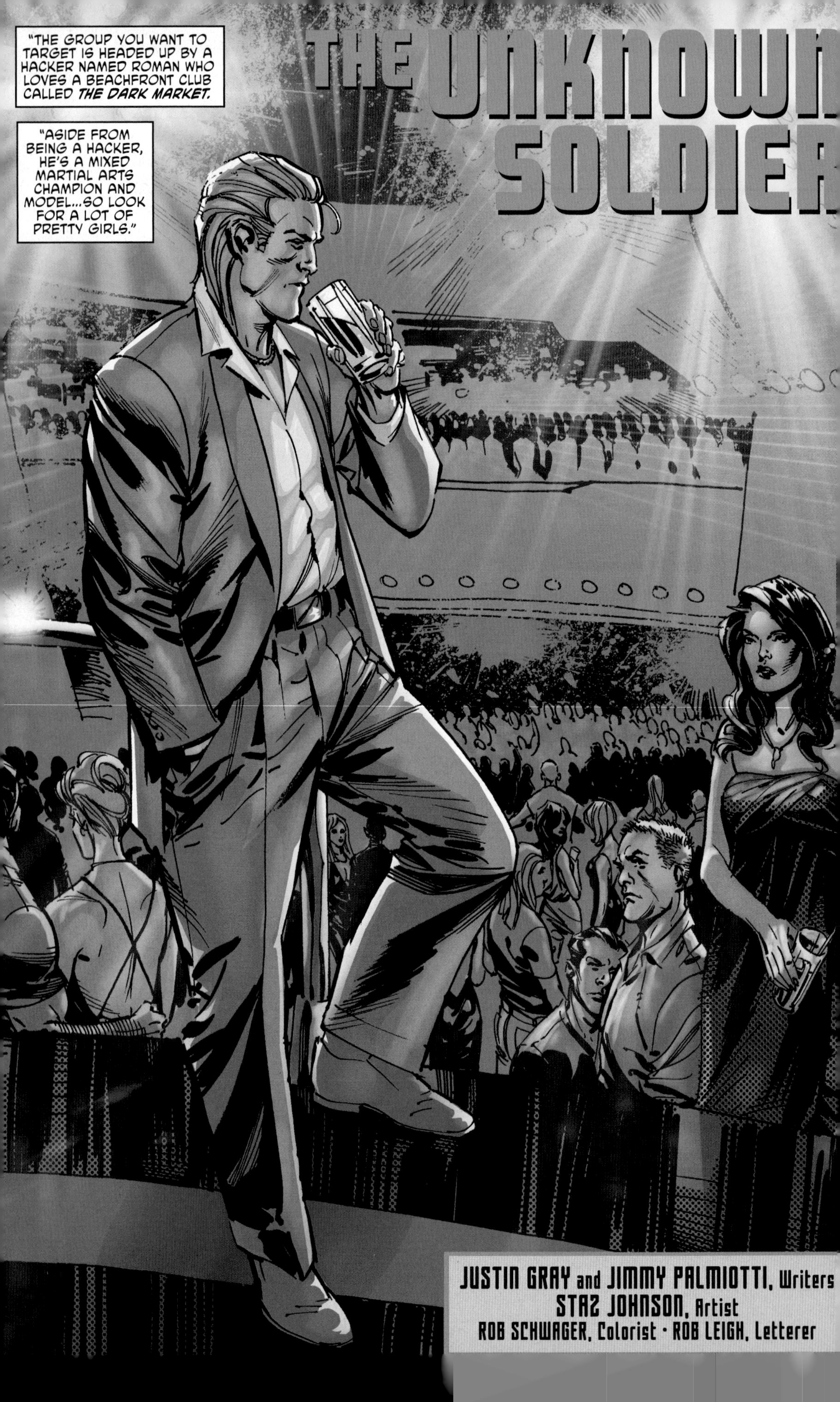

"THE GROUP YOU WANT TO TARGET IS HEADED UP BY A HACKER NAMED ROMAN WHO LOVES A BEACHFRONT CLUB CALLED *THE DARK MARKET.*
"ASIDE FROM BEING A HACKER, HE'S A MIXED MARTIAL ARTS CHAMPION AND MODEL...SO LOOK FOR A LOT OF PRETTY GIRLS."
THE UNKNOWN SOLDIER
JUSTIN GRAY and JIMMY PALMIOTTI, Writers
STAZ JOHNSON, Artist
ROB SCHWAGER, Colorist · ROB LEIGH, Letterer

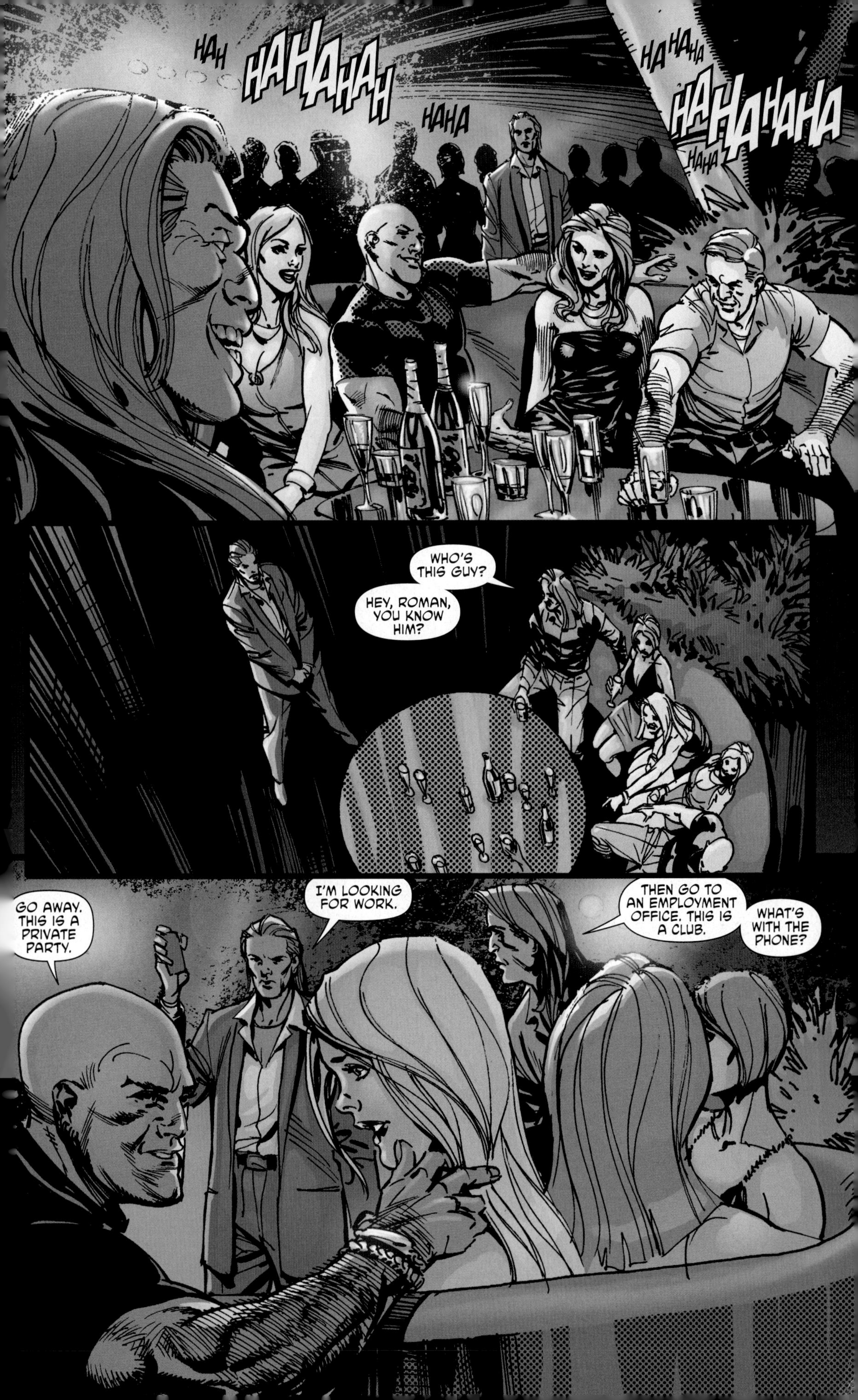
HAH
HAHAHAH
HAHA
HA HAHA
HAHAHAHAHA
HAHA
WHO'S THIS GUY?
HEY, ROMAN, YOU KNOW HIM?
GO AWAY. THIS IS A PRIVATE PARTY.
I'M LOOKING FOR WORK.
THEN GO TO AN EMPLOYMENT OFFICE. THIS IS A CLUB.
WHAT'S WITH THE PHONE?

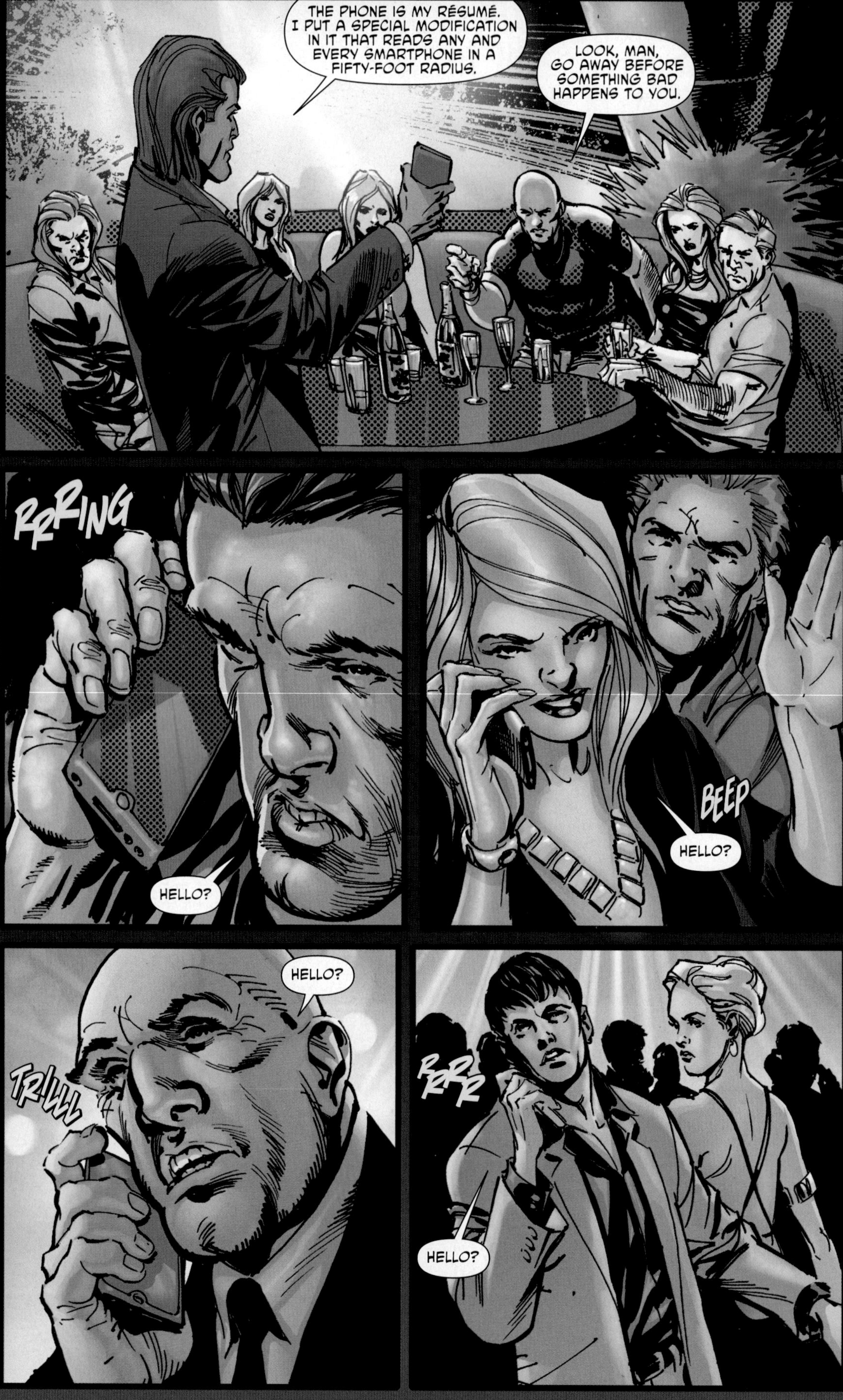
THE PHONE IS MY RÉSUMÉ. I PUT A SPECIAL MODIFICATION IN IT THAT READS ANY AND EVERY SMARTPHONE IN A FIFTY-FOOT RADIUS.
LOOK, MAN, GO AWAY BEFORE SOMETHING BAD HAPPENS TO YOU.
RRRING
HELLO?
BEEP
HELLO?
HELLO?
TRILLL
RRRR
HELLO?

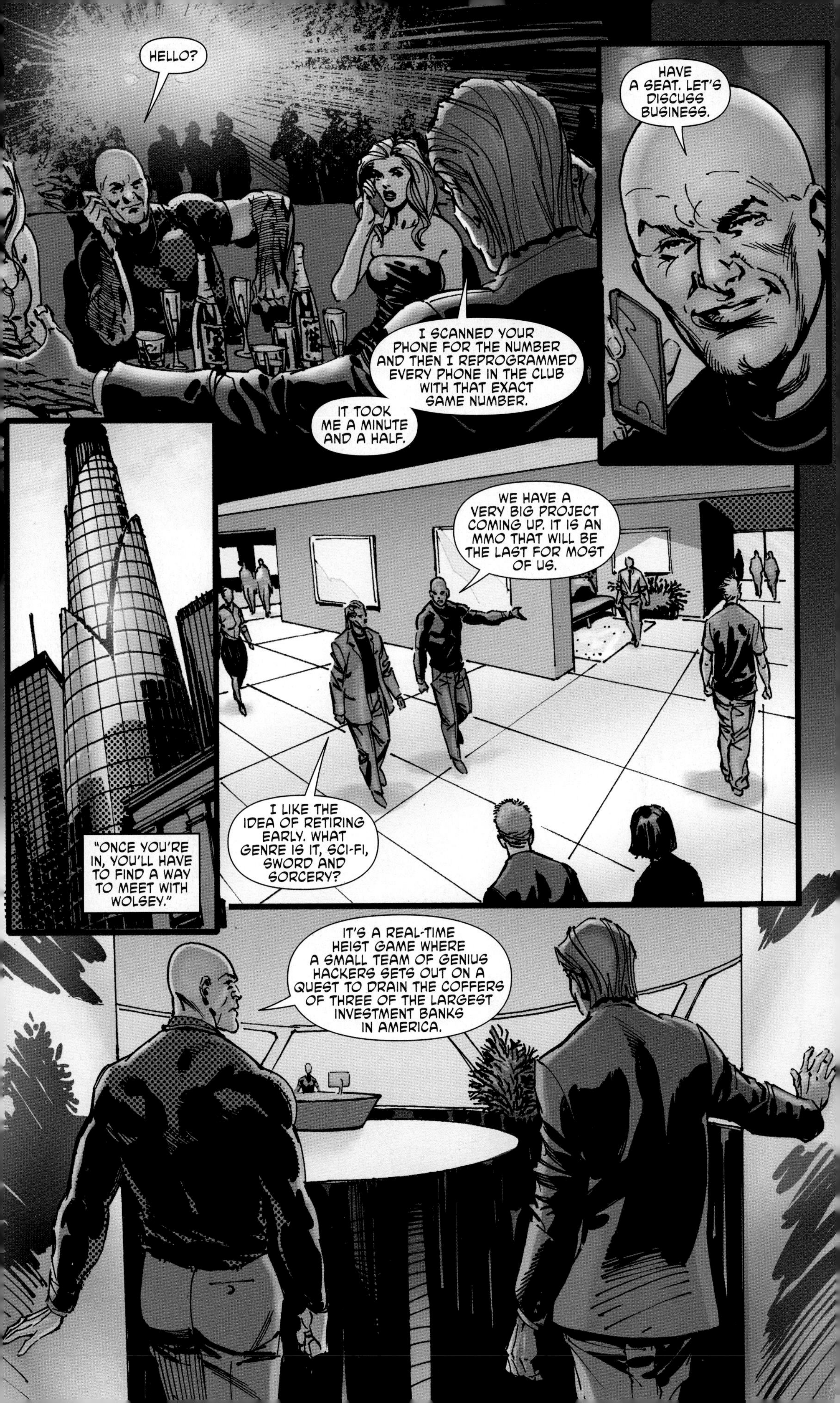
HELLO?
I SCANNED YOUR PHONE FOR THE NUMBER AND THEN I REPROGRAMMED EVERY PHONE IN THE CLUB WITH THAT EXACT SAME NUMBER.
IT TOOK ME A MINUTE AND A HALF.
HAVE A SEAT. LET'S DISCUSS BUSINESS.
"ONCE YOU'RE IN, YOU'LL HAVE TO FIND A WAY TO MEET WITH WOLSEY."
WE HAVE A VERY BIG PROJECT COMING UP. IT IS AN MMO THAT WILL BE THE LAST FOR MOST OF US.
I LIKE THE IDEA OF RETIRING EARLY. WHAT GENRE IS IT, SCI-FI, SWORD AND SORCERY?
IT'S A REAL-TIME HEIST GAME WHERE A SMALL TEAM OF GENIUS HACKERS SETS OUT ON A QUEST TO DRAIN THE COFFERS OF THREE OF THE LARGEST INVESTMENT BANKS IN AMERICA.

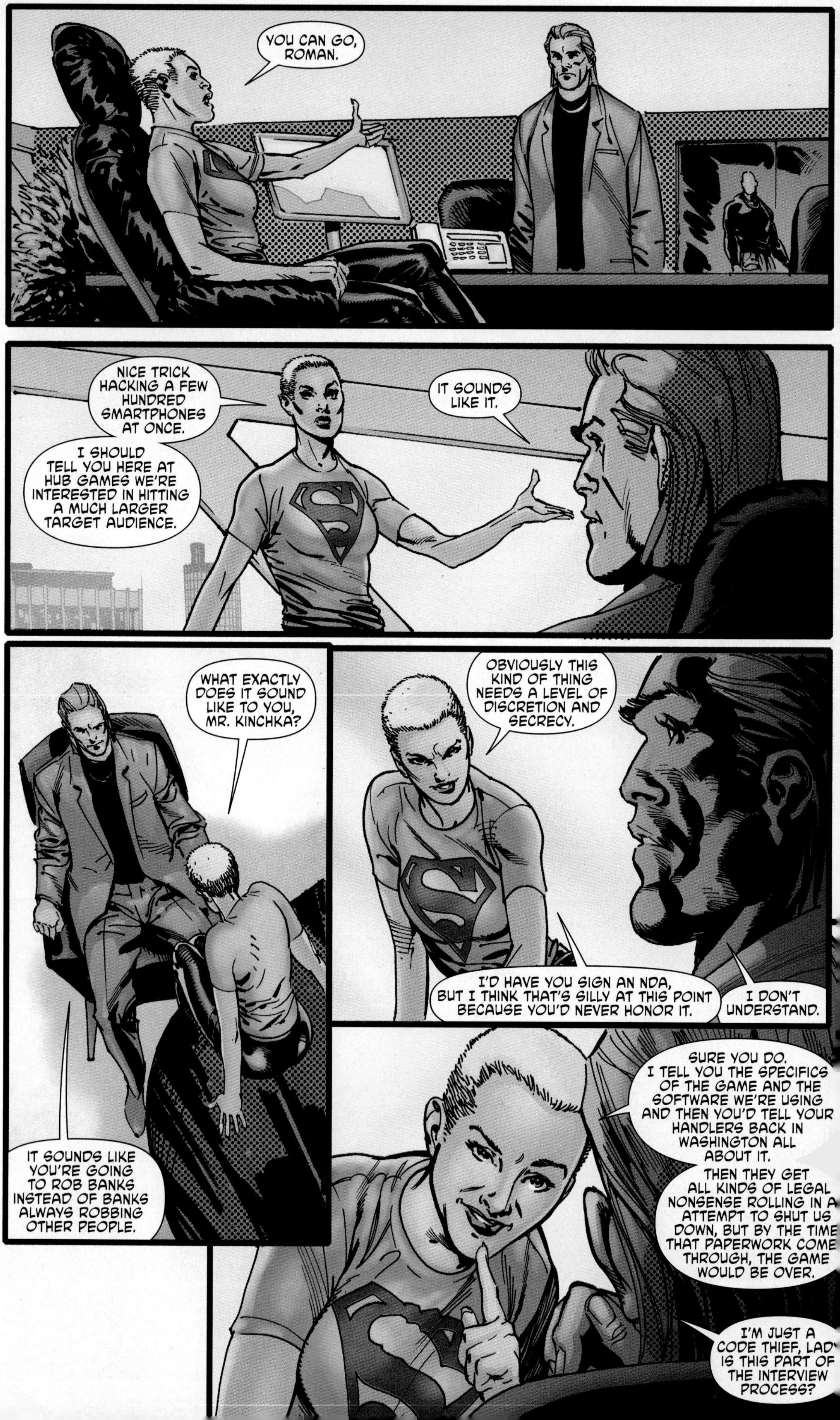

YOU CAN GO, ROMAN.
NICE TRICK HACKING A FEW HUNDRED SMARTPHONES AT ONCE.
I SHOULD TELL YOU HERE AT HUB GAMES WE'RE INTERESTED IN HITTING A MUCH LARGER TARGET AUDIENCE.
IT SOUNDS LIKE IT.
WHAT EXACTLY DOES IT SOUND LIKE TO YOU, MR. KINCHKA?
IT SOUNDS LIKE YOU'RE GOING TO ROB BANKS INSTEAD OF BANKS ALWAYS ROBBING OTHER PEOPLE.
OBVIOUSLY THIS KIND OF THING NEEDS A LEVEL OF DISCRETION AND SECRECY.
I'D HAVE YOU SIGN AN NDA, BUT I THINK THAT'S SILLY AT THIS POINT BECAUSE YOU'D NEVER HONOR IT.
I DON'T UNDERSTAND.
SURE YOU DO. I TELL YOU THE SPECIFICS OF THE GAME AND THE SOFTWARE WE'RE USING AND THEN YOU'D TELL YOUR HANDLERS BACK IN WASHINGTON ALL ABOUT IT.
THEN THEY GET ALL KINDS OF LEGAL NONSENSE ROLLING IN A ATTEMPT TO SHUT US DOWN, BUT BY THE TIME THAT PAPERWORK COME THROUGH, THE GAME WOULD BE OVER.
I'M JUST A CODE THIEF, LAD IS THIS PART OF THE INTERVIEW PROCESS?

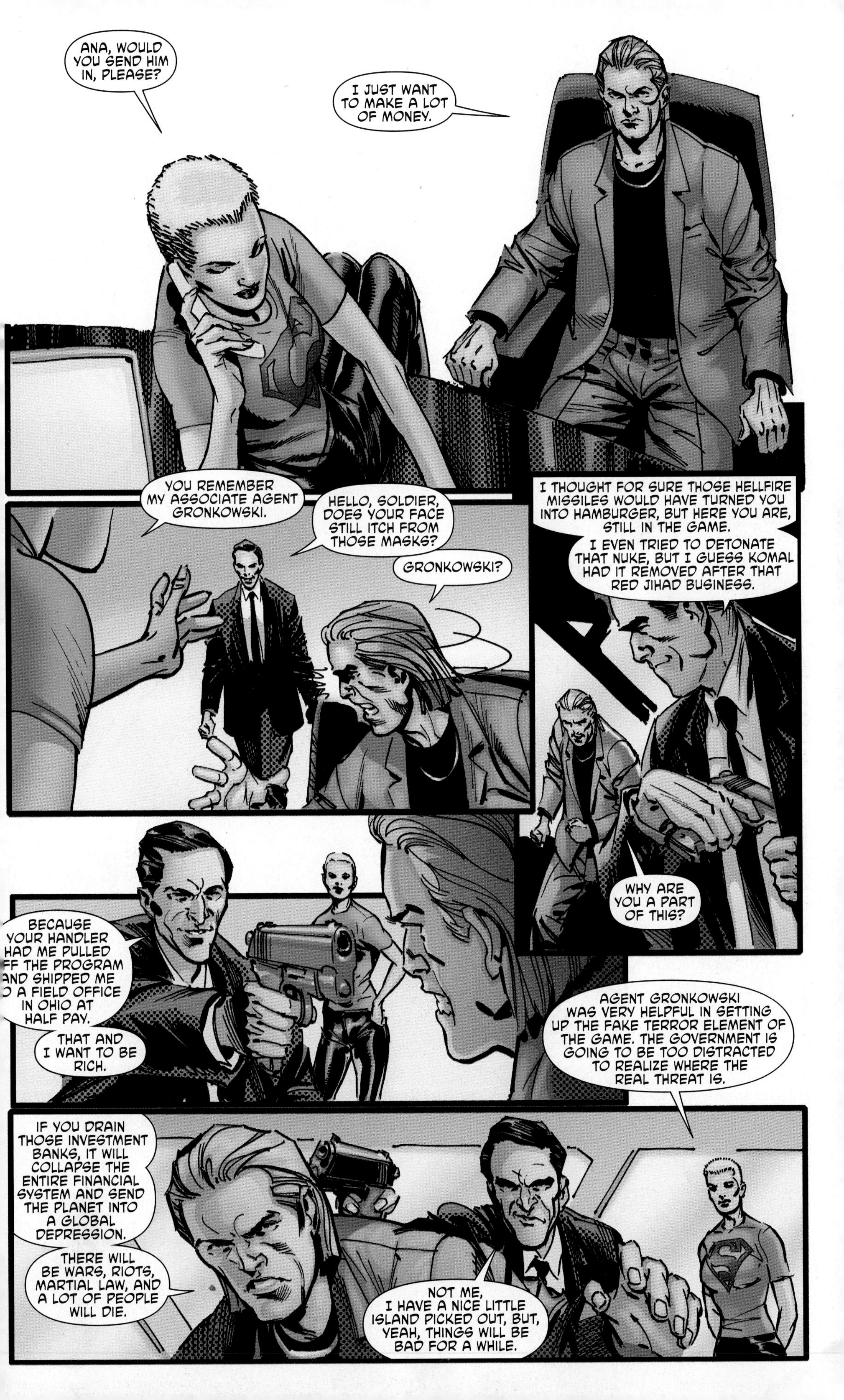
ANA, WOULD YOU SEND HIM IN, PLEASE?
I JUST WANT TO MAKE A LOT OF MONEY.
YOU REMEMBER MY ASSOCIATE AGENT GRONKOWSKI.
HELLO, SOLDIER, DOES YOUR FACE STILL ITCH FROM THOSE MASKS?
GRONKOWSKI?
I THOUGHT FOR SURE THOSE HELLFIRE MISSILES WOULD HAVE TURNED YOU INTO HAMBURGER, BUT HERE YOU ARE, STILL IN THE GAME.
I EVEN TRIED TO DETONATE THAT NUKE, BUT I GUESS KOMAL HAD IT REMOVED AFTER THAT RED JIHAD BUSINESS.
WHY ARE YOU A PART OF THIS?
BECAUSE YOUR HANDLER HAD ME PULLED FF THE PROGRAM AND SHIPPED ME A FIELD OFFICE IN OHIO AT HALF PAY.
THAT AND I WANT TO BE RICH.
AGENT GRONKOWSKI WAS VERY HELPFUL IN SETTING UP THE FAKE TERROR ELEMENT OF THE GAME. THE GOVERNMENT IS GOING TO BE TOO DISTRACTED TO REALIZE WHERE THE REAL THREAT IS.
IF YOU DRAIN THOSE INVESTMENT BANKS, IT WILL COLLAPSE THE ENTIRE FINANCIAL SYSTEM AND SEND THE PLANET INTO A GLOBAL DEPRESSION.
THERE WILL BE WARS, RIOTS, MARTIAL LAW, AND A LOT OF PEOPLE WILL DIE.
NOT ME, I HAVE A NICE LITTLE ISLAND PICKED OUT, BUT, YEAH, THINGS WILL BE BAD FOR A WHILE.

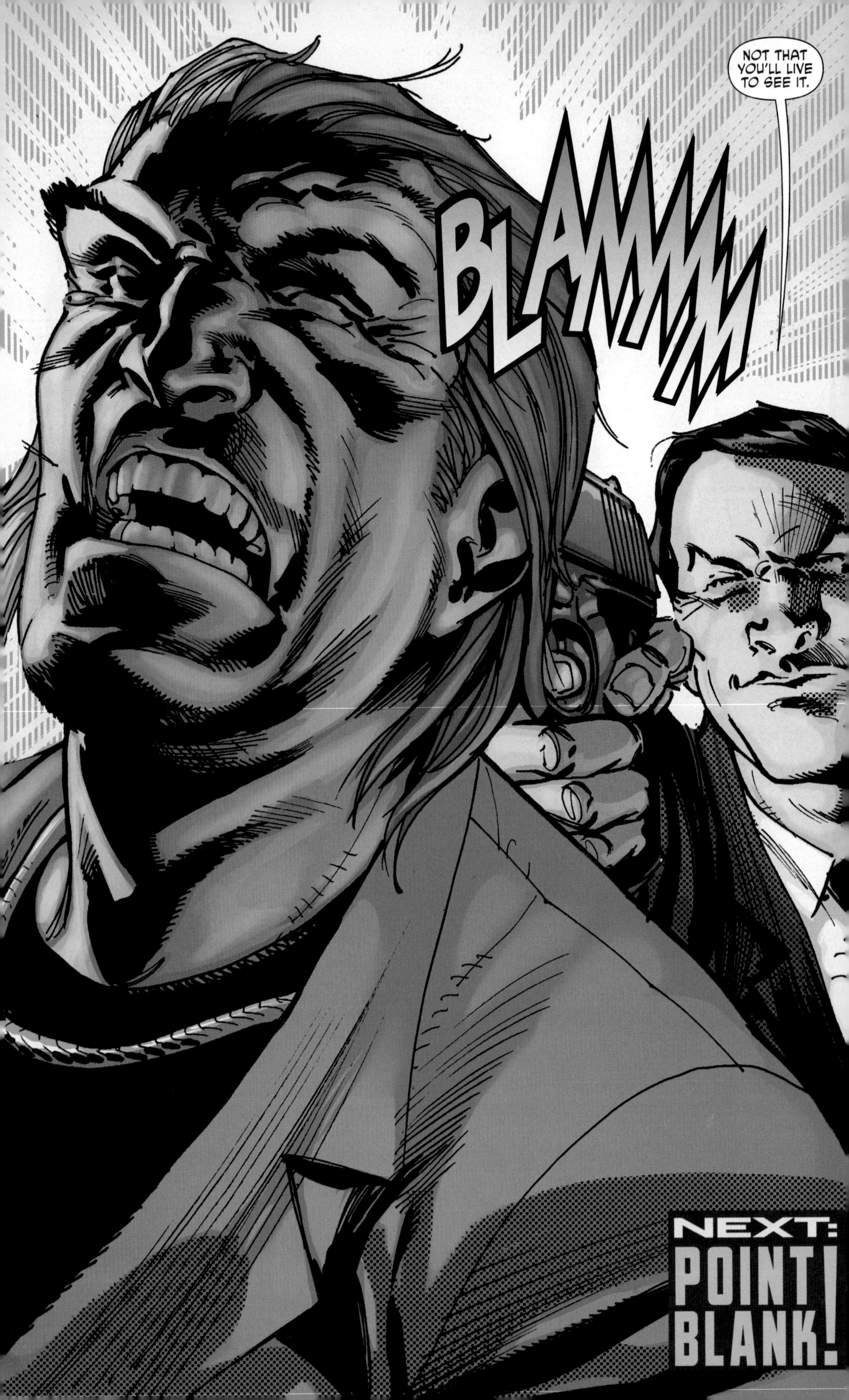
NOT THAT YOU'LL LIVE TO SEE IT.
BLAMMM
NEXT: POINT BLANK!

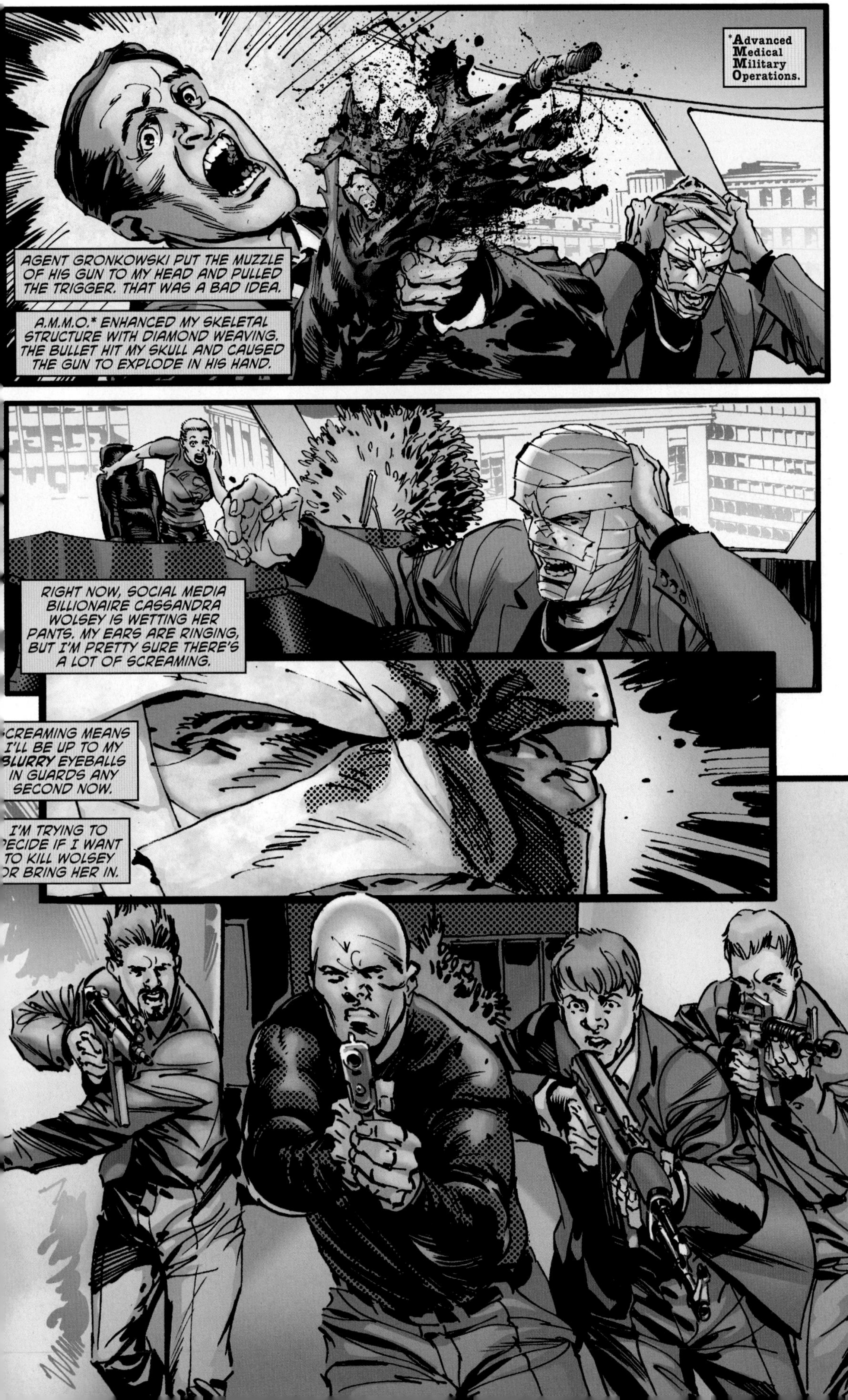
*Advanced Medical Military Operations.
AGENT GRONKOWSKI PUT THE MUZZLE OF HIS GUN TO MY HEAD AND PULLED THE TRIGGER. THAT WAS A BAD IDEA.
A.M.M.O.* ENHANCED MY SKELETAL STRUCTURE WITH DIAMOND WEAVING. THE BULLET HIT MY SKULL AND CAUSED THE GUN TO EXPLODE IN HIS HAND.
RIGHT NOW, SOCIAL MEDIA BILLIONAIRE CASSANDRA WOLSEY IS WETTING HER PANTS. MY EARS ARE RINGING, BUT I'M PRETTY SURE THERE'S A LOT OF SCREAMING.
SCREAMING MEANS I'LL BE UP TO MY BLURRY EYEBALLS IN GUARDS ANY SECOND NOW.
I'M TRYING TO DECIDE IF I WANT TO KILL WOLSEY OR BRING HER IN.

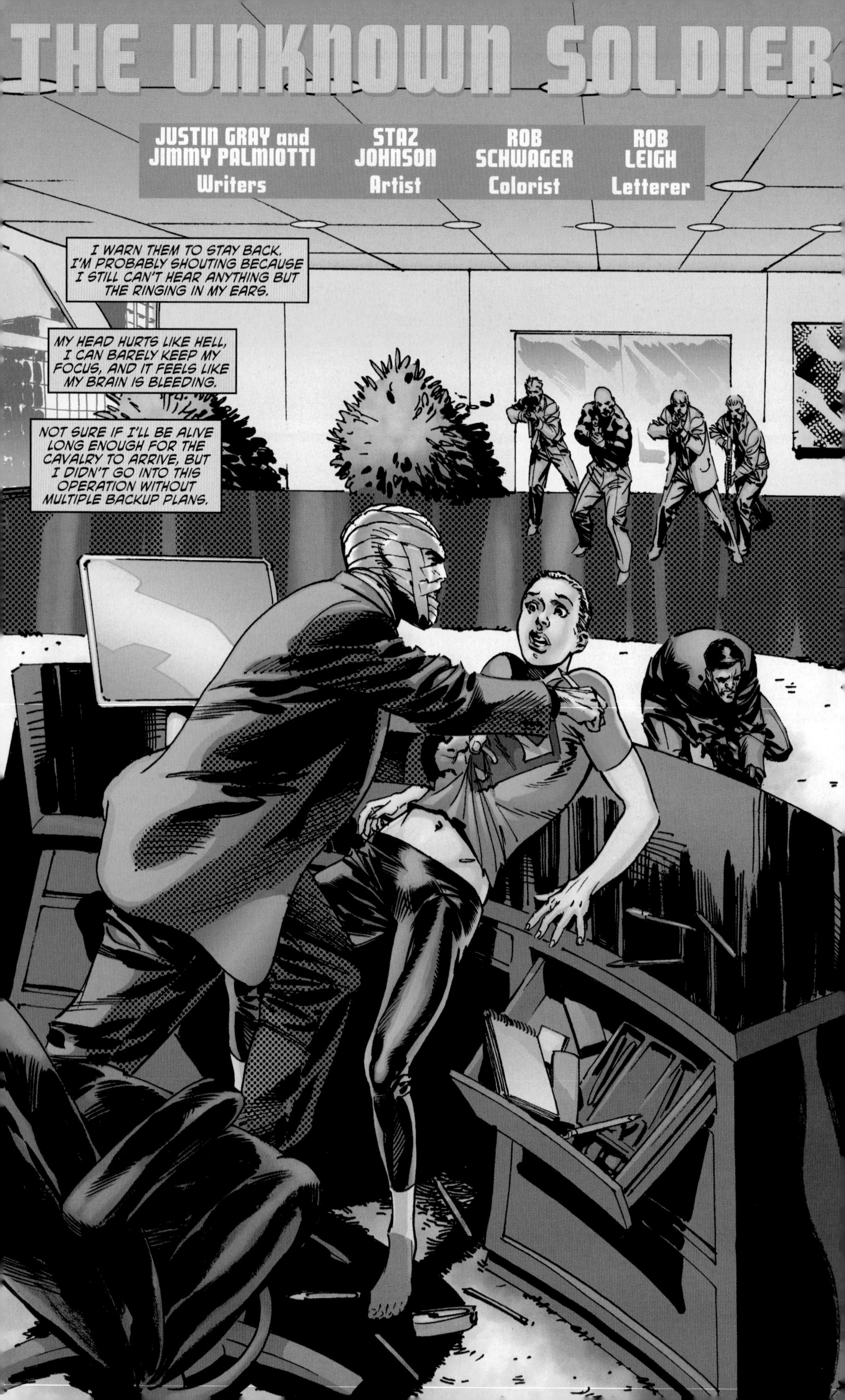
THE UNKNOWN SOLDIER
JUSTIN GRAY and JIMMY PALMIOTTI Writers
STAZ JOHNSON Artist
ROB SCHWAGER Colorist
ROB LEIGH Letterer
I WARN THEM TO STAY BACK. I'M PROBABLY SHOUTING BECAUSE I STILL CAN'T HEAR ANYTHING BUT THE RINGING IN MY EARS.
MY HEAD HURTS LIKE HELL, I CAN BARELY KEEP MY FOCUS, AND IT FEELS LIKE MY BRAIN IS BLEEDING.
NOT SURE IF I'LL BE ALIVE LONG ENOUGH FOR THE CAVALRY TO ARRIVE, BUT I DIDN'T GO INTO THIS OPERATION WITHOUT MULTIPLE BACKUP PLANS.

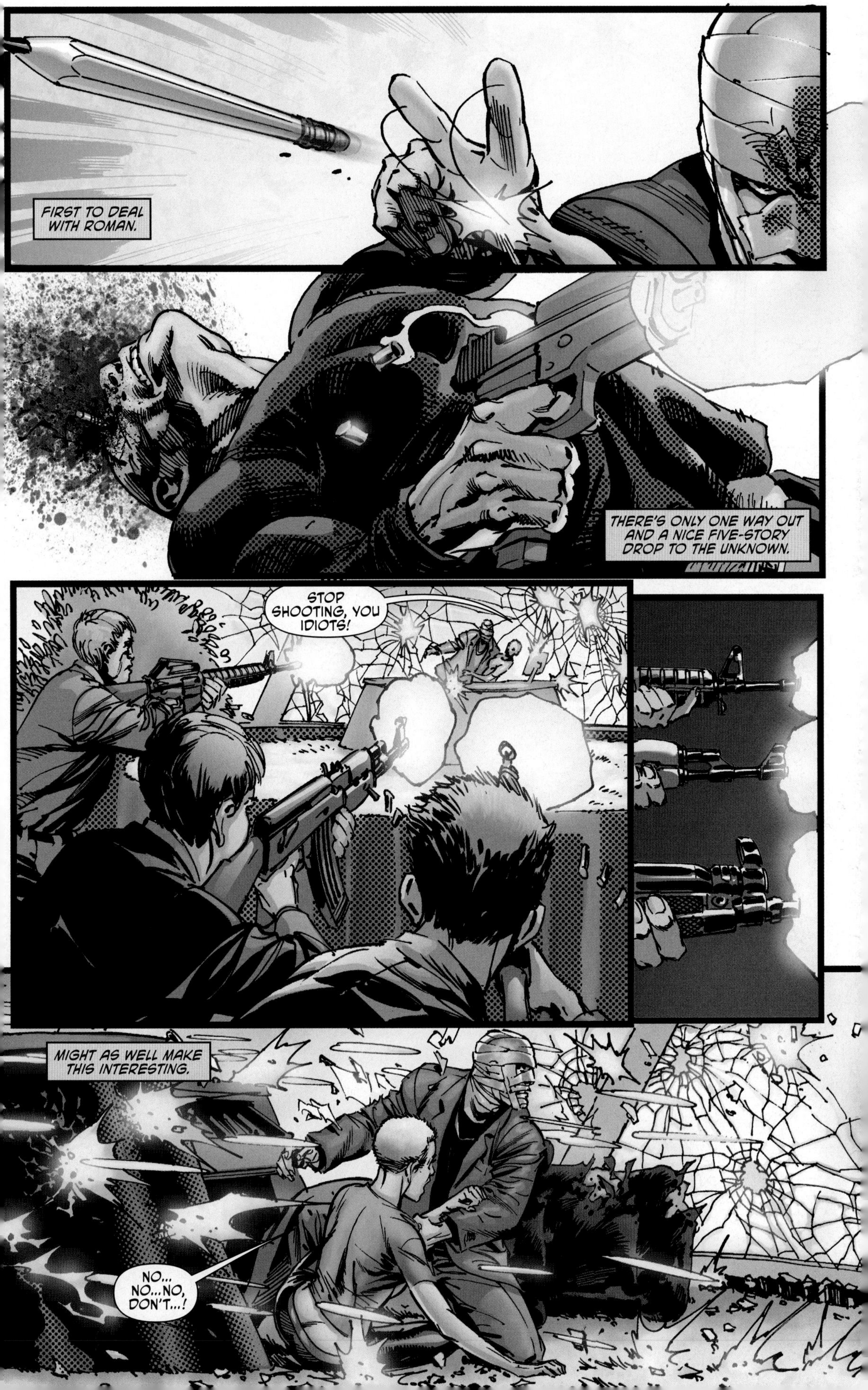
FIRST TO DEAL WITH ROMAN.
THERE'S ONLY ONE WAY OUT AND A NICE FIVE-STORY DROP TO THE UNKNOWN.
STOP SHOOTING, YOU IDIOTS!
MIGHT AS WELL MAKE THIS INTERESTING.
NO... NO...NO, DON'T...!

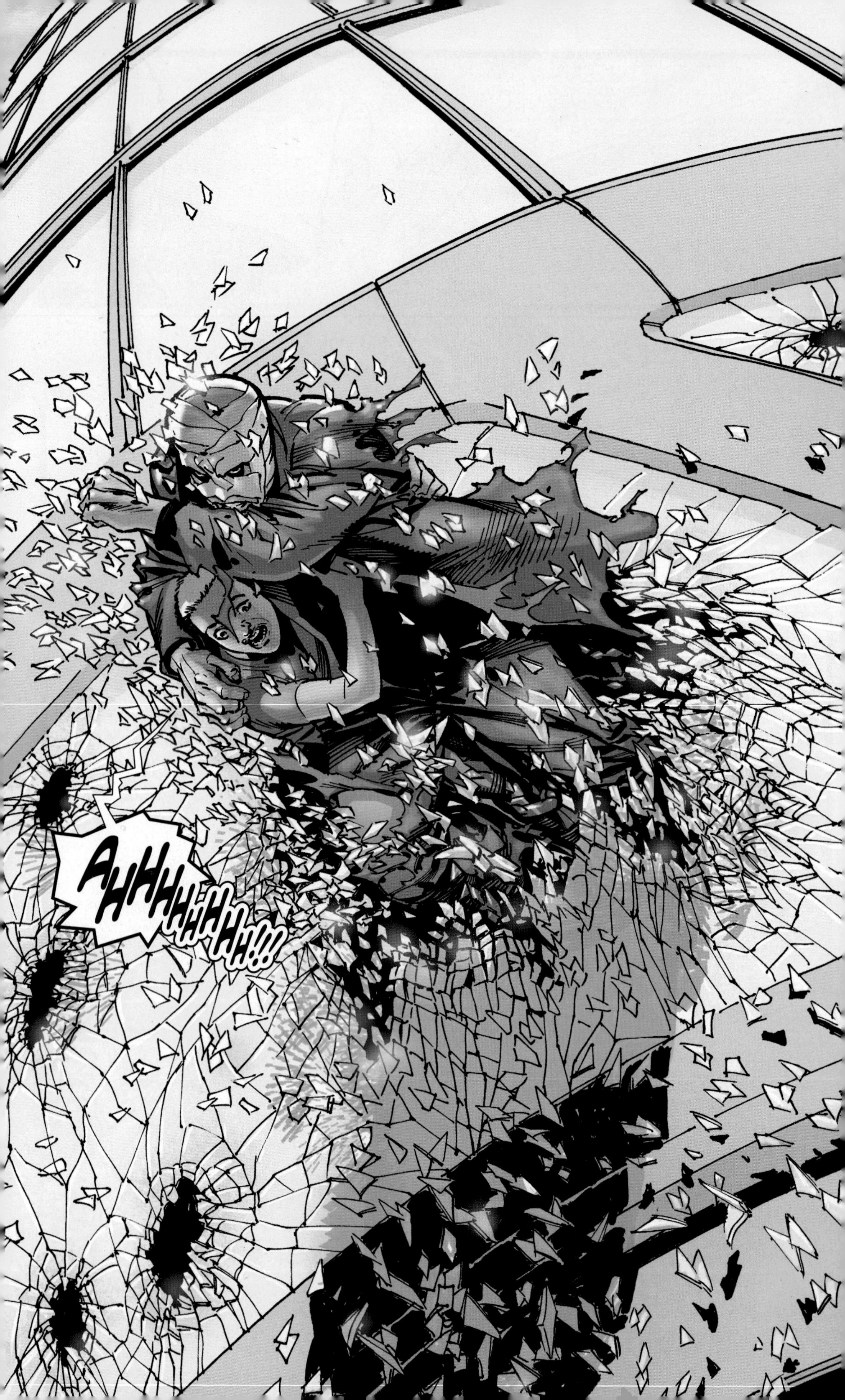
AHHHHHHHHH!!!

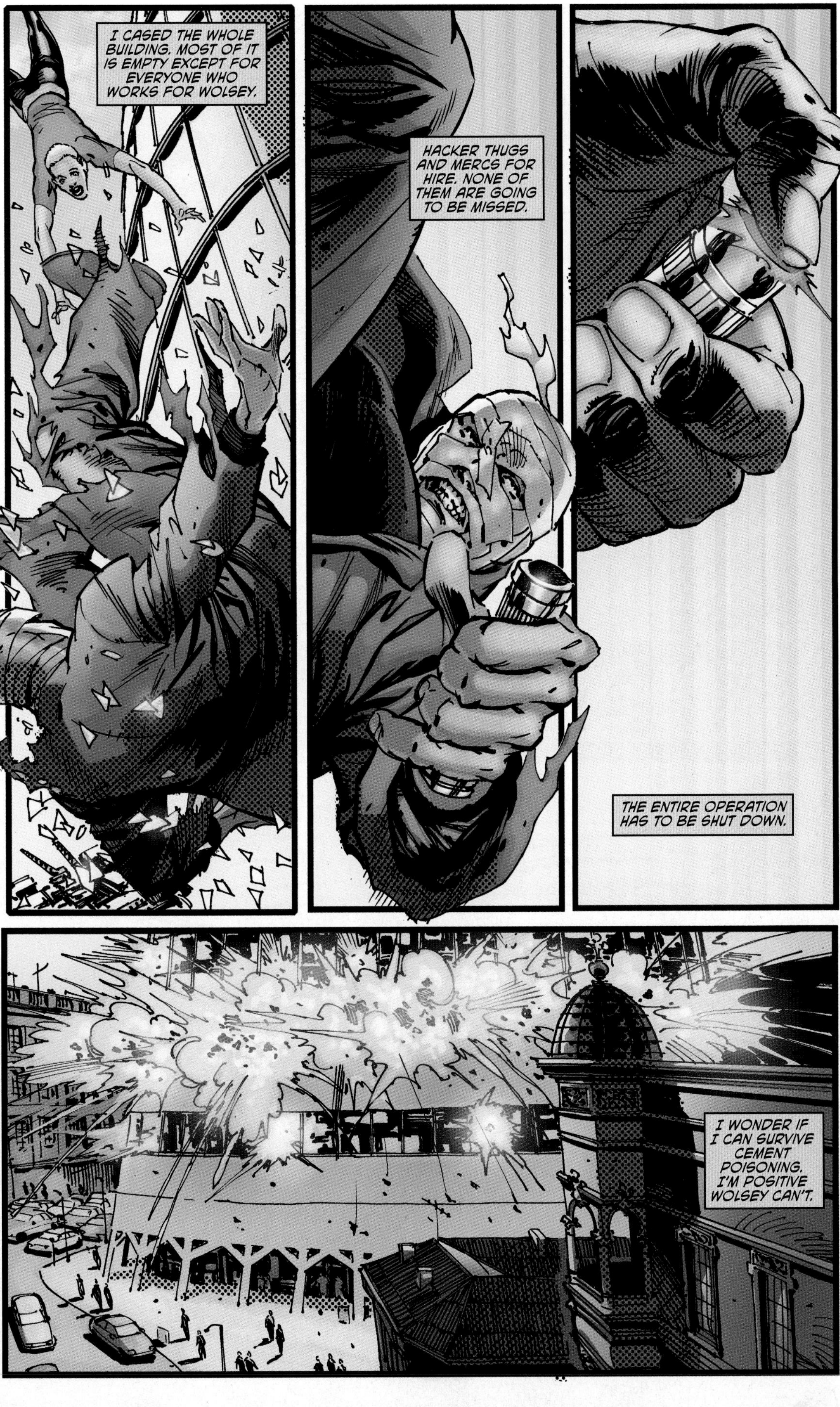
I CASED THE WHOLE BUILDING. MOST OF IT IS EMPTY EXCEPT FOR EVERYONE WHO WORKS FOR WOLSEY.
HACKER THUGS AND MERCS FOR HIRE. NONE OF THEM ARE GOING TO BE MISSED.
THE ENTIRE OPERATION HAS TO BE SHUT DOWN.
I WONDER IF I CAN SURVIVE CEMENT POISONING. I'M POSITIVE WOLSEY CAN'T.

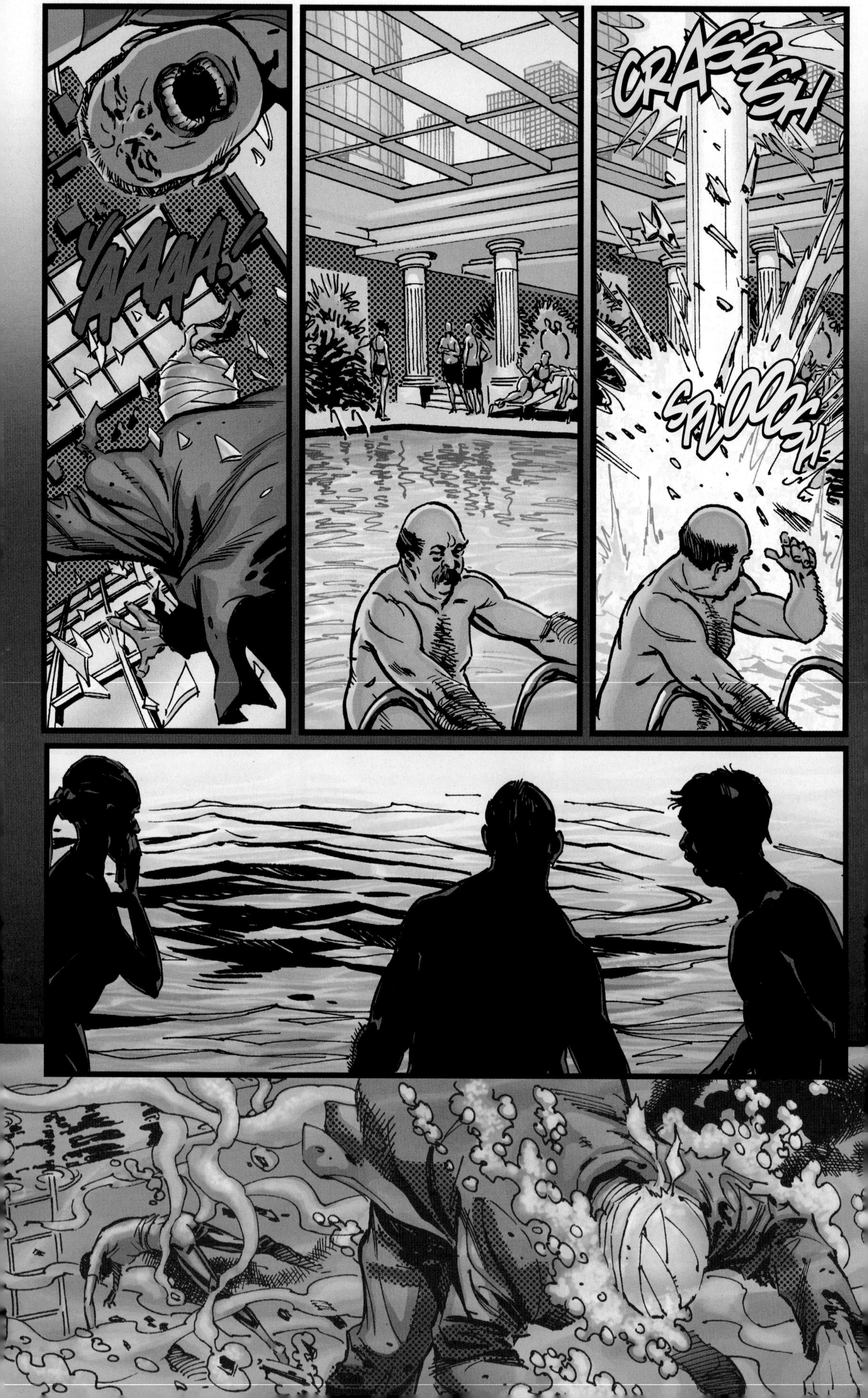

YAAAA!
CRASSSH
SPLOOOSH

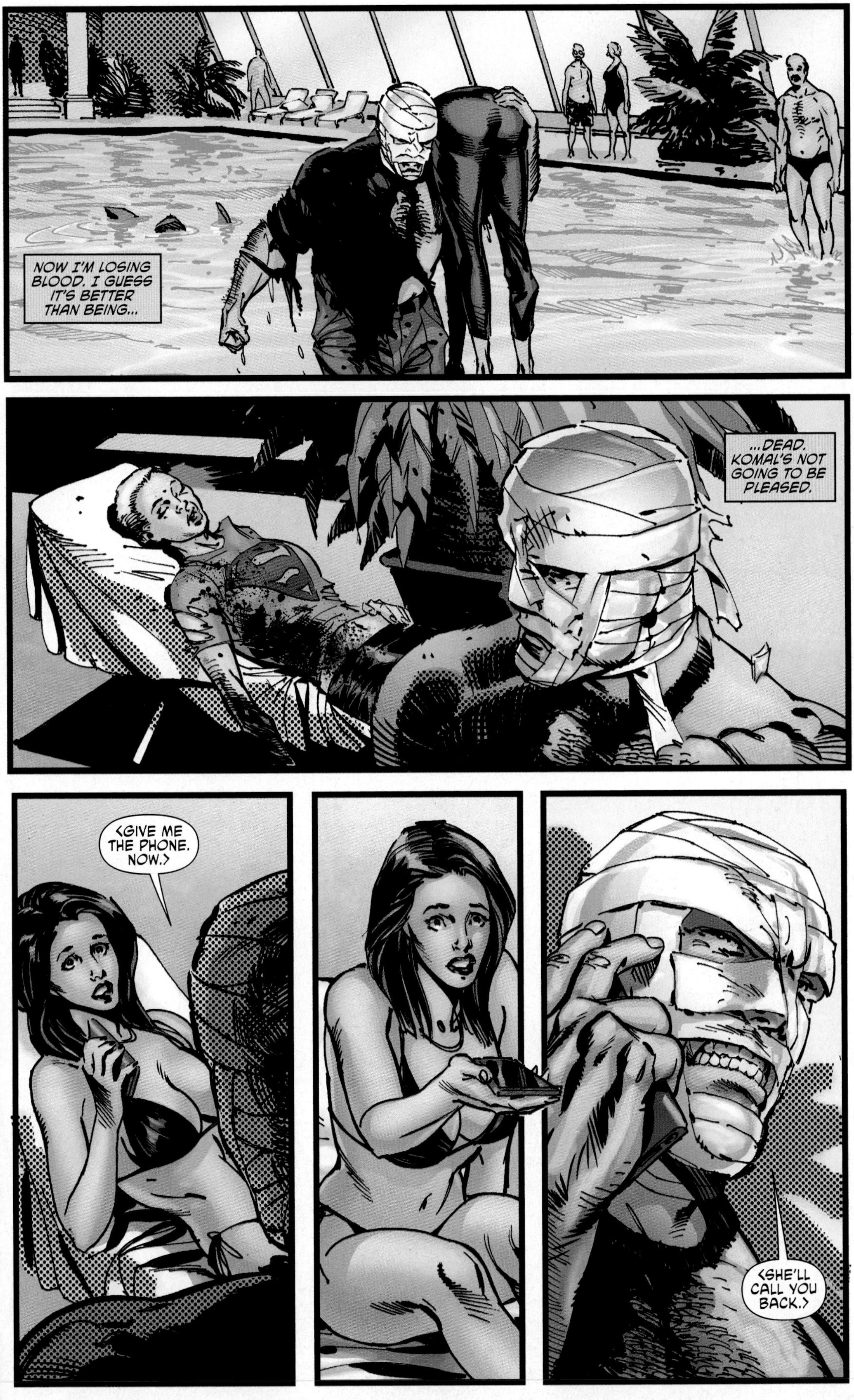
NOW I'M LOSING BLOOD. I GUESS IT'S BETTER THAN BEING...
...DEAD. KOMAL'S NOT GOING TO BE PLEASED.
<GIVE ME THE PHONE. NOW.>
<SHE'LL CALL YOU BACK.>

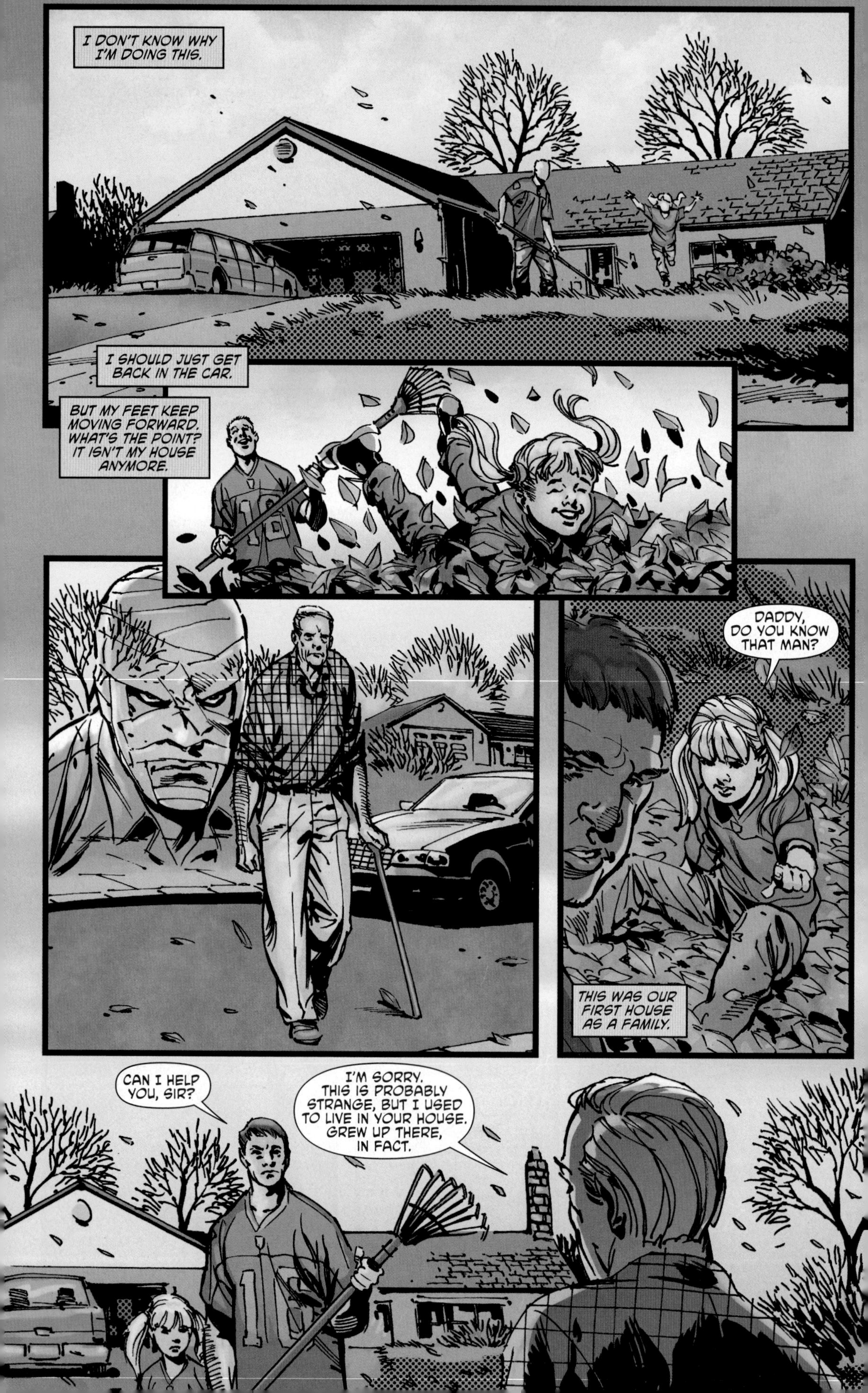
I DON'T KNOW WHY I'M DOING THIS.
I SHOULD JUST GET BACK IN THE CAR.
BUT MY FEET KEEP MOVING FORWARD. WHAT'S THE POINT? IT ISN'T MY HOUSE ANYMORE.
DADDY, DO YOU KNOW THAT MAN?
THIS WAS OUR FIRST HOUSE AS A FAMILY.
CAN I HELP YOU, SIR?
I'M SORRY. THIS IS PROBABLY STRANGE, BUT I USED TO LIVE IN YOUR HOUSE. GREW UP THERE, IN FACT.

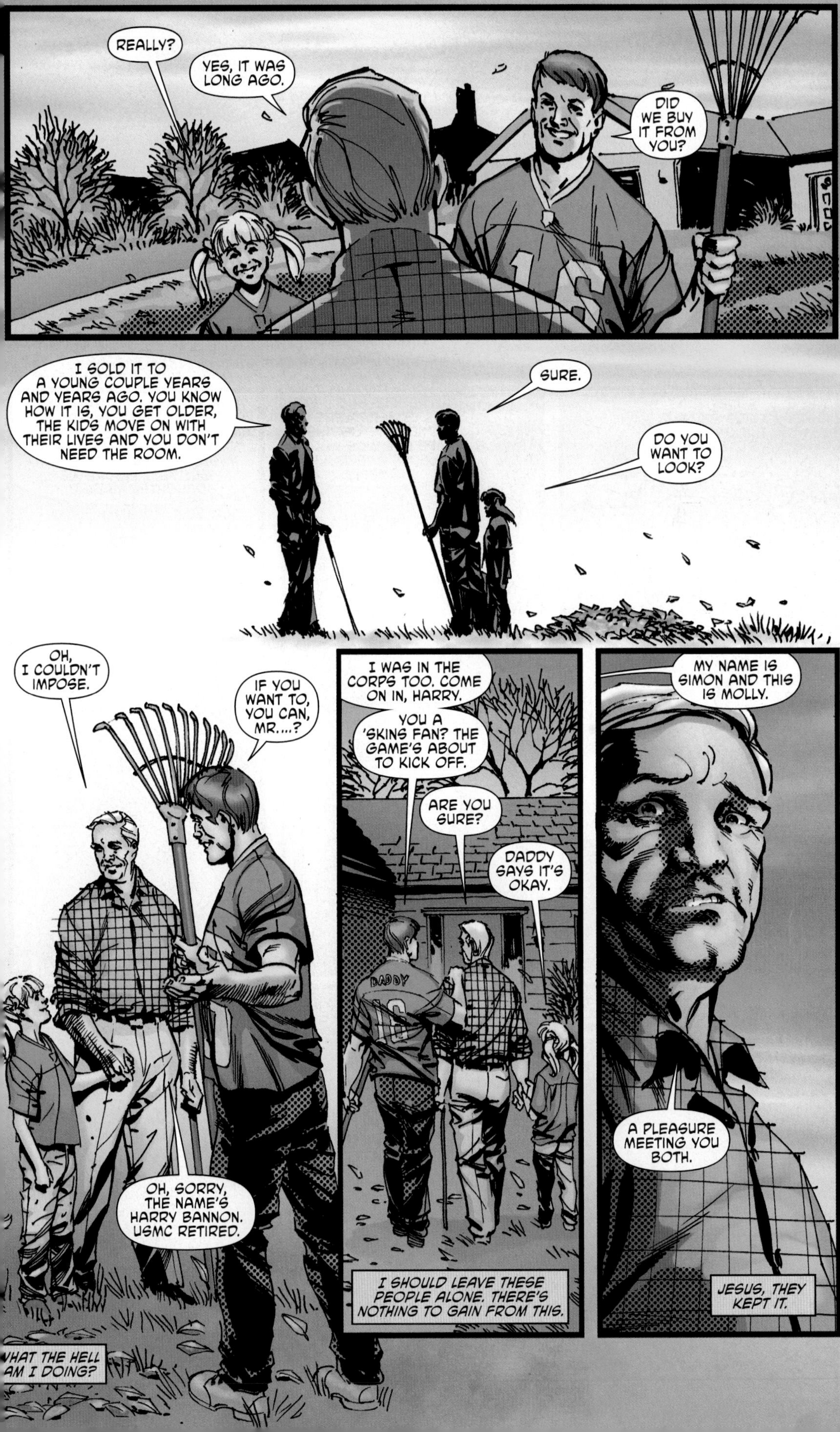
REALLY?
YES, IT WAS LONG AGO.
DID WE BUY IT FROM YOU?
I SOLD IT TO A YOUNG COUPLE YEARS AND YEARS AGO. YOU KNOW HOW IT IS, YOU GET OLDER, THE KIDS MOVE ON WITH THEIR LIVES AND YOU DON'T NEED THE ROOM.
SURE.
DO YOU WANT TO LOOK?
OH, I COULDN'T IMPOSE.
IF YOU WANT TO, YOU CAN, MR....?
OH, SORRY, THE NAME'S HARRY BANNON. USMC RETIRED.
WHAT THE HELL AM I DOING?
I WAS IN THE CORPS TOO. COME ON IN, HARRY.
YOU A 'SKINS FAN? THE GAME'S ABOUT TO KICK OFF.
ARE YOU SURE?
DADDY SAYS IT'S OKAY.
DADDY
I SHOULD LEAVE THESE PEOPLE ALONE. THERE'S NOTHING TO GAIN FROM THIS.
MY NAME IS SIMON AND THIS IS MOLLY.
A PLEASURE MEETING YOU BOTH.
JESUS, THEY KEPT IT.

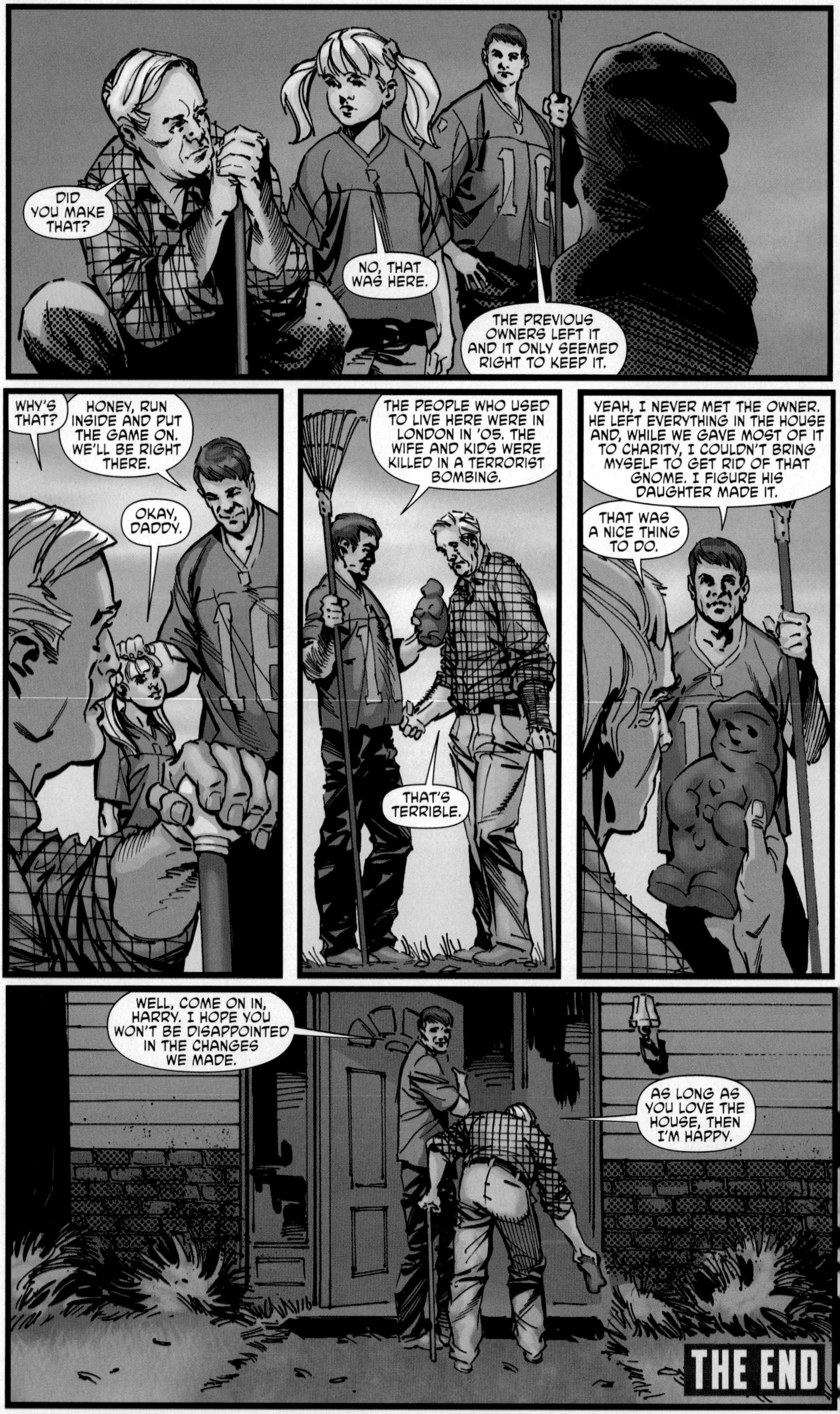
DID YOU MAKE THAT?
NO, THAT WAS HERE.
THE PREVIOUS OWNERS LEFT IT AND IT ONLY SEEMED RIGHT TO KEEP IT.
WHY'S THAT?
HONEY, RUN INSIDE AND PUT THE GAME ON. WE'LL BE RIGHT THERE.
OKAY, DADDY.
THE PEOPLE WHO USED TO LIVE HERE WERE IN LONDON IN '05. THE WIFE AND KIDS WERE KILLED IN A TERRORIST BOMBING.
THAT'S TERRIBLE.
YEAH, I NEVER MET THE OWNER. HE LEFT EVERYTHING IN THE HOUSE AND, WHILE WE GAVE MOST OF IT TO CHARITY, I COULDN'T BRING MYSELF TO GET RID OF THAT GNOME. I FIGURE HIS DAUGHTER MADE IT.
THAT WAS A NICE THING TO DO.
WELL, COME ON IN, HARRY. I HOPE YOU WON'T BE DISAPPOINTED IN THE CHANGES WE MADE.
AS LONG AS YOU LOVE THE HOUSE, THEN I'M HAPPY.
THE END

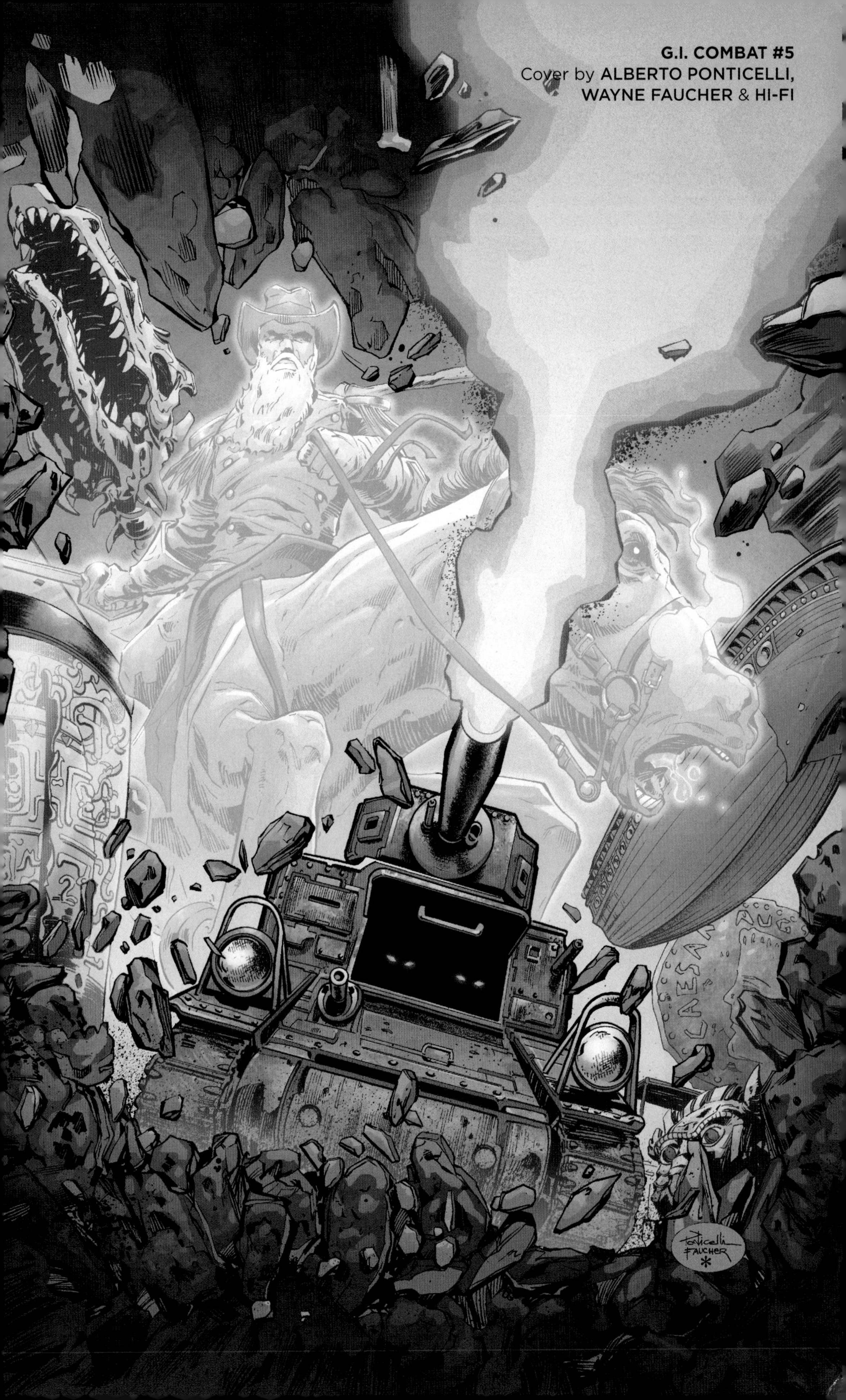
Ponticelli
Faucher

G.I. COMBAT #5
Cover by **ALBERTO PONTICELLI, WAYNE FAUCHER** & **HI-FI**

THE HAUNTED TANK
PETER J. TOMASI writer
HOWARD CHAYKIN artist

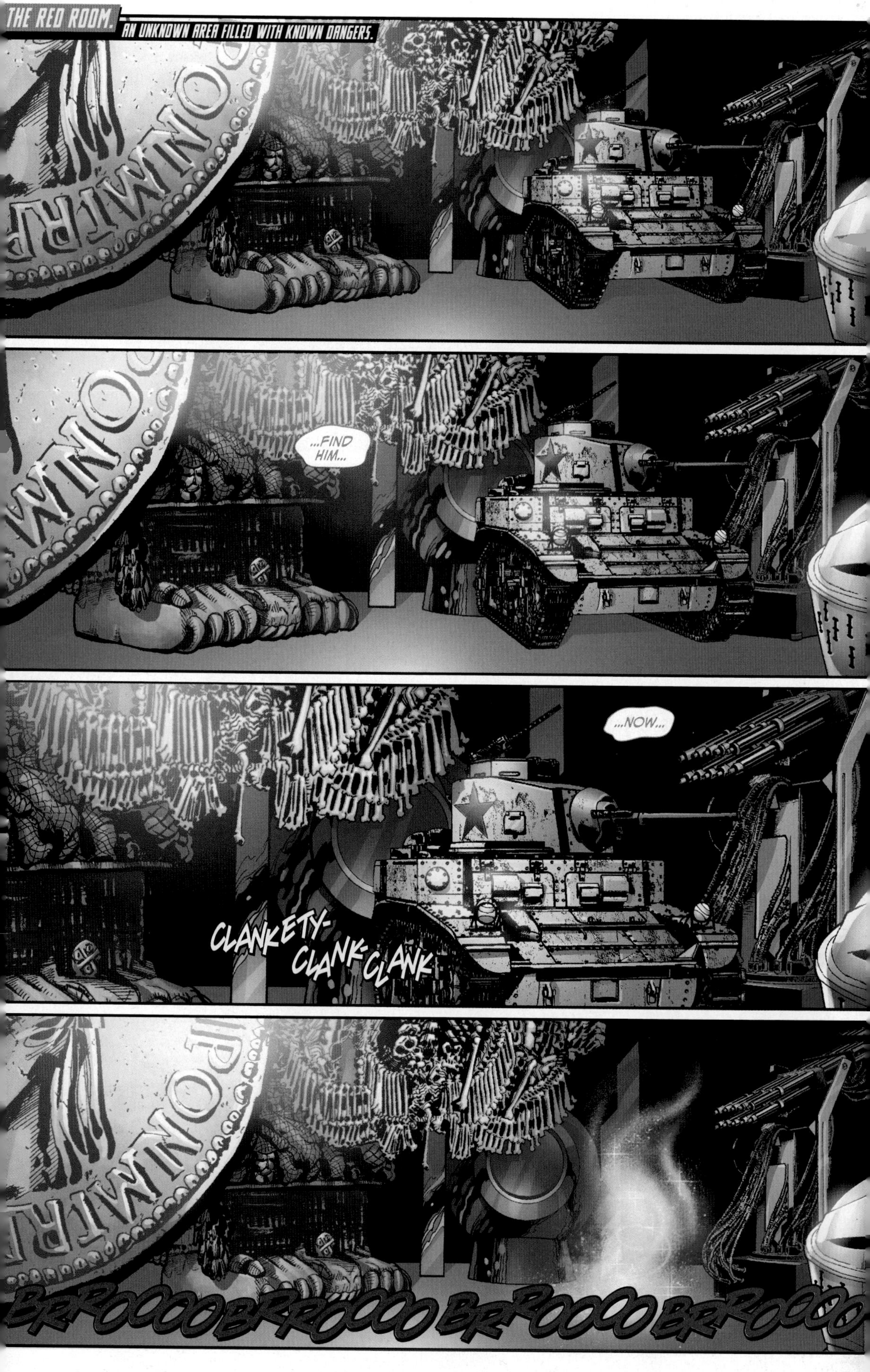
THE RED ROOM.
AN UNKNOWN AREA FILLED WITH KNOWN DANGERS.
...FIND HIM...
...NOW...
CLANKETY-CLANK-CLANK
BRROOOOO BRROOOOO BRROOOO BRROOOO

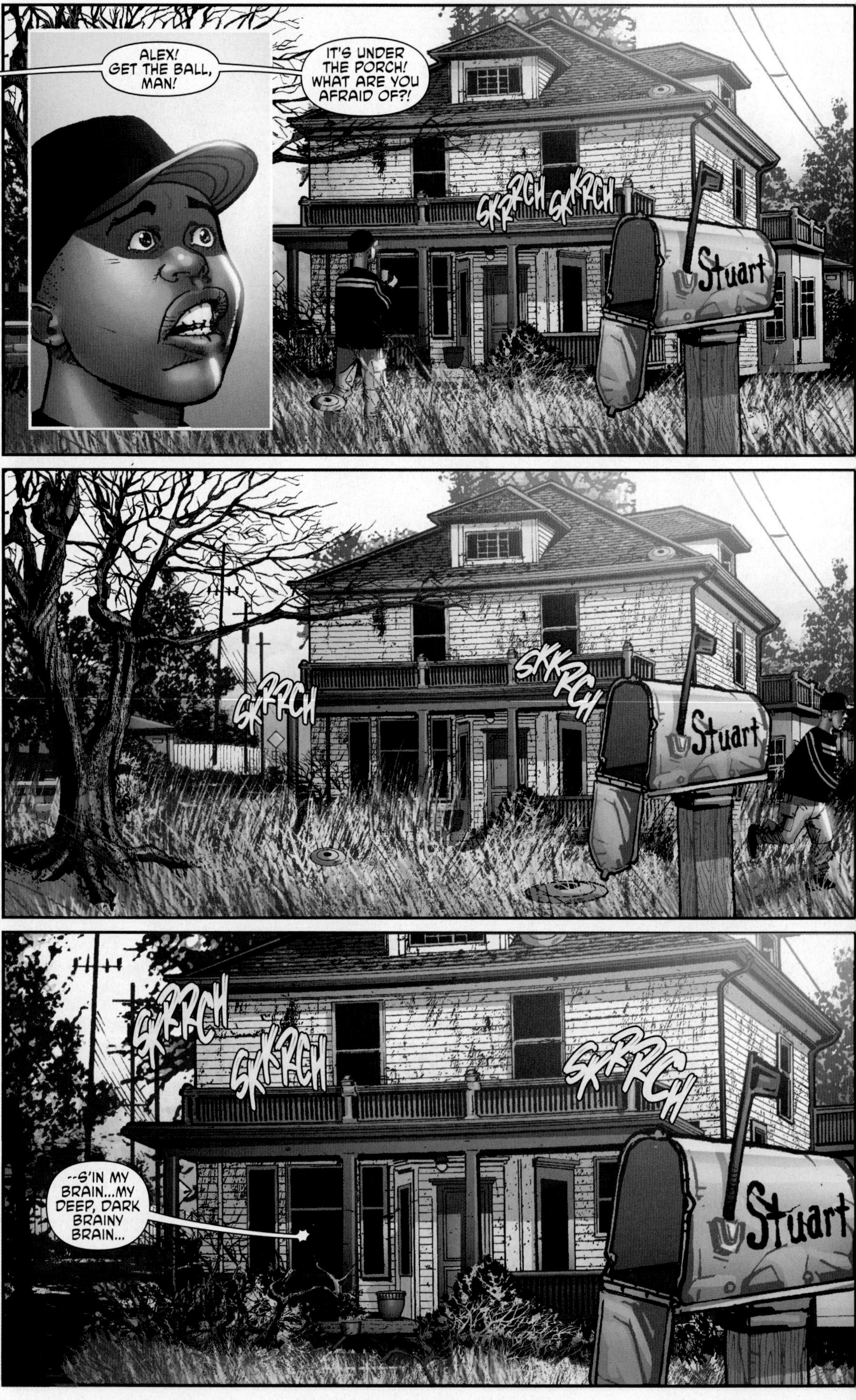
ALEX! GET THE BALL, MAN!
IT'S UNDER THE PORCH! WHAT ARE YOU AFRAID OF?!
SKRRCH SKKRCH
Stuart
SKRRCH
SKKRCH
Stuart
SKRRCH
SKKRCH
SKRRCH
--S'IN MY BRAIN...MY DEEP, DARK BRAINY BRAIN...
Stuart

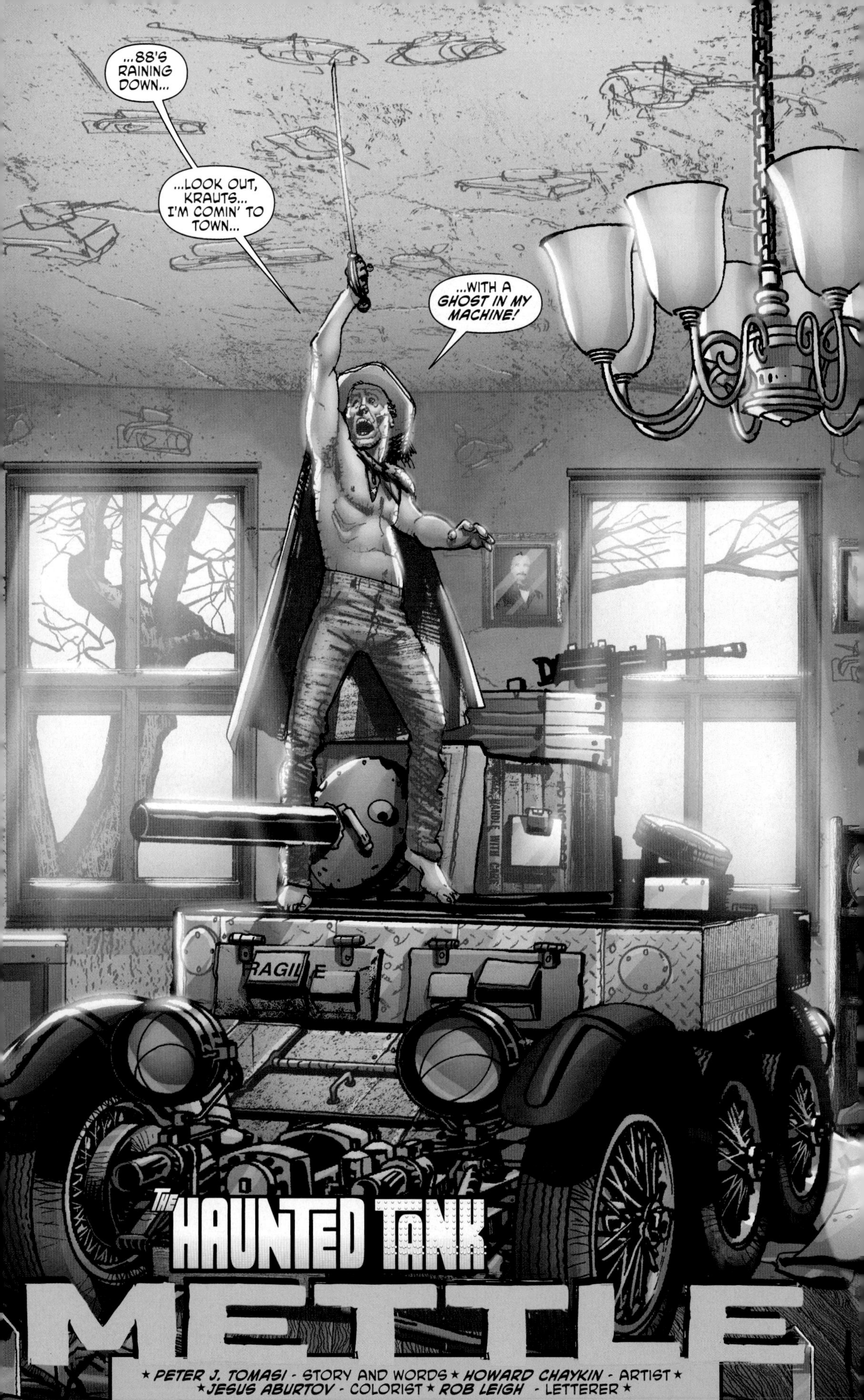

...88'S RAINING DOWN...
...LOOK OUT, KRAUTS... I'M COMIN' TO TOWN...
...WITH A GHOST IN MY MACHINE!
FRAGILE
HANDLE WITH CARE
THE HAUNTED TANK
METTLE
★ PETER J. TOMASI - STORY AND WORDS ★ HOWARD CHAYKIN - ARTIST ★
★ JESUS ABURTOV - COLORIST ★ ROB LEIGH - LETTERER ★

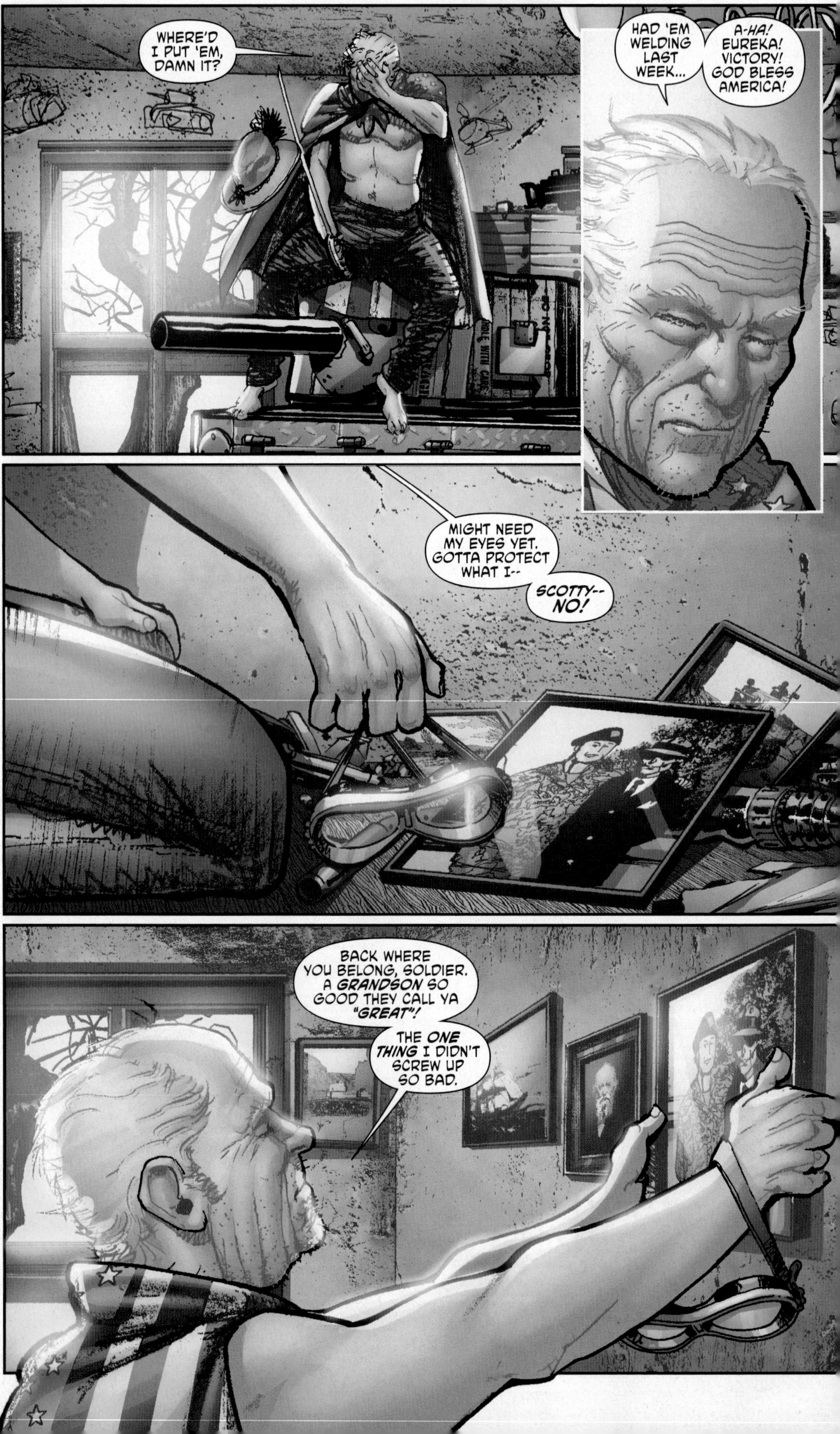
WHERE'D I PUT 'EM, DAMN IT?
HAD 'EM WELDING LAST WEEK...
A-HA! EUREKA! VICTORY! GOD BLESS AMERICA!
MIGHT NEED MY EYES YET. GOTTA PROTECT WHAT I--
SCOTTY-- NO!
BACK WHERE YOU BELONG, SOLDIER. A GRANDSON SO GOOD THEY CALL YA "GREAT"!
THE ONE THING I DIDN'T SCREW UP SO BAD.

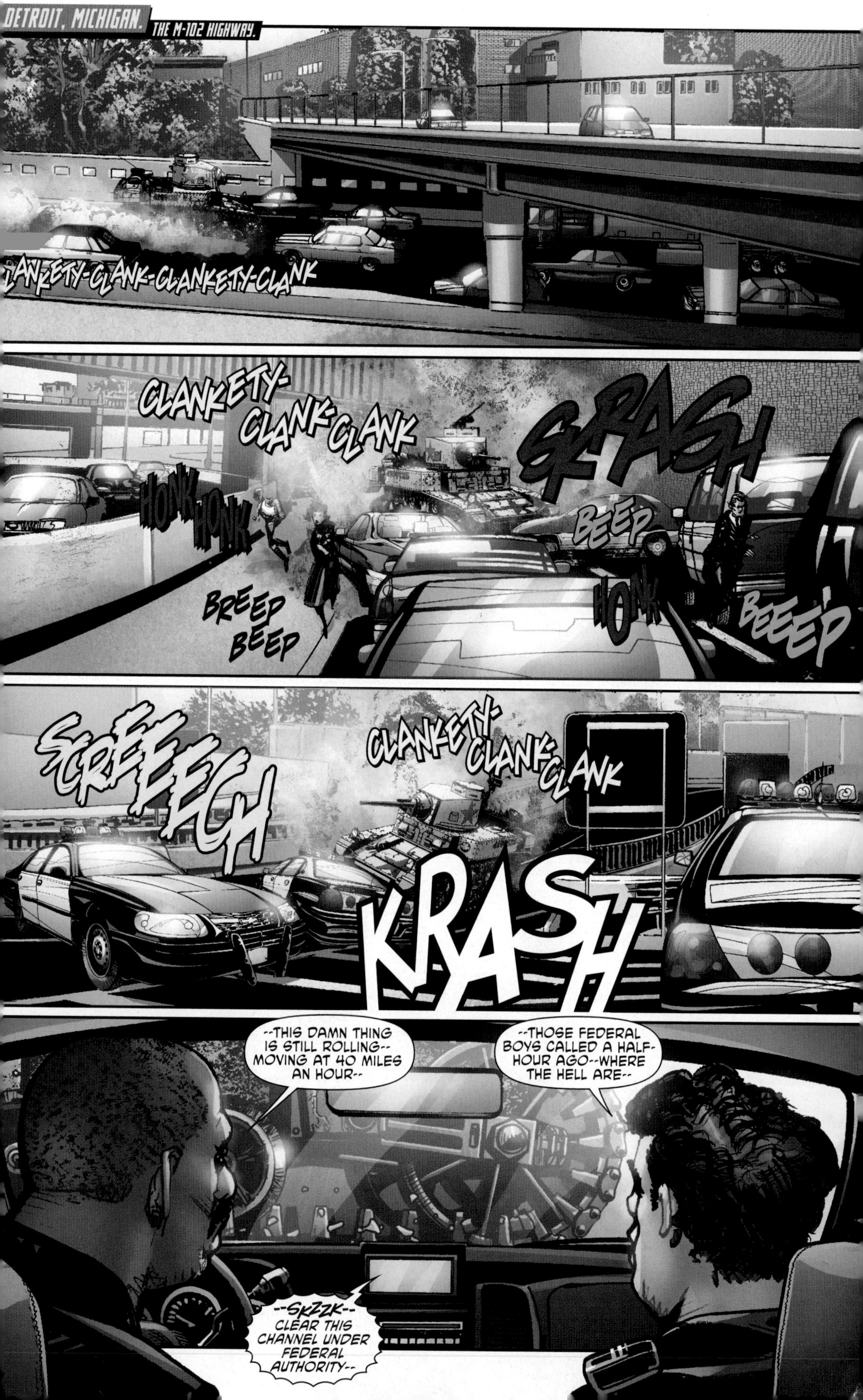
DETROIT, MICHIGAN.
THE M-102 HIGHWAY.
CLANKETY-CLANK-CLANKETY-CLANK
CLANKETY-CLANK-CLANK
SKRASH
HONK HONK
BEEP
BREEP BEEP
HONK
BEEEP
SCREEEECH
CLANKETY-CLANK-CLANK
KRASH
--THIS DAMN THING IS STILL ROLLING--MOVING AT 40 MILES AN HOUR--
--THOSE FEDERAL BOYS CALLED A HALF-HOUR AGO--WHERE THE HELL ARE--
--SKZZK--CLEAR THIS CHANNEL UNDER FEDERAL AUTHORITY--

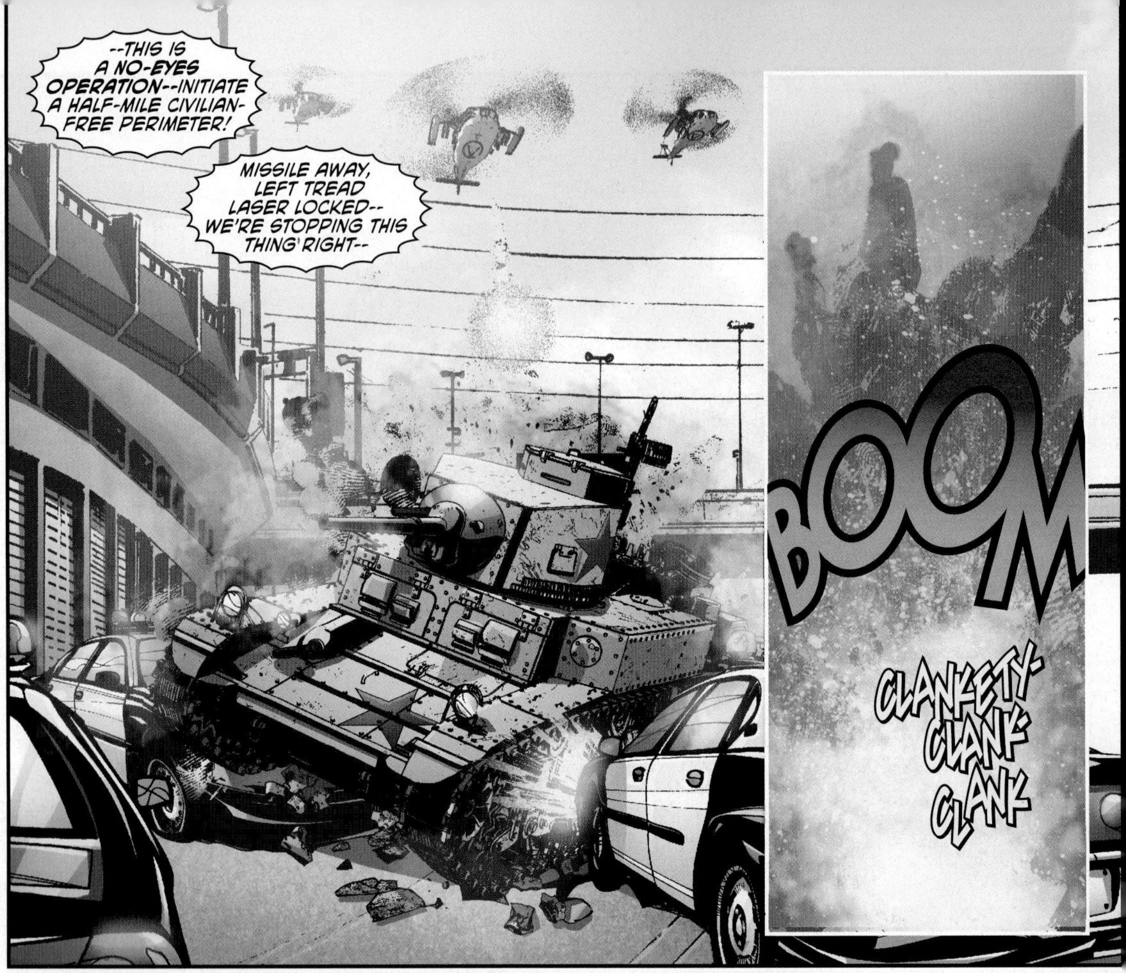
--THIS IS A NO-EYES OPERATION--INITIATE A HALF-MILE CIVILIAN-FREE PERIMETER!
MISSILE AWAY, LEFT TREAD LASER LOCKED--WE'RE STOPPING THIS THING RIGHT--
BOOM
CLANKETY-CLANK-CLANK CLANK
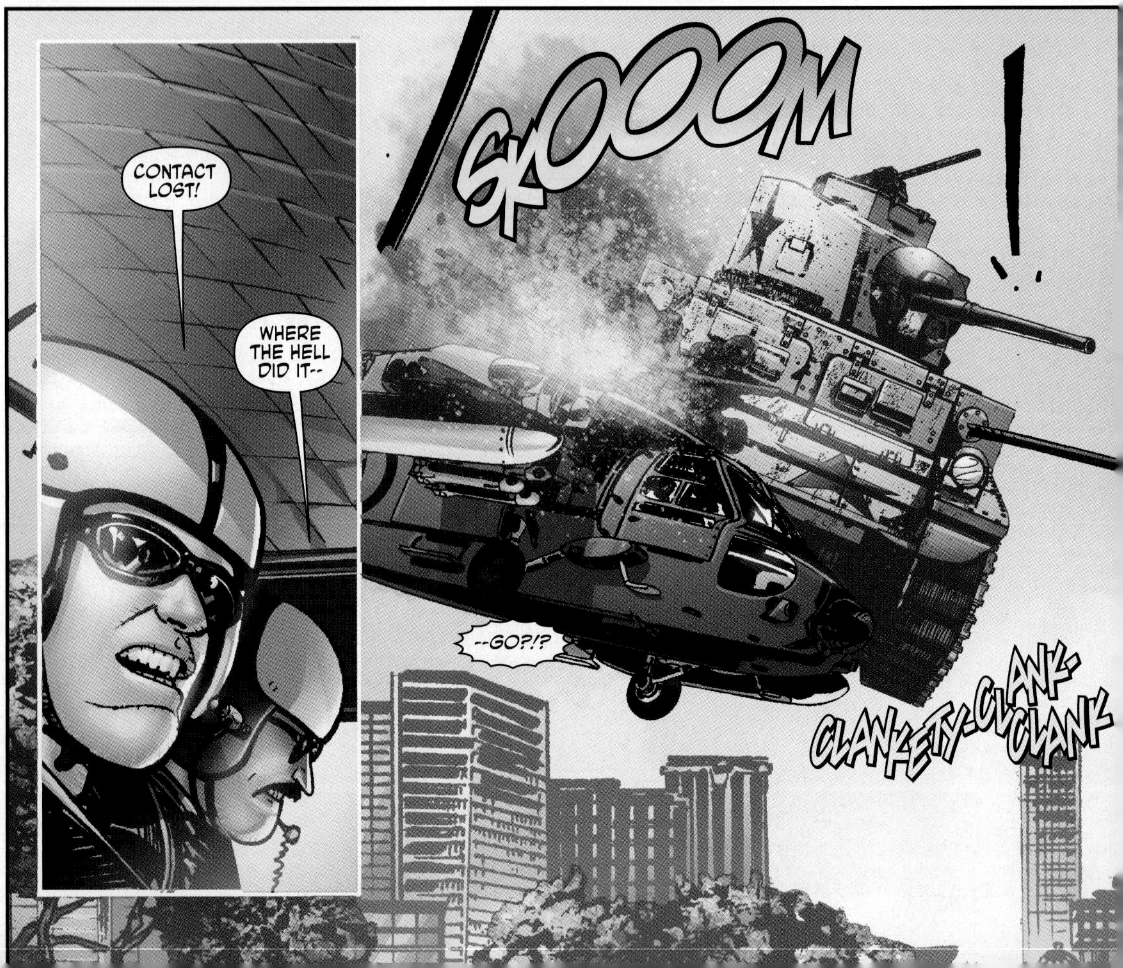
CONTACT LOST!
WHERE THE HELL DID IT--
SKOOOM
!
--GO?!?
CLANKETY-CLANK-CLANK

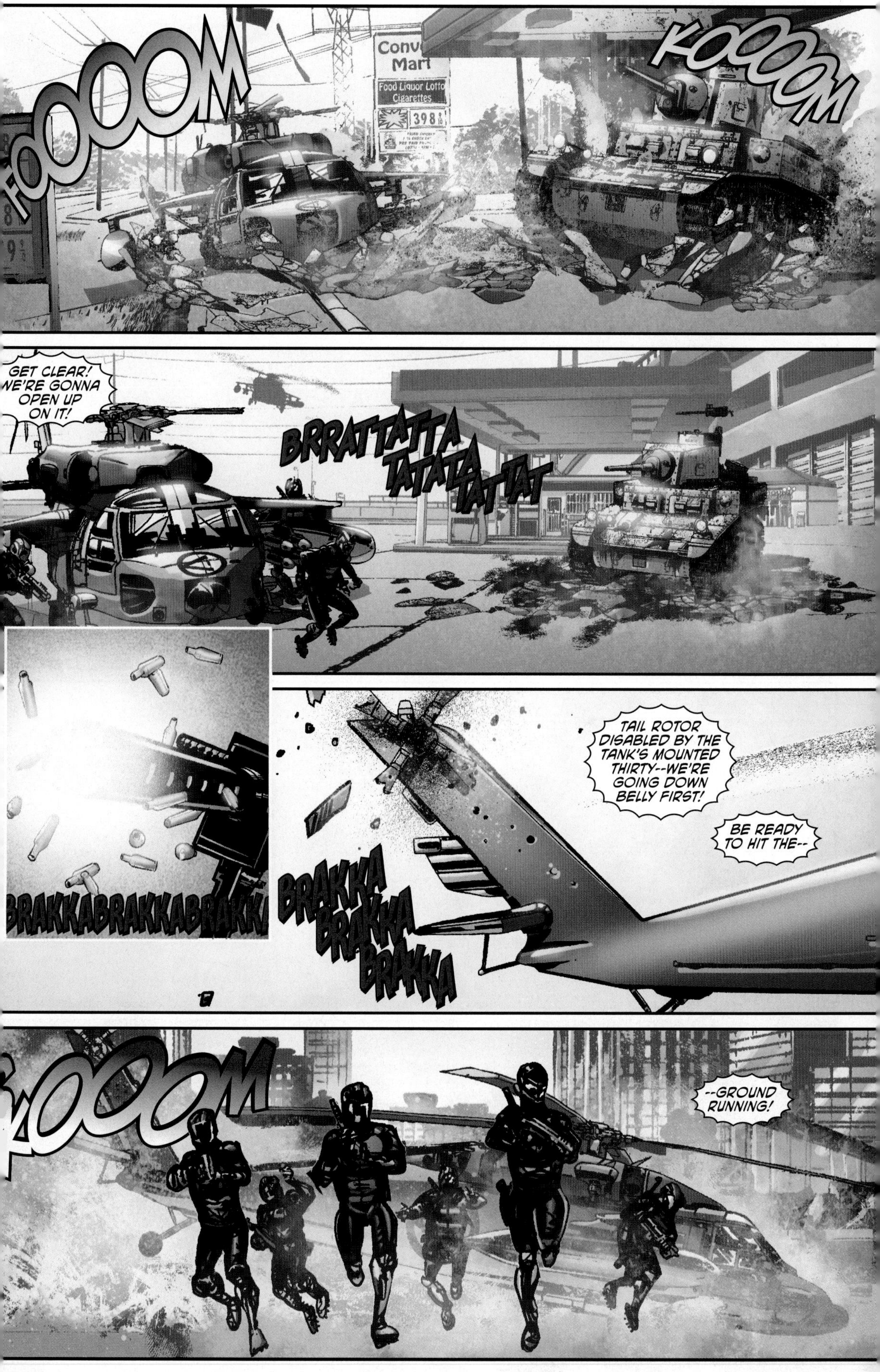
FOOOOOM
Conve
Mart
Food Liquor Lotto
Cigarettes
398
KOOOOOM
GET CLEAR! WE'RE GONNA OPEN UP ON IT!
BRRATTATTA TATATA TATTAT
BRAKKABRAKKABRAKKA
BRAKKA BRAKKA BRAKKA
TAIL ROTOR DISABLED BY THE TANK'S MOUNTED THIRTY--WE'RE GOING DOWN BELLY FIRST!
BE READY TO HIT THE--
KOOOOM
--GROUND RUNNING!

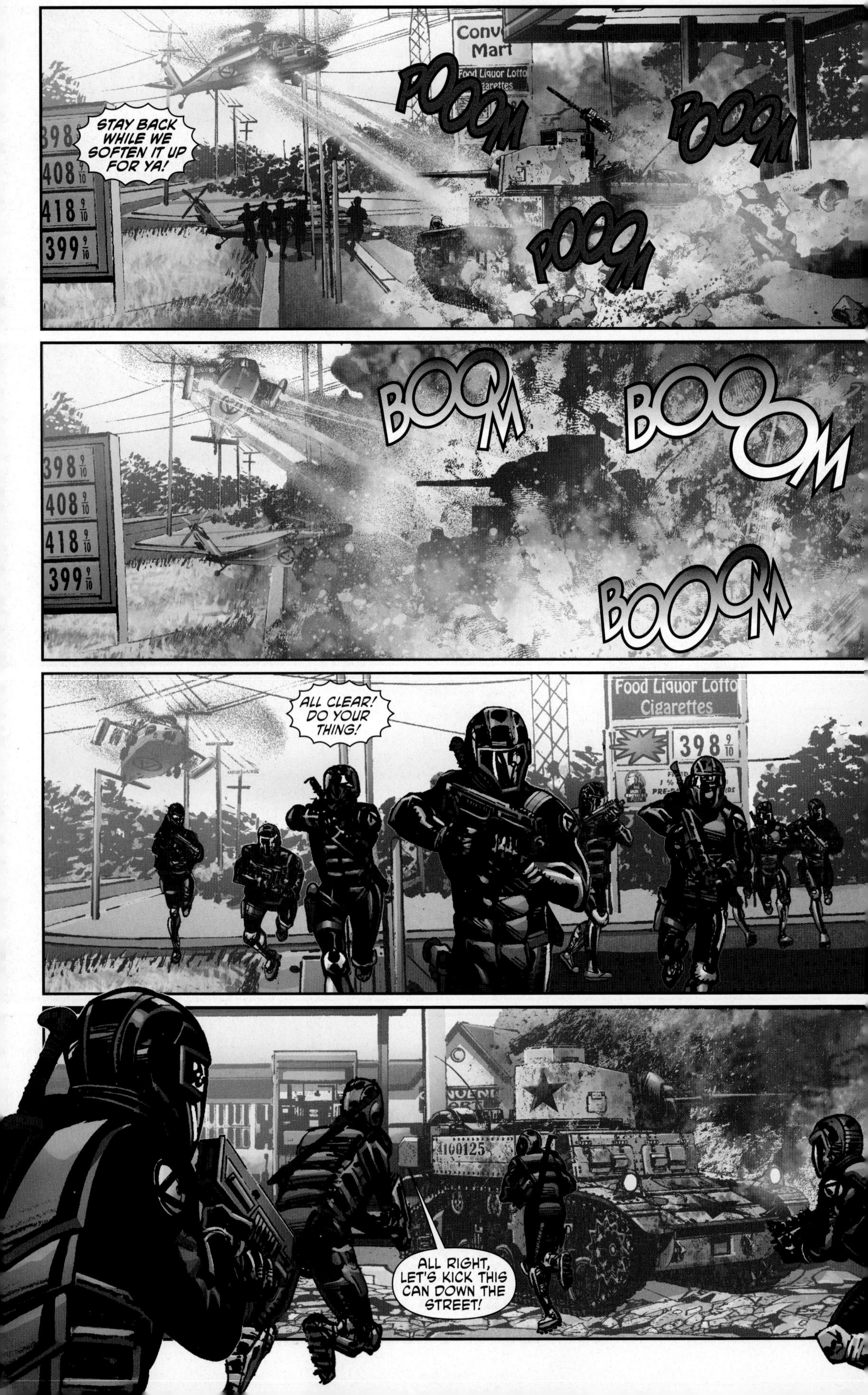
Conve
Mart
Food Liquor Lotto
Cigarettes
STAY BACK WHILE WE SOFTEN IT UP FOR YA!
POOOM
POOOM
POOOM
BOOOM
BOOOOM
BOOOM
Food Liquor Lotto
Cigarettes
ALL CLEAR! DO YOUR THING!
4100125
ALL RIGHT, LET'S KICK THIS CAN DOWN THE STREET!

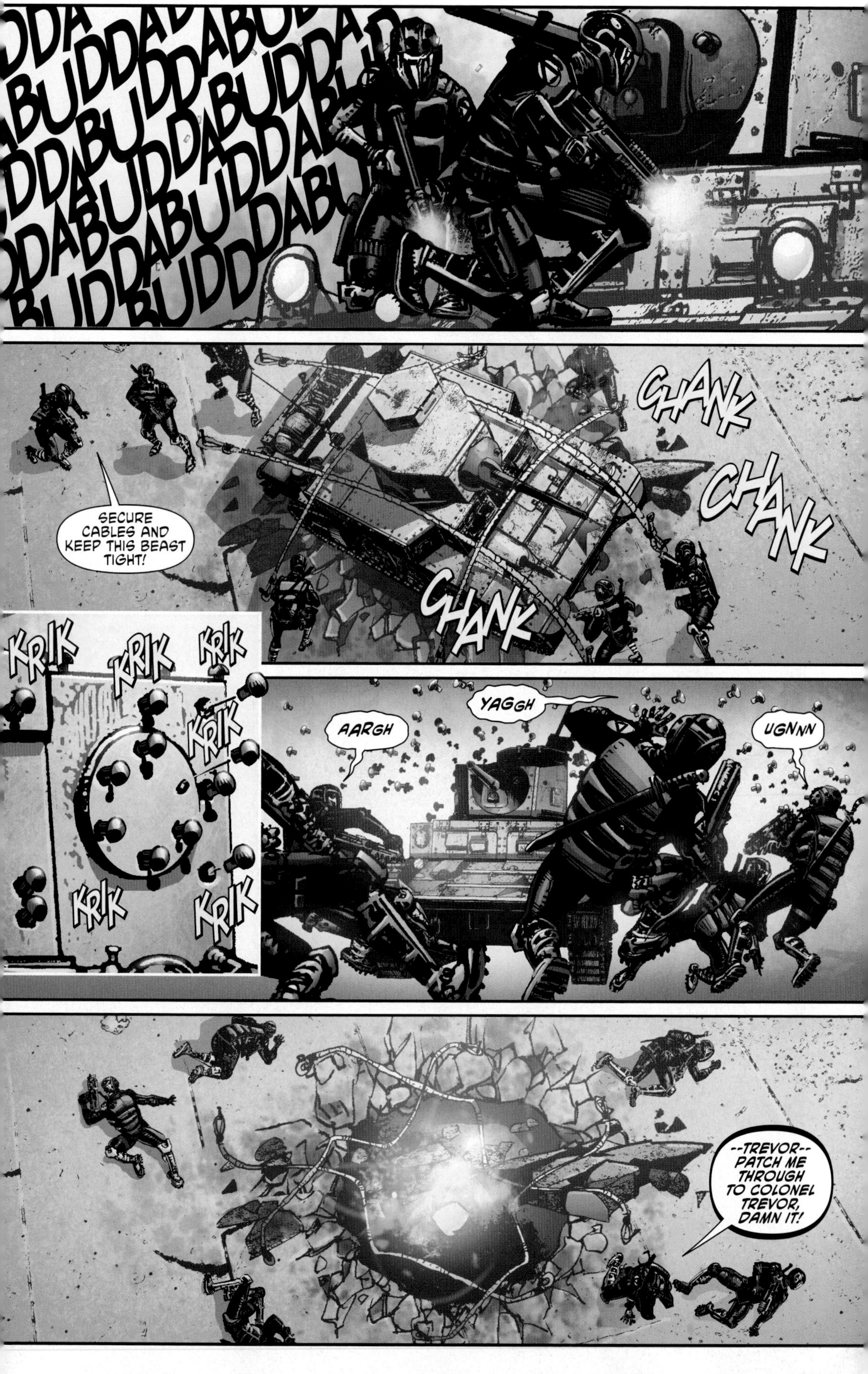

DABUDDABUDDABUDDABUDDABUDDABUDDABUDDABUDDABUDDABUDD
CHANK
CHANK
SECURE CABLES AND KEEP THIS BEAST TIGHT!
CHANK
KRIK
KRIK
KRIK
KRIK
KRIK
KRIK
AARGH
YAGGH
UGNNN
--TREVOR-- PATCH ME THROUGH TO COLONEL TREVOR, DAMN IT!

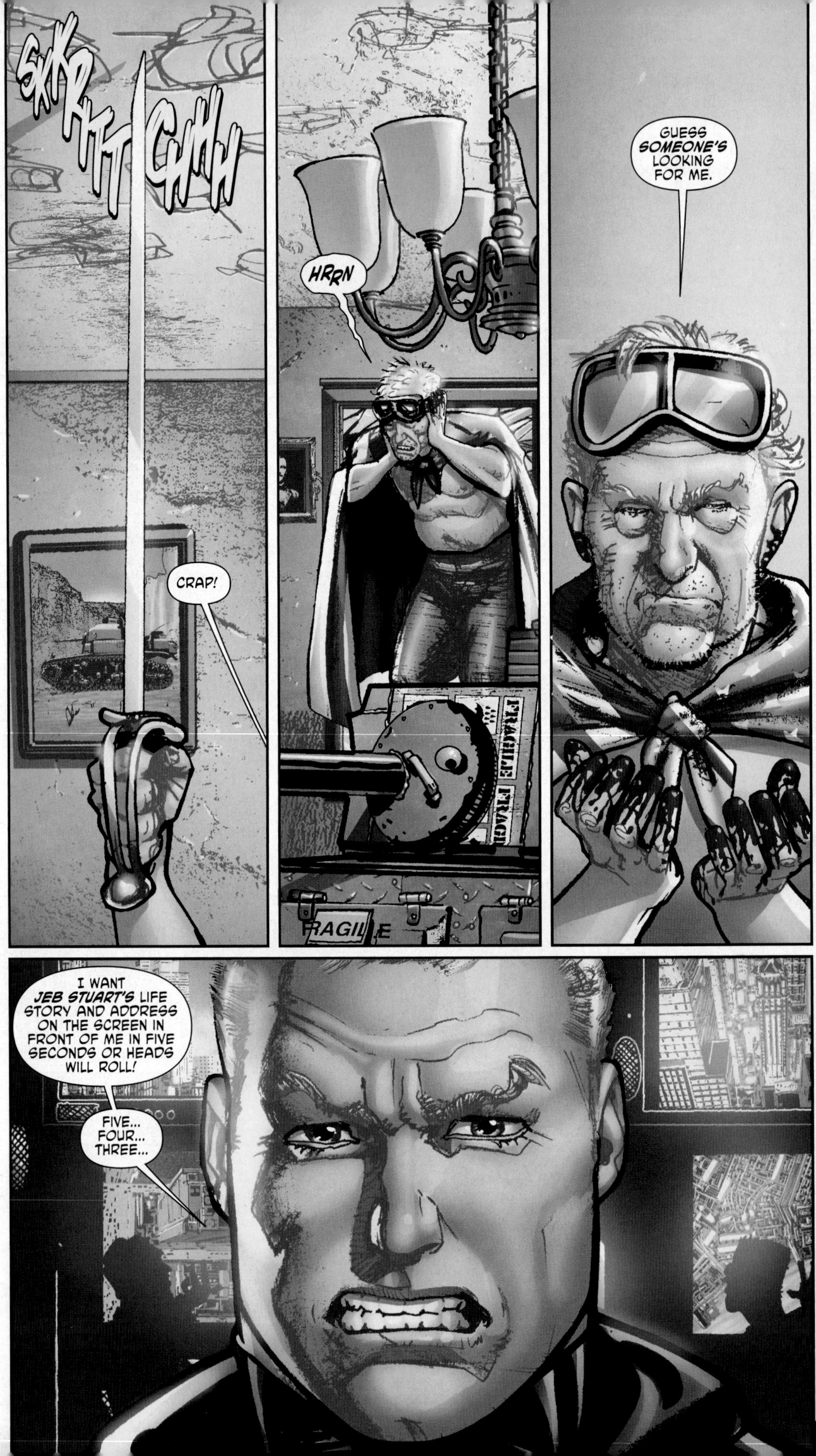
SKKRITTT CHHH
CRAP!
HRRN
FRAGILE
GUESS SOMEONE'S LOOKING FOR ME.
I WANT JEB STUART'S LIFE STORY AND ADDRESS ON THE SCREEN IN FRONT OF ME IN FIVE SECONDS OR HEADS WILL ROLL!
FIVE... FOUR... THREE...

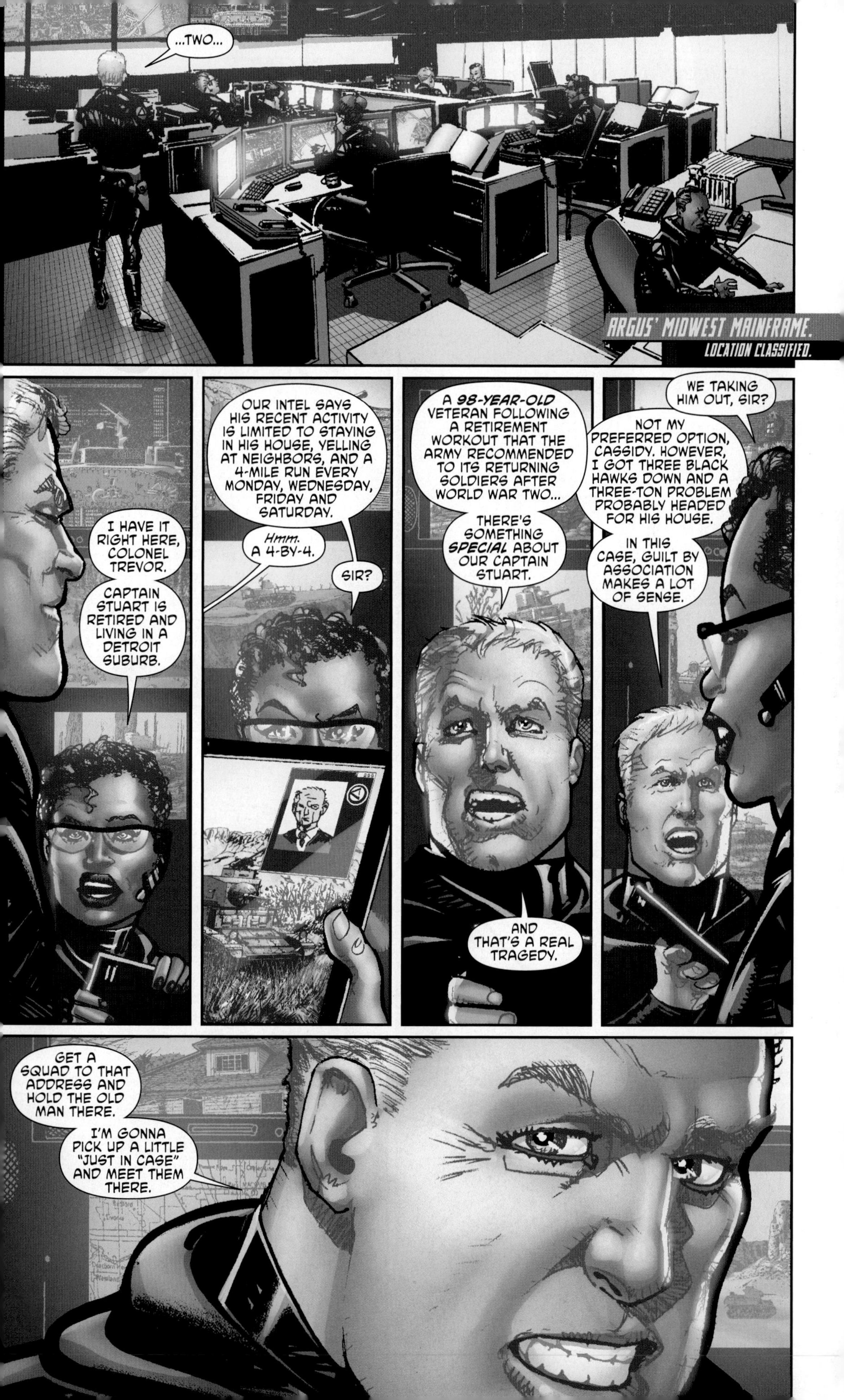

...TWO...
ARGUS' MIDWEST MAINFRAME.
LOCATION CLASSIFIED.
I HAVE IT RIGHT HERE, COLONEL TREVOR.
CAPTAIN STUART IS RETIRED AND LIVING IN A DETROIT SUBURB.
OUR INTEL SAYS HIS RECENT ACTIVITY IS LIMITED TO STAYING IN HIS HOUSE, YELLING AT NEIGHBORS, AND A 4-MILE RUN EVERY MONDAY, WEDNESDAY, FRIDAY AND SATURDAY.
Hmm. A 4-BY-4.
SIR?
A ***98-YEAR-OLD*** VETERAN FOLLOWING A RETIREMENT WORKOUT THAT THE ARMY RECOMMENDED TO ITS RETURNING SOLDIERS AFTER WORLD WAR TWO...
THERE'S SOMETHING ***SPECIAL*** ABOUT OUR CAPTAIN STUART.
AND THAT'S A REAL TRAGEDY.
WE TAKING HIM OUT, SIR?
NOT MY PREFERRED OPTION, CASSIDY. HOWEVER, I GOT THREE BLACK HAWKS DOWN AND A THREE-TON PROBLEM PROBABLY HEADED FOR HIS HOUSE.
IN THIS CASE, GUILT BY ASSOCIATION MAKES A LOT OF SENSE.
GET A SQUAD TO THAT ADDRESS AND HOLD THE OLD MAN THERE.
I'M GONNA PICK UP A LITTLE "JUST IN CASE" AND MEET THEM THERE.

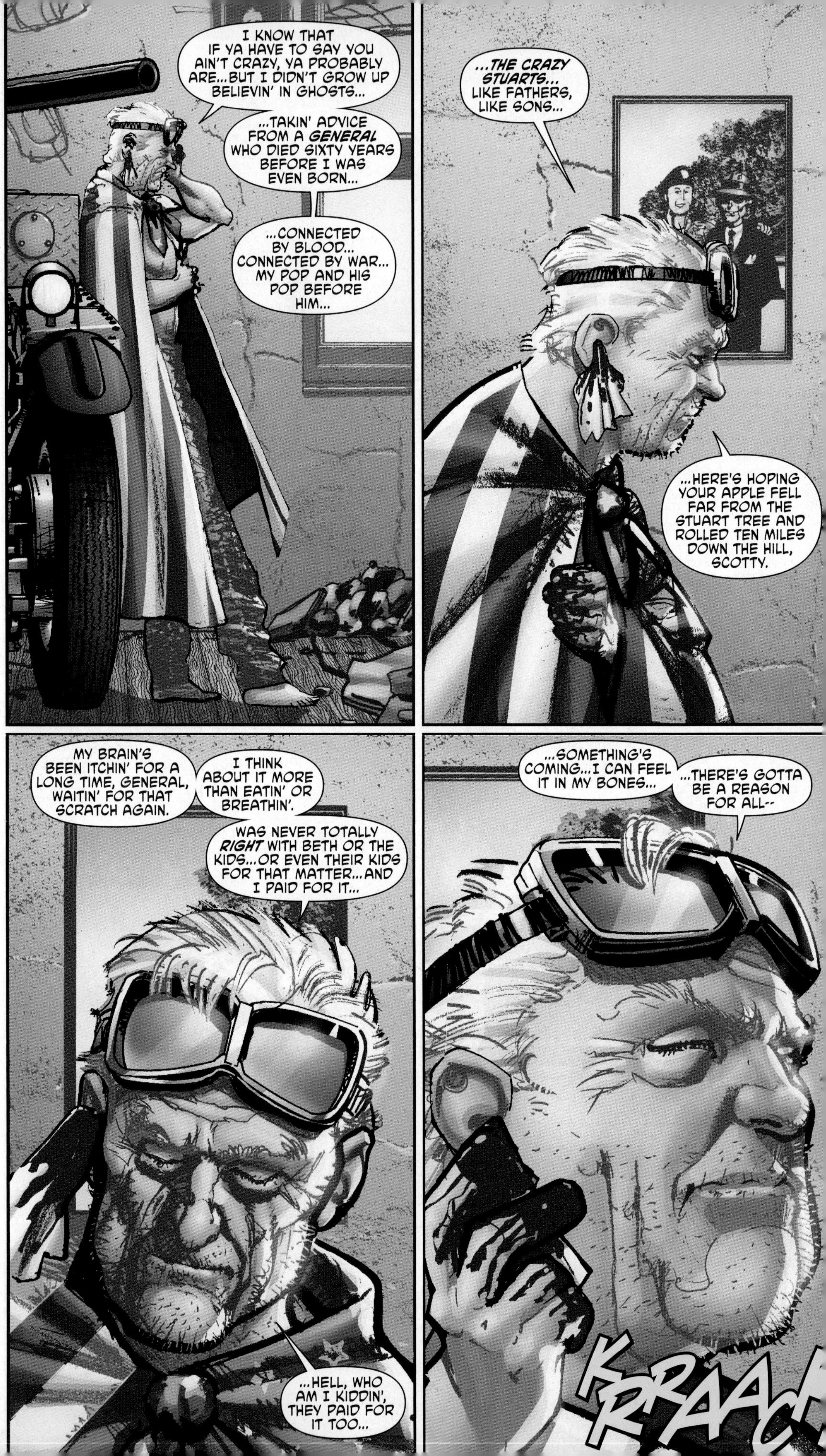
I KNOW THAT IF YA HAVE TO SAY YOU AIN'T CRAZY, YA PROBABLY ARE...BUT I DIDN'T GROW UP BELIEVIN' IN GHOSTS...
...TAKIN' ADVICE FROM A GENERAL WHO DIED SIXTY YEARS BEFORE I WAS EVEN BORN...
...CONNECTED BY BLOOD... CONNECTED BY WAR... MY POP AND HIS POP BEFORE HIM...
...THE CRAZY STUARTS... LIKE FATHERS, LIKE SONS...
...HERE'S HOPING YOUR APPLE FELL FAR FROM THE STUART TREE AND ROLLED TEN MILES DOWN THE HILL, SCOTTY.
MY BRAIN'S BEEN ITCHIN' FOR A LONG TIME, GENERAL, WAITIN' FOR THAT SCRATCH AGAIN.
I THINK ABOUT IT MORE THAN EATIN' OR BREATHIN'.
WAS NEVER TOTALLY RIGHT WITH BETH OR THE KIDS...OR EVEN THEIR KIDS FOR THAT MATTER...AND I PAID FOR IT...
...HELL, WHO AM I KIDDIN', THEY PAID FOR IT TOO...
...SOMETHING'S COMING...I CAN FEEL IT IN MY BONES...
...THERE'S GOTTA BE A REASON FOR ALL--
KRAAC

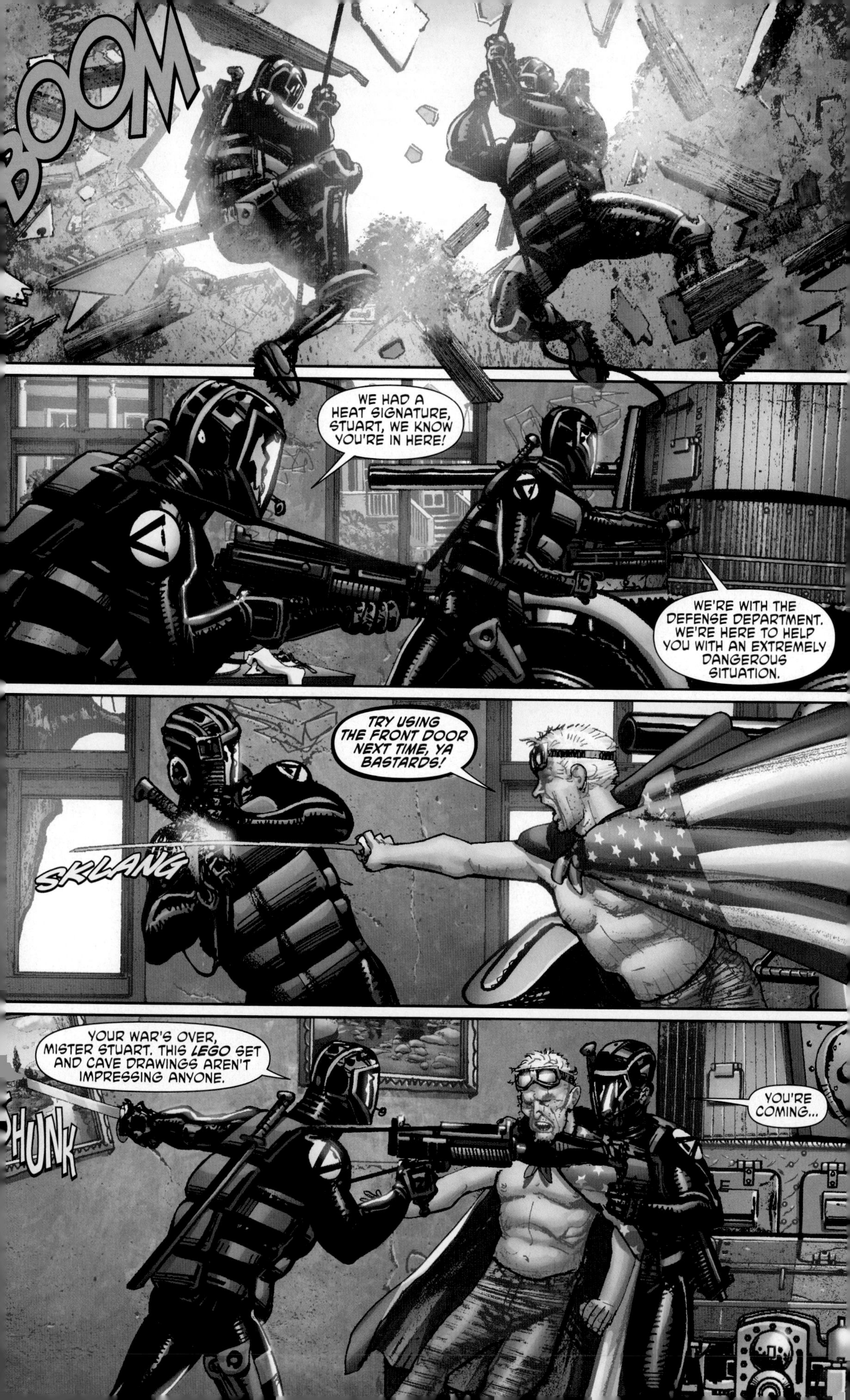
BOOM
WE HAD A HEAT SIGNATURE, STUART, WE KNOW YOU'RE IN HERE!
WE'RE WITH THE DEFENSE DEPARTMENT. WE'RE HERE TO HELP YOU WITH AN EXTREMELY DANGEROUS SITUATION.
TRY USING THE FRONT DOOR NEXT TIME, YA BASTARDS!
SKLANG
YOUR WAR'S OVER, MISTER STUART. THIS LEGO SET AND CAVE DRAWINGS AREN'T IMPRESSING ANYONE.
YOU'RE COMING...
THUNK

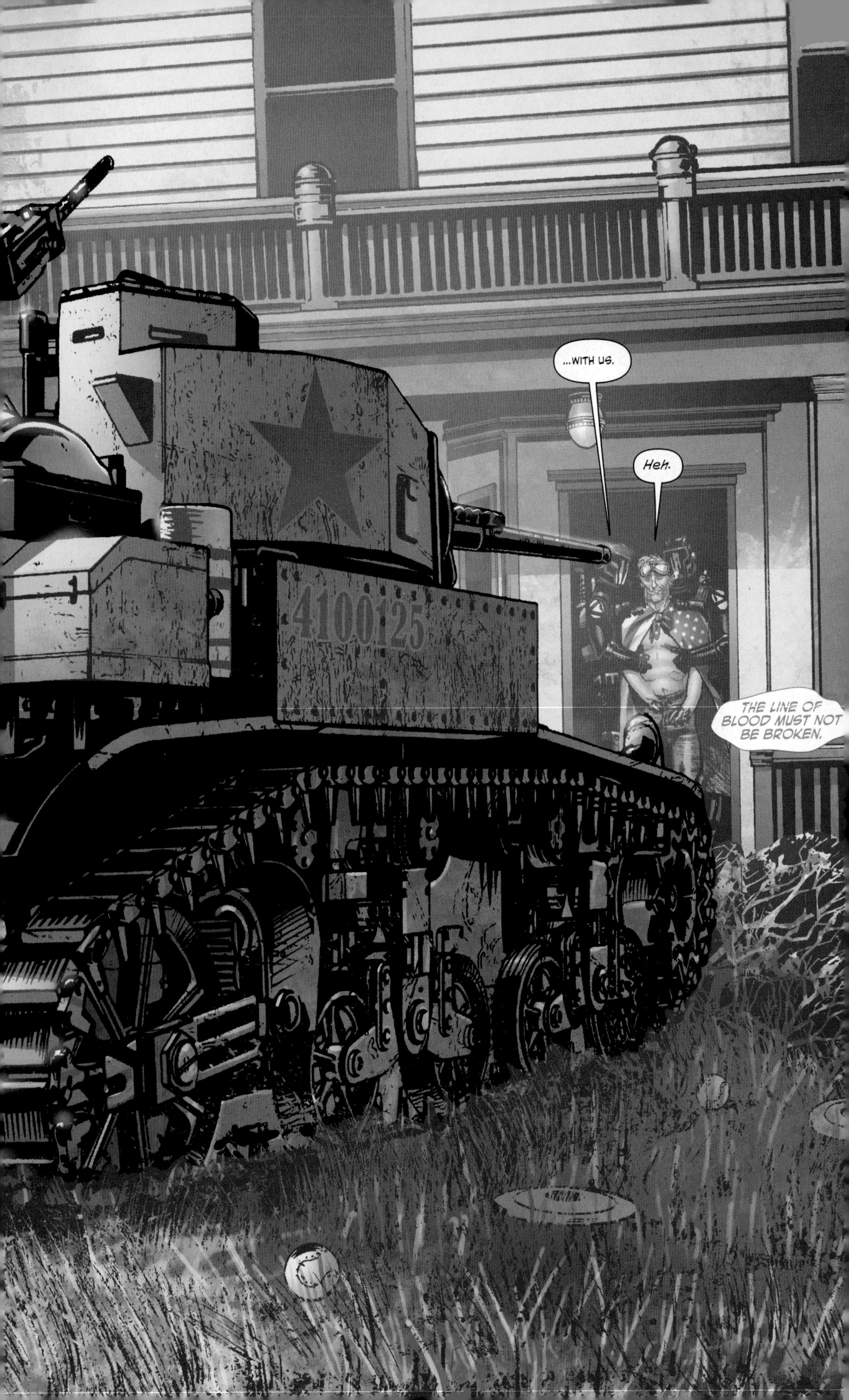
...WITH US.
Heh.
THE LINE OF BLOOD MUST NOT BE BROKEN.
4100125

AARGH

NGAAH

ZZZRAK!

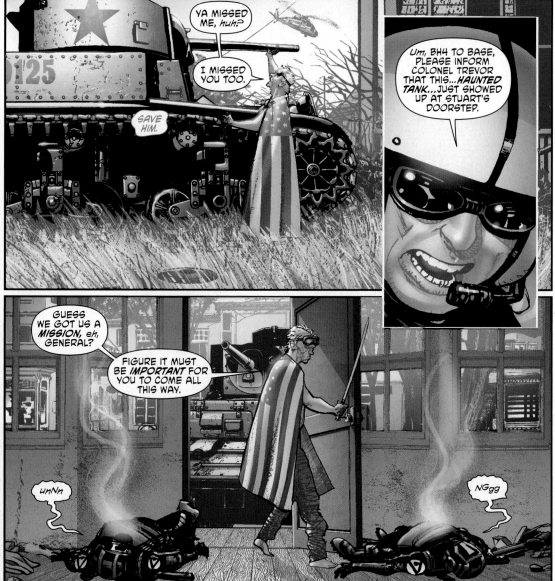

YA MISSED ME, huh?

I MISSED YOU TOO.

SAVE HIM.

Um, BH4 TO BASE, PLEASE INFORM COLONEL TREVOR THAT THIS...HAUNTED TANK...JUST SHOWED UP AT STUART'S DOORSTEP.

GUESS WE GOT US A MISSION, eh, GENERAL?

FIGURE IT MUST BE IMPORTANT FOR YOU TO COME ALL THIS WAY.

unNn

NGgg

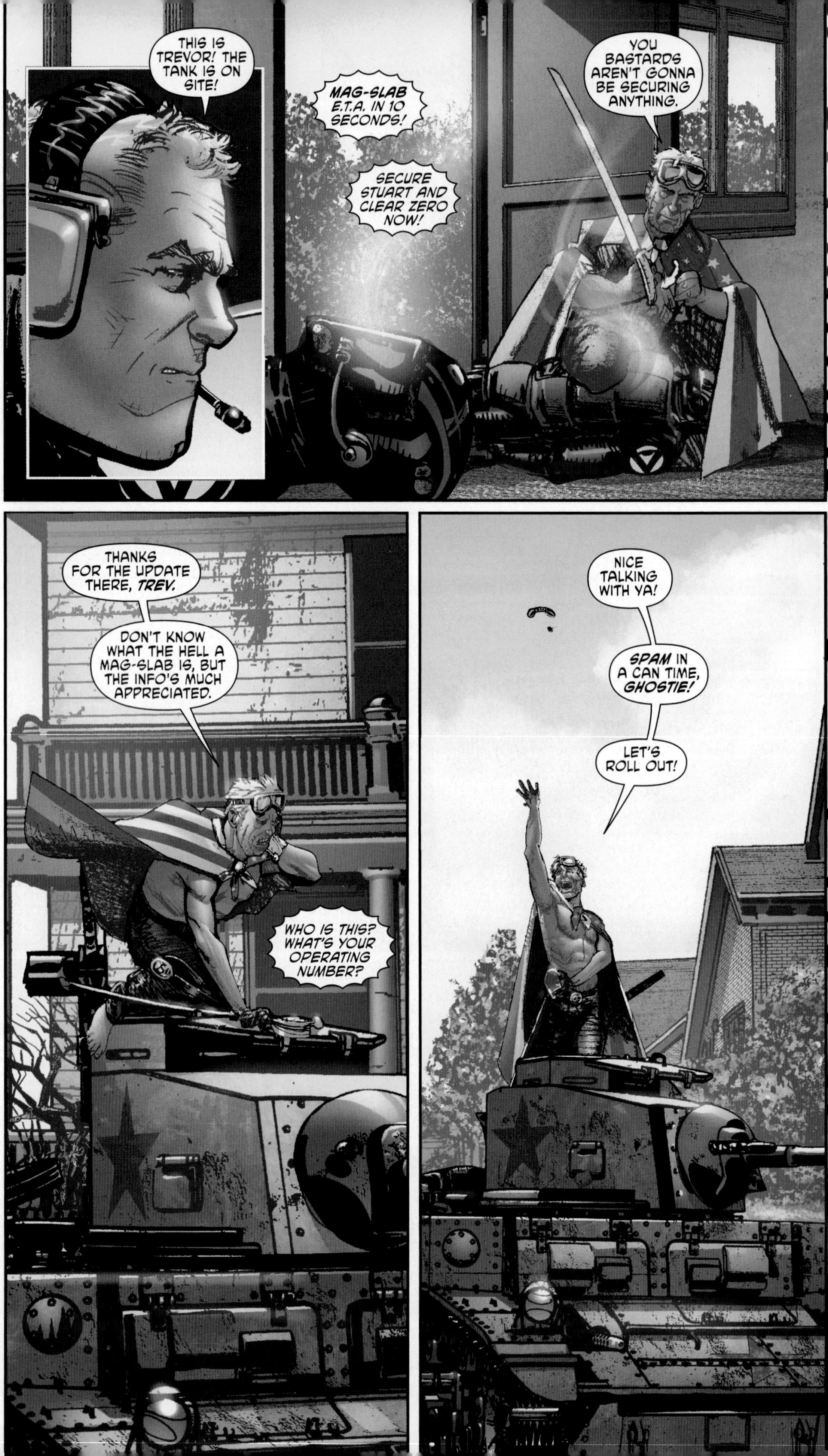

THIS IS TREVOR! THE TANK IS ON SITE!
MAG-SLAB E.T.A. IN 10 SECONDS!
SECURE STUART AND CLEAR ZERO NOW!
YOU BASTARDS AREN'T GONNA BE SECURING ANYTHING.
THANKS FOR THE UPDATE THERE, TREV.
DON'T KNOW WHAT THE HELL A MAG-SLAB IS, BUT THE INFO'S MUCH APPRECIATED.
WHO IS THIS? WHAT'S YOUR OPERATING NUMBER?
NICE TALKING WITH YA!
SPAM IN A CAN TIME, GHOSTIE!
LET'S ROLL OUT!

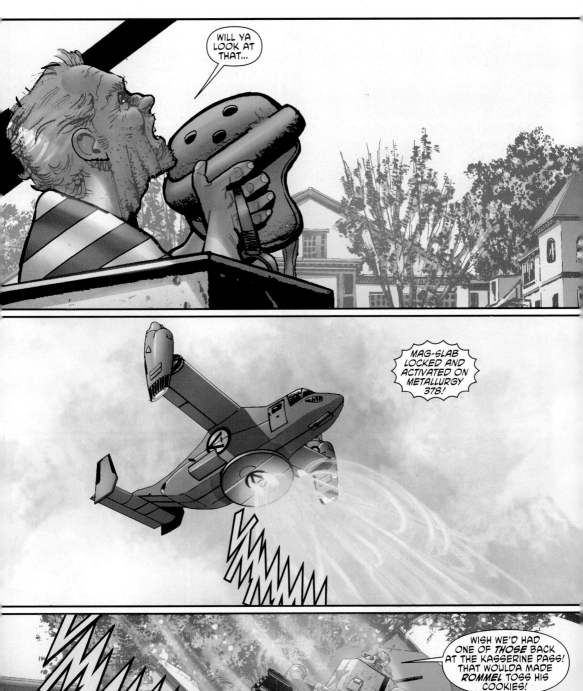

WILL YA LOOK AT THAT...

MAG-SLAB LOCKED AND ACTIVATED ON METALLURGY 378!

WISH WE'D HAD ONE OF *THOSE* BACK AT THE KASSERINE PASS! THAT WOULDA MADE *ROMMEL* TOSS HIS COOKIES!

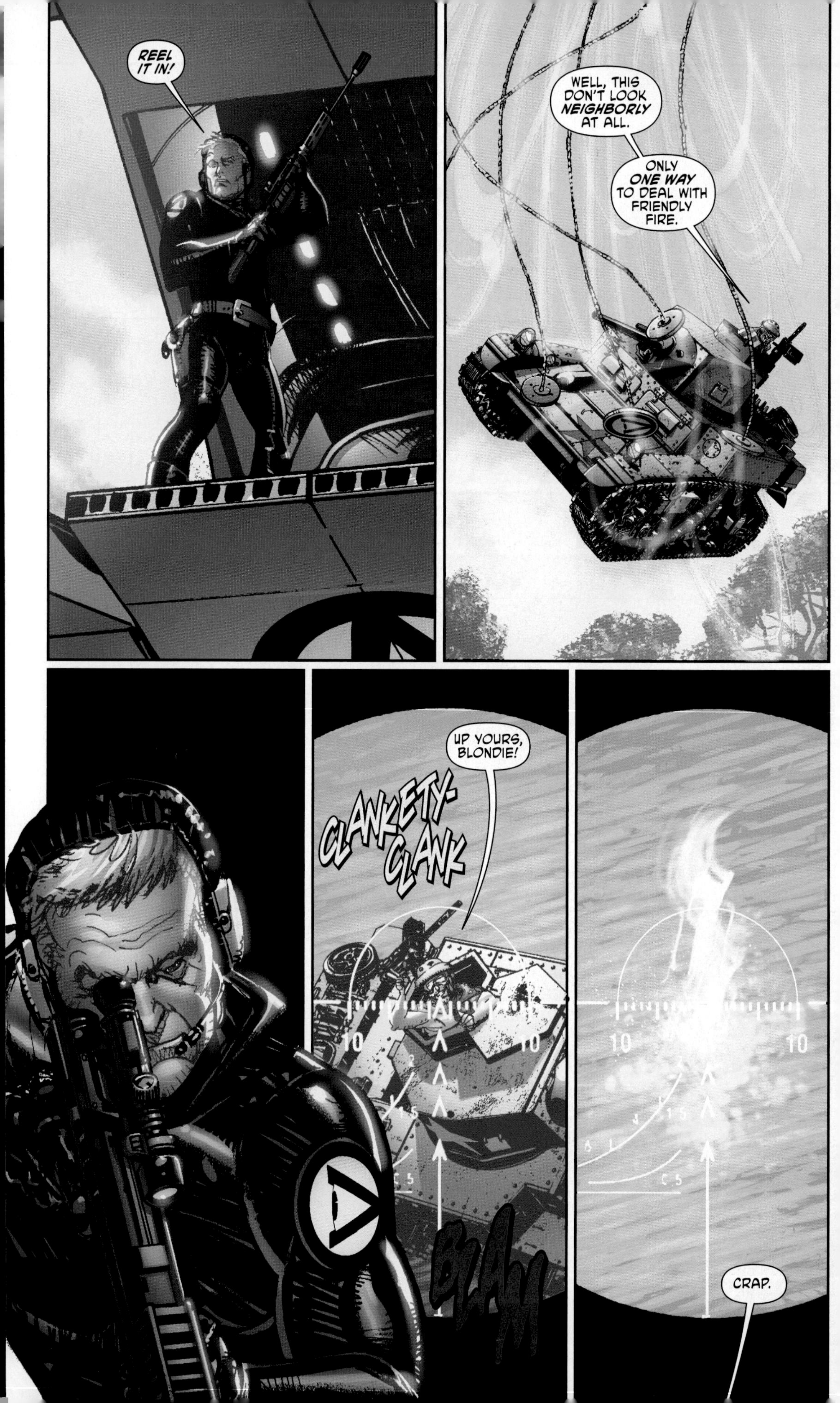
REEL IT IN!
WELL, THIS DON'T LOOK NEIGHBORLY AT ALL.
ONLY ONE WAY TO DEAL WITH FRIENDLY FIRE.
UP YOURS, BLONDIE!
CLANKETY-CLANK
BLAM
CRAP.

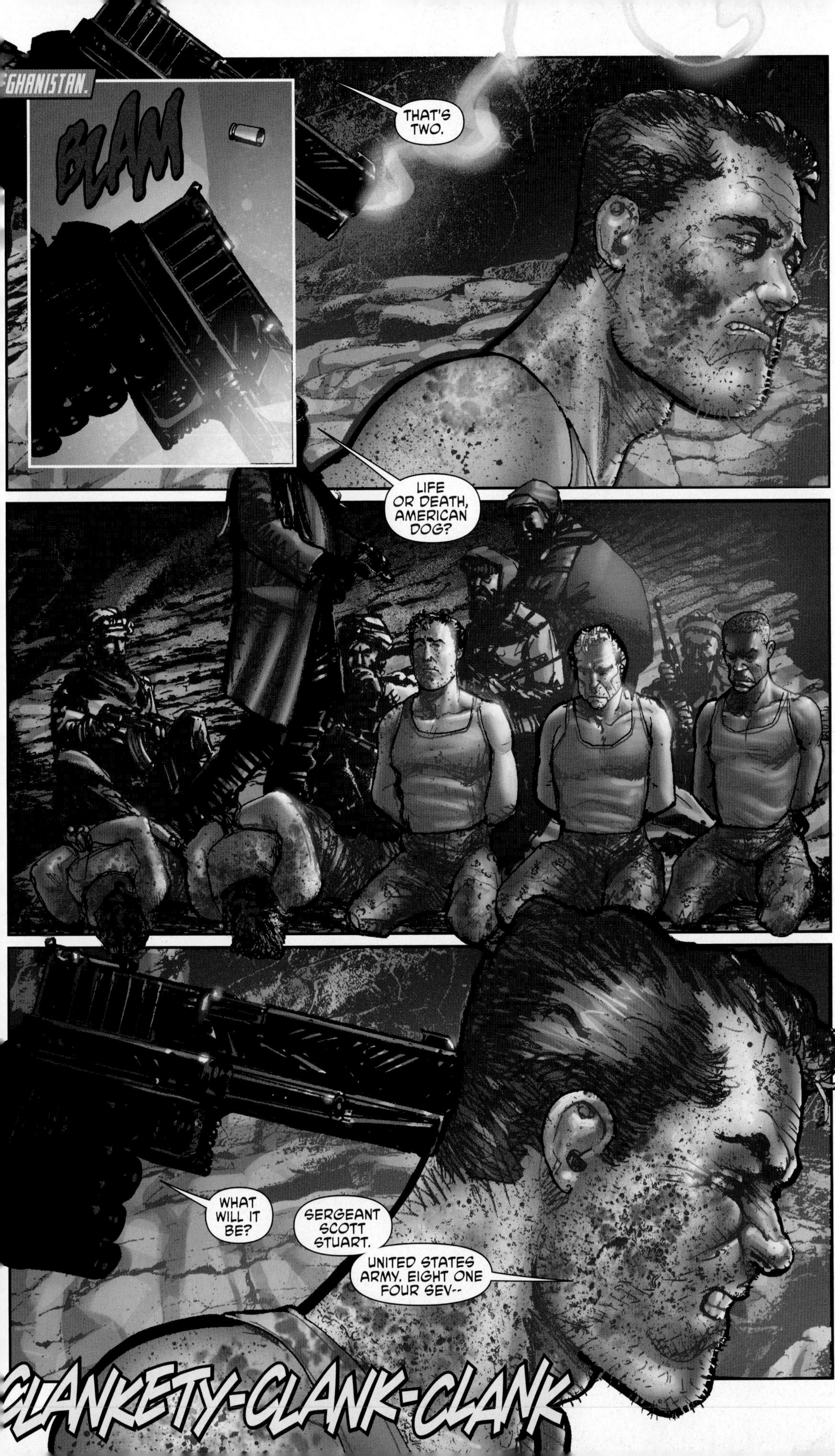
GHANISTAN.
BLAM
THAT'S TWO.
LIFE OR DEATH, AMERICAN DOG?
WHAT WILL IT BE?
SERGEANT SCOTT STUART.
UNITED STATES ARMY. EIGHT ONE FOUR SEV--
CLANKETY-CLANK-CLANK

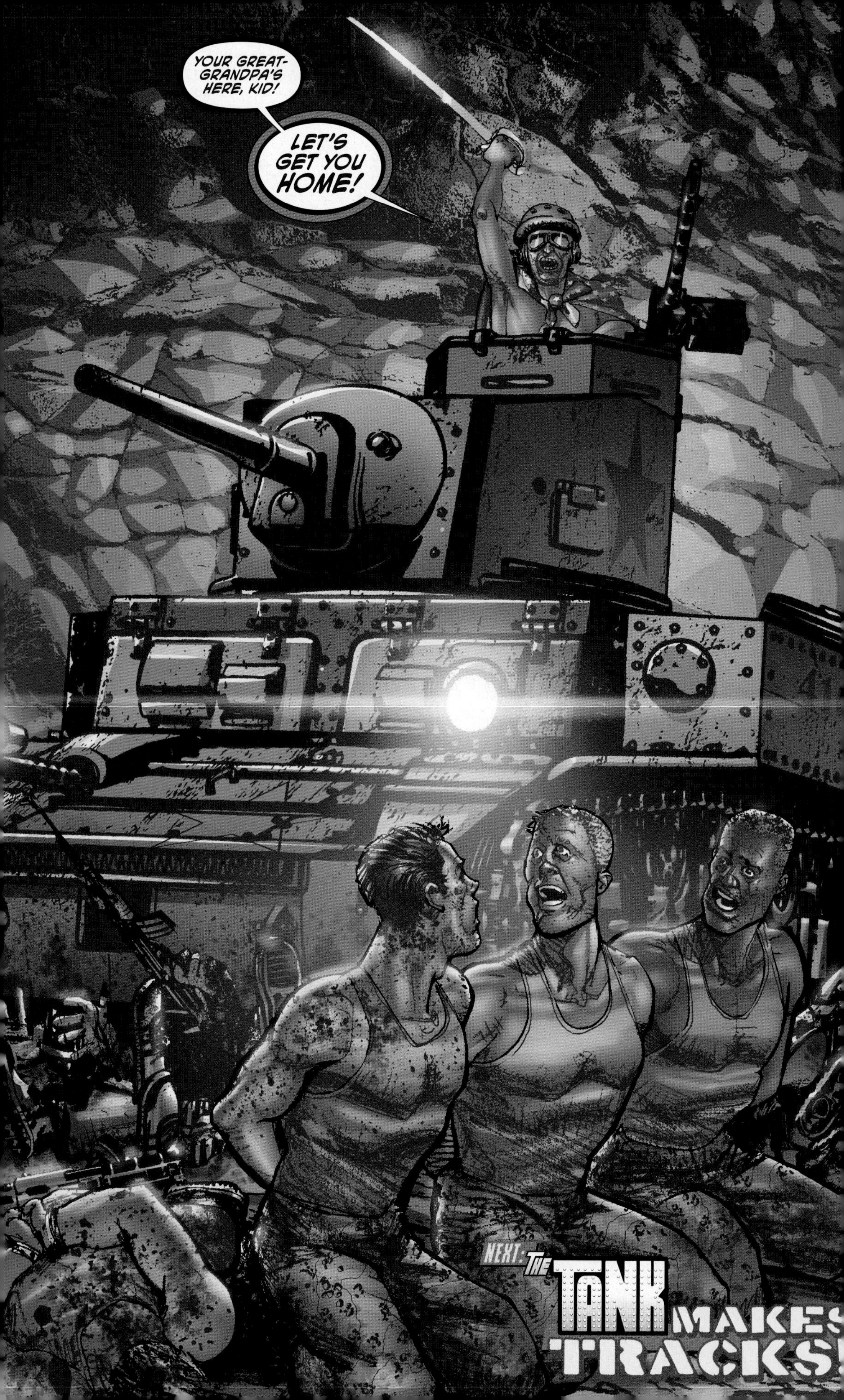
YOUR GREAT-GRANDPA'S HERE, KID!
LET'S GET YOU HOME!
41
NEXT: THE TANK MAKES TRACKS!

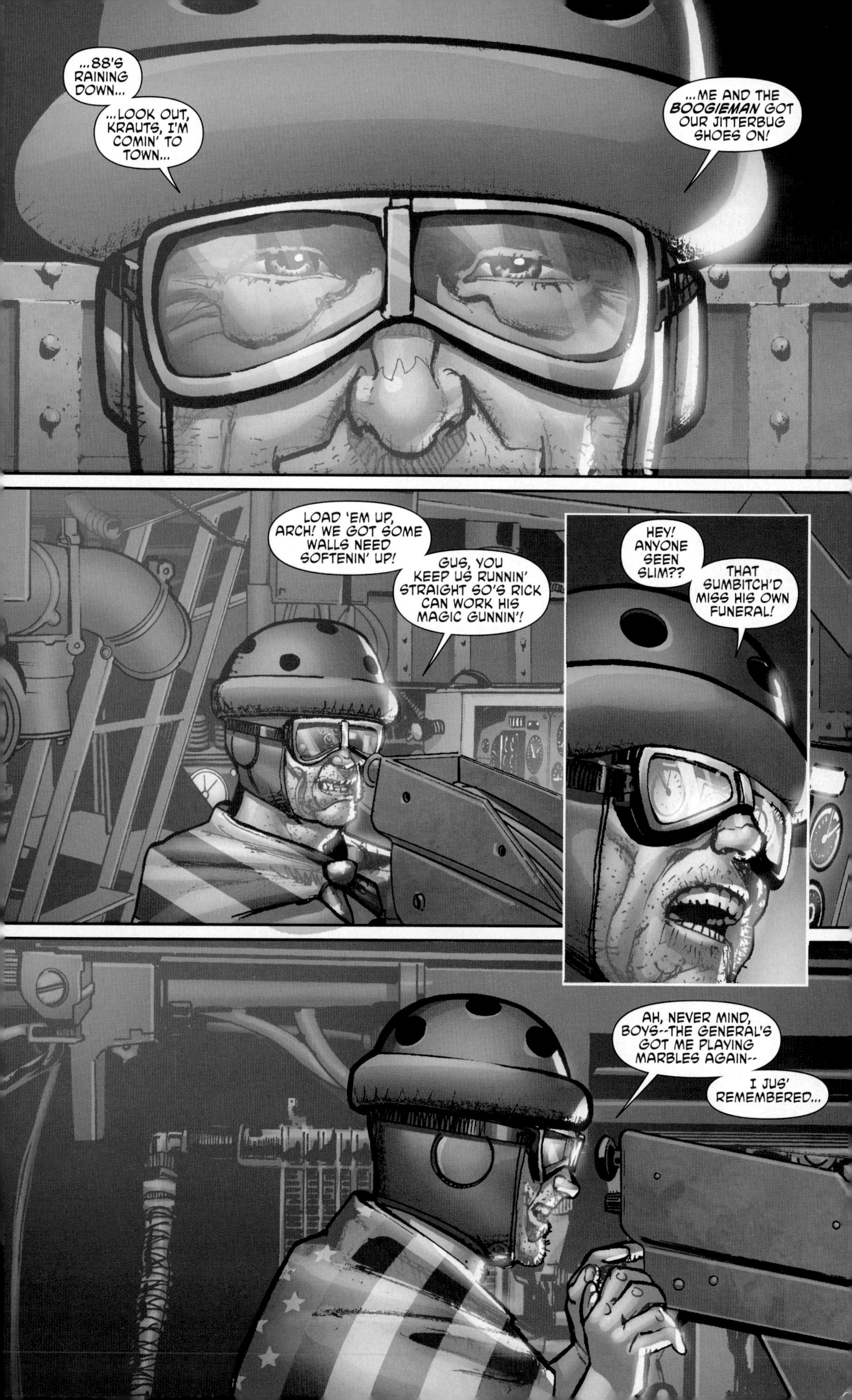
...88'S RAINING DOWN...
...LOOK OUT, KRAUTS, I'M COMIN' TO TOWN...
...ME AND THE *BOOGIEMAN* GOT OUR JITTERBUG SHOES ON!
LOAD 'EM UP, ARCH! WE GOT SOME WALLS NEED SOFTENIN' UP!
GUS, YOU KEEP US RUNNIN' STRAIGHT SO'S RICK CAN WORK HIS MAGIC GUNNIN'!
HEY! ANYONE SEEN SLIM??
THAT SUMBITCH'D MISS HIS OWN FUNERAL!
AH, NEVER MIND, BOYS--THE GENERAL'S GOT ME PLAYING MARBLES AGAIN--
I JUS' REMEMBERED...

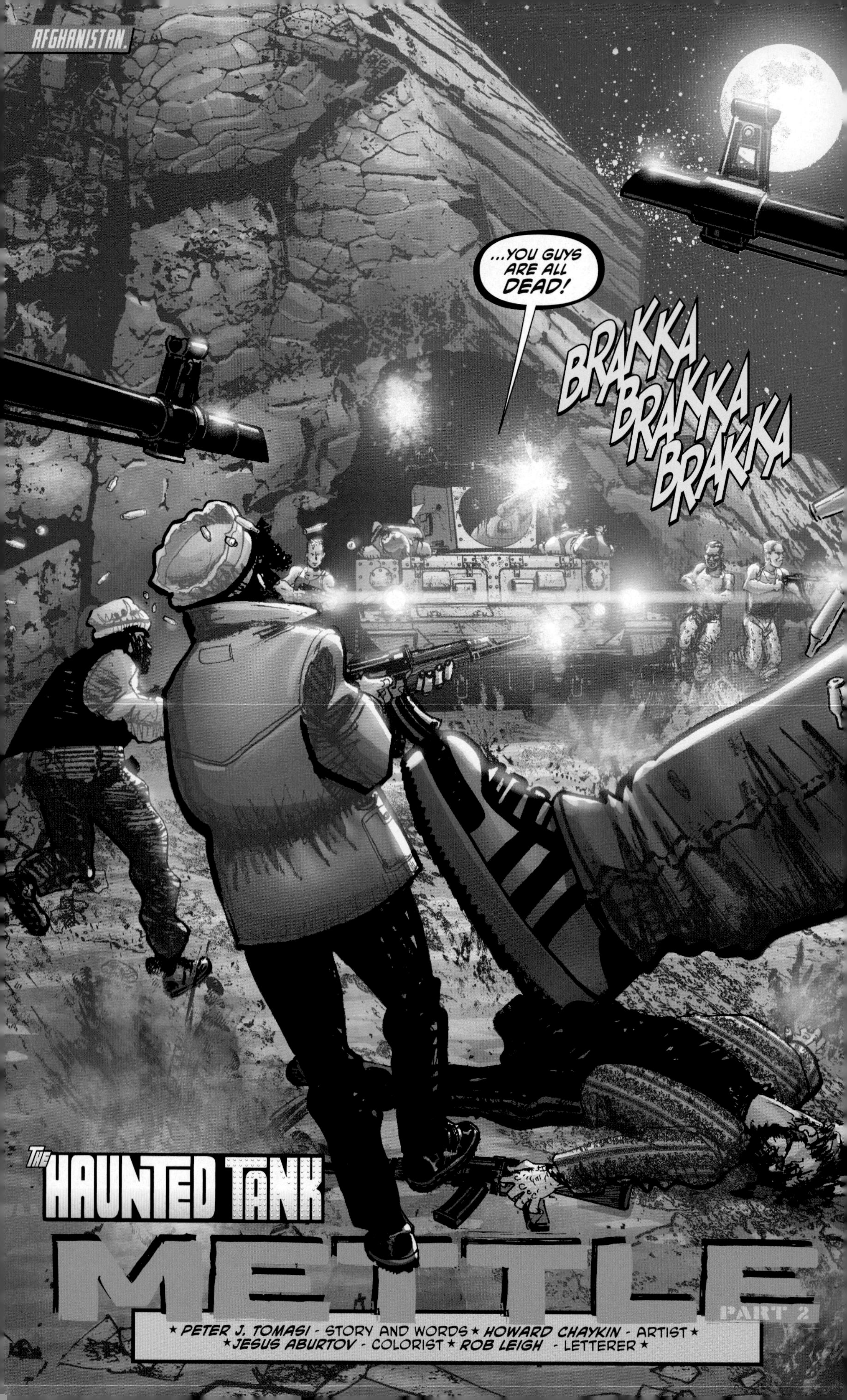
AFGHANISTAN.
...YOU GUYS ARE ALL DEAD!
BRAKKA BRAKKA BRAKKA
THE HAUNTED TANK
METTLE
PART 2
★PETER J. TOMASI - STORY AND WORDS★HOWARD CHAYKIN - ARTIST★
★JESUS ABURTOV - COLORIST★ROB LEIGH - LETTERER★

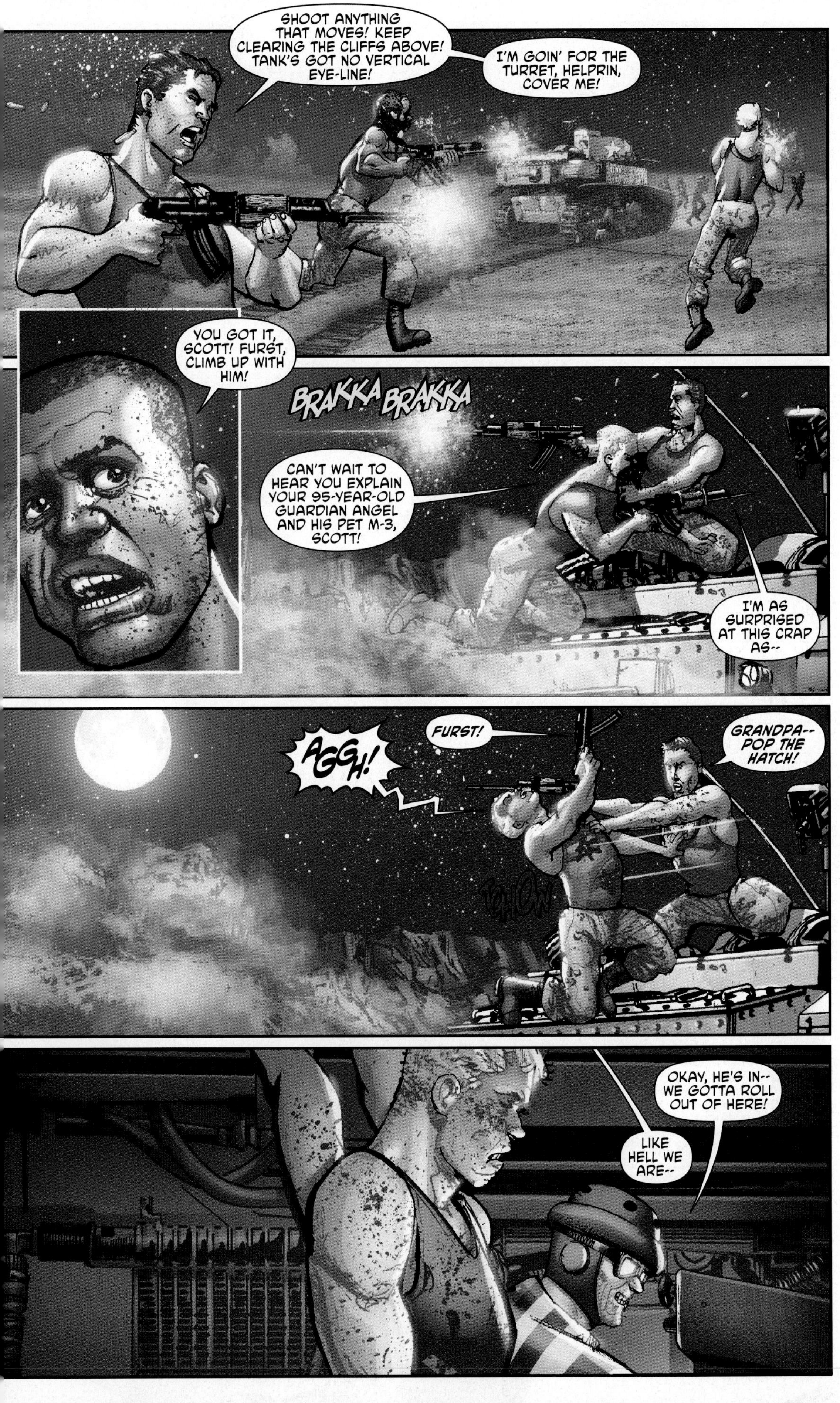
SHOOT ANYTHING THAT MOVES! KEEP CLEARING THE CLIFFS ABOVE! TANK'S GOT NO VERTICAL EYE-LINE!
I'M GOIN' FOR THE TURRET, HELPRIN, COVER ME!
YOU GOT IT, SCOTT! FURST, CLIMB UP WITH HIM!
BRAKKA BRAKKA
CAN'T WAIT TO HEAR YOU EXPLAIN YOUR 95-YEAR-OLD GUARDIAN ANGEL AND HIS PET M-3, SCOTT!
I'M AS SURPRISED AT THIS CRAP AS--
AGGH!
FURST!
GRANDPA--POP THE HATCH!
TCHOW
OKAY, HE'S IN--WE GOTTA ROLL OUT OF HERE!
LIKE HELL WE ARE--

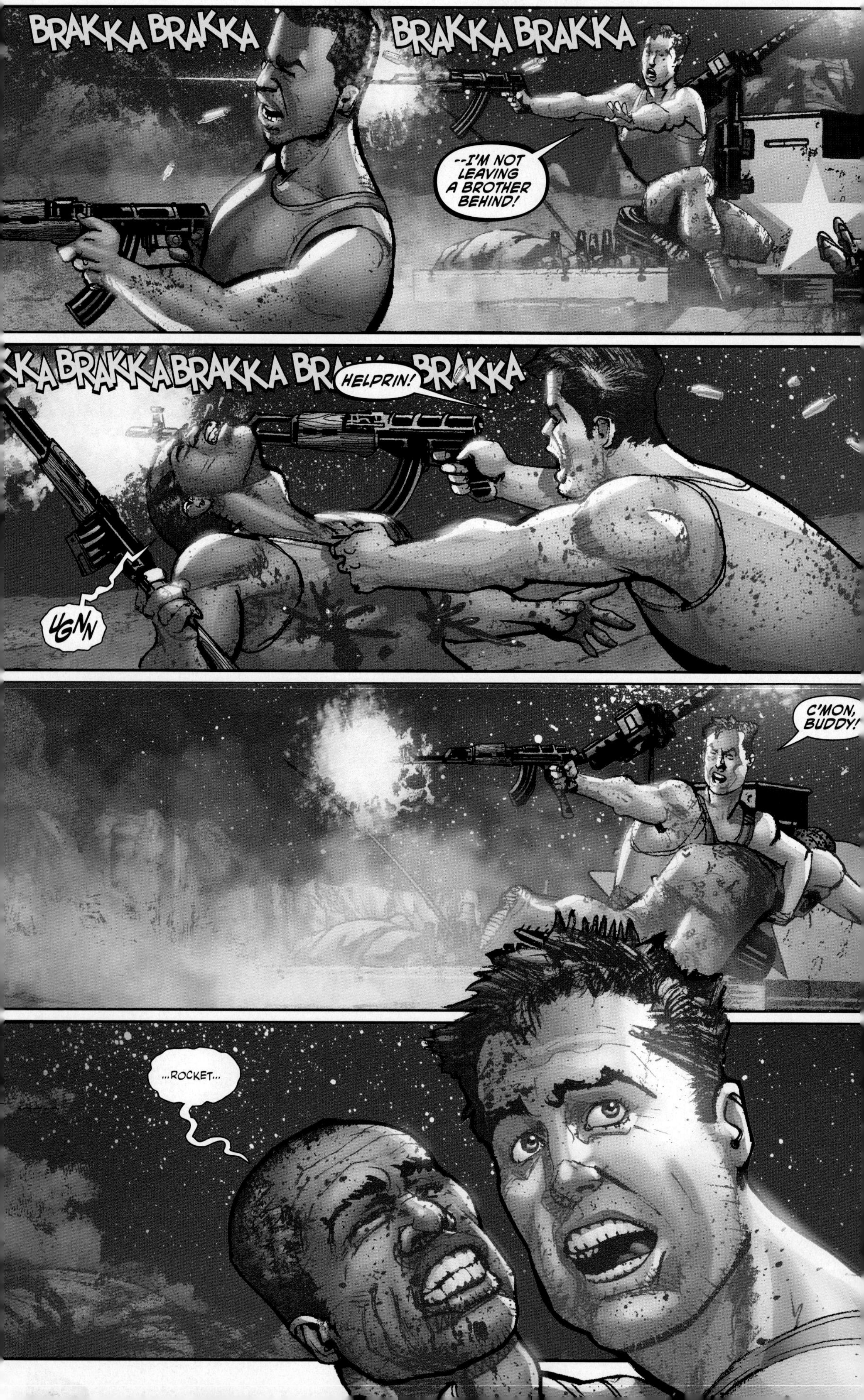
BRAKKA BRAKKA
BRAKKA BRAKKA
--I'M NOT LEAVING A BROTHER BEHIND!
KKA BRAKKA BRAKKA BR
HELPRIN!
BRAKKA
UGNN
C'MON, BUDDY!
...ROCKET...

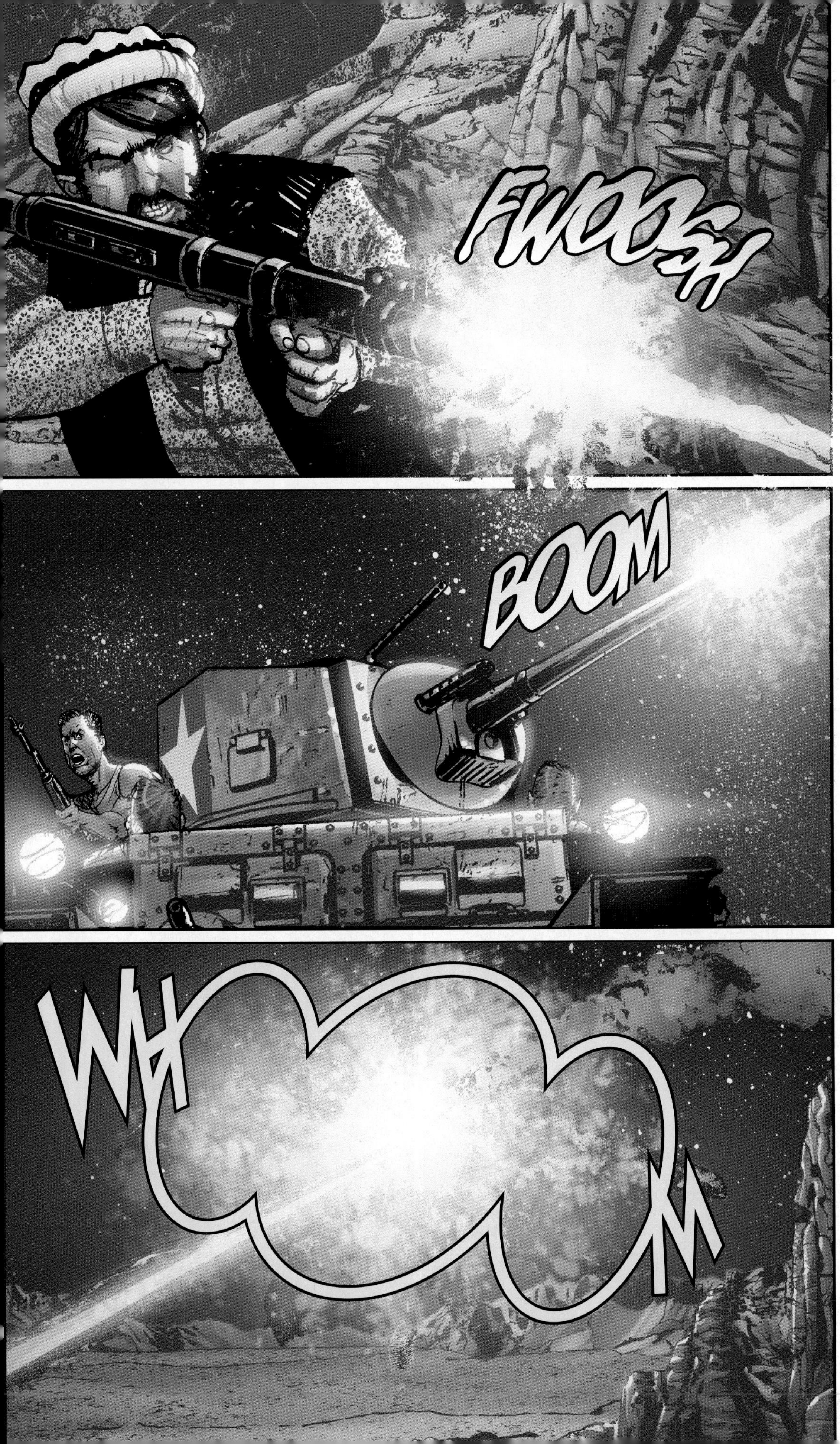
FWOOSH
BOOM
WHOOM

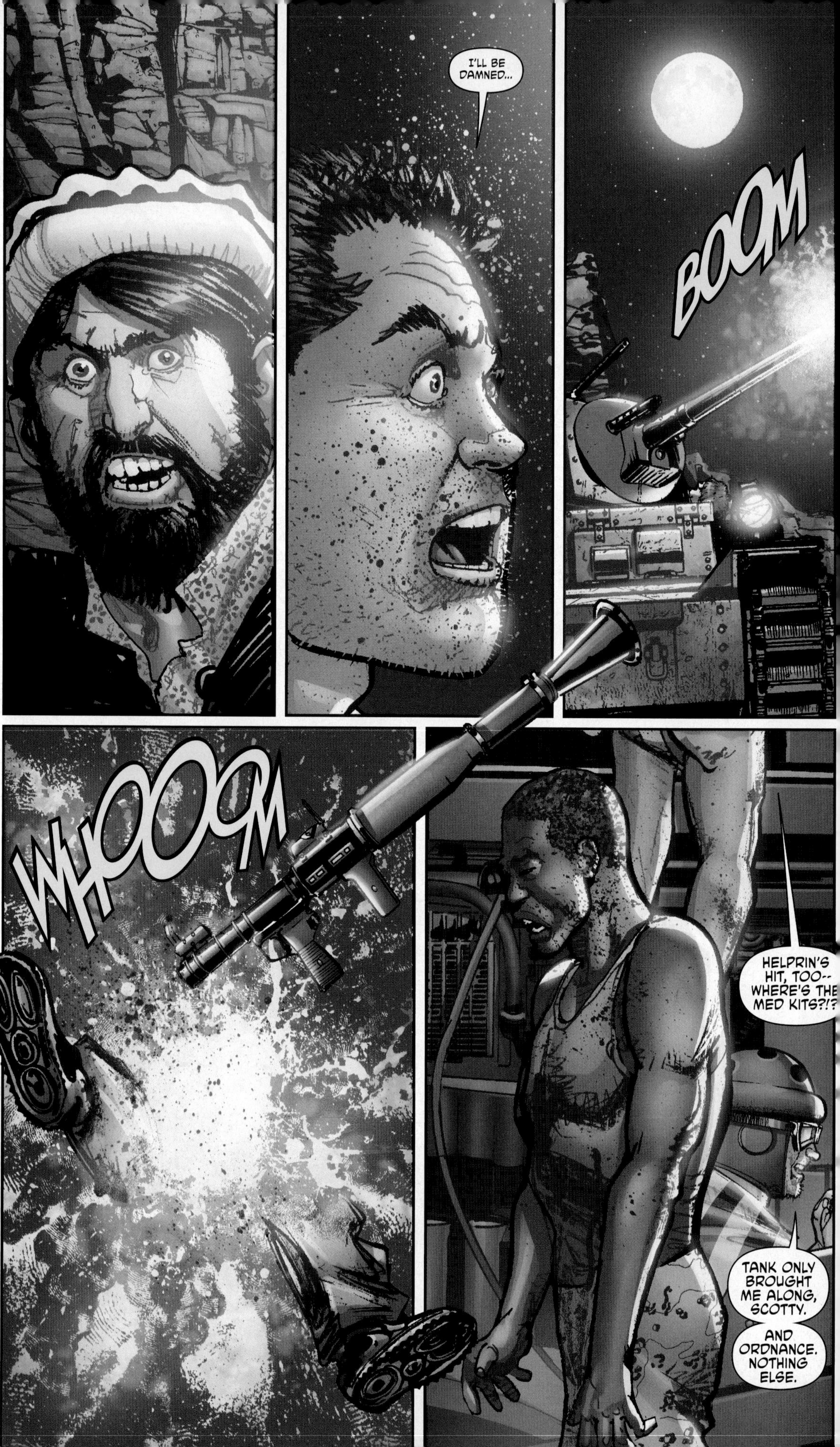
I'LL BE DAMNED...
BOOM
WHOOM
HELPRIN'S HIT, TOO-- WHERE'S THE MED KITS?!?
TANK ONLY BROUGHT ME ALONG, SCOTTY.
AND ORDNANCE. NOTHING ELSE.

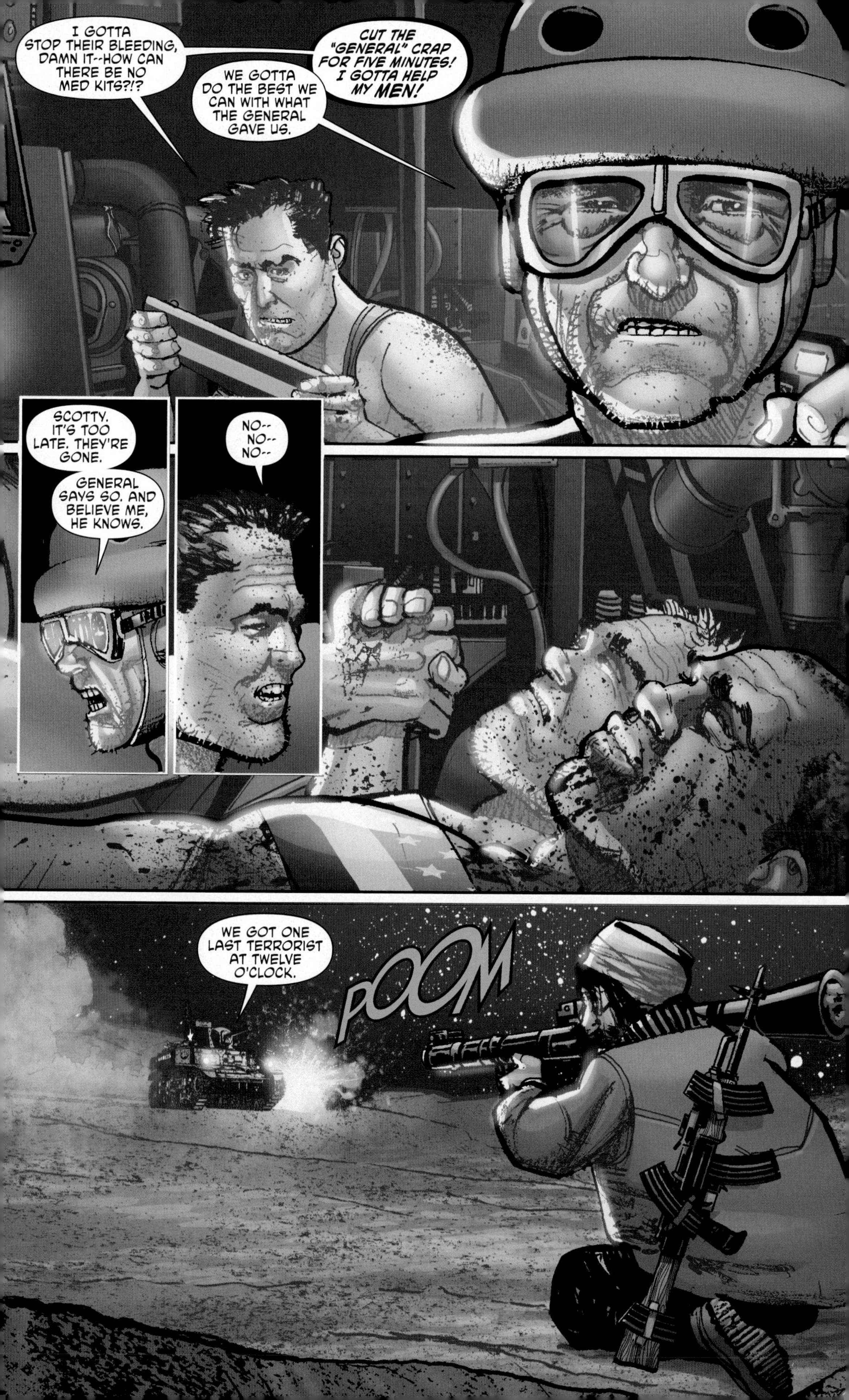
I GOTTA STOP THEIR BLEEDING, DAMN IT--HOW CAN THERE BE NO MED KITS?!?
WE GOTTA DO THE BEST WE CAN WITH WHAT THE GENERAL GAVE US.
CUT THE "GENERAL" CRAP FOR FIVE MINUTES! I GOTTA HELP MY MEN!
SCOTTY. IT'S TOO LATE. THEY'RE GONE.
GENERAL SAYS SO. AND BELIEVE ME, HE KNOWS.
NO-- NO-- NO--
WE GOT ONE LAST TERRORIST AT TWELVE O'CLOCK.
POOM

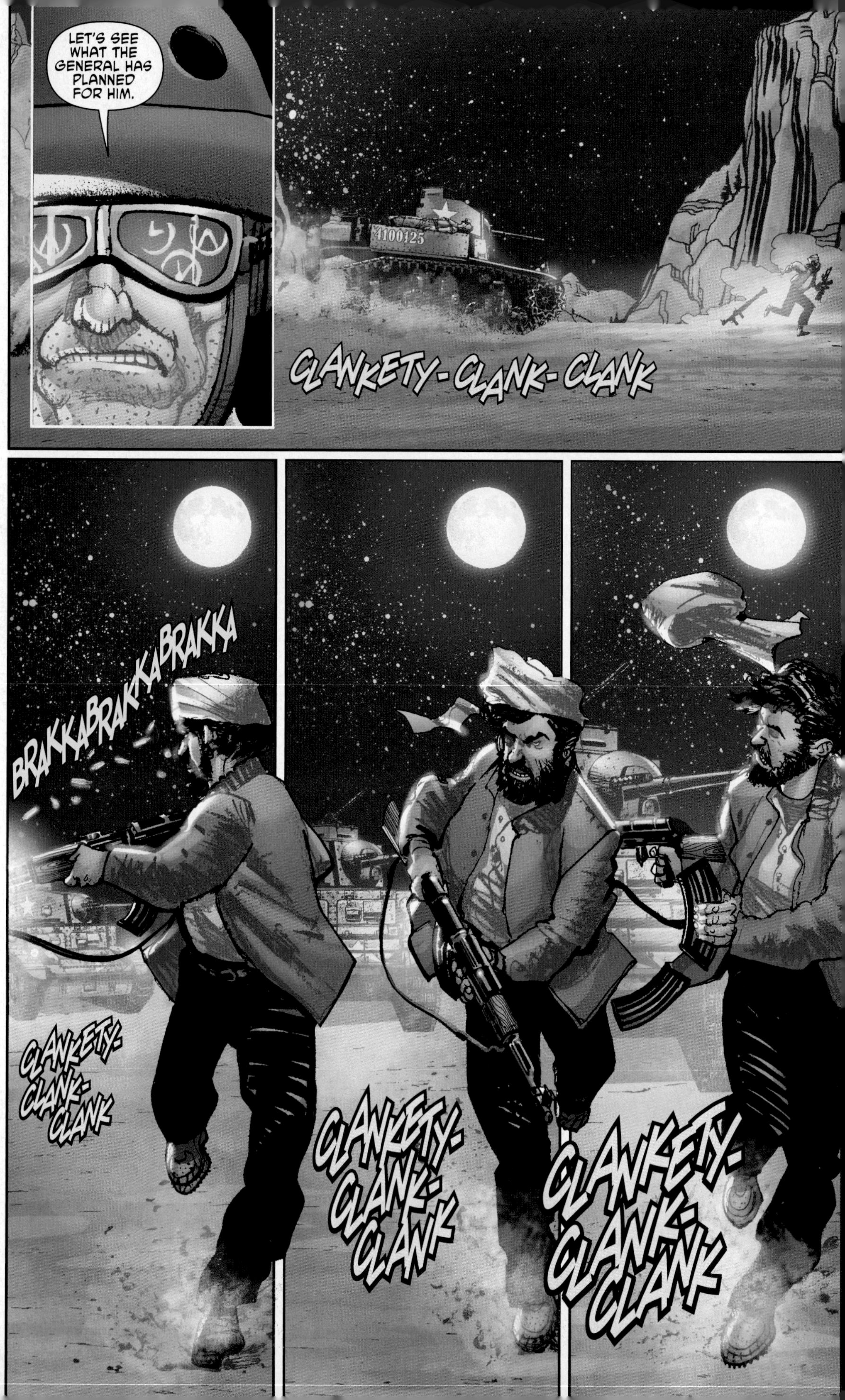
LET'S SEE WHAT THE GENERAL HAS PLANNED FOR HIM.
4100125
CLANKETY- CLANK- CLANK
BRAKKABRAKKABRAKKA
CLANKETY-CLANK-CLANK
CLANKETY-CLANK-CLANK
CLANKETY-CLANK-CLANK

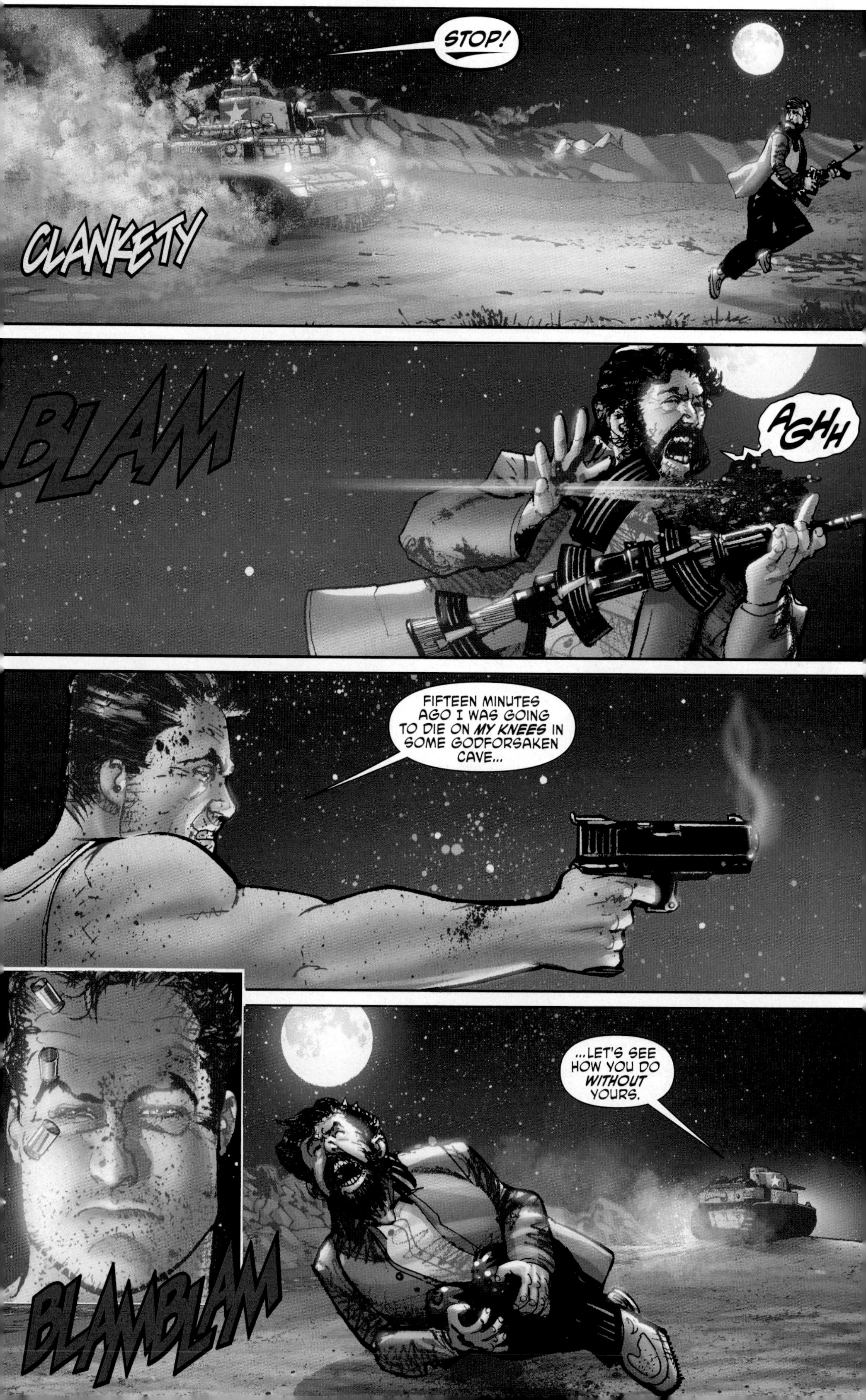
STOP!
CLANKETY
BLAM
AGHH
FIFTEEN MINUTES AGO I WAS GOING TO DIE ON MY KNEES IN SOME GODFORSAKEN CAVE...
...LET'S SEE HOW YOU DO WITHOUT YOURS.
BLAMBLAM

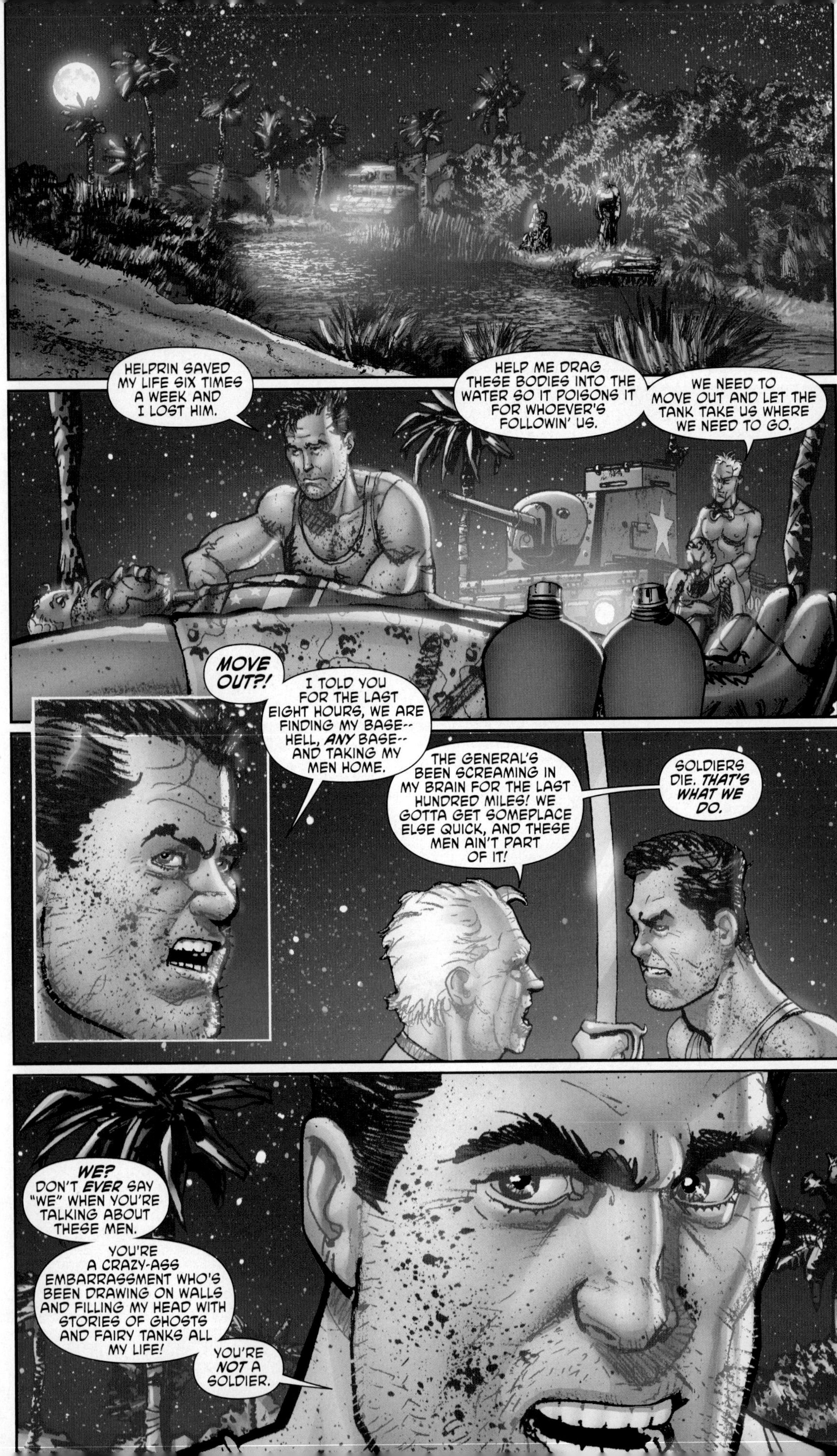
HELPRIN SAVED MY LIFE SIX TIMES A WEEK AND I LOST HIM.
HELP ME DRAG THESE BODIES INTO THE WATER SO IT POISONS IT FOR WHOEVER'S FOLLOWIN' US.
WE NEED TO MOVE OUT AND LET THE TANK TAKE US WHERE WE NEED TO GO.
MOVE OUT?!
I TOLD YOU FOR THE LAST EIGHT HOURS, WE ARE FINDING MY BASE-- HELL, ANY BASE-- AND TAKING MY MEN HOME.
THE GENERAL'S BEEN SCREAMING IN MY BRAIN FOR THE LAST HUNDRED MILES! WE GOTTA GET SOMEPLACE ELSE QUICK, AND THESE MEN AIN'T PART OF IT!
SOLDIERS DIE. THAT'S WHAT WE DO.
WE? DON'T EVER SAY "WE" WHEN YOU'RE TALKING ABOUT THESE MEN.
YOU'RE A CRAZY-ASS EMBARRASSMENT WHO'S BEEN DRAWING ON WALLS AND FILLING MY HEAD WITH STORIES OF GHOSTS AND FAIRY TANKS ALL MY LIFE!
YOU'RE NOT A SOLDIER.

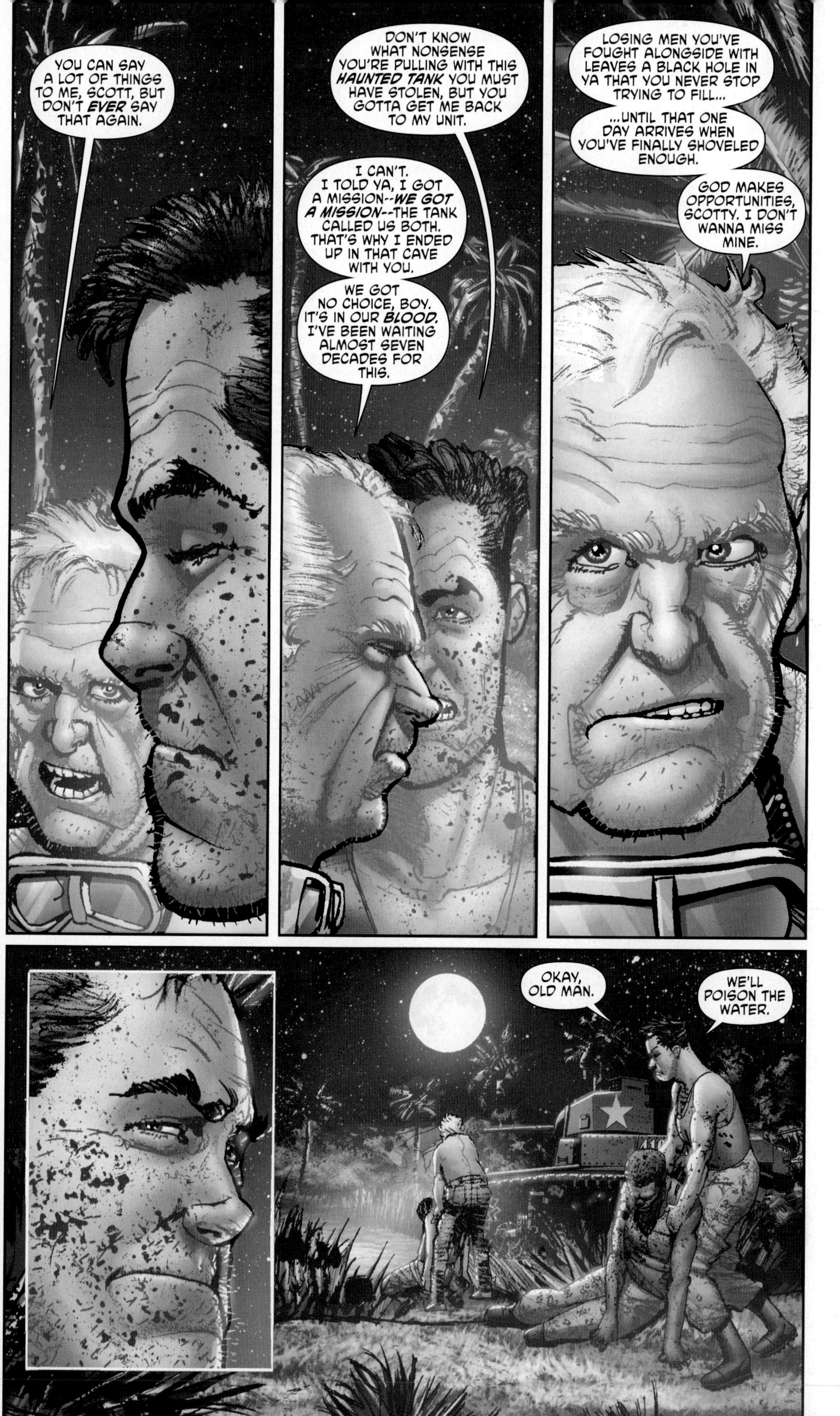
YOU CAN SAY A LOT OF THINGS TO ME, SCOTT, BUT DON'T EVER SAY THAT AGAIN.
DON'T KNOW WHAT NONSENSE YOU'RE PULLING WITH THIS HAUNTED TANK YOU MUST HAVE STOLEN, BUT YOU GOTTA GET ME BACK TO MY UNIT.
I CAN'T. I TOLD YA, I GOT A MISSION--WE GOT A MISSION--THE TANK CALLED US BOTH. THAT'S WHY I ENDED UP IN THAT CAVE WITH YOU.
WE GOT NO CHOICE, BOY. IT'S IN OUR BLOOD. I'VE BEEN WAITING ALMOST SEVEN DECADES FOR THIS.
LOSING MEN YOU'VE FOUGHT ALONGSIDE WITH LEAVES A BLACK HOLE IN YA THAT YOU NEVER STOP TRYING TO FILL...
...UNTIL THAT ONE DAY ARRIVES WHEN YOU'VE FINALLY SHOVELED ENOUGH.
GOD MAKES OPPORTUNITIES, SCOTTY. I DON'T WANNA MISS MINE.
OKAY, OLD MAN.
WE'LL POISON THE WATER.

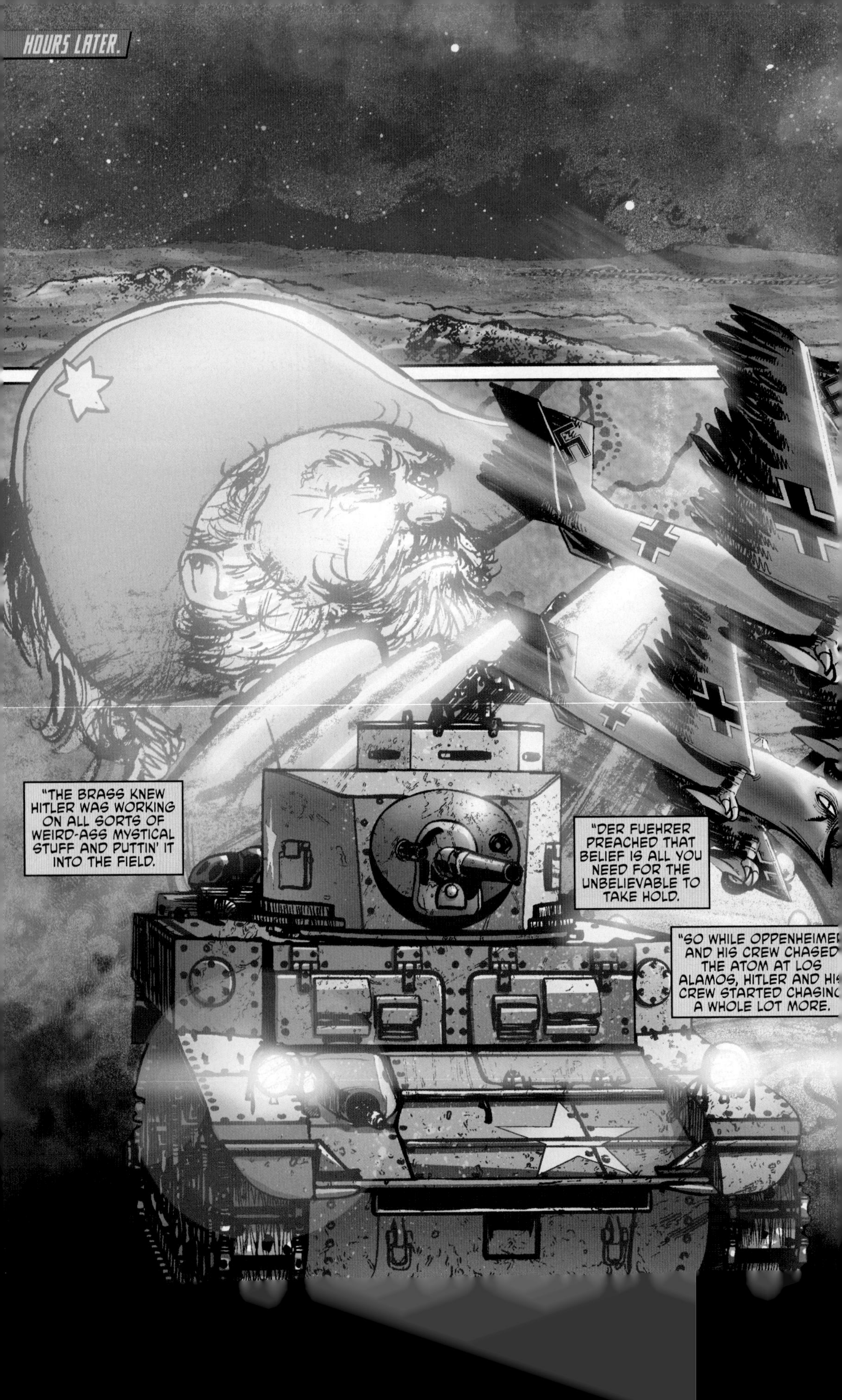
HOURS LATER.
"THE BRASS KNEW HITLER WAS WORKING ON ALL SORTS OF WEIRD-ASS MYSTICAL STUFF AND PUTTIN' IT INTO THE FIELD.
"DER FUEHRER PREACHED THAT BELIEF IS ALL YOU NEED FOR THE UNBELIEVABLE TO TAKE HOLD.
"SO WHILE OPPENHEIMER AND HIS CREW CHASED THE ATOM AT LOS ALAMOS, HITLER AND HIS CREW STARTED CHASING A WHOLE LOT MORE.

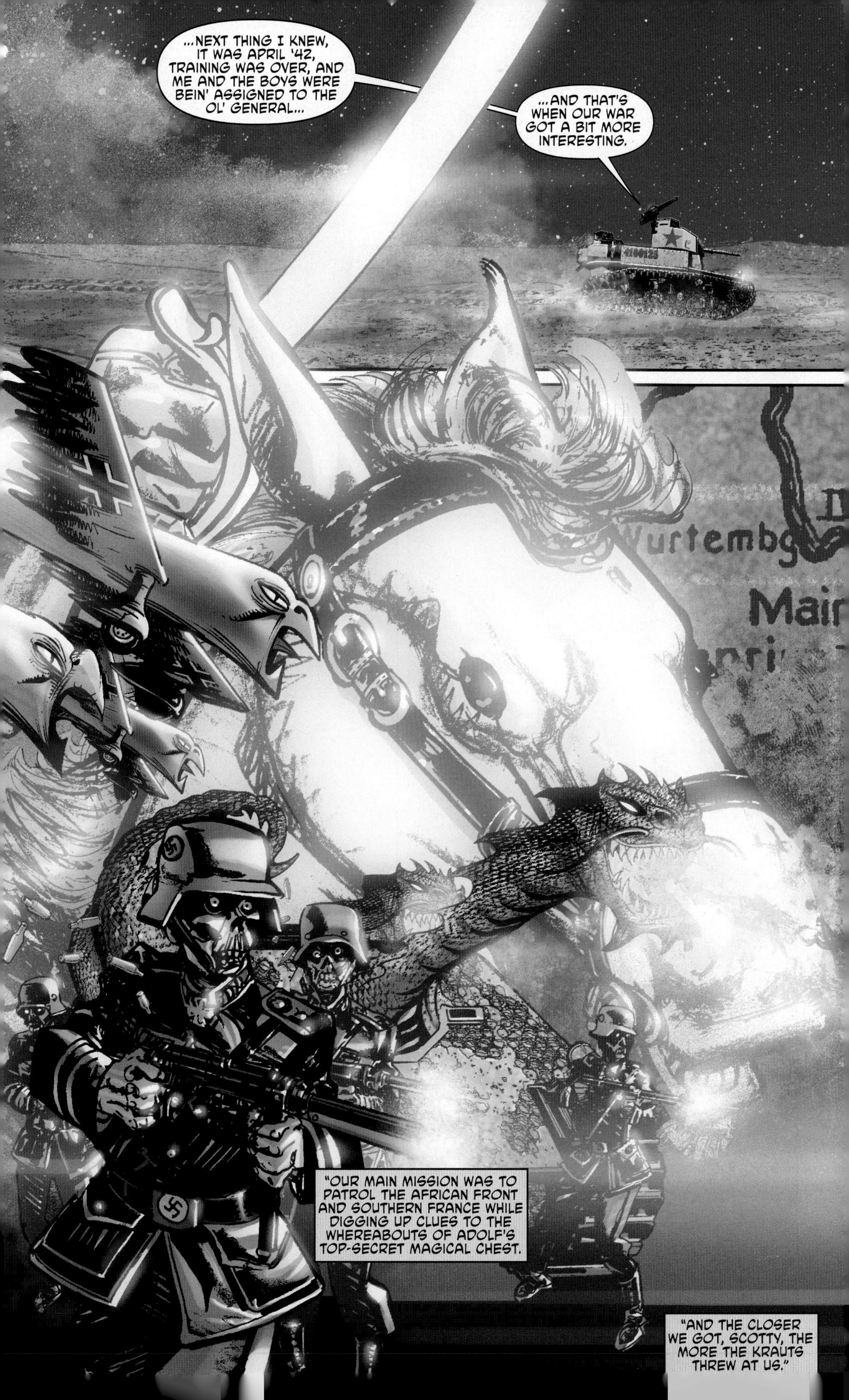
...NEXT THING I KNEW, IT WAS APRIL '42, TRAINING WAS OVER, AND ME AND THE BOYS WERE BEIN' ASSIGNED TO THE OL' GENERAL...
...AND THAT'S WHEN OUR WAR GOT A BIT MORE INTERESTING.
Wurtembg
Main
"OUR MAIN MISSION WAS TO PATROL THE AFRICAN FRONT AND SOUTHERN FRANCE WHILE DIGGING UP CLUES TO THE WHEREABOUTS OF ADOLF'S TOP-SECRET MAGICAL CHEST.
"AND THE CLOSER WE GOT, SCOTTY, THE MORE THE KRAUTS THREW AT US."

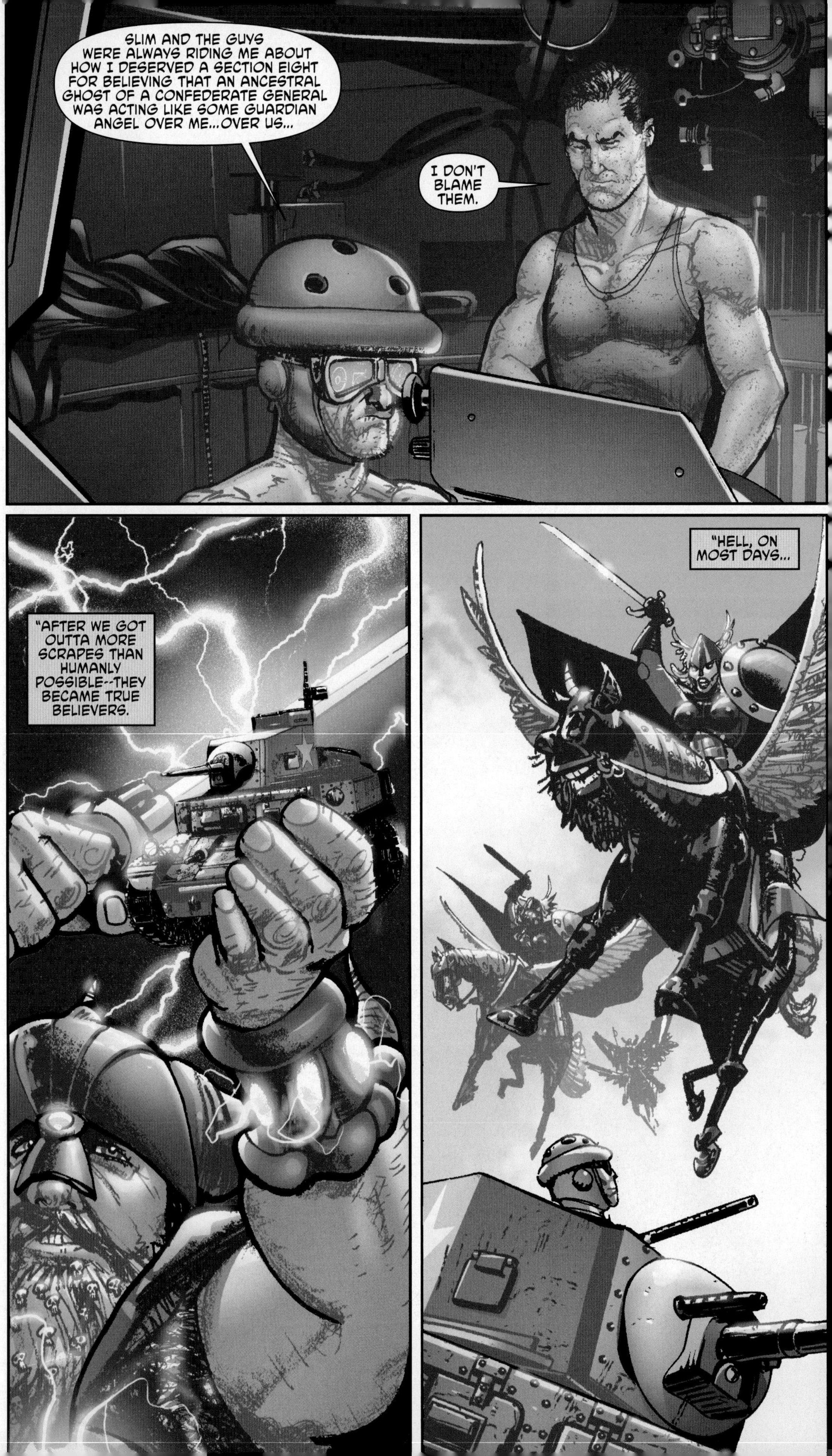
SLIM AND THE GUYS WERE ALWAYS RIDING ME ABOUT HOW I DESERVED A SECTION EIGHT FOR BELIEVING THAT AN ANCESTRAL GHOST OF A CONFEDERATE GENERAL WAS ACTING LIKE SOME GUARDIAN ANGEL OVER ME...OVER US...
I DON'T BLAME THEM.
"AFTER WE GOT OUTTA MORE SCRAPES THAN HUMANLY POSSIBLE--THEY BECAME TRUE BELIEVERS.
"HELL, ON MOST DAYS...

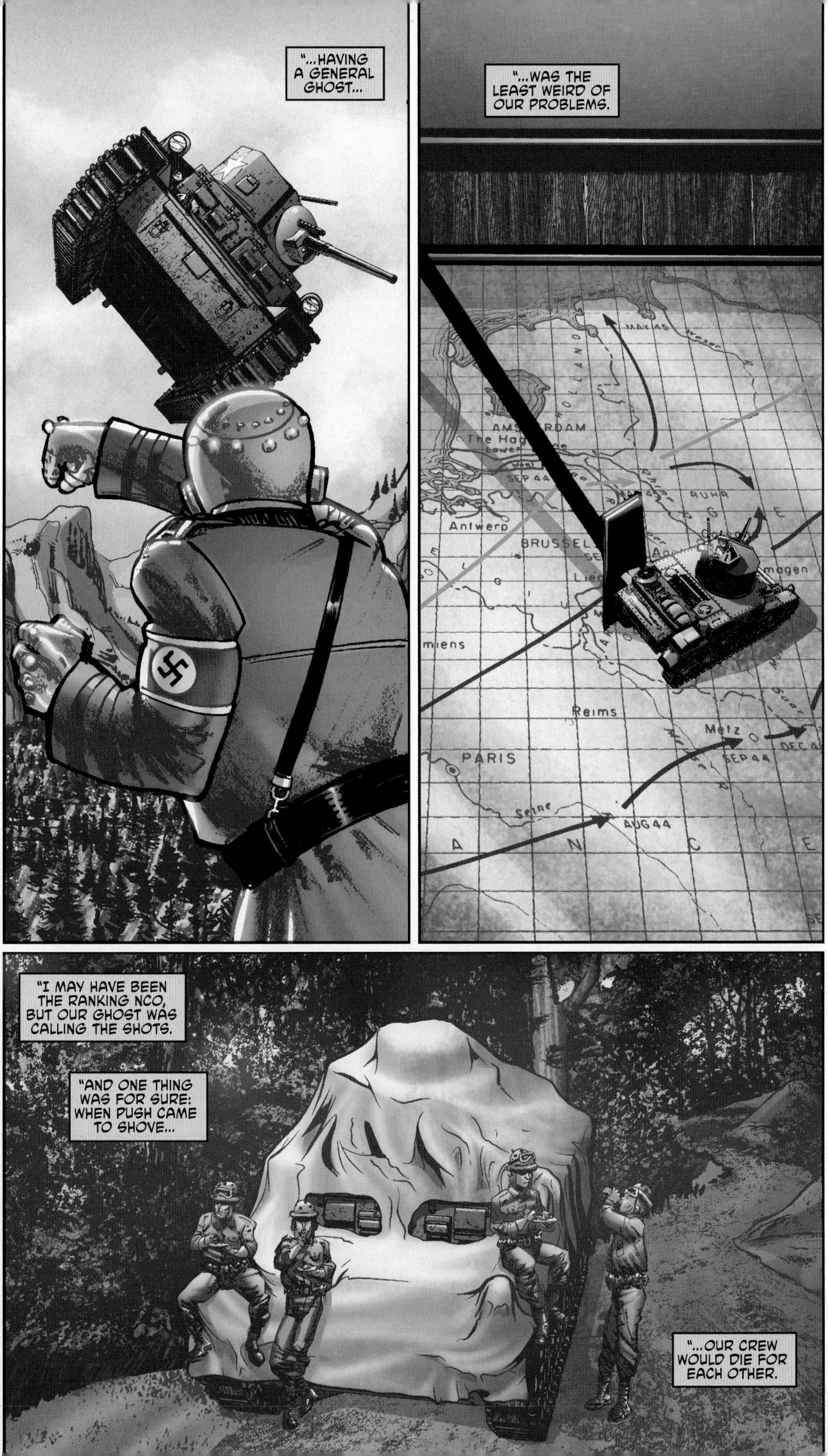
"...HAVING A GENERAL GHOST...
"...WAS THE LEAST WEIRD OF OUR PROBLEMS.
MAY 45
RUHR
SEP 44
Antwerp
Reims
Metz
PARIS
Seine
AUG44
"I MAY HAVE BEEN THE RANKING NCO, BUT OUR GHOST WAS CALLING THE SHOTS.
"AND ONE THING WAS FOR SURE: WHEN PUSH CAME TO SHOVE...
"...OUR CREW WOULD DIE FOR EACH OTHER.

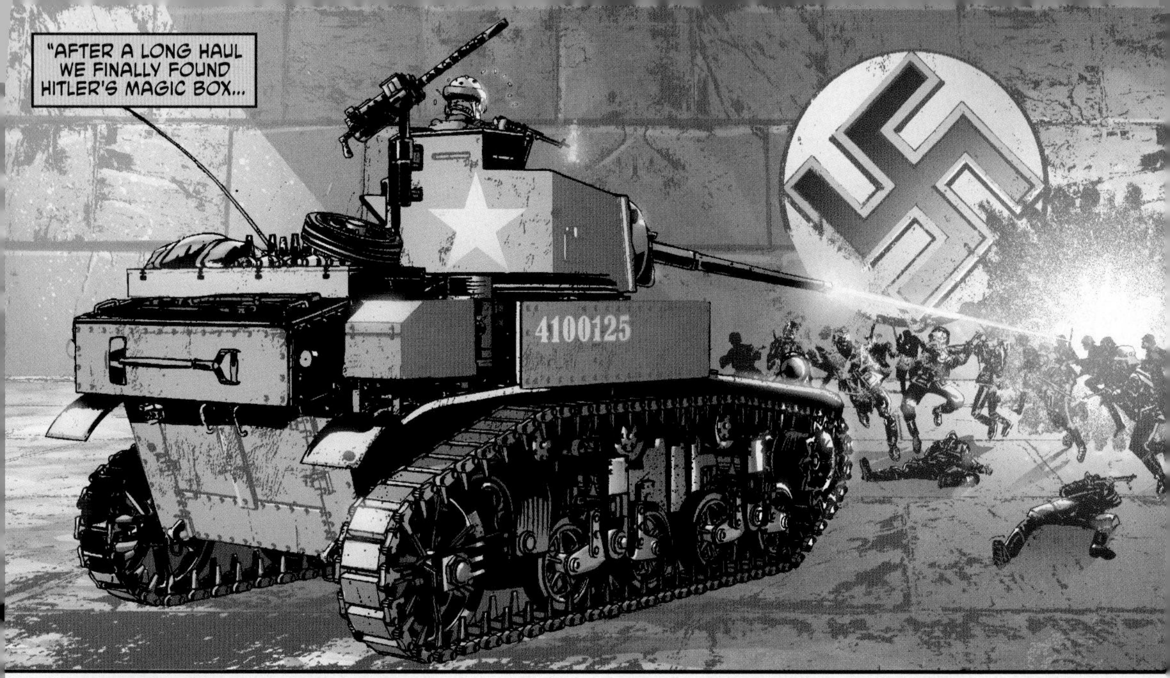
"AFTER A LONG HAUL WE FINALLY FOUND HITLER'S MAGIC BOX...
4100125

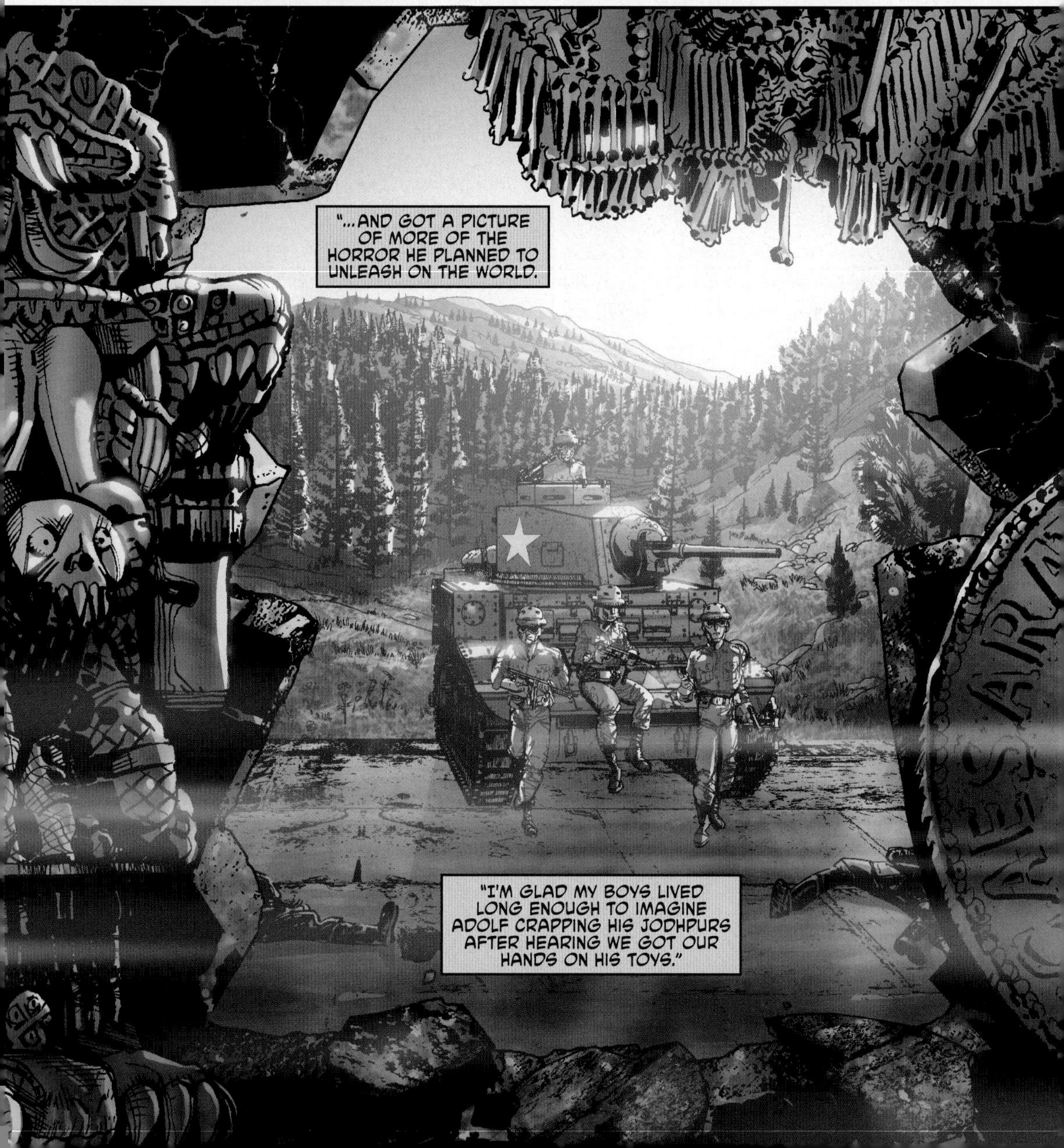
"...AND GOT A PICTURE OF MORE OF THE HORROR HE PLANNED TO UNLEASH ON THE WORLD.
"I'M GLAD MY BOYS LIVED LONG ENOUGH TO IMAGINE ADOLF CRAPPING HIS JODHPURS AFTER HEARING WE GOT OUR HANDS ON HIS TOYS."

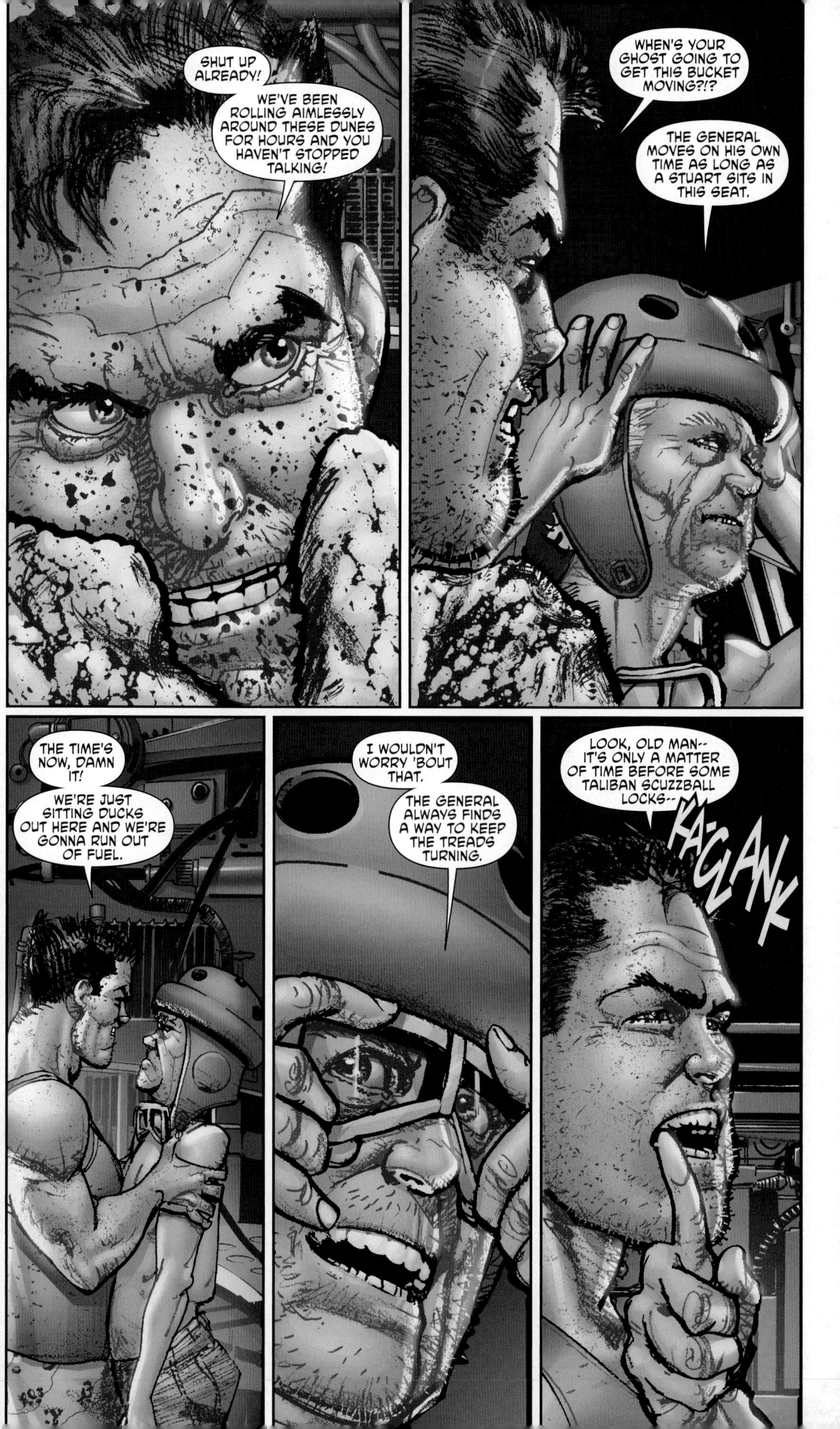

SHUT UP ALREADY!
WE'VE BEEN ROLLING AIMLESSLY AROUND THESE DUNES FOR HOURS AND YOU HAVEN'T STOPPED TALKING!
WHEN'S YOUR GHOST GOING TO GET THIS BUCKET MOVING?!?
THE GENERAL MOVES ON HIS OWN TIME AS LONG AS A STUART SITS IN THIS SEAT.
THE TIME'S NOW, DAMN IT!
WE'RE JUST SITTING DUCKS OUT HERE AND WE'RE GONNA RUN OUT OF FUEL.
I WOULDN'T WORRY 'BOUT THAT.
THE GENERAL ALWAYS FINDS A WAY TO KEEP THE TREADS TURNING.
LOOK, OLD MAN-- IT'S ONLY A MATTER OF TIME BEFORE SOME TALIBAN SCUZZBALL LOCKS--
KA-CLANK

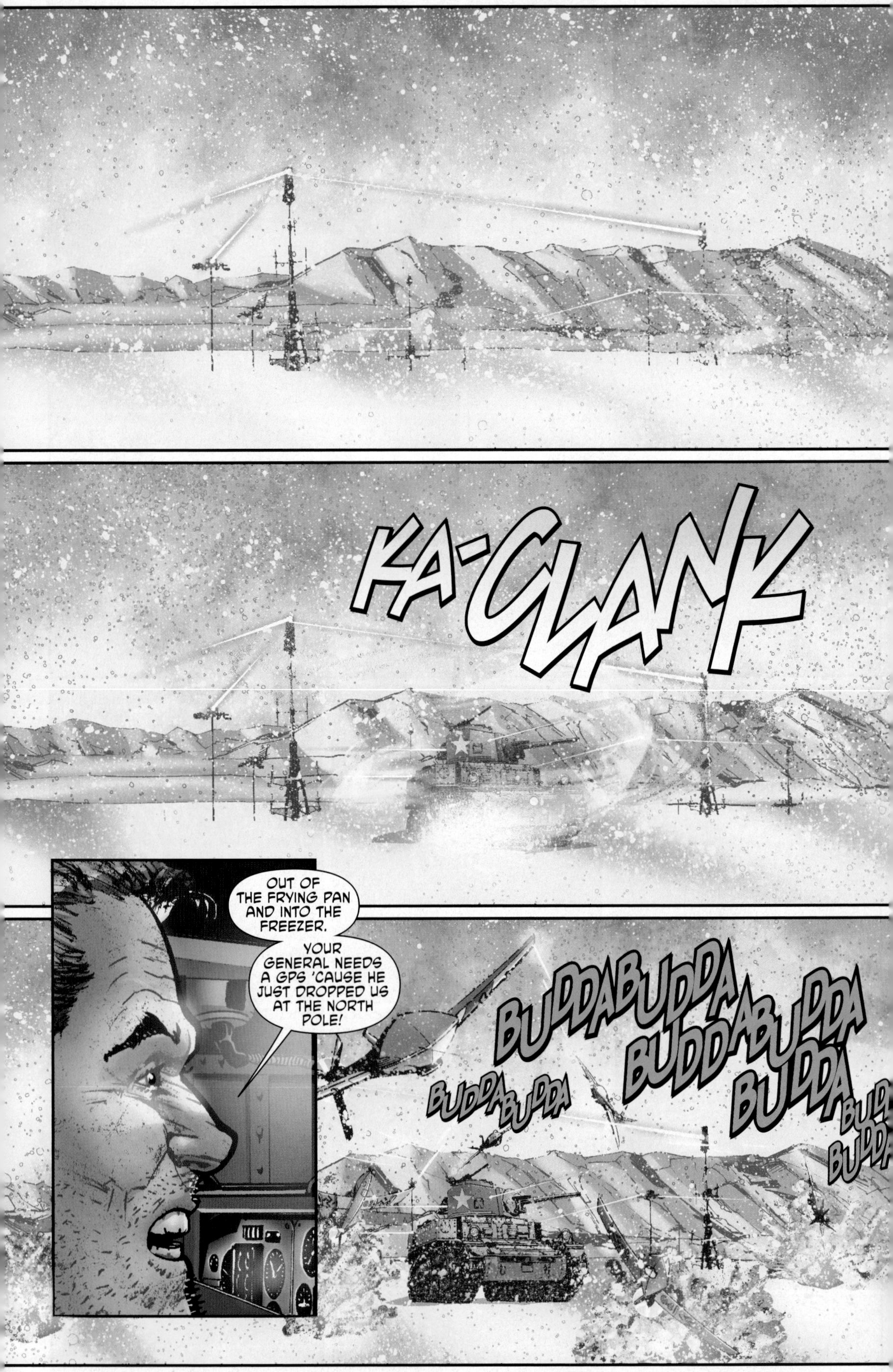
KA-CLANK
OUT OF THE FRYING PAN AND INTO THE FREEZER.
YOUR GENERAL NEEDS A GPS 'CAUSE HE JUST DROPPED US AT THE NORTH POLE!
BUDDABUDDA
BUDDABUDDA
BUDDA
BUDDABUDDA
BUDDA
BUDDA

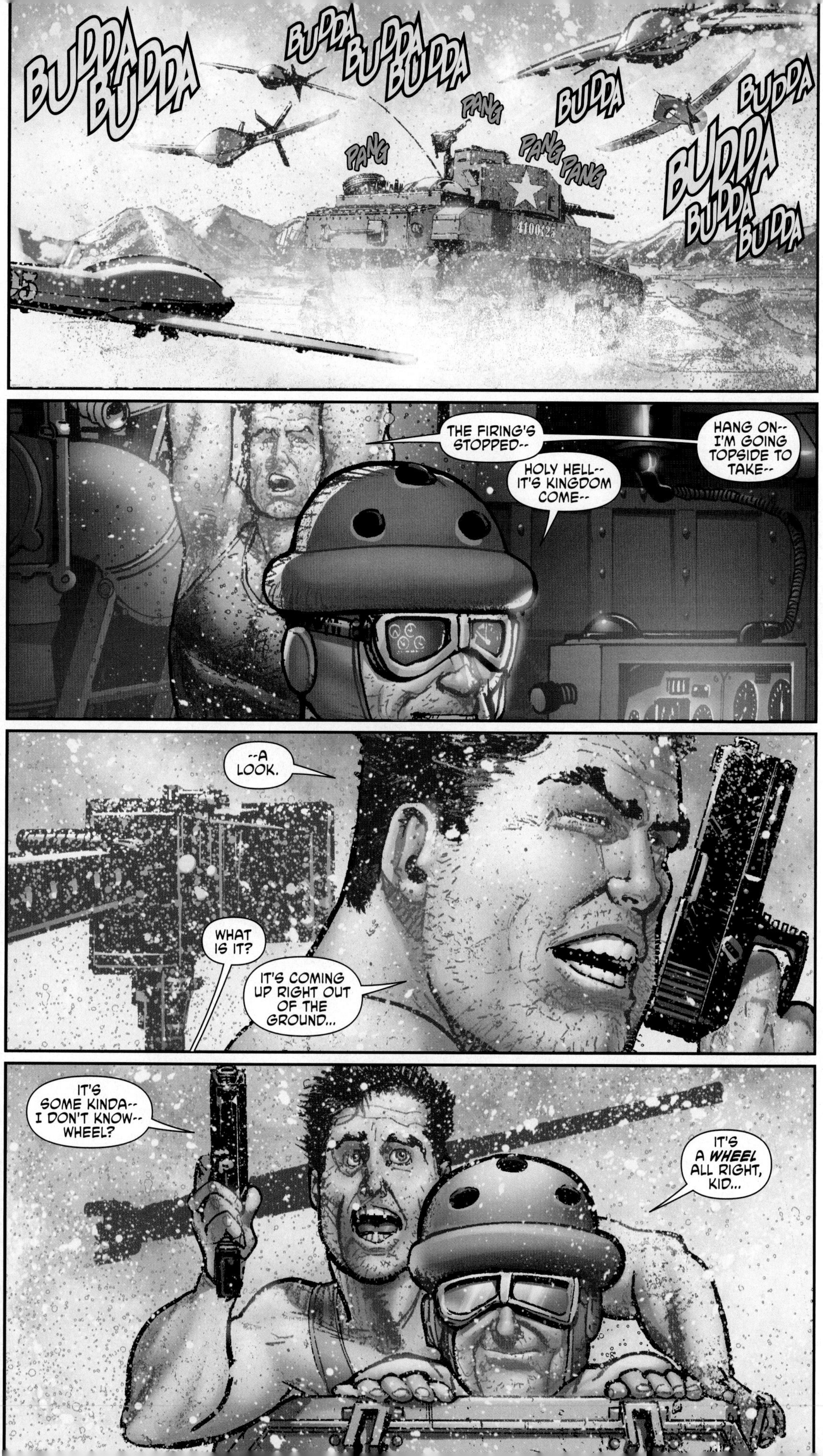
BUDDA BUDDA
BUDDA BUDDA BUDDA
PANG
PANG
PANG PANG
BUDDA
BUDDA
BUDDA BUDDA BUDDA
4100125
THE FIRING'S STOPPED--
HOLY HELL-- IT'S KINGDOM COME--
HANG ON-- I'M GOING TOPSIDE TO TAKE--
--A LOOK.
WHAT IS IT?
IT'S COMING UP RIGHT OUT OF THE GROUND...
IT'S SOME KINDA-- I DON'T KNOW-- WHEEL?
IT'S A *WHEEL* ALL RIGHT, KID...

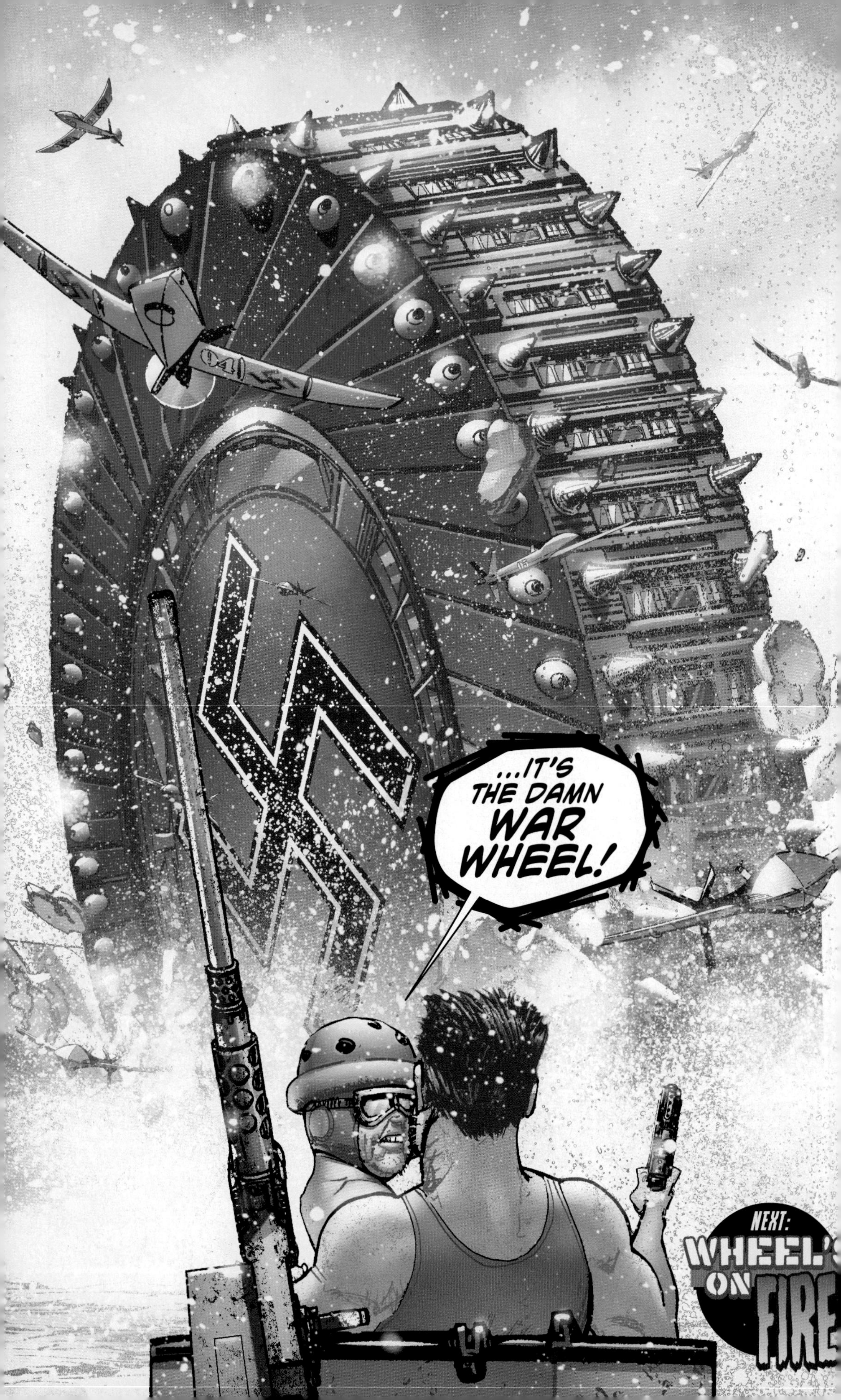
...IT'S THE DAMN WAR WHEEL!
NEXT:
WHEEL'S ON FIRE

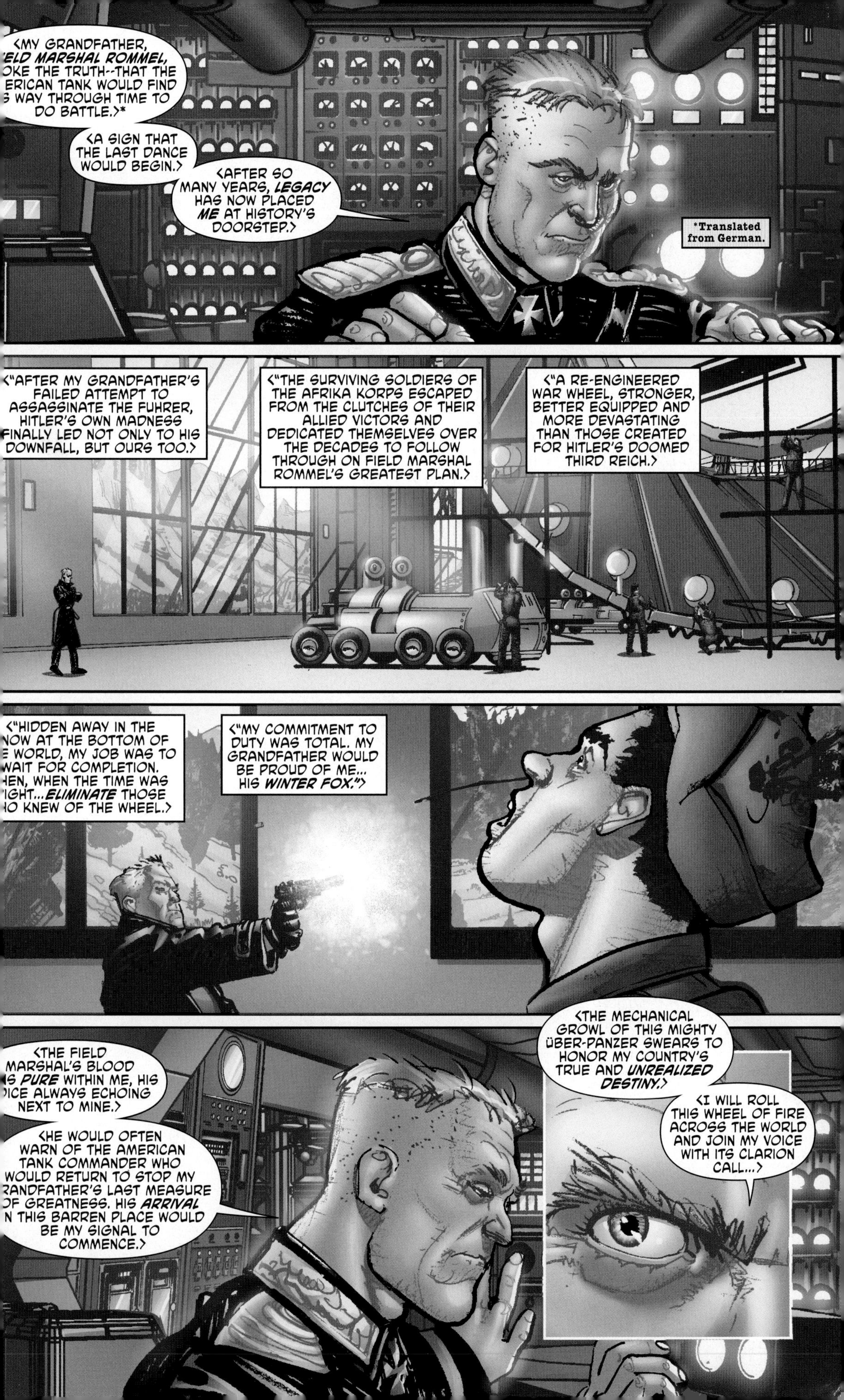

<MY GRANDFATHER, ELD MARSHAL ROMMEL, OKE THE TRUTH--THAT THE ERICAN TANK WOULD FIND S WAY THROUGH TIME TO DO BATTLE.>*
<A SIGN THAT THE LAST DANCE WOULD BEGIN.>
<AFTER SO MANY YEARS, LEGACY HAS NOW PLACED ME AT HISTORY'S DOORSTEP.>
*Translated from German.
<"AFTER MY GRANDFATHER'S FAILED ATTEMPT TO ASSASSINATE THE FUHRER, HITLER'S OWN MADNESS FINALLY LED NOT ONLY TO HIS DOWNFALL, BUT OURS TOO.>
<"THE SURVIVING SOLDIERS OF THE AFRIKA KORPS ESCAPED FROM THE CLUTCHES OF THEIR ALLIED VICTORS AND DEDICATED THEMSELVES OVER THE DECADES TO FOLLOW THROUGH ON FIELD MARSHAL ROMMEL'S GREATEST PLAN.>
<"A RE-ENGINEERED WAR WHEEL, STRONGER, BETTER EQUIPPED AND MORE DEVASTATING THAN THOSE CREATED FOR HITLER'S DOOMED THIRD REICH.>
<"HIDDEN AWAY IN THE NOW AT THE BOTTOM OF E WORLD, MY JOB WAS TO WAIT FOR COMPLETION. HEN, WHEN THE TIME WAS IGHT... ELIMINATE THOSE HO KNEW OF THE WHEEL.>
<"MY COMMITMENT TO DUTY WAS TOTAL. MY GRANDFATHER WOULD BE PROUD OF ME... HIS WINTER FOX.">
<THE FIELD MARSHAL'S BLOOD S PURE WITHIN ME, HIS OICE ALWAYS ECHOING NEXT TO MINE.>
<HE WOULD OFTEN WARN OF THE AMERICAN TANK COMMANDER WHO WOULD RETURN TO STOP MY RANDFATHER'S LAST MEASURE OF GREATNESS. HIS ARRIVAL N THIS BARREN PLACE WOULD BE MY SIGNAL TO COMMENCE.>
<THE MECHANICAL GROWL OF THIS MIGHTY ÜBER-PANZER SWEARS TO HONOR MY COUNTRY'S TRUE AND UNREALIZED DESTINY.>
<I WILL ROLL THIS WHEEL OF FIRE ACROSS THE WORLD AND JOIN MY VOICE WITH ITS CLARION CALL...>

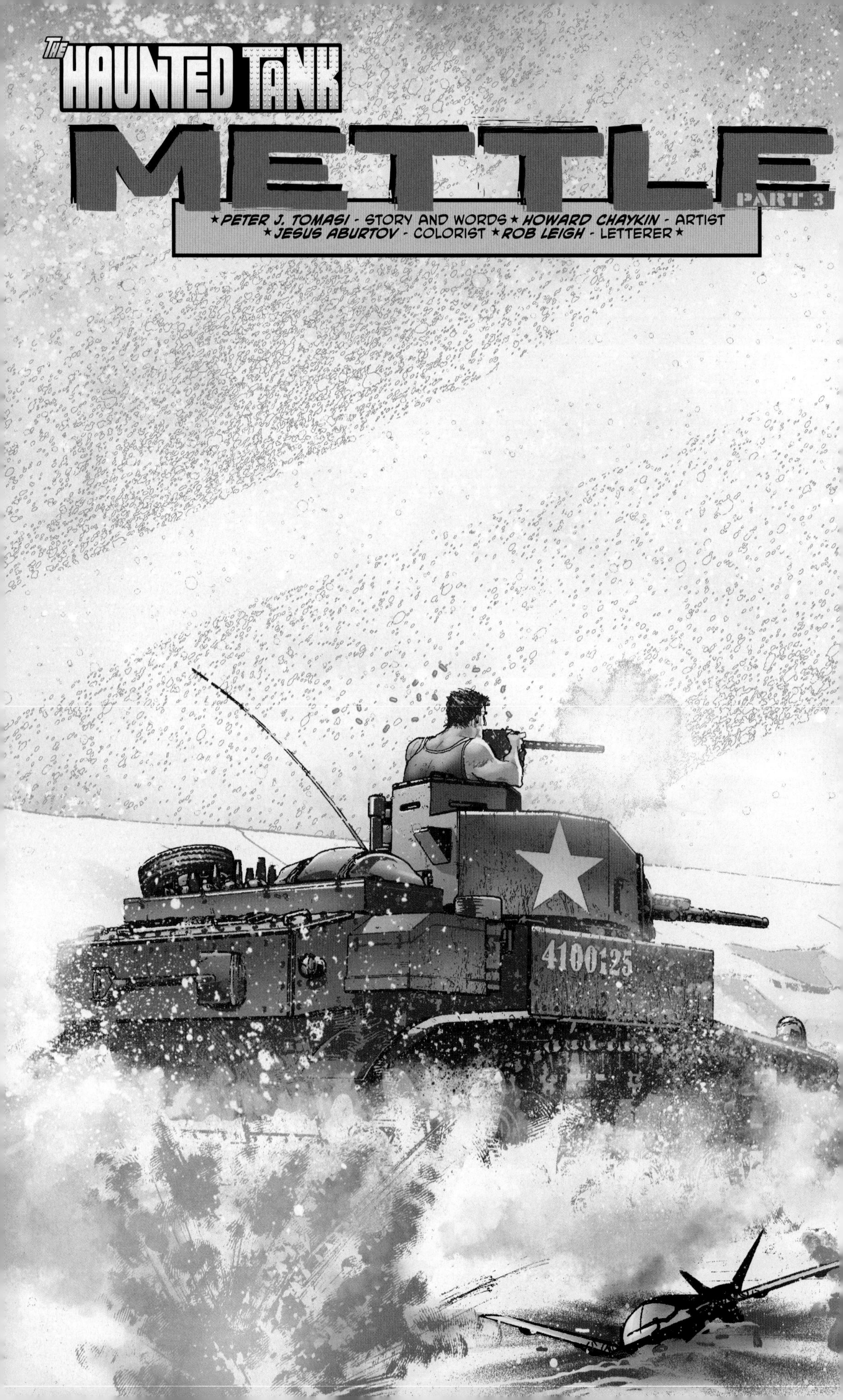
THE HAUNTED TANK
METTLE
PART 3
★PETER J. TOMASI - STORY AND WORDS★HOWARD CHAYKIN - ARTIST
★JESUS ABURTOV - COLORIST★ROB LEIGH - LETTERER★
4100125

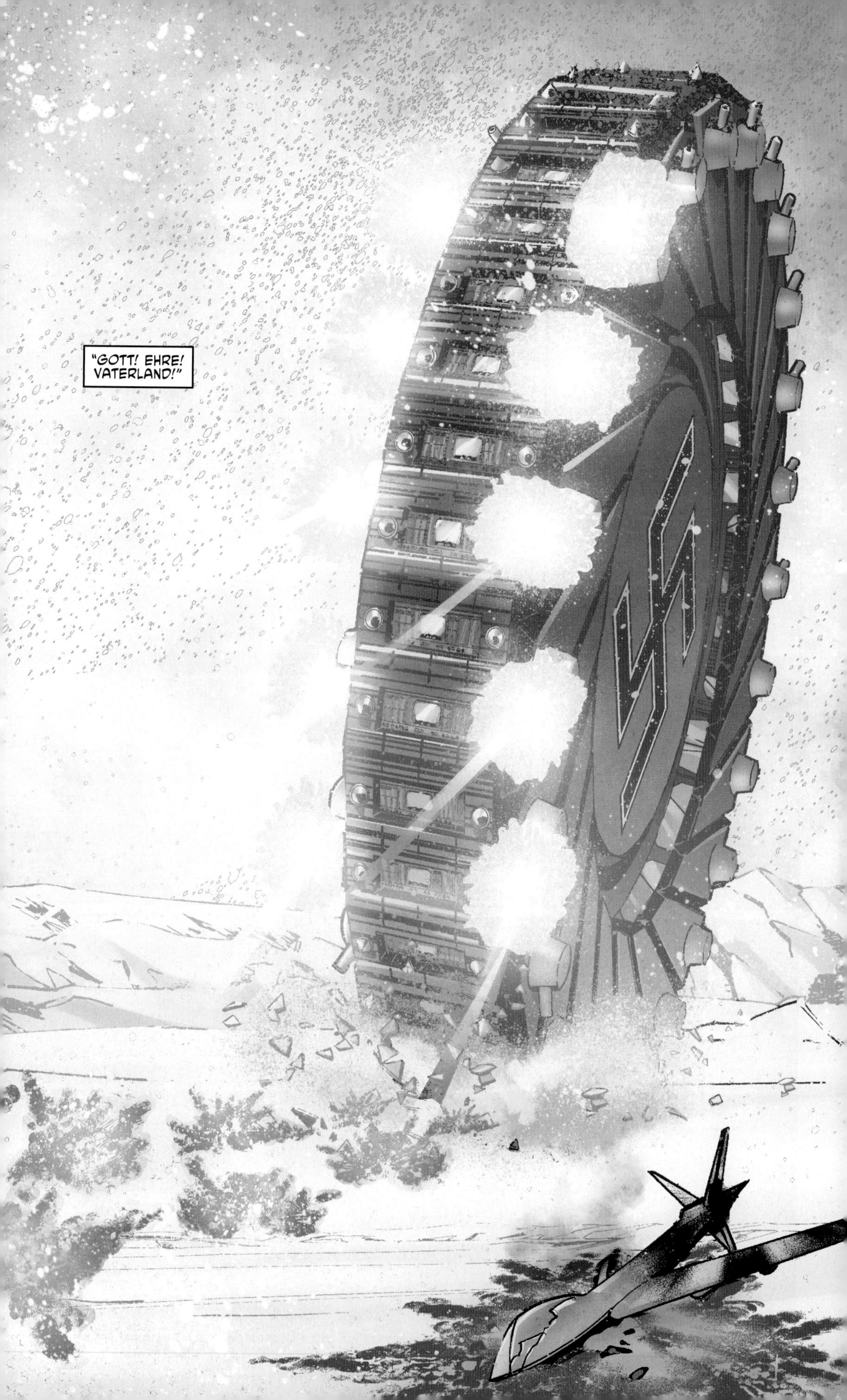
"GOTT! EHRE! VATERLAND!"

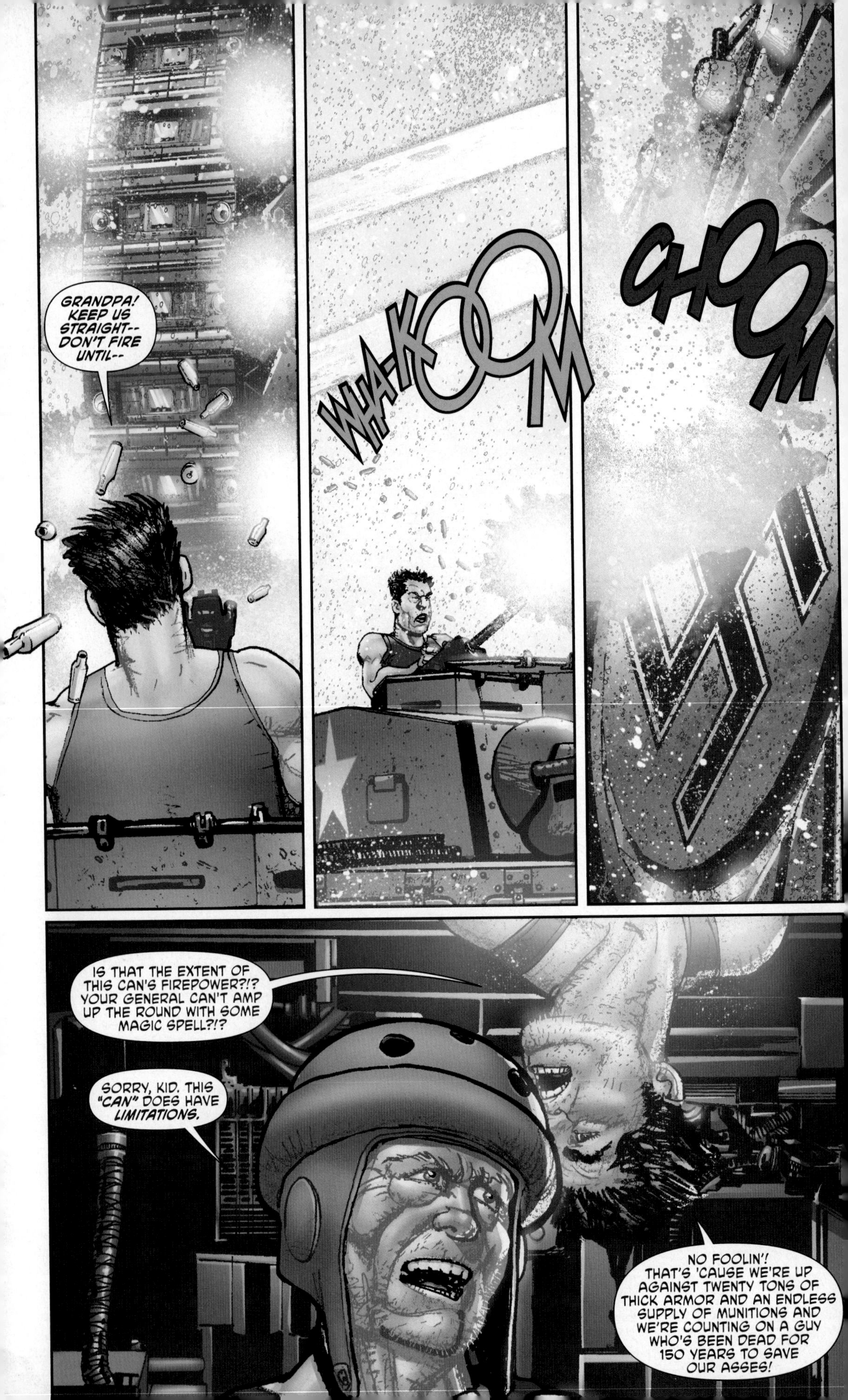
GRANDPA! KEEP US STRAIGHT-- DON'T FIRE UNTIL--
WHA-KOOOM
CHOOOM
IS THAT THE EXTENT OF THIS CAN'S FIREPOWER?!? YOUR GENERAL CAN'T AMP UP THE ROUND WITH SOME MAGIC SPELL?!?
SORRY, KID. THIS "CAN" DOES HAVE LIMITATIONS.
NO FOOLIN'! THAT'S 'CAUSE WE'RE UP AGAINST TWENTY TONS OF THICK ARMOR AND AN ENDLESS SUPPLY OF MUNITIONS AND WE'RE COUNTING ON A GUY WHO'S BEEN DEAD FOR 150 YEARS TO SAVE OUR ASSES!

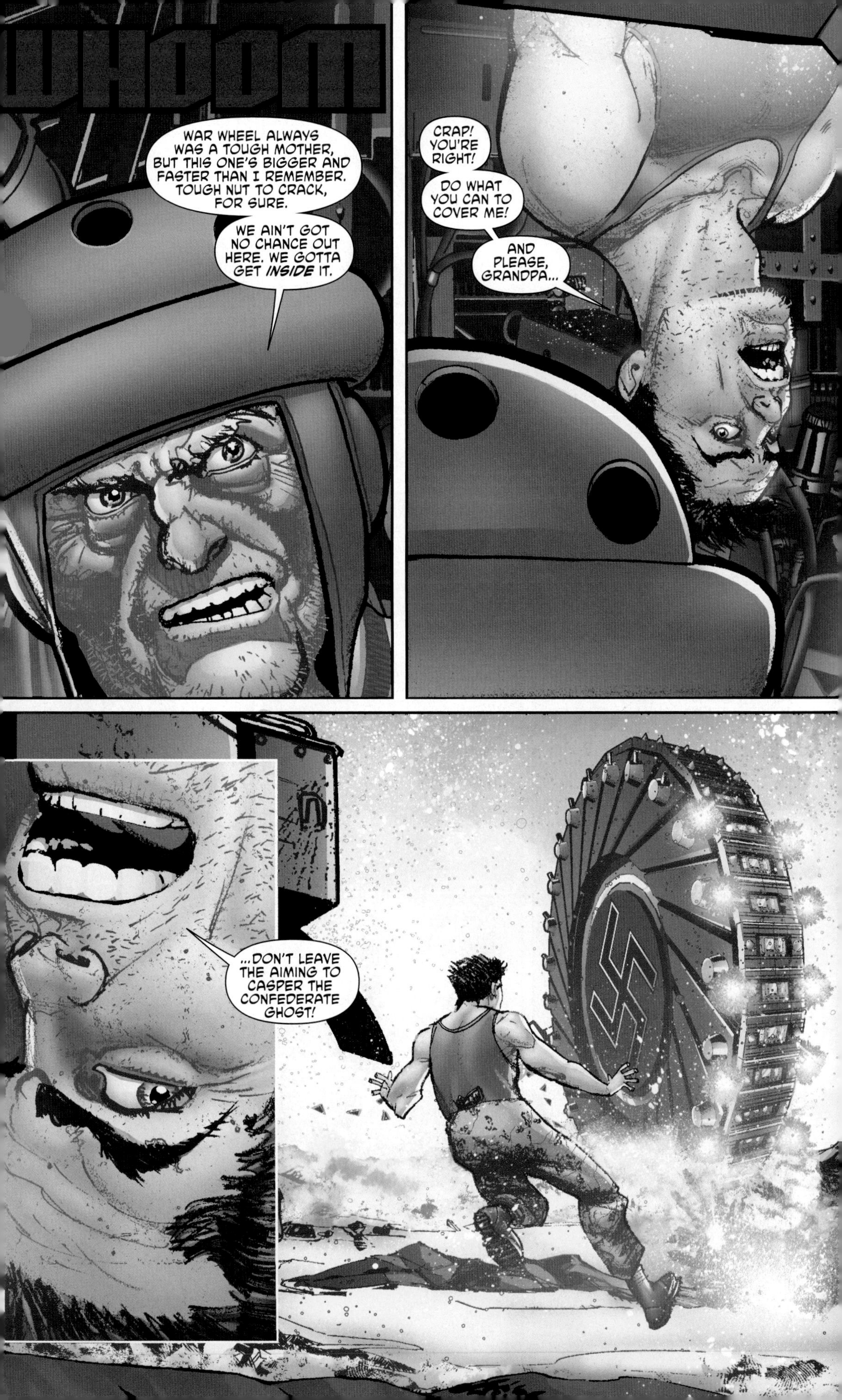
WHOOM
WAR WHEEL ALWAYS WAS A TOUGH MOTHER, BUT THIS ONE'S BIGGER AND FASTER THAN I REMEMBER. TOUGH NUT TO CRACK, FOR SURE.
WE AIN'T GOT NO CHANCE OUT HERE. WE GOTTA GET *INSIDE* IT.
CRAP! YOU'RE RIGHT!
DO WHAT YOU CAN TO COVER ME!
AND PLEASE, GRANDPA...
...DON'T LEAVE THE AIMING TO CASPER THE CONFEDERATE GHOST!

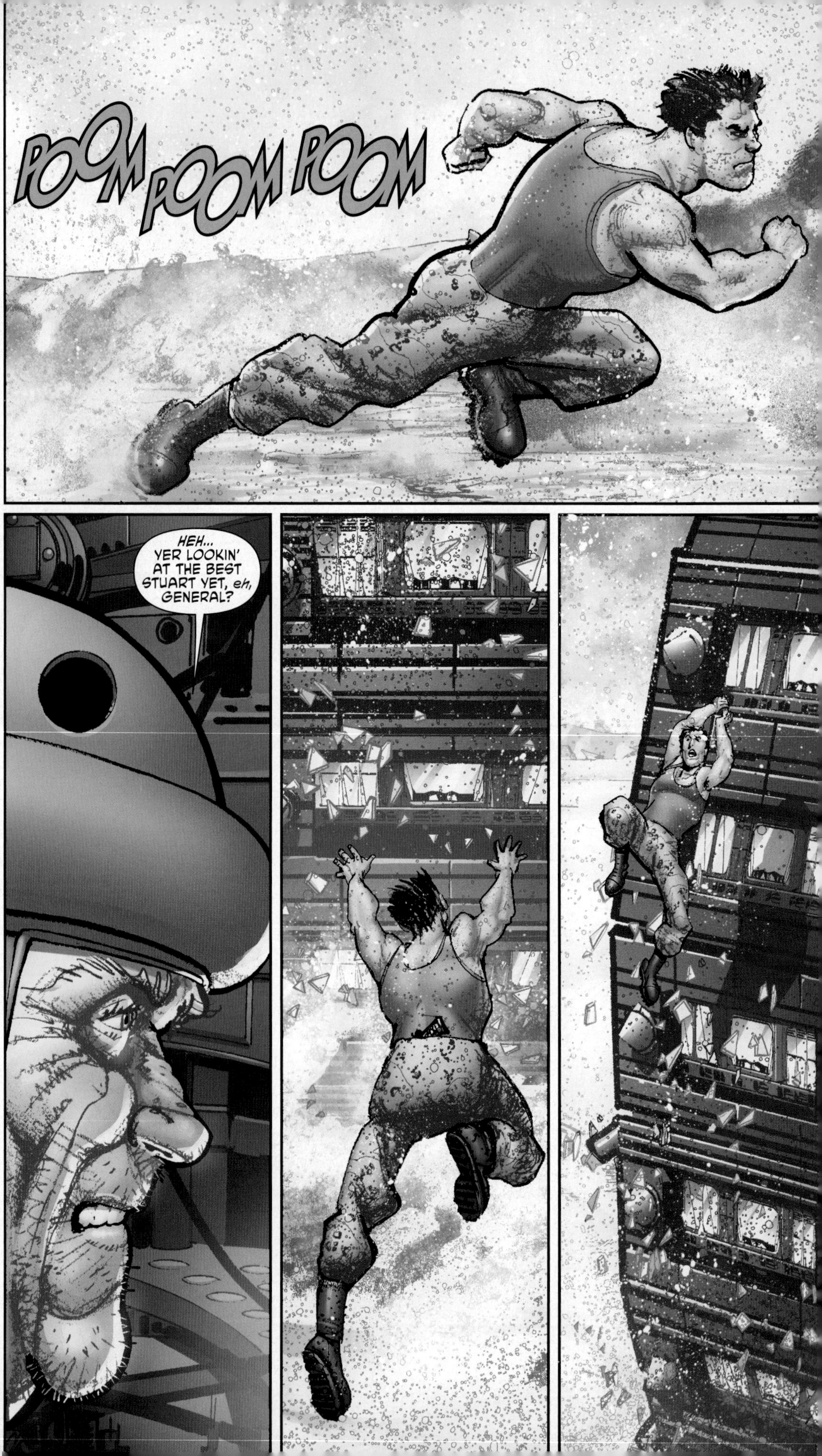
POOM POOM POOM
HEH... YER LOOKIN' AT THE BEST STUART YET, *eh,* GENERAL?

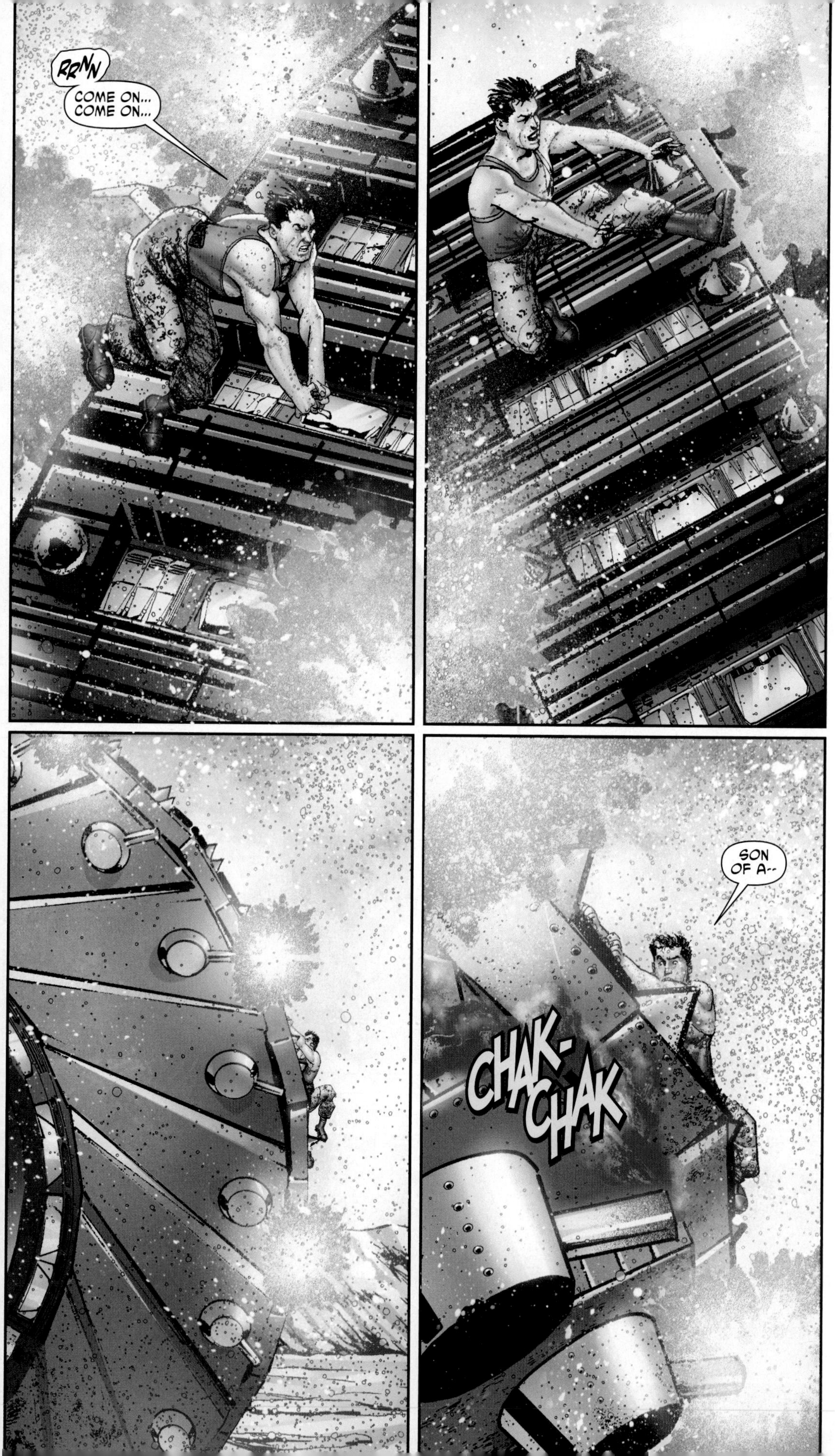
RRNN
COME ON...
COME ON...
SON
OF A--
CHAK-
CHAK

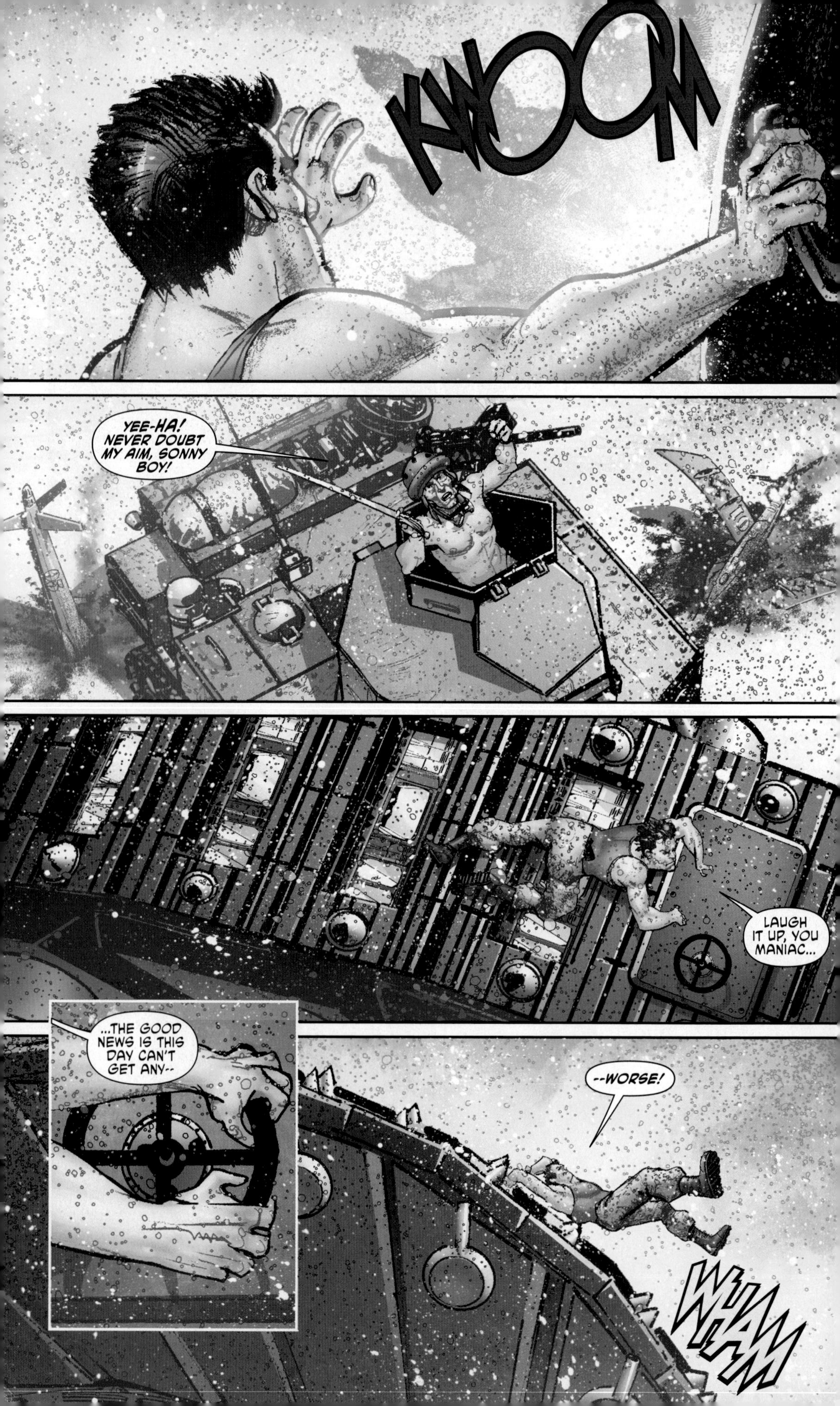
KWOOM
YEE-HA! NEVER DOUBT MY AIM, SONNY BOY!
LAUGH IT UP, YOU MANIAC...
...THE GOOD NEWS IS THIS DAY CAN'T GET ANY--
--WORSE!
WHAM

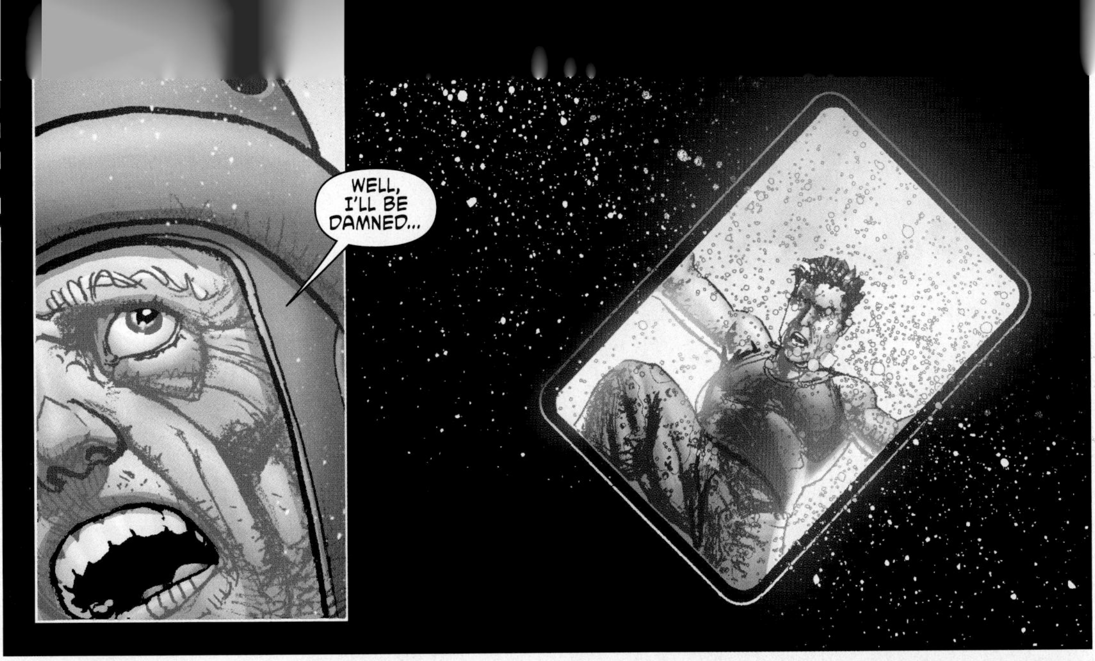
WELL, I'LL BE DAMNED...

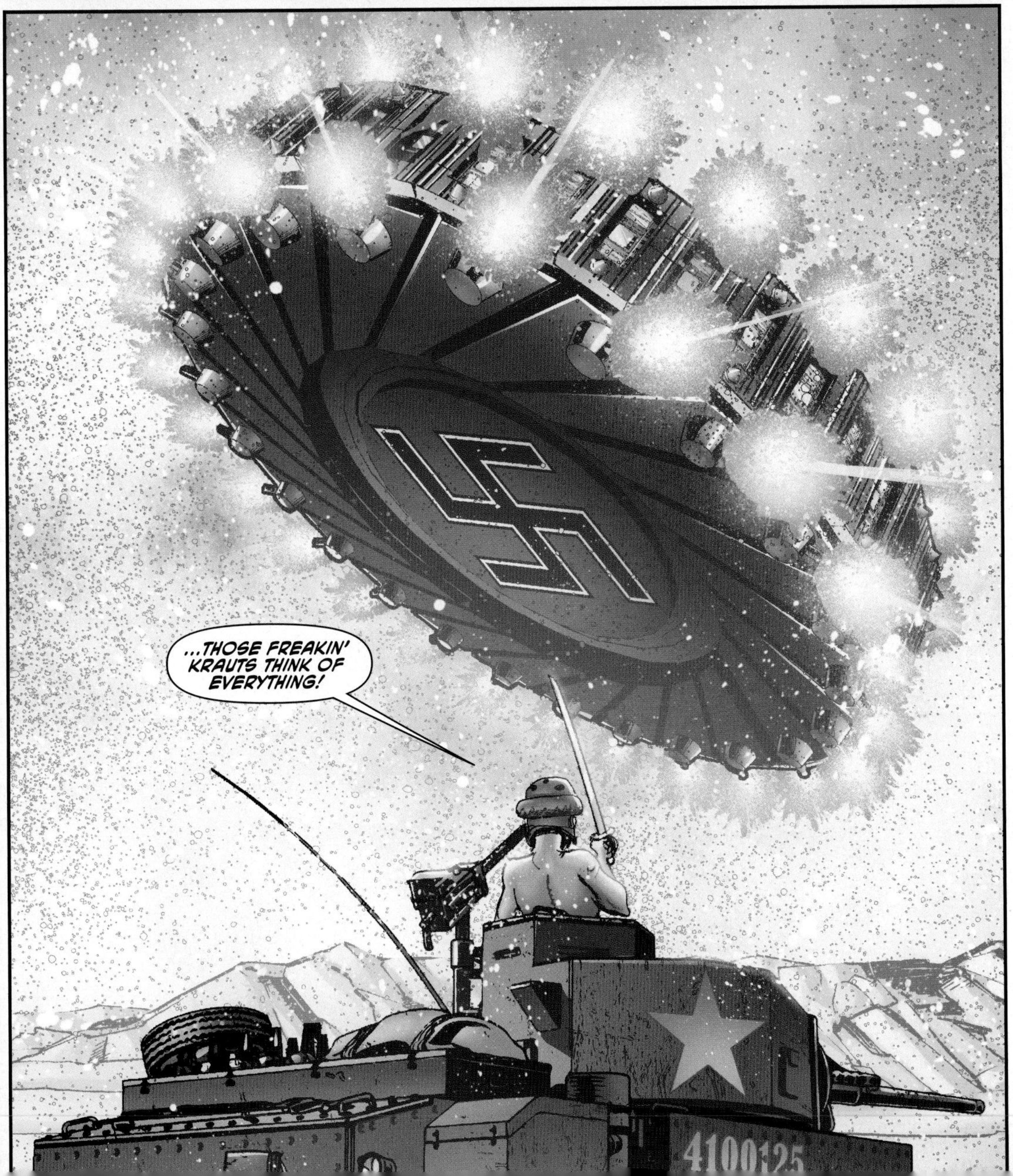
...THOSE FREAKIN' KRAUTS THINK OF EVERYTHING!
4100125

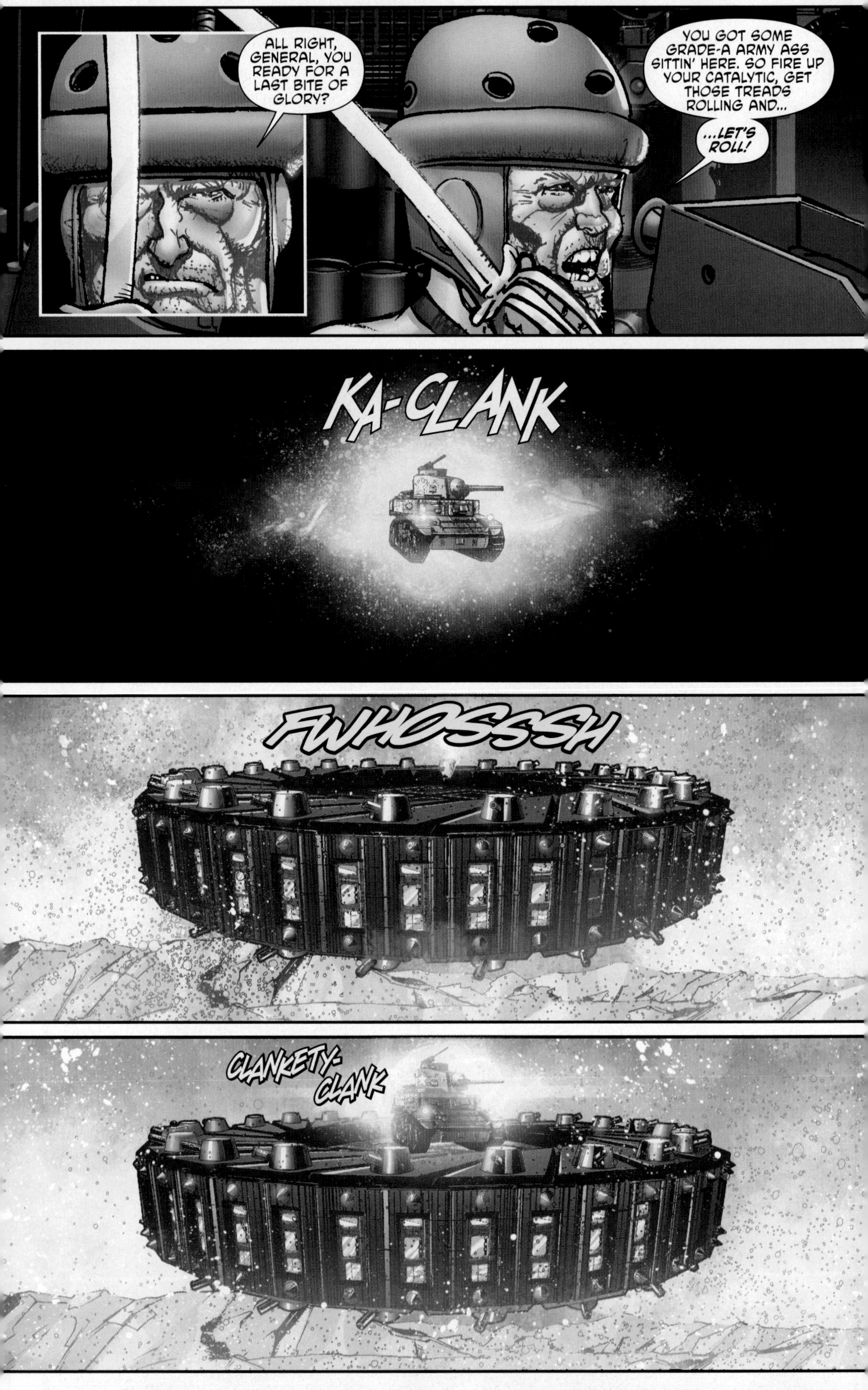
ALL RIGHT, GENERAL, YOU READY FOR A LAST BITE OF GLORY?
YOU GOT SOME GRADE-A ARMY ASS SITTIN' HERE. SO FIRE UP YOUR CATALYTIC, GET THOSE TREADS ROLLING AND...
...LET'S ROLL!
KA-CLANK
FWHOSSSH
CLANKETY-CLANK

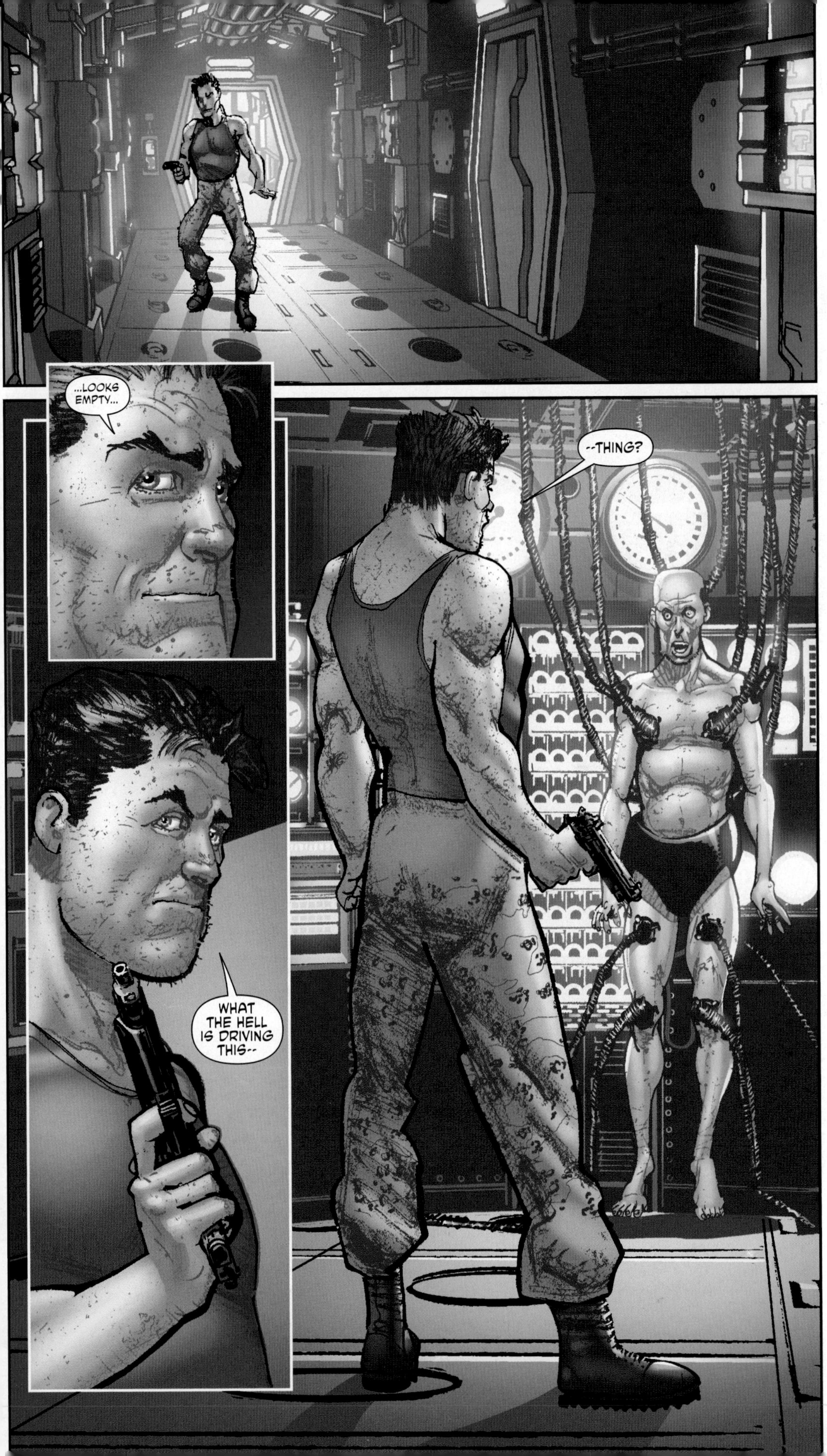
...LOOKS EMPTY...
WHAT THE HELL IS DRIVING THIS--
--THING?

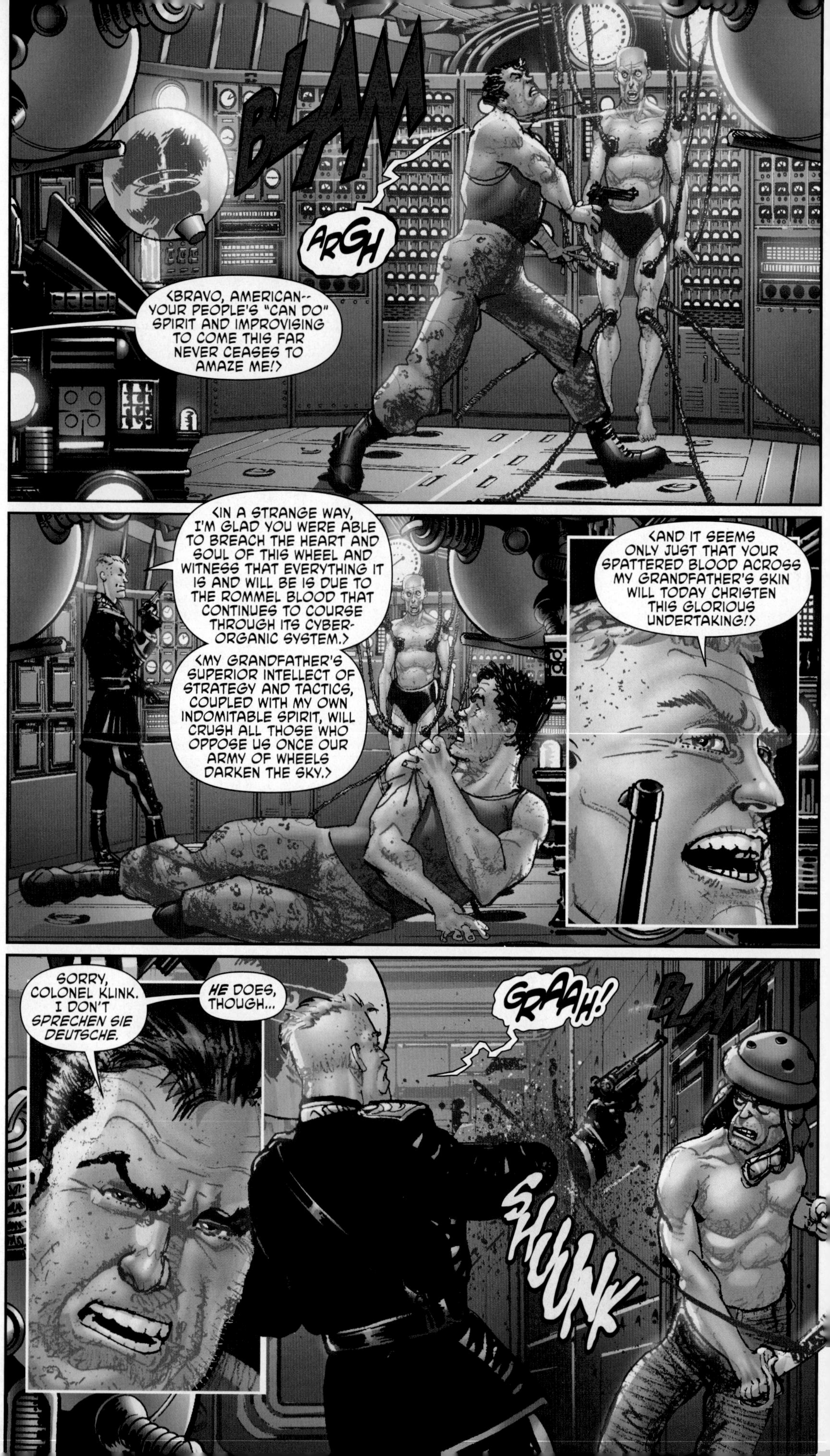
BLAM
ARGH
<BRAVO, AMERICAN-- YOUR PEOPLE'S "CAN DO" SPIRIT AND IMPROVISING TO COME THIS FAR NEVER CEASES TO AMAZE ME!>
<IN A STRANGE WAY, I'M GLAD YOU WERE ABLE TO BREACH THE HEART AND SOUL OF THIS WHEEL AND WITNESS THAT EVERYTHING IT IS AND WILL BE IS DUE TO THE ROMMEL BLOOD THAT CONTINUES TO COURSE THROUGH ITS CYBER-ORGANIC SYSTEM.>
<MY GRANDFATHER'S SUPERIOR INTELLECT OF STRATEGY AND TACTICS, COUPLED WITH MY OWN INDOMITABLE SPIRIT, WILL CRUSH ALL THOSE WHO OPPOSE US ONCE OUR ARMY OF WHEELS DARKEN THE SKY.>
<AND IT SEEMS ONLY JUST THAT YOUR SPATTERED BLOOD ACROSS MY GRANDFATHER'S SKIN WILL TODAY CHRISTEN THIS GLORIOUS UNDERTAKING!>
SORRY, COLONEL KLINK. I DON'T SPRECHEN SIE DEUTSCHE.
HE DOES, THOUGH...
GRAAAH!
BLAM
SHUUUNK

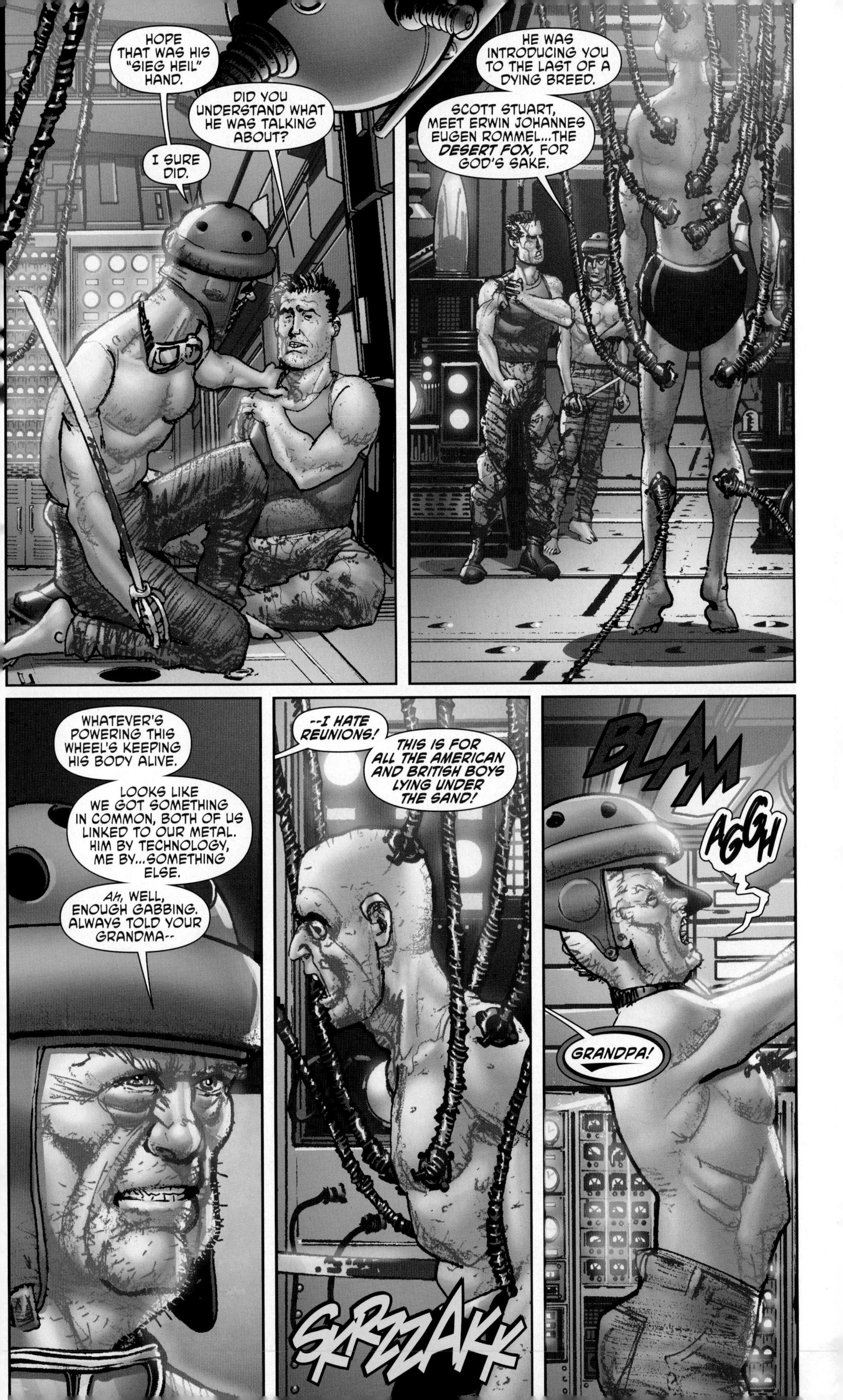
HOPE THAT WAS HIS "SIEG HEIL" HAND.
DID YOU UNDERSTAND WHAT HE WAS TALKING ABOUT?
I SURE DID.
HE WAS INTRODUCING YOU TO THE LAST OF A DYING BREED.
SCOTT STUART, MEET ERWIN JOHANNES EUGEN ROMMEL...THE *DESERT FOX*, FOR GOD'S SAKE.
WHATEVER'S POWERING THIS WHEEL'S KEEPING HIS BODY ALIVE.
LOOKS LIKE WE GOT SOMETHING IN COMMON, BOTH OF US LINKED TO OUR METAL. HIM BY TECHNOLOGY, ME BY...SOMETHING ELSE.
AH, WELL, ENOUGH GABBING. ALWAYS TOLD YOUR GRANDMA--
--I HATE REUNIONS!
THIS IS FOR ALL THE AMERICAN AND BRITISH BOYS LYING UNDER THE SAND!
SKRZZAKK
BLAM
AGGH
GRANDPA!

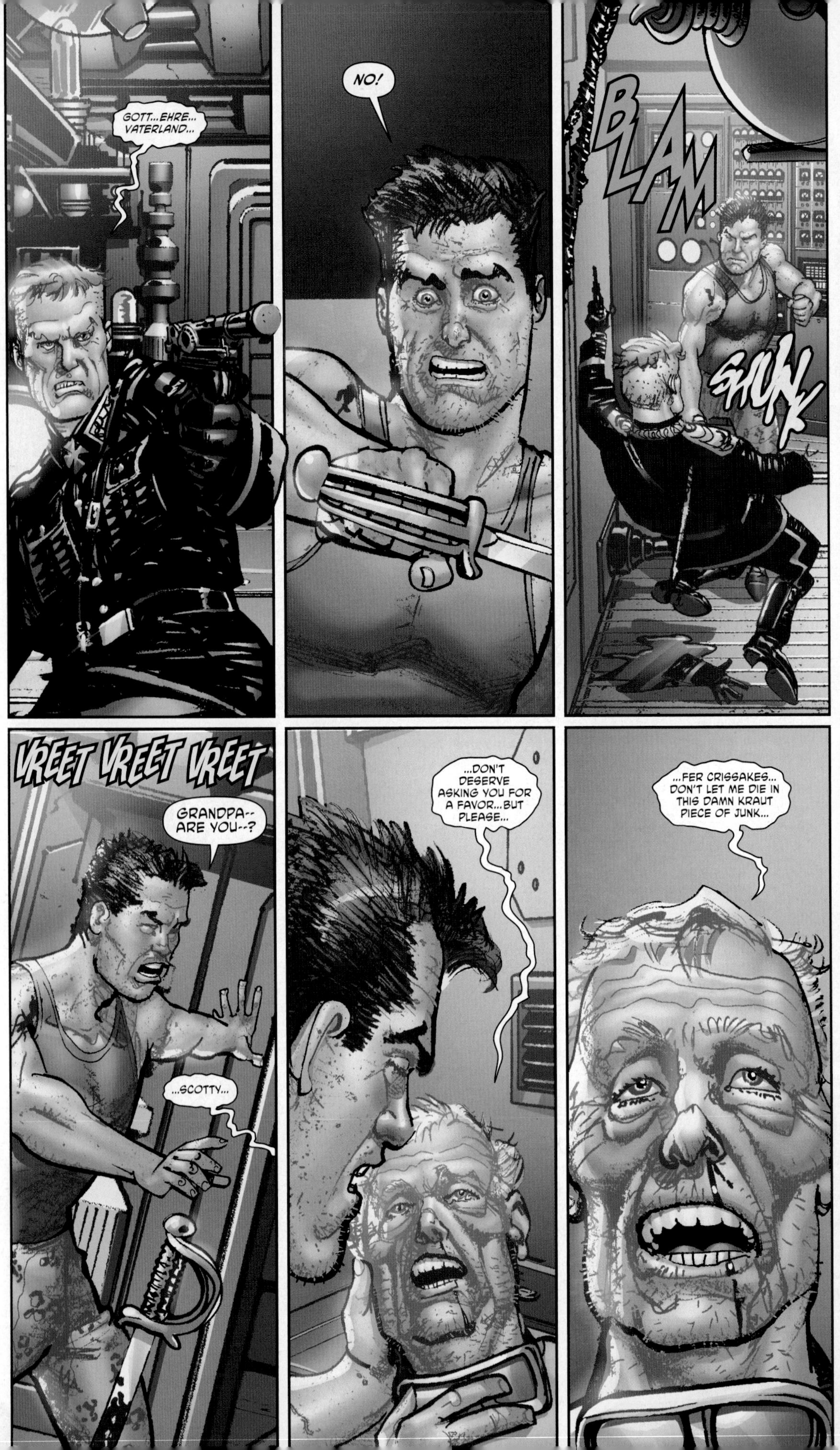
GOTT...EHRE... VATERLAND...
NO!
BLAM
SHUNK
VREET VREET VREET
GRANDPA-- ARE YOU--?
...SCOTTY...
...DON'T DESERVE ASKING YOU FOR A FAVOR...BUT PLEASE...
...FER CRISSAKES... DON'T LET ME DIE IN THIS DAMN KRAUT PIECE OF JUNK...

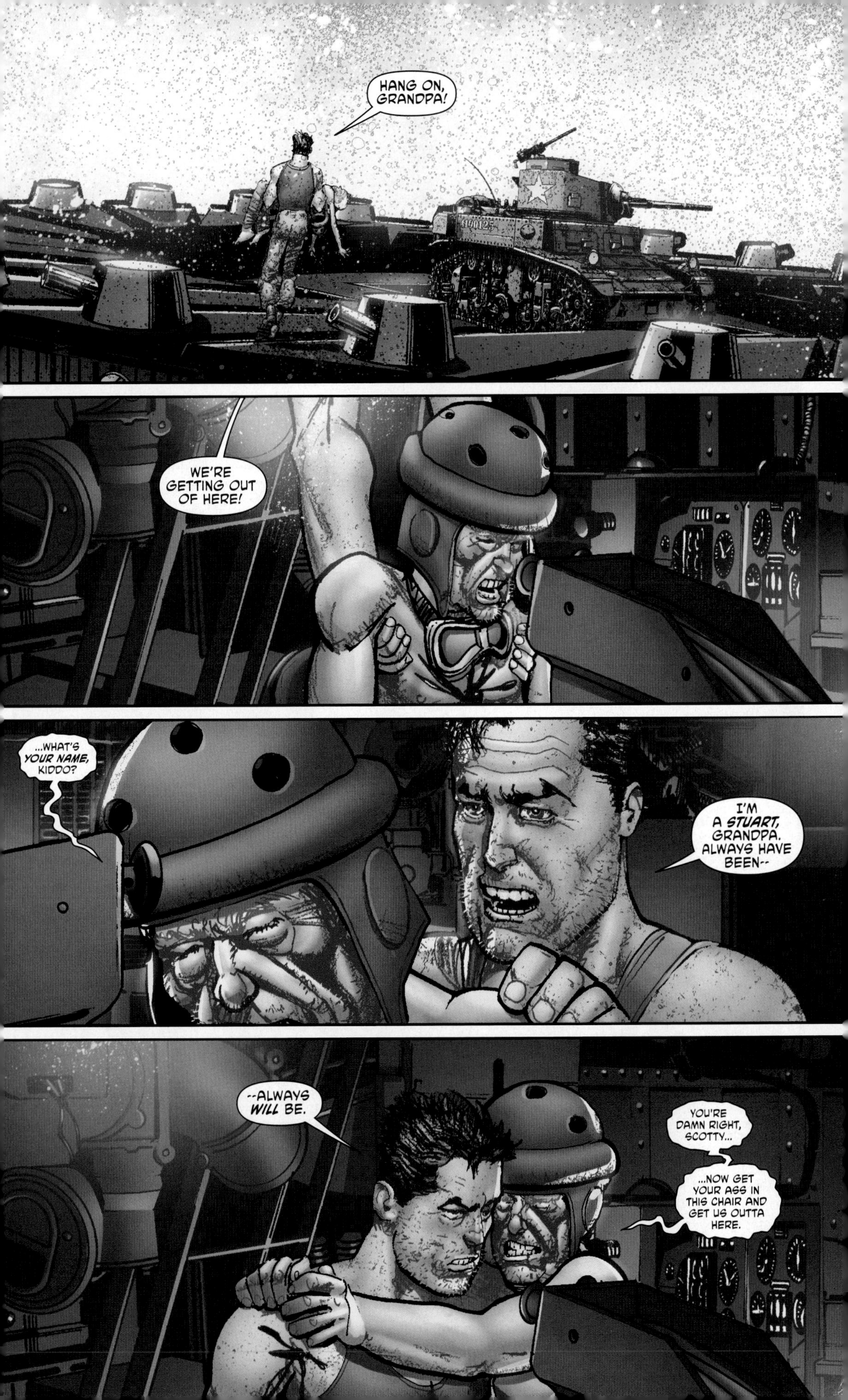
HANG ON, GRANDPA!
WE'RE GETTING OUT OF HERE!
...WHAT'S YOUR NAME, KIDDO?
I'M A STUART, GRANDPA. ALWAYS HAVE BEEN--
--ALWAYS WILL BE.
YOU'RE DAMN RIGHT, SCOTTY...
...NOW GET YOUR ASS IN THIS CHAIR AND GET US OUTTA HERE.

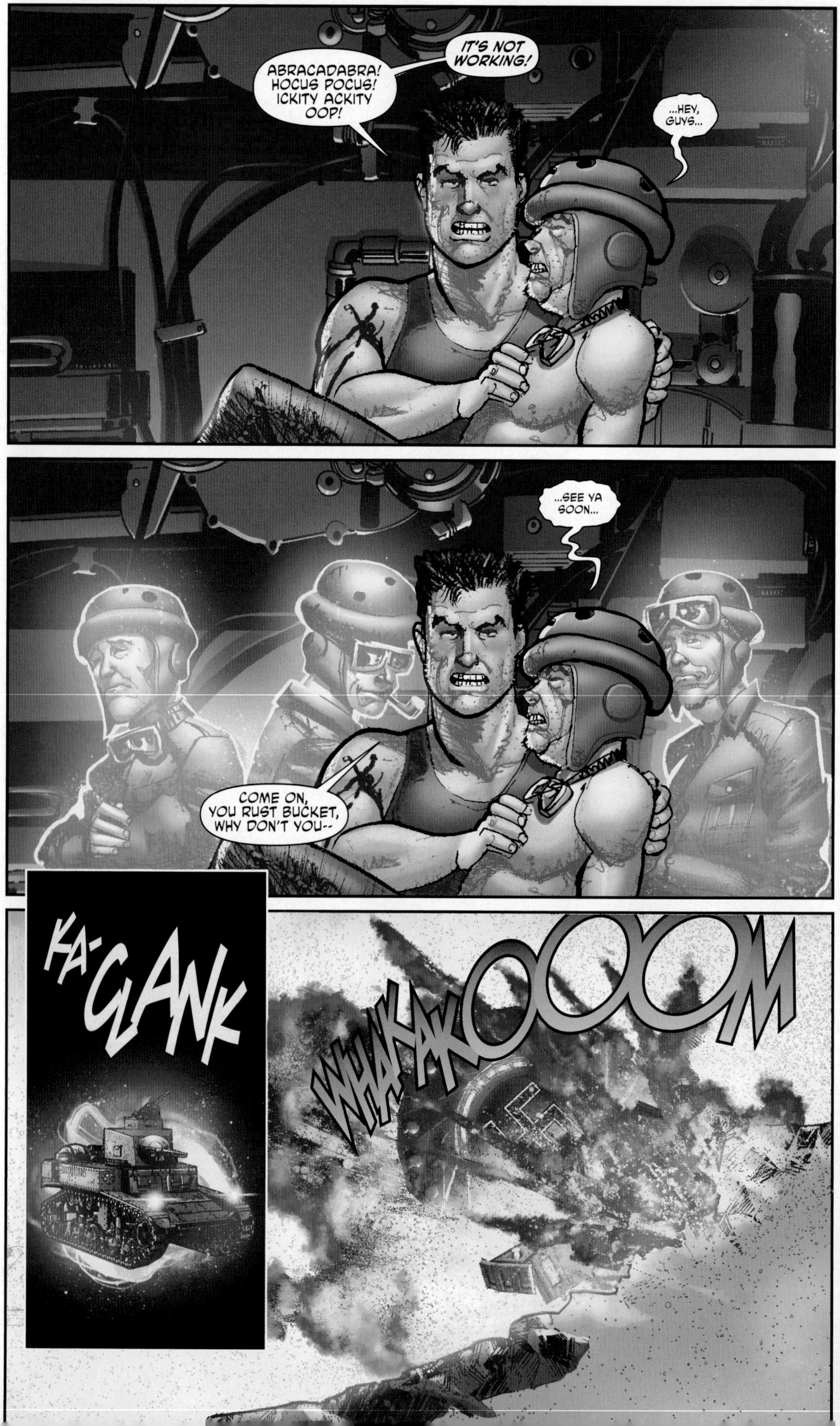
ABRACADABRA! HOCUS POCUS! ICKITY ACKITY OOP!
IT'S NOT WORKING!
...HEY, GUYS...
...SEE YA SOON...
COME ON, YOU RUST BUCKET, WHY DON'T YOU--
KA-CLANK
WHAKAKOOOOM

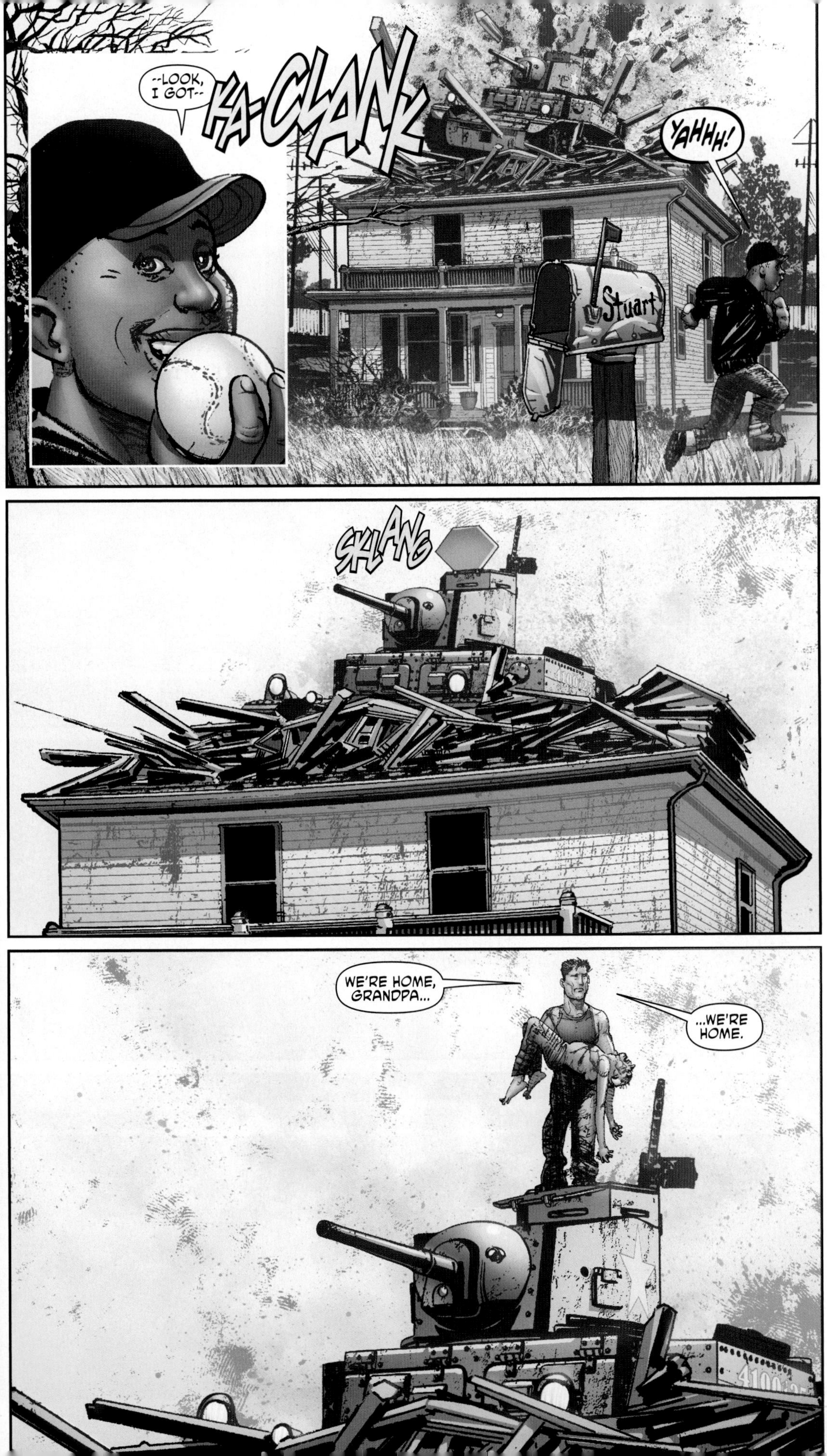
--LOOK, I GOT--
KA-CLANK
YAHHH!
Stuart
SKLANG
WE'RE HOME, GRANDPA...
...WE'RE HOME.

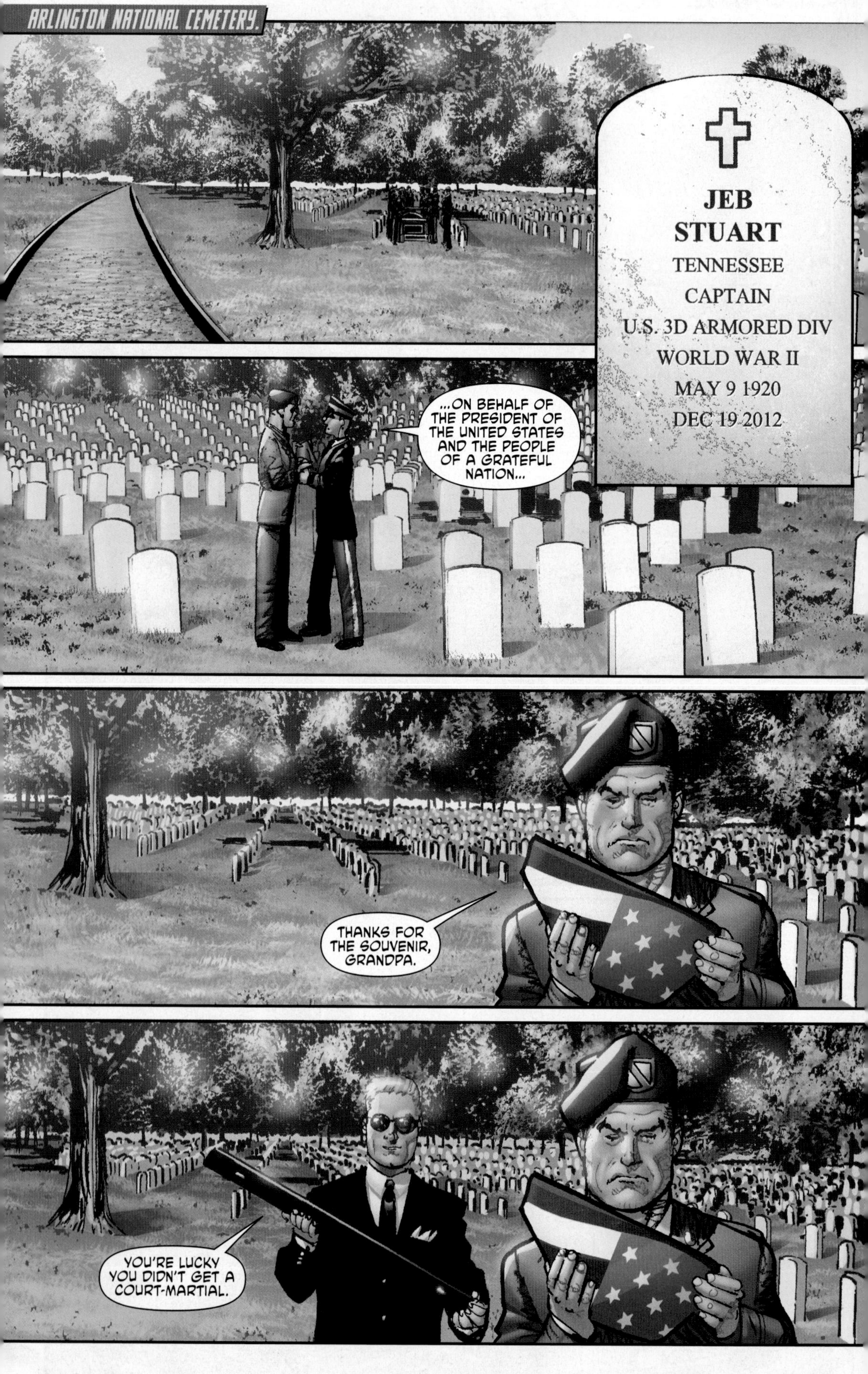
ARLINGTON NATIONAL CEMETERY.
JEB STUART
TENNESSEE
CAPTAIN
U.S. 3D ARMORED DIV
WORLD WAR II
MAY 9 1920
DEC 19 2012
...ON BEHALF OF THE PRESIDENT OF THE UNITED STATES AND THE PEOPLE OF A GRATEFUL NATION...
THANKS FOR THE SOUVENIR, GRANDPA.
YOU'RE LUCKY YOU DIDN'T GET A COURT-MARTIAL.

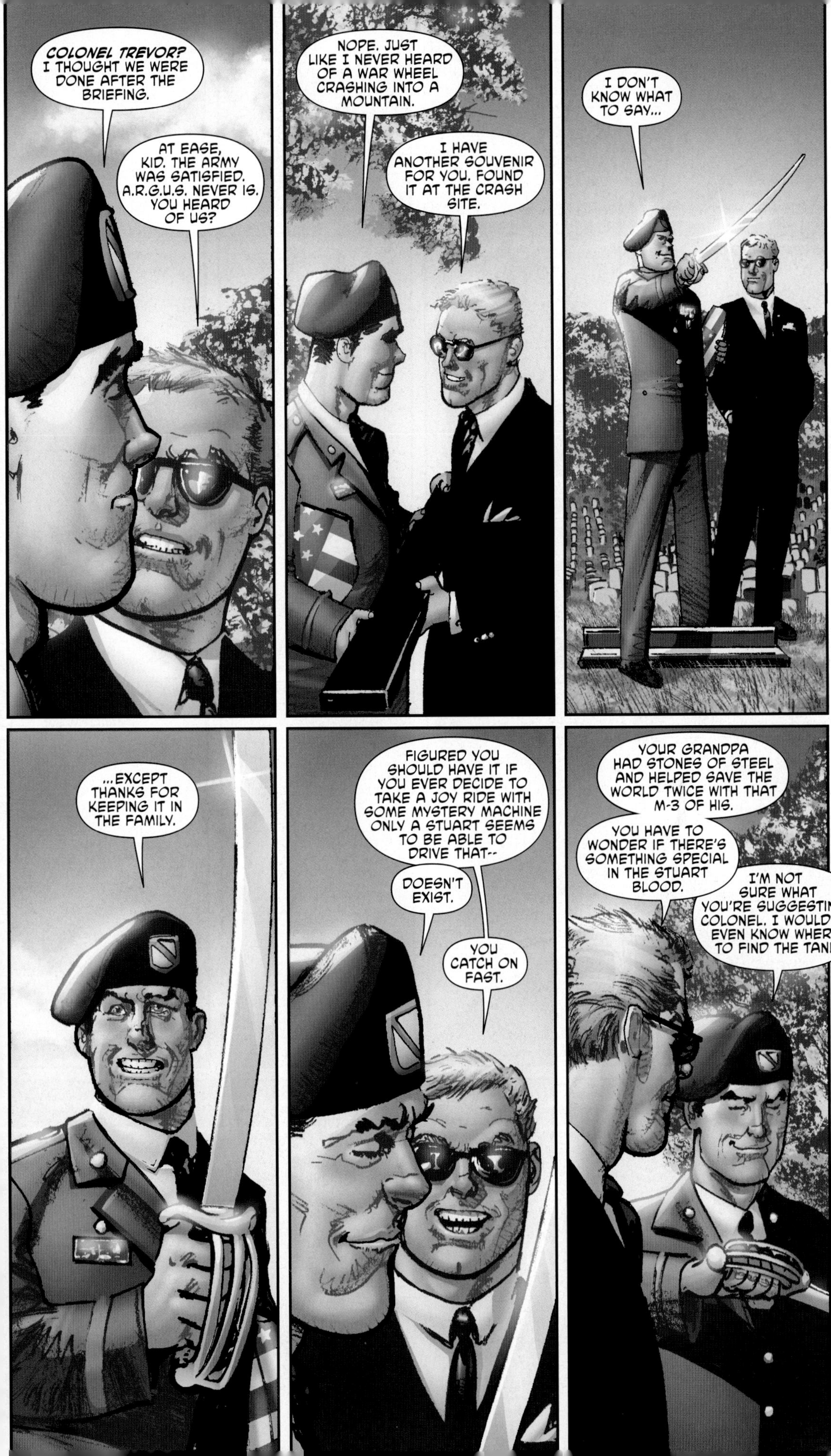
COLONEL TREVOR? I THOUGHT WE WERE DONE AFTER THE BRIEFING.
AT EASE, KID. THE ARMY WAS SATISFIED. A.R.G.U.S. NEVER IS. YOU HEARD OF US?
NOPE. JUST LIKE I NEVER HEARD OF A WAR WHEEL CRASHING INTO A MOUNTAIN.
I HAVE ANOTHER SOUVENIR FOR YOU. FOUND IT AT THE CRASH SITE.
I DON'T KNOW WHAT TO SAY...
...EXCEPT THANKS FOR KEEPING IT IN THE FAMILY.
FIGURED YOU SHOULD HAVE IT IF YOU EVER DECIDE TO TAKE A JOY RIDE WITH SOME MYSTERY MACHINE ONLY A STUART SEEMS TO BE ABLE TO DRIVE THAT--
DOESN'T EXIST.
YOU CATCH ON FAST.
YOUR GRANDPA HAD STONES OF STEEL AND HELPED SAVE THE WORLD TWICE WITH THAT M-3 OF HIS.
YOU HAVE TO WONDER IF THERE'S SOMETHING SPECIAL IN THE STUART BLOOD.
I'M NOT SURE WHAT YOU'RE SUGGESTING, COLONEL. I WOULDN'T EVEN KNOW WHERE TO FIND THE TANK.

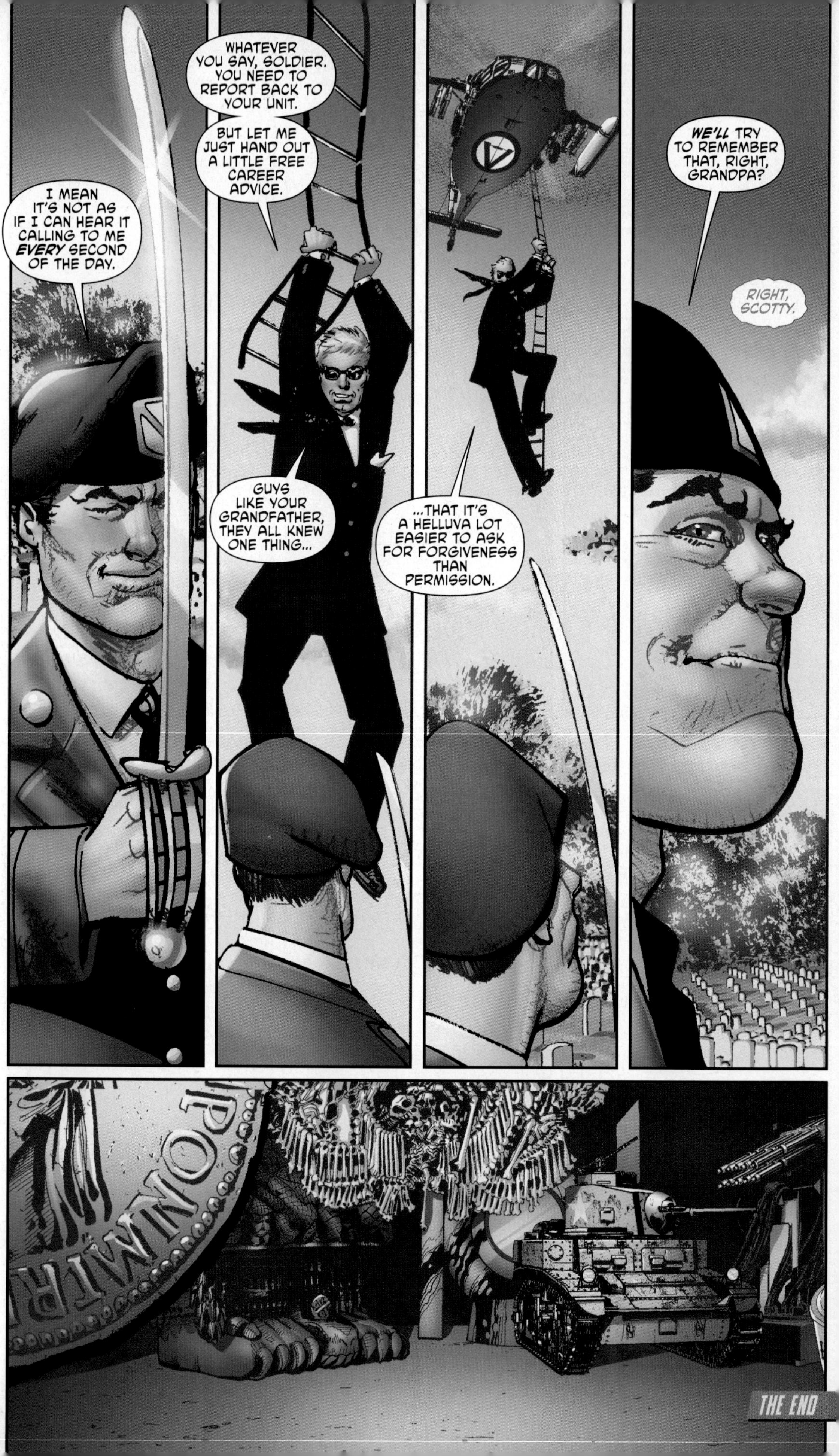
I MEAN IT'S NOT AS IF I CAN HEAR IT CALLING TO ME EVERY SECOND OF THE DAY.
WHATEVER YOU SAY, SOLDIER. YOU NEED TO REPORT BACK TO YOUR UNIT.
BUT LET ME JUST HAND OUT A LITTLE FREE CAREER ADVICE.
GUYS LIKE YOUR GRANDFATHER, THEY ALL KNEW ONE THING...
...THAT IT'S A HELLUVA LOT EASIER TO ASK FOR FORGIVENESS THAN PERMISSION.
WE'LL TRY TO REMEMBER THAT, RIGHT, GRANDPA?
RIGHT, SCOTTY.
THE END

G.I. COMBAT #1
Variant cover by **ARIEL OLIVETTI**

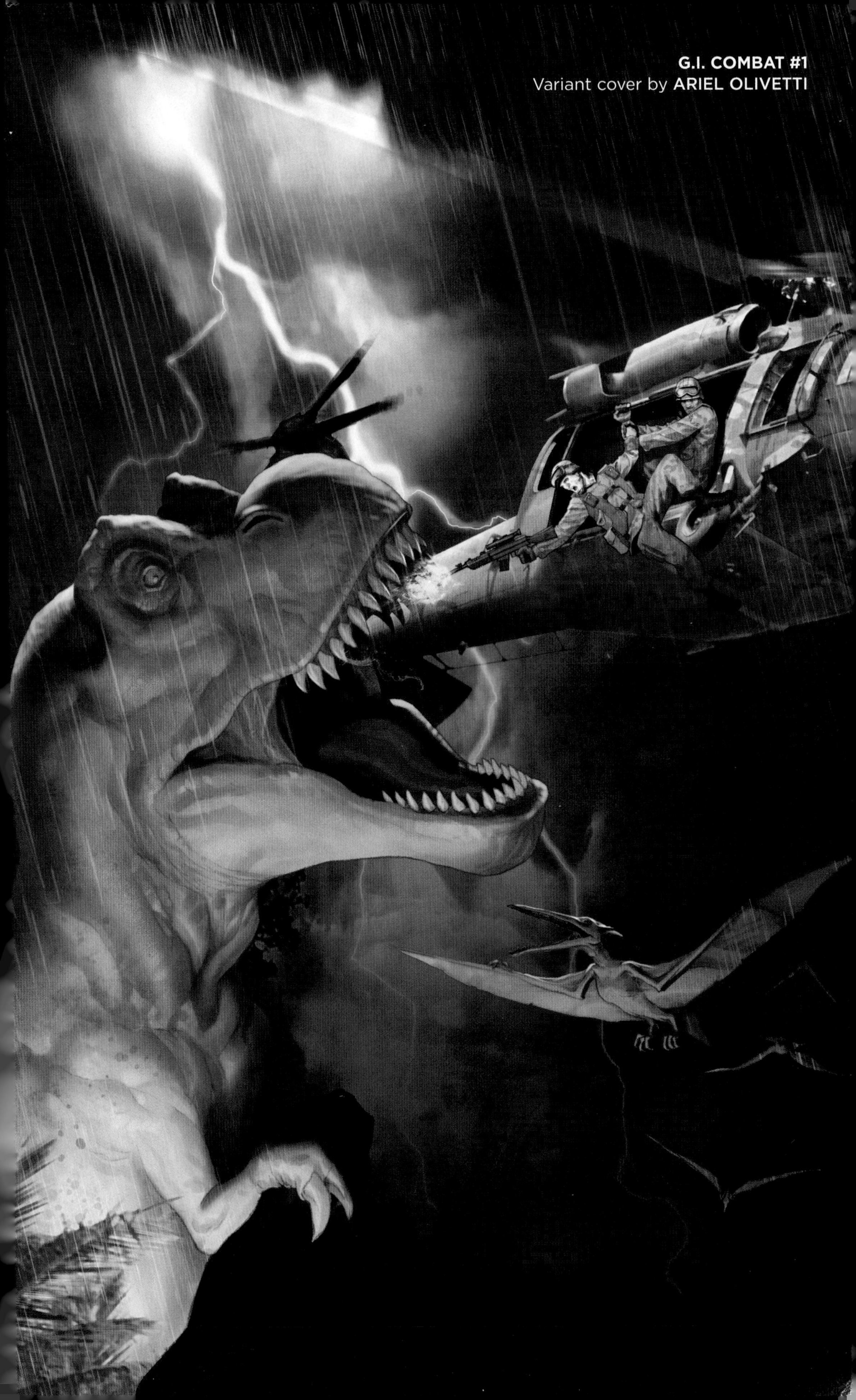

G.I. COMBAT #3
Cover by **ALBERTO PONTICELLI, WAYNE FAUCHER** & **HI-FI**

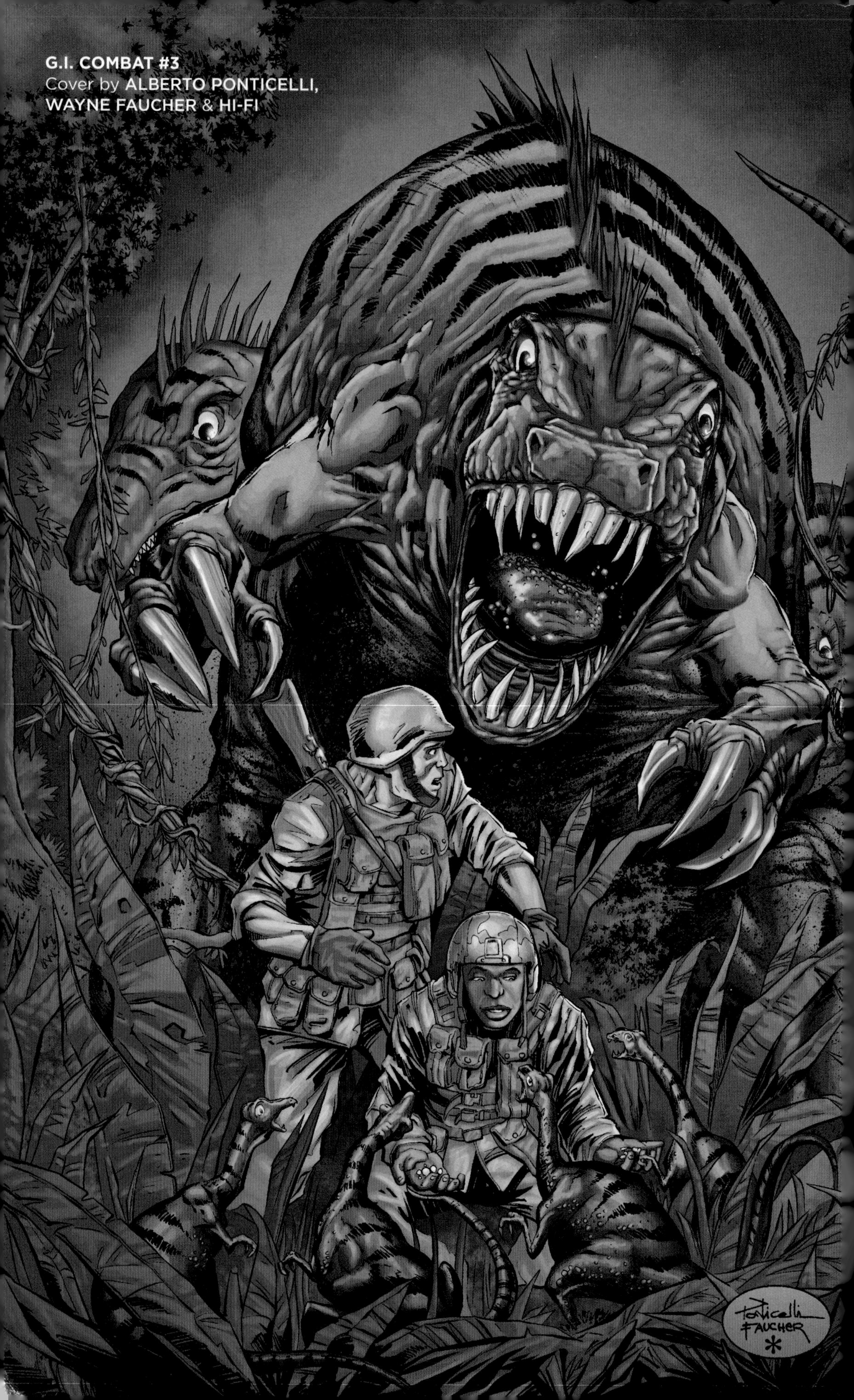
Ponticelli
FAUCHER

G.I. COMBAT #4
Cover by **ALBERTO PONTICELLI,**
WAYNE FAUCHER & **HI-FI**

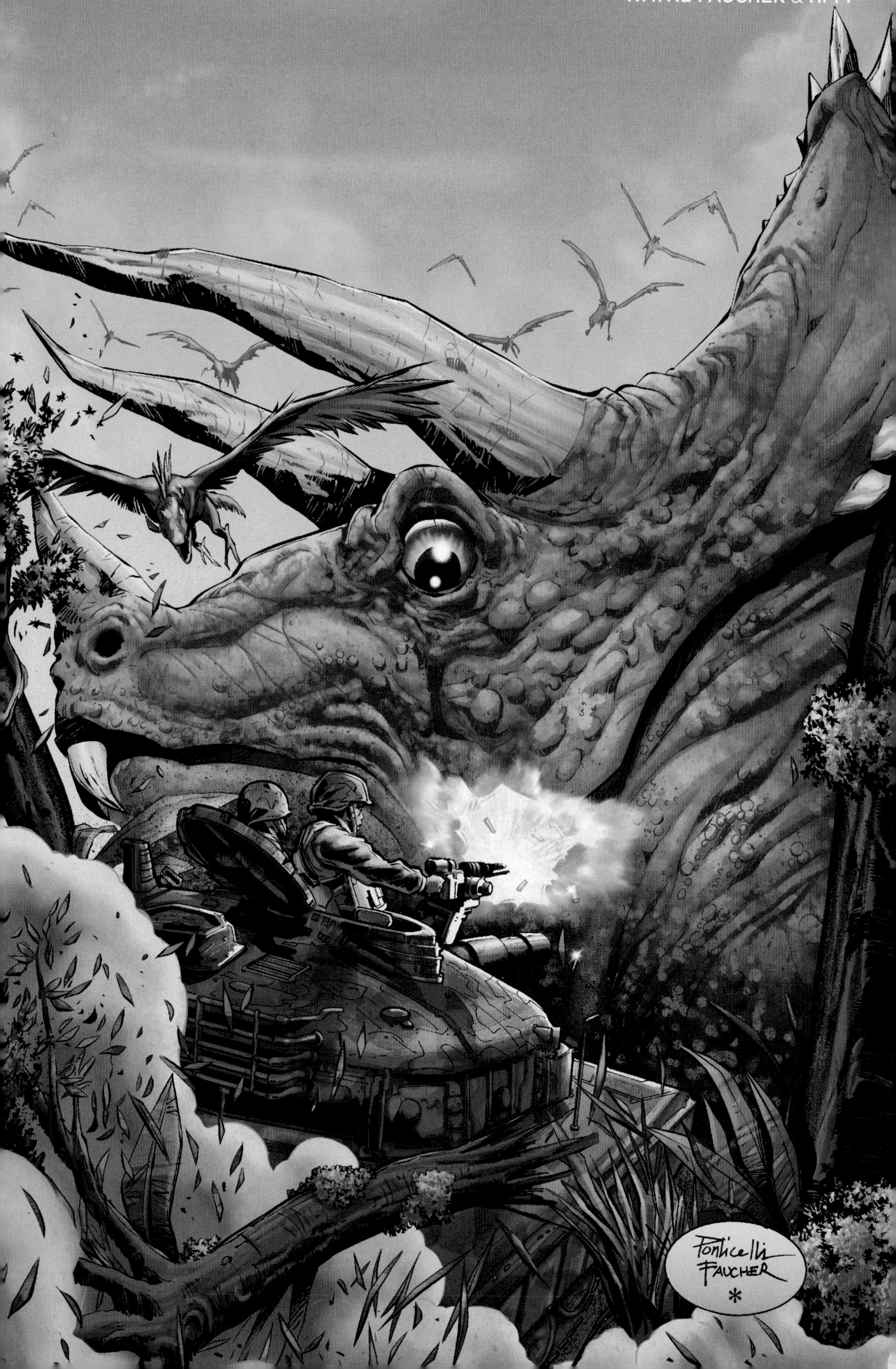
Ponticelli
FAUCHER

G.I. COMBAT #0
Cover by **VIKTOR KALVACHEV**

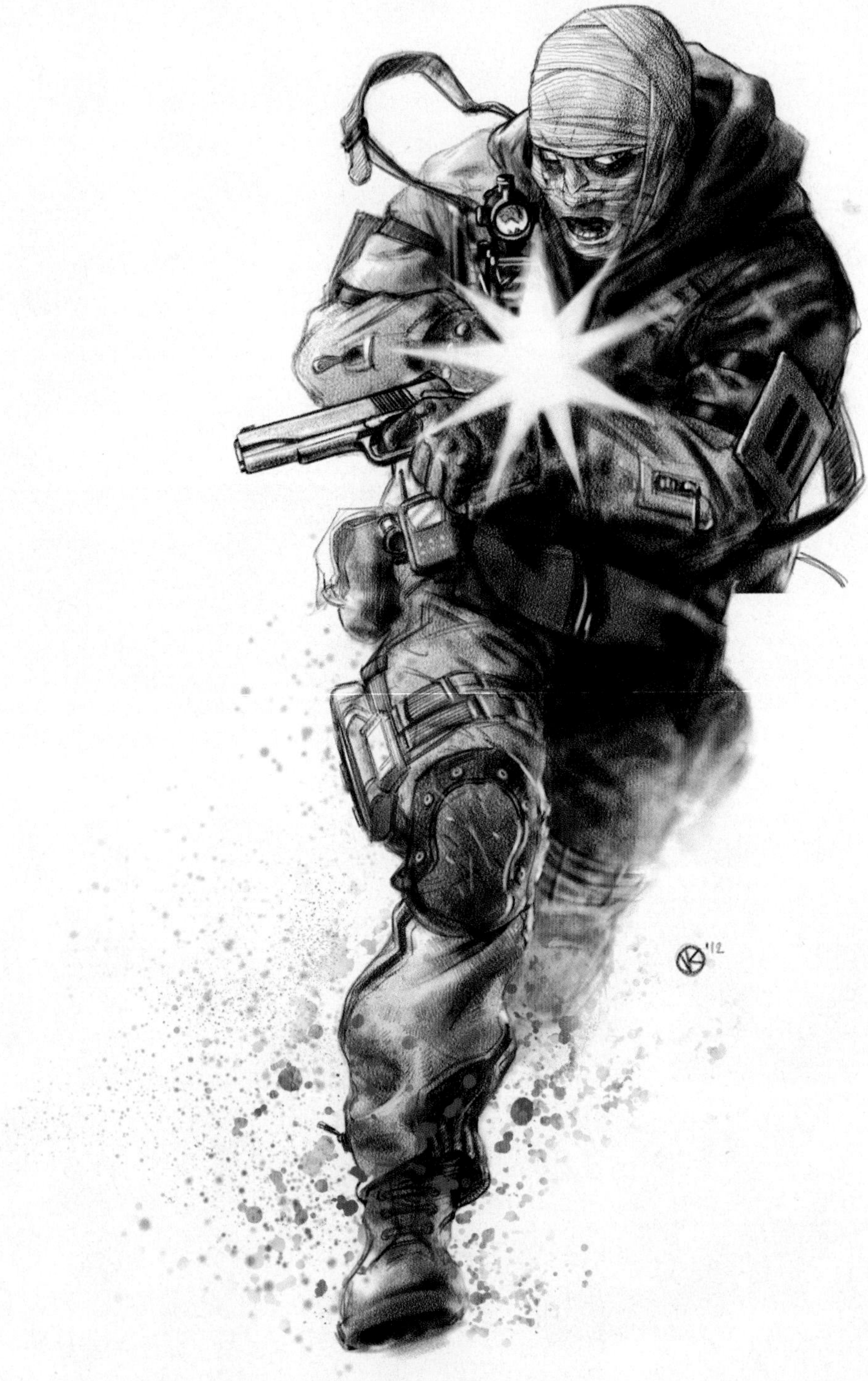

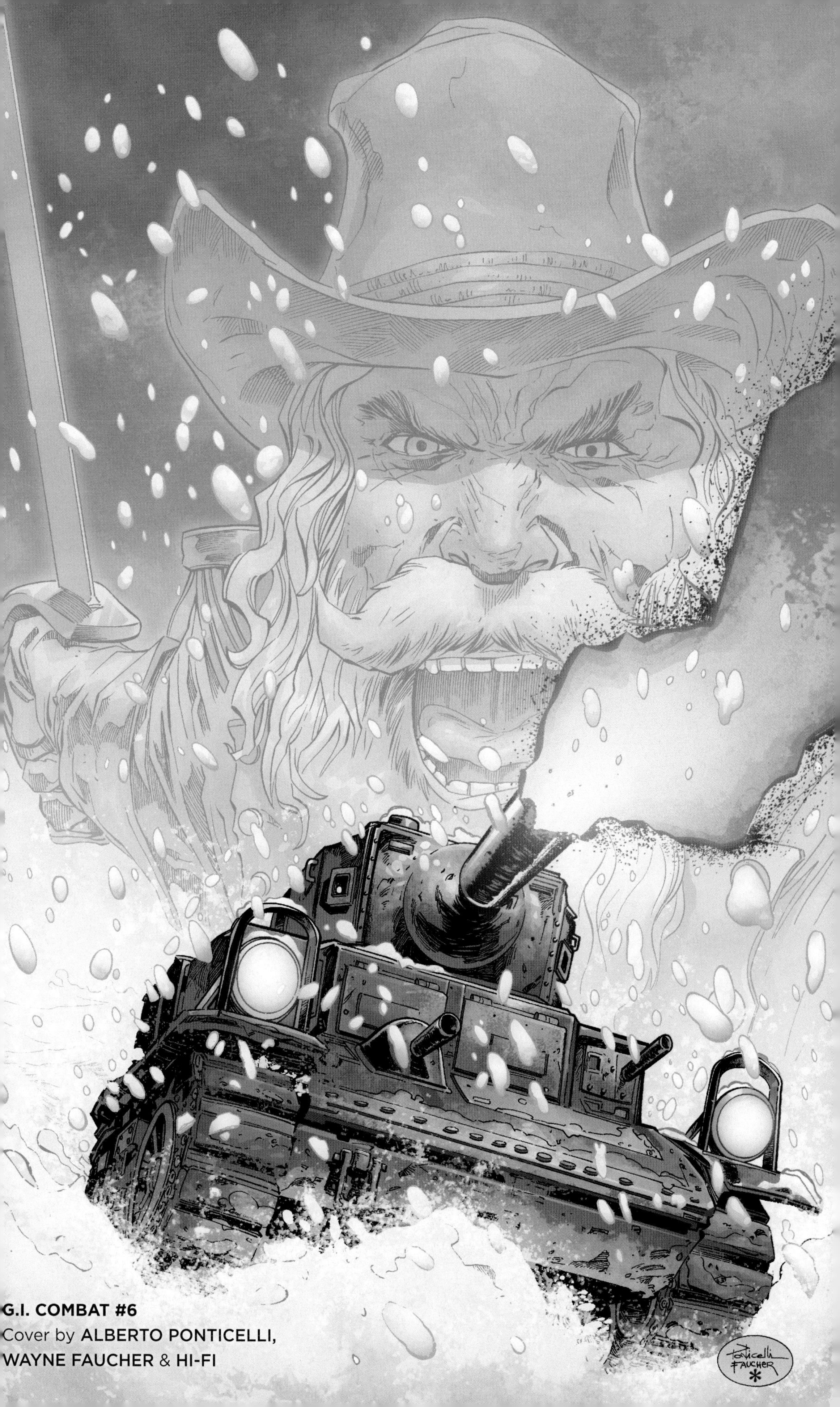
Ponticelli
FAUCHER

G.I. COMBAT #6
Cover by **ALBERTO PONTICELLI, WAYNE FAUCHER** & **HI-FI**

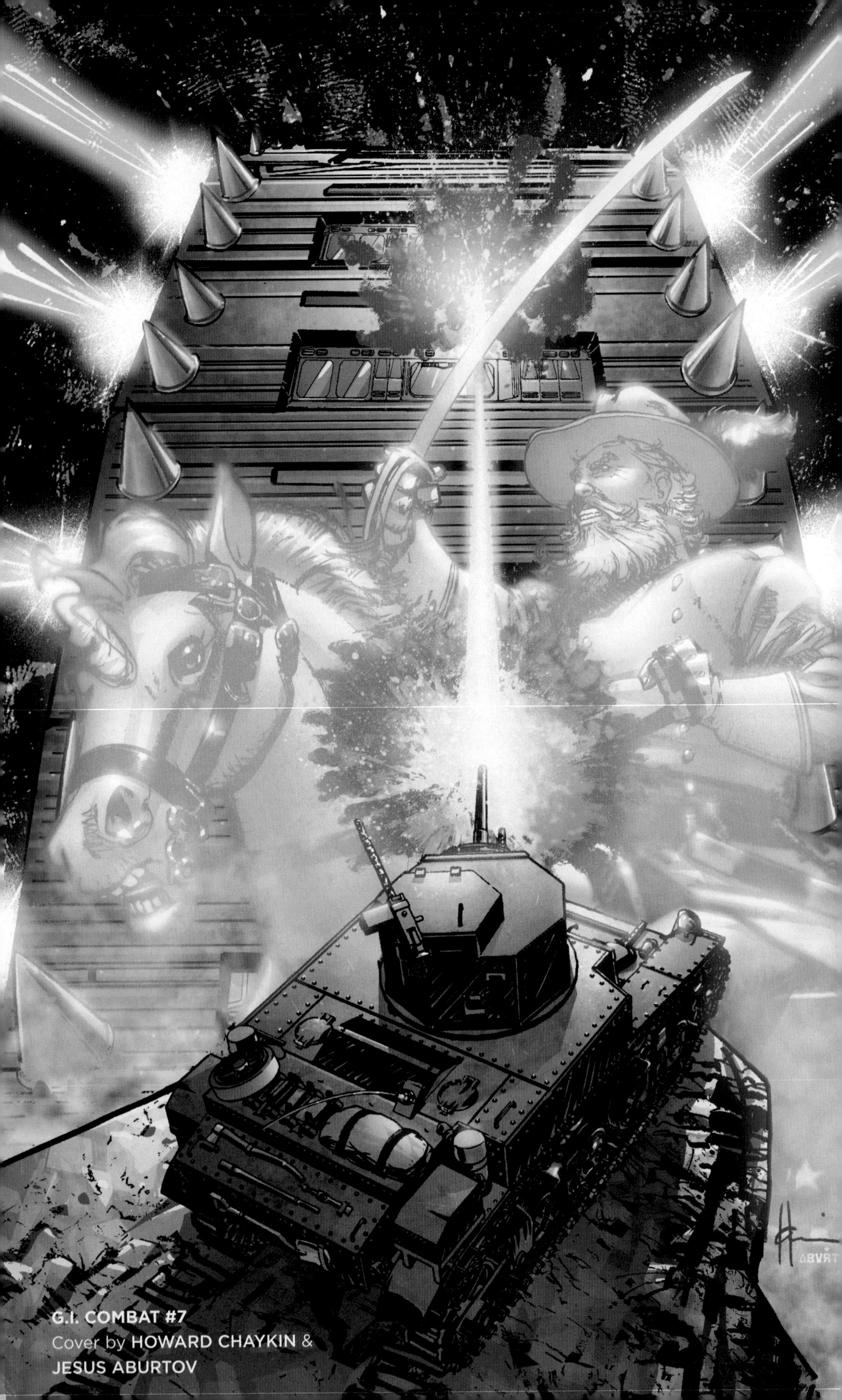
ABRT

G.I. COMBAT #7
Cover by **HOWARD CHAYKIN** &
JESUS ABURTOV

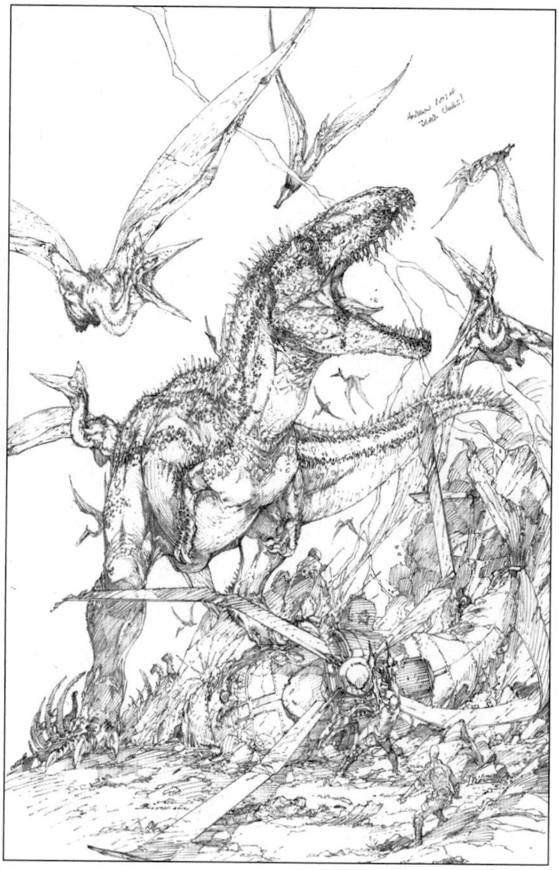

G.I. COMBAT #1 cover pencils by Brett Booth

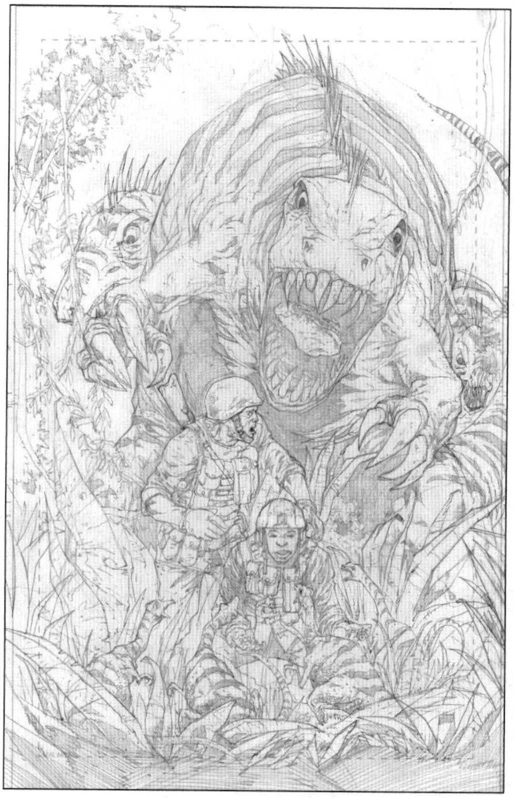

G.I. COMBAT #3 cover pencils by Alberto Ponticelli

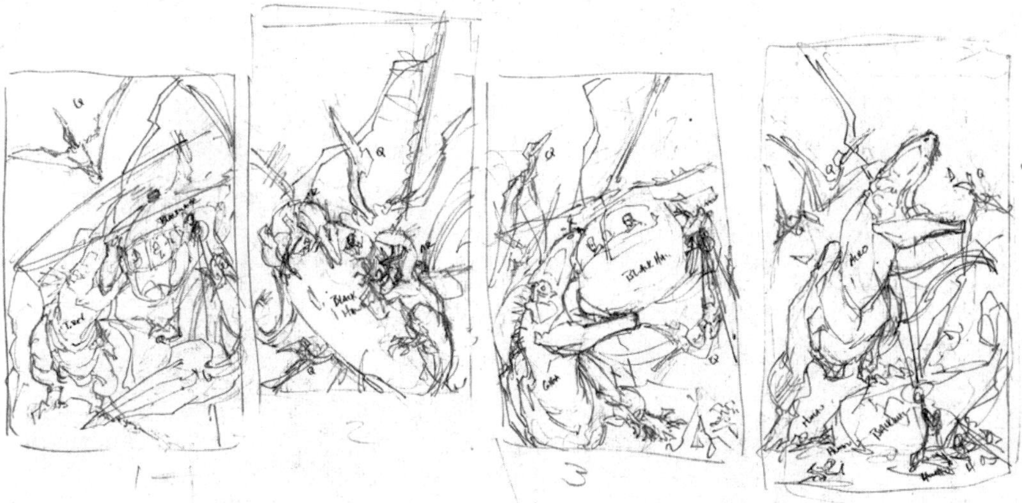

G.I. COMBAT #1 cover layouts by Brett Booth

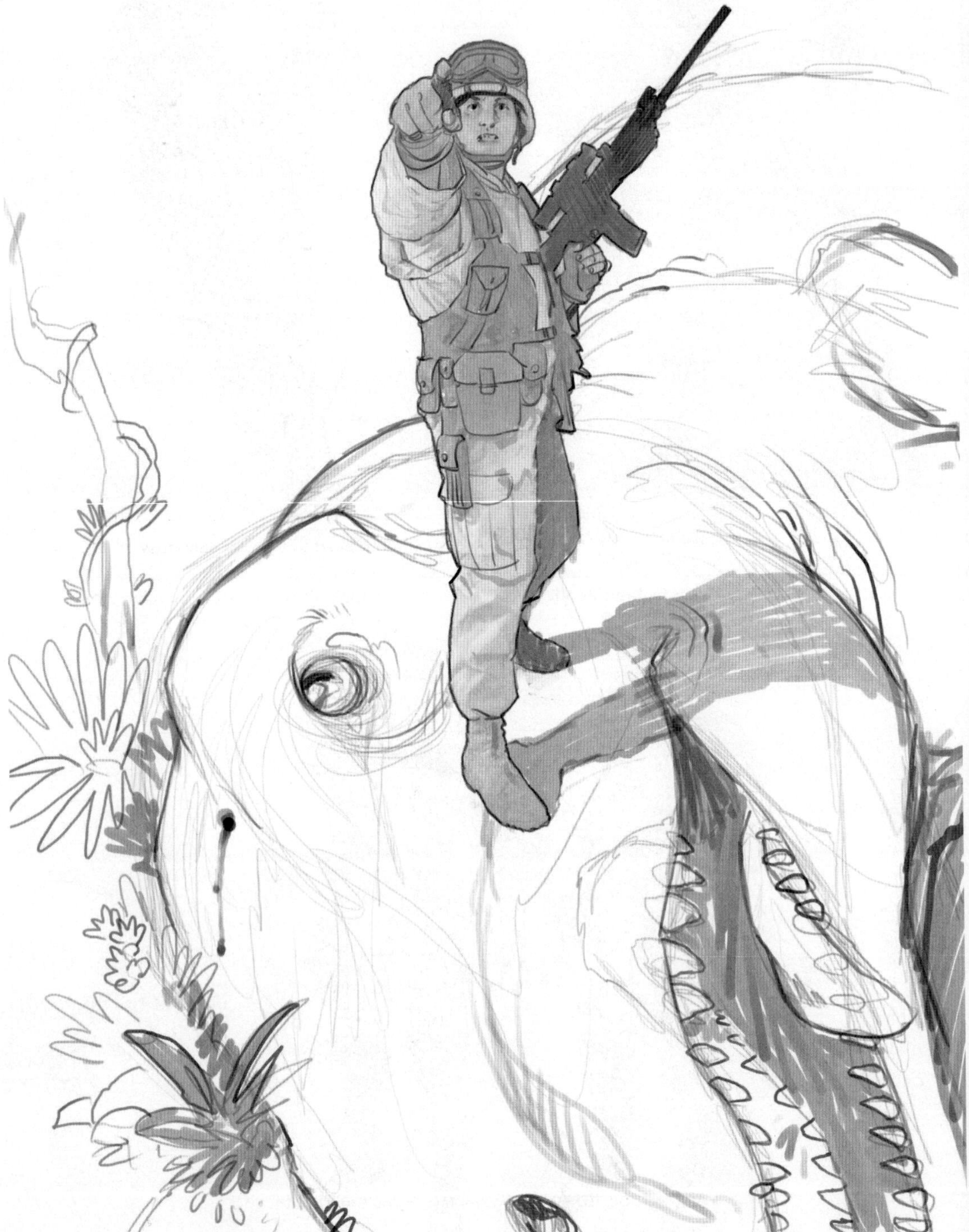

Sketch by Ariel Olivetti

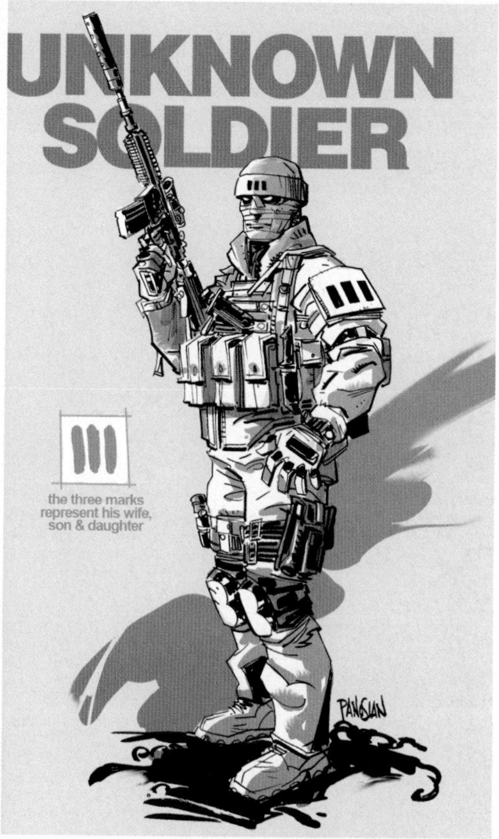
UNKNOWN SOLDIER
the three marks represent his wife, son & daughter
PANOSIAN
Final character design by Dan Panosian

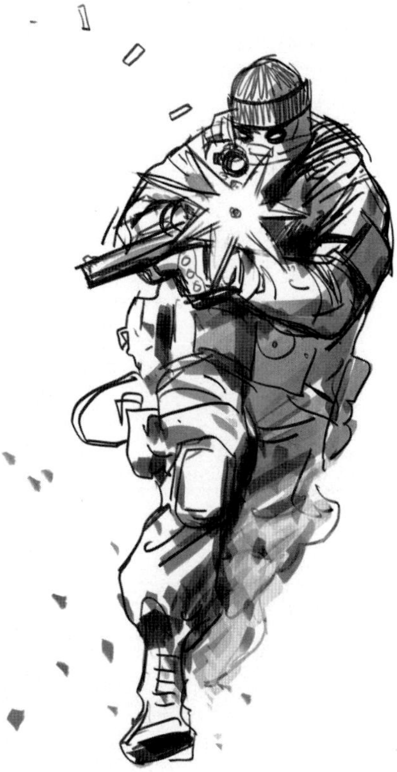
Cover sketch by Viktor Kalvachev

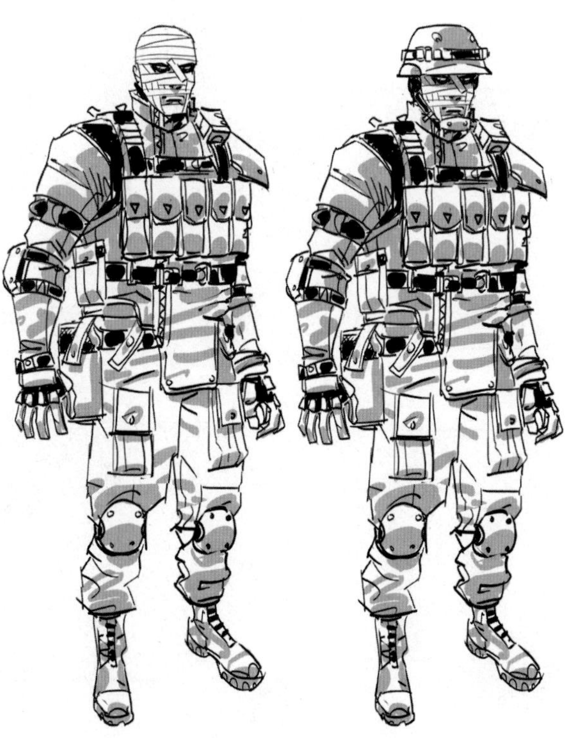
Character studies by Dan Panosian

“The Unknown Soldier” part 6 layouts by Staz Johnson

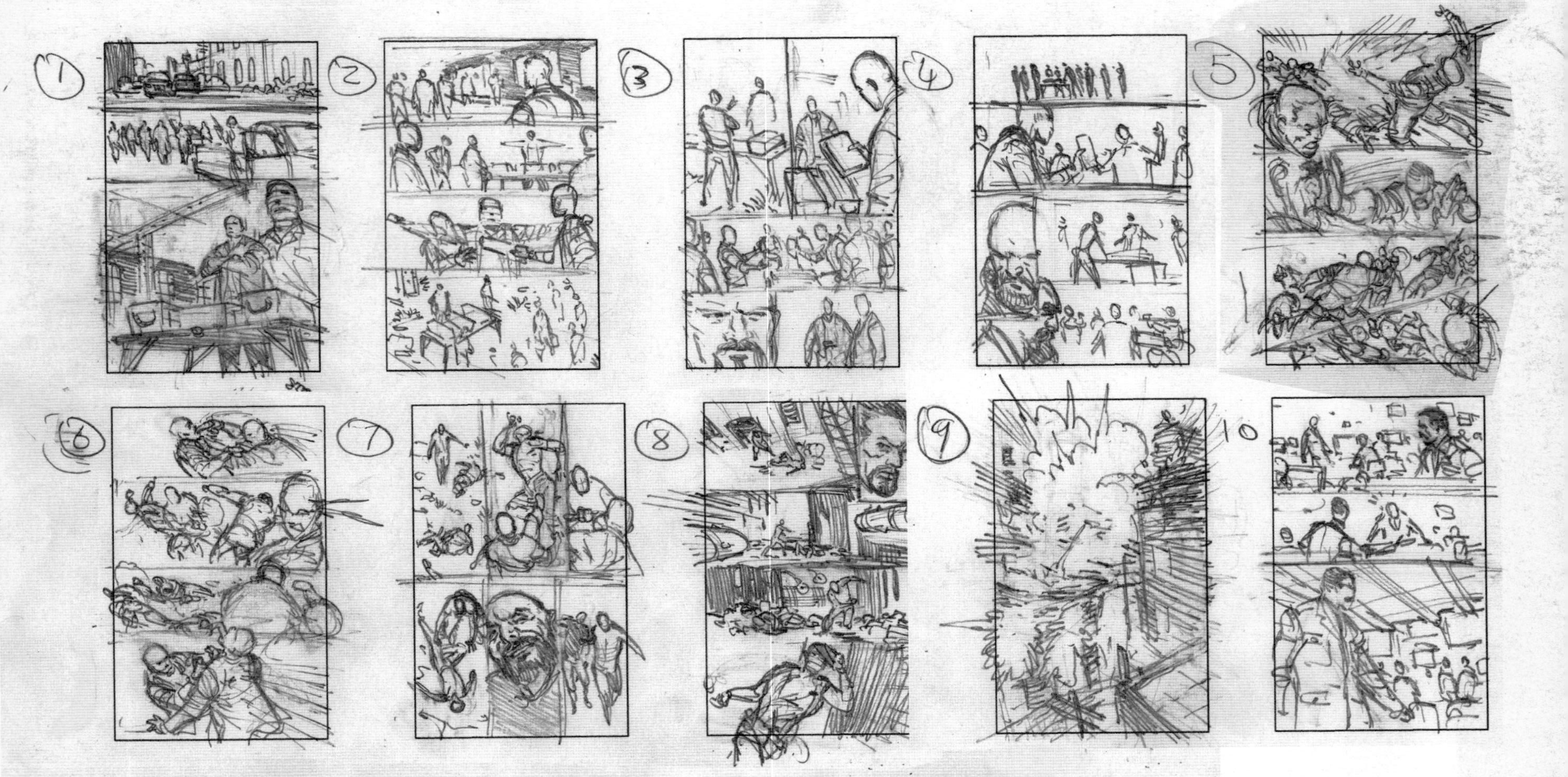

1

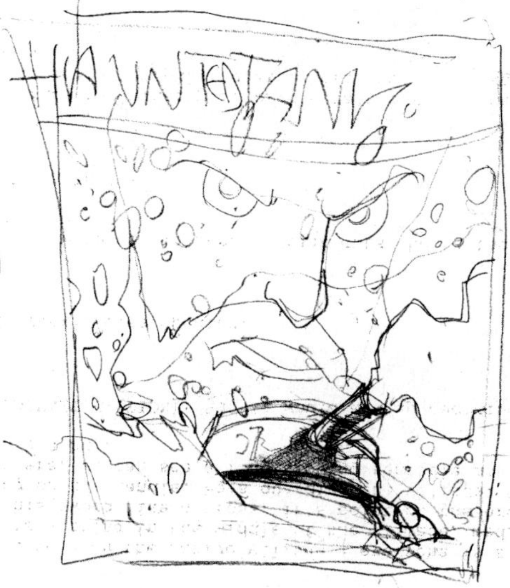

2

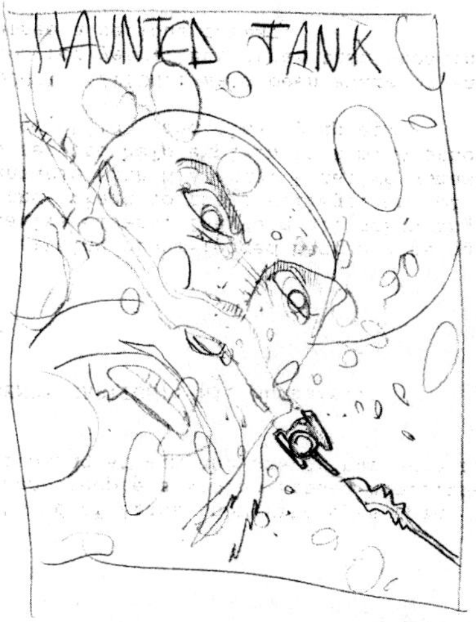
HAUNTED TANK

G.I. COMBAT #6 cover sketches by Alberto Ponticelli

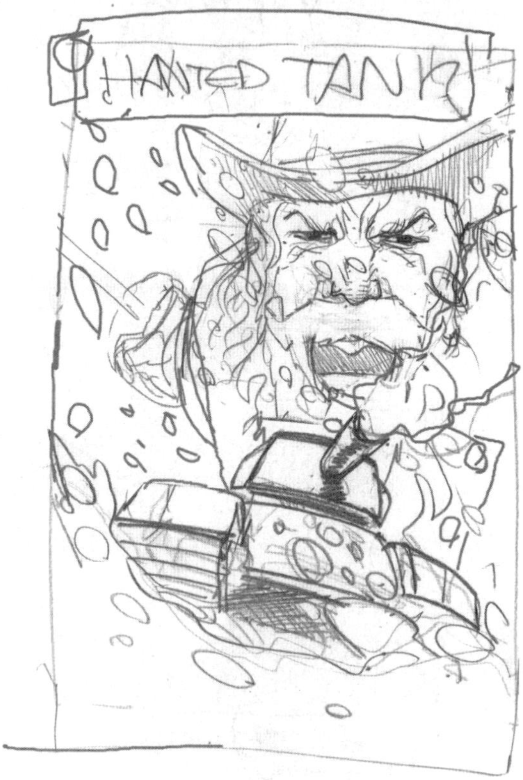

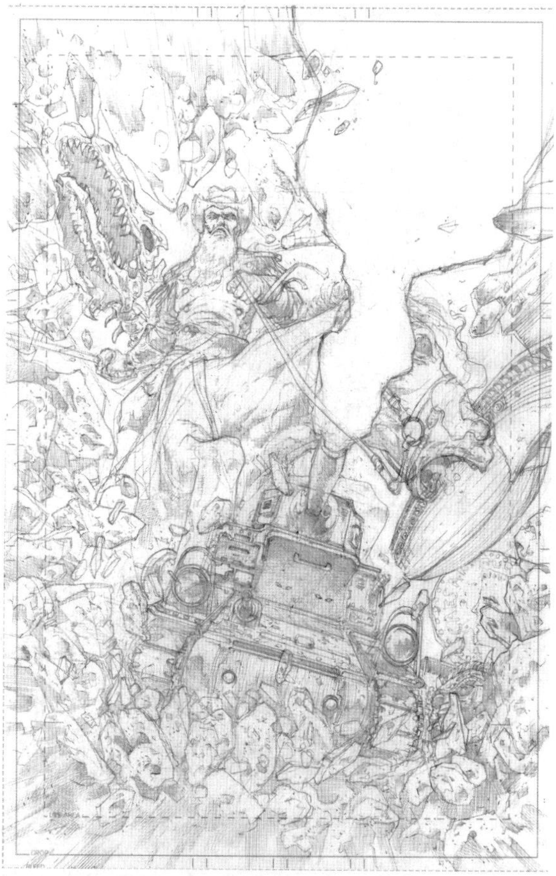

G.I. COMBAT #5 cover pencils by Alberto Ponticelli

G.I. COMBAT #5 cover sketches by Alberto Ponticelli

ALL BACK-GROUND STUFF IN SAME PERSPECTIVE
BOAT
HORSE LEG
DEBRIS BREAKING/ COMING OUT AT US

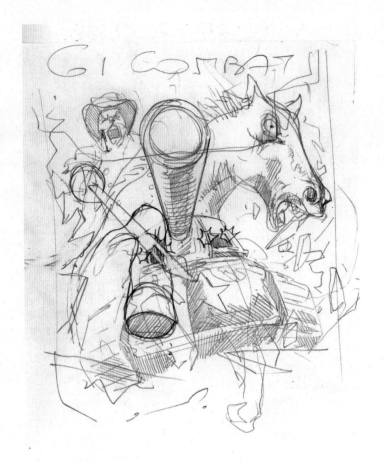

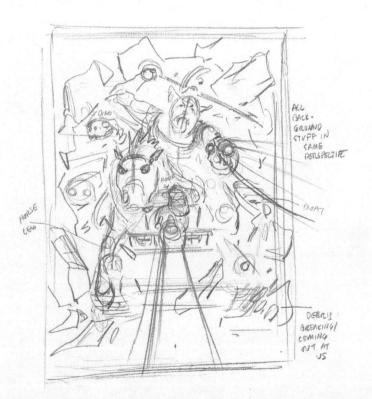